D1583091

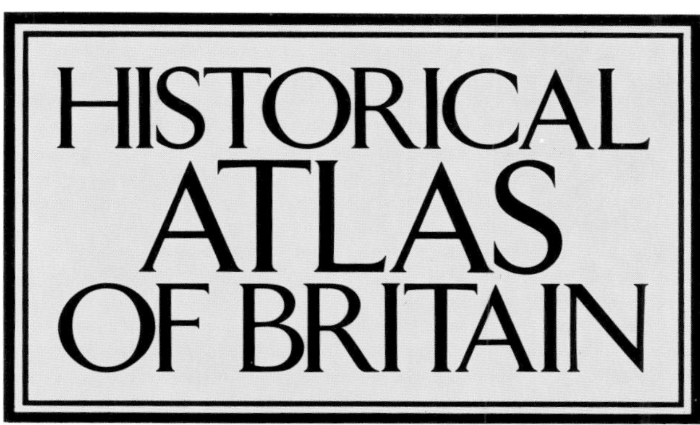
HISTORICAL
ATLAS
OF BRITAIN

MALCOLM FALKUS, JOHN GILLINGHAM

BOOK CLUB ASSOCIATES
LONDON

General editors
MALCOLM FALKUS
JOHN GILLINGHAM

Managing editor
JOHN GRISEWOOD
Assistant editor
JILLY GLASSBOROW
Production editors
NICK HEARD
MARTYN YEO

Design
JOHN STRANGE
Colour consultant
DAVE NASH
Picture research
CHARLOTTE PARRY-CROOKE
Sub-editor
CHRISTOPHER FAGG

Cartography
CREATIVE SERVICES STUDIO
PRODUCT SUPPORT (GRAPHICS) LTD. DERBY
Manager
RALPH ORME
Control
HUGH PENFOLD
Chief cartographer
MARION DUDLEY
Diagrams
TONY MOLD
MALCOLM PORTER

This edition published 1981 by
Book Club Associates
By arrangement with Grisewood and Dempsey Ltd

Designed and produced by Grisewood and Dempsey Ltd

Printed and bound by
Mohndruck Graphische Betriebe GmbH,
Gütersloh, West Germany

Phototypeset by Southern Positives and Negatives (SPAN),
Lingfield, Surrey

Colour separation of maps by
Fotolito Aldini s.r.l., Milan, Italy
Colour separation of transparencies by
Newsele s.r.l., Milan, Italy

CONTRIBUTORS

D. H. ALDCROFT
University of Leicester

A. S. ANDERSON
University of Leicester

K. R. ANDREWS
University of Hull

C. BABER
University of Cardiff

F. BARLOW
University of Exeter

R. J. BRADLEY
University of Reading

F. CAPIE
The City University, London

D. A. CARPENTER
Queen Mary College, London

R. R. DAVIES
University College of Wales, Aberystwyth

W. DAVIES
University College, London

C. J. DEWEY
University of Leicester

P. EARLE
London School of Economics

M. E. FALKUS
London School of Economics

J. B. GILLINGHAM
London School of Economics

T. GOURVISH
University of East Anglia

J. A. GREEN
The Queen's University, Belfast

R. A. GRIFFITHS
University College of Swansea

J. HATCHER
Corpus Christi College, Cambridge

N. HOOPER
Kings College, London

G. H. JENKINS
University College of Wales, Aberystwyth

D. KYNASTON
London School of Economics

P. LANE
Formerly Coloma College

C. M. LAW
University of Salford

C. H. LAWRENCE
Bedford College, London

B. P. LENMAN
University of St Andrews

D. McKAY
London School of Economics

D. NASH
Ashmolean Museum, Oxford

C. F. RICHMOND
University of Keele

I. ROY
King's College, London

A. P. SMYTH
University of Kent at Canterbury

P. STAFFORD
Huddersfield Polytechnic

D. R. STARKEY
London School of Economics

W. M. STERN
London School of Economics

F. M. L. THOMPSON
Director, Institute of Historical Research
University of London

D. C. WATT
London School of Economics

M. G. WELCH
University College, London

A. WILLIAMS
Polytechnic of North London

C. P. WORMALD
University of Glasgow

J. M. WORMALD
University of Glasgow

CONTENTS

Part 1
The Political History of Britain

Skara Brae – a Neolithic settlement on Mainland, Orkney.

CHAPTER ONE

The First Britons, 4000 BC to *c*.400 AD

Richmond Castle Yorkshire – an early Norman castle.

CHAPTER TWO

The Making of England, 400–1066

Henry IV and his wife Joan of Navarre.

CHAPTER THREE

Britain and Europe, 1066–1660

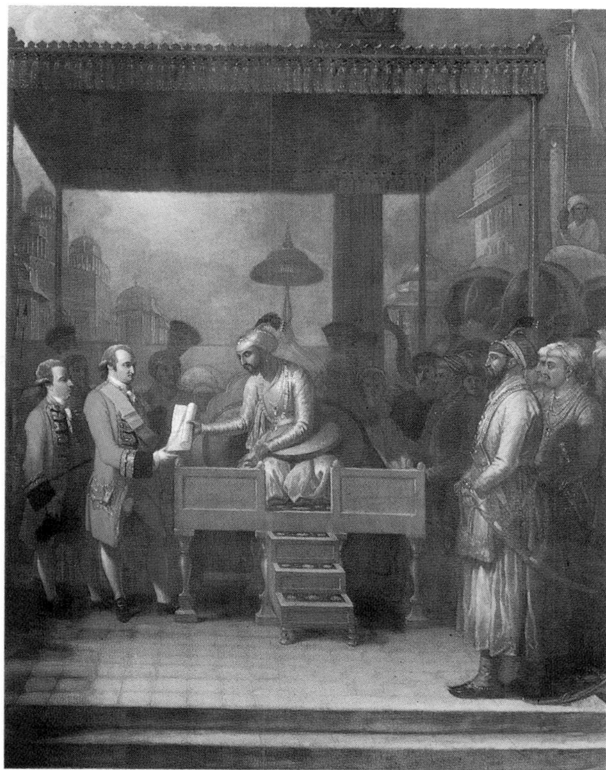

Robert Clive and the Mughal Emperor Shah Alam.

CHAPTER FOUR

The Expansion of England, 1660–1815

Power and confidence. British victories by land and sea.

Pilgrims at the shrine. A Rock festival, 1980s.

CHAPTER FIVE

Power, Peace and Prosperity, 1815–1914

CHAPTER SIX

Confrontation and Change: Britain Since 1914

Part 2
The Social and Economic History of Britain

Medieval commerce. A 15th century market.

CHAPTER SEVEN

'A Fair Field Full of Folk'

Transport revolution: The advent of railways.

CHAPTER EIGHT

The Great Transformation: The Rise of Industry and its aftermath

INTRODUCTION

In compiling and presenting *The Historical Atlas of Britain* the editors have tried to achieve three major goals. We have sought to produce – for the first time on this scale and at this level – an Atlas which yields within a single volume a comprehensive survey of British history from the earliest times until the present. We consider not only the component parts of the United Kingdom (indeed, the gradual unification of the nation is one of the principal themes) but also the various overseas possessions. If we have succeeded in producing such a survey, then a long-felt need will have been met.

Secondly, we have attempted, through our choice of contributors, to produce a work which will portray, both in the maps and in the accompanying texts, views and emphases which reflect recent historical scholarship. Thirdly, in choosing the topics, we have been guided by the need to concentrate on those aspects of the past which can most fruitfully be understood with the help of maps.

Readers will notice that we have placed considerable emphasis upon social and economic events, for in our view the general political picture must remain blurred unless this background is brought into focus. Although the Atlas concentrates upon Britain, many of the topics cover wider aspects also, while a chronology of major world historical events has been included so that British history can be placed in a broader perspective.

To select themes from so vast a score is no easy task. Not everyone will agree with the balance we have drawn between political, social, and economic changes, nor with the weights we have given to the different periods, regions, and subjects. We are aware that some important aspects of our past are barely touched upon, or omitted altogether, such as literature, music and other areas of our cultural heritage. But we would argue that we could not include everything, and that our selections have been governed throughout by those main objectives outlined above.

The organization of the Atlas is both chronological and thematic. Each topic is treated separately and is illustrated with maps, diagrams, pictures and text. For convenience the book has been divided into eight 'chapters', the first six dealing primarily with political changes and the last two concentrating on social and economic developments. But historical events do not occur in a vacuum, and neither the chapters nor the topics should be considered – nor have they been treated – as self-contained.

A collective enterprise such as this incurs many debts. Our foremost thanks must go to the contributors, who have taken time from their scholarly activities to present their knowledge in what is, for many, a novel medium. We are grateful, too, to John Grisewood and Michael Dempsey, who have provided the fullest co-operation and assistance, advice, encouragement, and a few headaches.

MALCOLM FALKUS JOHN GILLINGHAM

PART ONE:

THE POLITICAL HISTORY OF BRITAIN

Chapter One
THE FIRST BRITONS, 4000 BC - c. AD 400

In these five thousand years – a period three times as long as that covered by the rest of this atlas – the first Britons began to master their environment. Hunters, gatherers and fishers slowly gave way to pioneer farmers. By the time the Romans arrived to reduce almost the whole island to obedience and administrative order Britain had already taken on its familiar shape: a land of small communities based on an economy of mixed farming, cloth-weaving and metal-working, an island linked to the continent by politics and by trade.

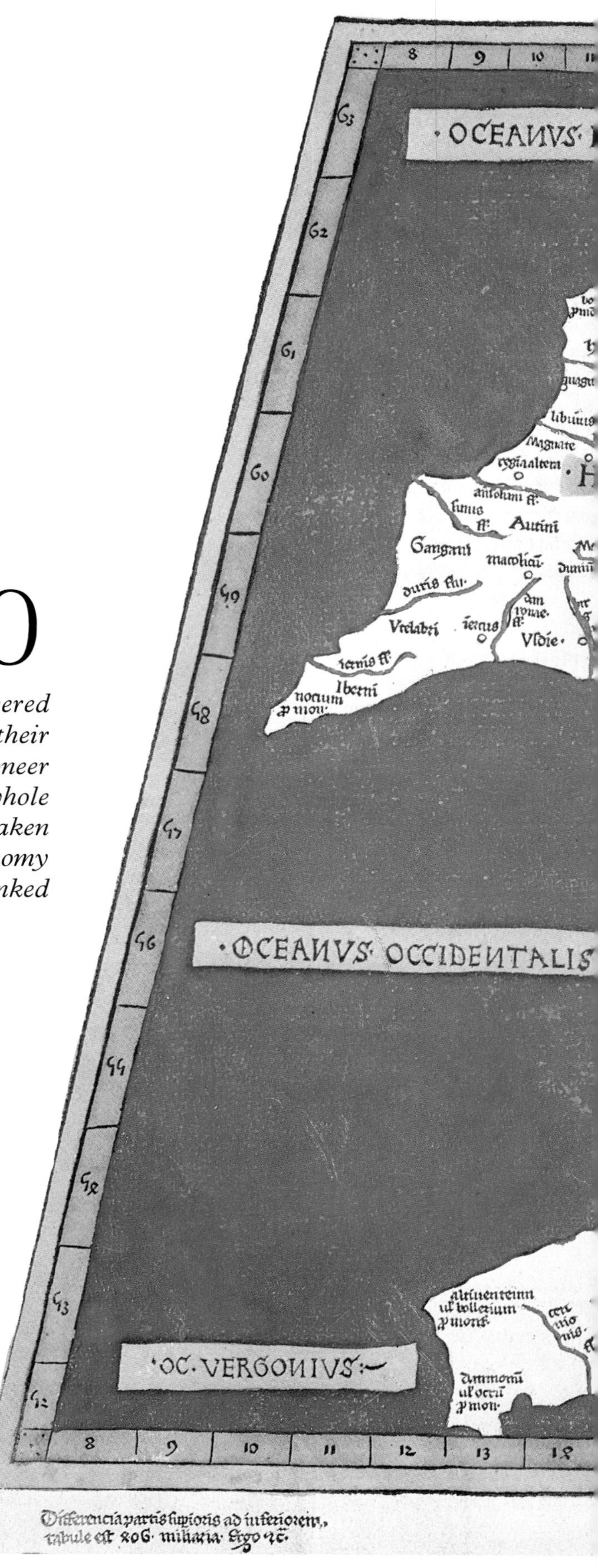

A map of the British Isles compiled from the coordinates given in Ptolemy's *Geography* (2nd century AD).

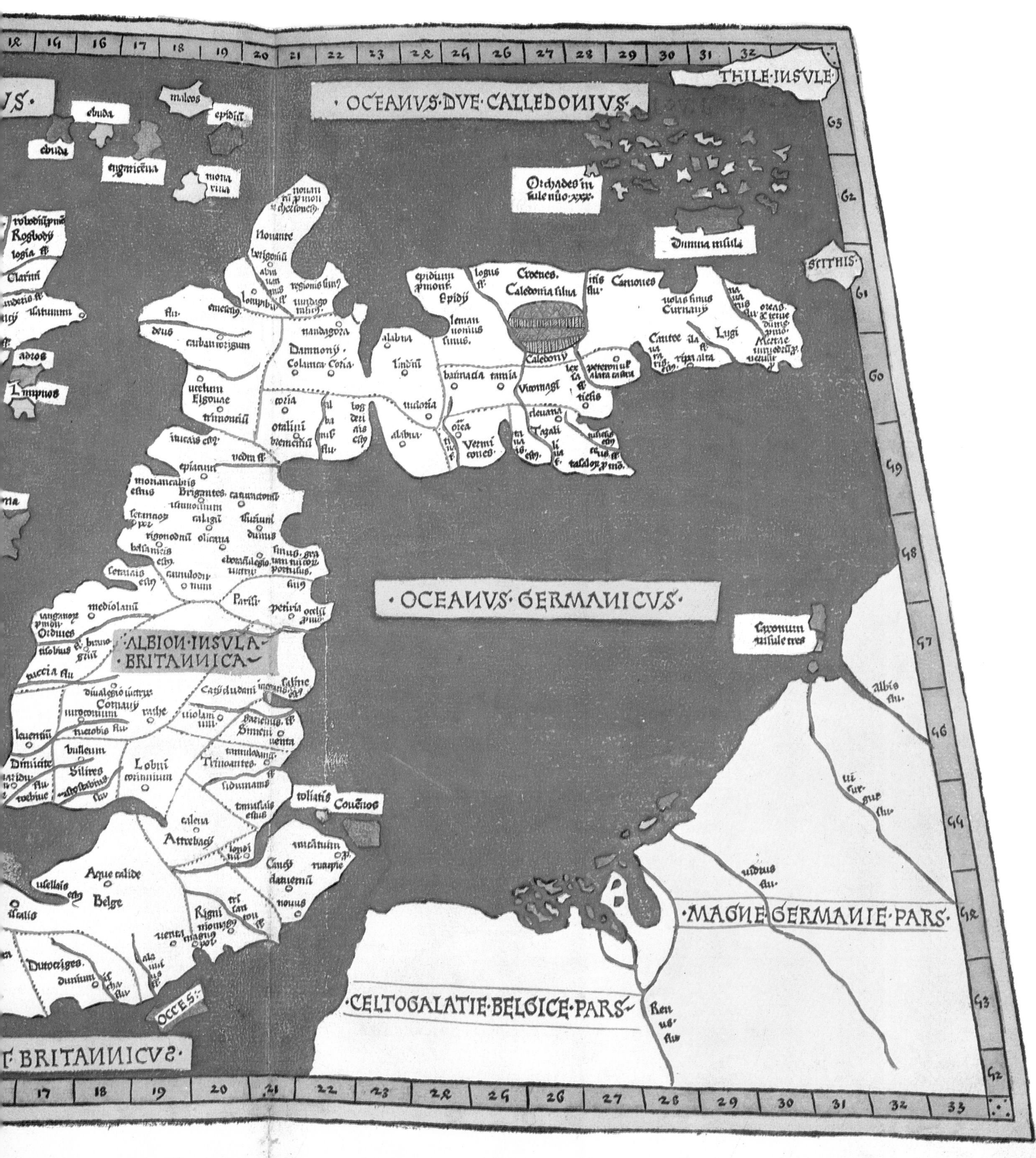
THILE·INSVLE
·OCEANVS·DVE·CALLEDONIVS·
·OCEANVS·GERMANICVS·
·ALBION·INSVLA·
·BRITANNICA·
·MAGNE·GERMANIE·PARS·
·CELTOGALATIE·BELGICE·PARS·
SCITHIS
OCCES
T·BRITANNICVS·

The First Farmers, *c.* 4000BC

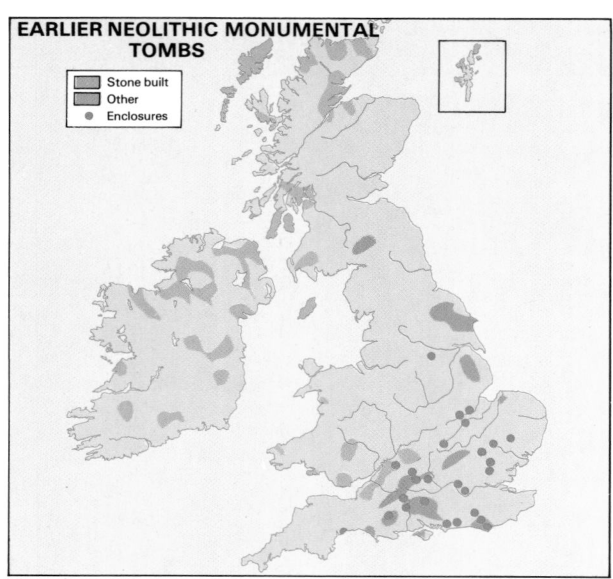

The location of communal tombs (left) during the earlier Neolithic tends to reflect areas in which sufficient of the population could be organized to undertake their construction. The restricted distribution of the enclosures suggests that these monuments were the culmination of long occupations of particularly fertile areas.

Henge monuments, successors of the earlier Neolithic enclosures, are widely distributed, suggesting a general expansion in the settled area.

The earliest stone circles are associated with monumental tombs or the later stages of henge monuments, but most are free-standing structures and seem to belong to the Bronze Age. Some almost certainly reflect astronomical alignments within their layouts. Stone alignments are less understood; they have been compared to the 'avenues' leading to ceremonial centres at Stonehenge and Avebury.

Scholars find the traditional division of the prehistoric period into Stone Age, Bronze Age and Iron Age difficult to use. It is no longer possible to make a satisfactory division at the point where iron working appeared. A more convincing distinction is between the Wessex Culture and its counterparts, which make up the earlier Bronze Age, and the developments which followed their gradual eclipse. For this reason the so-called Bronze and Iron Ages are treated together (below).

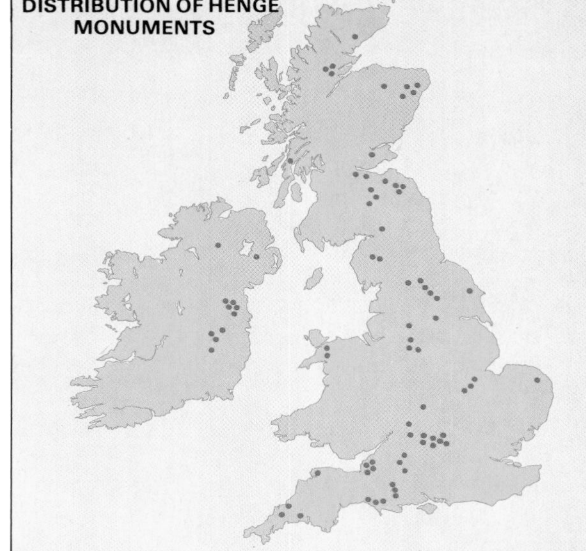

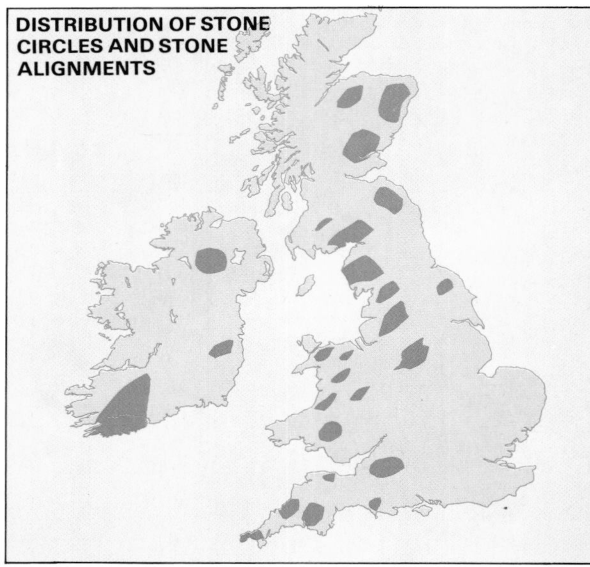

The earliest visible monuments of the British Isles belong to the *Neolithic* period, a time which also marks the widespread clearance of the native forest. But it should not be supposed that this represents the beginning of the prehistoric period. When the first farmers colonized Britain some time before 4000 BC they were probably outnumbered by an aboriginal population practising an efficient blend of hunting, gathering and fishing. But it is the nature of pioneer agriculture to leave little trace, and the prominent burial sites and ceremonial centres of the Neolithic belong to a rather later period, when these farming communities had mastered their environment, produced an economic surplus and developed the distinctive social organization celebrated by these monuments. Their settlements probably consisted of dispersed homesteads, made up of small rectangular buildings capable of housing a nuclear family. Many areas of light silty soils were cleared in this period, especially in low-lying ground close to important rivers. Some of these forest clearings remained in use for several centuries, while others regenerated rapidly. The economy was based on cereal cultivation and stock raising, with a special emphasis on cattle. The most prominent monuments of the same period covered only part of the settled landscape and the burial mounds in particular tend to be situated on higher ground, perhaps for greater visibility.

4000	3000	2000	1000	BC AD
Neolithic		Earlier Bronze Age	Later Bronze Age	Iron Age

Monumental communal tombs
Enclosures
Henge monuments
Flint mines
Stone axe quarries
Individual burials
Stone circles
Wessex Culture
Hill-forts
Celtic fields
Land boundaries
Yorkshire rich burials

The two main forms of monument in this early phase were ancestral tombs and earthwork enclosures. The first to be built were communal burial sites, which in highland areas included magnificent cairns and stone chambers. But these cannot be regarded simply as places of burial, since some of them were used in only one stage of the funerary process after the dead had first been exposed or buried elsewhere. Some sites contain the partial remains of up to 50 skeletons, but others may have acted as more temporary charnel houses. These monuments are best viewed as ancestral shrines.

The enclosures had a variety of separate functions ranging from settlement and defence to the disposal of the dead. Three recently excavated sites were massively defended and show evidence that they had been attacked. Most dramatically, at Hambledon Hill in Dorset two contemporary enclosures on one hilltop had quite contrasting functions. One had been a defended settlement, while the other site contained a number of relatively exotic objects and had been used for the exposure of the corpses. The whole hill was ringed by human skulls.

After these rather arresting developments, there fol-

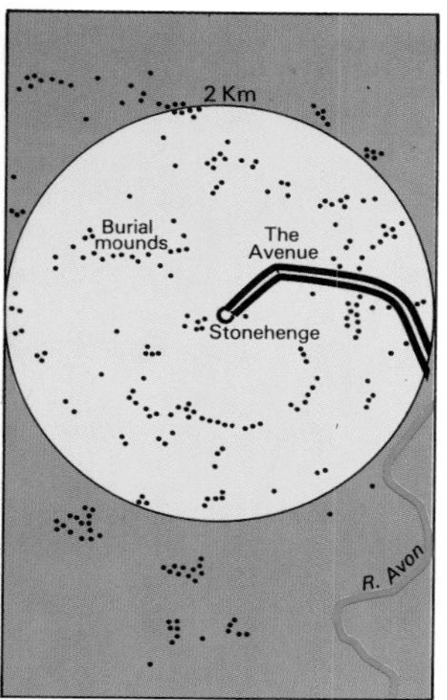

The Stonehenge area. An enormous series of contemporary burial mounds, or barrows, cluster within 2 km of this monument. The 'avenue', consisting of two parallel banks and ditches, leads from the entrance to Stonehenge to the bank of the River Avon – the main link with the Channel coast.

lowed a period of economic contraction and after 3300 there is less evidence for intensive agriculture and little sign of such elaborate treatment of the ancestors. Instead, a contrasting emphasis seems to have developed on individual burial and control over the production and distribution of exotic objects, including a variety of stone axes, finely finished flint implements and personal adornments. These are most often found in male graves or with a new range of ceremonial centres, the henge monuments. There was a substantial increase in the production of axes, which were distributed over considerable distances. A number of flint mines began operation in this period, while the manufacture of stone axes greatly increased in highland areas, such as Cumbria and North Wales. In some cases axes from these sources may have been distributed through henge monuments.

These henge monuments display a marked internal variety and fulfilled a range of functions varying from cremation cemeteries to temples. The most spectacular of these monuments were in Wessex and contained massive timber buildings which were later replaced by stone circles. Stonehenge itself began life as a cremation cemetery long before it assumed its present form.

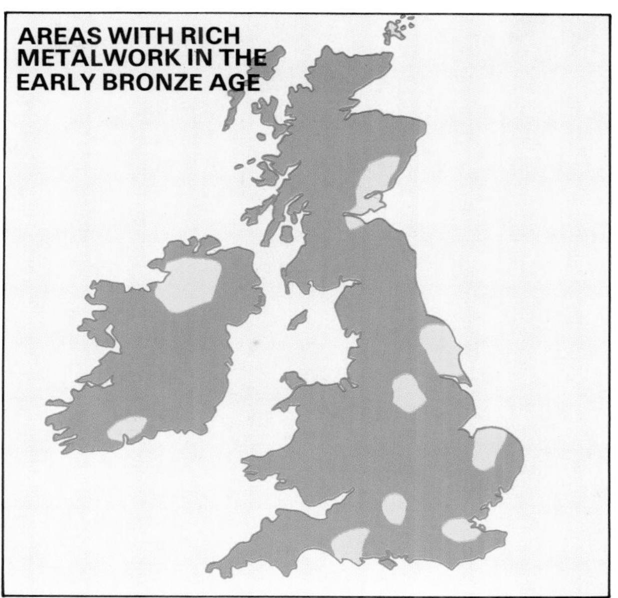

Avebury Rings, Wiltshire is one of the most important ceremonial centres of prehistoric Wessex.

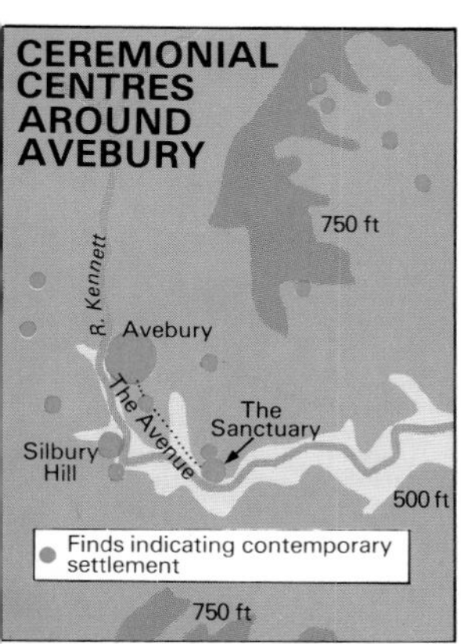

Avebury consists of at least four interconnected monuments. The henge monument at Avebury itself is connected to a smaller henge, known as the Sanctuary, by means of an avenue of paired stones. The fourth monument is Silbury Hill, the largest artificial mound of prehistoric Europe. The close relationship of these contemporary monuments with the River Kennett recalls that between Stonehenge and the Avon.

The main effect of the introduction of metals in the *Earlier Bronze Age* was to supply a further range of prestige objects and a more spectacular medium in which to display wealth and power. This applies as much to metal daggers as it does to the fine pottery of this phase. The essential political geography of earlier prehistoric Britain had been laid down in the later Neolithic, and the Bronze Age achievement was really an embellishment of this outline. Public works continued, with further phases of activity at ceremonial centres like Stonehenge and Avebury, and new sites were built, notably stone circles and alignments, some of which seem to have incorporated basic astronomical observations. The burial rite now emphasized individual graves, containing a great variety of exotic items, rather than communal tombs.

There are signs of considerable expansion. In one sense the growing political influence of certain areas with their ceremonial monuments and rich graves seems to have led to an expansion of exchange relations to take in the European mainland. At the same time such a lavish consumption of human energy and wealth seems to have been based on extensive food production and the clearance of larger segments of the landscape. By the middle of the second millenium BC Britain was receiving and supplying exotic goods which travelled over great distances before they were consumed in funerary ritual. The richest of these areas in Britain was in central southern England, the home of the so-called Wessex Culture.

The Age of Hill Forts, *c.* 1500BC–150BC

The map (below right) shows a series of particularly extensive Celtic field systems in relation to boundary earthworks and a major hill-fort, Segsbury. Note the way in which the fields incorporate, or are even aligned upon, Bronze Age barrows which were no longer in use. These systems seem to have developed in the first millenium BC. The white patches indicate areas where archaeological evidence is missing.

Hill-forts, ranging from defended farms to large-scale fortifications, were built in increasing numbers throughout the first millenium BC. Some of the local names for these sites are indicated. Raths and rounds were enclosed farms, brochs stone-built towers.

With the demise of the Wessex Culture came changes which were perhaps the most drastic to occur between the origins of agriculture and the immediate pre-Roman period. These, however, have only been given their due with the adoption of radio-carbon dating. Within the first part of this period, up to about 650 BC, four developments stand out: the intensification of overseas trade, particularly in weaponry; the development of fortifications, including the first building of hill-forts; a massive intensification of mixed farming, marked by surviving field systems and land boundaries; and the disappearance of the burial monuments and ceremonial centres characteristic of the previous centuries. All these features can be found from about 1300 BC. The period known as the 'Iron Age' really represents a development of these deep-rooted patterns.

There is little agreement on the reasons behind the collapse of the Wessex Culture, although climatic deterioration, wasteful farming methods and a shortage of imported materials may all have played a part. Certainly, this period sees a dramatic contrast with earlier developments, with prestigious sites like Stonehenge abandoned, the practice of barrow-building gradually discontinued, and a massive increase in the amount of human labour turned over to intensive farming. There are signs of reorganized mixed farming based on wheat, barley, cattle, and sheep. The latter increased in importance throughout the first millenium, as did winter-sown crops. The best evidence of expansion comes from surviving 'Celtic' field systems, which consist of regular networks of small rectilinear plots, sometimes expanding over very large areas. These are known quite widely but have been most extensively investigated on the chalk. Settlements were normally farmsteads rather than villages, although ther was a steady increase in the variety of settlement types Houses were usually circular, and grain for consumptio was kept in raised storehouses, while underground silo were used for seed corn. Livestock was overwintered in th open. There are signs of regional specialization, particularly in the Later Bronze Age, when the river gravels o southern England possessed a thriving weaving industry while areas of downland were converted to large tracts o pasture.

The last development corresponds with the intensification of exchange between different areas of the rura landscape and with the emergence of fortified centres. A few sites were directly integrated with a network o territorial boundaries, while others seem to have enclose an array of storehouses for surplus food. These early hill forts were undoubtedly impressive structures, with elaborate gateways, incorporating bridges and even bastions and reinforced with vast amounts of timber. A few of thes sites show an orderly arrangement of internal buildings suggesting an element of planning. These defended site gradually grew in number, dominating a rural hinterlan and perhaps acting as fortified villages. They may hav served as local markets and political centres. A basi division may be made between the larger sites and thos that were essentially defended farms, and the mor dispersed pattern in the West reflects the historica settlement pattern of this area. By the 1st century BC th larger sites could be regularly spaced across the landscape

With the initial reorganization of the landscape, ther was an increase in the exchange and consumption o metalwork, some of which was eventually destroyed o buried in a show of wealth. Much of this material, whic

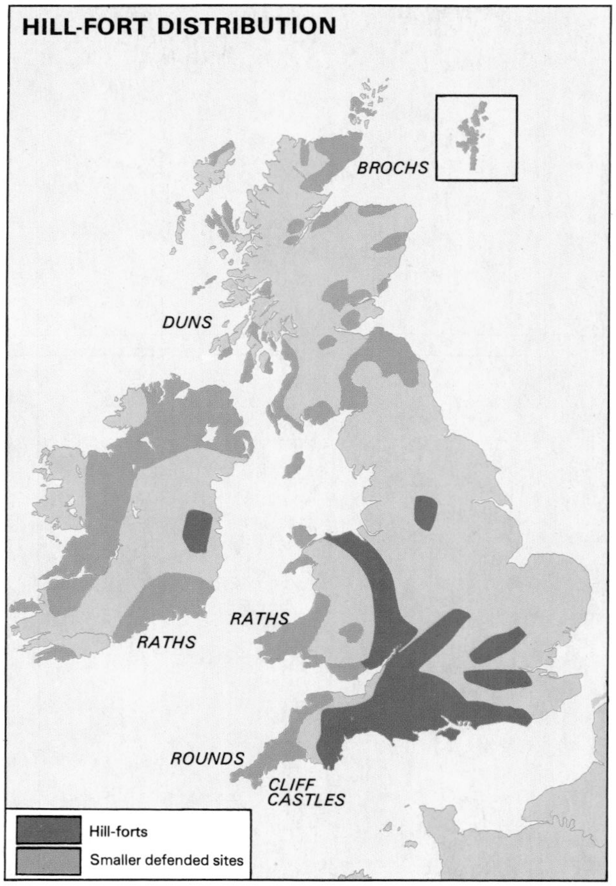

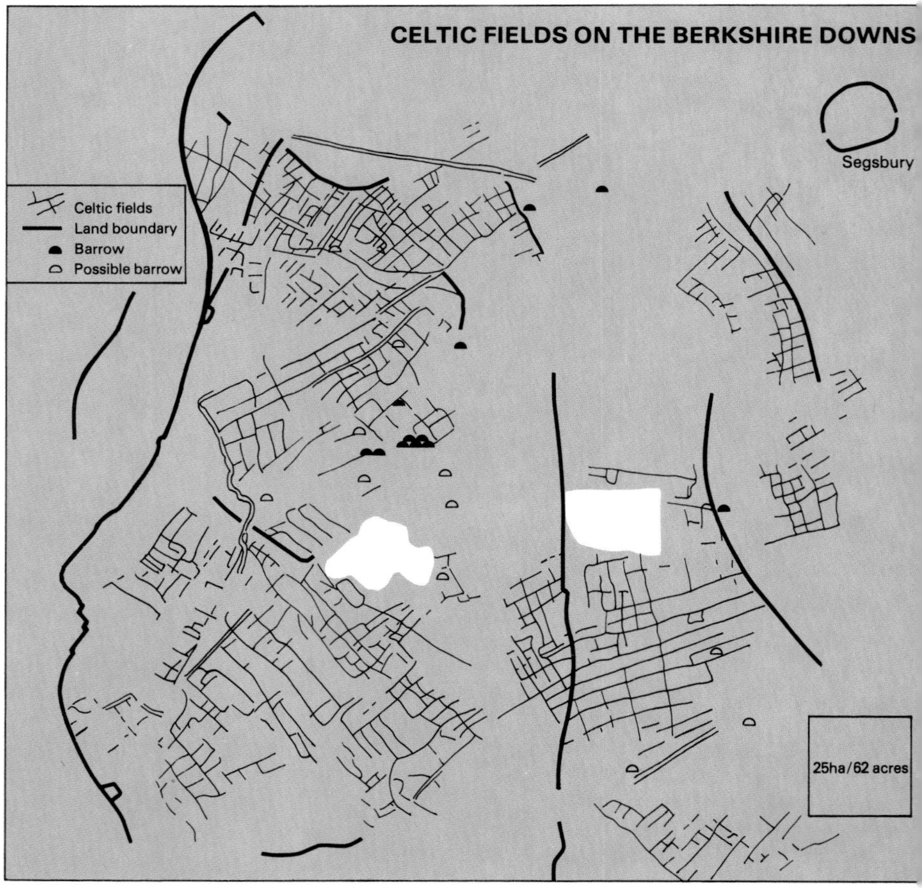

includes weapons and bronze vessels, was finally thrown into rivers. The contacts of communities in lowland Britain extended from Iberia to Scandinavia, but much of the wealth obtained from these areas was concentrated in the South East, where the quality of the agricultural land allowed the accumulation of an economic surplus. The Thames estuary was at the heart of this interchange. These patterns went on into the Iron Age. In both periods there is little evidence of elaborate burial rites, the main exception being the rich Iron Age burials of Yorkshire, which included dismantled chariots, and it is possible that much of the metalwork found in lowland England had been deposited in funerary ritual.

White Horse Hill above Uffington, Berkshire. The gigantic outline of a horse cut into the turf to show the chalky subsoil probably dates from Iron Age times. A prehistoric track – the Ridge Way – runs along the crest of the hill.

The Decline of Trade

It was in the sphere of long-distance exchange that the adoption of iron made its main impact on a society in which access to exotic goods may have played a part in establishing social position. The exchange networks of the Bronze Age necessarily reflect the difficulty of obtaining raw materials in areas which were remote from sources of copper and tin, notably the productive farmland of south-east England. It is small wonder that the adoption of iron, which can be found in most areas of Britain, began a gradual decline in the foreign contacts of British communities which was only halted with the expansion of the Roman Empire towards the end of the prehistoric period. The use of iron provided excellent agricultural tools, but at the same time it accompanied the fragmentation of the countryside into a series of independent units specializing in different forms of production. Political centralization could come about only with the renewal of long-distance trade.

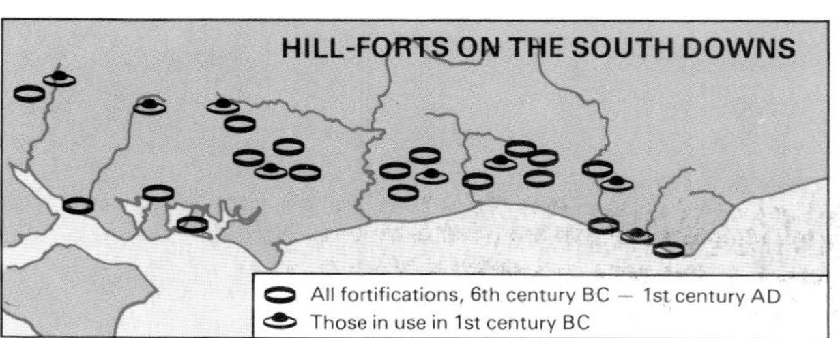

Towards the end of the first millenium BC, fortified sites came to be roughly spaced out across the landscape, each dominating a specific area.

Maiden Castle, Dorset. In the South-West, control remained centred on hill-forts like this. This traditional pattern reflected a degree of economic isolation brought about by the severing of links with Armorica – in contrast to the transformations wrought in the South-East by contact with Roman Gaul.

An early Iron Age crown.

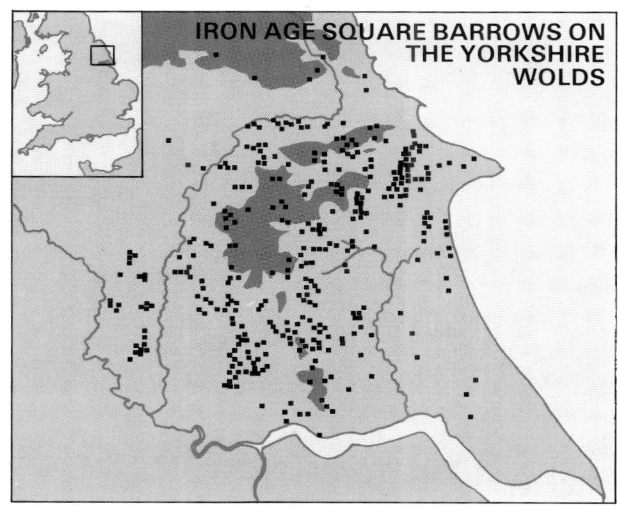

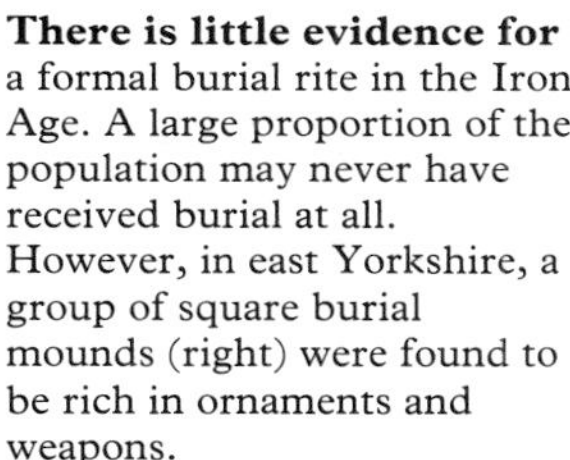

There is little evidence for a formal burial rite in the Iron Age. A large proportion of the population may never have received burial at all. However, in east Yorkshire, a group of square burial mounds (right) were found to be rich in ornaments and weapons.

Britain and Gaul in the late Iron Age, c.150BC–AD42

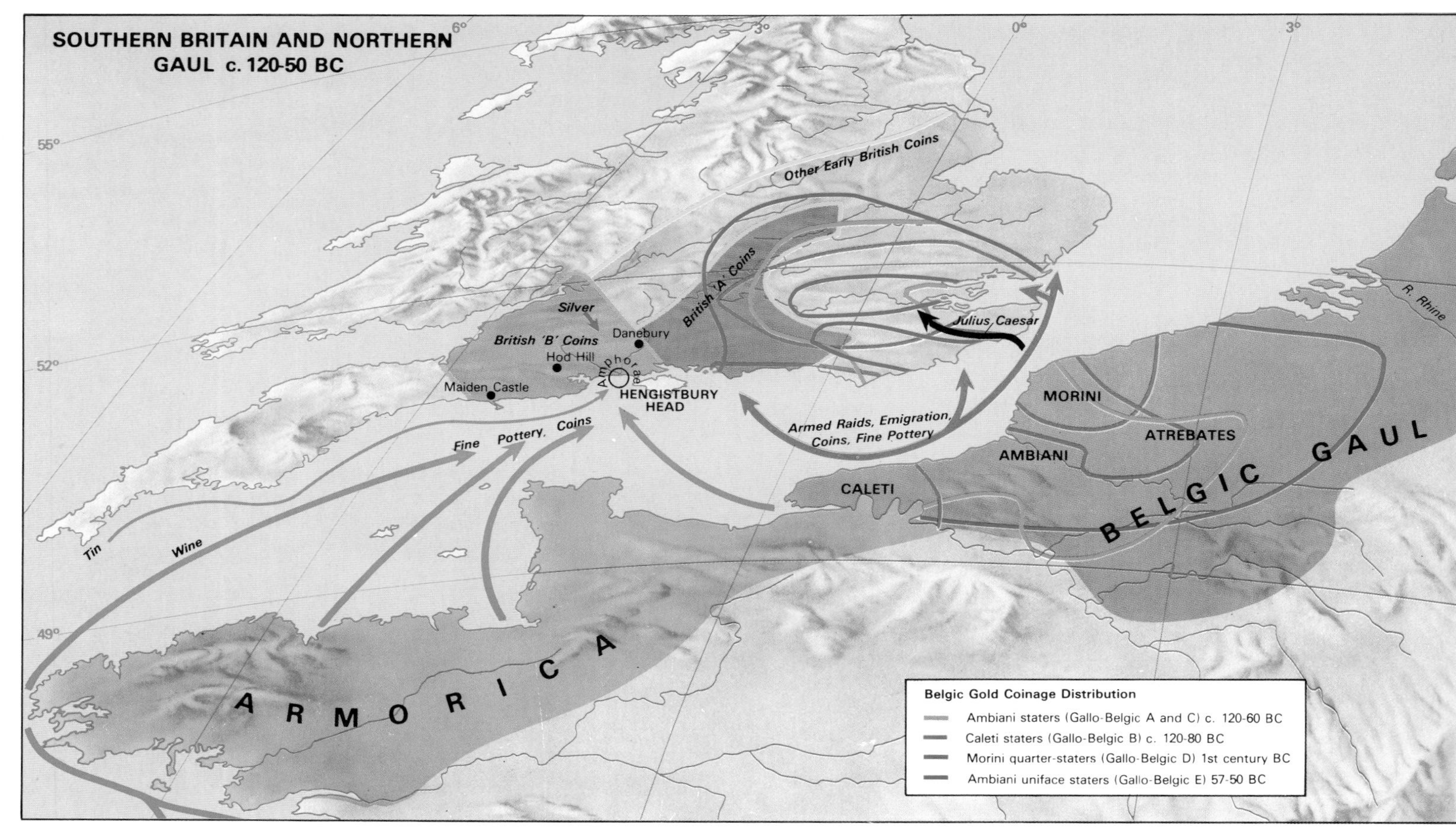

The two main systems of contact between Britain and Gaul. The South-West looked to western Gaul and Spain; the South-East was linked with the Belgic kingdoms of northern Gaul. Coin distributions reflect areas of Belgic political influence in Britain, especially in those which supplied mercenaries for service with Belgic nobles. Ambiani uniface gold staters were struck to meet the cost of the war with Caesar in northern Gaul. Belgic coins are largely absent from the territory of the non-Belgic Catuvellauni.

The political development of Britain in the late Iron Age was conditioned by its relation with the Continent, founded on its growing importance as a source of minerals and slaves for the markets in Gaul and the Roman world. The strongest political authorities were accordingly in southern Britain, rulers of small districts in command of at least one hill-fort at which ceremonial and administrative activities were conducted. Several such chiefs might constitute a cohesive regional group with a shared name, but with little marked internal hierarchical ranking.

There were two systems of contact between Britain and Gaul. A western system linked south-west Britain with Armorica, Spain and the Romans at Narbonne, while an eastern system linked south-east Britain with Belgic Gaul, eastern France and Massilia or Italy. By 100 BC the constraints of increasingly close relations with Gaul in both directions promoted a rising tide of violent political competition throughout south Britain, which issued in the formation of larger political units under more centralized authority.

In the South West this process was largely a domestic affair. Initially, many existing hill-forts had their defences improved. Subsequently, however, many were abandoned for a smaller number of conspicuous defended settlements commanding river crossings and coastal harbours. The key feature of the south-west zone between *c.*100 and 50 BC was the Durotrigian port of Hengistbury Head, where minerals such as tin from Cornwall and precious metals from the Mendips and Wales were assembled for manufacture, distribution and exchange with Armorican traders, from whom fine pottery, metalwork, and Italian wine were obtained. Regional centres like Danebury or Maiden Castle were important in the management of other districts in the hinterland.

At the same period, south-east Britain supplied Belgic Gaul with raw materials, slaves, and mercenary soldiers. It was also an area where ambitious Belgic nobles could make plundering raids, seize land for themselves and their followers, and acquire resident British communities as tributary subordinates. As a result, the rapid political expansion of the Belgic nobility between *c.*120 and 50 BC increasingly affected Britain, where Caesar says Belgic nobles came first to make war and then to settle, transferring their community names to their new dependencies. The Suessionian king Diviciacus was said to have had extensive domains in Britain in the 70s, and it was then that many British chiefs began to strike coinage on current Belgic models for distribution to their own subordinates. Belgic immigration principally affected the coastal zones of Kent, Essex and the Thames estuary, and north-west Hertfordshire, and probably involved rather small groups of nobles and warrior-peasants, whose political influence was disproportionately great.

The Roman conquest of Gaul in 58–50 BC led to the establishment of a permanent Roman military presence in Belgic Gaul and the Rhineland, and brought south-east Britain into direct contact with Roman markets for the first time. The alliances which Caesar formed during his raids in south-east Britain in 55 and 54, especially with the Trinovantes, were the basis on which subsequent relations between Britain and the Romans in Gaul were founded, and facilitated the importation of large numbers of wine amphorae into Essex and Hertfordshire. In *c.*15 BC Augustus recognized Tincommius of the Atrebates and Tasciovanus of the Catuvellauni as client kings, a status enjoyed by their successors until Claudius' conquest in AD 43. This period accordingly saw the formation of strongly centralized kingdoms in the south-east zone, and their increasing influence over remoter tribes in Britain. In the West, by contrast, Caesar's disruption of Armorican trade with Britain in 56 BC, and the absence of significant Roman economic activity in Armorica thereafter, meant that south-west Britain underwent no such transformation. Here, society retained a more traditional political structure centred on hill-forts such as Maiden Castle and Hod Hill.

In the south-eastern kingdoms, sprawling chiefly settlements or *oppida* were formed, often on new sites, defined by complex systems of linear earthworks, in which the political, ceremonial and economic activities of kings and district chiefs were focused. Prominent among them were Verulamium, Braughing, Camulodunum, Canterbury, Calleva, Winchester and one in the Chichester–Selsey area. Calleva, Verulamium and Camulodunum appear as mint-marks on coins.

The outstanding prestige of Camulodunum, and its associated trade with Gaul, is reflected in a succession of struggles among rulers of the Trinovantes and Catuvellauni for its control. The area finally fell to Cunobelinus, who achieved unprecedented dominance by uniting Catuvellauni and Trinovantes under his rule, and by encroaching on the Atrebates and parts of the Midlands and Kent. His southern contemporary and fellow client-king Verica, who had succeeded to the domains of Tincommius, seems to have lost Calleva to him, and retained only the territory of the Regni around Chichester. Cunobelinus governed these peripheral dependencies through subordinates, perhaps especially members of his own household: Andoco . . . in the Midlands, Epatticus and Caratacus at Calleva and Adminius in Kent.

The precarious unity of Cunobelinus' domains was broken on his death, when they were parted between his sons Togodumnus and Caratacus. At around the same time Verica fled his residual kingdom, and the period of ensuing political instability in south Britain provided Claudius with an opportunity to effect its annexation.

Traditional Celtic and Romano-Celtic coins. It is likely that Roman coin dies were among the gifts which Augustus presented to Tasciovanus and Tincommius in *c.*15 BC, in recognition of their new status as client-kings (right). Traditional Celtic designs were abandoned about this time (left). Subsequent coinage issued by these kings shows strong Roman influence.

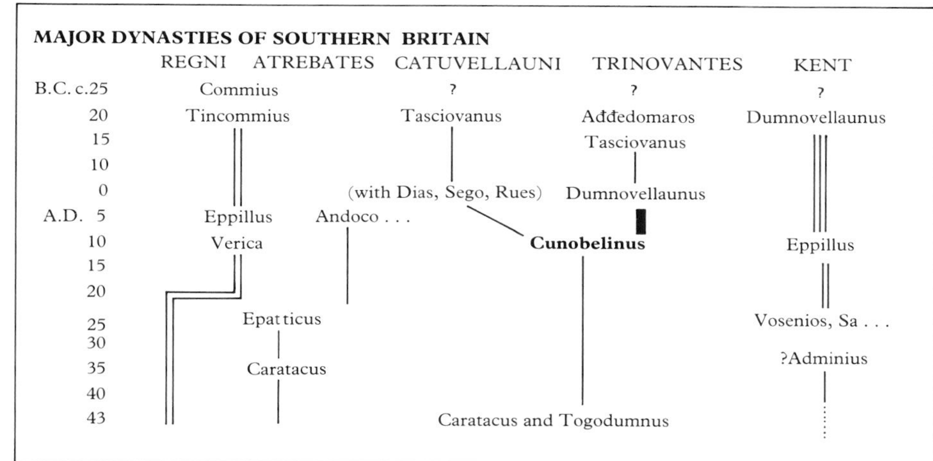

MAJOR DYNASTIES OF SOUTHERN BRITAIN

	REGNI ATREBATES	CATUVELLAUNI	TRINOVANTES	KENT
B.C. c.25	Commius	?	?	?
20	Tincommius	Tasciovanus	Ađđedomaros	Dumnovellaunus
15			Tasciovanus	
10				
0		(with Dias, Sego, Rues)	Dumnovellaunus	
A.D. 5	Eppillus	Andoco . . .		
10	Verica		Cunobelinus	Eppillus
15				
20				
25	Epatticus			Vosenios, Sa . . .
30				
35	Caratacus			?Adminius
40				
43		Caratacus and Togodumnus		

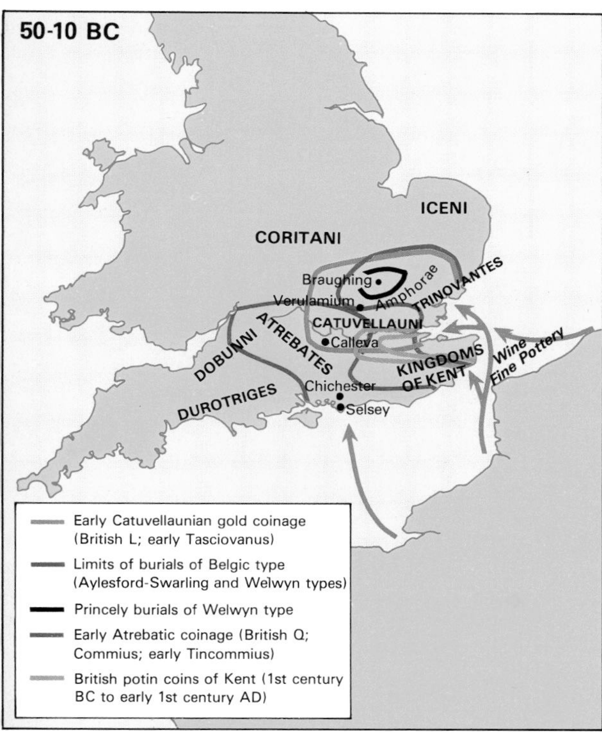

Left: Relations between southern Britain and Gaul after the Roman conquest of 58–50 BC. Roman policy was to enter into alliance with tribal rulers: as a result, powerful centralized kingdoms emerged in the South-East and trade flourished.

Right: Relations between the kingdoms of the South-East and the peripheral tribes. The major tribal groups outside the dominant kingdoms probably owed much of their wealth to their role in the procurement of slaves and raw materials. These were traded on to the stronger kingdoms, who in turn supplied them to the Romans at markets in Gaul.

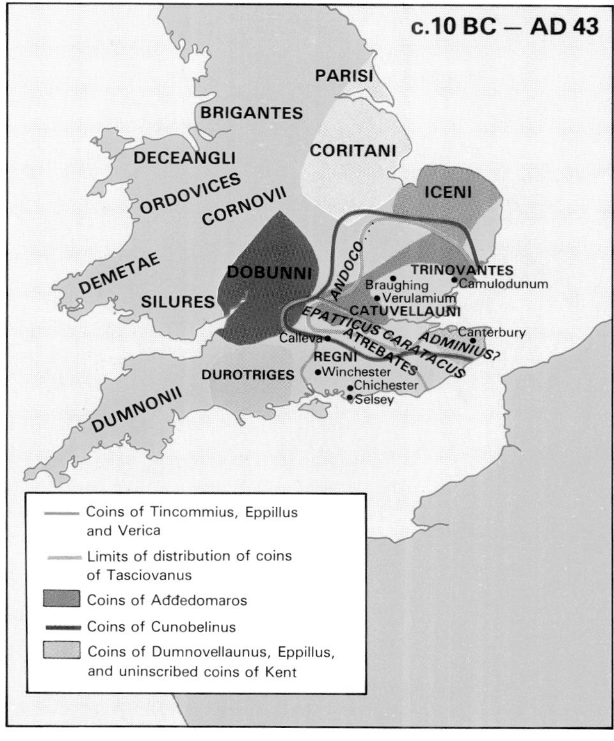

The Roman Conquest of Britain

The invasion of Britain in AD 43 was one of the most carefully planned and skilfully executed operations ever undertaken by the Roman army. In the summer of that year a large force of 40–50,000 men set out from the coast of Gaul towards Britain under the command of Aulus Plautius, recently governor of Pannonia on the Danube and one of the leading senators of the day. With him were four legions: Legio II Augusta from Argentoratum (Strasbourg) and commanded by Titus Flavius Vespasianus, the future emperor Vespasian, Legio XX Valeria from Novaesium (Neuss) and Legio XIV Gemina from Moguntiacum (Mainz), all three from the Rhine Command, while the remaining unit, Legio IX Hispana, seems to have accompanied Plautius from Pannonia. These regiments, all with experience of warfare in northern Europe, formed about half the invasion force, the rest being comprised of auxiliary units of lightly armed cavalry and infantry recruited mostly from the less civilized frontier provinces. The auxilia included units from Gaul, Thrace and Germany.

The timing and motivation for the invasion derived from several factors. In Britain, after many years of stable rule, the death of the powerful Catuvellaunian king Cunobelinus allowed his vast territories in south-east England to fall into the hands of his two headstrong and vehemently anti-Roman sons Togodumnus and Caratacus. In their lands south of the Thames, the Atrebates were among the first to feel the results of a new wave of Catuvellaunian expansion. The two tribes were traditional enemies and soon the aged king of the southern dynasty, Verica, was expelled from his last strongholds in Sussex and fled to Rome. Togodumnus and Caratacus now ruled all the most developed and wealthy areas of Britain. Confident of their ability to defy Rome with impunity, the Catuvellaunians demanded the extradition of the Atrebatic leader.

Despite their seemingly commanding position, the Britons' assumption that Rome could be intimidated proved misguided. Firstly, Verica was an ally of Rome, perhaps with the status of a client king, who could rely on the execution of treaty rights. Secondly, the Roman emperor Claudius had strong personal and political reasons for wanting to act against the new régime in Britain. Claudius, already in middle age when he assumed the purple in AD 41, had no military experience, having led a quiet literary life because of a physical deformity. However, he was the son of Drusus and brother of Germanicus, both distinguished generals, and was acutely aware of the need for military success to retain the loyalty of the army. In addition, the Rhine garrison had become dangerously large should a usurper ever come to power in the area, and to station troops along the Channel to defend against the aggressive Britons would have added to the problem. Accordingly, it was decided to use the surplus manpower as the backbone of an invasion force, to fulfil treaty obligations to an ally and finally to complete the work done by Julius Caesar nearly a century before.

The Invasion

Only one landing place of the Roman forces in AD 43 has been positively identified, at Richborough in Kent, where an enclosure of four hectares (10 acres), protected by a double ditch, was constructed as a beach-head. Somewhere nearby, a much larger camp of over 60 hectares (150 acres) must have existed to act as a collection point for the whole army, though this has yet to be found. Another possibility is that part of the invasion force landed in west Sussex to liberate the Atrebates. The Roman advance was only temporarily delayed by minor skirmishes in east Kent but

Bronze head of the Emperor Claudius (AD 41–54). Claudius visited Britain for only 16 days but in that time Camulodunum, the British capital of Colchester, was occupied and the surrender of the British tribes accepted.

Right: Tombstone of Marcus Favonius Facilis, from Colchester. It depicts a centurion of Legio XX Valeria who probably came to Britain as part of the invasion force in AD 43. It was probably thrown face downwards by Boudican forces in AD 60 – an act of desecration which, ironically, would have ensured its survival in an excellent state of preservation.

Below: The Claudian invasion of Britain, AD 43.

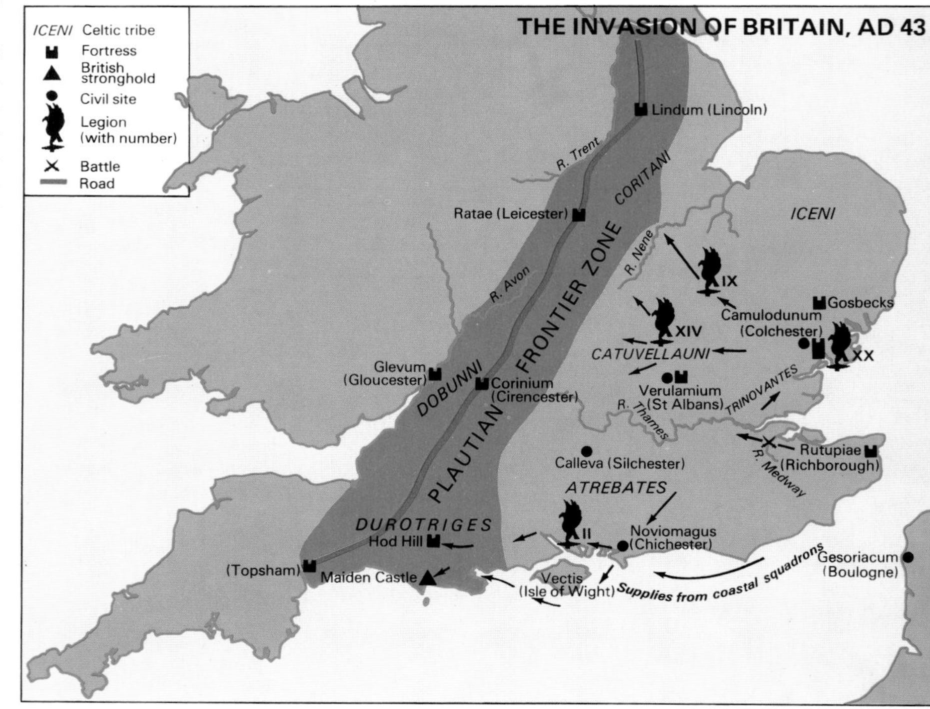

he British were soon encountered in strength at the rossing of the Medway. A two-day battle ensued which vas only won after hard fighting and the action of Batavian uxiliaries, from the Low Countries, who swam the river in ull armour to outflank the Britons and to gain a foothold on he other bank so that legionaries could be ferried across. 'ollowing this victory, the army advanced to the Thames vhere Aulus Plautius called a halt, to await the arrival of the mperor. By the time Claudius arrived, perhaps two nonths later, Togodumnus had been killed and Caratacus ad fled to Wales, from where he was to carry on resistance o Rome for several years. Claudius visited Britain for only 6 days, but in that time Camulodunum, the British capital, vas occupied and the surrender of the British accepted.

Now the conquest was resumed. Legio XX remained at Colchester while battle groups headed by Legio IX and egio XIV moved into the north and west Midlands espectively. In the South-West Legio II fought a fierce ampaign against Durotriges, centred on Dorset, and nother recalcitrant tribe. Vespasian captured the Isle of Vight and over 20 hill-forts, including Maiden Castle vhere a hastily dug cemetery of 28 graves, with one skeleton till having a Roman ballista bolt embedded in its back-one, testifies to the ferocity of the legionaries' assault.

In the wake of the conquest forces, permanent forts were uilt to control key points. Initially their positioning was etermined by concentrations of the native population – for xample, at Verulamium (St. Albans) and Gosbecks, near Colchester – but overall strategy and the protection of road ommunications were also important, for example, Corin-um (Cirencester). Such forts were frequently for a garrison f 500 auxiliaries, but could include a legionary component s at Hod Hill, Dorset. At Colchester a fortress was built to ouse Legio XX, while the other legions were at first split nto smaller groups (vexillations) and based at a series of esser fortresses, such as that at Longthorpe, near Peter-orough. Special attention was paid to areas behind the Trent and Severn, where a deep fortified zone stretching rom Lincolnshire to Devon marked the limit of the newly reated province established by Plautius.

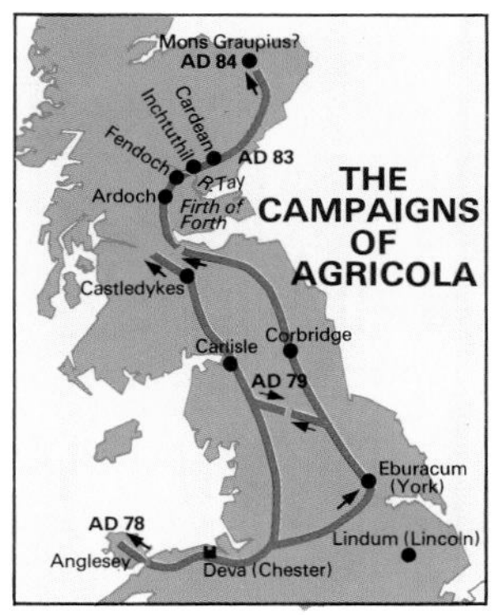

Following the recapture of Anglesey in AD 78, the governor, Cn. Julius Agricola, advanced northwards until he reached the Tay in 80. By 83 he had progressed as far north as the area of Aberdeen. Forts, including legionary fortresses at Inchtuthil, protected the Roman supply lines. In 84 the native Caledonians, under Calgacus, sustained a shattering defeat at Mons Graupius: 10,000 Caledonians were said to have perished for the loss of 360 Roman troops. Roman power in Britain was at its zenith.

Below left: Boudican remains at All Hallows, Kent.

The Boudican Revolt

The late 40s and 50s saw Roman attention turned towards Wales from where Caratacus was attacking the province. Despite his defeat and capture in AD 51, Wales remained a problem as a focus of resistance and a power-base for the Druids, who encouraged confrontation. The centre of their operations was Anglesey and it was there, when the Roman army was celebrating the capture of the island in AD 60, that news was received of the rebellion of Boudica in the South-East.

Since the invasion, two areas of lowland Britain had been granted the status of client kingdoms, being ruled by their own leaders and with a certain degree of autonomy, as a reward for co-operation with Rome. In the South, Verica's lands were ruled by his successor, Cogidubnus, and in East Anglia, the Iceni were ruled by Prasutagus. These lands were due to convert to direct Roman rule on the death of their kings but, when Prasutagus died, his wife Boudica resisted the officials sent to claim his property and she and her daughters were molested. In response, the Iceni rose in revolt and, accompanied by the disgruntled Trinovantes who had been angered by the activities of Roman colonists in Colchester, attacked nearby Roman settlements. A large part of the army was in Wales with the governor Suetonius Paullinus and the South-East was unprotected. A detachment of Legio IX, probably from Longthorpe, did try to relieve the beleaguered city of Colchester, only to be ambushed and almost totally annihilated. In the event, Colchester, London and Verulamium were destroyed, horrifying atrocities took place and thousands of Romans died. Momentarily it appeared as if the province would be lost, but Paullinus marshalled his troops and met the Boudican forces in battle, somewhere in the Midlands, probably in the vicinity of Mancetter, Warwickshire. The Roman historian Tacitus tells us that 80,000 Britons fell for the loss of only 400 Romans. Victory went to Paullinus, Boudica committed suicide and, following the battle, the Romans harried the rebel lands; the Iceni were crushed and security was once more regained.

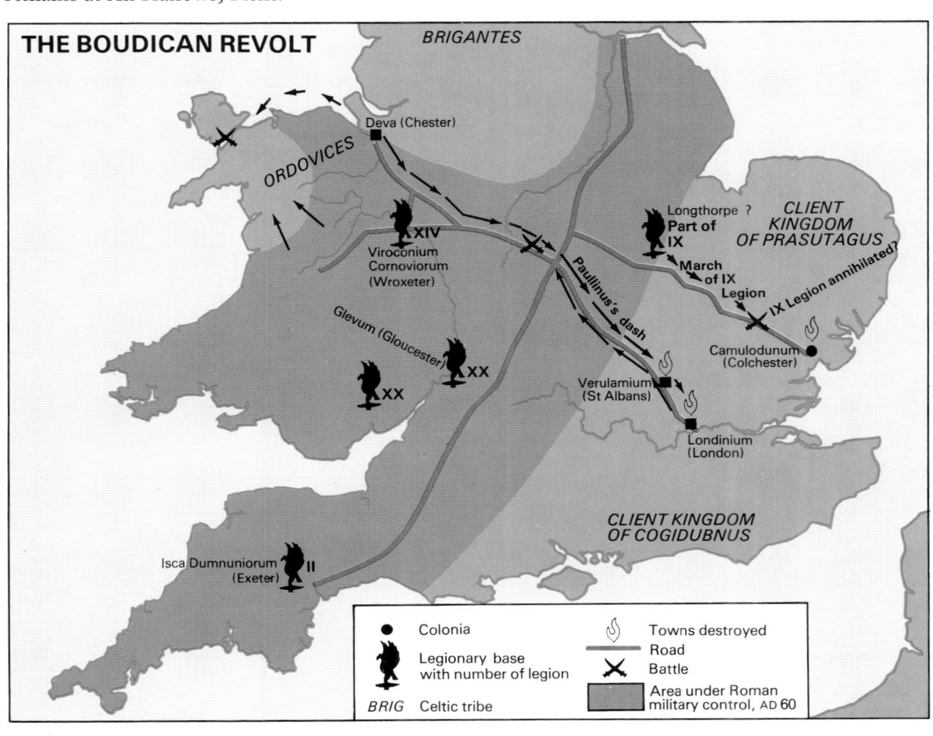

The Northern Frontier, AD85–211

The gains made in Scotland by Agricola were to be short-lived. In AD 85 trouble on the Danube frontier meant that one legion had to be transferred there, no doubt accompanied by several auxiliary regiments. This led inevitably to manpower shortages in the garrison of Britain. Accordingly, the forts north of the Clyde were abandoned; Inchtuthil was dismantled before it had been completed; the latest coin found there, probably minted in 87, gives a clue to the evacuation date. In southern Scotland many forts were strengthened and a network of occupation formulated that was to be maintained until the early 2nd century when, either by deliberate evacuation or by enemy action, many forts were burnt to the ground. Henceforth, *c.*105, a new frontier was established along the Stanegate, a road built by Agricola from Corbridge to Carlisle.

Hadrian's Wall

In 122 the Emperor Hadrian arrived in Britain, on a tour of the western provinces that had begun the previous year. His activities in Germany and elsewhere show him to have been very concerned with the effectiveness of Rome's frontiers. Accordingly, he ordered that the northern frontier in Britain be completely reorganized to include a physical barrier in the form of a continuous wall, to be built just north of the Stanegate.

This work, known today as Hadrian's Wall, was first planned to stretch from Bowness, on the southern shore of the Solway, eastwards to Newcastle, although at its east end it received an extension of a further four miles (6.4 km) to Wallsend, giving a total length of 80 Roman miles. As originally envisaged, the barrier was to consist of a wide masonry wall, 10 feet (3 m) in width, stretching from Newcastle to the River Irthing; from there to Bowness-on-Solway a turf wall was to be built, probably because of a shortage of limestone for mortar in this western sector. The Wall was to be equipped with small fortlets – milecastles – at every Roman mile, with two small turrets between each pair. The milecastles were of turf and timber on the turf wall and elsewhere of stone. They sometimes contained two small barracks, but frequently only one. The turrets were built of stone, even in the turf wall sector. In front of the entire work ran a large ditch, except in locations where precipitous cliffs or very hard rock made this impractical. If an emergency arose, large concentrations of troops could be quickly summoned from their forts on the nearby Stanegate.

Work began under the direction of the governor A. Platorius Nepos and progressed westwards from Newcastle. However, perhaps due to local native hostility, modifications had soon to be made to the original plan. One of these changes was a reduction in the width of the wall to just over 8 feet (*c.*2.5 m), possibly in order to speed up the progress of construction. Building work was being carried out in short lengths by detachments of the three British legions (II, VI and XX), and progress was somewhat unequal; the broad wall foundation had reached the Irthing, though the wall itself had only reached the North Tyne, when the order to change to the narrow wall was implemented. This was subsequently set on the wider foundation, where it existed, but the eastwards extension to Wallsend had a narrow foundation designed to support the new width of wall, a change undoubtedly based on the need for speed and economy. Another major alteration concerned itself with the tactical organization of the frontier and involved the transfer of entire regiments into new forts to be built on the Wall, so removing reliance on the old Stanegate system. The building of these 15 new garrison forts was accompanied by the establishment of a military zone behind the Wall, delineated on its southern side by an earthwork known as the *Vallum*, a ditch running between two parallel mounds of earth faced with turf. In addition, beyond Bowness-on-Solway, a further chain of milecastles and towers extended along the Cumberland coast; some of the features associated with this area may even pre-date Hadrian's Wall.

Several aspects of its original design reflect the purpose of the Wall. Although it formed a linear barrier to north-south travel, there was lavish provision of gateways, with a

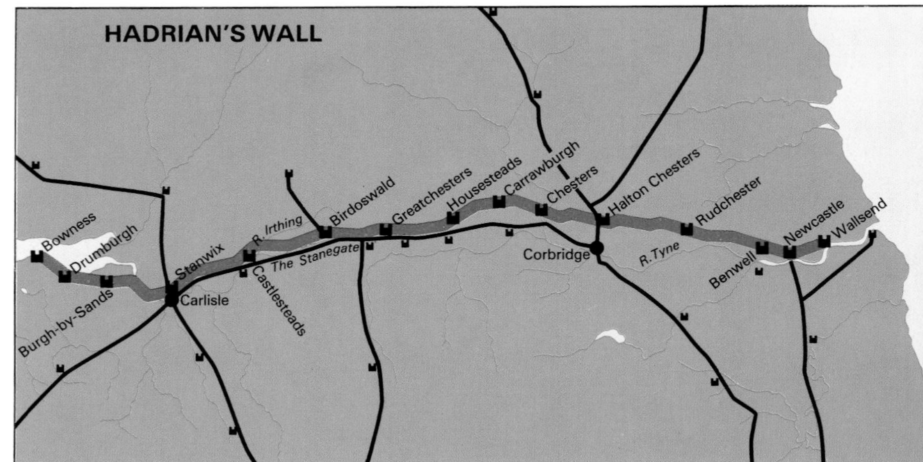

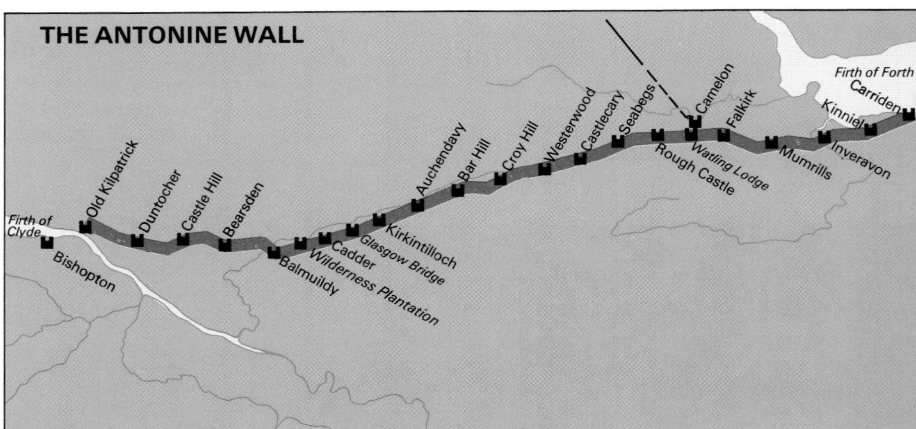

Distance slab from the Antonine Wall at Bearsden. The Antonine Wall was built in a series of lengths by the three British legions, the II, VI and XX. At the end of each section a Distance Slab was set up to record the work done by a particular legion – in this case the Legio XX Valeria Victrix.

Sestertius of the reign of Antoninus Pius (AD 138–161).

Hadrian's Wall – a surviving section.

An *aureus* of the Emperor Septimius Severus (AD 193–211). Severus and his son, Caracalla, led the last major Roman incursions north of Hadrian's Wall.

route through the Wall at each milecastle. Its main function was the control of movement of goods and peoples both north and south of the frontier. The Wall was, in fact, much too long to be efficiently manned as a defensive fighting platform: even when forts were built on the Wall, three of their gateways were usually situated to the north of the Wall to allow for rapid deployment of troops in advance of the frontier.

The Antonine Wall

The accession of Antoninus Pius in AD 138 led to a complete re-appraisal of the frontier situation in Britain. A new governor, Quintus Lollius Urbicus, was entrusted with the task of re-occupying southern Scotland and building a new wall across the Forth-Clyde isthmus. By 142 victory had been gained and Antoninus Pius hailed as *imperator*. As soon as lowland Scotland was secure, probably in the same year, work began on the new wall and was once again largely undertaken by the legions, although auxiliaries seem to have assisted in fort construction. In concept, it took its basic design from that of Hadrian's Wall, though for speed of construction the building material was to be turf rather than stone.

The new wall was 37 miles (60 km) long, roughly half the length of the Hadrianic frontier, and consisted of a turf rampart, perhaps 13 feet (4 m) high, and built on a heavy stone base 15 feet (4.6 m) wide – an improvement on Hadrian's turf wall – fronted by a wide berm and ditch. Behind the fortifications ran a road or military way for lateral communications. Like the modified Hadrianic barrier, the new wall was to have garrison forts attached. Originally there were six of these, spaced 8–9 miles (12.9–14.5 km) apart, and constructed before the wall, at Mumrills, Castlecary, Balmuildy, Old Kilpatrick and probably Bar Hill and Carriden. Between these forts there would appear to have been a series of small fortlets located at approximately one-mile (1.6 km) intervals and of similar plan and function to the Hadrian's Wall milecastles. Seven of the 'fortlets' are now known. However, before the work could be completed a change of plan occurred and more forts were added to the line, making 19 in all. Unlike the primary forts, many of the later additions were too small to hold complete regiments, and units must have been divided between the forts, which were now only just over 2 miles (3.2 km) apart.

In function the Antonine Wall was similar in character to its Hadrianic predecessor, built to control movement and to monitor events farther north. The initial advance into Scotland may have been undertaken to promote the personal prestige of Antoninus Pius, but the advantages of the new frontier, in direct proximity to the disturbed areas and in economy of length, are obvious. Archaeology has attested two main periods of occupation, and this agrees with epigraphic evidence. An inscription, dated to 158 and recording the rebuilding of the curtain wall on the Hadrianic barrier, must mark the end of the first Antonine Wall period, for it is unlikely that both walls would have been occupied at once. This withdrawal seems to have been temporary and the second occupation of the Antonine Wall began after only a short interval. However, *c.*163 it was abandoned again in favour of Hadrian's frontier, this time finally. The policies which had brought about the re-conquest of the lands around the Forth-Clyde isthmus were no longer of primary concern to Rome.

Punitive expeditions against the Scots by Severus himself in 208–9, and his son Caracalla in 210, were far-reaching. They followed disruption in the North at the end of the previous century. Two series of large temporary camps can be assigned to them. However, only two permanent forts, Carpow and Cramond, were built. No full-scale occupation of Scotland seems to have been contemplated.

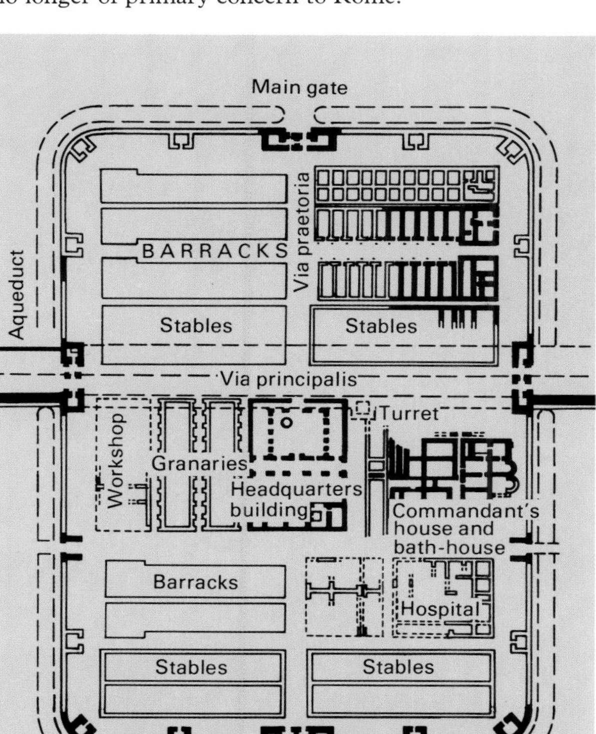

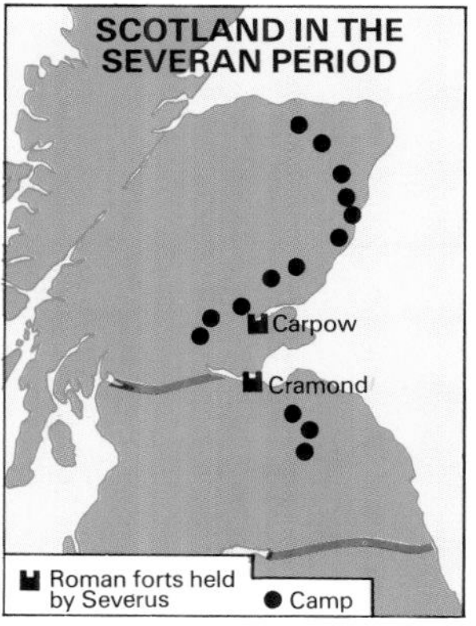

Left: Plan of the fort at Chesters on Hadrian's Wall. It is a typical fort of the 2nd century, rectangular and with rounded corners. The central range of buildings contained the HQ and commanding officer's quarters. Most of the rest of the fort area was taken up with barracks and stables.

Life in the Province

Britain, with its standing garrison of four, later three, legions and numerous auxiliary regiments, presented a considerable administrative challenge. Typically, those who were appointed to the office of governor were experienced men of the highest ability, schooled by years in previous legionary and governmental commands in the warlike provinces along the Danube which, like Britain, were viewed as frontier areas where the chance of action was high. Thus, right from the time of its incorporation into the Empire, Britain ranked as a consular province – a province governed by a senator who had already held the consulship.

As the emperor's appointed deputy the governor was responsible for both military and civil affairs. In Britain the frontiers frequently required close attention and this politico-military problem was further complicated during the 1st century by Rome's relations with the client kingdoms, which retained a certain autonomy under treaty arrangements with the government. Presumably the governor normally hoped to tackle his civil duties outside the campaigning season but, in practice, these responsibilities were ever present and certain domestic decisions concerning the populace must have been taken even when the governor was in the midst of war on the northern frontier. It was the governor's task to supervize the civil communities, to ensure that roads were built and properly maintained and that the imperial post functioned correctly. He was also responsible for military recruitment. In provincial legal matters he was the court of appeal and he exercised jurisdiction over all cases concerned with capital punishment or sentencing to the mines, or involving Roman citizens, although in criminal cases citizens could appeal directly to the emperor.

The only area in which the governor's decision was not supreme was in financial matters, a duty which was incumbent upon the *Procurator Augusti Britanniae*, who had the task of receiving revenue from taxes and imperial estates, paying the army and governmental representatives and managing the emperor's financial interests in the province. The best-known of procurators for Britain is C. Julius Classicianus, whose complaints to the emperor about the harsh treatment meted out to the Britons by the governor Suetonius Paullinus, after the Boudican rebellion, led to the governor's removal. Classicianus subsequently died while in office and his funerary monument, from London, can now be seen in the British Museum.

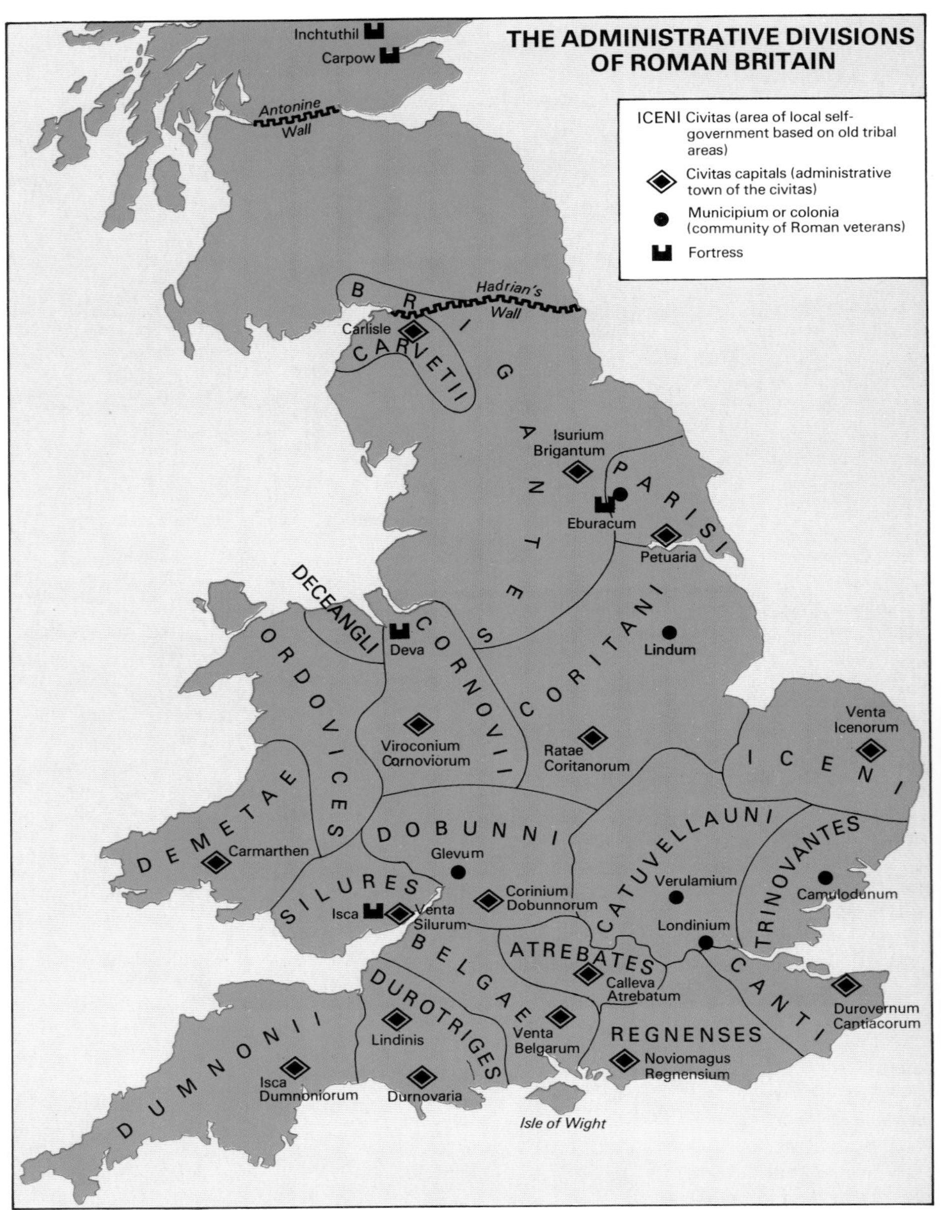

Most of Britain was divided into self-governing areas – the *civitates* – based largely on the tribal areas that existed immediately prior to the conquest in AD 43. The civitas capital was the administrative centre of each area. The *coloniae* and *municipia*, founded by Imperial charter, were self-governing communities of Latin or Roman citizens. They were intended to act as an example of Roman civilization to the non-citizen communities of the *civitates*.

Local Government

Military administration was relatively short-lived in south-east Britain, ending in many areas with either the removal of troops to dispositions farther north or west, or with the incorporation of a client kingdom into the province following the death of its ruler, although the death of Prasutagus of the Iceni, husband of Boudica, led to the reverse response. Gradually, a system of local self-government was introduced over large parts of the country, based on models already operating efficiently in Gaul. This was centred on self-governing communities of non-citizens – *civitates peregrinae*. In addition, Rome fostered the growth of self-governing towns of Latin or Roman citizens, whose architecture and life-style could serve as examples of Roman civilization to the native Britons.

In the 1st century three such communities of Roman veterans – *coloniae* – were established in Britain, partly to act as a civilizing influence but also to provide a military reserve. Colchester was the earliest, founded in AD 49, with Lincoln and Gloucester changing from legionary fortresses to *coloniae* later in the century. Each was surrounded by a *territorium* of land, administered by the town, as was the *municipium*, probably of Latin status, established at Verulamium in the 1st century. In these towns, founded by imperial charter, government was loosely modelled on the constitution of Rome. The ruling body, the *ordo*, a council of up to a hundred members – *decuriones* – had at its head either two or three pairs of executive officers. The senior pair, the *duoviri iuridicundo*, took charge of the law courts, and one or other would act as chairman of the *ordo*. Below them, two *aediles* had responsibility for the upkeep of public buildings and roads, aqueducts, water distribution systems and sewers. Some towns also had a third pair of officers, *quaestores*, who were responsible to the senior magistrates for financial affairs. Another group, also important in the municipal hierarchy, were the six priests – *seviri Augustales* – who conducted the ceremonies connected with the imperial cult. If a man came from one of the *coloniae* or a *municipium* then his legal place of origin was the town where his family was registered, but for most people in Britain in the 1st and 2nd centuries, who were not citizens, the situation was different; their legal *origo* was related to the tribal area from whence they came, rather than the area's main town.

Most of Britain was divided into *civitates* or areas of local self-government based largely on the old late Iron Age tribal areas. At the centre of the administration of each *civitas* was a town, the civitas capital. Little is known about the administrative organization of these units in Britain, but the existence of the basic institutions such as the *ordo* and its executive officers may be presumed from finds such as the inscription found at Brough-on-Humber, relating to M. Ulpius Januarius, who is recorded as being an aedile, probably of the civitas of the Parisi, the local tribe. The names of several *civitates* are known from inscriptions which include a tribal suffix e.g. *civitas Cornoviorum, civitas Dobunnorum* with their capitals respectively at Wroxeter and Cirencester. Within these tribal areas each town ranked as a *vicus*, with a certain measure of self-government, and the larger centres may have been formed of collections of *vici*, resulting in self-governing districts within towns. For administrative reasons even the countryside was divided up into areas known as *pagi*, but little evidence remains pertaining to their function and organization.

In the administrative centres of the province urban life developed rapidly, and in the larger towns series of straight streets were laid out running both parallel and at right angles to one another to form rectangular *insulae* of building land in the interstices. Public buildings, shops and private houses were soon erected, at first in wood, but by the 2nd century often in stone. By this time many buildings contained fine mosaic floors and painted walls reflecting the wealth of the inhabitants.

Religion

Roman state religion was firmly connected to the worship of the classical pantheon, headed by Jupiter, and the veneration of Rome and the imperial *numen*, the emperor's guiding spirit. However, in late Roman Britain new trends were becoming apparent with increased participation in the rituals of mystic religions of the Greek and Persian East. Prominent among these was the cult of Mithras, popular with the upper echelons of the army and represented by several temples in northern Britain. The best preserved is that at Carrawburgh on Hadrian's Wall, which appears to have been destroyed by Christians in the late 4th century. Another example, in London, has provided several fine examples of mithraic sculptural representations. Besides these imported beliefs, the worship of many native Celtic-derived deities flourished, such as is shown by the large temple complex dedicated to the god Nodens at Lydney, Gloucestershire.

Most important among the eastern religions was Christianity. Its influence within the Empire had been felt long before the 4th century, but it was of minor importance in Britain until the conversion of the Emperor Constantine in 312 led to the encouragement of the faith by the central government and halted the persecutions of Christians. Evidence for early Christianity in Britain is scarce, although one of the most famous British martyrs, St Alban, dates to the early 3rd century. For the later period archaeological finds have revealed more, with the discovery of a small church at Silchester in Hampshire, mosaic pavements displaying Christian symbols at Frampton and Hinton St Mary, Dorset, a 'house church' at the villa at Lullingstone and numerous Christian chi-rho symbols on a variety of artefacts. With an ever increasing following, it is not surprising that three bishops from Britain attended the religious Council of Arles in 314 and that more British bishops were present at the Council of Ariminum in 359.

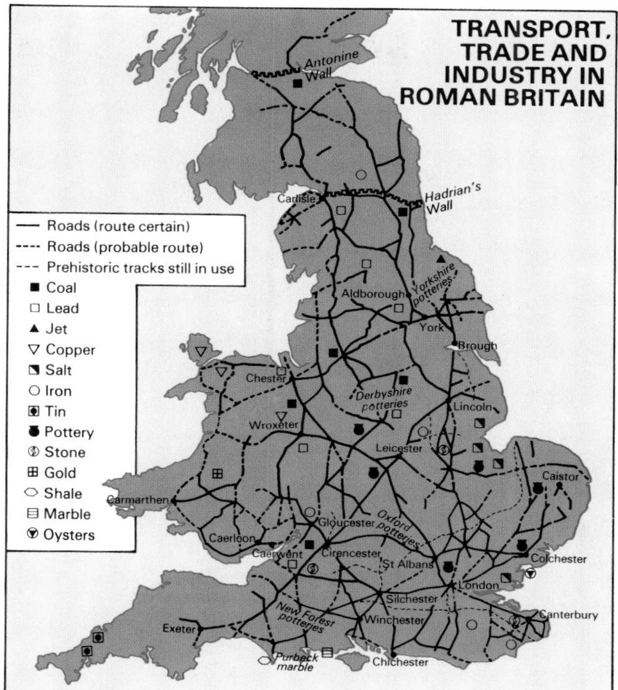

In the wake of the conquest forces trade and industry, in particular mining, began to flourish. Most production was on a small scale and with a localized distribution, but some concerns traded their goods over long distances – lead from British mines travelled to Rome and pottery produced in Dorset was used in large quantities in many areas of the country as far north as the Antonine wall. Many goods were transported by water, but undoubtedly the new system of Roman roads was a great incentive to commerce. Over 11,900 km of Roman roads are known in Britain, many dating to the first century.

A section of Roman road in Yorkshire. Planned by military engineers and built by soldiers, each road was laid along the most direct route possible. The road surface was built up in layers of gravel, flint and broken stones. Only a few roads were paved.

Mithras sacrificing a bull. From the Roman temple of Mithras at Walbrook, London. The cult of Mithras was popular with the upper echelons of the army.

Silchester, Hampshire was a typical Romano-British planned town. At the heart of any self-governing Roman community was the forum and basilica. Their construction was the physical manifestation of the community's existence. The forum was a large rectangular courtyard for public assemblies and trading, surrounded on three sides by shops and offices. The basilica, forming the fourth side, was a long, aisled hall, used for the administration of local government and justice.

The Last Century of Roman Britain

By the 4th century Britain had assumed a very different character from that of the early years of Roman rule. The spread of Roman culture and mass-produced consumer goods, such as pottery, had helped to obscure regional differences, and the grant of universal citizenship to all freeborn men within the Empire, in the early 3rd century, had even clouded social distinctions. In the countryside the early 4th century was a time of unrivalled prosperity, witnessing the refurbishing and elaboration of villa houses in many areas of southern Britain. Several theories have been proposed to account for this display of rural wealth, including the influx of foreign capitalists from less secure areas in Gaul and the Rhineland. Indeed, 4th-century Britain was a much safer place than many areas of the Continent, but no single satisfactory explanation for the 'golden age of the villa' covers all the possibilities.

In any event, the villa estates represented by opulent houses at such sites as Chedworth, Gloucestershire and Bignor, Sussex, were the properties of wealthy landowners well versed in the ways of Mediterranean civilization, whose lifestyles reflect the permeation and acceptance of Latin culture in the province. This assimilation can be readily observed in the styles of decoration of the villa buildings themselves, where walls were painted in typical Mediterranean manner and the floor mosaics display scenes based on Virgil or from Greek mythology. So numerous are the mosaics from the first half of the 4th century that four 'mosaic schools' have been identified, based on Cirencester, Dorchester, Brough-on-Humber and Chesterton, all serving their respective urban centres and environs.

Late Roman Defences

The late 3rd century was a time of mounting unrest in many parts of the Empire due to barbarian incursions, rampant monetary inflation and increasing bureaucratic interference. In 276 Franks and Alemanni crossed into the Empire and ravaged dozens of cities in Gaul, where most urban centres were completely unprotected. It was but one of many invasions which were to undermine the economy and discourage the once prosperous interaction between town and country in the western Empire, as rural areas became less secure. Britain, however, remained wealthy and free from major barbarian incursions until the late 4th century, largely because of her defences.

In Britain, most large towns had received stone defences in the 3rd century while, in the North, Hadrian's Wall and many of the forts in the Pennines were fully maintained to discourage attacks from Scotland. Around the coasts of Wales and north-west England forts were built to guard against raiders from Ireland, and along the south and east coasts further fortifications were constructed to defend the South East against Saxon attacks from across the North Sea. These forts were part of a command covering both sides of the English Channel, known as the Saxon Shore system and supervised from Boulogne. The earliest Saxon Shore forts, Reculver, Kent, and Brancaster, Norfolk, both dateable to the 3rd century, were built in traditional army style – rectangular, with rounded corners. Later additions to the system were constructed with thick, free-standing walls with towers projecting forward, in keeping with a new style of urban defences developed in Gaul.

Politically, late Roman Britain witnessed many upheavals. Late in 286 or early the following year, Carausius, commander of Classis Britannica, the British fleet, was accused of corrupt practices and his execution was ordered by Rome. He seized Britain and declared himself emperor. At first he also controlled northern Gaul, but in 293 the last of these Gallic possessions, Boulogne, was lost to a force

Reconstruction of a Roman villa at Rockbourne, Hampshire.

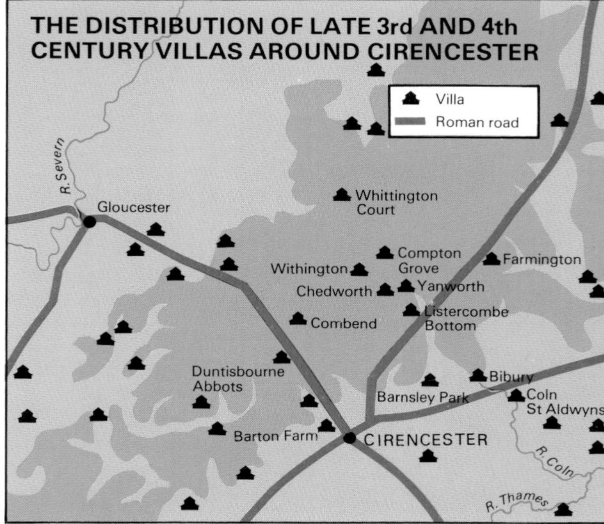

Right: Town and country. Roman villas around Cirencester in the late 3rd and 4th centuries. Here, as in many parts of Roman Britain, the dense distribution of villas around an urban centre indicates rural prosperity and the importance of local market towns.

under the Roman Caesar Constantius. Shortly afterwards Carausius was murdered by his finance minister Allectus who continued to rule Britain until 296 when he was killed in a battle with a Roman invasion force.

Once more part of the Empire, Britain received a further visit from Constantius in 305, when several forts in the North appear to have been refurbished. Later, in the winter of 342–3, the Emperor Constans arrived in Britain and some emergency must be suspected, as mid-winter would normally be considered inappropriate for crossing the Channel. A coin of Constans discovered at the Saxon Shore fort of Pevensey was found in a context which suggests that he may have been responsible for the fort being built. Also the addition of projecting towers to the defensive circuits of many towns may have been started on his instructions. These towers, used as artillery platforms and to increase the range of fire of the defenders, used to be considered as the work of Count Theodosius after 367–8, but several can now be shown to have been in use by 360 or earlier.

In 367 disaster struck when the Picts, Scots and Allacotti, working in concert, invaded northern Britain. The Roman commander in the North was captured and the Count of the Saxon Shore was killed. General confusion led to desertions from the army and the appearance of bands of

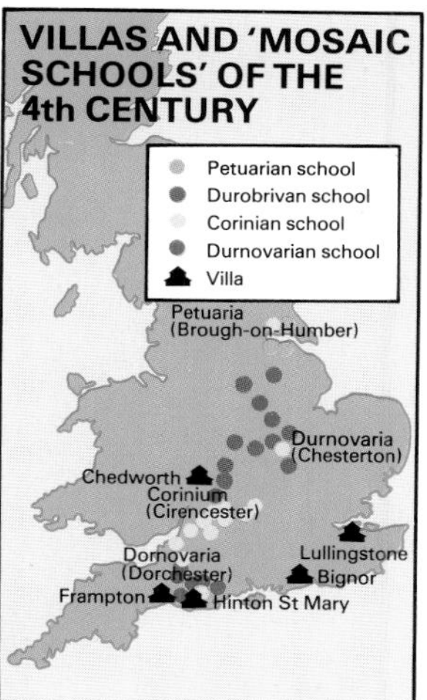

Far left: Mosaic floor from the 4th century Roman villa at Lullingstone, Kent. Its subject – the Greek hero Bellerophon with the four Seasons – is typical of the Mediterranean culture exported by Rome and assimilated by its provinces.

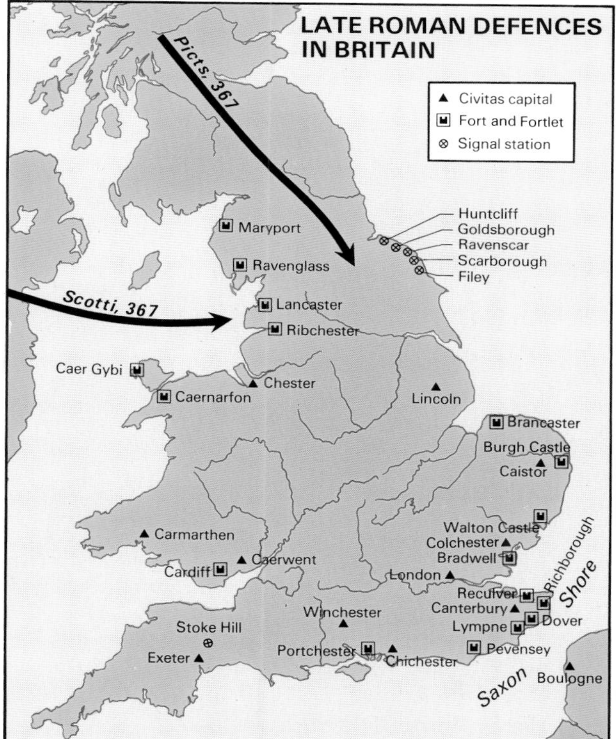

Far left: In 197, Septimus Severus divided Britain into two, Upper and Lower Britain. During the reign of Diocletian (286–305), Lower Britain, situated in the north of Britain, was divided into Britannia Secunda and Flavia Caesariensis; in the south, Upper Britain was reorganized into Britannia Prima and Maxima Caesariensis. In the north the capital of one of these new provinces was York and the other may have been Lincoln; of the southern provinces, Britannia Prima seems to have had its capital at Cirencester, and Maxima Caesariensis was administered from London. Each of these new provinces had its own governor who was responsible to the Emperor's representative, the *vicarius*, who had his staff and office in London.

Left: From the late 3rd century barbarian peoples exerted increasing pressure in the Empire. Britain, with its strong defences, remained safe from barbarian attacks until the late 4th century.

looters throughout the country. The Roman general Count Theodosius was dispatched from the Continent and was eventually able to restore order and repair defences. However, little evidence exists of destruction in the towns of Britain at this time and most must already have been well defended. In 383 Magnus Maximus, a commander in Britain possibly flushed with success gained in a campaign against the Picts in the previous year, declared himself emperor and withdrew a large part of the army of Britain to assist his Continental ambitions. In 398 another serious invasion occurred and the Roman general Stilicho was sent to restore the situation. This was probably the last time that the central government sent a force to Britain to deal with barbarian incursions. In 406 the troops of Britain once again elected their own emperor, named Marcus, who was deposed the following year and replaced by Gratian. However, a fresh invasion of barbarians from across the Rhine now threatened to cut Britain's communications with Rome; Gratian was deposed and a soldier, Constantine, elevated in his place, was entrusted with restoring the situation. To do this, Constantine removed the remainder of the garrison of Britain and crossed to Gaul.

In 408, the British, now defenceless, faced a serious barbarian invasion. Realizing that no help would come from Rome, the Britons expelled the Roman officials from the country and, establishing government on their own authority, organized forces with which to expel the invaders. In effect, from that time Britain ceased to be a part of the Roman Empire and faced the threat of the invading Saxons alone. In 410 the Emperor Honorius, acknowledging the position, wrote to the cities of Britain instructing them to look to their own defence.

Chapter Two
THE MAKING OF ENGLAND, c.400-1066 AD

When the Roman legions withdrew, Britain was settled and gradually conquered by a new people: the English. For more than five hundred years the native Britons (Celts) were hemmed in the north and west while the English kept the most prosperous parts of this island for themselves. Theirs was a vital and a lasting achievement – the establishment of the English language, of the Christian English Church and of the unification of England under one king.

Map of England, Scotland and Wales attributed to the English historian Matthew Paris.

The Coming of the English

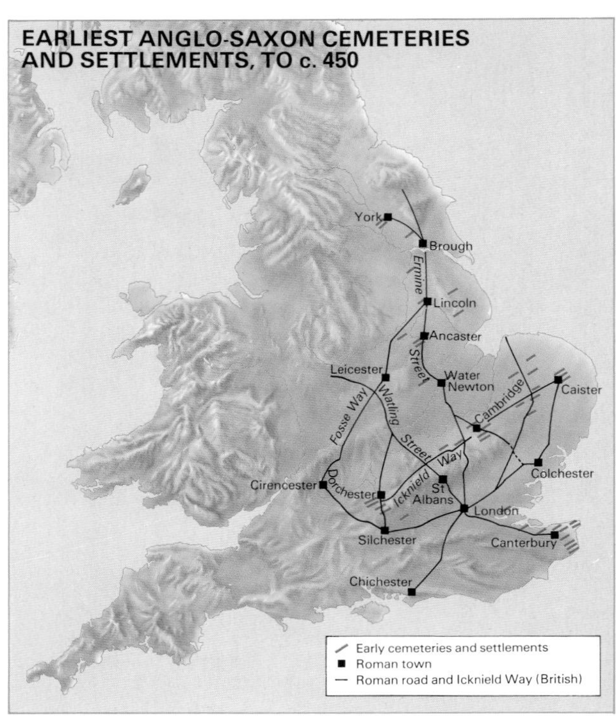

The distribution of Anglo-Saxon cemeteries and settlements *c*.450 suggests that the earliest Anglo-Saxon communities in Britain were those of mercenaries serving in the Roman army.

Far right: Bronze plaque with enamelled ornament from the ship burial at Sutton Hoo, Suffolk. The tomb, which may be that of an East Anglian king, reveals strong links in style and practice with the warrior culture of Sweden.

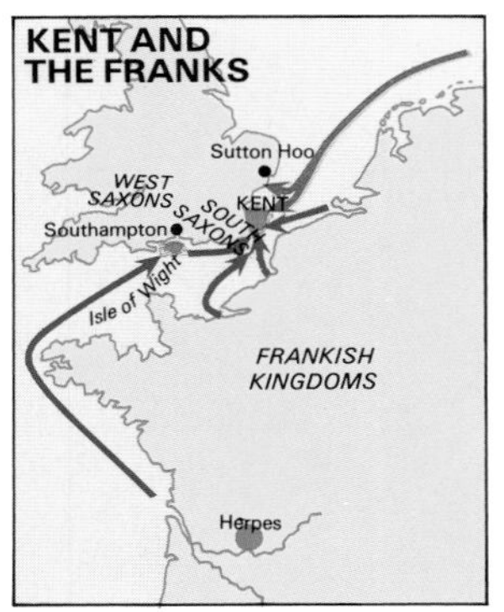

Relations between Kent and the Frankish kingdoms. The Kentish monopoly on trade with the Continent was finally broken when the West Saxons established a trading post at Southampton in the late 7th century.

The 5th century 'coming of the Saxons' was the beginning of a migration of peoples from Scandinavia and northern Germany to eastern Britain. We call these peoples the Anglo-Saxons, and they spoke Old English, a Germanic language ancestral to our own speech. The written sources describing their arrival are few and were recorded either far away in the Mediterranean area, or long after the event by Anglo-Saxon and British commentators. There have been attempts to reconstruct the process of Anglo-Saxon settlement in Britain from the many village names and other place-names of Old English origin which have survived to the present day. But place-name scholars are now less confident of their ability to date particular name forms to an early period of settlement. For this reason we need to rely more on the archaeological evidence from the settlements in which the Anglo-Saxons lived and the cemeteries in which they were buried, either unburnt, fully-dressed and accompanied by status symbols, or burnt and placed in a container.

A small number of Anglo-Saxons were living in Britain before the withdrawal of the Roman field army in AD 408. All of them appear to have been serving in the army and in most cases were probably accompanied by their wives. Such men may have fought against the Saxon pirates, who raided the eastern and southern coasts of Britain from the 3rd century onwards. The British authorities, threatened by invasions from the Picts in the first half of the 5th century, apparently hired Saxon mercenaries to replace the absent Roman army. The distribution of the earliest Anglo-Saxon cemeteries in eastern Britain from York to Kent makes more sense as the disposition of mercenaries accompanied by their families than as territories seized by sea invaders. They are located so as to guard the entry points of the Humber, the Wash and the Thames from coastal invasion, with defence in depth extending from the Wash to the Thames Valley around Oxford. The Picts were never again to be a threat, but the mercenaries stayed and, realizing their strength, rebelled. After this revolt came the sea-borne migrations of peoples continuing into the 6th century.

The Anglo-Saxon Bede, writing in the 8th century describes his ancestors as belonging to three groups: th Angles, Saxons and Jutes. His belief that the Anglians wer the principal settlers of the East and North (East Angli east Midlands and Northumbria), the Saxons of the Sout of Britain (Essex, Sussex, Middlesex and Wessex) and th Jutes the settlers of east Kent, the Isle of Wight an Hampshire, finds some support in the archaeology. Th *cruciform* brooch is the dominant type of female jewellery i the areas of north Germany and Scandinavia from whic the Angles and Jutes came, while the *saucer brooch* i associated with the Saxons. Bede's threefold division of th pattern of settlement is an oversimplification, as the overla between the distributions of the two brooch types indicates and it also ignores the contribution of other Germanic speaking peoples, such as the Franks, to the Anglo-Saxo settlement.

Kent's Cross-Channel Links

The *Anglo-Saxon Chronicle* of the 9th century gives a outline of the conquest of the south coast regions in the 5t century, beginning with Kent, followed by Sussex and the Hampshire, and the archaeological evidence agrees wit this. The westward coastal movement is checked *c*. 500, fo Dorset has no cemeteries before the later 6th century, and i is tempting to link this to the British victory at Moun Badon, which has been located by some at Badbury Ring (Dorset). Kent was the first Anglo-Saxon kingdom t accept Christianity from Augustine's mission in 597. Th missionaries from Rome did not choose Kent simpl because it provided the shortest sea crossing, but becaus its king was married to a Christian, the Frankish princes Bertha.

The strong influence of Frankish fashions on jewellery i Kent throughout the 6th and 7th centuries suggests tha this diplomatic link was nothing new. Compared to thei Saxon neighbours the people of east Kent were buried wit conspicuous wealth, and the distributions of objects i England imported from the Continent imply that trad between the Anglo-Saxons and the Franks was channelle

Above: Frankish bronze buckle and belt fitting, 6th century, from Herpes, Charente.

Below: Distribution of cruciform and saucer brooches in the 5th and early 6th centuries. The cruciform pattern was associated with the Angles and Jutes, the saucer pattern with the Saxons.

Below right: Anglo-Saxon cemeteries and settlements by the mid-6th century. The initial Anglo-Saxon settlement was reinforced by a series of sea-borne migrations. Slowly, the line of occupation moved westwards.

through Kent. A large collection of Kentish jewellery in the Frankish cemetery at Herpes in South-West France may imply a special connection between the wine-growing Saintonge region and Kent. The cemetery of Chessell Down on the Isle of Wight contains Kentish-made jewellery, and it seems probable that Kent was able to enforce its monopoly of cross-Channel trade by excluding the South Saxons and the West Saxons. The monopoly was certainly broken before the end of the 7th century when King Ine of the West Saxons established an important trading post at Southampton. Kent had retained its contacts with Scandinavia through the 6th century, however, as witnessed by the adoption of animal art styles developed by Scandinavian metalsmiths. Similarly, the design of the various artefacts discovered in the early 7th century Sutton Hoo ship burial in Suffolk, a burial possibly that of an East Anglian king, illustrates contact between eastern England and Sweden.

Farther north, other east coast kingdoms, Lindsey, Deira and Bernicia, gradually emerged from a multitude of Anglian settlements. According to later tradition the Bernician stronghold of Bamburgh was established in 547 but this date, uncertain as it is, remains almost the only 'fixed point' in an otherwise extremely obscure process.

As the Anglo-Saxons pushed slowly westwards, so the native British either gave ground or submitted to the newcomers. Roman Britain vanished; its place was taken by Anglo-Saxon England and British Wales.

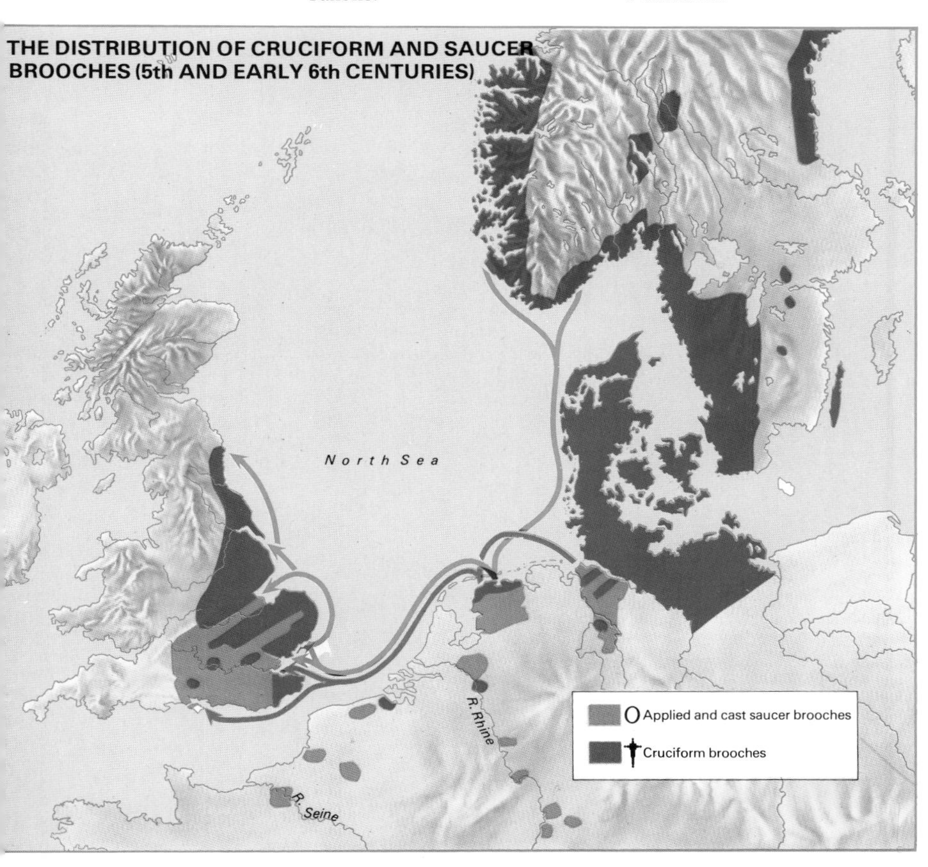

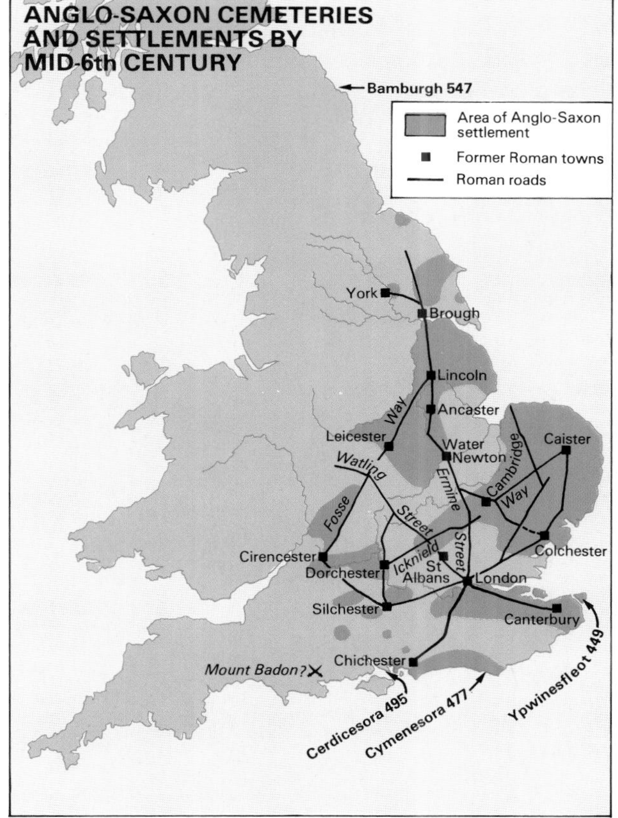

The Conversion of the Anglo-Saxons, 597–685

The familiar version of the coming of Christianity to Anglo-Saxon England is based on Bede's great *Ecclesiastical History of the English People* (731). According to this version the Romano-British Church was obliterated by pagan invaders, who first received the faith from the Roman mission, planned by Pope Gregory the Great and led by Augustine in 597. Its initial success was dramatic: the prompt conversion of King Aethelberht of Kent (?560–616), and of the kings of Essex and East Anglia; then the baptism of Aethelberht's son-in-law King Edwin of Northumbria (617–33), by his bride's Roman chaplain Paulinus. Sees were thus established at Canterbury, Rochester, London and York. But all four kingdoms soon relapsed into paganism, and only Kent was quickly re-converted. The evangelistic initiative passed to the Scottish church of Iona, founded by the Irishman, Columba, in 563. King Oswald of Northumbria (634–42) was converted while in exile among the Scots, and invited Iona to send him a mission: the result was Aidan's foundation of Lindisfarne in 635. The Irish bishops of Lindisfarne consolidated Northumbrian Christianity; their fellow-countrymen, Diuma and Ceollach, and their English pupils, Cedd and Trumhere, re-established it in Essex, and introduced it to Mercia and the Middle Angles, whose king, Penda (?610–55), was the last great pagan ruler. In none of these kingdoms was there any further significant relapse. But Iona was out of line with Rome on the methods of calculating the date of Easter. In 663, Bishop Colman was defeated on the issue at the Synod of Whitby, and withdrew to Iona, leaving the way clear for the organization of the English Church by Theodore of Canterbury (669–90).

But it is now recognized that, for all his qualities as a historian, Bede concentrated on what suited his didactic purposes, and was not always well-informed, especially beyond his native Northumbria. In the first place, he probably underplayed British Christian survival. The place-name Eccles and its compounds, denoting a Romano-British church building, suggest Anglo-Saxon contact with indigenous Christians, as do the pre-English names o monuments of the early Northumbrian churches at Me rose, Peebles, Carlisle and Whithorn. In Wessex, Wareha and Glastonbury were probably British churches take over intact. These places are mostly on the fringes o English settlement, and they barely overlap with place names reflecting Anglo-Saxon paganism, such a Woodnesborough, a few miles from Canterbury, o Harrow, dominating from its hill the infant church i London. But even in the heartland of Anglo-Saxo settlement there is some evidence of Christian continuit There are two Eccles in Norfolk and one in Kent. The cu of the British martyr, Alban, seems to have survived at i eponymous centre, and the fact that St Martin's, Cante bury, where the first missionaries settled, was known t have been a church in Roman times argues the persisten there of worship in some form. All this tends to quali Bede's impression of a complete break.

Secondly, Bede gives less than due emphasis to mi sionaries from elsewhere, notably the churches in the Par basin, Burgundy and northern Italy founded or inspired b the Irish Columbanus during the period 590–614. Birinu founder of the West Saxon see at Dorchester-on-Tham probably came from northern Italy, and his successo Aegilbert, certainly came (via Ireland) from Jouarre, ne Paris, the foundation of a Columbanian disciple. Of th next two Wessex bishops, now based at Winchester, Wi was educated in Gaul, and Leuthere was Aegilbert nephew. King Sigeberht of East Anglia was converted i Gallic exile, and his first bishop, Felix, was a Burgundia Several East Anglian princesses joined Columbania nunneries, including that at Chelles, a colony of Jouarr where Botolph, founder of Icanhoe in Suffolk, is said t have been trained. An abbess of Chelles is known to ha sent holy men and women to England, and these may ha included the first abbesses of Much Wenlock, Shropshir and Bath. For Wessex and East Anglia, at least, Gaul w more important than Rome or Iona.

Thirdly, other Irish pilgrims, unconnected with Ion whom Bede mentions in passing, if at all, are found i England. An Irish inscription of *c.*600 was discovered a Silchester in Hampshire. Foundations independent o other missions in the area were those of Fursa at Burg Castle in East Anglia, Maeldubh at Malmesbury in Wess and Diccuil at Bosham in Sussex. Also briefly recorded a Tuda, bishop of York in 664, Dagan in Kent, and Ronan i Northumbria. The general impression is that the co version of the English was a more haphazard process, owin more to individual initiative, than Bede's concern with th organized missions of Rome and Iona suggests. Thu much more crucial to the making of the English Churc than Whitby (only one of a series of Easter debates in th 'Celtic' and continental Churches of the 7th century) w Theodore's Council of Hertford (672), which began t bring order out of the relative chaos.

Meanwhile, the fact that peoples followed their kings i conversion is indicated by the appearance, within generation or two, of native bishops. The whole story i epitomized by Wilfrid (634–709), spokesman for th orthodox Easter at Whitby and first English bishop o Northumbria, whose vigorous churchmanship blende Irish, Roman, and Frankish values, who was the apostle o Sussex, the last pagan kingdom, and who was the first o many Englishmen to carry the Word back to their ancestr homelands on the Continent.

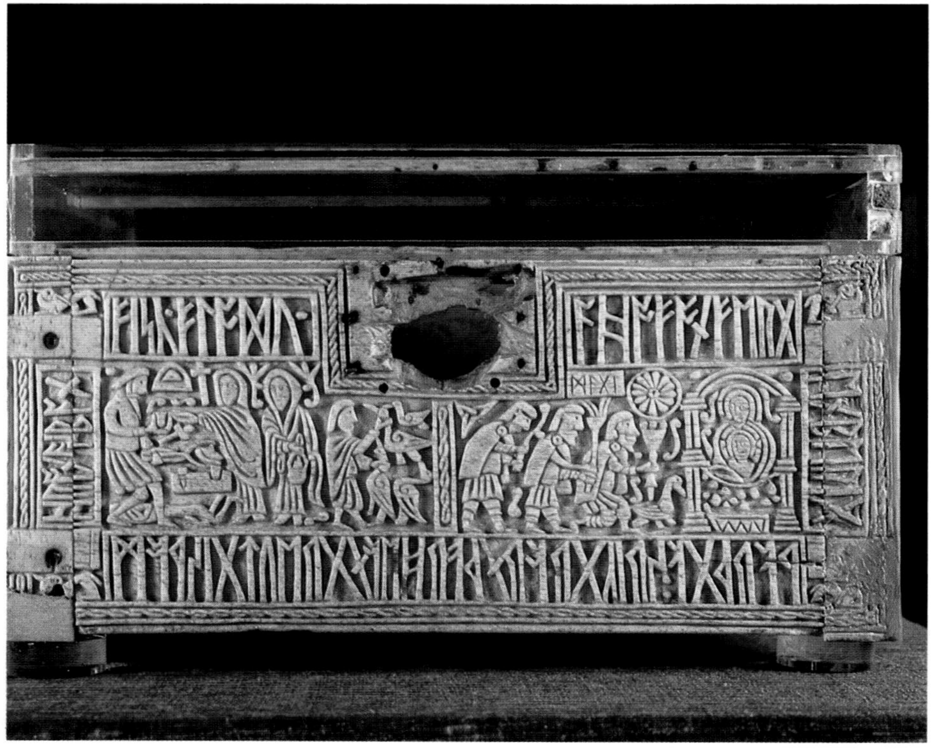

The Franks Casket of the 8th century from Northumbria. The runic inscription on the whale-bone panel reads, 'the fish flood lifted the whale's bones onto the mainland'. The left-hand panel shows a scene from the legend of Wayland the Smith, the right-hand panel the Adoration of the Magi. This fusion of barbarian craft traditions and Christian values and practice produced a Christianity that was distinctively aristocratic and vigorous.

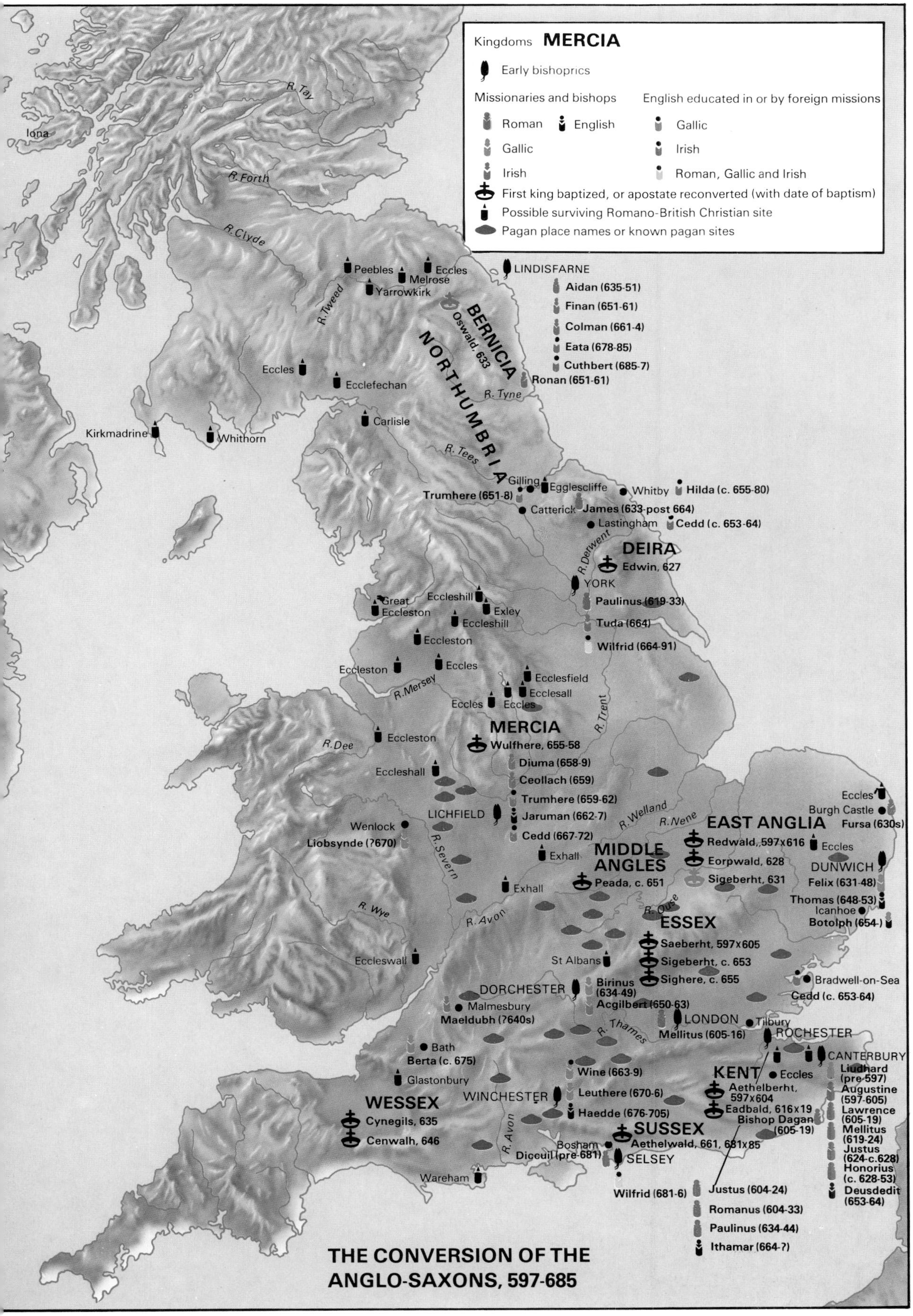

THE CONVERSION OF THE ANGLO-SAXONS, 597-685

Kingdoms **MERCIA**

Early bishoprics

Missionaries and bishops: Roman; English; Gallic; Irish

English educated in or by foreign missions: Gallic; Irish; Roman, Gallic and Irish

First king baptized, or apostate reconverted (with date of baptism)

Possible surviving Romano-British Christian site

Pagan place names or known pagan sites

Iona
R. Tay
R. Forth
R. Clyde
Peebles
Eccles
Melrose
Yarrowkirk
R. Tweed
LINDISFARNE
Aidan (635-51)
Finan (651-61)
Colman (661-4)
Eata (678-85)
Cuthbert (685-7)
Ronan (651-61)
BERNICIA
Oswald, 633
NORTHUMBRIA
Eccles
Ecclefechan
R. Tyne
Kirkmadrine
Whithorn
Carlisle
R. Tees
Gilling
Egglescliffe
Trumhere (651-8)
Whitby
Hilda (c. 655-80)
Catterick
James (633-post 664)
Lastingham
Cedd (c. 653-64)
R. Derwent
DEIRA
Edwin, 627
YORK
Paulinus (619-33)
Tuda (664)
Wilfrid (664-91)
Great Eccleston
Eccleshill
Exley
Eccleshill
Eccleston
Eccleston
Eccles
R. Mersey
Ecclesfield
Ecclesall
Eccles
Eccles
R. Trent
MERCIA
Wulfhere, 655-58
Eccleston
R. Dee
Diuma (658-9)
Ceollach (659)
Eccleshall
Trumhere (659-62)
LICHFIELD
Jaruman (662-7)
Cedd (667-72)
Wenlock
Liobsynde (?670)
R. Severn
Exhall
MIDDLE ANGLES
Peada, c. 651
Exhall
R. Welland
R. Nene
EAST ANGLIA
Redwald, 597x616
Eorpwald, 628
Sigeberht, 631
Eccles
Burgh Castle
Fursa (630s)
Eccles
DUNWICH
Felix (631-48)
Thomas (648-53)
Icanhoe
Botolph (654-)
R. Wye
R. Avon
R. Ouse
ESSEX
Saeberht, 597x605
Sigeberht, c. 653
Sighere, c. 655
Eccleswall
St Albans
Bradwell-on-Sea
Cedd (c. 653-64)
DORCHESTER
Birinus (634-49)
Acgilbert (650-63)
Malmesbury
Maeldubh (?640s)
LONDON
Mellitus (605-16)
Tilbury
ROCHESTER
R. Thames
Bath
Berta (c. 675)
Glastonbury
Wine (663-9)
Leuthere (670-6)
Haedde (676-705)
WESSEX
Cynegils, 635
Cenwalh, 646
WINCHESTER
R. Avon
KENT
Eccles
Aethelberht, 597x604
Eadbald, 616x19
Bishop Dagan (605-19)
CANTERBURY
Liudhard (pre-597)
Augustine (597-605)
Lawrence (605-19)
Mellitus (619-24)
Justus (624-c.628)
Honorius (c. 628-53)
Deusdedit (653-64)
SUSSEX
Aethelwald, 661, 681x85
Bosham
Diccuil (pre-681)
SELSEY
Wareham
Wilfrid (681-6)
Justus (604-24)
Romanus (604-33)
Paulinus (634-44)
Ithamar (664-?)

Bede's account, of a pagan England converted first by St Augustine and, later, by Irish missionaries from Iona, leaves aside the possibility of surviving Romano-British foundations. Place names formed with the root 'Eccles' (Latin ecclesia = church) indicate pre-English Christian centres. For all its shortcomings, Bede's *Ecclesiastical History of the English People* (731) remains fundamental.

St Martin's Cross, Iona. The community on Iona was founded by the Irish St Columba in 563, 34 years before Augustine's mission to Kent.

The Making of the English Church, 669–850

The conversion of the Anglo-Saxons began a period of astonishing creative energy in the infant Church. Among its manifestations were the missions to the Anglo-Saxons' pagan kinsfolk in Frisia and North Germany, begun from Northumbria by Wilfrid and his pupil, Willibrord, and consummated by the West Saxon, Boniface, and his disciples. Another was the transformation of native culture in the image of Mediterranean civilizations, epitomized by Bede and his environment. Where *Beowulf* speaks of wooden halls, Bede says, and archaeology confirms, that his abbeys of Monkwearmouth and Jarrow were 'in the Roman manner', that is of stone, and with glazed windows. Where *Beowulf* is based on the oral circulation of heroic tales, Bede's vast learning was derived from the library of late Roman scholarship collected by his founding abbot, Benedict Biscop, on many Mediterranean visits. Sufficient remnants survive of other pre-Viking churches and their sculpture, and of other early book-collections to show that Biscop's cultural ambition was not unique. Nor was this cultural osmosis all one-way. Anglo-Saxon identification with the new faith can be seen in Christian poetry, which expresses theological mysteries in the language and imagery of heroic sagas. Similarly, the sumptuous Lindisfarne Gospels (*c.*698) adapt the techniques and motifs of secular metalwork, such as we find at Sutton Hoo, to the medium of the Holy Book: what had glorified a proud aristocracy was now to honour God.

What made all this possible were two other features of Christian growth: the organization of a diocesan structure, and the remarkable proliferation of monasteries. The first of these was essentially the achievement of Archbishop Theodore, at and after his Council of Hertford in 672. By 750, Pope Gregory's original scheme for 12 southern dioceses, plus an archbishopric, had been realized. But in the North, where he had envisaged a similar pattern, there were never to be more than four sees, including the Yor archbishopric, until the 19th century. It is impossible to b certain about the precise boundaries of bishoprics befor the 11th century, by which time there had certainly bee changes in the South West, East and North. But it seem highly likely that boundaries were the same in the 8t century as in the 11th century where possible (for exampl in the South East and the west Midlands), and here the appear to coincide with political frontiers: the diocese o Selsey with the kingdom of Sussex, that of Worcester wit the Hwicce and so on. It is thus a reasonable guess th unknown boundaries, such as those between the Eas Anglian sees, or the bishoprics of Lindsey and the Middl Angles, reflected the administrative divisions of the la Saxon period, which were probably based, in their turn, o earlier political units. If this is right, the diocesan structu of the early English Church represented a compromis between Gregory's blueprint as enforced by Theodore, an the secular organization of Anglo-Saxon society.

Bede tended to refer to monasteries, unlike bishopric only in passing, and mentioned few, other than episcopa monasteries, outside Northumbria. But other sources sho that there was a very large number of religious communiti in England in 850. The thick cluster in the diocese o Worcester almost certainly reflects the unique survival of s many reliable charters in the Worcester archives, and n the fact that monasteries were exceptionally numerou there. For areas such as East Anglia or the Midlands, whe there are few, if any, charters, late and often legendar evidence for the foundation of communities, such as a list o burial-places of the English saints, seems therefore accept able. The survival of architectural and artistic remain comparable with those from known monasteries may als be evidence of an early community. The overall pictur may be misleading in particular details, but is mo unlikely, in the patchy nature of our evidence, to exaggera the number of monastic foundations. Unlike Monkwea mouth and Jarrow, few of these 'monasteries' would hav been easily recognizable to a medieval Benedictine, which one reason why Bede did not recognize them. Many we small communities, founded by a nobleman on his estat ruled by his relatives, and staffed by his dependents; the were 'family monasteries', with most of the functions of parish church. Historians prefer to call them by the vernacular term, *minster*. Others were major royal foun dations, like many of the double-monasteries of segregate monks and nuns, ruled over by a princessly abbess. What a had in common was that their government owed less t monastic regulations than to aristocratic notions of ki solidarity. But without the enthusiastic participation (an wealth) of the nobility, the achievement of the Englis Church is inconceivable. The survival of aristocratic value in so incongruous a context is the reverse of a coin whos obverse is a gospel-book decorated to look like a gre secular treasure.

The Lindisfarne Gospels: the beginning of St Matthew's Gospel. This illuminated Latin manuscript was written by Eadfrith of Lindisfarne shortly before 700. Artistically, it represents an astonishingly accomplished synthesis of Anglo-Saxon, Irish and Mediterranean influences.

The late 7th and early 8th century was the age of the Anglo-Saxon mission to heathen Germanic peoples, Frisians, Saxons and Thuringians. Outstanding among those who chose the strenuous and dangerous life of the missionary was the West Saxon Wynfrid, commissioned in 719 by Pope Gregory II to preach to the 'unbelieving gentiles'. Taking the Roman name Boniface, he carried out the task with zeal and political flair, earning himself, by the time of his death in 754, the title 'the Apostle of Germany.'

The period 669–850 was an age of reorganization and rapid developments, dominated by great churchmen like Theodore, Bede and Wilfrid. In Frisia and Saxony, English missionaries baptized their still pagan cousins, while in England, now equipped with a full diocesan organization, religious communities proliferated.

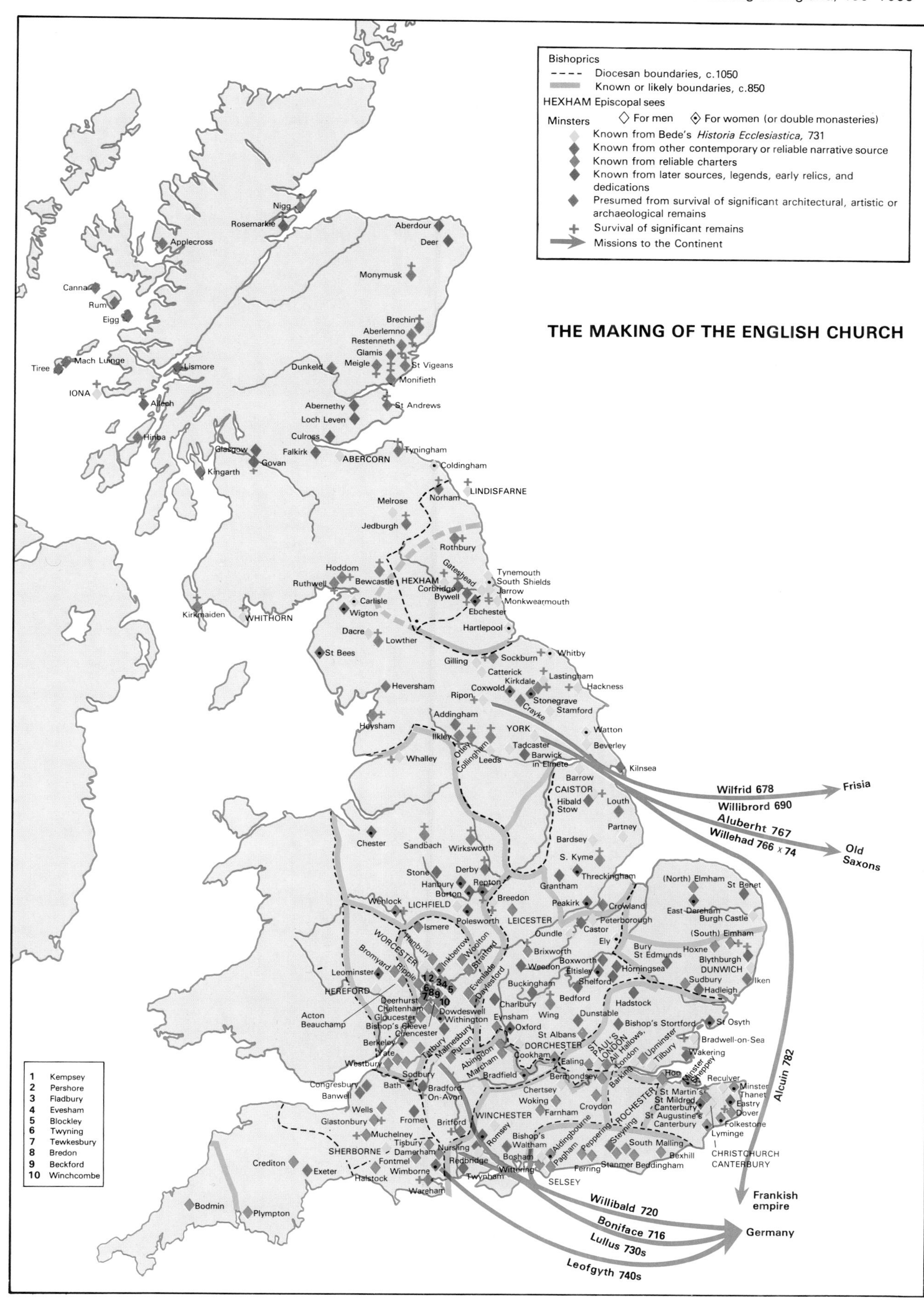

English Politics in the Age of Beowulf

Mercian penny minted during the reign of King Offa (757–96). The issue of a royal coinage bearing the name, even the portrait, of the king reflects the growing power and prestige of the Mercian monarchy.

A section of Offa's Dyke. This immense system of earthworks, forming the western frontier of the kingdom of Mercia, originally stretched from the Dee estuary to the mouth of the Wye, a distance of 120 miles (193 km).

We know less about politics than the Church in the 7th and 8th centuries, because Bede was an ecclesiastical historian for whom politics was important chiefly as a working-out of the ways of God. He wrote of a single English people because Gregory had envisaged, and Canterbury had achieved, a single English Church, albeit divided into two provinces. In an immensely influential passage, Bede described how a series of kings from the late 5th to the late 7th century had held 'empire' over all the kingdom south of the Humber (and thus, in the case of the three 7th-century Northumbrian overlords, over the whole English people). This empire may reflect a memory of the united Roman province of *Britannia*. Historians are increasingly aware of institutional continuity between Roman Britain and Anglo-Saxon England. It is probable that early English kings inherited a system of renders in kind by the surrounding population to local administrative centres, and it is possible that some early kingdoms, like Kent or Lindsey (which retain the basis of a Roman name), corresponded to Roman units.

But the dynamics of English politics in this period were determined less by Roman or ecclesiastical ideals of unity than by the heroic values of the contemporary epic poem *Beowulf*, a unique window on the thought-world of the warrior nobility. Kings in *Beowulf* reside in halls, where they dispense to their followers the treasure accumulated in plunder and tribute from their neighbours. Success in war attracts more followers with the prospect of more treasure,

and thus ensures further success. On the other hand, th mightiest kingdoms are vulnerable to the vengeance of the victims and to feuds within their royal house; hegemoni can collapse as quickly as they rise, with warriors seekir prosperous lords. There are many indications that this wa the pattern of early English politics. Charters and recor of royal council show that kings moved around from hall t hall rather than staying in a single capital. The roy tumulus of Sutton Hoo (which has many analogues with th royal burial described in *Beowulf*) shows what spectacula treasures were at a king's disposal. Assassinations and civ wars punctuated the royal succession in Northumbri Wessex and Mercia. The (for Bede) saintly King Oswald Northumbria (634–42) appears in a light more reminisce of the raids and revenges of *Beowulf*, when we see that h was killed at Oswestry on the far-eastern border of Merci and when we are told that the monks of Bardney in Linds refused to receive his remains because they resented h conquest of their country. The long series of battles alor their respective frontiers between Northumbria, Merc and Wessex may have been more like the tribal feuds *Beowulf* than the struggle for empire described by Bede.

More significant, therefore, than an intermittent empi in this period was the more gradual but also mo permanent absorption of the smaller kingdoms into th greater. Suggestively, the successful kingdoms were tho with an open frontier to the Celtic West, offering the be prospects of land and treasure to a king's potenti followers: Bernicia, which created the Northumbria kingdom by swallowing Deira in 651; Wessex, whic extinguished the Isle of Wight in 685; and above all Merci which, between the reigns of Penda (*c*.610–55) and Of (757–96) conquered all the other kingdoms of the Midlan and the South-East. The Mercians never lost their wester ambitions; Offa's stupendous dyke along the Welsh bord now seems to have been less a negotiated frontier than base for further raids in Wales and a barrier again reprisals, and both Offa and his successors penetrated we beyond it. But, for the key to the unprecedented Mercia success, we must perhaps look beyond western *Lebensraum*.

It is now clear that southern England was an increasing wealthy and commercially conscious society in the 7th an 8th centuries. The element *-wic* found in the early plac names of London, York, Ipswich and Southampton ha connotations of a trading centre, and there is literary and/ archaeological evidence that each was an internation market. Here, and at Canterbury, native coins were bein minted by the mid-7th century, initially in gold. Later cam the silver *sceattas*. The very wide distribution of *sceatt* throughout central and southern England shows how far money economy was penetrating. These coins never bear king's name, and were probably produced by trader themselves.

Mercian command of an increasing part of this tradin area must have contributed to Mercian power. Charte show Aethelbald (716–57) taking tolls at London. Off himself was the first king to issue a royal coinage on a reall significant scale. His new 'pennies', bearing his name an often his portrait, were minted in millions, and it is highl likely that, like his Carolingian contemporaries, he wa taking a cut of the profit of mintage. Even Mercian powe however, was not proof against the dynastic feuds tha broke out after the death of Cenwulf (796–821), an Wessex inherited its command of the South-East. But b the time Alfred faced the Vikings, English kingship ha developed from taking renders at royal manors, an treasures from defeated opponents, to the thorough exploi tation of the movable wealth of its subjects.

A passage from Beowulf, the Anglo-Saxon epic poem. The poem, elegaic in tone, was probably composed around AD 700. The single manuscript in which it is preserved was written about AD 1000.

Map showing English politics and economy, 597–850. Mercian power was enhanced by a parallel growth in trade within the area it controlled.

England and the Danes, 800–955

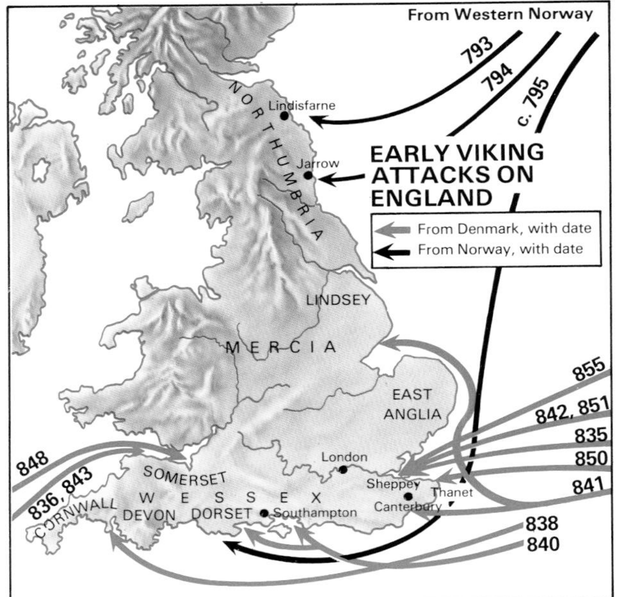

Viking attacks on England in the 8th and 9th centuries. This pattern of raiding was to culminate, in 865, in a full-scale Danish invasion under Halfdan and Guthrum and the extinction of all the former English kingdoms except Wessex.

The gradual build-up of Danish raids in the first half of the 9th century culminated in 865 with the invasion of the Great Army. Under the impact of this massive threat, a land that had once been several kingdoms – Northumbria, Mercia, East Anglia and Wessex – was swiftly reduced to sword-land ruled by Danish warriors, with Wessex alone surviving under Alfred as a focus for English resistance. This involved not only a permanent Danish settlement in eastern England but also the passing of the old order of Anglo-Saxon life and tribal kingship. The success of Alfred and, more significant still, of his son and grandsons, resulted in the conquest of the heathen Danes and in the unification of England – for the first time a unification achieved from within, unlike the earlier unity imposed from outside by Imperial Rome.

After its initial landing in East Anglia in 865 the Great Army made amazingly rapid progress. By 867 the Danes had captured York, killed the king of Northumbria and reduced its southern province (Deira) to submission. By 869 they had returned to East Anglia, slain its king, Edmund, and conquered his realm. The invasion of Wessex began in 871 but fortunately for Alfred, whose reign began in this year, the Danes were called back to Northumbria to put down a revolt (872–3). Then, in 874, King Burgred of Mercia gave up the struggle and the eastern part of his realm became Danish territory. Wessex was now the only fully independent English kingdom still surviving. In 875, however, Halfdan, one of the Danish leaders, made a tactical mistake, yielding to pressure from his men and settling his army in Northumbria. This left only a depleted Danish force under Guthrum to return to the conquest of Wessex. Even so, Guthrum's surprise attack in January 878 nearly worked. Alfred was forced to flee to Athelney in the Somerset marshes. But from this safe refuge he was able to organize the counter-attack which led to the victory at Edington (May 878).

'Then King Alfred ordered warships to be built to meet the Danish ships: they were almost twice as long as the others, some had 60 oars, some more; they were swifter, steadier and with more freeboard; they were built neither after the Fresian design nor after the Danish, but as it seemed to him that they could be most serviceable'. This passage from the *Anglo-Saxon Chronicle* for 896 is the only genuine evidence behind the legend of Alfred as 'the founder of the British navy'. Yet the implication is that it was not unusual for a king to order warships, merely that these ships had a remarkable design.

In the 14 years of relative quiet which followed, Alfred consolidated his hold on Wessex. In particular a programme of fortress (*burh*) building – the details of which are known from a later document known as the *Burghal Hidage* – did much both to strengthen the kingdom's defences and to develop urban life. When, in 892, the next major Danish attack came, Alfred's re-organized forces were generally able to contain the invaders. In 896 they withdrew. 'Thanks be to God', wrote the author of the *Anglo-Saxon Chronicle*, 'the (Danish) army had not too much afflicted the English people'. Alfred's patronage of literature, including the 'official' history of his own reign as told in the *Anglo-Saxon Chronicle*, and his own direct participation in the work of translating Latin books into English, are two further aspects of this remarkable king's many-sided talents.

On the death of Alfred in 899, his methods were continued by his son and successor, Edward the Elder (899–924) and by his daughter Aethelfled, 'Lady of the Mercians', who ruled English Mercia centred on the Severn Basin. Aethelfled's forts, stretching from Warwick (914) in the south of Mercia to Chester (907) and Runcorn (915) in the north-west, show a clear geographical and chronological extension of the West Saxon system, while the fortifications of her brother Edward concentrated on the frontier war of attrition against the Danish colonists. While Alfred is remembered for saving Wessex, it was Edward's achievement to have begun the re-conquest of England from the Danes, pushing the English frontier, nominally at least, as far north as the Humber.

Since the Danes had also been constructing *burhs* the reconquest was inevitably an arduous and expensive business. The key area in this struggle for control of England lay along the old frontier agreed between Alfred and the Danish Guthrum soon after 880. This frontier divided England roughly along a diagonal from Chester to London, following the Roman road of Watling Street in the Midland region from Tamworth to Passenham, and in the South-East it was marked by the meanders of the Great Ouse and the Lea. The crucial region along this frontier, where Edward devoted most of his energies in the wars from 917 to 920, lay south of Danish Northampton from Towcester to Bedford. The *Anglo-Saxon Chronicle* makes it clear that Danes and West Saxons alike dug in on either side of the frontier here in a desperate effort to hold their forts. The loss of this region cost the Danes dear. By 924 Edward had over-run the Five Boroughs of Lincoln, Derby, Nottingham, Stamford and Leicester. In the North Edward secured the English frontier against invasion from the Norwegian kingdom of Dublin by building forts at Rhuddlan (921), Thelwall and Manchester (919): but the Danes of York held on grimly both to their autonomy and to their Scandinavian kings.

Equally grimly Alfred's grandsons, Athelstan (924–39), Edmund (939–46) and Eadred (946–55), stuck to the task of securing the submission of the North. The 930s and 940s were turbulent decades and kings like Olaf Guthfrithsson and Eric Bloodaxe formidable opponents, but in the end the dogged persistence of the House of Wessex, and its continuity of policy, won the day. By the end of his reign Eadred was king over all England.

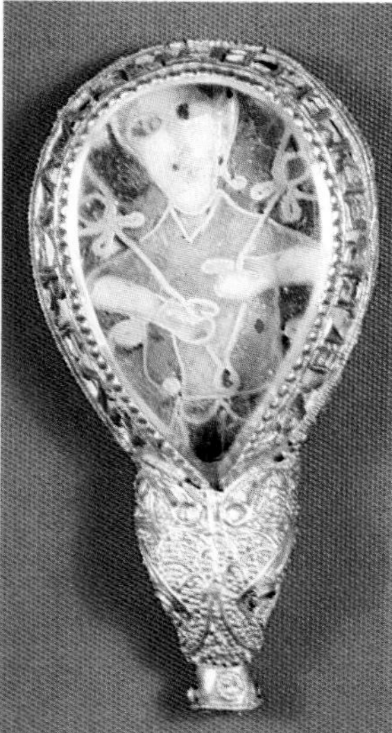

The Alfred Jewel. It is widely thought that Alfred the Great, who died in 899, owned this jewel for it bears the Anglo-Saxon inscription. 'Alfred had me made'. The jewel is gold decorated with cloisonné enamel. It was found near the Island of Athelney, Somerset, in 1693. The jewel might have been a pointer for following the lines of a manuscript.

England from King Alfred to Eadred, *c*.865–955. With dogged persistence, Alfred and his successors rolled back Danish power in the North. By the end of his reign, Eadred ruled over an England united within a vastly expanded Wessex.

ENGLAND FROM KING ALFRED TO EADRED c. **865-955**

- West Saxon fort in Burghal Hidage built *c.* 878-910
- Fort built by Aethelfled, 'Lady of the Mercians'
- Fort built by Edward the Elder
- Danish borough or temporary war camp
- One of the five boroughs of southern Danelaw
- Bishoprics
- Major Roman roads, perhaps still in use
- Ancient trackways
- Battlefields
- Northumbrian churches which survived the Viking wars
- Other ecclesiastical centres
- Other centres
- Forest
- Marsh

The Making of One Kingdom

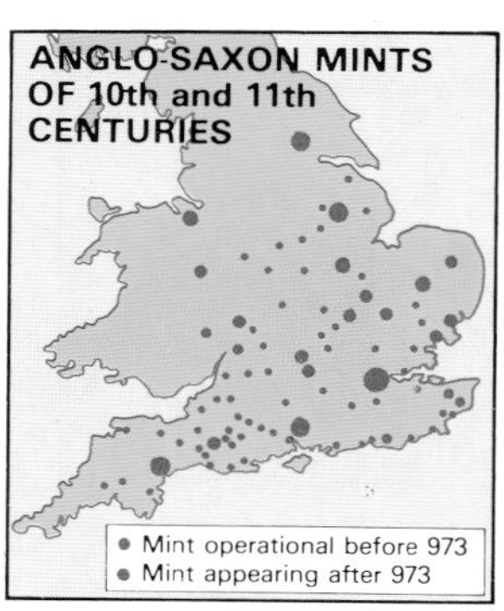

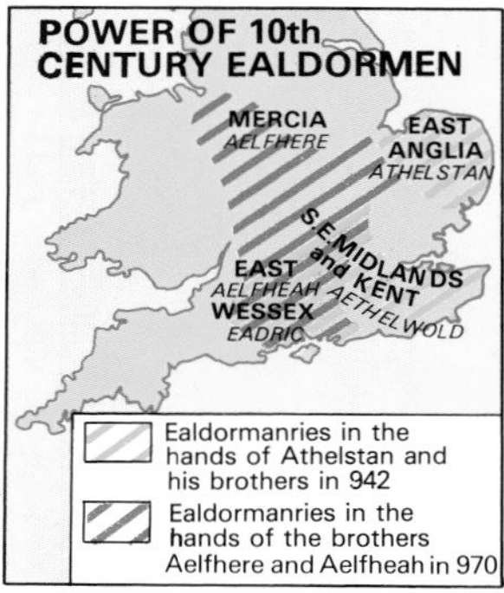

Top: Anglo-Saxon mints of the 10th and 11th centuries. The minting of coin in Anglo-Saxon England was decentralized. Mints reflect economic, administrative and royal needs, the largest being in the major trading and administrative centres. Thus Winchester, and especially London, were important throughout the period. The importance of Chester on the routes to Wales and Viking Ireland was eclipsed, by the end of the 10th century, by the growing size of York and Lincoln on the North Sea trade routes. New mints were established in the wake of the reform of the coinage instituted by Edgar in 973. Further mints, chiefly in Wessex, supplied the coin for royal dues and maximized the king's profit from the coinage.

Above: The power of 10th-century ealdormen. Tenure of office in the shape of the larger ealdormanries formed the basis of power for some noble families. The families of Athelstan 'Half King' of East Anglia and Aelfhere of Mercia had both originated in Wessex but the kingdom's expansion created opportunities north of the Thames.

The military conquest of Viking England was only the first stage of unification and in some ways it was the simplest. In 954 the West Saxon kings found themselves in nominal control of a realm which stretched as far north as Lothian. North of the Thames they had acquired, in Northumbria, Mercia and East Anglia, areas which had long histories as separate kingdoms. Somehow or other these different regions had to be welded into a single political society governed by the House of Wessex. In carrying out this task the king's chief local agents were the *ealdormen*. But, whereas in 9th-century Wessex each ealdorman had governed a single shire, in the 10th century trusted ealdormen could now find themselves in charge of much larger units – ealdormanries which perpetuated the shape and structure of the former independent kingdoms. Such men had already benefited from the profits, in land and plunder, of the wars of reconquest; now the task of governing newly acquired territories offered fresh challenges and greater opportunities. Stepping into the shoes of former kings, some of the nobles (thegns) who attended the West Saxon royal court were richer and more powerful than any earlier English aristocracy.

On the other hand, to some nobles affairs at the West Saxon court were of little interest. Relatively few thegns from north of the Trent, for example, bothered to attend. Most independent of all were the rulers of the far North, the earls of Bamburgh. Although they made a token submission to the West Saxon kings they were, in practice, treated as the hereditary lords of the English lands north of the Tees (formerly Bernicia). Defence of the border against the advancing Scots was left entirely in their hands. Symptomatic of the extent to which, even a century later, this region still lay beyond the reach of the kings of England, is the fact that it was left out of the Domesday Survey.

Yorkshire, however, was surveyed – a fact which reflects the rather more strenuous efforts made by previous Englis kings to bring the southern part of Northumbria (th Viking kingdom of York) under their effective contro They appointed governors (ealdormen), commonly thegn from the north Midlands, i.e. men whose own family estate lay outside Northumbria. But these outsiders had a har time of it. The king himself possessed very little land c power in Northumbria and, in consequence, could giv them little support. One ealdorman was murdered, anothe driven into exile.

Moreover the kings never divided this region into smalle administrative units. By and large the later boundaries c the huge county of Yorkshire preserved the boundaries c the Viking kingdom – a sure sign of the kings' inability t make much impression on the old forms of political life.

Farther south things were rather different. At some stag during the 10th century the local West Saxon system c shires was extended into Mercia. The centring of many c these shires on the English and Viking *burhs* underlines th military origins of the system, though full shire adminis tration in Mercia was probably the result of gradua developments over the 10th and 11th centuries. Older unit were not immediately supplanted and ignored, nor wer they forgotten. In 1016 the *Anglo-Saxon Chronicle* sti referred to the men of Hereford as the Maegonsaetan; in th 990s a Winchester scribe described West Mercia as th Hwicce; and the shire of Rutland probably represents a old Mercian unit.

Even so, the West Saxon dynasty was clearly much mor in control of Mercia than of the lands farther north. Th death of his sister Aethelfled in 918 had allowed Edward th Elder to move in, though not without having to overcome rebellion in favour of Aethelfled's daughter. But it i possible that Mercia might have been established as a sub kingdom for a branch of the Wessex dynasty, and certai

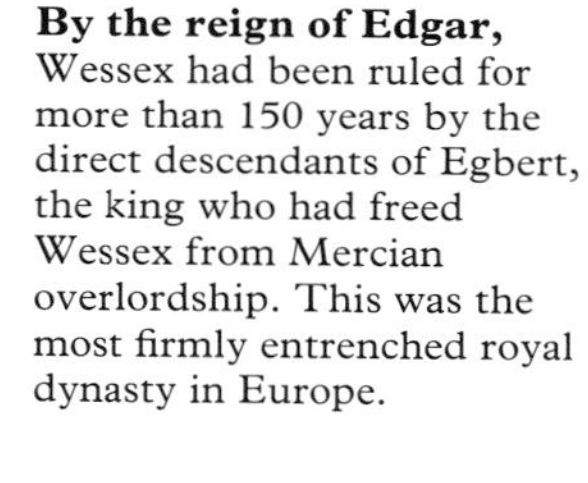

By the reign of Edgar, Wessex had been ruled for more than 150 years by the direct descendants of Egbert, the king who had freed Wessex from Mercian overlordship. This was the most firmly entrenched royal dynasty in Europe.

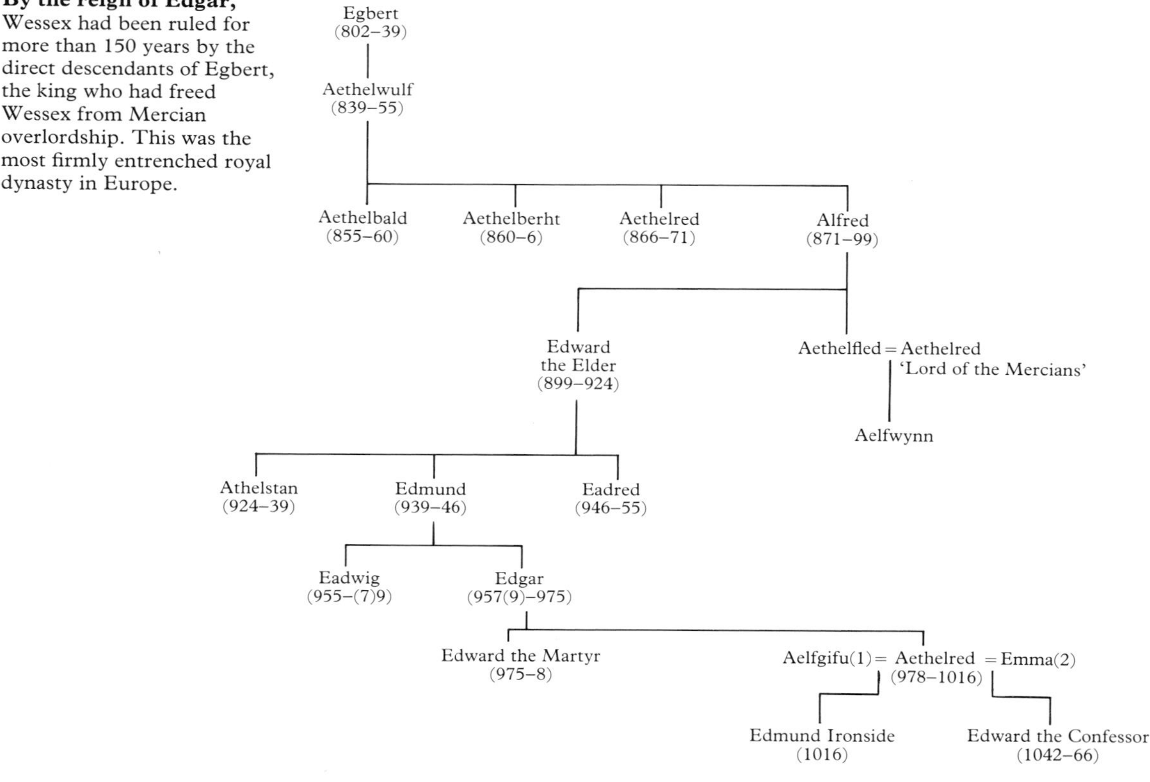

that whenever there were succession disputes within the royal family, as in 956, 975 and 1035, the Mercians, often in alliance with Northumbria, preferred to give their support to the rival who opposed the 'Wessex' candidate. Indeed, for a short while, between 957 and 959, there was once again a king of Mercia: Edgar, younger brother of Eadwig, King of Wessex. Only the accident of Eadwig's death led to the swift reunification of the Kingdom of England under Edgar.

Nonetheless, accident or not, a kind of unity was upheld and increasingly taken for granted. Leadership in the wars of reconquest had so enhanced the prestige of Alfred's descendants that no other English dynasty had a hope of competing for the crown. Weak though it was in some areas, the administration was strong enough to impose a uniform, royal coinage on England and to reap financial advantage from the country's growing economic prosperity. At the end of the century, when the Vikings came again, the prize at stake was nothing less than the Kingdom of England. This is a measure of the achievement of the House of Wessex.

The administration of England in the 10th century. The Danelaw boundary drawn by Alfred and Guthrum proved to have less significance than the older units of Mercia and East Anglia, ancient kingdoms which were preserved in the administrative geography of 10th-century England. During the course of this century, Mercia was divided into large, neat shires, each dependent on a county centre. The shires of Sussex, Essex, Kent, East Anglia and York, on the other hand, reflect earlier divisions. The royal court was itinerant, but it stayed generally south of the Thames Valley with Winchester and, increasingly London as favoured residences.

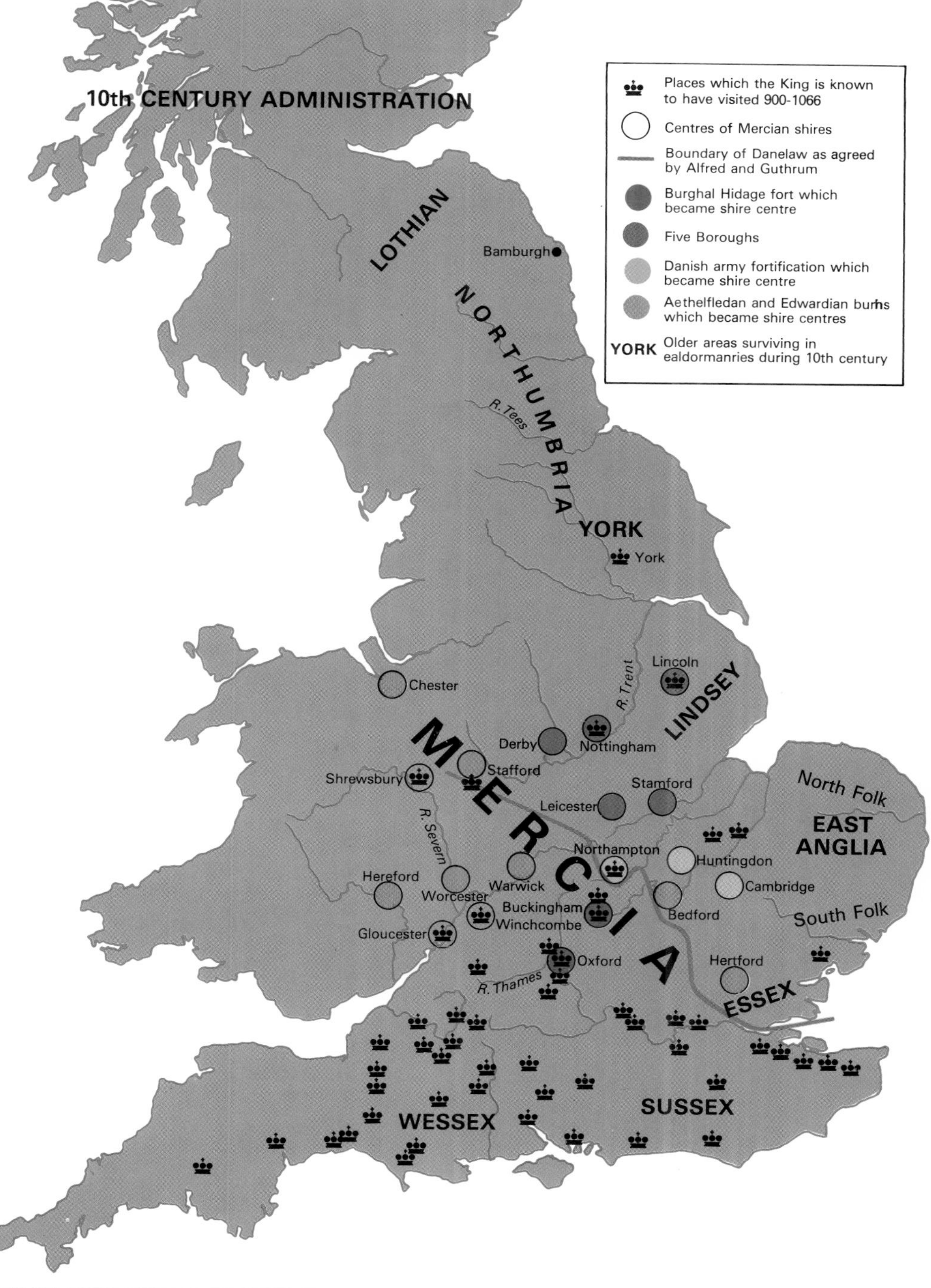

A page from the Anglo-Saxon Chronicle. Originally compiled during Alfred's reign, the chronicle was continued at several different centres for another 200 years. In the 10th century it concentrates on the deeds of the kings and, at times – as in the manuscript containing a poem celebrating Athelstan's victory at Brunanburh – it helps to enhance the prestige of the ruling dynasty.

An. dccclxxi. Her cōm se here to Readingum on west seaxe. ⁊ þæs ymbe .iii. niht ridon
twegen eorlas up. þa gemette æþelwulf ealdor
man hie on englafelda. ⁊ him þær wið gefeaht.
⁊ sige nam ⁊ heora wearð oþer þær ofslægen
þæs nama wæs Sidrac. Ða ymb .iiii. niht æþered
cyning. ⁊ ælfred his broþer þær mycle fyrd
to readingum gelæddon. ⁊ wið þone here ge-
fuhton. ⁊ þær wæs mycel wæl geslægen on gehwæþere
hand. ⁊ eaðelwulf ealdorman wearð ofslægen.
⁊ þa deniscan ahton wælstowe geweald. ⁊ þæs
ymb .iiii. nyht gefeaht æþered cyning ⁊ ælfred
his broþor wið ealne þone here on æsces dune.
⁊ hi wæron on twam gefylcum on oðrum wæs
bagsecg. ⁊ healfdene þa hæðenan cyningas. ⁊ on
oðrum wæron þa eorlas. ⁊ þa gefeaht se cyning
æþered wið þara cyninga getruman. ⁊ þær
wearð se cyning bagsecg ofslægen. ⁊ ælfred
his broþor wið þara eorla getruman. ⁊ þær

The 10th-Century Reformation

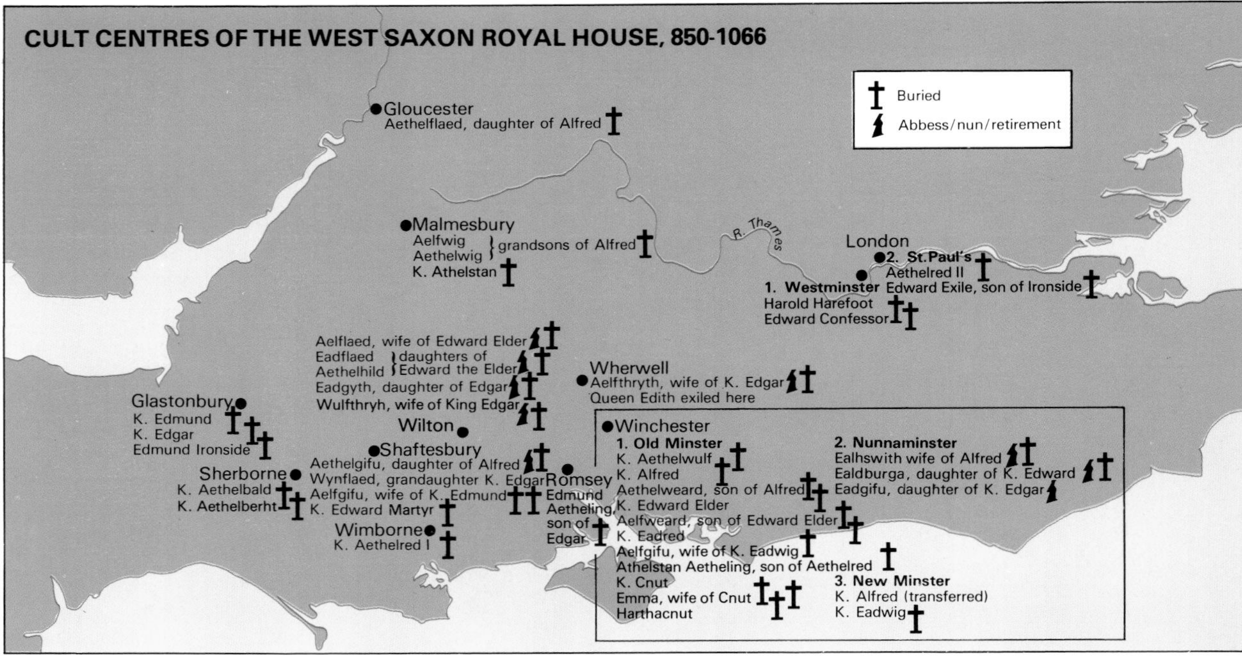

Royal cult centres in Wessex. The king was nominally protector of all the reformed monasteries. However, royal patronage still concentrated on the royal monasteries of Wessex. These served the royal dynasty by offering prayers for the family and its dead, by providing places of burial, as well as refuges for widows, repudiated wives and unmarried daughters. Similar functions were sought by the nobility from their own foundations.

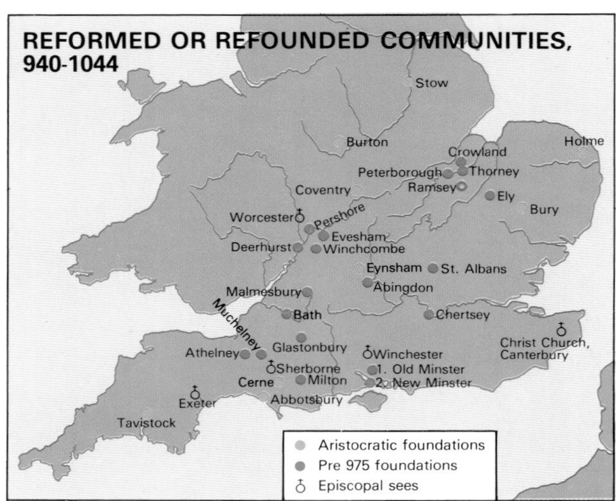

Distribution of reformed communities. These show a marked geographical concentration. In so far as the royally protected monasteries formed centres of royal influence, they tended to reinforce rather than extend the area of that influence. The major thrust of the movement belongs to the period before the death of Edgar in 975.

In England, as in Europe, the 10th century saw the triumphant spread of Benedictine monasticism. The so-called 'Monastic Revival' or 'Reformation' was not a simple reform of laxity. It was concerned at the institutional level with the protection of communal life through an insistence on corporate endowment and celibacy; at the spiritual level with an emphasis on the monks as 'soldiers of Christ', whose unending round of prayer assisted the souls of the dead and safeguarded the well-being of society as a whole.

The movement had an important educational dimension at a time when the Christianization of Europe was still superficial. It was everywhere aristocratic in its recruits, providing career openings for the sons of noble families. Their large and well managed estates assured the monks a noble life-style, political importance and prosperity.

English monasticism had suffered at the hands of Vikings. Many important monastic centres in Eastern England, Ely and Peterborough (*Medeshamstede*), had disappeared; others, including Canterbury itself, showed signs of decay, of both learning and organized life, by the late 9th century. Some communities, like Glastonbury, did survive, and Alfred and his son Edward the Elder made efforts to revive West Saxon monasticism at Athelney and New Minster, Winchester. Where they still existed communities were often small, consisting in most cases of married clerks with an ill-protected, non-corporate endowment.

The English reforming movement began in the reign of Athelstan (924–39) but gathered momentum during those of his brothers Edmund (939–46) and Eadred (946–55) and especially during that of Edmund's son Edgar (957/9–75).

The leaders of the English reform were Dunstan, Aethelwold and Oswald. All three were of noble birth. Dunstan and Aethelwold both began their careers at the court of Athelstan. Aelfheah, bishop of Winchester, encouraged Dunstan to become a monk, while Oswald followed the same course at the instigation of his uncle Oda, archbishop of Canterbury. Dunstan was at Glastonbury before 939 and became abbot there in about 943. Continental developments certainly influenced the English movement. Oswald went to Fleury to train as a monk and Aethelwold wished to travel there to learn monastic discipline. When Dunstan was expelled from the royal court in 956 his exile was spent in the monastery of Ghent. Monks from both foundations were in England in the late 10th century. But Aethelwold became abbot of Abingdon instead of going to Fleury, and the English movement followed its own course on the fringes of the continental reform and its learning.

In its early stages the reform was very dependent on the king. All three reformers were advanced to key bishoprics, Dunstan to Worcester, London and Canterbury, Aethelwold to Winchester, and Oswald to York/Worcester. Expelled from the courts of Athelstan and Eadwig, at the heart of royal counsel under Eadred and Edgar, the career of Dunstan shows how deeply politics affected the monastic movement. Royal patronage was crucial to success. It was Eadred, for example, who gave the decayed monastery of Abingdon to Aethelwold in 954, Edgar who gave him Ely and backed with force his attempts to expel married clerks from Winchester.

The surviving history of Edgar's reign is dominated by

the reform. The strength of his kingship is suggested by the obeisance of the Welsh kings in 973 after his imperial coronation at Bath. Yet that coronation had been masterminded by the reformers, a tangible benefit from the close alliance between king and monks. The king's protection was extended to all the new monasteries and the monks were favoured candidates for bishoprics. But direct royal patronage in the form of land grants went chiefly to the old royally connected foundations in Wessex, in the heart of royal power.

Many noble families who had derived wealth from 10th century political changes were patrons of the new movement. Most great religious houses outside Wessex, such as Worcester, Evesham, Ramsey, Peterborough, Ely and Burton, were episcopal and noble, rather than royal, foundations. Reforming monk-bishops often expelled the clerks who had traditionally served their cathedrals and replaced them with monks. As a result Winchester, Canterbury, Sherborne, Exeter and Worcester became monastic cathedrals. Some monasteries acquired land very rapidly and by questionable means. This led to resentment between local nobles and monks, and a violent 'anti-monastic' reaction on Edgar's death. But this attack was not against monasticism as such and had no permanent effect. Eleventh-century houses, such as Coventry and Stow, show the continuing noble interest in the benefits derived from monastic foundations.

The geography of the revival reflects its patronage: the numerous West Saxon royal foundations; the Severn Valley houses linked largely with Oswald's wealthy bishopric of Worcester; the Fenland and East Anglian group patronized by local nobles and benefiting from the tireless energy of Aethelwold of Winchester. The failure of the reform to penetrate the North of England underlines not only the poverty of both Church and king in this area, but also the minimal involvement of the northern nobility.

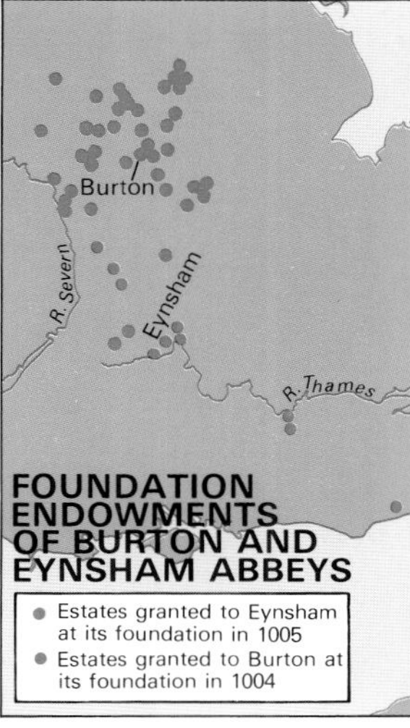

Left: The foundation endowments of two abbeys. A Benedictine house needed lavish endowment; the reform could not have happened without the wealth of 10th-century kings and nobles. Here, the endowments reflect the geographically scattered nature of Anglo-Saxon noble estates.

Below: Church links abroad. Fleury and Ghent provided the major continental influence on the English movement. There were extensive contacts in north France, west Germany and along the pilgrim route to Rome.

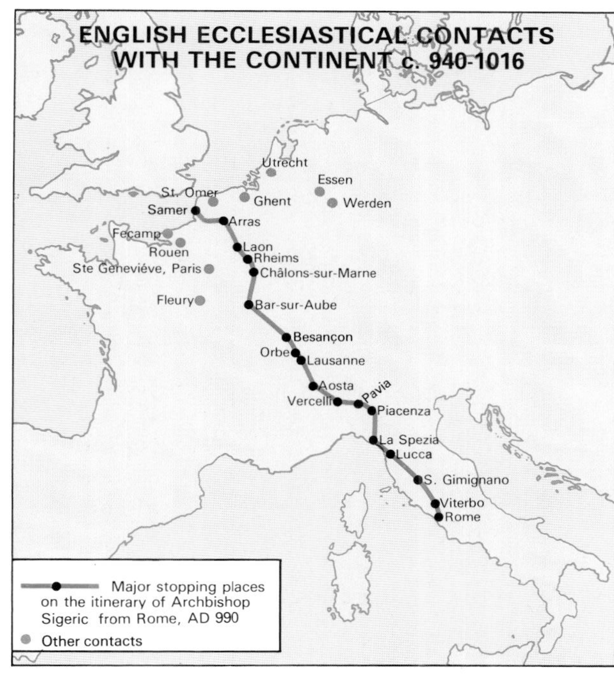

Wales in the Early Middle Ages

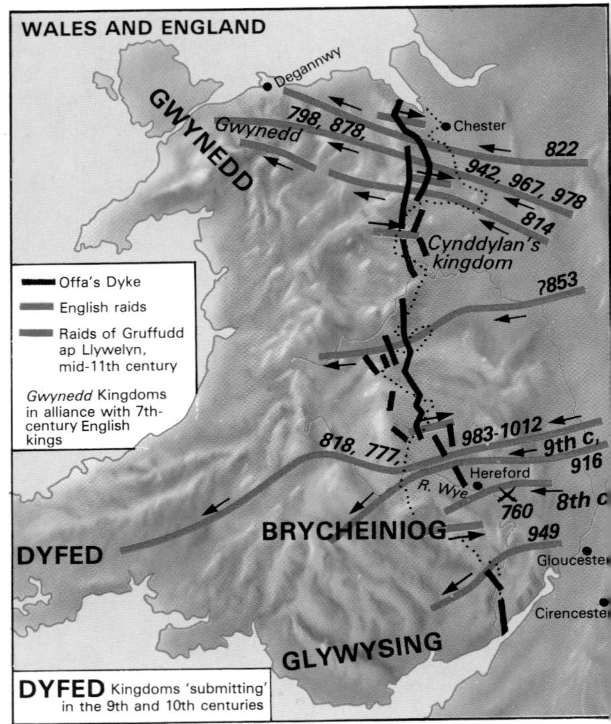

Wales is a mountainous country in which there are no large stretches of workable lowland, as there are in England and Ireland. This combination makes both communications and intensive cultivation difficult and consequently impedes both the progress of military conquest and the accumulation of sufficient resources to support any large army. The political history of early medieval Wales was very clearly conditioned by all these factors for, during much of the period, kingdoms were small and separate. Though in time a few came to predominate, there was neither any administrative development capable of supporting larger kingdoms, nor any political consolidation sufficient to unite the whole area. Population seems to have remained low and resources very limited: it was a poor country in comparison with its neighbours. We find little evidence of trade, therefore – other than the passage of the Vikings along the coasts – and none of markets in the centuries when England and Europe were experiencing a great commercial expansion; even as late as the 11th century there was no visible trend towards urbanization.

The Roman conquest of Wales had had uneven effects: only the South-East was fully drawn into the Roman economic network of towns, villas and large-scale estates. In the 1st and 2nd centuries much of the mountain of the North and Midlands was straddled by a network of forts, but only a few of these were retained as military posts into the 4th century. The most notable development during the centuries after the termination of Roman government was the emergence of a number of small kingdoms, several of which were already evidenced in the 6th century. The more successful of these – those that survived until the Norman Conquest or beyond – were the ones whose power was focused in the broader stretches of exploitable lowland, located in the four corners of Wales. These were Gwynedd, Dyfed, Glywysing and, to a lesser extent, Powys. The long-term trend from the 6th to the 11th century was for the gradual elimination of the less successful kingdoms, a process intensified in the 9th and 10th centuries. (In the

Right: The expansion of the major Welsh kingdoms from the 6th to 11th centuries.

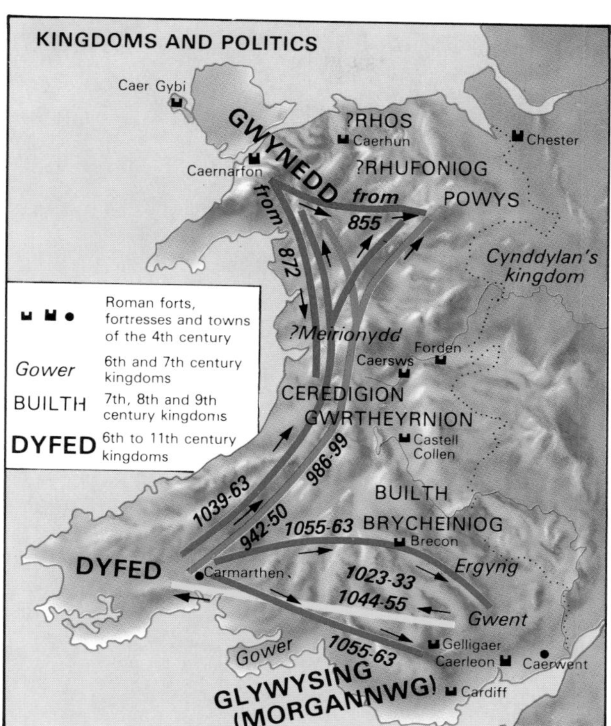

English attacks on Wales, 777–1012. Under pressure, some Welsh kings entered alliances with English kings. Later these alliances, interpreted as 'submissions', formed the basis of English claims to overlordship.

Recorded ecclesiastical sites in Wales up to the 12th century. The preface *llan-*, meaning 'sacred enclosure', is widespread, testifying to the vigour of pre-Norman Celtic Christianity in Wales. Beginning with Romano-British Christian influences, Wales later received missionaries from south Gaul, Brittany and north Britain.

South-East an early kingdom of Gwent was absorbed by a new larger kingdom of Glywysing in the 7th and 8th centuries, but in the 11th century intruding dynasties revived Gwent and the contracting Glywysing became known as Morgannwg). The great names of early Welsh history, Rhodri Mawr (d.878), Hywel Dda (d.950), Maredudd ab Owain (d.999) and Gruffudd ap Llywelyn (d.1063), were all kings of the West – of Gwynedd and Dyfed – who were notable, among other achievements, in extending political conquest well outside the bounds of their own kingdoms; Gruffudd even briefly succeeded in ruling all Wales between 1055 and 1063.

Even more notable is the fact that these political successes were not sustained over two generations, and such conquests did not upset the essential three-fold division which crystallized in the 9th and 10th centuries – that between Gwynedd, Dyfed and Glywysing/Morgannwg. The fourth of the principal kingdoms, Powys, had no part in this final phase, for not only was its dynasty absorbed by Gwynedd in the 9th century, but it also suffered heavily from constant English attack. In effect, much of Powys must have become English by the early 9th century, and it is notable that the frontier Dyke constructed by the Mercian king Offa in the late 8th century places the north-eastern lowlands of Wales on the English side of the border.

The fate of Powys is a reminder that, though Wales was a land of small kingdoms, it was not isolated from the world around it. In the 7th century kings of Gwynedd and Powys had allied with the early English; in the later 9th and 10th centuries kings of Gwynedd and of the South were to do the same; and in the later 10th and 11th centuries Welsh kings were glad to use English mercenaries for their own political purposes. But relations were not always good; just as Powys suffered from constant Mercian raiding, so the raids battered at Brycheiniog and the South-East, and plunged into the heart of Dyfed and Gwynedd, in the 8th, 9th and 10th centuries – unaffected by the construction of Offa's Dyke, or the border agreement concluded by King Athelstan on the river Wye in 927. Indeed, for nearly a century from the late 9th century, English kings claimed that kings of Wales had 'submitted' to them, a claim to some extent practically effected by Edward the Confessor in his dealings with Gruffudd. Such submissions may well have involved the payment of tribute by the Welsh. English influence was not entirely military, however, and such diverse aspects as law-codes and sculpture, not forgetting the place-names of the border, all bear the mark of English contacts.

Contacts with Ireland

From its position in the Irish Sea, Wales also looked westwards. Irish settlement of the early 5th century, especially in the South-West, was only a prelude to sustained contacts with Ireland, expressed in the sharing of religious cults and further influence on sculptural styles. Moreover, though there is no good evidence of Viking settlement in Wales, it is quite clear – from place names and coin hoards, and more sculpture – that Viking trade routes from Ireland to England along northern and southern coasts did not merely pass by mainland Wales.

In the later 10th and 11th centuries the Vikings attacked Welsh churches frequently, especially St David's. Much has been written of the Celtic Church and of the 'Age of Saints' in Wales, but little of it depends on early recorded evidence, since this is scarce. The modern picture has been too much influenced by the retrospective glances of the writers of the 11th- and 12th-century Saints' Lives and their romantic view of the past. But although we know almost nothing about Welsh saints, a range of pre-Norman sources tells us of the existence of some 40 religious foundations – churches served by communities. A further 30 very small churches and monasteries, located almost entirely in Gwent, and especially on the river Wye and its tributaries, could be added from the (for Wales) uniquely detailed charter evidence from the South-East. This pattern, however, was probably not typical of the whole of Wales.

The Making of Scotland, 550–1018

In North Britain the series of complex developments which culminated in 1018 with the emergence of a strong south Scottish kingdom under Malcolm II, began with invasions from Ireland in the 5th and 6th centuries. These Gaelic-speaking Irish invaders from Dál Riada in Antrim were the original 'Scots'. The modern name 'Scotland' stands as a monument to their slow-maturing achievement. Their first step was to push the Picts – the oldest indigenous historical inhabitants of Britain north of the Clyde-Forth line – out of Argyll, Arran and Bute. Here, in the coastal lands west of the 'Spine of Britain' (Druim nAlban), the Dál Riada established themselves in three distinct tribes. Of these the more important were the Cenél Loairn (controlling the southern entrance to the Great Glen) and the Cenél Gabráin (occupying Kintyre and Cowal and the northern approaches to the Clyde). With the warriors and settlers came Christian missionaries. In the 6th century Brendan of Clonfert and others established monasteries at Elachnave and Lismore in the Firth of Lorne, together with houses on Rum, Eigg and Tiree. The coming of Columba to Hinba and Iona *c.*563 gave leadership and direction to the infant Scottish Church. He undertook several expeditions up the Great Glen to Brude mac Maelchon, king of the Picts and overlord of the Northern Isles. Columba may not have personally succeeded in converting the Pictish nation to Christianity, but he undoubtedly paved the way for major Scottish influences on the Picts, not least in the flowering of Pictish sculpture on the Symbol Stones which originated in the 7th century, in the region of the Dornoch and Moray Firths. The Pictish royal succession was matrilineal, and so Scottish and other neighbouring kings fathered sons on Pictish princesses. This, together with their acceptance of Columban Christianity, left the Picts vulnerable to increasing Dál Riada influence which led ultimately to their absorption by the Scots in the 9th century. Yet the rise of Dál Riada was slow, and the 'Pictish twilight' saw great kings such as Brude mac Bile (died *c.*692) who ruled from Orkney to the Forth.

South of the Clyde-Forth line lay the British kingdoms of Strathclyde (though its capital, Dumbarton, lay just north of the Clyde) and of the Gododdin in Lothian. But in the later 6th and 7th centuries British Lothian was overrun by some other recent arrivals, the Angles of Northumbria. Under the leadership of Ecgfrith (671–85) the Angles even pushed into Pictish territory beyond the Forth, possibly penetrating well to the north and east of Stirling. But after the disastrous defeat and death of Ecgfrith at the hands of forces led by Brude mac Bile at Nechtanesmere in 685 the Anglo-Pictish boundary was stabilized at the Forth. Farther west, meanwhile, the English had advanced to the shore of the Solway, bringing down another British kingdom, Rheged, in the process. Eventually (*c.*720) an English bishopric was established at Whithorn in southern Galloway. Long before this date contact had been made between the English and the Scots. In military terms the southward expansion of the Dál Riada had been checked in 604 when the Northumbrians beat Aedán mac Gabráin in battle at Degsastan (perhaps in Liddesdale). But culturally the Christian Scots had much to give to the pagan English.

If, by the 8th century, a precarious balance between Picts, British, Scots and English had been achieved, it was soon to be overturned by the arrival of the Vikings. By the opening of the 9th century heathen Norse colonists had overrun Orkney and Shetland. By *c.*850 they occupied Caithness, Sutherland, and the west coast as far south as Islay. Iona had fallen into the hands of the Norsemen, and Argyll and Kintyre, the political heart of Dál Riada, were now constantly exposed to Viking attack. The Vikings came in such numbers that their place-names left a permanent mark on the Scottish landscape; and in the Icelandic sagas Orkney and even Caithness came to be regarded as an integral part of Scandinavia. Faced with invading Norsemen on the one hand, and eager to exploit the weakness of the Picts on the other, the Scots under Kenneth mac Alpine moved from Kintyre and Cowal into the Central Lowlands. From new centres such as Scone they dominated the old southern Pictish realm south of the Mounth. At the same time, the Scots of Cenél Loairn moved from the mouth of the Firth of Lorne up the Great Glen to overrun the northern Pictish kingdom centred on the Moray Firth. They then appear in *Orkneyinga Saga* as the enemies of the Norse earls of Orkney who ruled as far south as the river Oykell in Sutherland. *Orkneyinga Saga* records two battles

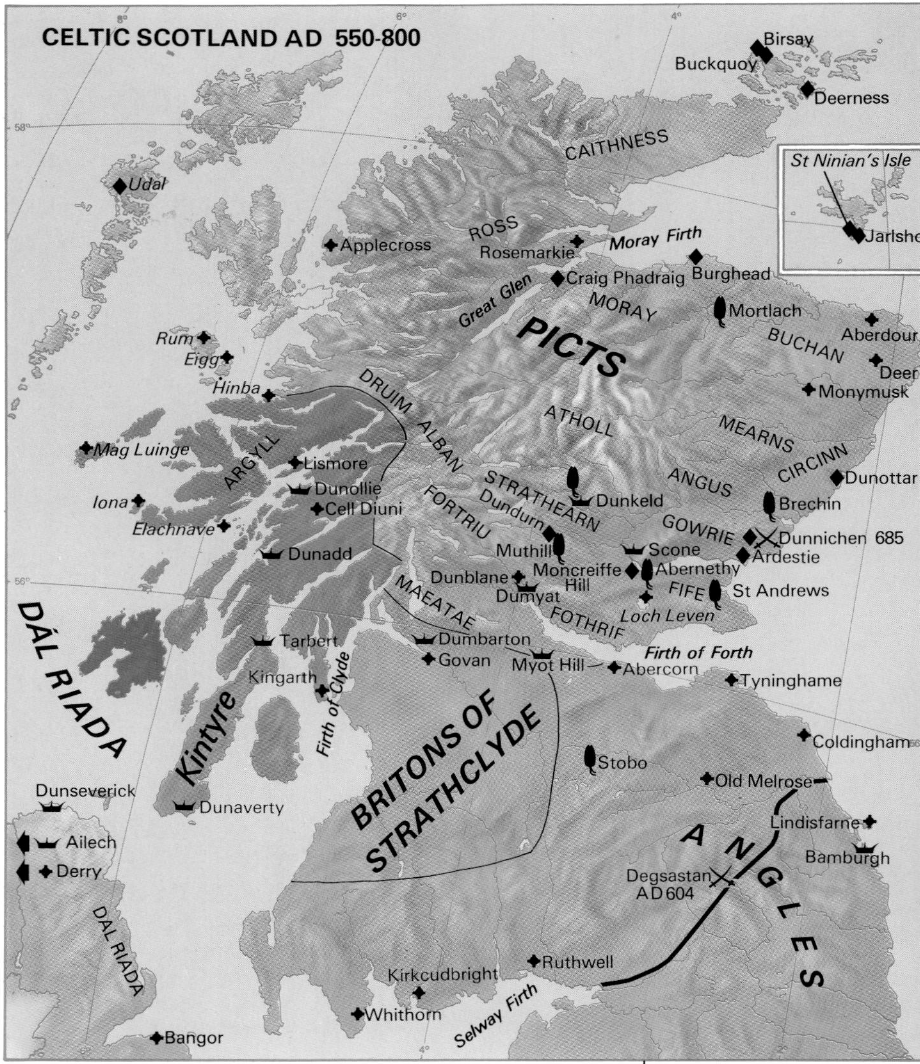

Celtic occupation of Scotland, 550–800. Beginning with the invasions of the Dál Riada from Antrim in Ireland, a new pattern of occupation began to emerge. The indigenous Picts were driven northwards and eastwards, while original British kingdoms centred on Strathclyde and the Borders came under pressure from migrating English (Angles) who established themselves from the Solway in the West to the Forth.

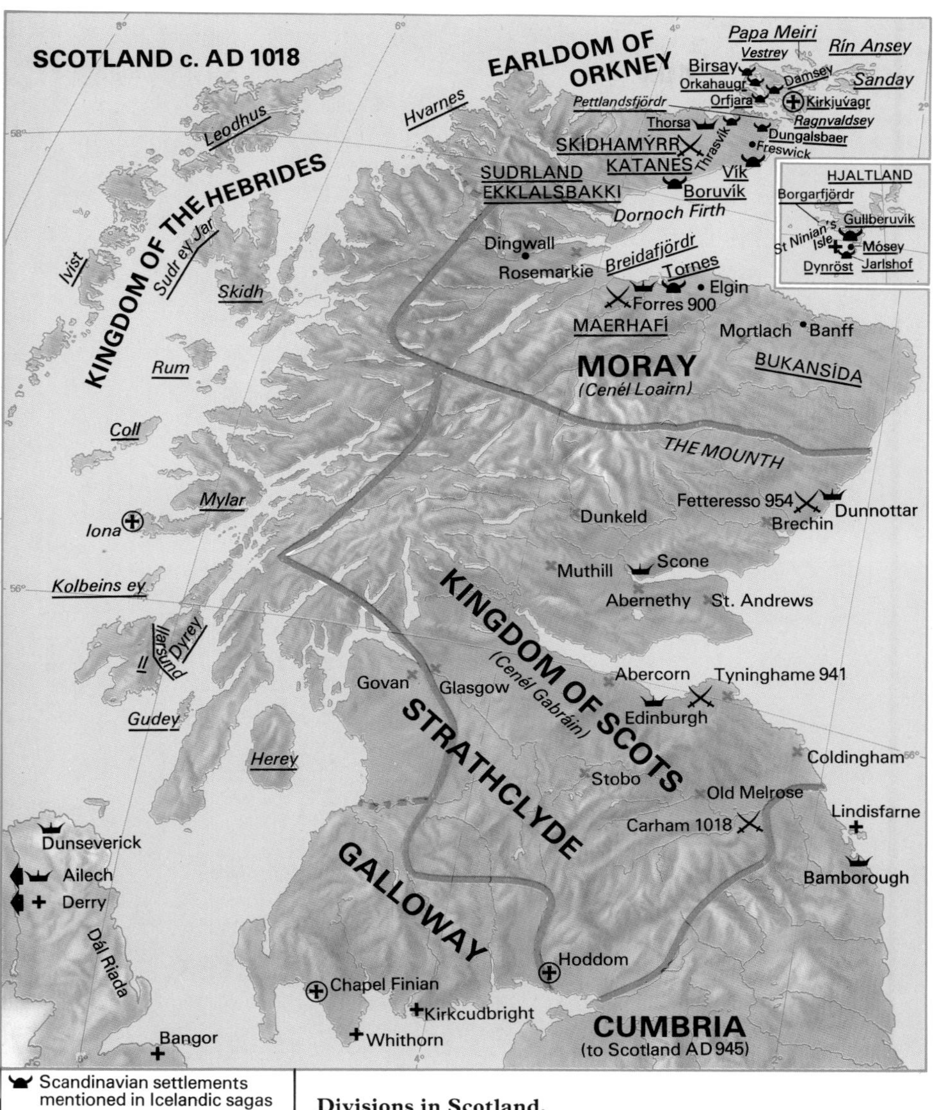

Divisions in Scotland, *c.*1018. Viking invasions from 850 overturned the balance of powers in Scotland. Forceful Scots kings turned events to their advantage in creating a strong Scots kingdom.

Pictish cross at Glamis Manse, Angus. Contact with Irish missionaries such as St Columba and his successors brought about a flowering of Christian Pictish culture.

in the 10th century between the Norsemen of Orkney and the Scots of Moray at Skitten (*Skídhamýrr*) in Caithness. This northern Scottish kingdom retained its own rulers and something of its autonomy right into the 11th century; Scottish chronicles show that several Scots kings from south of the Mounth were slain while invading Moray. But it was during this period that the dynasty of Kenneth mac Alpine deliberately set itself on a course which ultimately resulted in the formation of the kingdom of modern Scotland. Faced with a hostile dynasty in Moray, and lured south by the confusion caused by the Danish wars in England, the Cenél Gabráin pursued a policy of expansion across the Forth into Lothian, Strathclyde and Cumbria. Strathclyde fell early in the 10th century, its native British dynasty making way for a branch of Kenneth Mac Alpinés house.

At the same time, Galloway and the Northumbrian lands west of the Pennines were taken over by a further influx of Norse settlers. The emergence of the Danish kingdom of York then left the northern English isolated and beleaguered. In a complex series of wars and diplomatic manoeuvres the southern Scots took full advantage of this opportunity. In the mid-10th century they forced the English to abandon Edinburgh. Some 20 years later (*c.*973) Kenneth II secured parts of Lothian. When his son Malcolm defeated the Northumbrians at Carham in 1018 he completed this annexation and pushed the Scottish border to the Tweed. At about the same time (*c.*1015) the Scottish sub-kings of Strathclyde disappear from the pages of history. The Highlands and Islands had yet to be annexed but, apart from disputes over Cumbria, by 1018 southern Scotland had achieved permanent form.

The Irish Sea in the Viking Age, 800–1170

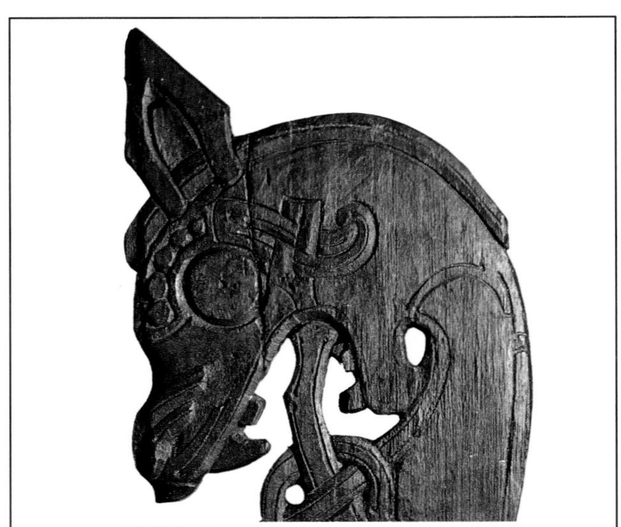

Carved wooden post ornament of the Viking Age. The restless energy of the Viking interlaced animal-art decoration testifies to a culture at once vigorous, barbaric and technically ingenious.

Opposite: The Irish Sea in the Viking Age. Viking power, based on mastery of the sea, was further consolidated under warlord rulers in Dublin and York.

- Major sea-route of 9th and 10th centuries
- Major sea-route of 11th and 12th centuries
- Minor sea-routes of all periods
- Regions colonized by Norsemen over substantial period of time
- Coastal area under Norse influence
- Churches, towns or settlements showing Norse influence in archaeology or place names
- Scandinavian fortress
- Ecclesiastical centres
- Ecclesiastical centres with Norse connections
- Other centres
- Battles

For three centuries, from 800 to 1100, the political and economic life of the Irish Sea was dominated by Scandinavian military activity and trade. A Viking stronghold was established at Dublin in 841 and by the 850s it had become the home of a dynasty of kings descended from an ancient Scandinavian line. Olaf the White, from the House of Vestfold in Norway, consolidated his Dublin base by bringing all the Norse colonists about the Irish coast into subjection to him. He further added to his realm in the 860s by subduing the Norse colonists of the Hebrides and Galloway, while also raiding extensively over Ireland and Scotland. Olaf's companion in the kingship of Dublin, Ivar, was joint leader of the Great Army which invaded England in 865 and which conquered York and south-eastern Northumbria in 866. The Scandinavian circle about the Irish Sea was closing in the opening years of the 10th century when Norwegian settlers poured into north-west England, colonizing the coastal lands between the Wirral and Galloway. These Scandinavian newcomers showed little regard for previous political alignments in the British Isles. Yet, from 850 until 954, the Norsemen themselves achieved a remarkable degree of political cohesion when, for a unique century in the history of these islands, they established a united realm based on Dublin and York.

York became a merchant city, whose Scandinavian street names still survive, with a harbour filled with ships from Ireland and Germania – as is vouched for by William of Malmesbury. Dublin was essentially an armed stronghold which gave protection to Viking traders and slave raiders who plied the Atlantic route, and its farming hinterland was less extensive and less significant than that of York. Communication between Dublin and York involved, as well as direct sailing across the Irish Sea, land journeys over the Pennines from the Wirral via Manchester and Leeds; along Ribblesdale and Wharfedale; and along the old Roman road from York to Carlisle. The Chester route is attested by Hingamund's invasion of the Wirral from Dublin in 902; by King Sitric's sacking of Davenport in Cheshire in 920; and by the Viking coin hoard at Bangor in North Wales. For the Ribblesdale route we have evidence of the impressive Cuerdale hoard in Lancashire which dates to the opening years of the 10th century, while the Carlisle road route to York was travelled by Eric Bloodaxe when that last Scandinavian king of York was struck down in an ambush on Stainmore in 954.

But land journeys over the Pennine passes were extremely hazardous and involved abandoning ships on the west coast of Britain. The most popular route between Dublin and York involved a sea journey via the Firths of Forth and Clyde, with an overland route across Lowland Scotland running roughly along the line of the Antonine Wall. There is documentary evidence to connect this sea-route with the reign of almost every over-king of York and Dublin. It was a journey which may have involved portage between the Forth and the Clyde. We have evidence in Norse saga for portage across Kintyre in the 11th century and Irish annals comment on the portage of Viking longships in the 10th century. The popularity of the Lowland Scottish route from York to Dublin drew Scottish rulers into close participation in the activities of the Viking warlords of York, as evidenced by Scottish involvement with King Guthfrith's invasion of Northumbria in 927, and by Scottish participation on the side of Olaf Guthfrithsson in the battle of Brunanburh in 934.

In spite of the collapse of the Danish monarchy in 954, Dublin enjoyed a considerable economic boom in the late 10th century, minting its own coins and harbouring a large colony of tradesmen and merchants behind its walls. This period, too, saw the flowering of remarkable Viking Christian sculptures on the Isle of Man at centres such as Kirk Michael, and on the shores of Cumbria as exemplified by the splendid cross at Gosforth. The prosperity enjoyed by Norse coastal settlements in the Irish Sea from the late 10th century onwards coincided with a shift in trade routes away from the old Dublin-York axis. The fall of York may have given Dublin a freer hand to trade with the ports of southern England and Normandy. She built up a lucrative trade with Bristol and Normandy during the 11th and 12th centuries, and it is largely to the 11th century that we may date Scandinavian place-name influence on the Welsh shores of the Bristol Channel where the Norsemen established staging posts on the run to Bristol, Cardiff and Newport.

The Dublin kingdom which had remained aggressively pagan eventually surrendered to Christianity, as shown first by the pilgrimage in 980 of King Olaf Cuaran to Iona – and later by the defeat of Sigurd and his pagan hordes from the Orkneys at the hands of the Irish high-king, Brian Boru, in the battle of Clontarf on Good Friday 1014. By the middle of the 11th century Dublin had even acquired its own Norse bishop and diocese, and it retained its Scandinavian culture and independence until it was finally destroyed by Anglo-Norman invaders in 1169. It was inevitable, as soon as Angevin power asserted itself in Britain, that the Hiberno-Norse trading monopoly in the Irish Sea was doomed. It may have been Bristol's trade with Waterford and Dublin which, more than anything else, attracted Strongbow and his followers to Ireland, and it was significantly the Hiberno-Norse towns which were the first to fall to the invaders.

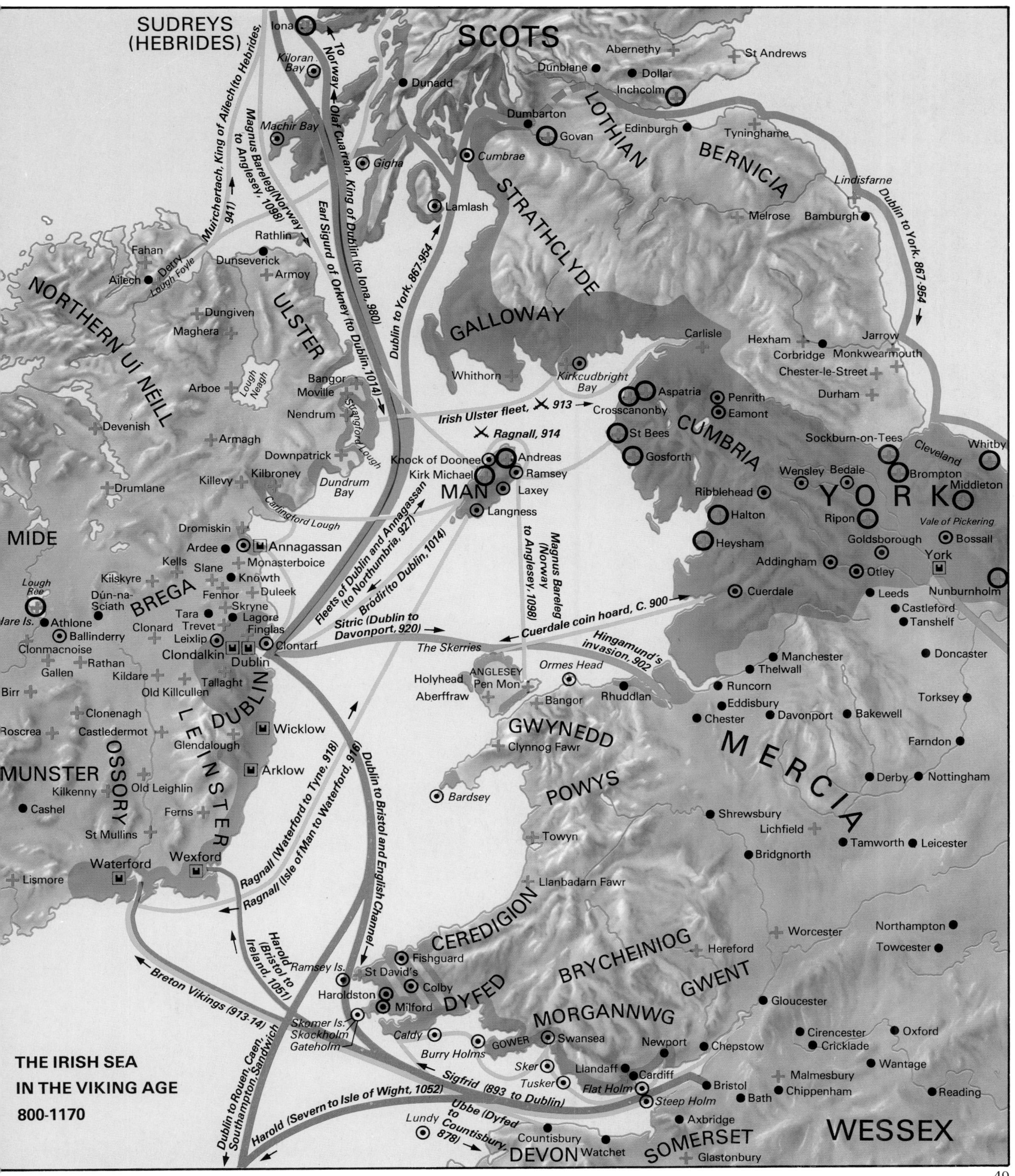
THE IRISH SEA
IN THE VIKING AGE
800-1170
SUDREYS (HEBRIDES)
SCOTS
LOTHIAN
BERNICIA
STRATHCLYDE
GALLOWAY
CUMBRIA
YORK
MAN
NORTHERN UÍ NÉILL
ULSTER
MIDE
BREGA
DUBLIN
LEINSTER
OSSORY
MUNSTER
GWYNEDD
POWYS
MERCIA
CEREDIGION
BRYCHEINIOG
GWENT
DYFED
MORGANNWG
SOMERSET
DEVON
WESSEX
Iona
Dunadd
Dublin

The Reign of Aethelred the Unready

Opposite page: Viking and Scandinavian attacks on Aethelred's kingdom. The earliest raids were by Vikings from settlements around the Irish Sea. Direct attacks from Scandinavia grew in scale and frequency during the 990s. The map indicates that the North escaped relatively lightly but this may reflect the largely southern interest of contemporary commentators.

A coin of Aethelred's reign. The wealth of England, expressed here in the coinage, was a magnet to Viking attack and conquest.

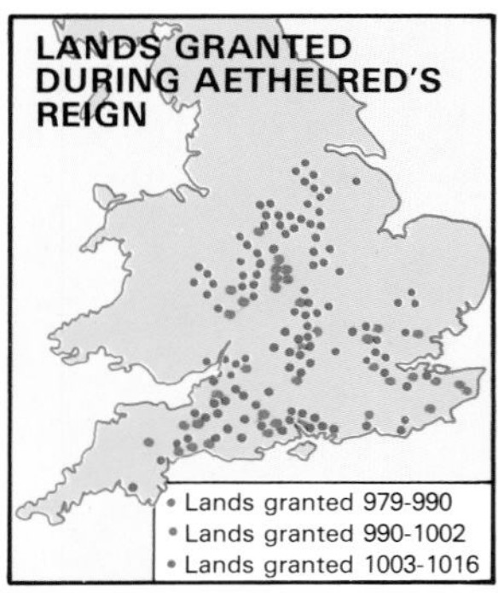

The distribution of Aethelred's land grants, 979–1016. Despite severe external attack, the political and administrative pattern of Aethelred's reign long followed that of the earlier 10th century. After 1003, however, the traditional concentration of royal grants in and around Wessex changed. Royal patronage shifted into the Midlands and eastern England, partly in response to Viking attacks.

In popular history Aethelred cuts a poor figure: Aethelred 'the Unready', the king who lost England to the Vikings. To some extent this is a view which goes back to his own time, to the *Anglo-Saxon Chronicle*. But whereas the *Chronicle* had given an 'official' – and favourable – account of Alfred's reign, it looks at Aethelred's reign from a very different standpoint, presenting a detailed picture of royal incompetence, internal treachery and cowardly collapse. It was not that simple. The *Chronicle* was written during the last few years of the reign when English defeat was obvious. Its account is deeply scarred by the recriminations of defeat and by the contemporary need for scapegoats. Study of the events reveals a much more complex picture.

Aethelred was crowned at Kingston-on-Thames in 979, but the circumstances in which the young king came to the throne were far from happy. Edgar's death in 975 had been followed by a bitter succession dispute between the rival factions which supported his two surviving sons (by two different wives) Aethelred and Edward. Edward was the elder of the two and he was initially victorious, but he was then murdered and Aethelred's mother, Aelfrida, was widely believed to be responsible. News of English political troubles may have spurred the renewal of Viking attacks. But attacks on Wales from the Viking settlements in the Irish Sea had never ceased during the 10th century, and the late 10th century saw a general revival of Viking raiding in Western Europe.

During the 980s, raids along the Welsh coast were extended to south-west England. At the same time attacks on London and south-east England began, apparently from the North Sea and Scandinavia. The 990s saw the operation of great armies under the leadership of Olaf, later King of Norway, and Swein, King of Denmark.

During this period the response to Viking attack was constructive, if traditional. Aethelred had appointed ealdormen to take charge of key military areas: Leofwine in the West Midlands; Leofsige in Essex; Aelfhelm in York. An attack on Essex in 991 was met by the local ealdorman Brihtnoth at a famous encounter at Maldon; in 992 a fleet assembled at London had some success against the Viking army; the time-honoured methods of ransom, Danegeld, and baptism of Viking leaders continued to be followed.

During the brief respite in the year 1000, Aethelred launched a double attack on the Isle of Man and Cumber land, suggesting a mistaken assumption that the majo threat still came from the Vikings in the Irish Sea. In fac the major onslaught came directly from Scandinavi especially from Swein and Denmark. From 1003 to 100 and again in 1013, Swein led devastating attacks o England, while Thorkell the Tall campaigned in the Sout and East between 1009 and 1013. Aethelred continued t combine the payment of tributes with attempts at militar organization. A series of huge gelds was paid to victoriou Viking armies: 24,000 pounds in 1002, 36,000 pounds i 1007, and 48,000 pounds in 1012. By 1006 the stresses o internal political intrigue and external attack had brough the exile of Leofsige and murder of Aelfhelm.

In 1007 Aethelred ordered the building of ships and re created the large ealdormanry of Mercia for Eadric in a attempt to co-ordinate English defences. But the flee assembled at Sandwich in 1009 fell prey to bad weather, not to internal treachery, and English efforts had little effec against Thorkell's determined campaign of 1009–13. Thi culminated in the capture and murder of Aelfheah archbishop of Canterbury. Swein came to England i August 1013 secure in the expectation of conquest. A Gainsborough he received the submission of Northumbri Lindsey and the Five Boroughs; Oxford, Winchester an south-west England soon followed. Finally, towards th end of the year, the last resistance collapsed. Swein wa recognized as king and Aethelred fled to Normandy.

Swein died in 1014 and the Viking fleet immediatel raised his son Cnut as king, but the English councillo recalled Aethelred. In 1015 Aethelred's eldest son Edmun revolted against his father in an attempt to usurp th throne: an act which may well betray fears of his younge half-brothers and their mother, Aethelred's second wif This, coupled with the king's illness and the enmit between Edmund and ealdorman Eadric, divided the fin stages of the English effort.

Aethelred died in 1016 and, in spite of Eadric of Mercia' defection to Cnut, Edmund – though defeated in battle a Ashingdon – contrived to hold Cnut to a stalemat Division of England, giving Edmund Wessex and Cnut th North, was nullified by Edmund's premature death i 1016. And so the Viking conqueror Cnut was left to ru England.

The site of the Battle of Maldon, Essex (991). Danish invaders found themselves confronted by a local English defence force led by the ealdorman Brihtnoth. At the end of a bloody encounter Brihtnoth and his retainers lay dead: their courage and loyalty were immortalized in a famous Old English poem.

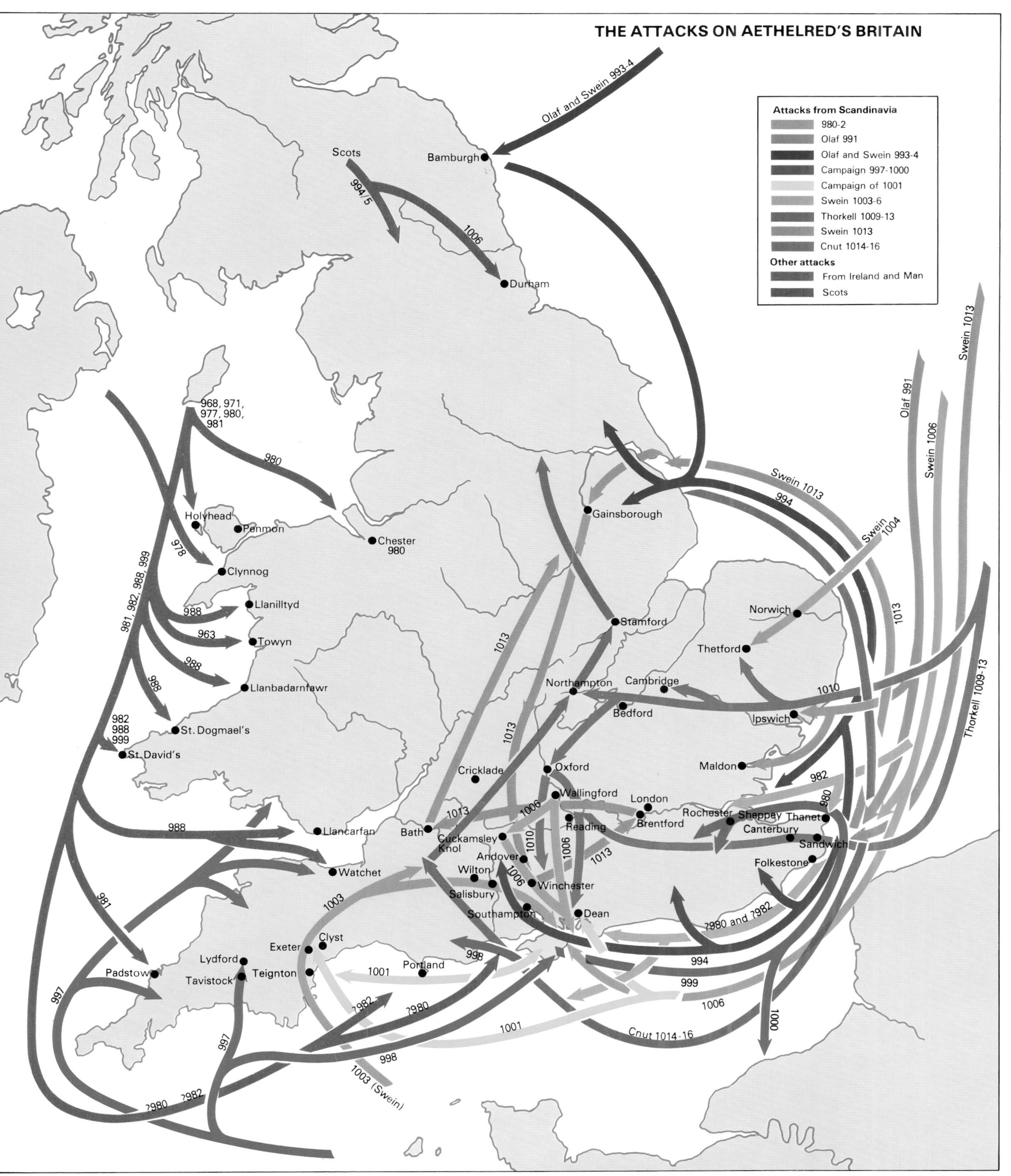

THE ATTACKS ON AETHELRED'S BRITAIN
Attacks from Scandinavia
980-2
Olaf 991
Olaf and Swein 993-4
Campaign 997-1000
Campaign of 1001
Swein 1003-6
Thorkell 1009-13
Swein 1013
Cnut 1014-16
Other attacks
From Ireland and Man
Scots
Olaf and Swein 993-4
Scots
Bamburgh
994/5
1006
Durham
968, 971, 977, 980, 981
980
Holyhead
Penmon
Chester 980
978
Clynnog
981, 982, 988, 999
Llanilltyd
988
963
Towyn
988
Llanbadarnfawr
988
982 988 999
St. Dogmael's
St. David's
988
Llancarfan
Watchet
981
Padstow
Lydford
Tavistock
Teignton
Exeter
Clyst
1003
1001
Portland
998
?982
?980
1001
997
997
998
1003 (Swein)
?980
?982
Gainsborough
Swein 1013
994
Swein 1004
Stamford
Norwich
Thetford
Northampton
Cambridge
Bedford
Ipswich
1010
1013
1013
1013
Cricklade
Oxford
Maldon
Wallingford
London
Brentford
Reading
Rochester
Sheppey
Thanet
Canterbury
Sandwich
Folkestone
982
980
1013
Bath
Cuckamsley Knol
1006
1010
1006
1013
Andover
Wilton
Salisbury
Winchester
1006
Southampton
Dean
?980 and ?982
994
999
1006
Cnut 1014-16
1000
Olaf 991
Swein 1006
Swein 1013
1013
Thorkell 1009-13

Cnut's North Sea Empire and the Rise of the House of Godwine, 1016–57

An early representation of Cnut, his crown held by an angel.

Cnut's conquest of England in 1016 laid the foundation of a northern empire. After his coronation in 1018, and his marriage with Emma, Aethelred II's widow (a marriage which secured the goodwill of her brother, the Duke of Normandy), Cnut's position as king was impregnable. A year or so later, he acquired the kingdom of Denmark after the death of his brother Harald. In Norway, however, the pro-Danish jarls of Hlathir (Lade), who had ruled the kingdom on Swein's behalf, had been driven out by Olaf Haraldson (St Olaf), and Cnut regained control only after the two battles of Holy River (1026–7) and Stiklastadir (1030), in the second of which St Olaf was killed.

Although trade had long existed between England and Scandinavia, the kingdoms of Cnut's empire had little in common besides allegiance to the King, and no general administrative structure existed to unite them. English traders and missionaries travelled to Scandinavia and Scandinavian traders to England; many Danes settled in England and to some Cnut gave high administrative rank. It was at this period that the English title 'ealdorman' was replaced by the Danish 'earl (jarl)', though this change of name did not mean any change in the nature of the office or the powers of its holder. Conversely, Cnut's English wife, Aelfgifu of Northampton (herself an ealdorman's daughter), was made regent of Norway for their eldest son, Swein. But her reign was unpopular and, even before Cnut's death, she was driven out in favour of St Olaf's son, Magnus. On the English side of the North Sea few of Cnut's Danish earls outlasted the 1020s. At the end of the reign, the kingdom was dominated by three earls – an Englishman of the old aristocracy (Leofric of Mercia), an English newcomer (Godwine of Wessex) married to a Dane, and a Dan (Siward of Northumbria) married to an Englishwoman. N earl of East Anglia is recorded between the exile of Thorke the Tall in 1020 and the appointment of Harold in 1044–5 though Thuri 'earl of the middle peoples', recorde between 1041 and 1044–5, presumably held an earldom i the east Midlands.

Cnut's empire collapsed on his death. The rebellion o Magnus of Norway led to prolonged war between Norwa and Denmark, and this prevented Hardacnut, Cnut' chosen heir and son by Emma, from crossing to England. I his absence, his half-brother Harold was chosen, first a regent, and later as king, and Emma was forced to go int exile.

After Harold's death (1040) Hardacnut re-united th two kingdoms; but when Hardacnut himself died in 1042 England reverted to the old West Saxon line. The short an troubled reigns of Cnut's sons saw the rise of powerfu dynasties in England, notably the family of Earl Godwin From obscure origins in Sussex, this family rose in tw generations to the pinnacle of power. A turning-point in it fortunes was the marriage in 1043 of Godwine's daughte Edith to King Edward the Confessor. The advancement c her kinsmen followed immediately; an earldom was spe cially created for her eldest brother Swein (1044), he second brother, Harold, became earl of East Angli (1044–5) and her cousin Beorn Estrithson received a earldom in the east Midlands, apparently as Harold' subordinate.

Swein Godwineson was the family's black sheep and hi wilder exploits – including the abduction of the abbess c Leominster and the murder of his cousin Beorn – led to hi

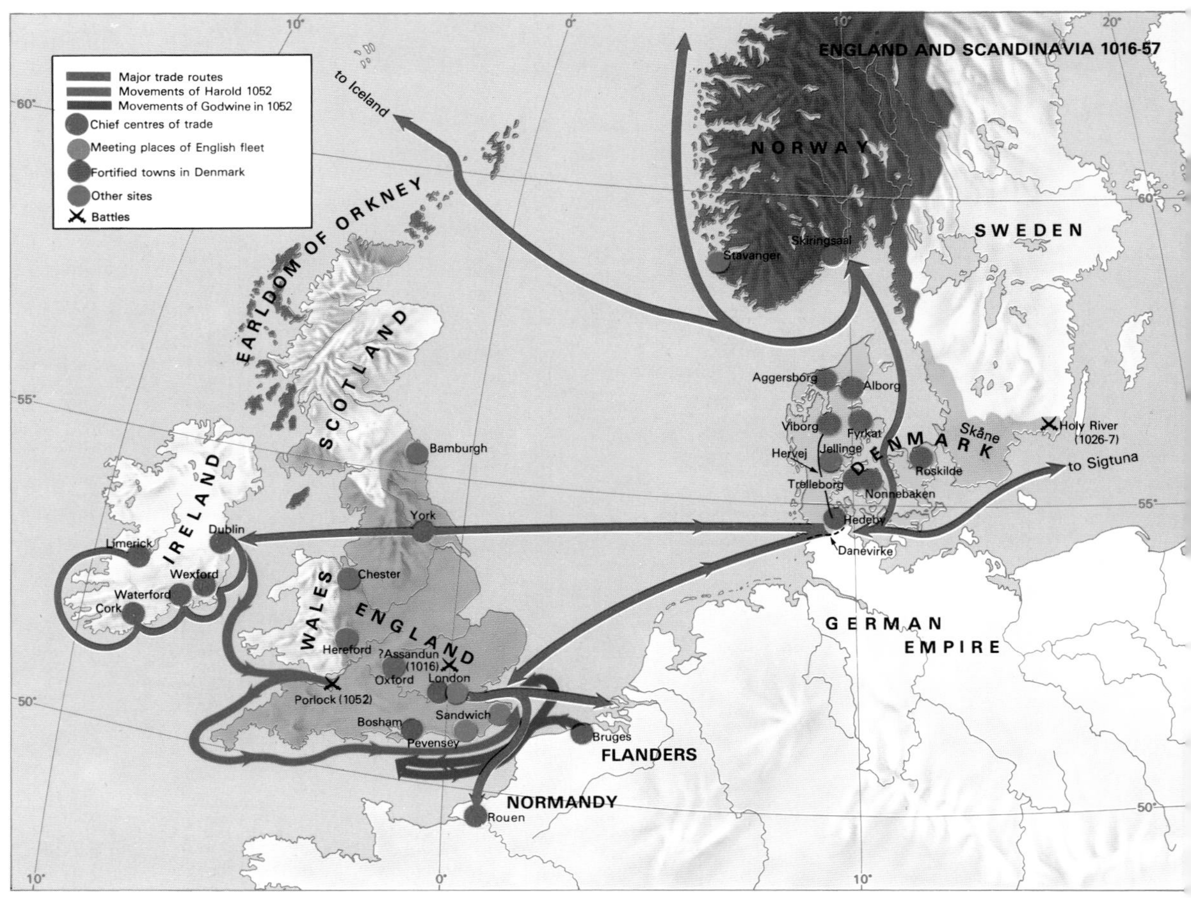

The political union of England, Denmark and Norway made possession of an effective fleet an essential adjunct of royal power. Cnut used the land-tax *(geld)*, first raised by Aethelred II, to maintain a force of ships' crews *(lithesmen* or *butsecarles)* based at London, and each campaigning season began with an assembly of ships at Sandwich. This system remained in operation until 1051, when Edward the Confessor abolished the geld and paid off the ships' crews; though the older naval force raised from the shires (the *scipfyrd*) continued till 1066.

anishment in 1049, though he was later pardoned. Edward bviously resented his dependence upon Godwine and, in 051, the Earl and his family were deprived of their titles nd exiled. But the King had over-reached himself. In 1052 Godwine's family engineered a successful return, forcing he King to restore their land and titles.

Godwine died in 1053 and was succeeded (Swein being ead) by Harold, who became earl of Wessex, yielding his East Anglian earldom to Aelfgar, son of Leofric of Mercia. n 1055, on the death of Siward, Tostig Godwineson, the third brother, became earl of Northumbria; and when, in 1057, both Leofric of Mercia and Earl Ralph of Hereford died, Harold added Hereford to the earldom of Wessex, Gyrth succeeded Aelfgar (now earl of Mercia) in East Anglia, and Leofwine received an earldom in the east Midlands. From this time onwards, Harold was the real ruler of England. His campaigns against the Welsh, culminating in the conquest of north Wales, added to his prestige and he was justly described by contemporaries as *subregulus* (underking) and *dux Anglorum*.

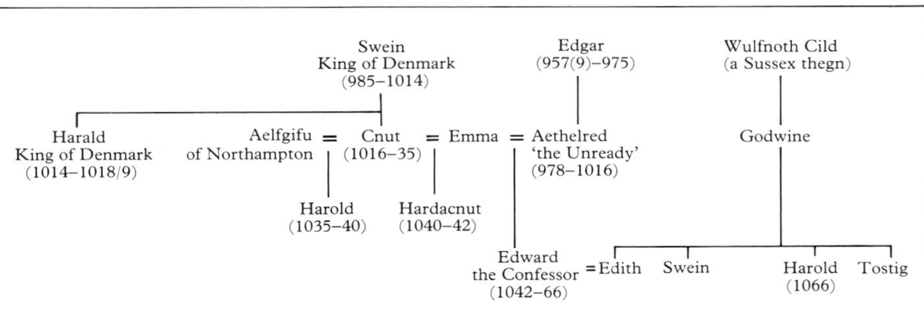

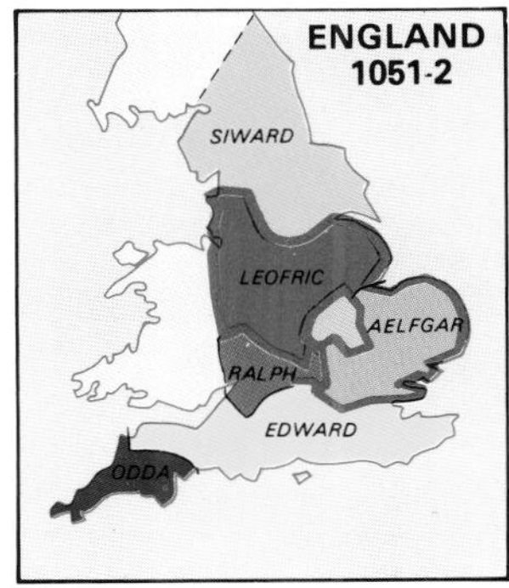

Below left: The Anglo-Danish earldoms *c.*1020. The itle of earl (jarl), like its predecessor earldorman, described men of varied power. It was borne by great nobles set over entire provinces (as in the case of Thorkell the Tall of East Anglia) and by 'subordinate' earls, such as Hakon of Worcestershire, in charge of a single shire. Dominant by the end of Cnut's reign were the earls of Mercia and Wessex. Leofwine's son, Leofric, added the Five Boroughs to his earldom of Mercia; Godwine of Central Wessex acquired the shires of Sired and Aethelweard.

Above left: Relationships between the Danish and Wessex royal houses and the Godwine family.

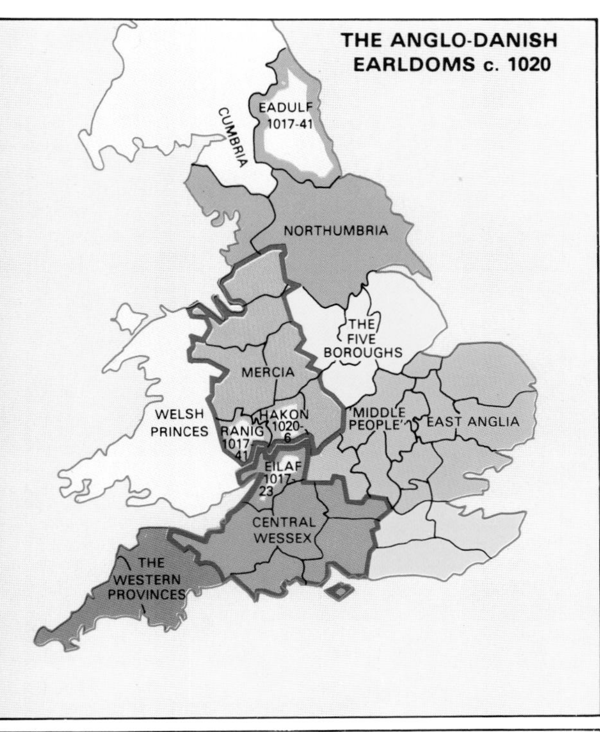

Earldom of Godwine

Earldom of Thorkell the Tall (1017-20)

Earldom of Aethelweard (1017-20)

Earldom of Sired (1019-22)

Earldom of Leofwine (1018-23)

Earldom of Erik of Hlathir (1017-23)

Lordship unknown before 1030

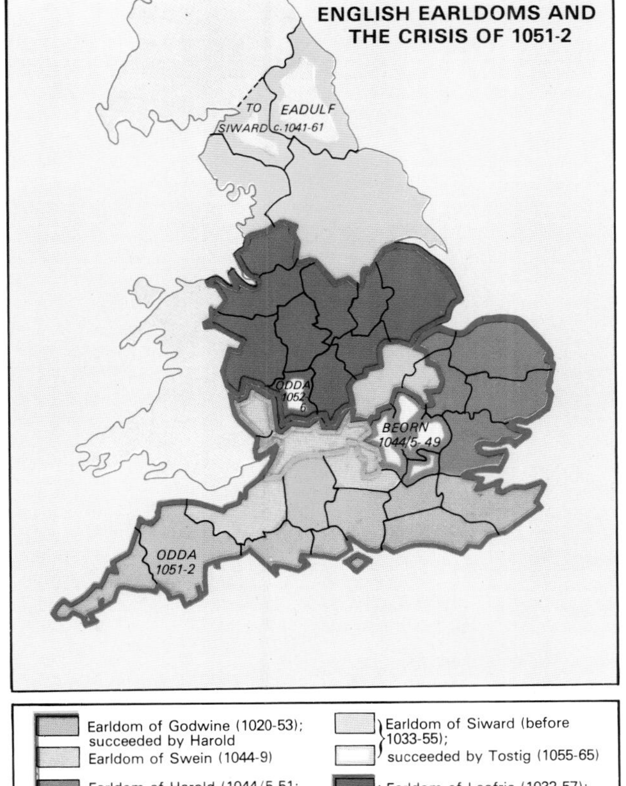

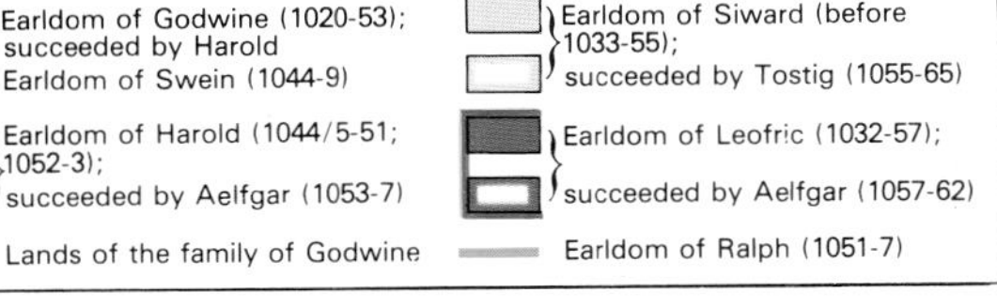

The struggle for power, 1051–2. On the disgrace of Godwine in 1051, Edward redistributed the Godwine earldoms (see map left) as in the small map above. He entrusted the western shires to his kinsman Odda. Swein's earldom was dismembered and East Anglia was given to Aelfgar, son of Leoric of Mercia. On the triumphant return of Godwine and his sons, the earldoms of Wessex and East Anglia were returned to Godwine and Harold. Earl Odda was compensated with an earldom in Worcestershire.

1066: The Year of Three Kings

Coinage issued by Edward the Confessor (top), Harold and William.

Distribution of the English earldoms 1057–1066. The sons of Godwine, led by Harold, were at the height of their power in the years 1055–65. As well as the earldoms held by the family in the South, Tostig was earl in Northumbria. But Tostig and Harold seem to have been jealous of each other, and family unity was probably not as impressive as it might seem. After the northern revolt of 1065, Northumbria passed to Morkere, brother of Eadwine of Mercia, but this turbulent province was not a source of strength.

The death of Edward II ('the Confessor') in January 1066 left England without an adult male representative of the royal line. William the Bastard, Duke of Normandy, claimed that Edward had promised him the kingdom as early as 1051, while Harold Godwineson, Earl of Wessex and for many years the King's right-hand-man, said that Edward had granted him the throne on his deathbed. The Scandinavian kings could be expected to fish in these troubled waters, as Harald of Norway did in September 1066, followed by Swein Estrithson of Denmark after the Conquest. A further factor was Harold's brother Tostig, exiled in 1065, who attempted to regain his earldom by force of arms.

With the death of Edward, William and his magnates took steps to build a fleet and gather an army in Normandy; in England, Harold and his nobles decided to station an army along the south coast and a fleet off the Isle of Wight. But Tostig was first off the mark, raiding the south coast until frightened off by Harold, and the east coast until Earl Edwin defeated him in Lindsey. Tostig fled to Scotland, where he sheltered until joining Harald of Norway.

Harold watched the Channel from May until early September. If William had sailed when he had hoped to, he would have run into a warm reception. According to the *Anglo-Saxon Chronicle* Harold had mustered 'greater nava and land levies than any king ever before in this century' By using a two-month shift system he was able to keep ar army and a fleet in position throughout the summer William was lucky. The prevailing wind direction kept hi fleet bottled up in port until after the provisions of the English forces had been exhausted. In September Harolc disbanded his levies and returned to London, where he heard that the Norwegians had landed in Yorkshire. Withir two weeks he raised an army and force-marched it from London to York but, before he could arrive, Edwin and Morkere stood against Harald of Norway at Gate Fulford some two miles south of York. Their defeat after a harc battle meant that they could play little part in the following events, and left the invaders free to march on York, where the men of the shire agreed to help in the conquest of England Five days later King Harold and his army pounced on the Norwegians at their camp at Stamfordbridge, taking them by surprise. The battle raged all day, and by nightfall or 25th September, Harald of Norway and Tostig lay deac and the shattered remains of their army were in full flight

Harold had defeated one of the foremost warriors of the age and, tradition had it, was at a celebration feast when the news arrived that William had landed with his army a

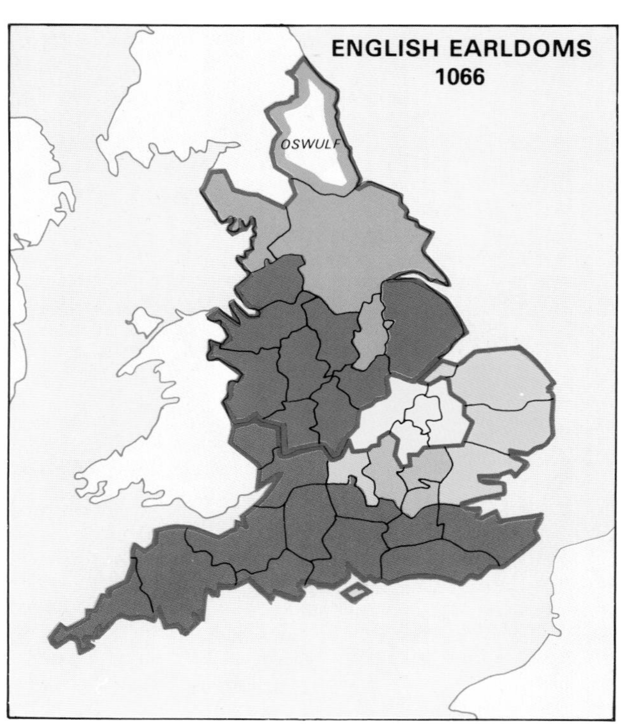

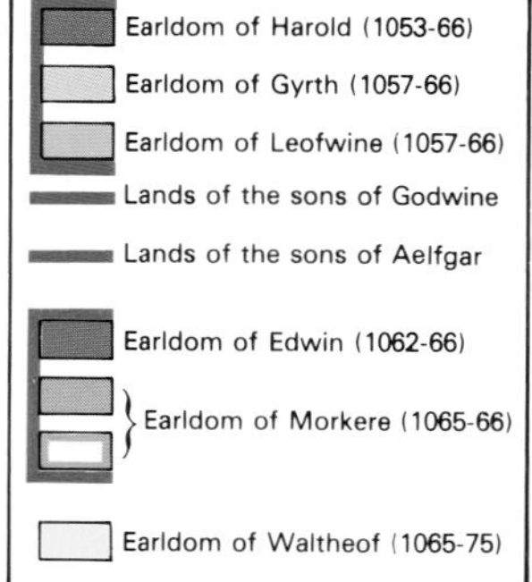

Harold's campaigns of 1066.

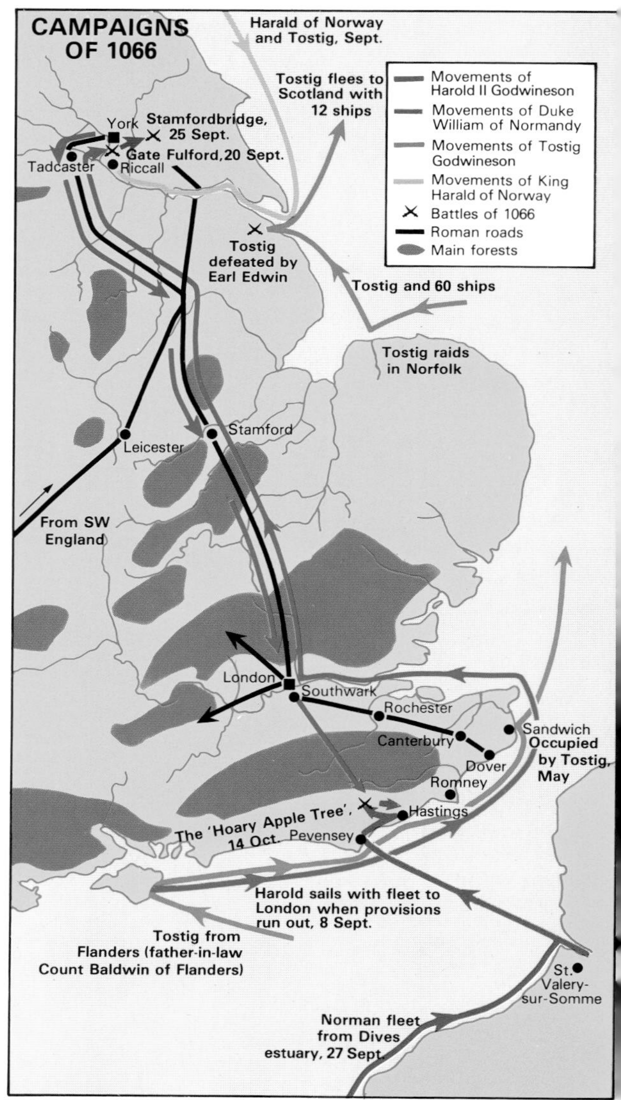

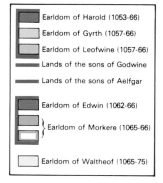

Pevensey on the morning of 28th September. The winds which had detained William on the coasts of Normandy had blown Harald of Norway across the North Sea, and had then changed to carry William's fleet to the undefended south coast of England. William's achievement in keeping together his polyglot army through the summer, and in welding it into an effective fighting force, cannot be over-emphasized.

The Norman Invasion

Once more King Harold was all energy: within 13 days at the most he had completed the settlement of the restless North, marched 190 miles (304 km) back to London, raised more troops and marched a further 50 miles (80 km) to a point in striking distance of Hastings, where the Normans had established their base.

Harold has been accused of 'reckless and impulsive haste', and the chroniclers agree that he fought with an army smaller than it need have been. It seems that Harold sought to take the Normans by surprise, a tactic that had worked three weeks before. But the Norman scouts warned of the English approach on the morning of 14th October and it was the English who were taken by surprise.

The English dismounted on the cross-ridge at Battle to fight on foot in their traditional manner. It is generally said that each army numbered about 7000 men, but the figures may have been lower. The English may have deployed some 4000 men, mainly nobles, and the Normans perhaps 5000 infantry, including archers and crossbowmen, and about 2000 knights. The battle began at 9 a.m. and lasted all day. The English shieldwall managed to survive the attacks of the Norman knights and archers until the death of Harold at dusk. Then the English survivors fled into the forests of the Weald.

The deaths of Harold and his brothers Gyrth and Leofwine did not win for William the Crown of England. It was not until he had made a threatening march round London, ravaging on the way, and perhaps an abortive attempt to force the passage of London Bridge, that the English leaders began to submit in any numbers. During this time there was a movement to make the royal prince Edgar king, but he was only a boy and had little support outside London. So William was accepted and crowned king on Christmas Day 1066 – but he had only defeated in battle the strength of southern and central England. In the following years his rule would be severely tested by revolts throughout the West Country, West Mercia and Northumbria.

A section of the Bayeux tapestry. This work was commissioned by William's half-brother Odo, bishop of Bayeux and probably produced in a Canterbury workshop. Here we see Harold's death through first being struck in the eye by an arrow and then cut down by a cavalryman's sword.

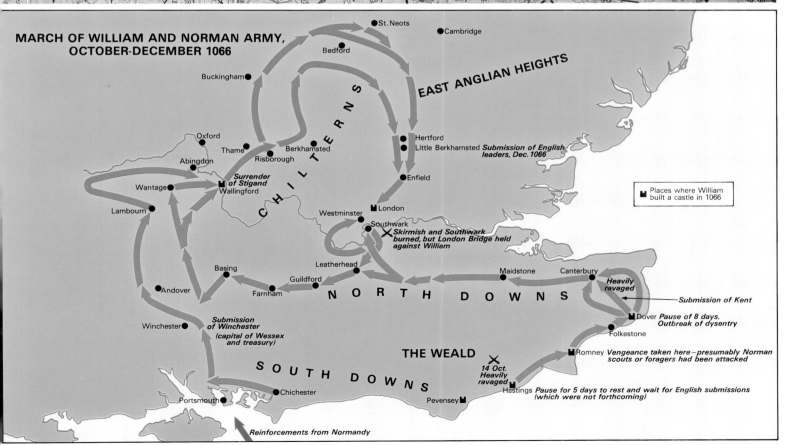

MARCH OF WILLIAM AND NORMAN ARMY, OCTOBER-DECEMBER 1066

St. Neots
Cambridge
Bedford
Buckingham
EAST ANGLIAN HEIGHTS
CHILTERNS
Oxford
Thame
Berkhamsted
Risborough
Abingdon
Hertford
Little Berkhamsted *Submission of English leaders, Dec. 1066*
Enfield
Wantage
Surrender of Stigand
Wallingford
Lambourn
Westminster
London
Southwark
Skirmish and Southwark burned, but London Bridge held against William
Places where William built a castle in 1066
Basing
Leatherhead
Guildford
Farnham
Andover
Maidstone
Canterbury
Heavily ravaged
NORTH DOWNS
Submission of Kent
Dover *Pause of 8 days. Outbreak of dysentry*
Folkestone
Winchester
Submission of Winchester (capital of Wessex and treasury)
THE WEALD
Romney *Vengeance taken here–presumably Norman scouts or foragers had been attacked*
14 Oct. Heavily ravaged
SOUTH DOWNS
Hastings *Pause for 5 days to rest and wait for English submissions (which were not forthcoming)*
Chichester
Portsmouth
Pevensey
Reinforcements from Normandy

Revolt and Repression, 1066–86

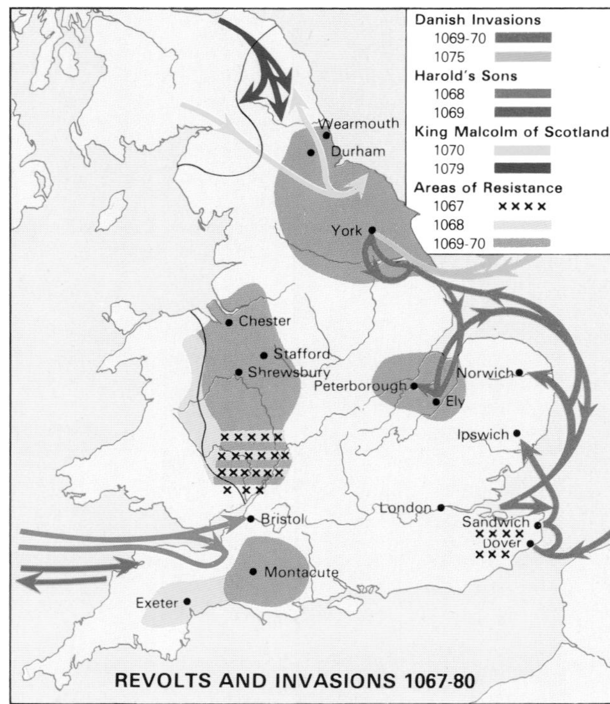

The threat to William: revolts and invasions, 1067–80.

Richmond Castle, Yorkshire. This, one of the earliest Norman castles to be built, is also one of the best-preserved. Its magnificent site, high above the River Swale, was a naturally strategic point from which to command both the river crossing and Swaledale beyond.

The battle of Hastings was one of the decisive events in English history. It settled the fate not just of a ruler, but of an entire ruling class. The political preoccupations, the style of warfare, even the language of the new élite, marked a break with the past. However, when William was crowned king at Christmas 1066, most of these changes were yet to be felt, for the conquest of England was still in its early stages. For the next two decades he and his followers had to overcome internal resistance and invasion from outside in order to extend and consolidate their hold. Resistance began in 1067 with the revolt of Edric the Wild in Herefordshire, and a rising in Kent in which the English called on Eustace of Boulogne, a man who had fought for William at Hastings but had interests of his own to press in England. The following year saw the resistance and subjugation of Exeter, followed by the submission of the South-West, so that an expedition from Ireland, led by King Harold's illegitimate sons, met with resistance at Bristol and the surrounding area.

The real crisis came in 1069, when trouble arose in many quarters. The major theatre was the North, an area as yet barely touched by Norman rule. There a general rising was headed by Edgar 'the Aetheling', of the old line of the kings of Wessex. The rebels were joined by a Danish fleet sent by King Swein, who also had claims to the throne of England, and after taking York the combined force moved into north Lincolnshire. Meanwhile, news of the rising put heart into the resistance elsewhere, and Edric the Wild's revolt spread north as far as Chester and Stafford. There was also a rising in Dorset and Somerset and, to cap it all, another expedition of Harold's sons. The way William tackled this crisis exhibited to the full that decisiveness and ruthlessness which were characteristic of his generalship. Sending lieutenants to the South and West, he himself marched north, laying waste the area round York, and the rebels retreated to their ships in the Humber estuary. There followed that systematic destruction known as the 'Harrying of the North': in the dead of winter William marched as far north as the river Tees, then crossed the Pennines to subdue Chester and Stafford, before returning south. The rebellion was not yet over, however, because the Danish fleet sailed from the Humber to join Hereward, a Lincolnshire thegn whose resistance in the Isle of Ely became a legend. Their joint forces attacked Peterborough Abbey, but when the Danes retired from the struggle in 1070 it marked the beginning of the end for Hereward, who eventually surrendered.

Although 1069–70 was the most serious challenge to William's rule, the remainder of his reign was far from trouble-free. The 1070s saw two new developments. The first was the active intervention of the Scottish king, Malcolm Canmore, whose incursions over the border led William in 1072 to mount a daring and risky expedition by land and sea which eventually met the Scottish king at Abernethy on the river Tay. There Malcolm did homage and handed over one of his sons as a hostage. A further invasion in 1079 was followed by another Norman expedition and a renewal of homage. The second development was a breakdown of that unanimity of purpose among the Normans which had contributed greatly to their success. In 1075 the Norman Earl of Hereford joined Ralph the Breton, Earl of East Anglia, and they associated with their revolt a third earl, the Englishman Waltheof. In the event their rebellion was contained easily enough, and a Danish fleet, called on by Earl Ralph, arrived too late to be of any use and had to be content with attacking York again.

One of the crucial factors in explaining why relatively few Normans could hold down large areas is their use of castles.

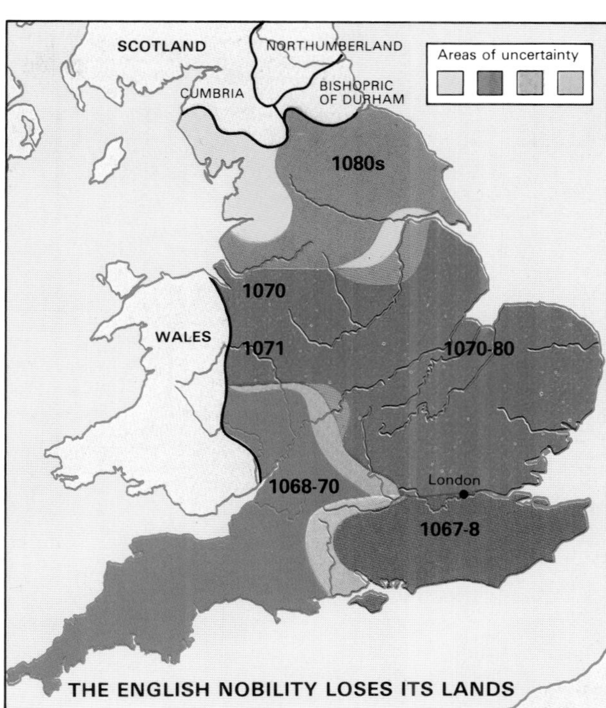

Although the possible existence of castles in England before 1066 has been debated, it is clear that castle-building, already developed by the Normans, was to be one of the important changes wrought by the Conquest. One of William's first actions on landing in 1066 had been the building of a castle at Hastings, graphically depicted in the Bayeux Tapestry. This was followed up by the planning of castles at strategic points on roads and in centres of population. Early post-Conquest castles were characteristically simple earth-and-timber fortifications which, where possible, made use of existing natural or man-made defences. Often the castle consisted of a motte, or mound, surmounted by a wooden palisade, and a surrounding bailey, or enclosure. Such fortifications could be thrown up quickly (William is said to have built one of the two castles at York in eight days). Documentary evidence for the building of castles is usually lacking, and there may have been many more in existence by 1086 than are shown on the map.

In the same year, 1086, the Domesday survey reveals just how complete had been the dispossession of a native nobility in favour of the Normans. Although many Englishmen still had lands, there were only two remaining in the first ranks of the magnates. Yet there are signs that at the start William did not envisage, nor could he have achieved, such a complete transfer. In the early days it seems Englishmen could offer their submission and receive back their lands from him, and leading Englishmen like the earls Edwin and Morkere were to be found in his entourage. But military considerations as well as the need to reward his followers soon prompted the distribution of lands in the South-East, grants of land in Sussex probably dating from the winter of 1067–8. A second area of military importance where dispossession started early was the Welsh Marches. William FitzOsbern was evidently exercising extensive powers in Herefordshire and the neighbouring counties of Gloucestershire and Worcestershire before his death in 1071. Elsewhere there are signs that Normans were acquiring lands by peaceful means, through marriage or as tenants. The crisis of 1069–70 and the final fall of Earl Edwin in the following year seems to have brought this early phase to an end. Further lordships were set up in Cheshire and Shropshire, and the whole of the Midlands and East Anglia fell into Norman hands, though the details of this process remain obscure. In the North it would appear that settlement was later, possibly a few years before the Domesday survey, while in the North-East Norman penetration was still minimal.

Castle-building was vital to the completion and consolidation of the Norman Conquest. As the Normans tightened their grip on England, there was a parallel dispossession of the landowning English nobility (top right). The landowners of the South-East were the first to go; not until the 1080s were those who lived north of the Humber in much danger.

Above right: A scene from the Bayeux tapestry showing a castle being built.

Chapter Three
BRITAIN AND EUROPE, 1066-1660

The Norman Conquest ushered in a period when the French political and cultural connection was of paramount importance: language, literature and art were all profoundly influenced. From 1066 until the 15th century the king of England was also a French prince; from 1340 indeed the kings of England claimed to be king of France, a title that was not relinquished until the 17th century. For more than four hundred years the requirements of continental warfare acted as the chief motor of governmental development and only at the end of this period did Englishmen begin to look beyond Europe to a wider world.

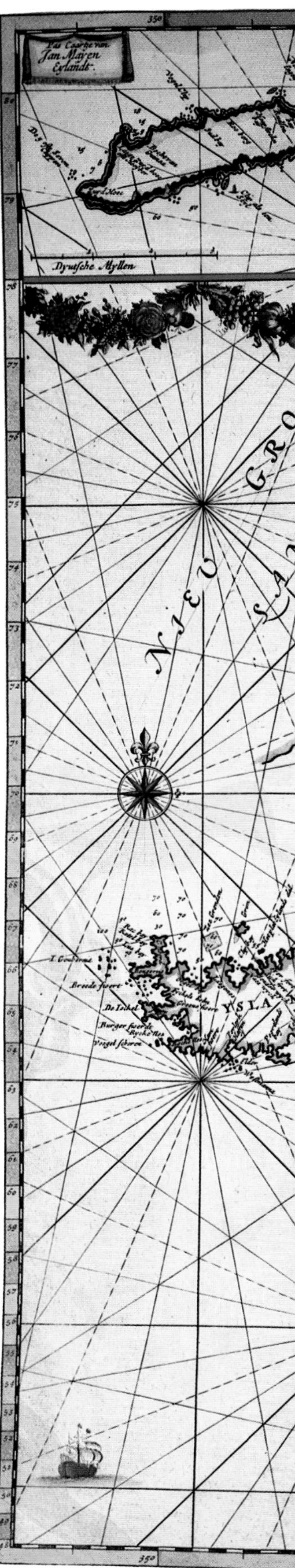

Map of Europe by the 17th-century Dutch map-maker Joannes Van Kuelen.

Pascaerte
Van't Noordlyckste Deel van
EUROPA
Beginnende vande Canael tot aen
Spitsbergen, en van Ysland tot aen
Nova Zemla;
Alles op Wassende graden Geleyt:
't Amsterdam
By Joannes van Keulen Boeck-verkooper
en Graad-boogh maecker, aen de Nieuw-
brugh inde geCroonde Loots-man.
Met Privilegie voor 15 Jaar
SPITS BERG EN
NOVA ZEMLA
Waygats of Straet Nassau
Nieuw Holland
NIEUW WALCHEREN
LAPLAND
RUSLAND
OOST FINLAND
NOORWEGEN
FINMARCKEN
SCHOT LAND
Lyflandt
Coerlandt
Pomeren
Pruißen
Beeren Eylandt

The Anglo-Norman Empire, 1066–1154

William the Bastard was, after 1066, King of England, Duke of Normandy and Count of Maine. So it is not unreasonable to speak of his cross-Channel kingdom, or even empire, for, like some other princes in the French kingdom, he barely acknowledged his subordination to the French monarch and exercised all royal powers within his duchy, and once he himself became king used that title wherever he might be.

Those of William's successors who held land on both sides of the sea behaved likewise: William II never, and Henry I seldom, used the ducal title. Except in one respect, this kingdom was more compact and coherent than most principalities in northern Europe. It is even possible to regard the stretch of sea which separated the two parts more as a great internal waterway than as a barrier. Henry I organized regular ferry services from Portsmouth and Southampton to Dieppe for the north and to Barfleur for the south of his duchy. Yet, typical of the time, the kingdom had uncertain boundaries. The kings of England maintained claims to lordship over Welsh and Scottish princes, while the dukes of Normandy strove to dominate a complete ring of marcher counties.

Another feature this kingdom shared with other territorial accumulations of the time was its joint ownership by a family or dynasty. Although in Normandy, even more than in England, impartibility (the passing on of an undivided inheritance) had been the rule and primogeniture (the first-born's right of succession) was becoming the custom, all members of the family had some claim on the patrimony. Whenever the ruler died or was incapacitated a conflict of interests arose: the dominant male tried to reduce or suppress rival claims, others sought to get as large a share of the inheritance as possible. During this period, therefore, a series of partitions and wars of succession occurred, first between the three surviving sons of the Conqueror – Robert, William Rufus and Henry – and then, after Henry's death, between the two residual female lines. Most barons and churchmen of the time, possessing kindred and lands on both sides of the Channel, wanted the whole Anglo-Norman kingdom to be united under one acceptable ruler. Yet the cross-Channel kingdom broke up three times (in 1087, 1100 and 1144) and for 26 of the 88 years between 1066 and 1154 England and Normandy were ruled separately. Moreover, during the weak rule of Robert in Normandy (1087–96, 1100–6), and Stephen in England (1135–54) and Normandy (1135–44), border provinces fell away, and everywhere disinherited kinsmen revived territorial claims, so that baronial families fought against one another and often among themselves.

The kingdom was at its largest and most powerful under Henry I (1100–35). A shrewd statesman and fine soldier, he had by 1120 defeated in pitched battles his brother Robert (Tinchebrai, 1106) and the King of France (Brémule 1119), brought the border principalities of Boulogne, Bellême, Maine and Brittany under his control – of the old Norman conquests only the French Vexin still eluded him – married his daughter Matilda to the German emperor and his only legitimate son, William, to the heiress of Anjou, while his nephew was Count of Blois and Chartres. In Britain most of Wales was under English rule and the king of Scots was a client.

The death of Henry's son and heir in the White Ship disaster (1120) caused the extinction of the Norman dynasty in its male line of descent and led to a dispute over the succession. This dispute was between Henry's daughter Matilda and his nephew Stephen of Blois. Matilda's second marriage was to Geoffrey, the heir of Anjou, and they were succeeded by their son Henry Plantagenet. Stephen

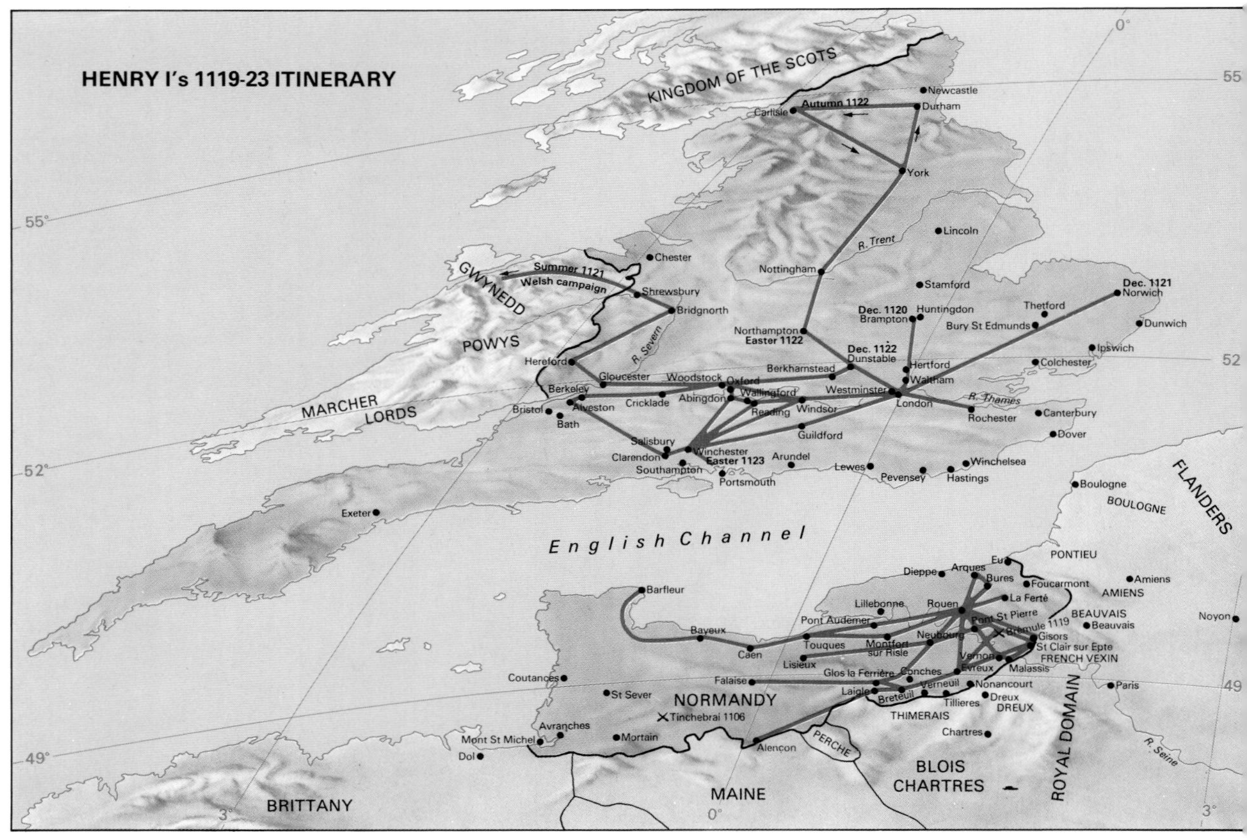

The Cross-Channel kingdom with a schematic representation of Henry I's itinerary of 1119–23. Medieval kings, itinerant by economic and political necessity, had favourite areas and residences, usually near hunting preserves and frontiers which had to be guarded. In Engand, Henry spent most of his time in the Thames Valley and 'central Wessex'. In Normandy he paid special attention to the Seine Valley south of Rouen (the Vexin and Evrécin), a vulnerable area close to the French royal domain. The main axis of the kingdom was Woodstock, Windsor, Clarendon (three hunting lodges), Southampton-Portsmouth, Barfleur, Bayeux, Rouen, Gisors/Evreux.

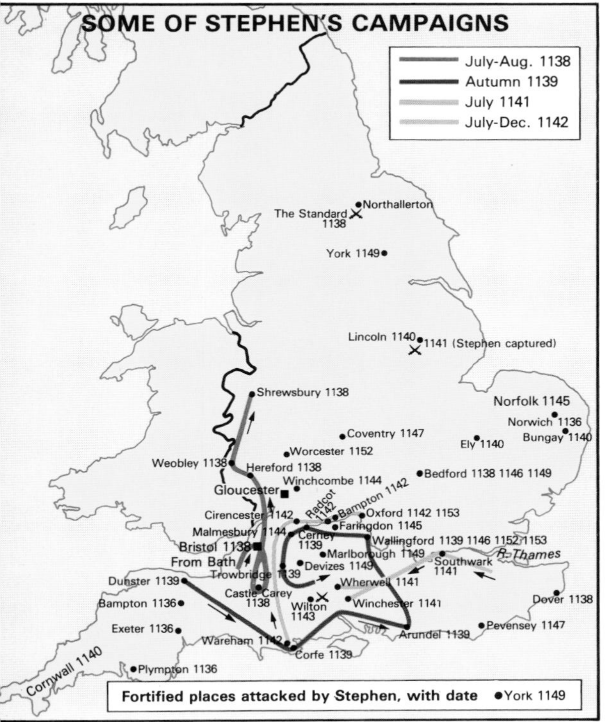

declared Matilda to be illegitimate and claimed the throne as the son of Adela Countess of Blois, a daughter of the Conqueror. By 1144 Stephen, who had initially been successful, had lost Normandy to Geoffrey Plantagenet. By 1154, when his own eldest son died and he surrendered the succession to Henry Plantagenet, the area of his effective rule had been reduced to little more than the shires to the east of Winchester and Oxford and to the south of the Trent.

The triumph of Henry, by then Duke of Normandy, Count of Anjou, and, in the right of his wife, Duke of Aquitaine, meant the absorption of the Norman into the Angevin dynasty and the birth of a new, rather different cross-Channel kingdom.

Far left: Some of the fortified places attacked by King Stephen and his captains in England. The main areas under the control of Angevin supporters in 1142 were Norfolk, north of the Tees and the South-West. Stephen's strategic aim was to uncover Bristol and Gloucester, the main bases of the enemy; the Angevin task was to maintain the covering arc of strongholds, especially those in the Thames Valley.

Left: Geoffrey Plantagenet. His son Henry in 1154 found himself ruler of an empire stretching from the Scottish border to the Pyrenees.

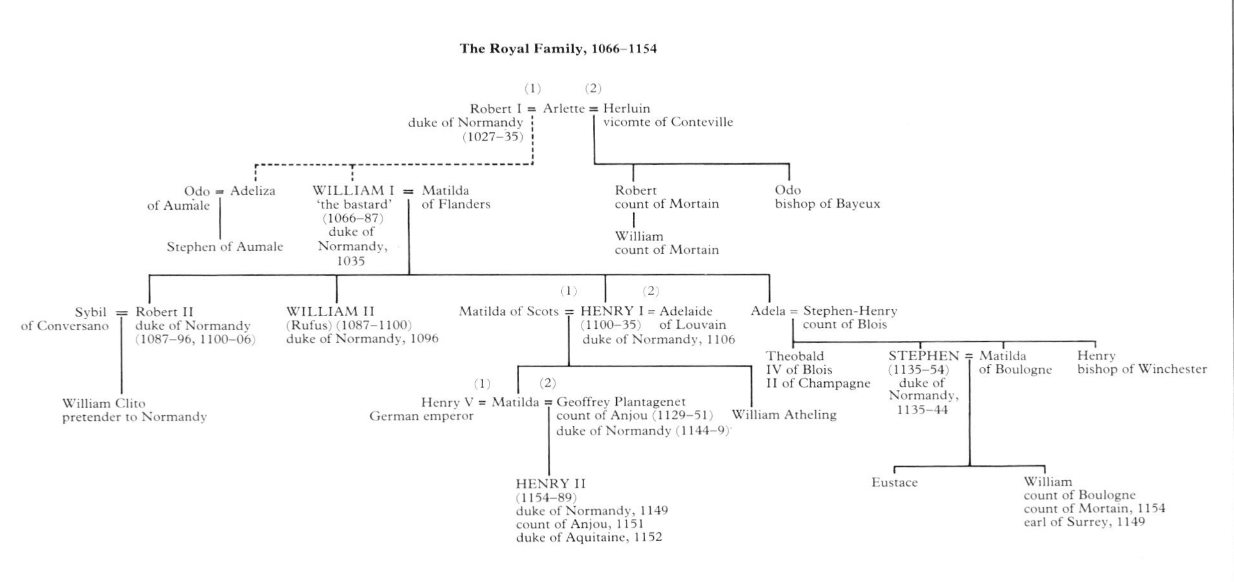

The Angevin Empire: The Reign of Henry II, 1154–89

Opposite: In this war Henry II's enemies included his wife, his three elder sons, Kings Louis VII of France and William of Scotland, Counts Philip of Flanders and Theobold of Blois. Though rebels were to be found in most parts of his dominions they were notably absent in Ireland, Wales, La Marche, the Limousin and Gascony. The greater number of English castles shown on the map reflects our greater knowledge of events there, but Henry's itinerary shows that he concentrated his attention on the Continent.

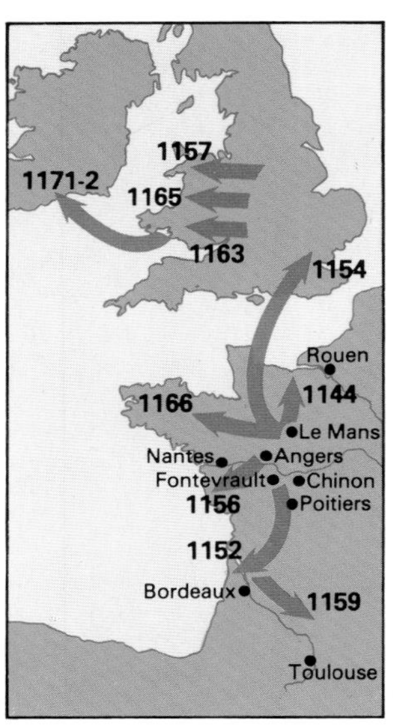

The Making of the Angevin Empire

In December 1154 a Frenchman from Anjou was crowned Henry II of England and found himself ruler of an empire stretching from the Scottish border to the Pyrenees: the Angevin Empire. As its name implies, Anjou, rather than England, was the heartland of this vast assemblage of lands. Henry had been born at Le Mans, he died at Chinon and was buried at Fontevrault – all places that lay within his Angevin patrimony. Throughout the 10th and 11th centuries his forefathers, the counts of Anjou, had belonged to a group of princes who were alternately enemies and allies in the struggle for land and power in northern and western Gaul. As a dynasty they had done well, particularly at the expense of the House of Blois, but noticeably less well than two of their main rivals, the Normans (who had conquered England) and the Poitevin dukes of Aquitaine (who had conquered Gascony). All this changed in the mid-12th century. In a few explosive years the Count of Anjou shot ahead of his competitors and became the most powerful ruler in Europe.

The key to this rapid expansion of Angevin rule is to be found in two crucially important marriages: Henry's own marriage to Eleanor of Aquitaine, and the marriage of his father, Count Geoffrey Plantagenet, to Matilda, daughter of Henry I and probable heiress to Normandy and England. After her father's death in 1135, Matilda was ousted by her cousin, Stephen of Blois, but Count Geoffrey pressed her claim to Normandy and eventually, in 1144, he was able to take it over. In 1150, just a year before his premature death, Geoffrey handed Normandy to their eldest son, Henry Plantagenet. This enterprising young man had already made several bids to secure England, but not until after Stephen's death (1154) was he able to do so. By this time he had himself married Eleanor, Duchess of Aquitaine. This wedding took place in May 1152, just eight weeks after Eleanor's first marriage, to King Louis VII of France, had been annulled. Henry's younger brother, Geoffrey, claimed Anjou as his share of the family fortune but Henry would yield nothing; Anjou was now the strategically vital land bridge between Aquitaine and the Anglo-Norman realm. By December 1154 the 21-year-old king was the richest prince in Europe, wealthier even than the emperor, and completely overshadowing the king of France, the nominal overlord of his continental dominions.

This did not mark the end of Angevin expansion. In 1156 a rebellion in Nantes gave Henry the chance to compensate his brother by installing him there as the new count. As King of England, Duke of Normandy and Duke of Aquitaine he had inherited the claims of his predecessors to lordship over neighbouring territories and these claims led to expeditions into Wales (1157, 1163 and 1165), into Brittany (1166) and against Toulouse (1159). Though not all of these campaigns were successful, he nonetheless registered substantial gains. The Welsh princes acknowledged his overlordship and remained loyal throughout the revolt of 1173–4. Cahors and the Quercy were captured in 1159. Brittany was occupied and its heiress betrothed to his third son, Geoffrey. In 1157 Henry had, by diplomatic pressure, forced the young king of Scotland, Malcolm IV, to restore Cumberland, Westmorland and Northumbria to the English Crown. Finally there was the move into Ireland, first by some lords from the Welsh March (1169–70) and then by Henry himself in 1171–2. The notorious quarrel which culminated in the murder of Thomas à Becket (1170) had done little or nothing to halt the tide of expansion.

Fortunate marriages and the accidents of birth and death had helped to bring the empire together; they could equally well pull it apart. By the late 1160s Henry II had decided that after his death his dominions should be partitioned between his three eldest sons, Henry, Richard and Geoffrey. The revolts of 1173–4, 1183 and 1189 were very largely caused by the frustrations of younger men who had been given titles but no certainty of power. As it happened the premature deaths of Henry and Geoffrey, combined with Richard's unwillingness to make room for John, meant that when the 'Old King' died (1189), his dominions remained undivided. Nonetheless the Angevin Empire was still not a traditional part of the European political scene and was not expected to survive as a unit.

Thomas à Becket, Archbishop of Canterbury, is murdered in his own cathedral in 1170. This illustration is from a manuscript by Matthew Paris, the 13th century historian of medieval England.

Centres of Trade and Learning

Within this empire England had an important place; it provided a royal crown and considerable wealth. But the other parts of the Angevin dominions were just as, if not, more, important. The prosperous communities which lived in the valleys of the Seine, Loire and Garonne river systems were centres of learning, art, architecture, poetry and music. Western France produced two of the essential commodities of medieval commerce: wine and salt. These could be exchanged for English wool, and this trade must have brought great, if unquantifiable, profits to the prince who ruled over both producers and consumers and whose lands included the major ports of north-western Europe: London, Southampton, Bristol, Rouen, Nantes, La Rochelle, Bordeaux, Bayonne – ports open to the new large ships, known as cogs, which contributed much to the general economic growth of the second half of the 12th century.

For a while, during the reigns of Henry II and Richard I, the kings of England, because they ruled much more than England, played a dominating role in the politics of western Europe. One aspect of this is the assistance they gave to the kingdom of Jerusalem, a kingdom overshadowed by Saladin's growing power, and also a kingdom ruled by a junior branch of the house of Anjou. Henry II's subsidies to his cousins are a further indication of the importance of family connection and responsibility in this world. Richard's contribution to the Third Crusade was massive in every sense. As commander-in-chief of the men who took a fleet and an army not just across the Channel but to the other end of the Mediterranean, he was responsible for a feat of organization on a scale unequalled by any other king of England.

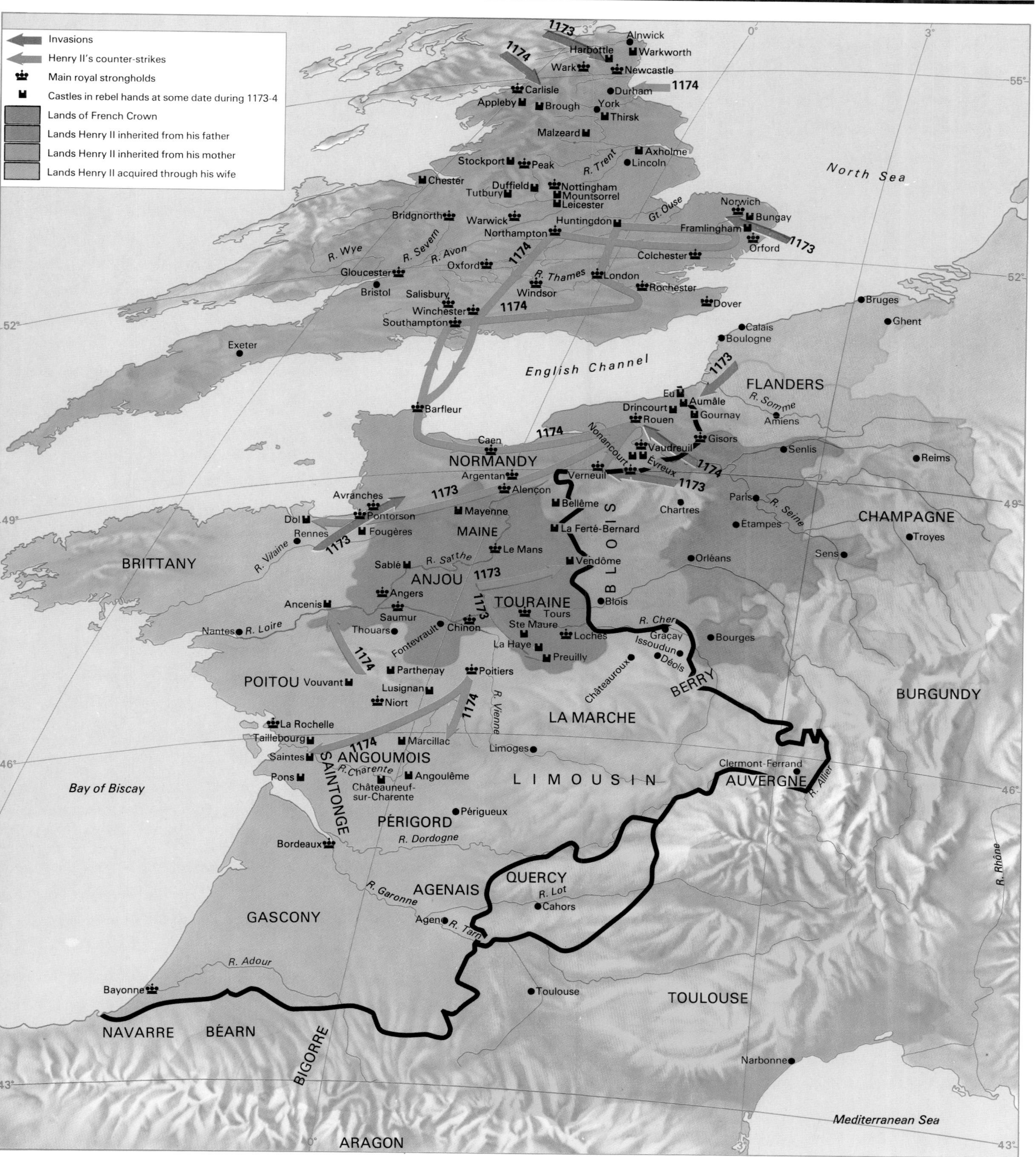
Invasions
Henry II's counter-strikes
Main royal strongholds
Castles in rebel hands at some date during 1173-4
Lands of French Crown
Lands Henry II inherited from his father
Lands Henry II inherited from his mother
Lands Henry II acquired through his wife
North Sea
English Channel
Bay of Biscay
Mediterranean Sea
NORMANDY
BRITTANY
MAINE
ANJOU
TOURAINE
POITOU
BLOIS
FLANDERS
CHAMPAGNE
BURGUNDY
BERRY
LA MARCHE
LIMOUSIN
AUVERGNE
ANGOUMOIS
SAINTONGE
PÉRIGORD
QUERCY
AGENAIS
GASCONY
TOULOUSE
NAVARRE
BÉARN
BIGORRE
ARAGON
1173
1174

The Church Under Norman Rule

The Church in Norman England. Diocesan re-organization and the distribution of Cistercian monasteries are the two main features illustrated here. Many Cistercian houses were located in those parts of the kingdom untouched by the monastic movement of the 10th century.

Inset: The ecclesiastical structure of Durham Cathedral Priory *c*.1154. Great abbeys like Durham were endowed with estates on which were village churches and dependent chapels. Sometimes they were given churches without the manors. All these were 'proprietary churches', *Eigenkirchen*. The bulk of the revenues from such churches was diverted into the abbey's coffers, leaving only a small portion for the resident vicar.

The Norman kings saw in the Church a stabilizing influence in the kingdom and an aid to their territorial expansion within Britain. They appointed only compatriots and a few other Continentals to bishoprics and abbeys and used Church reform as an instrument of imperial rule. The Scottish Church was, with papal approval, put under the archbishop of York; as Norman rule pushed into Wales, new bishoprics of the Anglo-Norman type were created; and some Irish kings and churches solicited the help of Archbishops Lanfranc and Anselm of Canterbury (1070–1109). These great churchmen established a sort of patriarchate over the British Isles.

William I's bishops were in general antipathetic to the special customs of the Anglo-Saxon Church and, under Lanfranc's leadership, made a vigorous attempt to remodel it according to ideal Norman standards. Lanfranc imposed, on a Church which already had a firm territorial organization, a novel hierarchical structure, claiming for Canterbury a primacy over Britain, and specifically over York. The diocesan bishops were subjected to their metropolitan, and dioceses were ordered to be divided into archdeaconries which, in turn, were divided into rural deaneries. The rural and urban parishes, which were left in the hands of native clergy, still mostly coincided with the manors; but they continued to subdivide because the dependent chapels which were built for hamlets and new settlements acquired in time their own baptismal fonts and cemeteries. Withi the towns, tiny parishes proliferated.

Other changes were made which showed that a new ag had begun. Several of the early Norman bishops not onl transferred their sees (diocesan headquarters) into a 'city or other more convenient centre, but also started to rebuil their cathedrals in their own variety of the romanesqu style, setting an example which was followed enthusiastic ally throughout the kingdom and beyond.

There also occurred a new monastic movement. The ol mostly royal, Benedictine abbeys prospered under Norma rule, and even in 1154 were still pre-eminent. Rebuil increasingly rich, surrounded by satellite cells and paris churches, and associated with native saints and kings, the stood for traditional standards. But in the 11th centur there arose, mainly out of disenchanted monks and loos associations of hermits inhabiting the wastelands of Europ in search of an evangelical way of life, a variety of ne orders. These new orders can be roughly divided int canons living under a rule (usually of St Augustine) an 'primitive' Benedictine monks. The canons-regular be came committed to an active ministry among the people an were immediately recognized by all classes as useful. In th reigns of Henry I and Stephen, over 100 Augustinia priories, as well as hospitals, hospices and almshouses wer founded in England, mainly in towns.

The new monastic orders were patronized eagerly by th

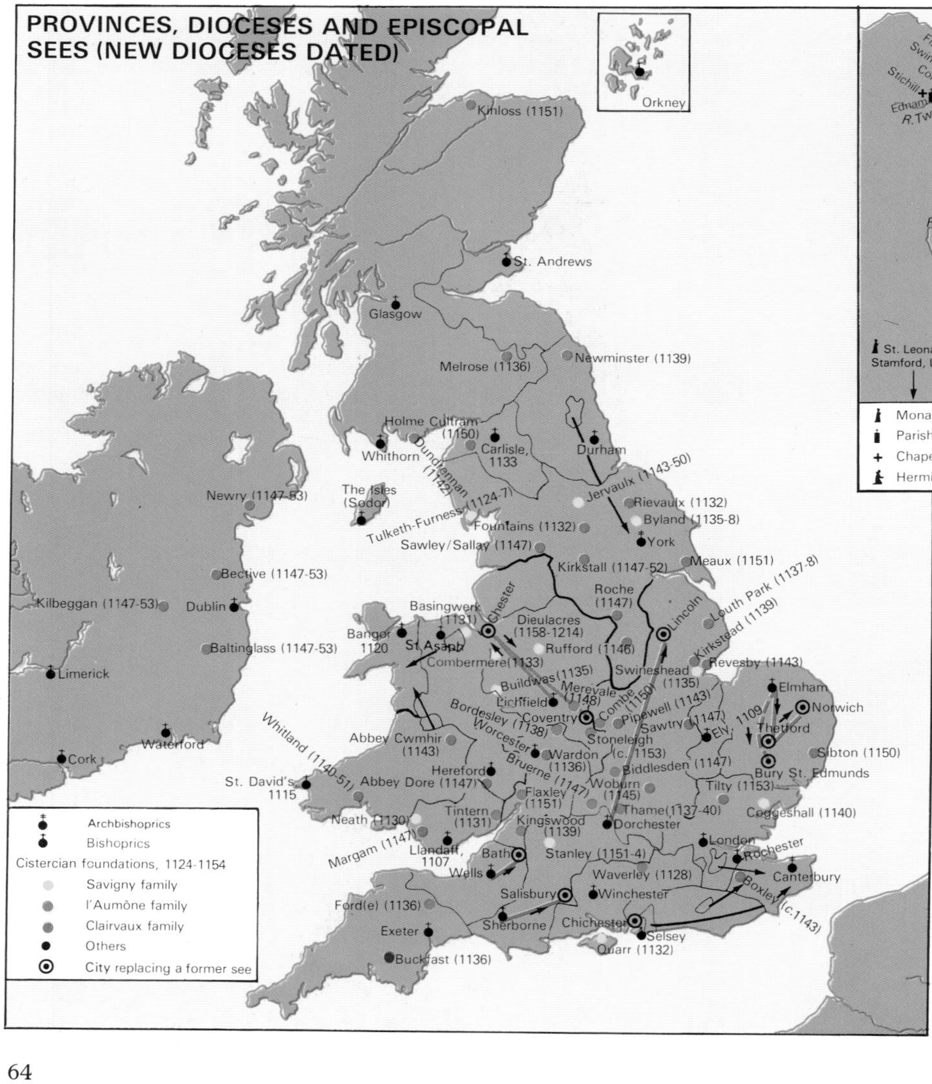

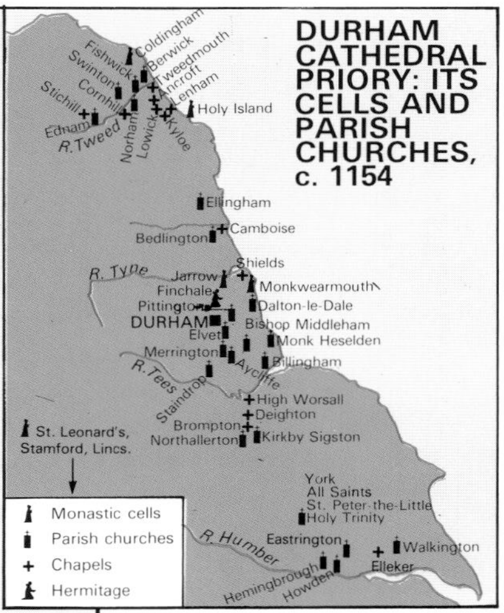

great landowners. Stephen, before he became king, in troduced monks from Savigny in his County of Mortain t Tulketh in 1124. By 1147, when the order amalgamate with the Cistercians, 13 houses had been set up in Englanc The Cistercian or White Monks spread throughout th land. From L'Aumône were founded Waverley (1128) an Tintern (1131), and from Clairvaux, where St Bernard wa abbot, Rievaulx and Fountains (1132). By 1154 there wer about 40 Cistercian monasteries in England, Wales and th north borderlands, mostly placed on previously un cultivated land and in those parts of the kingdom which th 10th century monastic movement had not penetrated.

Better provision was made for women who wanted t follow a religious life. Some 30 Benedictine nunneries wer founded, mostly in the Midlands and North, and the on new native English order, the creation of Gilbert o Sempringham and extending to six convents in the north eastern shires by 1154, used canons to minister to th communities of nuns. Thus, during the Norman period religious life in England was not only better organized bu also enriched and diversified.

The English Church, 1150–1300

Between the advent of the Angevins in 1154 and 1300, the diocesan and parochial organization of the English Church assumed the form that, with only minor variations, it was to retain until the end of the Middle Ages. The major development in this period was the growth of papal activity in English ecclesiastical affairs, as the sweeping powers the Gregorian popes had claimed were translated from theory into a centralized system of Church government. At the same time, England, in common with the rest of western Europe, experienced social and economic changes which posed new pastoral problems. Rapid urban growth, the expansion of international trade, the rise of a new bourgeoisie deriving its wealth from commerce, and the creation of an international community of learning, all tended to break down the isolation of local communities and to produce a society that was more mobile, more critical and, at the upper levels, more affluent than before.

One aspect of this social change was the wide-ranging intellectual renaissance of the 12th century. This was associated with the recovery by Western scholars of the whole body of Greek and Arabic philosophy and science, and the revival of classical Roman jurisprudence. These discoveries revolutionized both the content and the methods of learning. The nerve-centres of the new scholastic movement were the cathedral schools of northern France and, in the case of law, the urban schools of northern Italy. For some time England remained something of an intellectual backwater but, by the last two decades of the 12th century, the new learning was on offer at a number of English cathedral schools and other centres which had managed to secure the services of an outstanding teacher. The reasons for the concentration of numbers of teachers of Arts, Law and Theology, at Oxford, which was not a cathedral city but lay within the huge diocese of Lincoln, are obscure. At some date before 1209 they imitated the example of their colleagues at Paris and formed themselves into a scholastic guild or university. The evidence suggests that the sister university at Cambridge originated in a migration of scholars from Oxford between the years 1209 and 1214, when the Oxford masters had suspended lectures owing to a dispute with the city authorities. In the course of the following hundred years both universities attracted extensive royal privileges and established themselves alongside Paris as foremost nurseries of English prelates.

The higher schools educated a clerical elite that was destined for rapid preferment. They barely touched the problem of the parish clergy, most of whom were recruited quite locally from the ranks of the free peasantry and who were educationally little above the level of their rustic parishioners. The need to improve standards of pastoral care was made more urgent by the rise of a literate town-dwelling laity. English bishops wrestled with the problem in a variety of ways, but much of their effort was frustrated by the immensity of the problems and the resistance of the proprietory interests of lay and ecclesiastical patrons. This was the gap that the friars came to fill with outstanding success.

Mobile missionaries, vowed to a life of poverty, mendicancy, and apostolic preaching, with an international organization, and cosmopolitan in their recruitment, the friars represented a revolutionary departure from the old monastic tradition. They addressed themselves primarily to the town populations and centres of learning. The first party of Dominicans, or Friars Preachers, arrived in England in 1221 and made straight for Oxford. They were followed in 1224 by the Franciscans, or Friars Minor, who founded their first houses in Canterbury, London, and Oxford. The Carmelites and the Austin (Augustinian) friars first appeared in the 1240s. All four orders established their own theological schools in the English universities, but their mission was above all to the towns, where they were received with enthusiasm.

The universal mission of the friars as preachers and confessors had been authorized by the papacy. During the 13th century, the English Church experienced other and less welcome developments in papal activity. One of these was the expanding system of direct papal provision of clerks to canonries and parish livings. Another was the taxation of the income of beneficed clergy, either to finance the Crusades or to subsidize the policies of the Roman Curia. For the purposes of assessing these periodic levies, three successive valuations of English livings were carried out, the first in 1254, the second in 1276, and the last in 1291. Each valuation was more stringent than the one before. Taxation brought in its train a new species of curial agent – the resident papal collector. From the appointment of Stephen of Anagni in 1228, it is possible to trace a continuous series of resident collectors in England, who bore the title of *nuncio*, and who were almost all Italians. Unpopular though these developments were with the clergy, they occurred with the sanction of the king; he received the lion's share of the clerical tenths levied at the command of the Pope and took advantage of the system of papal provisions to obtain benefices for royal clerks.

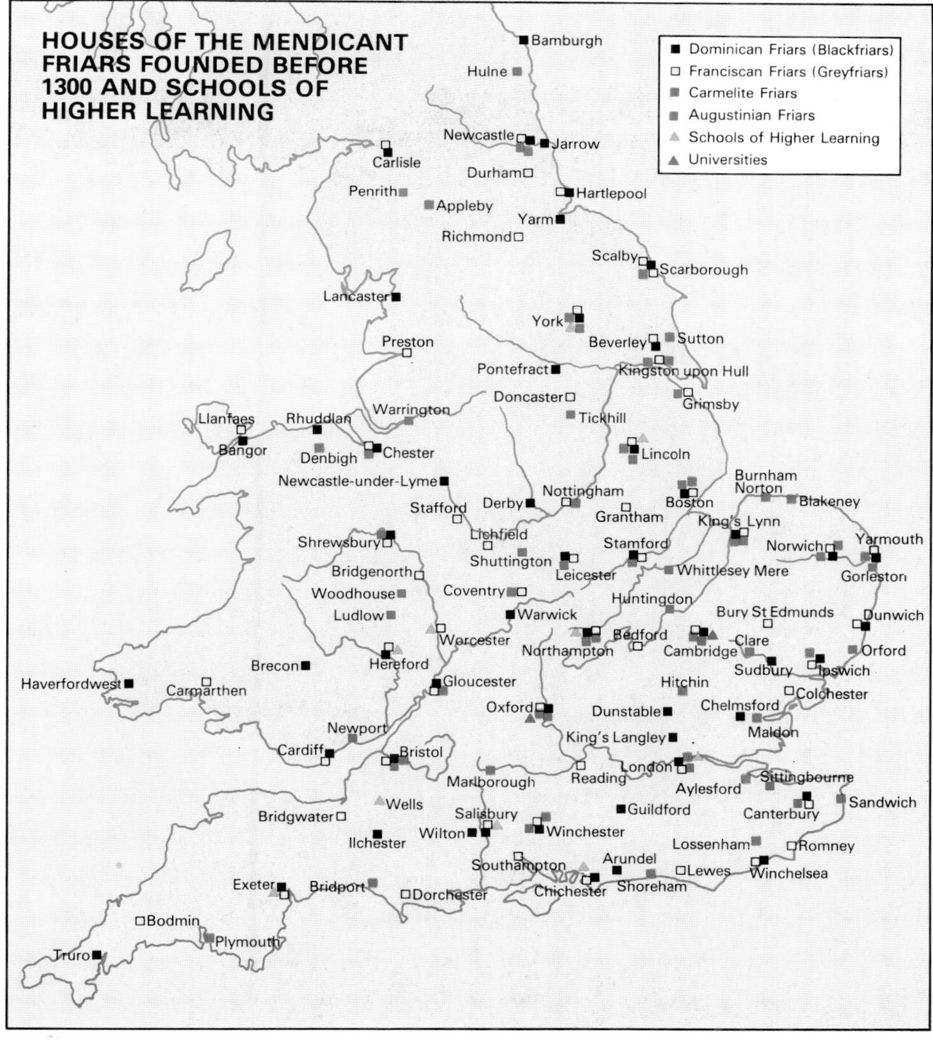

The Struggle against the Capetians, 1189–1224

In 1189 when Richard I came to the throne, England was just one of the lands ruled by the most powerful king in western Europe. The weight of Richard's arms was felt from the Atlantic Ocean to the eastern Mediterranean; only rarely – and then briefly – did he visit England. But he was not an English king who neglected England. He was the head of a royal dynasty whose network of family alliances encompassed France, Germany, Spain, Sicily and the Holy Land. By the mid-13th century the position was radically different. The Capetian kings of France, Philip Augustus (1180–1223) and Louis VIII (1223–26), had whittled away the Plantagenet dominions until they comprised no more than England and Gascony.

In these developments the decisive turning-point was the death of Richard I in April 1199. Although Angevin lands in Normandy and Touraine had earlier been lost to the king of France while Richard was held prisoner in Germany (December 1192–March 1194), these losses had not been permanent. Richard's skilful diplomacy, fine generalship and, above all, his greater resources had been thrown into the task of recovering them. By the end of 1198, only the great border castle of Gisors was still in Philip's hands – a loss more than compensated for by the building of Château-Gaillard and territorial acquisitions in Berry.

On Richard's death different parts of the Angevin Empire chose different heirs. The barons of England and

Below: Scenes from the life of Richard I. On the left Richard is shown in prison in Germany, captured by the Duke of Austria while returning from crusade. On the right a crossbowman (top right) in the castle of Chalus deals the King a mortal wound.

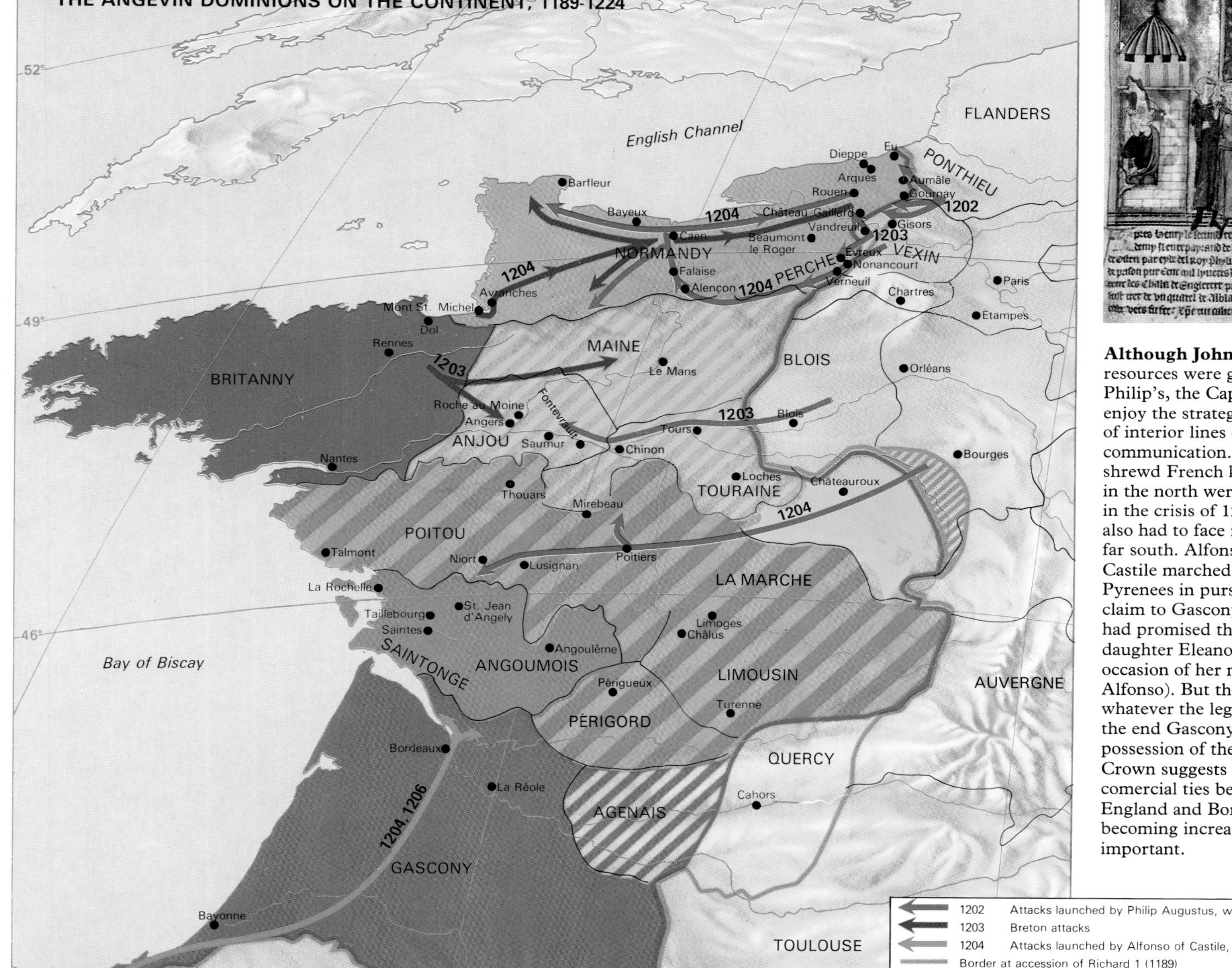

Although John's financial resources were greater than Philip's, the Capetian did enjoy the strategic advantage of interior lines of communication. As if the shrewd French king's attacks in the north were not enough, in the crisis of 1204–6 John also had to face invasion in th far south. Alfonso VIII of Castile marched across the Pyrenees in pursuit of his claim to Gascony (Henry II had promised the duchy to his daughter Eleanor on the occasion of her marriage to Alfonso). But the fact that, whatever the legal position, in the end Gascony remained a possession of the English Crown suggests that the comercial ties between England and Bordeaux were becoming increasingly important.

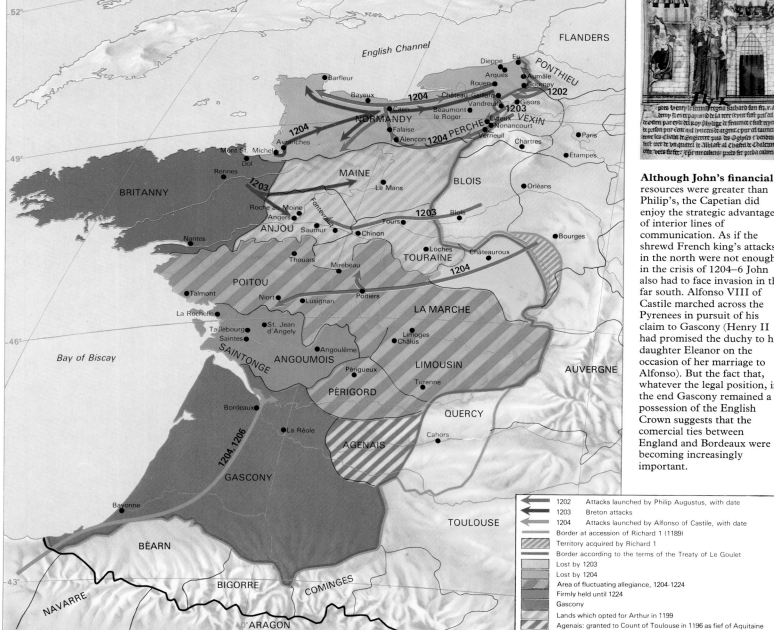

ENGLAND, WALES AND IRELAND AT THE END OF THE REIGN OF KING JOHN

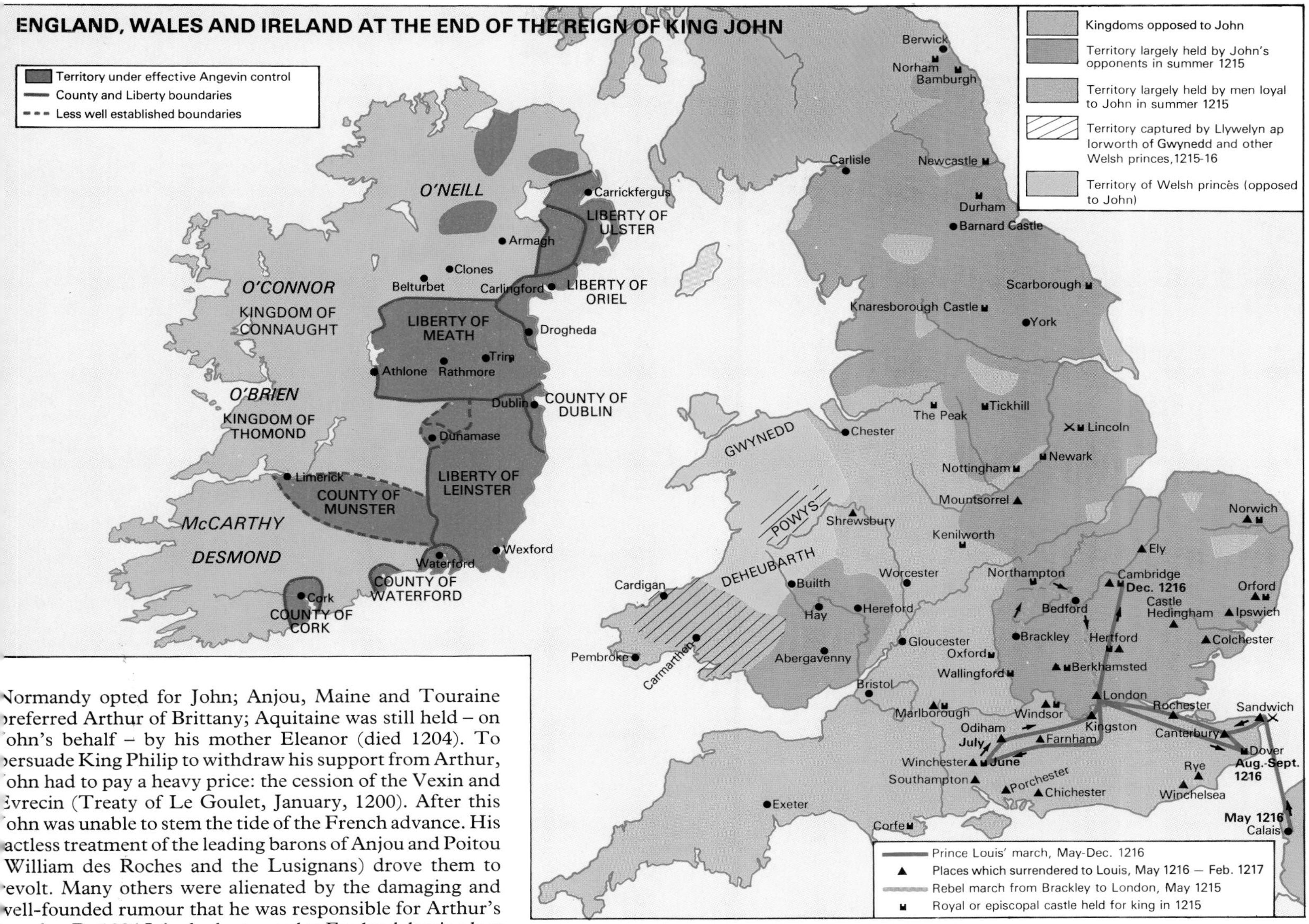

Normandy opted for John; Anjou, Maine and Touraine preferred Arthur of Brittany; Aquitaine was still held – on John's behalf – by his mother Eleanor (died 1204). To persuade King Philip to withdraw his support from Arthur, John had to pay a heavy price: the cession of the Vexin and Evrecin (Treaty of Le Goulet, January, 1200). After this John was unable to stem the tide of the French advance. His tactless treatment of the leading barons of Anjou and Poitou (William des Roches and the Lusignans) drove them to revolt. Many others were alienated by the damaging and well-founded rumour that he was responsible for Arthur's murder. By 1204 John had retreated to England, having lost Normandy, Anjou, Maine, Touraine and all of Poitou except for La Rochelle. Naturally, both John and Henry III dreamed of recovering their lands. In 1206, and again in 1214, John led expeditions to Poitou, but the defeat of his allies at the Battle of Bouvines (July 1214) entailed both the failure of his continental strategy and the onset of rebellion in England.

After his return from Poitou in 1206 John stayed mostly in England. Not since Stephen's reign had the country seen so much of a king, but there was little pleasure or profit to be got from a king who constantly suspected that men were plotting against him. Undoubtedly John faced genuine problems. An unprecedentedly high rate of inflation was eroding the real value of royal revenues; the King was driven to adopt novel and unpopular fiscal expedients. The relationship between king and barons was such that most barons, at some time or other, found themselves in debt to the Crown; John exploited this to enforce their loyalty. For a time it worked, but from 1212 onwards revolt was in the air.

But would-be rebels had genuine problems too. Leadership or, at the very least, a figure-head for revolt was normally provided by a discontented member of the royal family. After the elimination of Arthur, John faced no such rivals. His own sons were too young. The only possible candidate was Louis, son of Philip Augustus, but after the wars of the last 50 years a Capetian prince was barely an attractive anti-king. Thus the rebels were forced to devise a new kind of focus of revolt: a programme for reform. Instead of swearing allegiance to an alternative ruler, they could swear to abide by the terms of Magna Carta. But John would observe Magna Carta only for as long as he had to, so in the end the rebels had to invite Louis to take the throne. At first he achieved some striking successes but, when death removed John from the scene (in October 1216), support for Louis dwindled. In 1217 he accepted the Treaty of Lambeth and withdrew. Although as a peace treaty Magna Carta had failed, it rapidly came to symbolize the rights of the subject against the Crown and to create a new model for rebellion. From now on drawing up a reform programme became standard opposition procedure.

Preoccupied with the need to consolidate its hold on England, Henry III's minority council gradually lost control of Poitou. When Louis VIII invaded the province in 1224, only La Rochelle put up a show of resistance. Thereafter only Gascony remained. In 1254 it was declared to be an inalienable possession of the Crown. A new and more insular period of English history was beginning.

One consequence of the loss of the territories on the Continent was that John paid more attention to Scotland, Ireland, Wales and the North of England than any of his predecessors. In the troubles of 1215–16 Ireland remained quiet, but the Northerners, the King of Scotland and the Welsh princes were all numbered among his enemies. When the rebels captured London (May 1215), John was forced to make concessions.

England and Gascony, 1224–1325

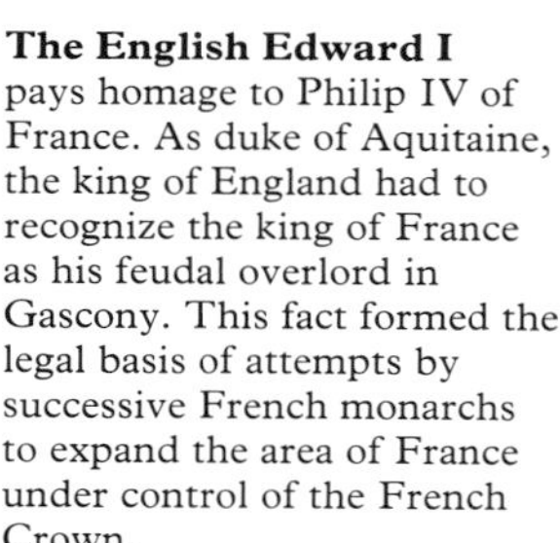

The English Edward I pays homage to Philip IV of France. As duke of Aquitaine, the king of England had to recognize the king of France as his feudal overlord in Gascony. This fact formed the legal basis of attempts by successive French monarchs to expand the area of France under control of the French Crown.

With the fall of Poitou in 1224, little remained t Henry III of the empire which his ancestors ha held in France except the land between th Gironde, the Dordogne and the Pyrenees. This land wa called Gascony. With many changes of boundary i remained in English hands till 1453. Henry and hi successors were never styled Dukes of Gascony, however They preferred the title Duke of Aquitaine, even thoug Gascony only formed the south of that duchy; the nort (Poitou) was controlled by the French royal family.

Given the speed with which the French conquere Normandy, Anjou and Poitou between 1202–24, England' retention of Gascony might seem surprising. Before 125 the province, in the French view, remained among th lands forfeited by King John in 1202. The Englis nervously anticipated attempts to execute this sentence. I 1259, under the Treaty of Paris, the English position wa accepted, and Henry III did homage to Louis IX fo Gascony. (In return he resigned his claims to Normandy Anjou and Poitou). But the treaty created friction over bot territory and rights of jurisdiction. As a result, the duch was confiscated by Philip IV in 1294, and a French arm

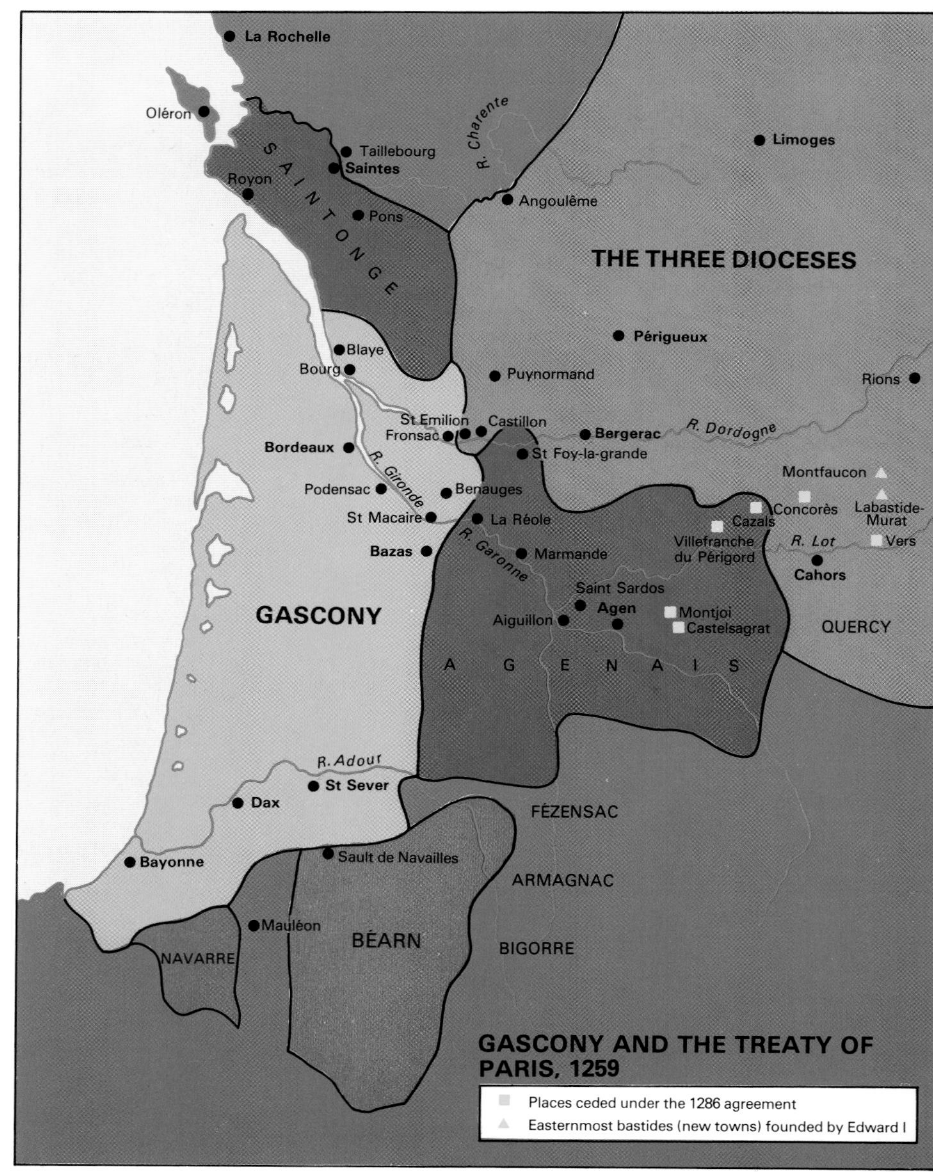

Right: English Gascony *c.*1290, after the implementation of the Treaty of Paris (1259). Under the terms of the treaty, Louis IX promised to cede to Henry III and his heirs the fiefs and domains in the three dioceses of Limoges, Perigueux and Cahors. After the death of Louis' brother Alphonse, the Agenais – with Alphonse's lands and fiefs in Quercy and Saintonge – was also to be given to the king of England. Transfers of lands and rights in the three dioceses began immediately, but there was prolonged conflict over fiefs and domains claimed as inalienable from the Crown of France in return for compensation. In 1306–7, the revenue from the three dioceses, although appreciable, was much less than that from the Agenais. Alphonse died in 1270. In 1279 (under the Treaty of Amiens) the Agenais and his possessions in Saintonge were acquired by the king of England. In 1286, lands worth £750 were promised in return for Edward I's claims in Quercy. In Saintonge and the Agenais, as well as in the three dioceses, the king of France retained numerous domains and fiefs. No continuous frontier was possible and dispute was inevitable. In 1324, Charles IV's foundation of a bastide at Saint Sardos, in the heart of the Agenais, precipitated war.

ccupied Bordeaux and a large part of the province until eace was made in 1303. After a second confiscation, by harles IV in 1324, the peace of 1325 allowed the French to etain La Réole and the Agenais.

How could our poor people subsist . . .'

n part the survival of English rule was due to the oderation of Louis IX and Charles IV, and the misfor- unes in Flanders of the more ambitious and unscrupulous hilip IV. (These had forced him to agree to the restoration f 1303). Gascony and England, however, were riveted ogether by one powerful mutual interest – the trade in ine. In Gascony burgesses and nobles alike engaged in the ultivation of the vine and the production of wine. The ine was largely exported, the great bulk of it from ordeaux whose population *c.*1300 was larger than that of ondon. In the 1300s 100,000 tonnes were sometimes xported annually (double the amount exported in 1956). ngland was the greatest single market for this wine. It took on what seems a conservative estimate) a quarter of the nnual exports. When the English connection was in- errupted, so was trade. With the war of 1324, English mports of Gascon wine fell by half. Of course Gascons ould find other markets, but England was the most natural nd convenient. All those engaged in wine production had, herefore, a vested interest in the English connection. nglish sympathy was consequently widespread: in the 300s half the wine exported came from within the diocese f Bordeaux; but the other half came from the area beyond the 'Haut Pays'), especially from the Agenais. Trade etween England and Gascony was two-way. The Gascons oncentrated on wine production and imported cloth, eather and corn, much of it from England. The heart of the nglish connection was expressed by a 14th-century ordelais, 'how could our poor people subsist when they ould not sell their wines or procure English nerchandise?'.

Kings of England were determined to keep Gascony. Henry III was there in 1253–4 and Edward I between 286–9. Armies were sent in 1294 and 1296. In the second alf of the century the province became increasingly aluable as its revenue multiplied several times over. There vere three reasons for this. The first reason was the oncession of territory under the Treaty of Paris. Difficulties over the implementation of the terms of this reaty have obscured the fact that the English eventually ained lands of great value, in particular the Agenais, which vas finally handed over in 1279. Many bastides (new towns) ad been founded here in the previous 30 years. In the year 306–7 the revenue from the Agenais was some £6000, 30 er cent of the total revenue from Gascony. The second eason was that from the 1260s large numbers of bastides vere founded in Gascony. These must have added to the ucal revenue. The third reason was that, between the 230s and the 1300s, there was probably a vast expansion in he revenue from the customs on wine exports. (Doubtless he bastides contributed to an increase in wine production). n the 1240s the great custom of Bordeaux had been farmed or as little as £300. In 1307 its value was over £6000. In otal in the year 1306–7 the revenue from Gascony was early £17,000. There are no comparable figures from an arlier period. However, in the 1250s, when Henry III's on Edward was endowed with lands worth £10,000 a year, e was given not only Gascony but also Ireland, the county f Chester, the King's lands in Wales, Bristol and umerous English manors. It seems unlikely that Gascony vas valued at more than a few thousand pounds. Henry III onstantly sent money to sustain his officials in Gascony. The multiplication of revenue did not necessarily save Edward I from such expenditure. But it certainly gave him and his successors growing incentive, and growing means, to retain and defend the province. English policy after 1337 should be seen against this background.

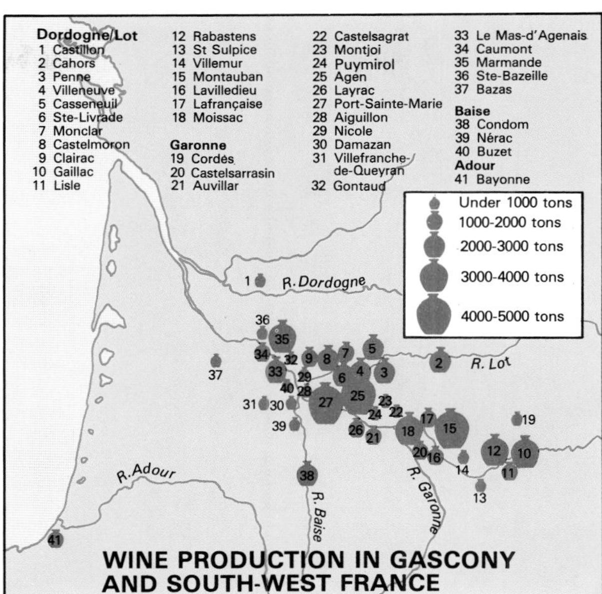

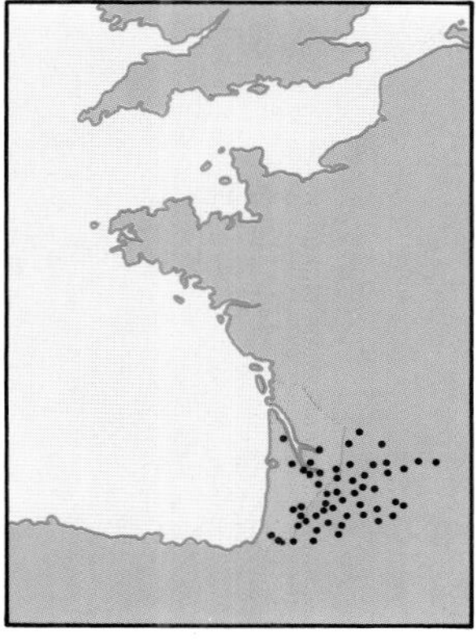

Below: Bastides in Gascony and the South-West of France. Those indicated were founded between 1180 and 1360, the great majority belonging to the period 1250–1330.

Above left: This map is based on details given in the Bordeaux customs accounts for 1306–7. In that year, half the wine exported from Bordeaux came from the diocese of Bordeaux itself. Although the accounts do not detail Bordeaux production, we have extremely detailed local figures for the 'Haut Pays', the area beyond the diocese.

Stages of the wine harvest in medieval France, from an early woodcut illustration.

Revenue from Gascony, 1306–7

Agenais	£6026
Périgord; Limousin; Quercy	£863
Saintonge	£752
Bordelais	£7887
(£6267 from customs)	
Bazadais	£512
Landes	£799
Total	£16,840

Parliament, Taxation and Defence of the Realm

Underlying the domestic and foreign policies of the long reigns of Henry III and Edward I can be detected the gradual elaboration of the idea that kings did not rule only with the help of advisers whom they themselves chose. The 'community of the realm' ought to be consulted and, at times, drawn in to share in decision-making. Although the 'community of the realm' was an abstract concept hardly susceptible of precise definition, it was at least clear that if it disliked a king's policy, it was capable of being passively awkward. Whereas the tax of a fifteenth granted in 1290 brought in £117,000, the ninth granted in 1297 – a tax which in theory should have brought in even more – in fact produced only £35,000. Evidently, if taxes were to be collected efficiently, the king needed the

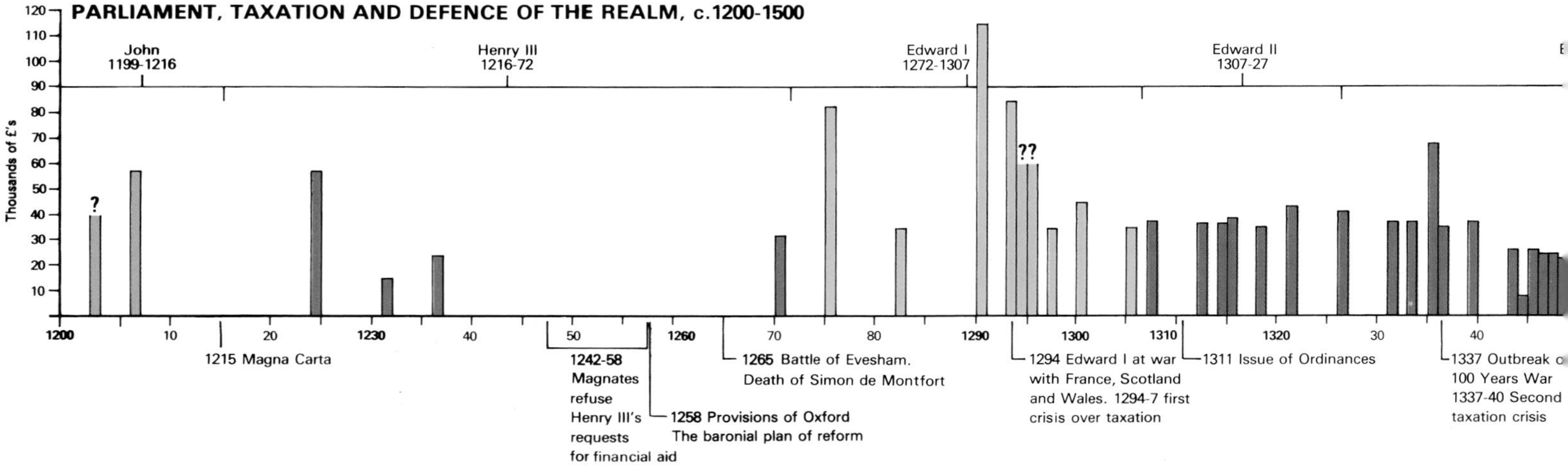

co-operation of the tax-payers, and to obtain this he had to consult them or their representatives. From the late 12th century onwards, kings had grown accustomed to bargaining with individual shire-communities, so it was an obvious step to require these local communities to choose men to speak for them when the king wanted to summon an assembly to represent the community of the whole realm. This is the process known as the growth of Parliament. As the example of 1290/1297 suggests, it was the king's financial needs more than any other factor, which stimulated this development.

In Magna Carta it was stated that when a king wanted an aid (a tax) he would have to obtain the consent of 'the common counsel of the realm'. By the second half of the century it was no longer taken for granted that Parliaments of barons always adequately represented the community. In certain circumstances they continued to do so – but not when taxation was on the agenda. The history of the Parliament of April–July 1290 is very revealing. The Commons (knights, burgesses and yeomen) did not meet until mid-July when Parliament had already been sitting for ten weeks and had got through a great deal of business, including some important legislation. Why then were the knights and burgesses called at all? Because the king wanted a grant of taxation and a Parliament without the Commons, though it could do much, could not give the king this. In these circumstances it is clear that there was likely to be a close connection between war – the most expensive of royal activities – and the growth of Parliament.

The first crisis in parliamentary history occurred in the late 1290s when Edward I's high-handed policies landed him in the position of having to fight three wars at once – in Wales, in Scotland and in France. Whereas in the first 90 years of the century kings had received nine aids (see the diagram below), the next nine came in 20 years. With thi sharp increase in financial pressure the Commons becam increasingly important. The second crisis came in the costl early years of Edward III's great war against France Thereafter Parliament without the Commons was incon ceivable. By the end of the 14th century the Commons wer devising new parliamentary procedures, impeaching min isters and intervening in the conduct of foreign policy – though they did this only when royal leadership was weak At the same time it is clear that aids were granted with ver much greater regularity during the Hundred Years' Wa than in the previous century. The Commons normally *di* consent to taxation. This is why they survived an flourished; if they had usually refused, there would hav

Above: Aids granted to the king, 1200–1500. The aid was a tax assessed on revenues and movable wealth. Devised in the late 12th century it was at first used only in special cases like the Crusade or the ransom of Richard I. In the 13th century it was used to meet the costs of war. But it always retained its character as an 'extra-ordinary' tax – and was never granted in a routine annual basis, unlike the customs duties on wool and cloth which came to be regarded as part of the king's ordinary revenue.

Note: in this table aids were assigned, so far as possible, to the year in which they were collected, not the year of their grant.

been no point in summoning them. Occasionally they did say no. They did not object to war – as their generosity to Henry V demonstrates. They objected only to unsuccessful war – as is clear from the stand taken by the 'Good Parliament' of 1376, by the rebels in 1381, and by the low level of support given to Henry VI. As the Commons knew, successful war could be very profitable. The two long gaps in this hundred years (1358–70; 1421–27) reflect the fact that Edward III's and Henry V's triumphs provided a respite for the English – though not the French – taxpayers. After the English had been swept out of France in the 1450s, taxation once again reverted to a more sporadic pattern. Yet, the Commons in Parliament were so firmly established that no king could think of doing without them.

Although nearly all of these wars had been fought abroad, war taxation had normally been justified, in parliamentary language, as money raised for 'the defence of the realm'. More deserving of this description was a purely local financial institution: the murage grant. The first such grant dates from 1220 – a time when invasion fears were still very real – and their distribution through time and space can serve as a rough index of insecurity, an indication of the areas where, and the periods when, townspeople felt sufficiently threatened to apply for a grant. The contrast – at all times – between the Welsh and Scottish borders is worth noting. So, too, is the relative lack of concern displayed by towns in the 15th century – with the exception of those towns within range of French raids.

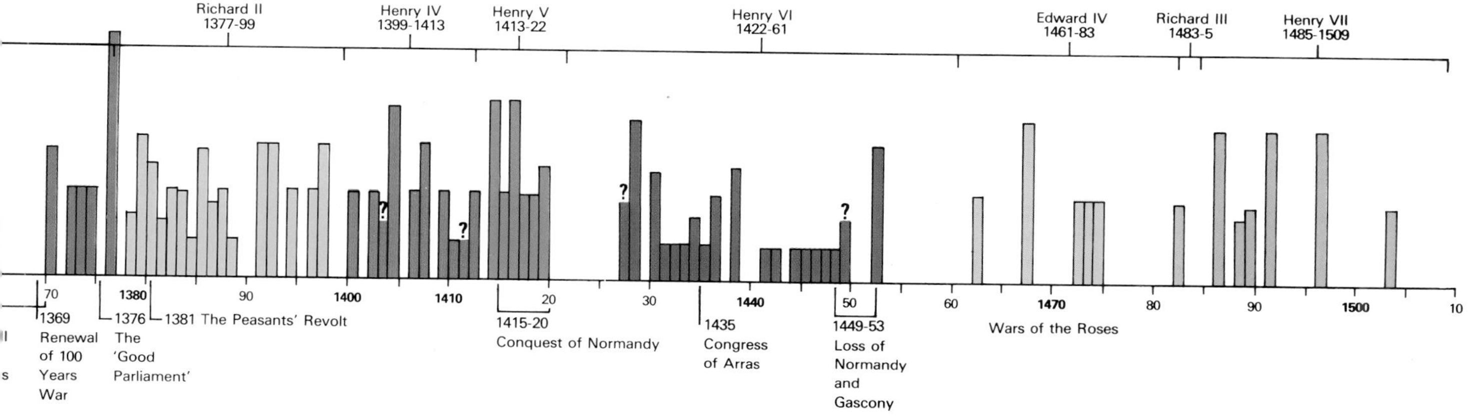

Murage Grants, 1220–1490. A murage grant was a licence to levy a toll (murage) on goods coming into a town for sale in order to finance the building and repair of the town walls. At first grants were made only for a year at a time but by the second half of the 14th century they were commonly made for ten years, and with the king's approval they could always be renewed. In the 15th century ten towns (six of them in the south coast counties) received other forms of financial contribution to defence costs.

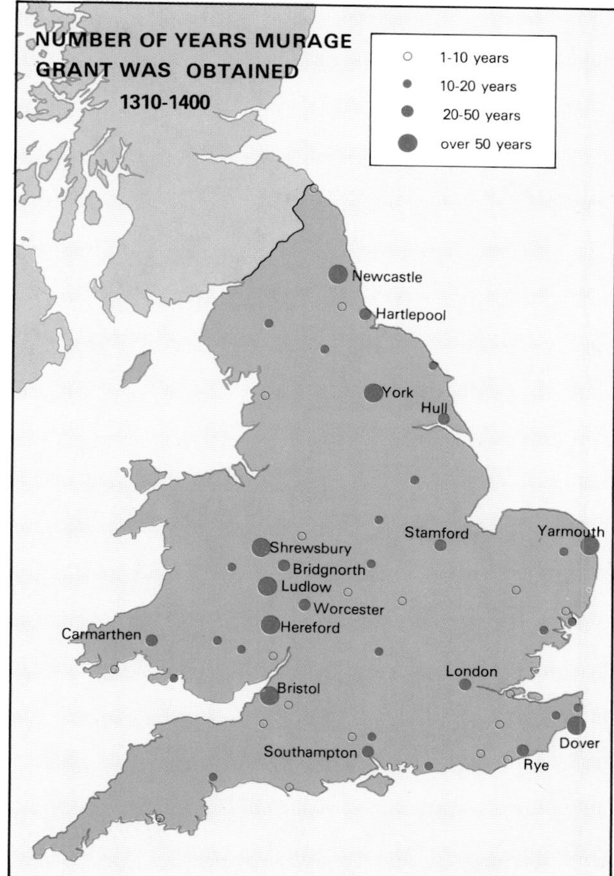

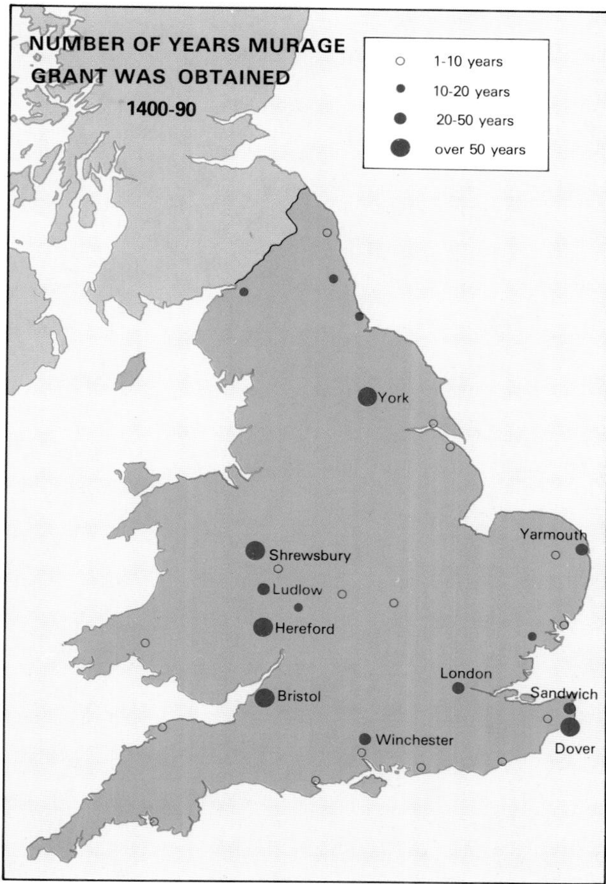

Wales and the Anglo-Norman Conquest, *c.* 1050–1400

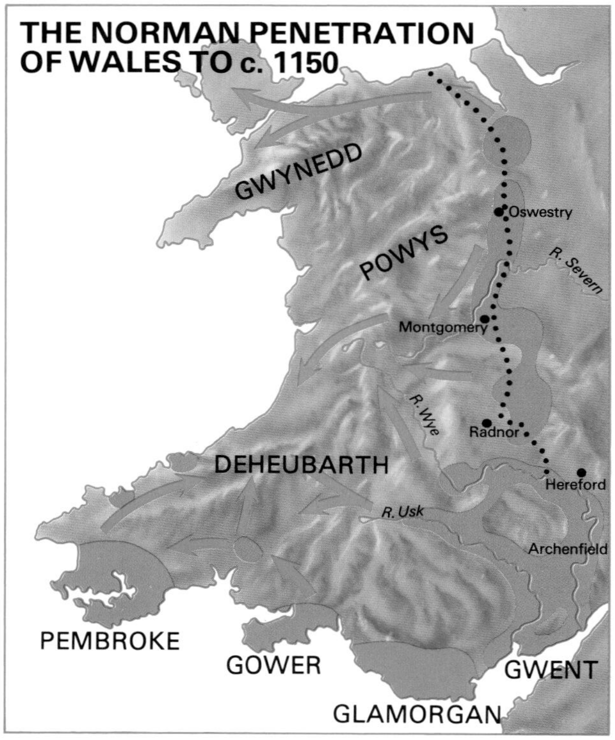

•••• Offa's Dyke
Area firmly in Norman control and intensively settled by Normans and their followers
Routes of penetration into areas where Norman control proved to be insecure

Norman colonization of Wales was largely confined to the lowlands and river valleys, with some degree of overlordship of neighbouring uplands. The Normans often penetrated much farther into Wales, but were unable to hold on to their conquests in the face of Welsh counter-attacks.

Below right: Harlech Castle, one of eight royal castles built in Wales between 1277 and 1330. Harlech itself was built between 1283 and 1290. At times, nearly a thousand workmen were employed on the site. The whole operation – the biggest programme of castle-building ever undertaken by an English king – was enormously expensive. It has been described as 'the premium that Edward paid to insure his Welsh conquests against the fire of rebellion.'

Wales was not a single political unit in the 11th century. It was a collection of small kingdoms which expanded and contracted in proportion to the ambitions and military fortunes of individual rulers. Some of these native Welsh rulers periodically acknowledged the supremacy of the kings of England; but English overlordship had not yet been given a precise definition nor was it sustained by any lasting degree of military control. The borders of Wales also remained ill-defined. Offa's Dyke and the river Wye were generally regarded as boundaries: but in many places (for example around Montgomery and Radnor) English settlers had penetrated well beyond the Dyke; elsewhere, Welshmen had settled in areas, such as Oswestry and Archenfield, which would later be regarded as parts of England. On occasion their military raids took them even farther eastwards – Hereford was burnt by a Welsh army in 1055.

Such was the fluid situation in terms of boundaries and political control which the Normans found in 1067. At first it looked as if the Normans would conquer Wales with the same speed and thoroughness as they had mastered England. But that was not to be the case. The Norman conquest of Wales proved to be a prolonged and uneven process, characterized on the one hand by periods of rapid advance, as in the years 1067–75 and 1100–35, and on the other by periods of major retreat, such as the years 1094–1100 and 1135–54, when the native Welsh princes recovered the military initiative and with it control of much of the lands hitherto lost to the Normans. In fact, the Norman Conquest of Wales took over two centuries to complete, for it can only be said to have been completed with Edward I's conquest of Gwynedd in 1282–3. It was also a piecemeal conquest, undertaken on the initiative of individual Anglo-Norman baronial families (such as those of Braose, Mortimer and Clare) and generally only loosely and spasmodically supervized by the kings of England. The lands which these families and their followers conquered were in effect 'private' lordships (Brecon and Glamorgan are examples) and lay outside the normal framework of English governance and justice.

Furthermore, the Norman Conquest of Wales was a limited process in that as a conquest in depth it was largely confined, at least until the 13th century, to the lowlands. It was only in the lowlands that the Normans established castles, manors, and boroughs and instituted a measure of routine civilian governance. Only in these lowland areas (notably in lowland Gwent, Glamorgan, Gower and Pembroke) was there a major colonization by alien settlers. Elsewhere in the upland regions of Wales, even in areas nominally under their control, the Anglo-Norman lords had to be content with a loose military superiority over native rulers and with the collection of tributes from the native population.

Many reasons can be adduced for the limited and piecemeal character of the Norman Conquest of Wales; but one of the major reasons certainly lay in the growing strength and resilience of the native Welsh kingdoms. The consolidation of the three kingdoms or principalities of Gwynedd, Powys and Deheubarth served as a major buffer against further Norman enterprise, especially in north and west Wales. In particular Deheubarth, under Rhys ap Gruffudd or the Lord Rhys (d.1197), and Gwynedd, under Llywelyn the Great (d.1240) and his grandson Llywelyn ap Gruffudd (d.1292), were transformed, at least temporarily, into cohesive political units capable of pursuing consistent policies. They managed to wrench much of the military initiative from the Anglo-Norman barons and to recover control of large parts of Wales. Indeed, Llywelyn the Great and his grandson went even farther: by force and persuasion, they gradually brought all other Welsh native dynasties under their authority and thereby forged native Wales (*pura Wallia*) into a single political unit. Their achievement was reluctantly acknowledged by Henry III of England in the Treaty of Montgomery (1267) when

Llywelyn ap Gruffudd's territorial gains and his newly claimed title of 'Prince of Wales' were formally confirmed.

Yet within 16 years of that treaty, the Anglo-Norman conquest of Wales was, belatedly, completed. In two devastating campaigns in 1277 and 1282–3, Edward I overran Gwynedd and secured the defeat or submission of the native princes of Deheubarth. The third Welsh principality, Powys, was already in effect an English dependency and was henceforth treated as an English barony. In spite of revolts in 1287 and 1294–5, the Edwardian conquest of north and west Wales proved final. It was followed by a military governmental settlement which shaped many features of Welsh life until the 16th century. A series of magnificent castles (such as Harlech, Caernarfon and Conway) ensured the permanence of the military victory. The newly acquired lands in Wales (the Principality as they came to be known) were largely retained in Crown hands and were divided into shires on the English model. Legally, native Welsh law was still tolerated in certain spheres but the forms and substance of English common law were introduced in the Statute of Wales (1284).

Wales had at last been conquered; but it had not been unified. The old distinction between the native principalities of Wales and the Anglo-Norman lordships was now replaced by the distinction between Crown lands (especially the five counties of the North and West and the county of Flint in the North-East) and the numerous large lordships known collectively as the March of Wales. These lordships were controlled by some of the major baronial families of England and in terms of administration and law were largely independent of each other and of the Crown. To this fragmentation of authority was added a division of race, that between the native Welsh and the settler English population. That division was manifested in many aspects of the life of Wales in the 14th century, but it came to focus on two areas of resentment in particular: the commercial privileges of the burgesses of the English towns in Wales and the alleged exclusion of Welshmen from high office in secular and ecclesiastical administration. It was that resentment which Owain Glyndŵr harnessed in the revolt which swept over much of Wales between 1400 and 1408. His revolt was the last major armed uprising against the Anglo-Norman Conquest of Wales.

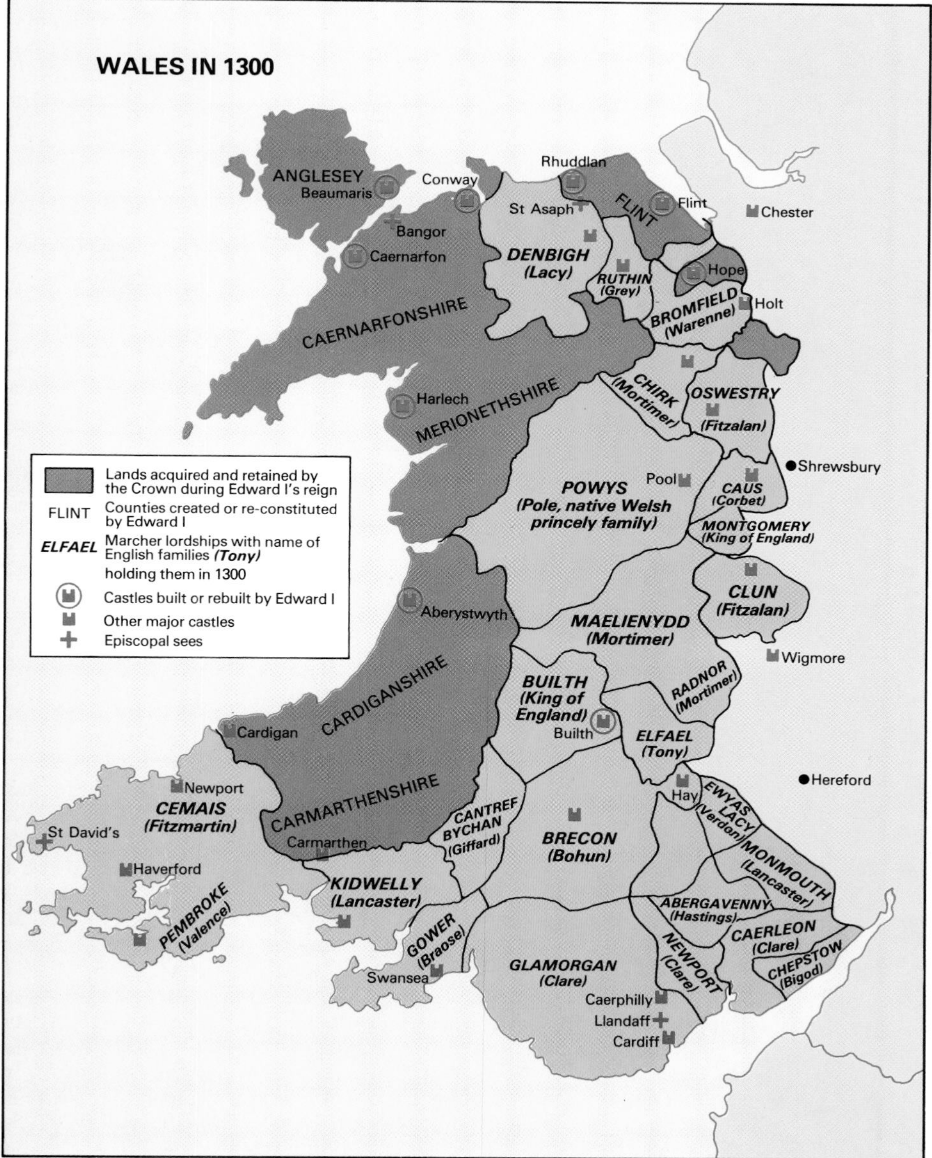

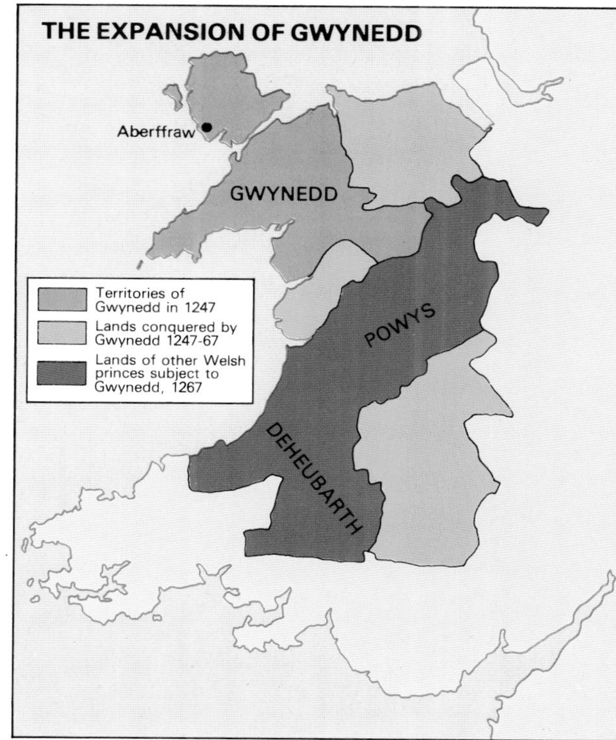

Left: Wales after the English conquest. By 1300, Wales was divided into Crown lands on the one hand and, on the other, numerous lordships – the March of Wales – controlled by Anglo-Norman families.

The expansion of Gwynedd, 1247–67. During the 13th century, the growth of the native Welsh principality of Gwynedd transformed the political situation. It brought the whole of north Wales under its control, compelled the Welsh princes of Powys and Deheubarth to acknowledge its feudal superiority and conquered several of the major lordships in the eastern March.

Edward III and the War in France, 1337–96

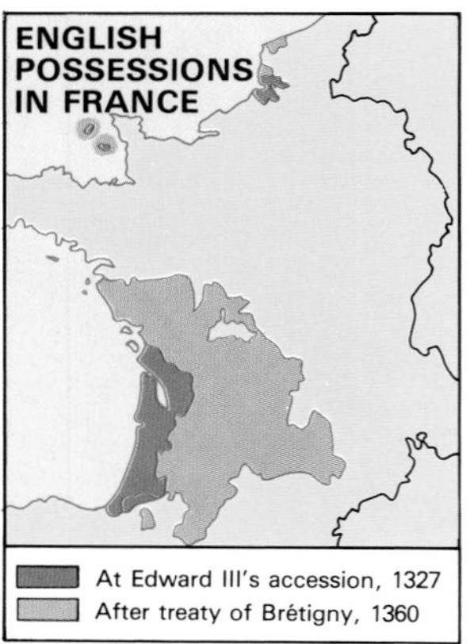

Above: Location of English possessions in France 1327–60. The Treaty of Brétigny (1360) marked the widest extent of English-held territory in the 14th century.

The 100 Years' War (so called from the early 19th century) was neither one continuous conflict nor even a single dispute lasting 100 years. It was part of a disjointed series of wars between England and France that went back to the Norman conquest. Edward III's expedition to the Low Countries in 1338 marked a new phase of the struggle, and the expulsion of the English from Gascony in 1453 stripped England of its last mainland possession except Calais. It is this phase of the conflict (1337–1453) which is known as the 100 Years' War.

England's war aims were not consistent and, particularly in the 14th century, its war diplomacy was primarily dictated by the search for a solution to immediate problems, especially of how to maintain independent rule in Gascony in the face of a unifying French kingdom. But Edward III also claimed the Capetian throne in 1337, though he abandoned the claim in 1360 (Treaty of Brétigny) for practical concessions. Dynastic ties, commercial and strategic considerations, even differing attitudes to the papacy (established at Avignon, 1308–78), helped to extend this Anglo-French conflict to the Iberian peninsula, the Empire and Low Countries, and to Scotland and Ireland. The wars were fought intensively during 1338–47 and again in the late 1350s; the renewal of war in 1369 led to more modest campaigning, with both kingdoms sufficiently exhausted to seal a 28-year truce in 1396.

ized, traditionally raised French forces. The English men-at-arms and archers had a decisive advantage which brought great victories in the first decades of the wars, even against overwhelming odds (as at Crècy and Poitiers, where John II of France was captured).

The war at sea was a minor affair, and its tactics showed little novelty or imagination. It was usually beyond the capability of 14th-century commanders to stage a naval engagement, and the battle of Sluys (which the English won) was incidental to Edward's second expedition. The English never kept a fleet permanently in being, but the Valois, learning from their Castilian allies, later established dockyards at Rouen which gave them an edge (as their victory off La Rochelle in 1372 showed).

The English commitment to the wars was, however, immense, despite the Black Death (1348) and later plagues. The expeditionary forces were occasionally large and raised with impressive regularity. The financial outlay was prodigious and willingly borne so long as the war was successful; but as England's military advantage narrowed after 1369, so its government resorted to newer expedients (such as poll taxes). The costs of war were indeed high. Whether England emerged in credit or not is a question which contemporaries simply would not have understood. Conquered castles and estates were enjoyed by fortunate soldiers, and ransoms were profitable during the victorious

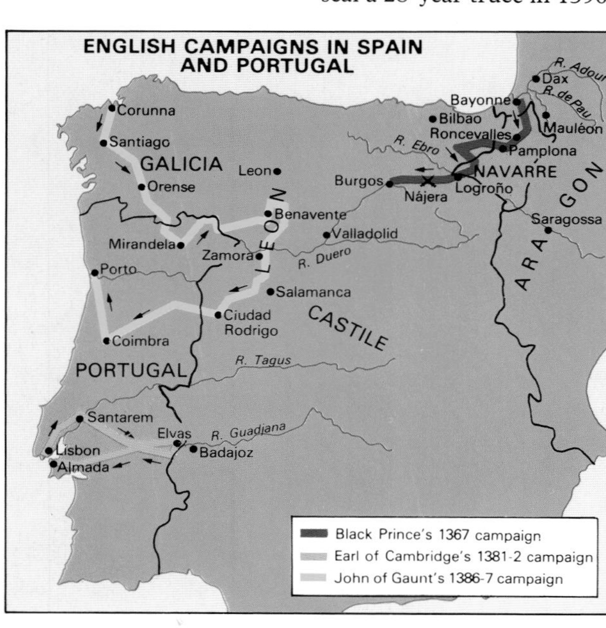

English intervention in Spain and Portugal occurred when the Black Prince entered the dynastic struggle in Castile. The Earl of Cambridge and John of Gaunt campaigned in support of the latter's claim to the Castilian throne through his wife, Constance of Castile. The French were ranged on the opposite side. English military failure, and a Castilian marriage for Gaunt's daughter, brought these episodes to an end.

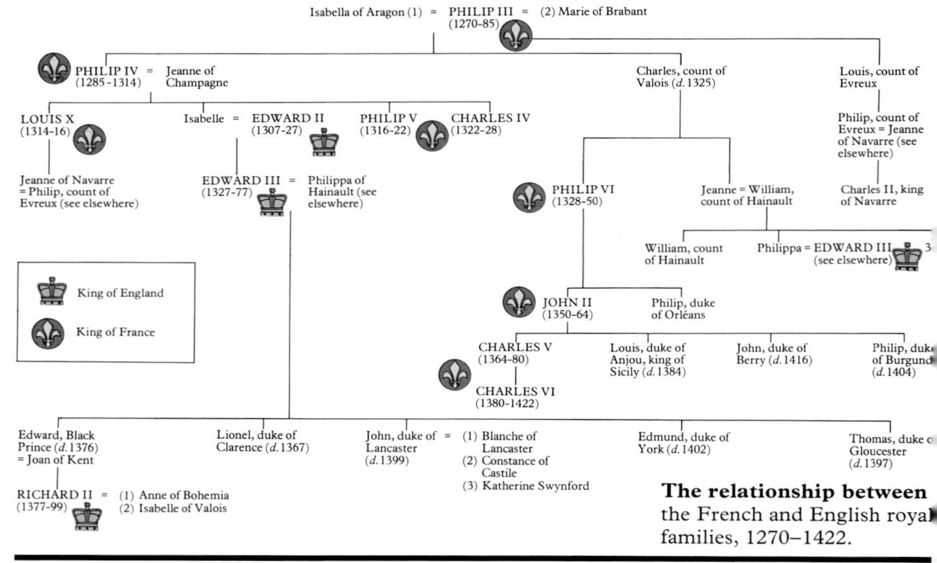

The relationship between the French and English royal families, 1270–1422.

The initial advantage lay with England, a relatively united and compact kingdom. Its prosperity, especially from the wool trade, and its 'imperial' wars in Scotland and Wales were an invaluable preparation for larger scale operations on mainland Europe. The existence of virtually independent French principalities dictated England's strategy. Thus, Edward III's earliest campaigns in the Low Countries (1339–40) relied on the support of the Flemish cities, and in the 1340s a succession dispute in Brittany enabled English forces to intervene there; while Gascony gave easy access to France for an English monarch who was also Duke of Aquitaine.

Edward I's and Edward II's wars had developed a unique ability on the part of the English Crown to raise large forces. Abandoning the feudal levy, the new, paid, contract armies, recruited by indentured captains, were better disciplined and more dependable than the loosely organ-

years (John II alone produced about £500,000). But the wars diverted thousands from their normal pursuits; supplies and equipment were devoted to operations that were often entirely destructive; and wool exports steadily declined. What is remarkable is that England was able to engage in these enterprises for decades without serious strain and at the same time defend the Scottish border, keep Ireland calm and avoid a Welsh uprising. The achievement owed much to the inspiration of the King and his eldest son, the Black Prince, who embodied a régime far removed from the harshness of Edward I and the incompetence of Edward II. Edward III, of a mind with his nobility, made practical adjustments to preserve the realm's unity of purpose.

But time was not on England's side. English arms won few victories after 1369, and public opinion grew critical of the old king and of the ministers of the new one, Edward's grandson, Richard II.

EDWARD III AND THE WAR IN FRANCE

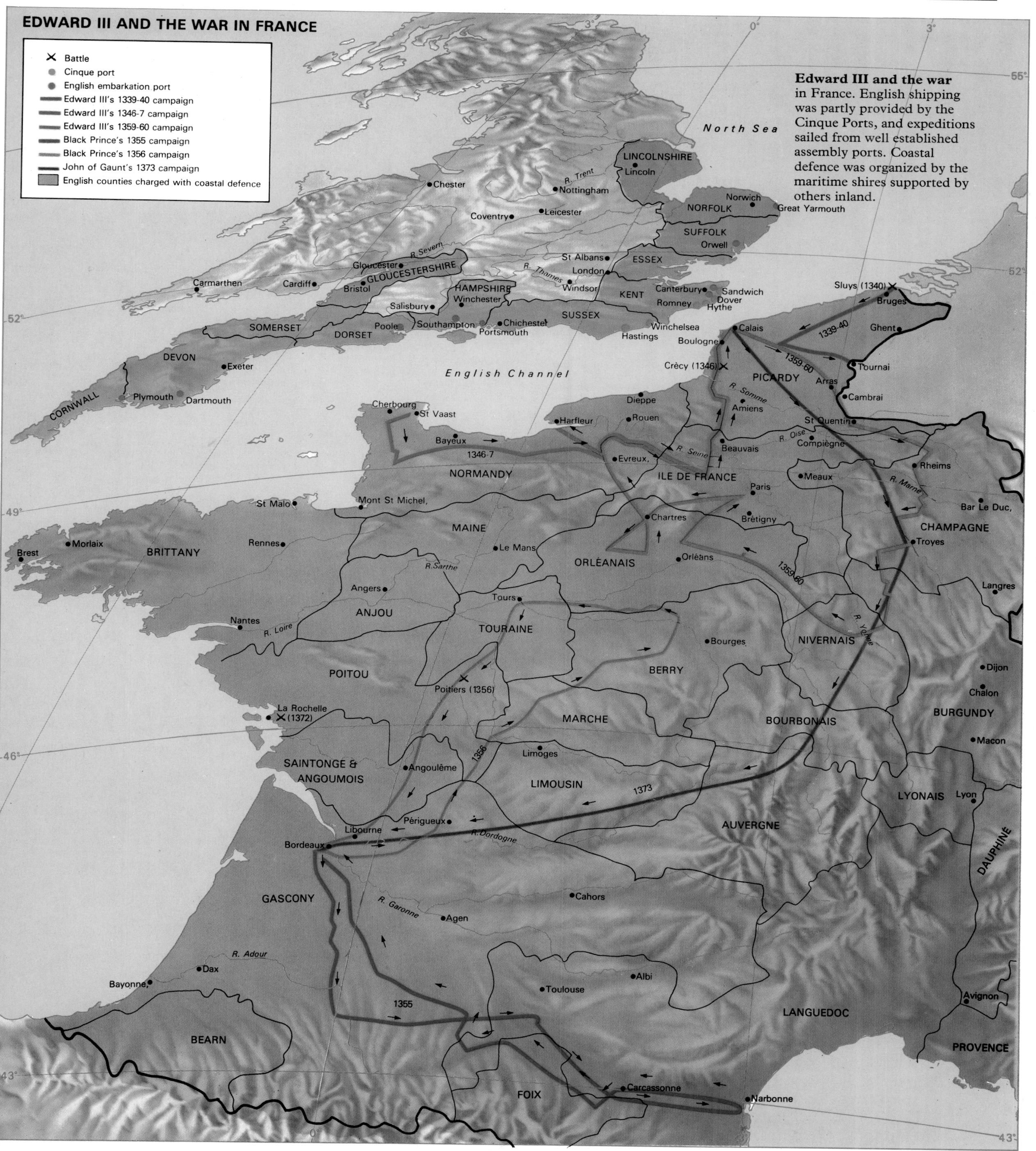

Edward III and the war in France. English shipping was partly provided by the Cinque Ports, and expeditions sailed from well established assembly ports. Coastal defence was organized by the maritime shires supported by others inland.

Discontent and Dethronement: England and Wales, 1376–1415

The pressures of war and the tensions of a personal monarchy made the reigns of the last Plantagenet (Richard II) and the first Lancastrian (Henry IV) a period of exceptional domestic upheaval. The institution of monarchy emerged largely unscathed, but criticism of ministers reached a new level of effectiveness, one dynasty was replaced violently by another, and proposals were canvassed for the realm's dismemberment. The period also saw the most widespread popular uprising of the Middle Ages.

The frustrating wartime experience of the 1370s was new to a country that had tasted victory for a generation. French raids were frequent, loss of control of the Channel harmed trade and annoyed the merchants, expensive *chevauchées* in France seemed profitless, the old King was senile, the Black Prince's health was failing – and yet the financial burden hardly eased. Many, especially the parliamentary Commons, began to question the honesty as well as the wisdom of politicians. Fortified by anticlericalism, the outcry swept the King's clerical ministers from power in 1371. In the 'Good Parliament' of 1376, allegedly corrupt and incompetent men were charged by the Commons and tried before the Lords in a novel procedure that henceforth enabled persons in high places to be held publicly responsible for their actions. The situation was hardly improved by the accession of Richard II (aged 10 in 1377).

This was the background to the Peasants' Revolt. Widespread violence was sparked off by another poll tax, this time at one shilling a head, three times the rate of 1377 and 1379. People responded with evasion, violence towards collectors and justices, and ultimately, in June 1381, rebellion. Agricultural workers from east and south-east England were joined by townsmen and Londoners. The dislocation of war and plague, the lingering inconveniences of manorialism, anticlericalism, and the resentments of town-dwellers were sharpened in a region with direct access to the turbulent Low Countries and northern

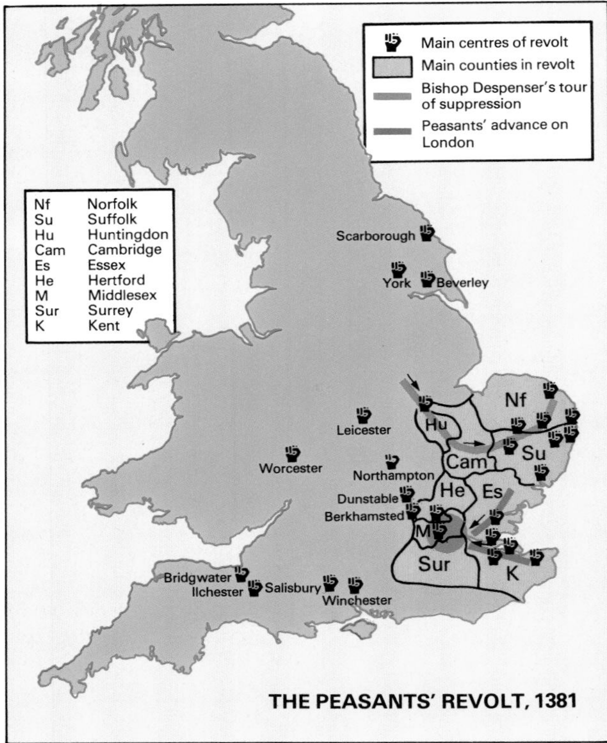

THE PEASANTS' REVOLT, 1381

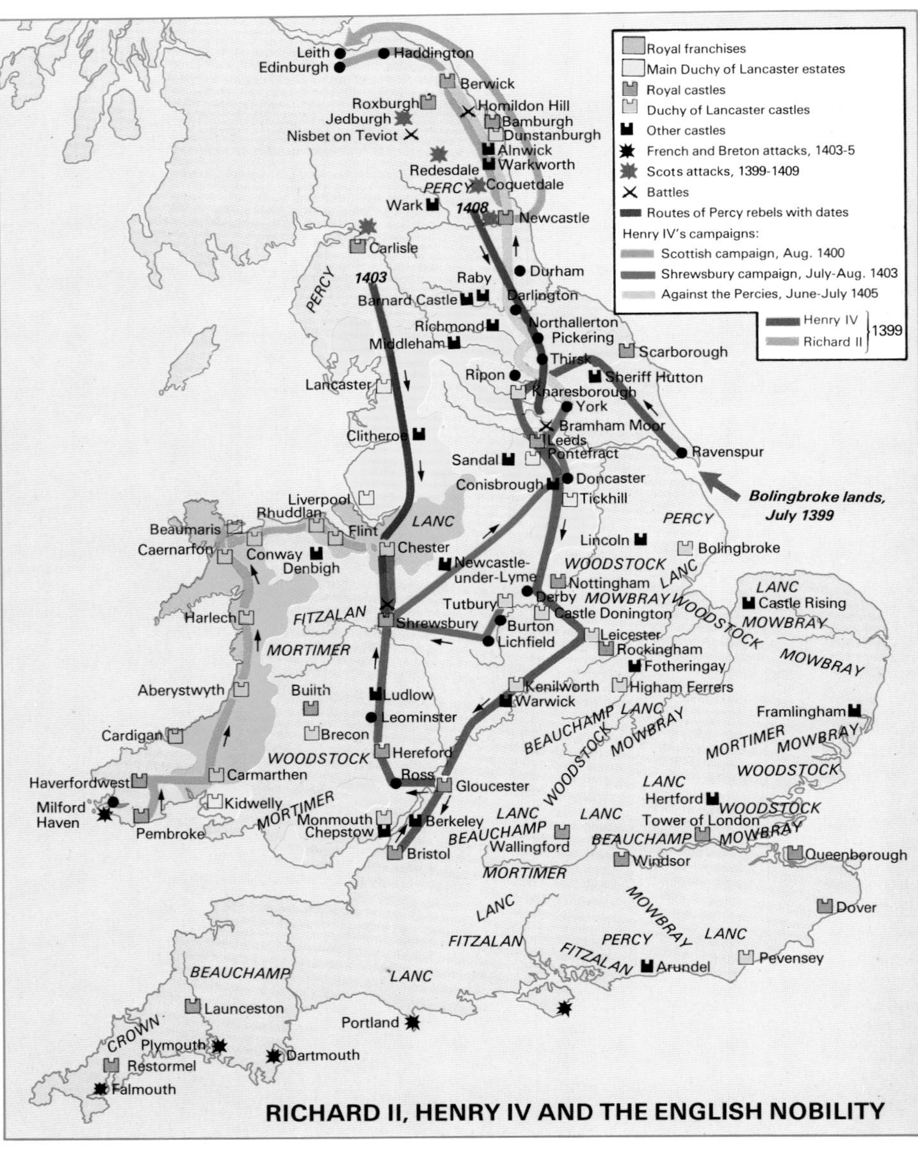

RICHARD II, HENRY IV AND THE ENGLISH NOBILITY

.eft: The illustration hows the last moments of Richard II's reign. The king as been persuaded – by Henry Percy Earl of Northumberland – to leave he relative security of Conway Castle and come to neet Bolingbroke at Flint. From Chester writs are sent ut summoning Parliament which was to witness the ormalities of Richard II's leposition.

Below: The progress and ailure of Owain Glyndŵr's evolt, 1400–8. The rebellion was the most serious and ersistent threat to Henry V's throne. In the struggle gainst Glyndŵr Prince Henry later Henry V) gathered aluable experience in a hard chool of warfare.

France. The populace of London offered a pool of potential sympathizers, while pressure on the government in Westminster and the capital held out the best hope for a remedy of grievances. The rebels accordingly converged on London from Kent (where Wat Tyler and John Ball emerged as leaders) and Essex. They threw open prisons, sacked the homes of ministers, ransacked the Tower, and tried to frighten the King into far-reaching concessions that would have broken the remaining bonds of serfdom and revolutionized landholding in Church and State. The poorly organized rebels soon dispersed by 15 June.

Hopes placed in the young King were disappointed. Quarrels within the ruling circle, including the King's uncles, engendered further mistrust, and lack of military success tarnished the reputation of the council and even the King. Richard was growing into a self-willed monarch. His choice of friends and advisers did nothing to assuage the political tensions. In 1386, Parliament and several magnates attacked his ministers and even threatened Richard with Edward II's fate. The King's refusal to yield led not only to further indictments (or 'appeals') of his advisers by five 'appellant' lords (Warwick, Arundel, Gloucester, Bolingbroke and Mowbray) but also a skirmish at Radcot

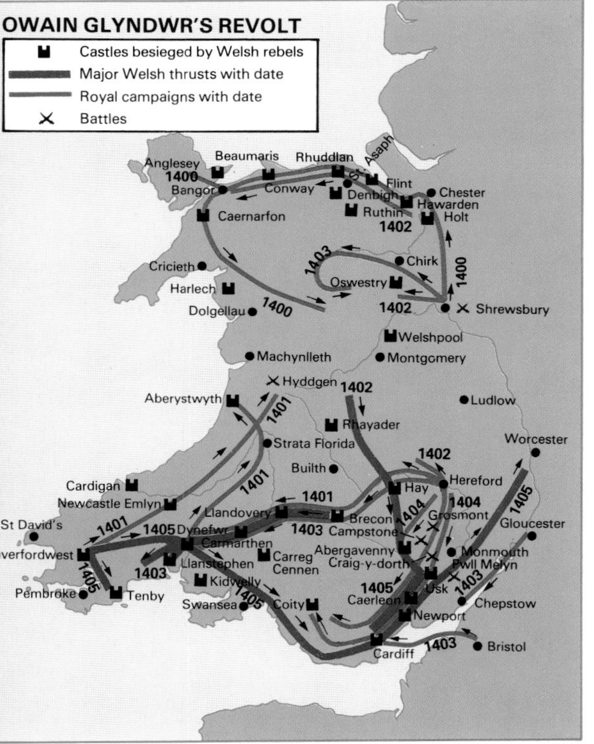

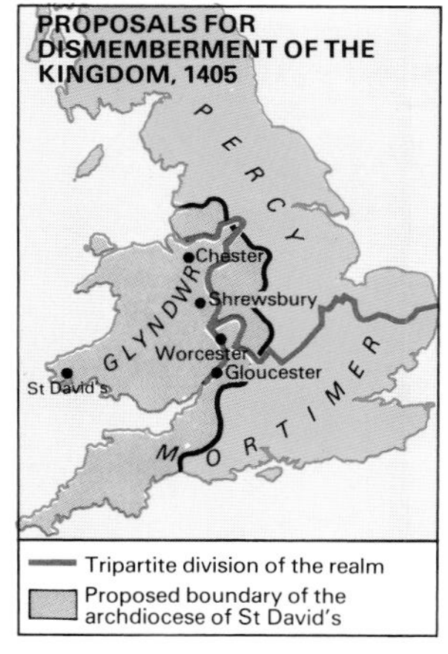

The Glyndŵr-Percy proposals for the tripartite division of England, 1405. These grandiose schemes would have given the Welsh prince a dominion that included areas whose Welsh connections were very tenuous.

.eft: The Crown's private states provided Richard with reservoir of men, money and atronage. They included the rincipality of Wales, the arldom of Chester and the Duchy of Cornwall. The Lancastrian estates of Richard's uncle, John of Gaunt, were added to the Crown estate in 1399 by Gaunt's son, Henry IV. Other ristocratic estates were the asis of provincial political nd social power.

Bridge in December 1387. At the 'Merciless Parliament' of 1388 the King was forced to submit. These events poisoned relations between the vengeful Richard and his opponents, who included some of the most powerful magnates in the realm, with estates in southern England that together rivalled in size the remoter franchises of the Crown in Wales, Cheshire and Cornwall. In a period of illusory calm (1390–6) the King nurtured feelings of revenge and carefully constructed a party of loyalists, based on his household and the distant franchises. His successful expedition to Ireland in 1394–5 fortified his power in another royal lordship and demonstrated what his household organization and resources could achieve. The truce with France in 1396 and Richard's marriage to Isabella of Valois halted the debilitating war, enabling the King to concentrate on his position at home. Warwick was exiled, Arundel executed, Gloucester murdered, and Bolingbroke and Mowbray eventually exiled. Ruthlessly deploying the monarch's personal powers, Richard's last two years have been justifiably termed tyrannous. His second visit to Ireland in May 1399 presented Bolingbroke with the opportunity to return to England to retrieve his position (and the Lancastrian estates recently seized by Richard).

The dethronement of Richard II was a momentous decision. Despite the precedent of 1327, it was the first occasion when the rightful heir was ignored. Richard's heir presumptive was the 7-year-old Earl of March; but Bolingbroke, the King's cousin, son of John of Gaunt, Duke of Lancaster seized the Crown after being assured of support from the Percy family, which Richard had alienated. No amount of distortion, concealment and argument could disguise what was a dynastic revolution; and this lay at the root of most of the domestic upheavals of Henry IV's reign.

Richard's die-hard supporters were foiled in their plot to assassinate the new king at Windsor and were apprehended at Cirencester in December 1399. The danger from such 'Ricardians' led to Richard's death in mysterious circumstances at Pontefract Castle. The Percy earls of Northumberland and Worcester, virtual kingmakers in 1399, were sufficiently disenchanted by 1403 with the King's efforts to conciliate all shades of opinion to plot several risings. Northumberland's son Hotspur, while marching to join the Welsh rebels, was defeated and killed near Shrewsbury in 1403. An alliance with Archbishop Scrope of York raised the North of England, but Henry again acted quickly and executed the prelate in 1405. Northumberland's last strike, with Scots aid, collapsed in 1408 at Bramham Moor, where the Earl himself was slain.

The Welsh rebellion had deeper-seated causes. The distress experienced by a plague-ridden society, oppression by alien landowners striving to buttress their incomes, a tendency to close doors to promotion and patronage to aspiring Welshmen, even resentment at Richard's removal, combined to throw the country into revolt. The absenteeism of English lords was crucial in the early stages, even though the diversity of rebel motives and divisions in Welsh society meant that this was no national, patriotic rising. From his estates in north-east Wales, Owain Glyndŵr laid waste alien institutions like the castle and borough, sought aid from Ireland, Scotland and France, formulated grand schemes for an independent Wales, and allied with the Percies to dismember Henry IV's realm (1405). Secure in the North and West, Owain yet had problems of manpower, supply and finance, and the failure in 1405 of his march on Worcester caused his star to wane.

By 1408 the greatest dangers were past: by perseverance, patience, decisiveness and a readiness to live in the saddle as he pursued his enemies across England – and to Edinburgh beyond – Henry overcame them all. By wise conciliation he obtained parliamentary support without surrendering any significant part of his prerogative. He enjoyed, too, the unique advantage of his father's vast Lancastrian estates as well as the Crown's franchises; whilst the support of his four sons (Henry, Thomas, John and Humphrey) was a maturing asset. Only two further threats occurred after his death in 1413. When in 1414 the anticlericalism of certain courtiers turned to Lollardy, Henry V did not hesitate to condemn even his old friend, Sir John Oldcastle; and the last revolt before 1450 to be justified by the usurpation of 1399 – that in favour of the Earl of March (1415) – was suppressed just before King Hal embarked for France.

Henry V and Lancastrian France

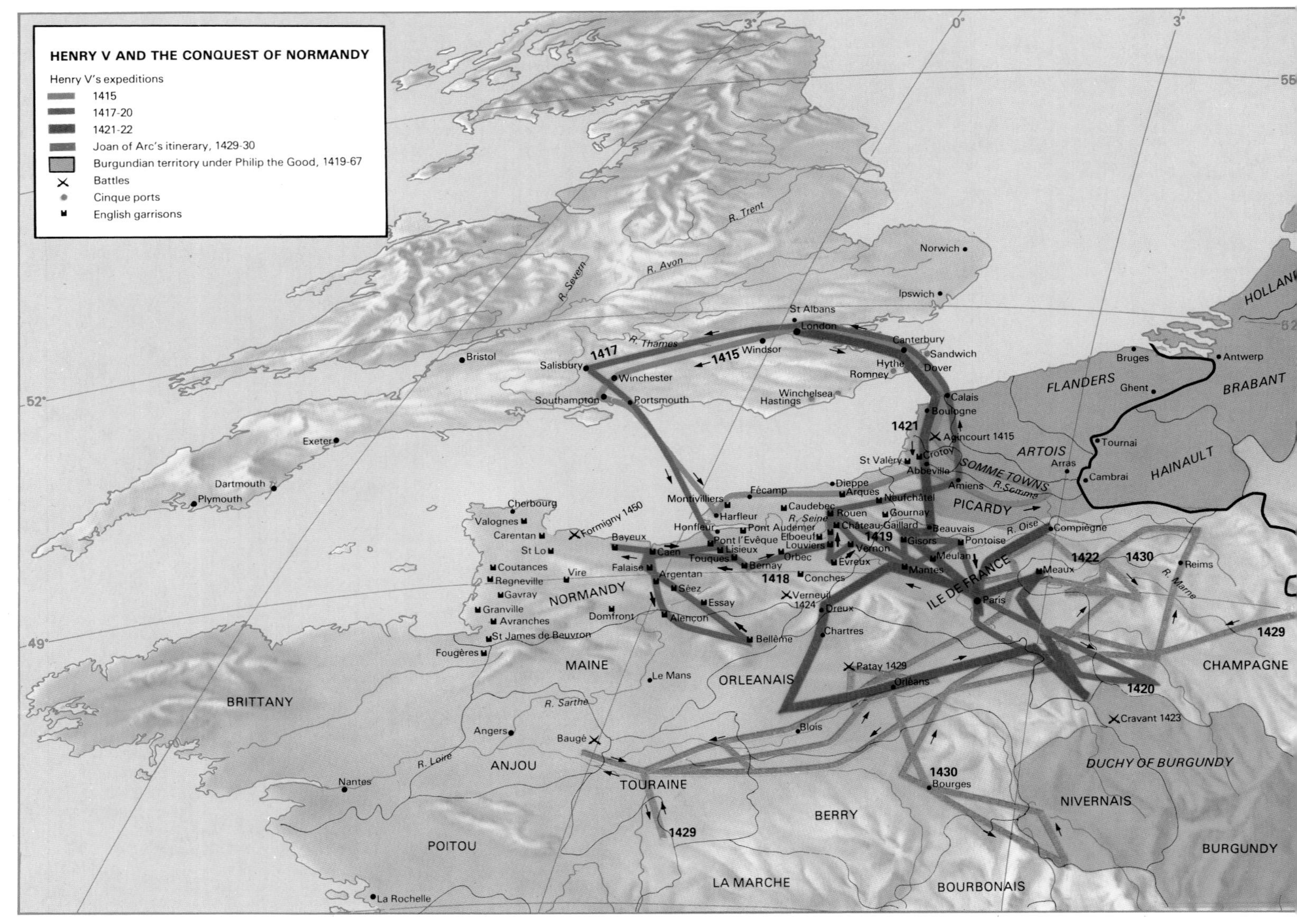

Henry V and the conquest of Normandy. Normandy and adjacent provinces were the main theatre of war during Henry's reign (1413–22) and beyond. Henry and Bedford pushed the frontier east and south (1417–29) and defeated the French at Agincourt (1415), Cravant (1423) and Verneuil (1424). This was the high point of English power in France. The resurgence begun by Joan of Arc contained the English (who were defeated at Patay, 1429). The defection of England's ally Philip of Burgundy in 1435 dealt a major blow to England's hopes. The final French victories came at Formigny (1450) and Castillon (1453). Only Calais remained of Henry V's empire.

Henry IV could claim considerable success in establishing his dynasty on firm foundations; and international acceptance was won by alliances in Germany, Scandinavia, Brittany and Burgundian Flanders. In 1413 Henry V inherited a realm that was sufficiently peaceful, loyal and united for him to campaign extensively in France (from 1415) and to spend half of the next seven years abroad. Experienced in war and government as a prince, he proved a capable, fearless and authoritarian king who was impatient of his father's careful ways. Even during his absence from England, his kingship was firm and energetic, enabling him to conduct a war that was as much a popular, national enterprise as Edward III's early campaigns. His reign was the climax of Lancastrian England.

Henry prepared for war by conciliating the Ricardians and renewing foreign alliances. The condition of France, with its frequently insane monarch and quarrelsome nobles, encouraged him to cherish dreams of conquest. By 1415 he felt able to demand full sovereignty over territories beyond Edward III's vision and even to revive Edward's claim to the French crown. Henry's ambitions coincided with his subjects' yearnings, as had those of Edward III before him. Large armies were raised, the realm voted taxation on a generous scale, the King skilfully expounded his aims publicly, and even laid the foundations for a nav to dominate the Channel. This enthusiasm hardly evaporated at all before his death.

The King's strategy was Edward III's: to ally wit French nobles to undermine French unity and press hi own dynastic claims. But quite soon the invaders' aim broadened into conquest and colonization on an unprecedented scale. The 1415 expedition had tested the wate and the victory at Agincourt strikingly vindicated Henry' tactics. In 1417–20, therefore, he became intent o conquering Normandy, and the Treaty of Troyes (142 with Charles VI made him Regent of France and heir to th Valois throne in place of the Dauphin Charles. This treat dictated Anglo-French relations for more than generation.

Though Henry V never became king of France (he pre deceased Charles VI in 1422), his baby son, Henry VI o England and Henry II of France, inherited the dua monarchy; to maintain it required unremitting effort Under the new King's uncle, the Duke of Bedford, 'constructive balance of firmness and conciliation' sough to make the conquered lands and further campaigns (i Anjou and Maine) pay for themselves. But French resur

Bottom: Henry V (left) and the Earl of Warwick at the siege of Rouen in 1419. They stand in the English camp with its palisades, batteries and tents. Beyond them can be seen the fortifications of Rouen itself. Illustration from the contemporary *Pageant of the Birth, Life and Death of Richard Beauchamp, Earl of Warwick 1389–1439.*

English and Burgundian territories in France, 1415–22. Throughout the war, Burgundian support, whether direct or indirect, was vital to English success.

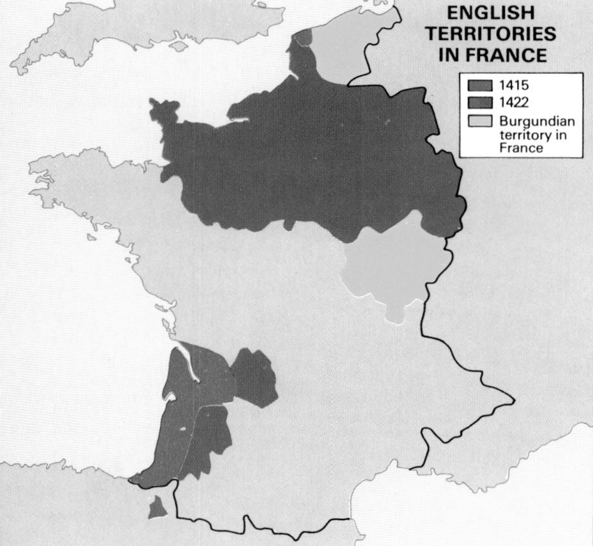

gence inspired by Joan of Arc and the coronation of Charles VII in 1429 foiled this plan. The Normans grew restless under their governors, England's Breton and Burgundian allies began to waver, and the English Parliament had to find more and more cash for the war in northern France, where garrisons and field armies were an increasingly heavy burden. The English were in a military as well as a financial trap – and without the genius of Henry V to direct them.

During the 1430s the search for peace gathered speed, particularly in England. The Congress of Arras (1435) and the discussions at Gravelines in 1439 were unproductive, largely because opinion in England was divided as to the wisdom of peace and the desirability of significant concessions. But the recovery of Charles VII's fortunes, the defection of Burgundy, the death of Bedford in 1435, and the mounting cost of English expeditions in defence of Lancastrian France were decisive factors. The government at last freed the Duke of Orléans (a captive in England since Agincourt) to promote the cause of peace among fellow French princes, though without much success; in 1445,

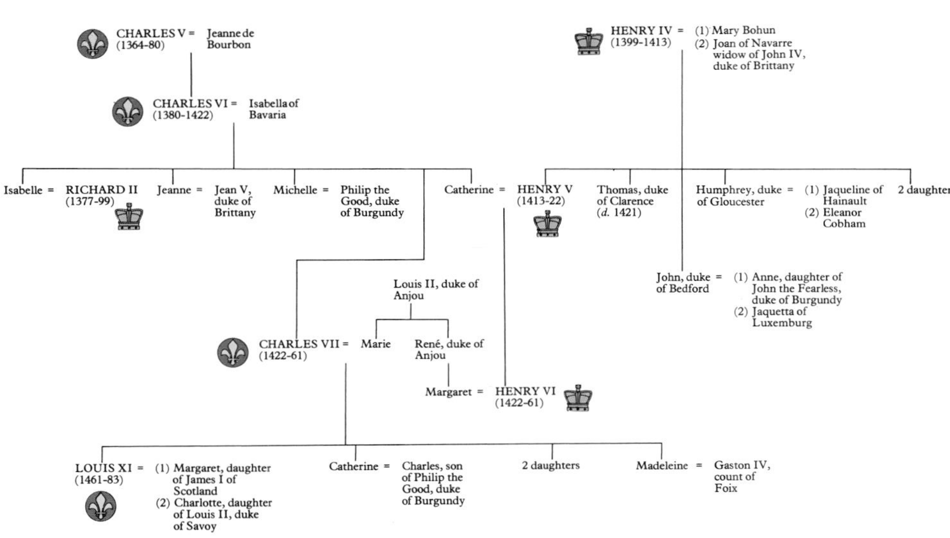

The descent of the French and English royal houses.

Henry VI married the French queen's niece, Margaret of Anjou, but that produced only a truce; and a meeting of kings was planned but never took place. Eventually Henry VI promised to surrender hard-won territory (Maine) as an earnest of his desire for peace. His failure to win the support of his subjects for this move – especially those who had lands in France and had borne the brunt of the fighting – led to the exasperated French attacking Normandy in 1449. Their onslaught was so spectacularly successful that the English had been cleared from the duchy by 1450. Gascony, which had seen few major campaigns under Henry V and Henry VI, was invaded by the triumphant French armies, so that by 1453 the English territories in the South-West were entirely lost. This was the most shattering blow of all, for Gascony had been English since the 12th century. Only Calais remained of Henry V's 'empire'. The long-established wine and cloth trades with south-west France were temporarily disrupted. The deprived and disillusioned soldiers and others who returned to England regarded the discredited Lancastrian government as responsible for their plight, for the surrender of what Henry V had won and the just claims he had forwarded. At home Henry VI would soon have to face the consequences of defeat.

Lollardy and Literacy

In the late 14th century, for the first time in English history, the established authorities began to be seriously alarmed about the spread of heresy. This was the heresy known as 'Lollardy' – 'lollard' being a continental term of abuse for a religious zealot whose attitudes appeared to be suspect. Lollardy's founding father, John Wyclif, spent most of his adult life as a typical university don. Except when employed by the government as a consultant in its dealings with the papacy, he remained at Oxford, lecturing, preaching and writing (1356–80). In time he came to develop unorthodox views – but this too was not uncommon. What was extraordinary was that he refused to withdraw them when required to do so by the Church. As a result he was obliged to leave the university in 1381. He retired to Lutterworth, where he was rector, and died there in 1384.

Wyclif's Doctrines and Beliefs

Among Wyclif's uncomfortable doctrines were beliefs that the true Church consisted only of those predestined to salvation and that the secular powers should compel the clergy to live a frugal life by divesting them of their landed property, leaving them with only tithes and voluntary offerings. Further, he believed that in the Eucharist (Mass) the substance of bread remained after consecration, i.e. that transubstantiation did not occur. Finally, he argued that Holy Scripture, every word of which was divinely inspired, did not require the clergy's 'expert' interpretation and thus ought to be made available to everyone. This led to the Lollard Bible, an English translation made in the 1380s by some of Wyclif's early academic supporters. Much of this coincided with the contemporary spirit in religion which was puritan, biblical, evangelical, anarchic, anti-sacerdotal and hostile to the established order. Eventually, influential Churchmen, active against Lollardy among academics at Oxford from the start, prevailed upon the government to take action: the statute *De Haeretico Comburendo* was enacted in 1401 and in the next 12 years two Lollards were put to death by burning.

With the accession of Henry V in 1413 all hope of radical reform in the Church disappeared; this disappointment led in 1414 to the rising of the committed Lollard leader Sir John Oldcastle, Henry V's former friend, who had escaped from the Tower in 1413. The government, informed of the reckless enterprise beforehand, easily dealt with the small number of insurgents who had converged on London.

Lollardy's long final phase as a sturdy underground movement of Bible-reading craftsmen should not be underestimated. Such men, mobile, independent and literate in the vernacular, were the backbone of 15th-century Lollardy; its level-headed piety appealed to these self-made men who had little time for the official and popular pieties of pilgrimage and devotion to images and relics. In their widely scattered households Lollardy survived (and thrived). These heretics had a wide network of contacts, their own priests, schoolmasters and schools, and an extensive vernacular literature. They were, in other words, a committed and organized group antagonistic to the Church. However, the Church was not unduly concerned about them because, as they won no recruits among the politically important, they consequently remained politically negligible.

Although their view of the nature of the Eucharist was unconventional, Lollards shared with their orthodox contemporaries an active piety and a critical attitude towards the priesthood. The clerical order was no longer (if it ever had been) highly regarded; now it was the man, not

The map attempts to plot these three phases: 1. Places where Lollard views are known to have been preached in the 1380s and 1390s and where the preachers' patrons and protectors lived. London is included to represent the royal household, some of whose members (and not the least important) were sympathetic to Lollardy at this time. 2. Places where participants in Oldcastle's rising came from. 3. Some of the places where the authorities detected Lollards between 1415 and 1522.

the cloth, which counted. Some Englishmen so distruste the clergy that they made sure their chantry foundatio were administered by laymen – like that of Willia Cannings in St Mary Redcliffe, Bristol, where the May could dismiss unsatisfactory chaplains. All however wou have applauded Margaret Paston's ambition for her son: will love hym bettere to be a good seculare man than to be lewit prest'.

Orthodox charity, like conventional piety, can neither b measured nor conveniently mapped. But one's impressio is of both the great number and the great range communal as well as individual acts of charity of the lat Middle Ages, from the gifts of bread and money to poor fo who attended funerals, to the foundation and maintenan of imposing urban hospitals, such as St Mary-in-th Newarke at Leicester, or St Bartholomew at Gloucester, the 10 hospitals and almshouses of early 16th-century Hu Nor should the good works of parish confraternities b overlooked: the care of the old, sick, and impoverishe being as important a function as the drinking of beer ar the upkeep of an altar with its priest, images and lights. O further point is that providing for education was one of t seven spiritual acts of mercy ('instructing the ignorant' and therefore one's own eternal salvation was involve

In the churches laymen in the 15th century built for themselves there was no architectural distinction between nave and chancel as is clearly shown in this photograph of Ewelme church, Oxfordshire. The other buildings at Ewelme are also representative, of the active devotion of the age: the almshouse and the school (to the left of the tower).

scholars were beadsmen too. Eton was far more than just a school.

Spirituality and literacy were connected: devotional reading was probably the most important sort of reading that there was. There were at least two levels of literacy (reading and writing) and two languages in which to be literate (Latin and the vernacular). As, in the late 14th century, French increasingly gave way to English as the vernacular of the upper classes, so their ability both to read and write it became widespread. Most merchants and businessmen were able both to read and write their own language; many craftsmen and artisans and some farmers could at least read it. Women of high social status were generally better readers than writers; most other women could do neither. Latin remained the language of administration, whether royal, noble, gentle, urban or ecclesiastical; it was also the language of the liturgy, of canon law, and of theology. Thus 'clerks' had to have a good working knowledge of Latin if they were to make successful careers. Careerist lawyers also needed French (the language of the Courts) as well as Latin.

By the 15th century instruction in Latin grammar, in its early stages at least, was in English. This meant that all those who went to grammar school were already capable of reading and writing in the vernacular. That literacy was increasing is made clear by the numbers of schools known to have existed. (In the 12th century there were about 30; in the 13th century about 70; in the 14th century about 100, and by 1530 about 120).

It appears, then, that William Caxton, like the experienced man of business that he was, responded to demand when he printed so many English books between 1474 and his death in 1491. Yet other Englishmen were slow to seize the opportunity: all the other printers in England before 1509 seem to have been foreigners; certainly all those in London were. Moreover, printers abroad were printing English books and importing them into England, and several foreign booksellers were established in London by 1509. The map above attempts to show how sluggish was the development of printing in England in this period.

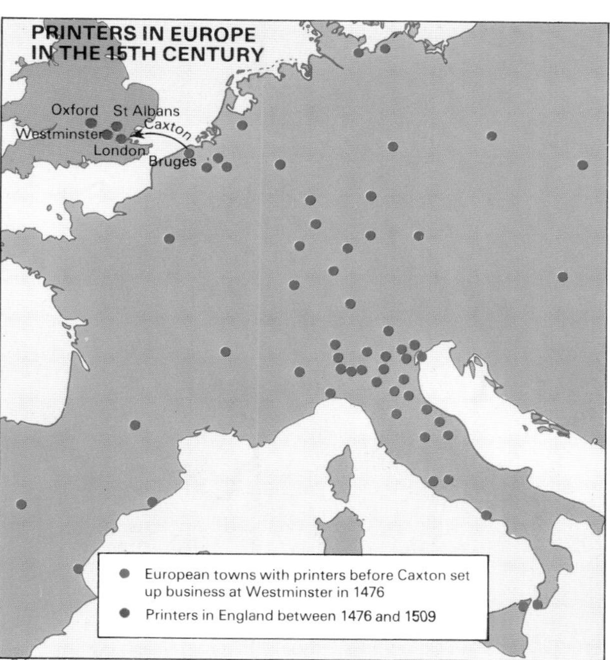

Printers in Europe and England during the 15th century. Despite a marked growth of literacy in England – in the vernacular as well as in learned languages – printing was slow to establish itself. The English printing trade was largely dominated by foreigners.

A portrait of John Wyclif, Lollardy's founding father.

The Wars of the Roses

'The Wars of the Roses' is in many ways a misleading label to apply to the whole period between the first battle of St Albans (1455) and the battle of Stoke (1487). It tends to suggest an unbroken series of wars caused by a single problem – either by the dynastic quarrel between Lancaster and York or, more sociologically, by a malignant disease of the body politic known as 'bastard feudalism'. 'Bastard feudalism' is another misleading label. Stripped of its negative overtones, it simply refers to a system of relationships linking Crown, lords, gentry and yeomen. As a system it was as characteristic of society in the 14th or 16th centuries as it was in the 15th century. Effective kings governed through 'bastard feudalism'; ineffective kings were overthrown by means of it. It posed no threat to the Crown as such.

In reality there were three separate wars. The first began in the 1450s, came to a crisis in 1459–61, and then continued to simmer in the North until 1464. The second lasted from 1469 to 1471. The third began in 1483 and ended in 1487. The first was caused by Henry VI's complete inadequacy as a ruler, by his inability either to hold France or govern England. Though to lose one kingdom may be a misfortune, to lose two looks like carelessness. The rebellion of Jack Cade in 1450 affords the most devastating commentary on the shortcomings of the ruling clique at court, but there was no way in which a gentry-led popular rising could provide an alternative government. This first became a serious possibility when Richard Duke of York, angered by his own exclusion from court, entered into political alliance with the powerful Nevilles, Richard Neville Earl of Salisbury and his son Richard Earl of Warwick. York and the Nevilles won the first battle of St Albans but, since they were not aiming to overthrow Henry VI, merely to dominate his council, they always remained vulnerable to a determined assertion of authority by the King or – to be more realistic – by the Queen, Margaret of Anjou. The Yorkists were eventually forced to accept that only by deposing Henry could they have any security. This dynastic issue, first seriously raised in 1460, was effectively settled in March 1461 when Edward IV won the fiercely contested battle of Towton.

The second war was caused by the Earl of Warwick's discontent. Convinced that he had placed Edward on the throne, he demanded a greater voice in council than any competent king could allow. It was only his defeat and flight to France in the spring of 1470, giving rise to the extraordinary spectacle of an alliance between Warwick and Margaret of Anjou, that permitted the resurrection of the Lancastrian dynasty (October 1470–May 1471). But after his victory at Tewkesbury, Edward IV killed off the surviving Lancastrians and then ruled in peace until his unexpected death in April 1483.

The third war was triggered off by Richard of Gloucester's murderous ambition. His *coup* shattered the Yorkist regime at court and in the country. All those who stood in his way (his nephews, Hastings, the Woodvilles and the lords and gentry involved in Buckingham's rebellion, October 1483) were either killed or driven into exile. From then on Richard III had to rely upon the support of an ever-diminishing group of northerners. Most of the Yorkist exiles congregated at the Breton 'court' of Henry Tudor, up till now a forlorn and obscure figure with no hope of ever making good his distant claim to the 'Lancastrian' throne. Thus, when Henry returned to England in 1485, he represented the Yorkist quite as much as the Lancastrian interest. In consequence, hardly anyone was prepared to fight for Richard III. After Bosworth (August 1485) a few northerners continued the struggle but

The 18 months between September 1459 and March 1461 saw no less than six battles and witnessed more violent swings of the political pendulum than any other period of similar length in English history. A high proportion of the nobility and gentry found themselves caught up in these violent events. But this was the climax of the Wars of the Roses and in marked contrast to the Bosworth campaign when both nobles and gentry were notable for their absence.

Having been driven into exile in September 1470, Edward IV returned to England on 14 March 1471, landing – as Bolingbroke had done – at Ravenspur. The odds seemed to be heavily stacked against him, but in the following weeks of non-stop activity Edward displayed generalship of the highest order. By capturing and retaining the initiative he made it difficult – and in the event impossible – for the three opposing forces, Warwick's, Margaret's and Fauconberg's, to take concerted action. One by one they were defeated. Fauconberg's campaign includes the only town-siege in the Wars of the Roses and highlights two other points: the turbulence of Kent in this period and the military importance of the Calais garrison.

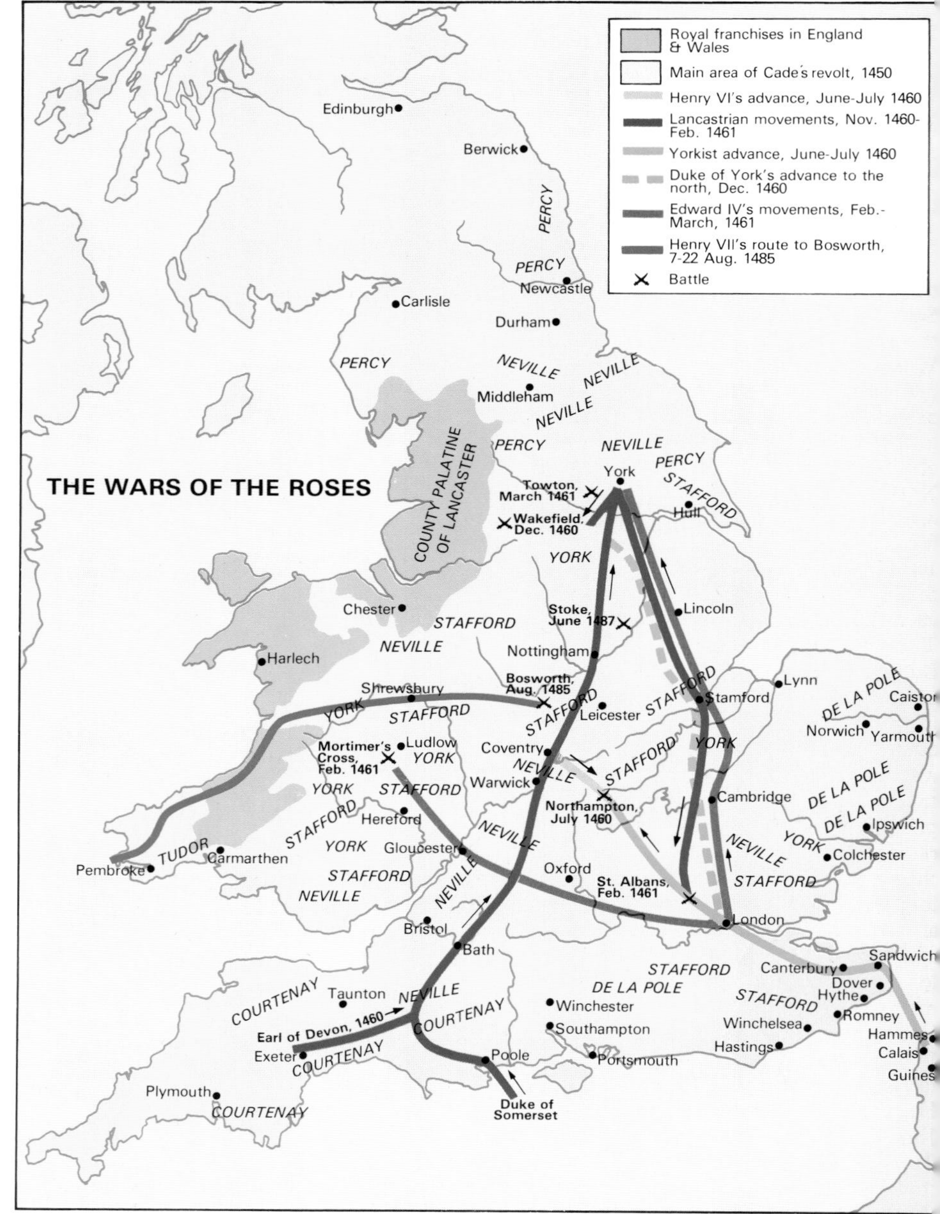

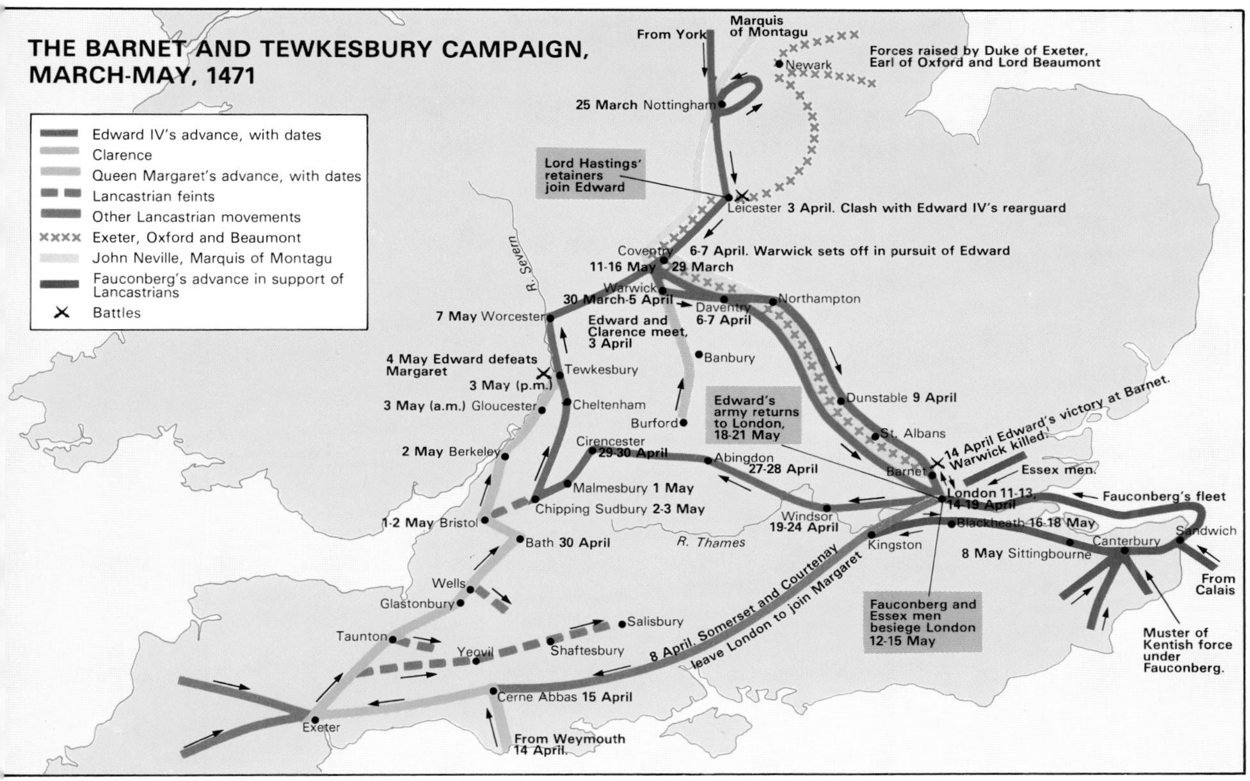

The Lancastrian Henry VI (1422–61 and 1470–71) and his strong-willed Queen, Margaret of Anjou. The Yorkists were defeated at the battle of Wakefield in which the Yorkist claimant, Richard Duke of York, was killed. A year later York's son, Edward, defeated the Lancastrians at Towton and Edward was crowned as Edward IV. Henry briefly regained his throne in 1470 before being driven off in the campaign shown above.

the suppression of Lovell's Rising (1486), the victory of Stoke (June 1487) and Henry VII's subsequent progress through Yorkshire and Durham marked the end of the Wars of the Roses.

As wars go, the Wars of the Roses had not been nasty, brutish and long – despite the popular, Shakespearian myth to the contrary. They were short and intermittent periods of violence in a basically peaceful society. Only in the far North, on the Scottish border, and in the Calais garrison was there anything approaching a permanent military force. In a period of more than 30 years the total time spent actually at war was about one year. This was not a long drawn-out struggle of attrition, fortification and devastation in the manner of most medieval wars. Except at Towton, the armies were fairly small and casualties light. By and large, economic, social and religious life went on unhindered. The temporary havoc which the wars caused in the aristocratic establishment was real enough – particularly in 1459–61 when a high proportion of the nobility was involved – and for many individuals this was deeply tragic. But it made little difference to the structure of politics. It is true that Tudor noblemen were reluctant to rebel, but so too were the lords of Lancastrian England – they put up with an incompetent king for an astonishingly long time. It is not true that the Tudor monarchs pursued an avowedly anti-aristocratic policy or waged a royal war against private armies. In order to rule they depended on lords and the whole structure of 'bastard feudalism' just as much as their predecessors had done. It is true that Henry VII did not create many new peers, but neither did Edward IV after 1471, the Lancastrian kings before 1437 nor, to go farther back still, did Edward I. In style of government Henry VII was rather like a more efficient version of King John. There was no significant break with the past here. The old view that the wars were the last dying convulsion of the Middle Ages, the divide between 'Medieval' and Modern', is a view which cannot be sustained.

The Political Structure of Early Tudor England

Behind the formal governmental machinery of Council and administration at the centre and of regional Councils and J.P.s in the localities, there lay a complex pattern of power in early Tudor England. This was firmly rooted in 'bastard feudalism' and at its heart was the royal household, whose organization in turn derived from the layout of the royal palace (right). Away from the centre the influence of the royal household was carried into the localities by the leading servants of the Chamber and Privy Chamber, who were part courtiers, part royal bastard feudal retainers. Servants in the king's household, they were masters of their own houses. Such a house, by its opulence and decoration of royal badges, symbolized the importance of both its builder and his royal master; it was also the focus of a dual power over its neighbours in which the interests of king and servant were inextricably mixed. But the Tudors' consequent monopoly of bastard feudalism was only regional. For as the main map shows the royal servants were very unevenly distributed.

The Power of the South

The origins of this structure of royal administration (like so much else in Tudor England) went back to the Yorkist Edward IV (1461–83). He had ruled most of England indirectly through a handful of great regional magnates, but in the necklace of counties around London he had recruited lesser men – the leading knights and gentry – into his household and had governed the 'Home Counties' directly through them. These household knights rose against Richard III in the ill co-ordinated series of Home Counties risings known as Buckingham's Rebellion and were de-

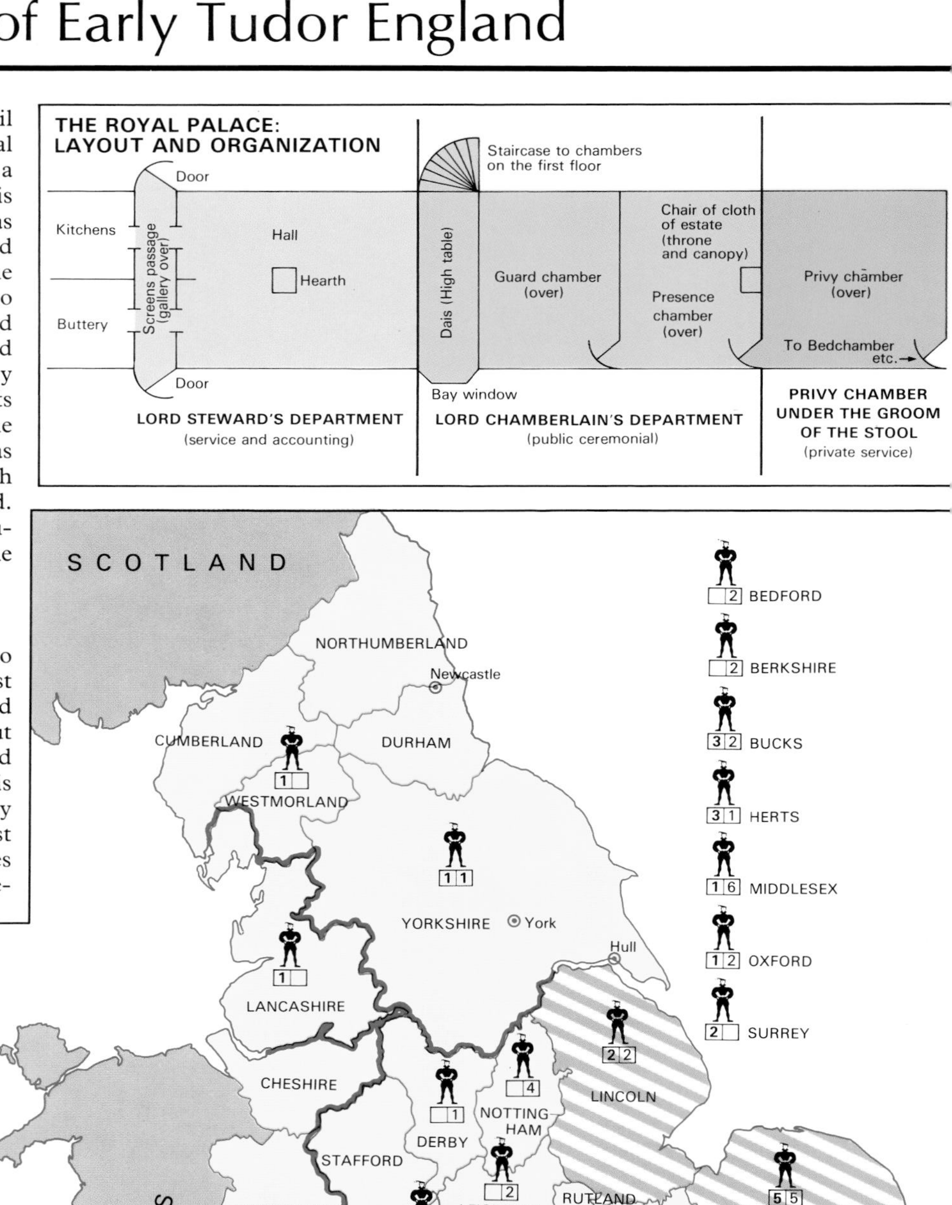

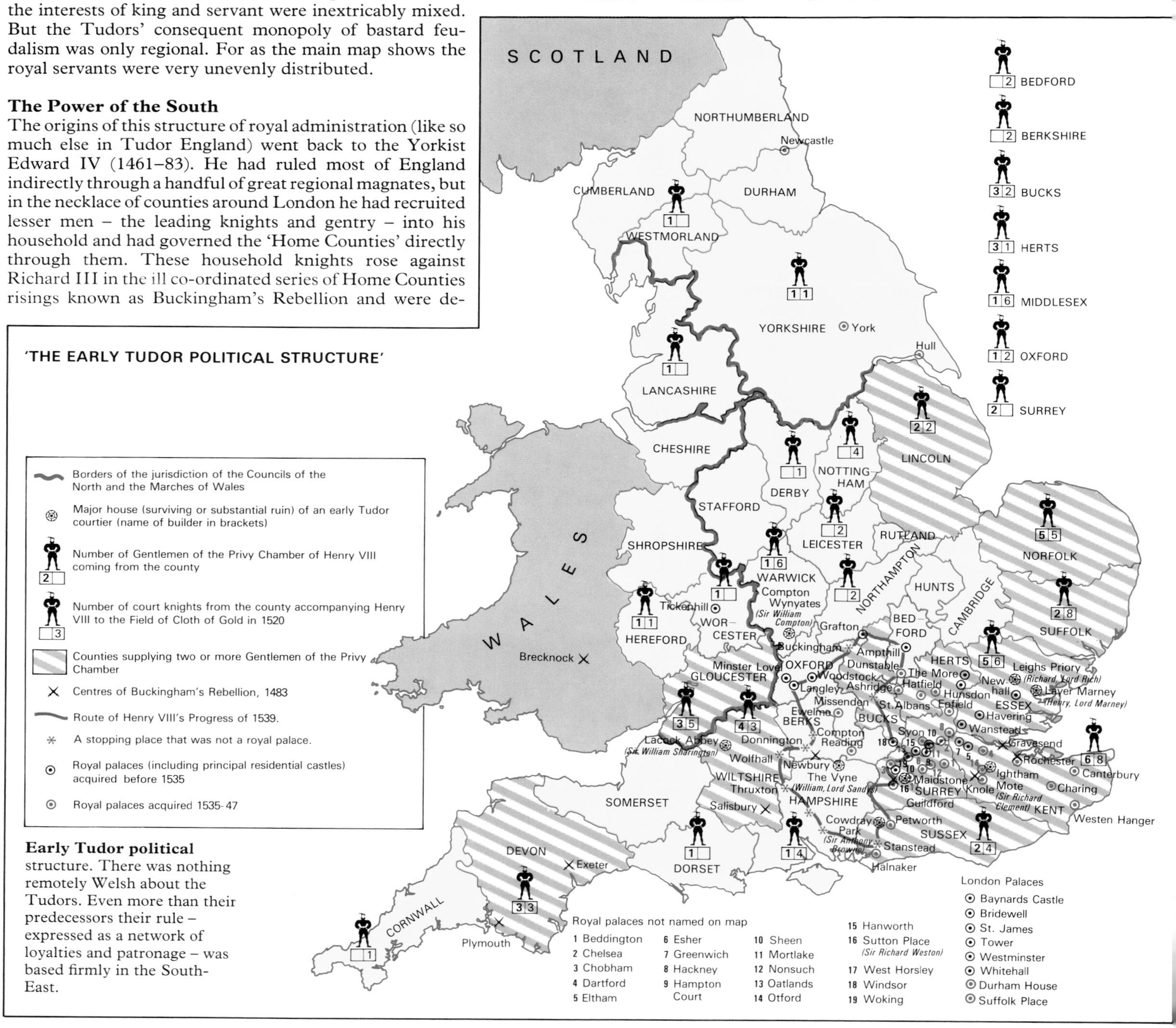

Early Tudor political structure. There was nothing remotely Welsh about the Tudors. Even more than their predecessors their rule – expressed as a network of loyalties and patronage – was based firmly in the South-East.

.eft: Plan of a typical ·oyal palace. From the 15th ·entury onwards, all royal palaces were built to the same general pattern.

ˈeated. But the survivors transferred their loyalties to the Ǝarl of Richmond, soon to be Henry VII, and it was their ˈamilies that were to supply the great majority of Henry VIII's Privy Chamber.

This southern bias in the king's servants was reinforced ɔy the king's own itineraries. For, with the building of Whitehall, Westminster became the political as well as the ıdministrative capital from which the king rarely strayed ·ar: royal progresses (in fact private summer hunting ɔarties) – like that of 1539 (see main map) – were tightly ·ircumscribed, while Henry VIII's palace building – ·hough it was prodigious – was densely clustered round London.

Nowhere probably was there anything more involved ·han political accident and personal caprice; nevertheless ·he drift south had a major effect on the stability of the Tudor regime. For the South-East was overwhelmingly dominant in both wealth and population. If secure here, the Tudors were secure indeed! Of course, none of this was ıbsolutely new. But there was a real shift of emphasis. Ǝarlier kings had ordinarily relied on the South, but in noments of crisis they had turned to dynastic power bases ·lsewhere – in Wales or the Midlands. For the Tudors, ıowever, the South itself was their stronghold. Nothing ·hows this more clearly than the case of Kent. Previously ·he county had been the perpetually fertile seedbed of ·ebellion – the Peasants' Revolt (1381), Cade's Rebellion 1450), Clarence's Rising (1469), Buckingham's Rebellion 1483); under the Tudors it became instead the bedrock of ·he dynasty. It did revolt once, in 1554. But Wyatt's Revolt s the exception which proves the rule, since both its leaders - men such as Wyatt and Culpepper – and its loyalist ɔpponents – like Sir Thomas Cheyney and Lord Abergavenny – were drawn from the Tudor courtier following ·hat had split under the twin threats of Mary's religious ·eaction and her Spanish marriage.

Two things have been left out so far: the role of the ıobility and the government of England outside the ·tronghold of the South.

The nobility – in regard to central politics and the court – were unusually quiescent. The reasons were part accidental minorities and personal disabilities), and part deliberate royal or ministerial policy). In the event, a few families were destroyed (Stafford) or severely weakened (Percy), ɔut most continued untroubled the sort of local dominance llustrated by the case of the De Veres, Earls of Oxford. They began rebuilding churches and decorating them with ·heir badge of the mullet in their moment of political glory ınder John, the 13th Earl, who commanded Henry VII's vanguard at Bosworth and could subsequently be referred ·o as 'the principal personage in the kingdom'. Nevertheless, the work continued almost as actively in the ·wilight that followed John's death and the family's disappearance from central politics.

The 'rest of England' – a blank on this map – appears ılled with rebellion on the map on page 88. It would be a nistake to think that this was the usual state of affairs. Most ɔf the time the leading families got on with their usual ɔusiness of running the shires and quarrelling with their ıeighbours. They maintained a decent loyalty to the Crown ınd were always willing to invoke its power in local disputes. Equally, they ignored its edicts whenever they ·rossed their own interests and it was politic to do so. In ·hort – save that they did not participate directly in central ɔolitics – things were not all that different from the South.

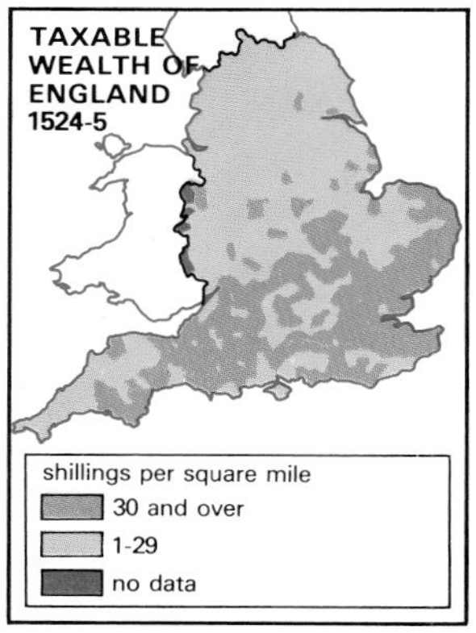

Wealth and population: the dominance of the South-East. To set these maps in context, they should be compared with the similar maps on pages 176–7.

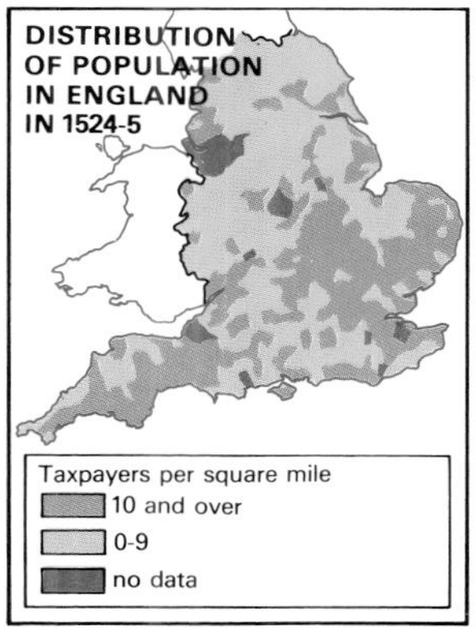

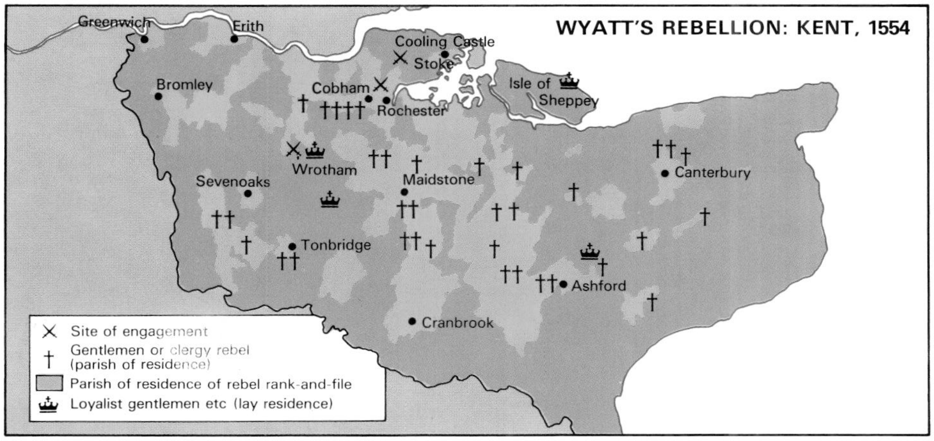

Wyatt's rebellion, 1554. The rebel rank-and-file came from the same parishes as the rebel gentlemen.

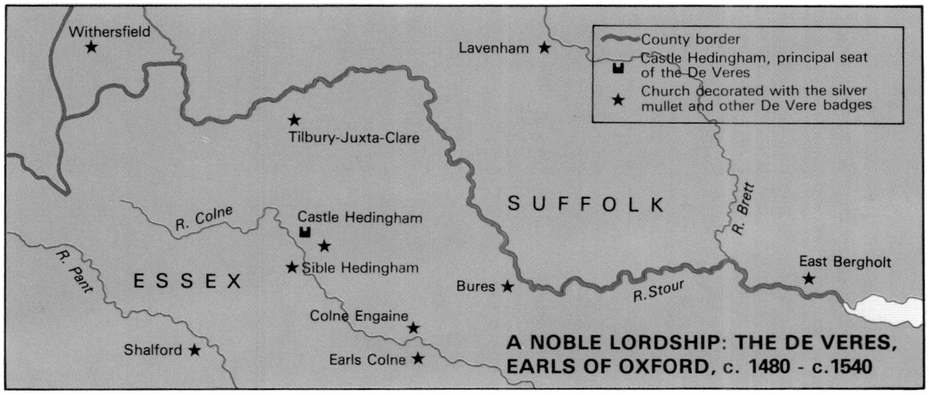

A noble lordship: the De Veres, Earls of Oxford *c.*1480–*c.*1540. The distribution of churches decorated with the De Vere badge gives a helpful indication of the extent of their local lordship in the heart of a prosperous East Anglian cloth manufacturing area.

Reformation, Rebellion and Attack

The organization of the post-Reformation English Church. Although the English Reformation and consequent re-organization of the Church were political measures carried through by the ruling elite, the men and women who were prepared to die for the new faith were overwhelmingly urban and lower class.

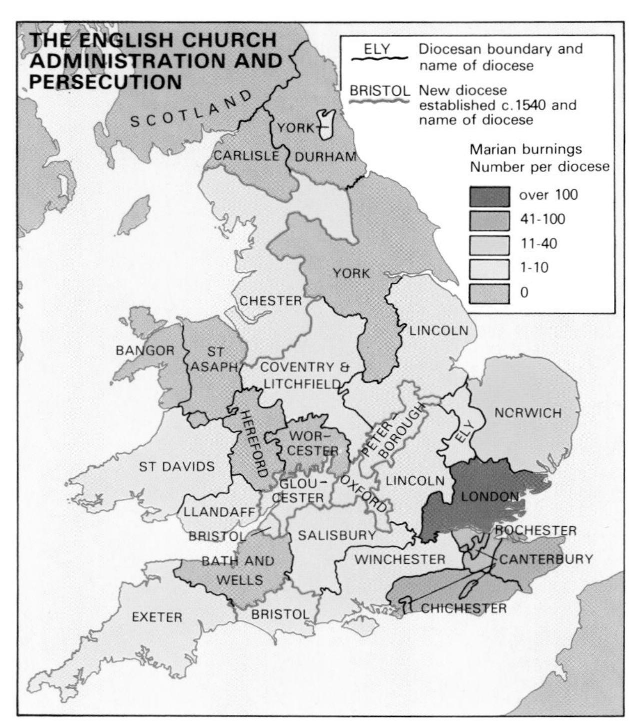

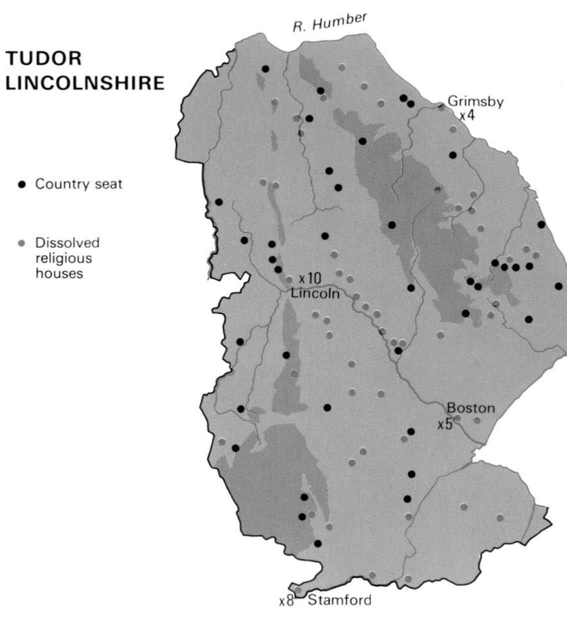

Far right: Tudor Lincolnshire. Here, as elsewhere in the countryside, monastic lands fell into the hands of local gentry, whose power and influence were much increased as result.

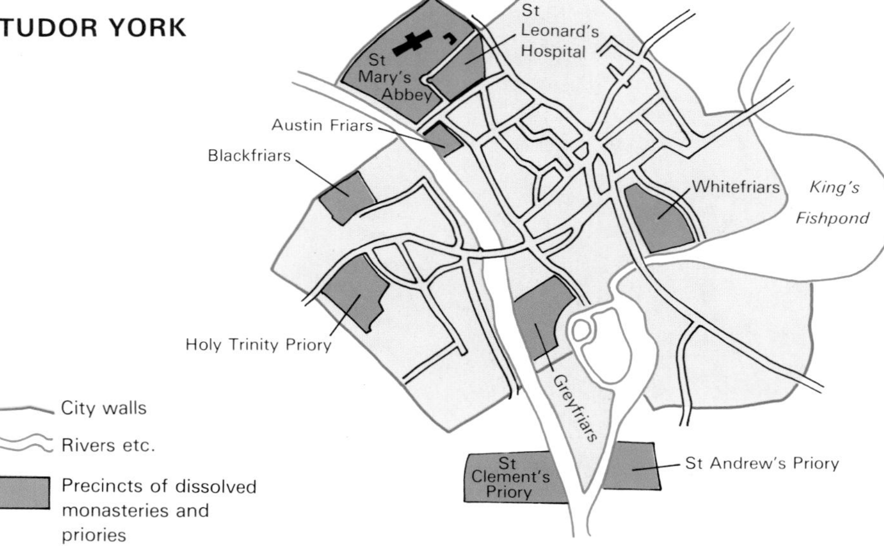

The impact of the dissolution of religious houses on Tudor York. The abrupt disappearance of these major urban landlords – and spenders – sharply affected the economic life of most towns.

The English Reformation was peculiar in three ways: that so complex a Church emerged from it; that resistance (though often vigorous) was always contained; and that foreign intervention was held at bay.

The map above shows the organization of the Church as it stood after the spate of legislation of the 1530s (partly reversed under Mary but restored in 1558–9). The two English Provinces of the old universal Catholic Church had become the independent national Church of England, legislated for by Parliament and ruled by the monarch, who alone appointed the two Archbishops and 24 bishops (five new sees had been added to the 19 pre-Reformation bishoprics). The bishops remained (despite attacks principled and unprincipled) and indeed remained great magnates: they continued to sit in Parliament as peers of the realm; they clung to most of their wealth (though th balance swung from land to impropriated tithes, while the surviving landholdings themselves became more con centrated); and they still maintained great households. Bu the seat of their influence shifted: from the Court an Council (only one bishop – Whitgift – sat on the Eliza bethan Privy Council) to the localities.

In contrast, one of the other chief elements of the pre Reformation Church – that formed by the 800 religiou houses containing about 9000 monks, nuns and friars – wa swept away. The consequences for education and poo relief were less serious than used to be supposed. New an re-founded schools, together with a nationally organize system of poor relief (reinforced by secular, specialize hospitals in the towns), were probably a more tha adequate substitute for the patchy monastic efforts of th past. However, the removal of the 27 mitred abbots fro the House of Lords was important, and the impact on th localities was massive. In the towns, the destruction of th friaries led to wide-scale urban blight that was heale quickly only in a minority of prosperous and expandin cities. And in the country, where within a generation or tw the bulk of the monastic land (about 10 per cent of the tot area) had passed into the hands of established gentr families, there was – as the map of Lincolnshire shows – massive shift of power, regionally and socially, which le the country house unchallenged as mistress of th landscape.

The Reformed and Recusant

But the Reformation was not only about power an property; it was also about ideas. Here there are tw different approaches. One is represented on the map above which shows the distribution of Protestant martyr (Marian burnings) who suffered under the restore Catholicism of Mary. The martyrs were overwhelmingl urban and lower class, and both clergy and women wer heavily represented. Thus to concentrate on them, or on th earlier heretical movements like Lollardy, turns th Reformation into a movement of dissent, a philosophy o

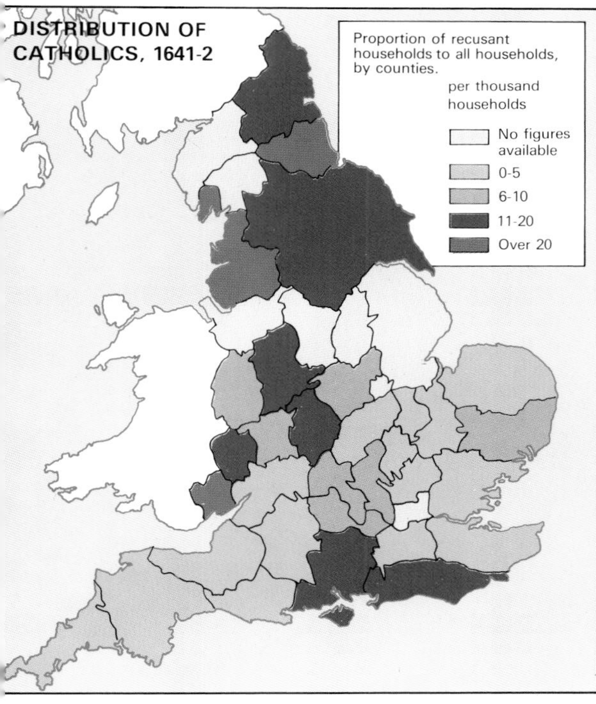

Used cautiously the figures for 1641–2 are probably a good guide to the distribution of Roman Catholic households in Elizabethan England. Roughly speaking Catholicism was strong in those areas where the influence of the Tudor court had always been weak, north and west of a line drawn from the Bristol Channel to the Humber.

the outsider. But (as at other times in Church history) steadfastness under persecution is no guarantee of importance in prosperity. And a very different emphasis emerges from the maps which deal with opposite ends of the religious spectrum that appeared after the restoration of Protestantism in 1558–9.

In the middle of this spectrum was the established Church. In doctrine it was thoroughly reformed (communion was commemorative, not sacrificial; salvation was decreed by God through predestination, not secured by man through free will), but in organization (the retention of bishops) and ceremonial (the continued wearing of vestments) much of the old remained. These 'rags of popery' the hotter Protestants (the so-called 'Puritans') were determined to strip off. But they were not thereby 'wild men'; instead the Puritans included many of the leading gentry (including great Court families such as the Cecils, Harringtons and Fitzwilliams). Such families controlled slabs of Church patronage as well as broad acres, and many Puritan congregations were little more than an expression of this double power. At the other religious extreme, the Roman Catholic recusants who refused to conform to the Elizabethan establishment were also dominated by the gentry. If this fact is combined with the pattern of distribution of recusants then a striking generalization becomes possible. The distribution of recusants is the negative image of the distribution of Henrician courtier

Right: Lacock Abbey, Wiltshire. The original foundation was dissolved in the 16th century and fell into the hands of Sir William Sharington.

Below: The distribution of congregations suggests that Puritanism owed much to the leadership and patronage of the local gentry.

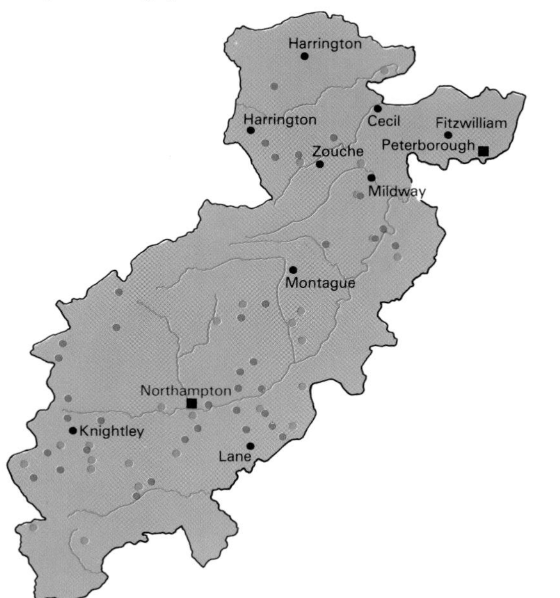

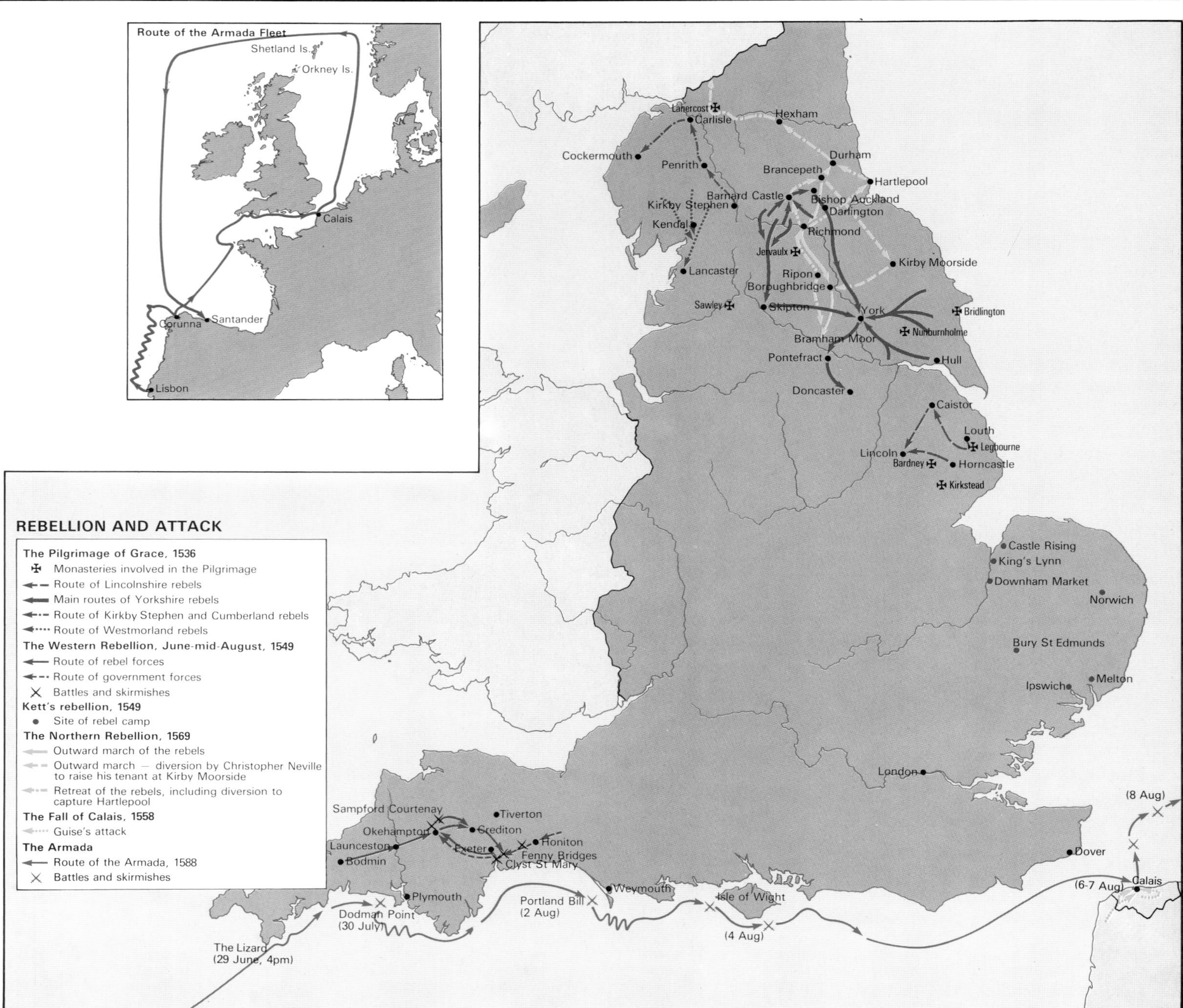

families. But these courtier families (with a few important exceptions) had themselves been largely responsible for the patronage and protection of early neo-Protestantism. So both religious change and resistance to change seem to come from the top, and they also seem to reinforce, rather than to undermine, existing patterns of social control.

The role of the gentry was just as important in the most extreme form of resistance: rebellion. Only one Tudor rebellion – Kett's revolt of 1549 – was anything like a straightforward rising by the people against their betters. It shows therefore a correspondingly exceptional geography, consisting not of marches on London or provincial capitals but of a series of stationary encampments from which an alternative county government was dispensed. Two other risings – the Cornish revolt of 1497 and the Western Rebellion of 1549 – were also essentially popular revolts, but this time directed against the policies of the central government: taxation in 1497 or religious innovation in 1549. Otherwise, in the Pilgrimage of Grace (1536), Wyatt's Rebellion (1554) or the Northern Rising (1569), mass social and religious grievances were articulated by leaders who were drawn from the political nation and whose own concerns were principally political. And it was this fact, as much as the government's own strength or the solidity of its south-eastern heartland, which accounts for both the containment of rebellion and the comparative leniency of the ensuing repression.

A similar mixture of good luck and some good management kept foreign intervention marginal: it was the reverse of these qualities (rather than criminal neglect) that led finally to the loss of Calais in 1558; while the defeat of the Spanish Armada in 1588 was their supreme embodiment.

Wales, c. 1410–1660

In the wake of the Glyndŵr rebellion, and throughout the 15th century, Welshmen deeply resented, and protested furiously against, the penal legislation which had effectively reduced them to the status of second-class citizens in their own land. Demands for English denizenship multiplied rapidly as the more enterprising gentry, in defiance of penal statutes, began to build up compact freehold estates and worm their way into public office. Dutiful bards nourished their dreams of emancipation by promising the arrival of a deliverer who would grant them their own charter of liberties. Several damp squibs were soon forgotten when Henry Tudor, a Welshman, secured the throne of England following a dazzling victory at Bosworth Field in 1485. Save for some studied gestures and short-term expedients, Henry VII never truly addressed himself to his early vows of ridding his countrymen of their 'miserable servitudes' and he failed to satisfy Welsh aspirations.

The Welsh gentry's demands for equal political status with Englishmen and the removal of economic disabilities were not met until the politico-religious crisis of the 1530s prompted Thomas Cromwell to impose a uniform structure of government throughout the whole of the realm. The Acts of Union (1536–43) made Wales part and parcel of England. But not only was Wales 'incorporated, united and annexed' to England, it was also unified politically within itself. The Welsh marcher lordships – a traditional thorn in the Crown's flesh – were swept away, and Wales was placed under shire government comprising 13 counties controlled by sheriffs and justices of the peace. The right of representation in Parliament was conferred on these shires, Welshmen were granted equality before the law, and the ancient landholding system of gavelkind was abolished in favour of primogeniture. English common law was made applicable to the whole of Wales, and justice and administration were vested in the officers of the Courts of Quarter Sessions, the Great Sessions and the Council of the Marches. Furthermore, English became the language of the law and administration in Wales and it was required that all officials should speak English.

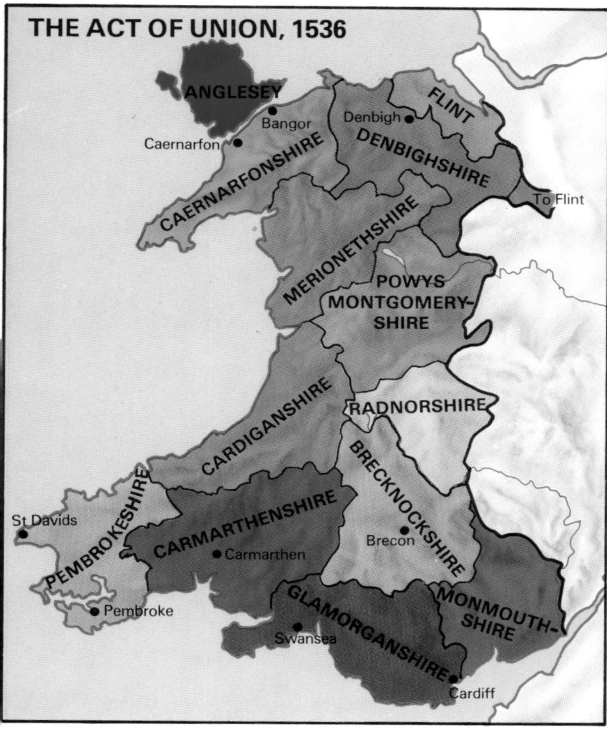

The administration of Wales following the Act of Union, 1536. Under the terms of this and subsequent Acts, Wales was completely absorbed into the English administrative and legal systems. The administrative framework established then persisted, save for some minor alteration, until April 1974.

'The Happy Union'

Scarcely a dog barked in protest as this legislation was put into effect. Indeed, by Elizabeth's reign, Welsh commentators were voicing their gratitude to the Tudors for bringing order, stability and prosperity to Wales. Fulsome paeans to the 'happy union with the valorous English' rang down the decades. Closer contact with England and the irresistible glitter of London's lights offered the Welsh gentry an opportunity to make their fortunes and to acquire a taste for good living. Inevitably, many of them developed a fondness for things English, bade their household bards farewell, and judged their native tongue to be nothing more than a barley-bread language, fit only for peasants. Mortified poets declared that 'the world has gone all English'. Even so, the anglicising process was a slow one and, until the Civil Wars, many of the Welsh gentry still took a lively interest in Welsh scholarship and literature. Some of them – notably William Salesbury, Humphrey Lhuyd and John Davies – were typical renaissance polymaths, cultivated men who were eager to modernize Welsh learning and letters and to sponsor reforming movements.

Throughout this period the remoteness and poverty of Wales made it one of 'the dark corners of the land'. The bulk of the population, nestling in scattered farms and tiny hamlets, lived on the very margins of subsistence and were vulnerable to the same kind of economic pressures which afflict countries of the Third World today. Men's horizons were inevitably narrow. Renaissance scholars found great difficulty in transferring the courtly ideals of Italian scholars to the rustic pastoral scene in Wales. Religious reformers, too, wondered at the lingering credulity of the Welsh and toiled unavailingly to galvanize support either for Catholicism or Protestantism. The absence of a strong middle class and the dearth of urban centres meant that Puritanism laid but slender roots. Nevertheless, by the end of Elizabeth's reign, Protestantism was something more than an imposed and grudgingly accepted religion. The publication of the New Testament and Prayer Book in Welsh in 1567 and that of the Bible in Welsh in 1588 were major landmarks. They made Welsh into the language of religion, and triggered off the campaign to make the doctrines of the Reformation intelligible and acceptable to Welsh people. Thanks to the catchy verses of Rees Prichard, the heroic labours of Vavasor Powell and the resonant prose of Morgan Llwyd, Puritanism was able to prepare the seed-bed of early Nonconformity in Wales. During the Civil Wars, and subsequently under the Act for the better propagation and preaching of the Gospel in Wales (1650–53), missionary enterprise, backed by the power of the sword, sought to penetrate the Welsh heartland. But most Welsh people despised the tub-thumping gospellers, and their disillusion with Puritan rule was voiced by the poet, Henry Vaughan, when he wrote 'out of that unfortunate region ... where destruction passeth for propagation, and a thick black night for the glorious day-spring'.

Small wonder that the bells rang throughout Wales to welcome the Restoration of the 'Merry Monarch' in 1660.

Frontispiece of the first Welsh Bible. The publication of the Welsh Bible in 1588 was the crowning achievement of Protestantism in Elizabethan Wales. It was the work of a learned Denbighshire vicar, William Morgan (*c.*1545–1604).

Scotland before 1603

The map of Scotland gives startling visual expression to the peculiar nature of the history of this remote and impoverished country during her six centuries as an independent kingdom. The blank space on the maps, where burghs did not grow up and where English armies never penetrated, was in reality no blank but the area of a community with a high level of oral, musical and intellectual culture, a language of richness and beauty, a powerful and timeless consciousness of its heroes and achievements. Yet its way of life is less easily 'mappable' than that of the Lowlands. Even in the remoter parts of the Southern Uplands, monasteries could be established, and grow fat on sheep farming, but virtually none existed in the economically hostile North. The post-Reformation Church, with all the zeal of the convert and missionary, might howl its protests against people believed to worship gods almost as malign as the God of Rome, but its grip on the Highlands remained tenuous. The monarchy, enforcing its claim to sovereignty over the West in the 13th century, was still struggling to assimilate and tame the last of the old provinces, the Macdonald Lordship of the Isles, in the 15th century. Its success, in the 12th and 13th centuries, in creating manageable administrative units, the sheriffdoms, in the lowland areas, contrasts sharply with its lasting failure to break down the vast Highland sheriffdom of Inverness. This is a measure of the problem – as the Crown saw it.

By contrast, eastern and southern Scotland enthusiastically followed the fashionable pursuits of burgh-building and economic expansion, administrative development, and the creation of a Church in all respects a recognizable part of the Church Universal, with its cathedrals and monasteries springing up to the glory of God and Scottish man, and even belatedly its own metropolitan sees. Determinedly 'European', it was a society which flourished politically, and was by no means poor within its own terms, however impoverished by the standards of the great European powers. The two very different elements which existed within the one realm created great division at home, for the Lowlander increasingly regarded the Highlander as an anachronism, to be feared and despised; but, ironically, they combined to create the unpredictable and astonishing success of this little kingdom as a whole.

The reasons which made the Highlands a thorn in the flesh of an expansionist monarchy and Church alike also made them one of the safeguards against annexation from without. It was not only their French ambitions which saved the Scots from the imperialist designs of the English kings, Edwards I and III. For the English, winning battles against the Scots was almost always easy; the problems of conquering and then controlling, from London, a country whose farther reaches were geographically both remote and difficult were insoluble. At the same time, the relative poverty even of the Lowlands, along with her northern position, gave Scotland no appeal in her own right in the eyes of ambitious continental rulers; her only bargaining counter abroad was her potential as a French ally against the English.

From that weakness came strength. Scotland was that most unusual phenomenon, a kingdom which experienced very little war. Apart from the Wars of Independence, she was almost entirely at peace; her only military involvement was with England, and then rarely. The Anglo-French and Flemings came to Scotland as settlers, not conquerors; and once the monarchy had given up its unrealistic dreams of extending its southern border, it was able to concentrate undisturbed on bringing the western seaboard into its realm. Centuries of relative peace were the crucial determinant. The considerable power of the Crown derived largely from the fact that it did not make demands of its subjects for men or money to support its military schemes; peripatetic kings – for only in the late 15th century did the largest burgh, Edinburgh, shake off the rival attractions of Perth and Stirling and become the undisputed capital – acted as overseers rather than ever-present rulers, leaving the localities with a rare degree of peace to manage their own affairs successfully. Their toe-hold in Europe, their usefulness to the French, was made the basis for regarding themselves as one of the notable European powers, with a positive part to play. That attitude was followed by others. The merchants of the thriving east-coast burghs, and also of the few in the West, benefited from years of peace, as they extended their trade with the Low Countries, the Baltic, Spain and even England. Churchmen and academics used their universities at home as first-degree colleges, and flocked abroad to the greater centres of learning and, in the 16th century, religious debate. The Kirk after 1560, with its vision of itself as part of the Universal Church – indeed, one of the 'purest' parts – was expressing an outward-looking self-confidence which had long been a major feature of Scottish society. So also, when in 1603 he went south to rule what he unquestionably regarded as his rightful inheritance, was James VI.

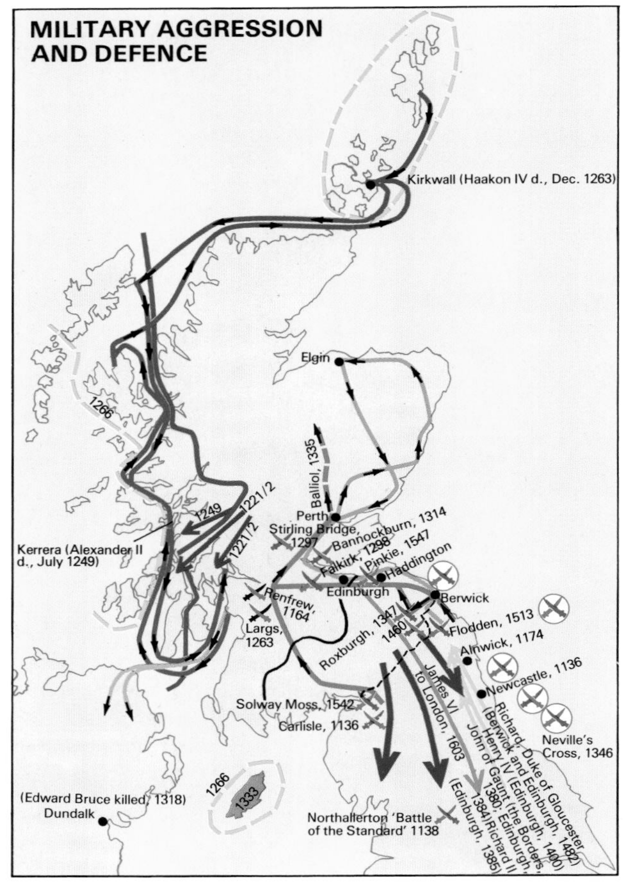

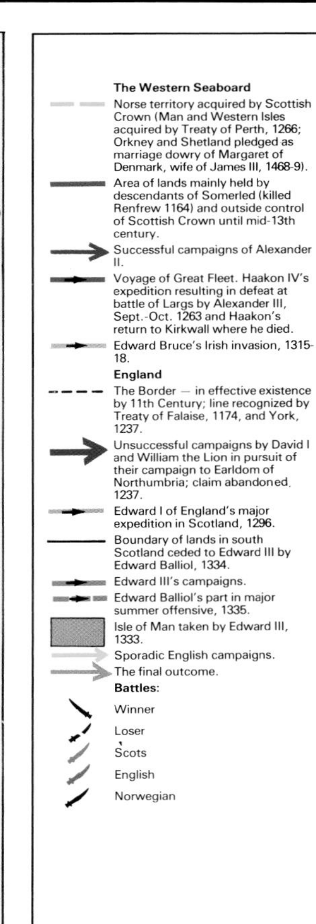

Above: Military aggression and defence in Scotland, 1126–1547. Although sea-borne forces could move freely around the Western Isles, and English invaders – especially under Edward I and Edward III – could occasionally dominate the Lowlands, the Highlands always remained an inaccessible refuge and base for counter-attack.

Below: The organization of the Scottish Church from the 13th to 17th centuries.

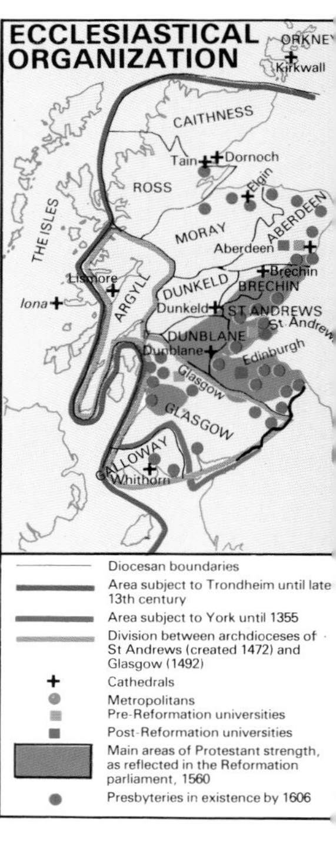

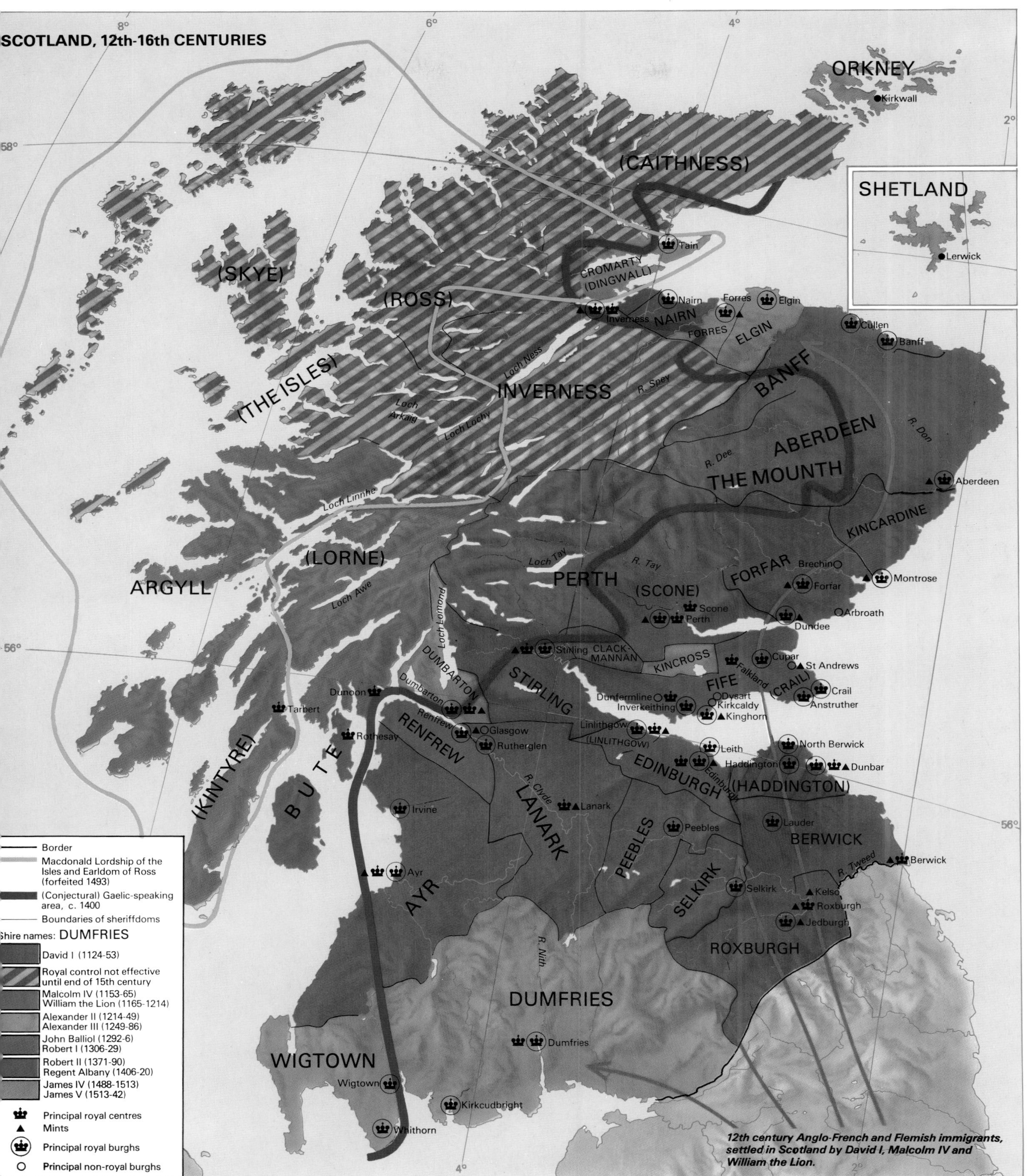
SCOTLAND, 12th-16th CENTURIES
ORKNEY
Kirkwall
SHETLAND
Lerwick
(CAITHNESS)
Tain
CROMARTY (DINGWALL)
(SKYE)
(ROSS)
(THE ISLES)
Nairn
Forres
Elgin
Inverness
NAIRN
FORRES
ELGIN
Cullen
Banff
BANFF
INVERNESS
Loch Ness
R. Spey
Loch Arkaig
Loch Lochy
ABERDEEN
R. Dee
R. Don
THE MOUNTH
Aberdeen
Loch Linnhe
KINCARDINE
(LORNE)
Loch Tay
R. Tay
FORFAR
Brechin
Forfar
Montrose
ARGYLL
PERTH
(SCONE)
Scone
Perth
Arbroath
Dundee
Loch Awe
Loch Lomond
Stirling
CLACKMANNAN
KINCROSS
Cupar
St Andrews
DUMBARTON
STIRLING
FIFE
Falkland
(CRAIL)
Crail
Anstruther
Dunoon
Dumbarton
Dunfermline
Inverkeithing
Dysart
Kirkcaldy
Kinghorn
Tarbert
Renfrew
Glasgow
Linlithgow
(LINLITHGOW)
Rothesay
RENFREW
Rutherglen
Leith
North Berwick
Haddington
Dunbar
EDINBURGH
Edinburgh
(HADDINGTON)
(KINTYRE)
BUTE
R. Clyde
Lanark
LANARK
Irvine
Peebles
Lauder
BERWICK
PEEBLES
R. Tweed
Berwick
Ayr
SELKIRK
Selkirk
Kelso
Roxburgh
Jedburgh
AYR
ROXBURGH
R. Nith
DUMFRIES
Dumfries
WIGTOWN
Wigtown
Kirkcudbright
Whithorn
12th century Anglo-French and Flemish immigrants, settled in Scotland by David I, Malcolm IV and William the Lion.
Border
Macdonald Lordship of the Isles and Earldom of Ross (forfeited 1493)
(Conjectural) Gaelic-speaking area, c. 1400
Boundaries of sheriffdoms
Shire names: DUMFRIES
David I (1124-53)
Royal control not effective until end of 15th century
Malcolm IV (1153-65)
William the Lion (1165-1214)
Alexander II (1214-49)
Alexander III (1249-86)
John Balliol (1292-6)
Robert I (1306-29)
Robert II (1371-90)
Regent Albany (1406-20)
James IV (1488-1513)
James V (1513-42)
Principal royal centres
Mints
Principal royal burghs
Principal non-royal burghs
8°
6°
4°
2°
58°
56°

England's Oceanic Expansion

The English overseas movement in these years laid the foundation of a colonial empire in North America and the West Indies and of a commercial empire in the East. This movement was part of the general expansion of Europe, but before 1550 the English played only a small part, while the Portuguese developed a rich trade with Asia via the Cape, and the Spaniards conquered Central and most of South America, as well as the West Indies. Men of Bristol exploring north-westwards from 1480, probably seeking new fishing grounds, may have discovered America before 1497, when the Italian John Cabot sailed from Bristol hoping to reach the East by way of the West. He made landfall in the region of Newfoundland. Subsequent voyages from Bristol achieved little, but the idea of an Arctic passage to the Orient became an especially English concern.

Oriental trade was in fact the great magnet of English oceanic enterprise throughout. The first thrust to achieve it was the voyage of Sir Hugh Willoughby and Richard Chancellor to the north-east in 1553. Willoughby died on the coast of Lappland, but Chancellor reached Moscow and started a valuable trade. Anthony Jenkinson then journeyed through Russia south-east to Bokhara on the way to China, and later again to Persia. Neither route proved commercially useful and the first major breakthrough came in 1581 with the establishment of regular trade with the Turkish Empire. Prosperous trade in Asiatic goods developed at Aleppo, among other places, but finally in 1600 the creation of the East India Company brought the English into the Indian Ocean to set up direct trade with Persia, India and the East Indies, handled by trading stations ('factories'). Throughout the East, the Company was in competition with the Portuguese and the Dutch, but in the first 60 years it established a secure position and made considerable profit. This was strictly a commercial enterprise, without territorial or political dominion.

In the north-west Atlantic English seamen (again in quest of oriental trade) were the chief explorers: Martin Frobisher's voyages to south-eastern Baffin Island (1576–78), John Davis's west of Greenland to 73°N (1585–87), William Baffin's to Lancaster Sound (1616) and Henry Hudson's into Hudson Bay (1610–11) are the most important, culminating much later in the Hudson's Bay Company (1670), the first to challenge the French fur empire of Canada.

Trade and Plunder

In the rest of the Atlantic the English began as interlopers in Portuguese and Spanish spheres of influence. They unsuccessfully poached on the Portuguese trade along the Guinea coasts, chiefly for gold, in the 1550s and 1560s. In the 1560s John Hawkins tried to break into the slave trade between West Africa and Spanish America, also without success. These intrusions were resisted by force and English reprisals followed, so that trade and plunder became inseparable. The 1570s saw raids on Panama and reconnaissance of the unoccupied zone south of Brazil and Peru. This was the object of the expedition led by Francis Drake in 1577, in which he captured a Spanish treasure ship, claimed 'Nova Albion' for Queen Elizabeth and returned via the Moluccas (Spice Islands). In North America Sir Humphrey Gilbert was the first Englishman to launch a colonial venture, but died on the return voyage (1583). His half-brother Sir Walter Ralegh then organized a more powerful effort and created two successive colonies at Roanoke Island (1585–7), but these failed and, during the war with Spain (1585–1603) the English concentrated on privateering.

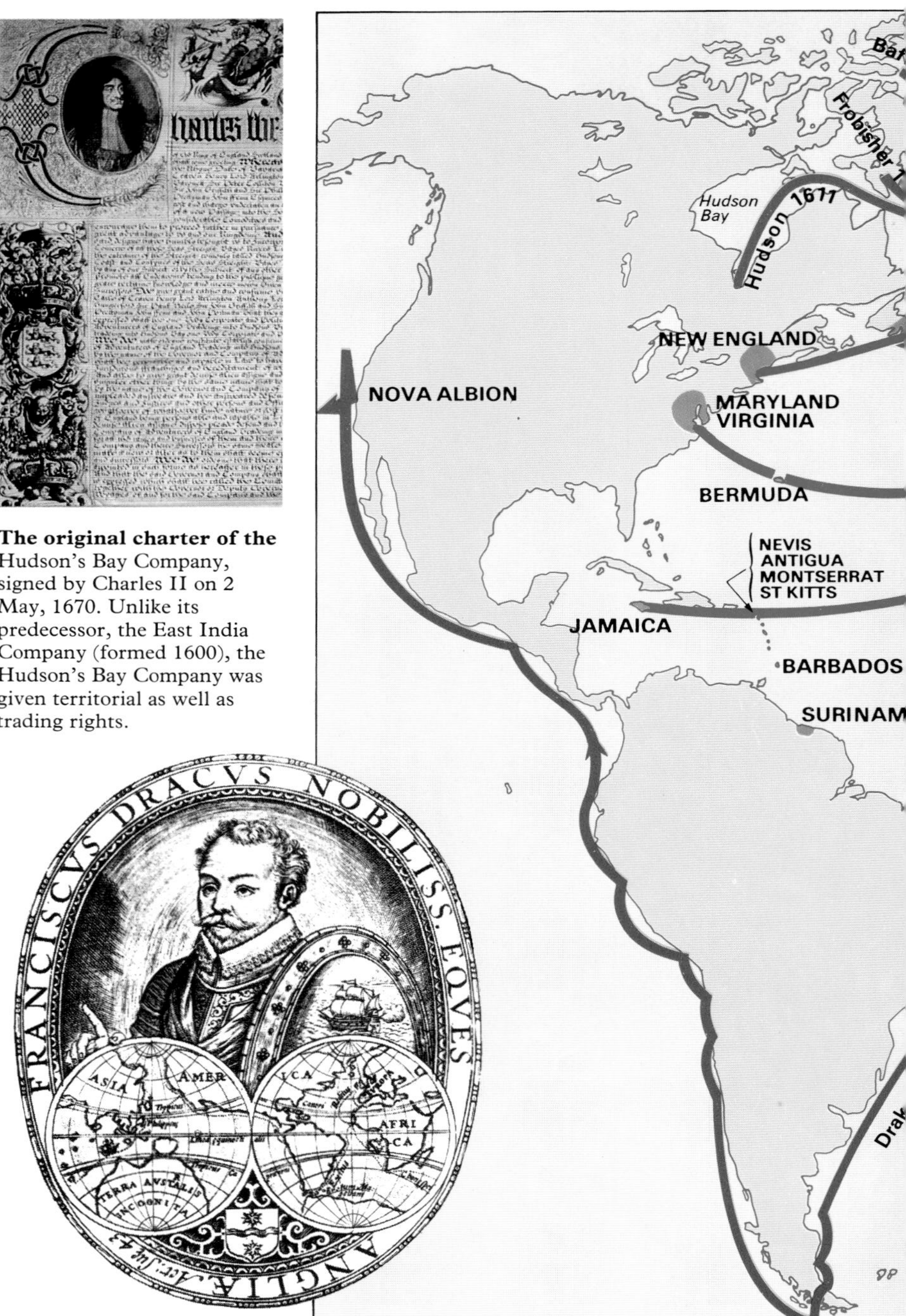

The original charter of the Hudson's Bay Company, signed by Charles II on 2 May, 1670. Unlike its predecessor, the East India Company (formed 1600), the Hudson's Bay Company was given territorial as well as trading rights.

Contemporary illustration celebrating Francis Drake's circumnavigation of the world, December 1577–October 1580.

At the end of the war with Spain, colonial projects were resumed in earnest, with stronger backing from the Court and the City of London. Spain was now much weaker while England had gained substantial commercial maritime power, and continued to do so. In 1607 the first permanent colony, Virginia, was established and after great initial difficulties began to thrive as a tobacco supplier. The adjacent colony of Maryland was founded in 1632. The occupation of the Bermudas (1609–10) was a by-product of the Virginia enterprise. Farther north the New England colonies were pioneered by Nonconformist Puritans, the first of whom, the so-called Pilgrim Fathers, founded New Plymouth near Cape Cod in 1620. In 1628–9 a stronger group created Massachussetts, from which Connecticut, Rhode Island and New Haven developed as offshoots

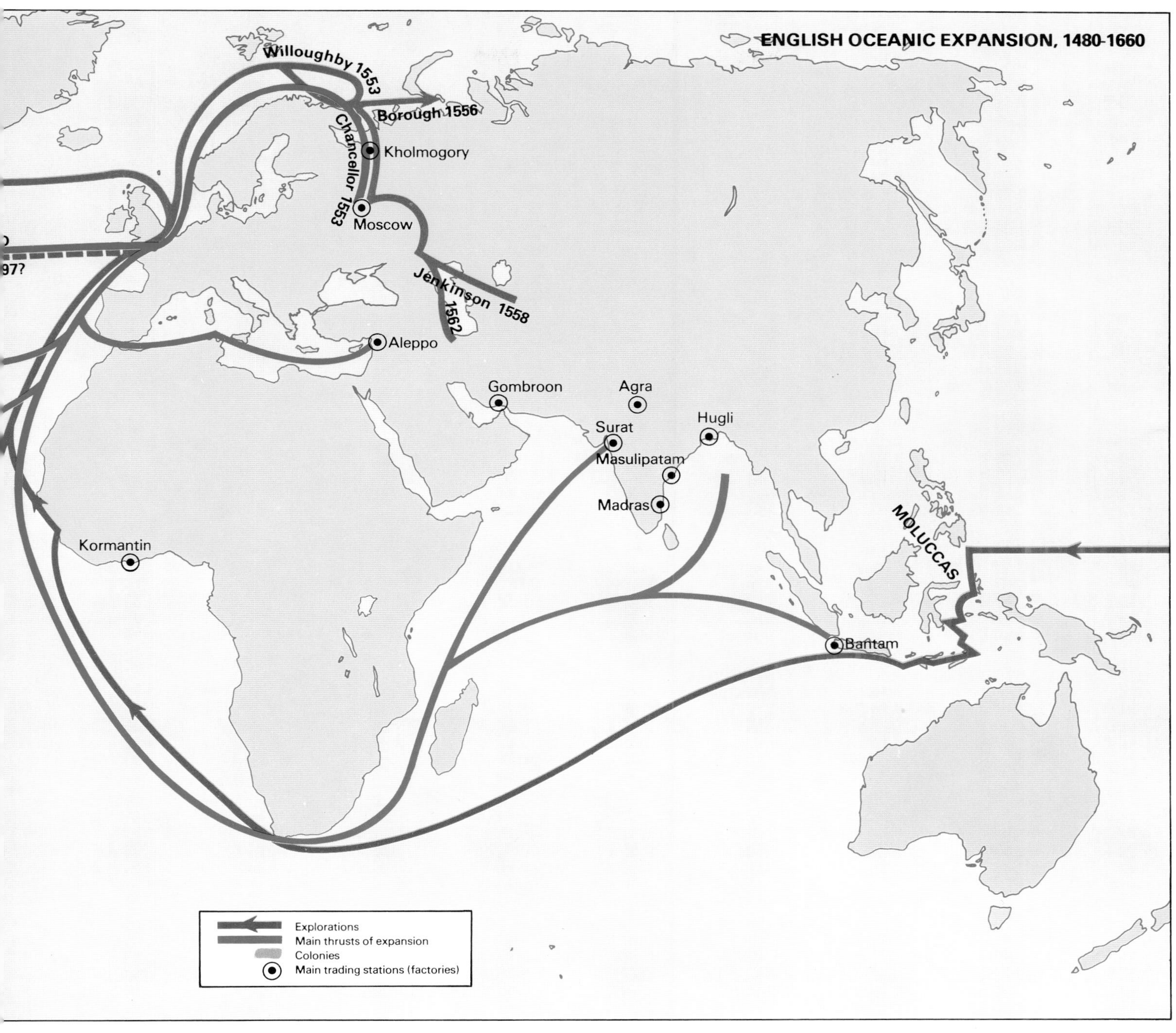

English oceanic expansion: the origins of an empire, 1480–1660.

ubsisting by farming, fishing and fur-trading, the New ngland communities were more self-sufficient than the outhern communities, politically and economically. In ewfoundland settlement proceeded hesitantly, the fishery being far more important and valuable at this time han the potential benefits of colonization.

The English penetrated the Caribbean in the first place as rivateers, pirates and smugglers, and such activities emained important throughout this period. Around the nd of the Spanish war, however, they began to trade for obacco with the Spaniards and native Indians, and this led n to attempts to create small tobacco colonies in Guiana .1612–25). These all failed, but a new war with Spain rengthened the English presence in the Caribbean once again and encouraged the tobacco promoters to take over St Kitts (1624) and Barbados (1625). Plantations on Nevis, Antigua and Montserrat in the Leeward Islands soon followed, and after yet another war with Spain the English added Jamaica to their tiny West Indies empire in 1655. By this time these colonies had begun the transition from tobacco to slave-grown sugar, which was to make them soon the most valuable possession of England overseas. In the 1650s Surinam was already a thriving sugar colony, but this was given up to the Dutch in 1667. The first permanent English post in West Africa was set up at Kormantin in 1631, mainly for the gold trade. The English share of the slave trade began around this time, but remained very small until after 1660.

The Civil Wars, 1638–51

The Civil Wars broke out, not because of opposition in England to Charles I's eleven years' rule without Parliament – though that was considerable – but because his Scots subjects were able successfully to resist the political and Church reforms imposed from London. United in a bond of association, the 1638 National Covenant, the Scots scattered the King's forces at the crossing of the Tyne at Newburn and occupied the North of England. The King was forced to call Parliament and to accept its demands for reform. Some form of political compromise might have been worked out had not the Irish rebellion broken out, in autumn 1641. Many Puritans suspected the King and his Catholic Queen to have been behind the revolt of the native Catholic Irish and the leaders of the Westminster Parliament took defensive measures. These measures, however, alienated the more conservative elements in England, who rallied to the King, and provided the basis of the Royalist party. The two sides, Cavaliers and Roundheads, drifted into civil war in the summer of 1642. The King was stronger in the North and West of England, and found support in Wales and among Catholics: the Parliamentarians' strength lay particularly in London and the south-eastern counties, as well as cloth-working areas. The Scots Covenanters were to be drawn into the conflict on the side of Parliament in 1644. The first campaign of the war, culminating in the drawn battle at Edgehill in October 1642, was indecisive, and the Royalists made their headquarters at Oxford for the rest of the war.

In organizing their military effort for a long war both sides found that the county was not a viable unit, and attempted to unite groups of shires in associations to support larger forces and contribute to national strategy. Most of these attempts failed, though they are worth recording, for they illustrate the natural regionalism of the conflict in England, and the theatres of war which developed. Only in the northern counties, united under the Earl of Newcastle for the King and under the Eastern Association for Parliament, did the system enjoy some military success. Warfare at the local level was more a matter of establishing and protecting permanent garrisons, securing territory and supplies, and raiding enemy quarters. The inset map is a close-up of one locality, Oxfordshire and the surrounding area, where the main field army of the King was quartered and which received the thrusts of the Parliamentarian forces for over three years. Th disposition of the royal forces in the towns, fortified hous and villages around Oxford in the first winter of the war shown. This base area was bounded by natural barriers the Chilterns in the east, the Berkshire Downs in the sou and the Cotswolds in the west, while the royal headquarte itself was protected by a screen of outlying strongholds, ar the rivers, extensive woodlands and undrained levels Oxfordshire. The extent of the quarters is remarkable. Th relatively small numbers of cavalry required all of o county and the richest part of another for their mainte ance; and the troops of the frontier posts of Banbur Boarstall House and Donnington Castle raided deep in Puritan countryside such as Warwickshire and Bucking hamshire, maintaining control over a radius of up to 2 miles (32 km) from the stronghold – a day's ride for th squadron of Horse kept by each garrison for this purpos Representative of these garrisons is Donnington, a med eval castle transformed into a vital strategic position in th Civil War, controlling one of the main roads from the We to London, by the construction of a five-pointed sta fortress, still recognizable in the early 19th century print

Military supplies came to the King from the industri Midlands, and, after their capture in 1643, from Bristol an western ports. For its part, London financed a major sha of Parliament's war effort. The quarters of both side fluctuated in the course of the war, as the tide of batt ebbed and flowed. Earlier garrison centres were abandone by the King, as new ones were acquired. By late 1644 th Parliamentarians had taken permanently both Reading an Abingdon, putting pressure on the remaining districts fro which the King drew support.

In the North and West, after initial successes, Royali forces had to yield ground. Newcastle was defeated, wit Prince Rupert, at the biggest battle of the war, Marsto Moor, close to York, by the combined forces of the Scot Fairfax's Yorkshire army and the Eastern Associatio army, whose cavalry was commanded by Oliver Cromwel Released from service in the North, some components o these parliamentary forces were joined with the remnants o earlier armies under Essex and Waller, to form the Ne Model Army, better paid and officered than any previousl This army, under Fairfax and Cromwell, was able to defe the King's forces piecemeal, at Naseby and Langport (Ju

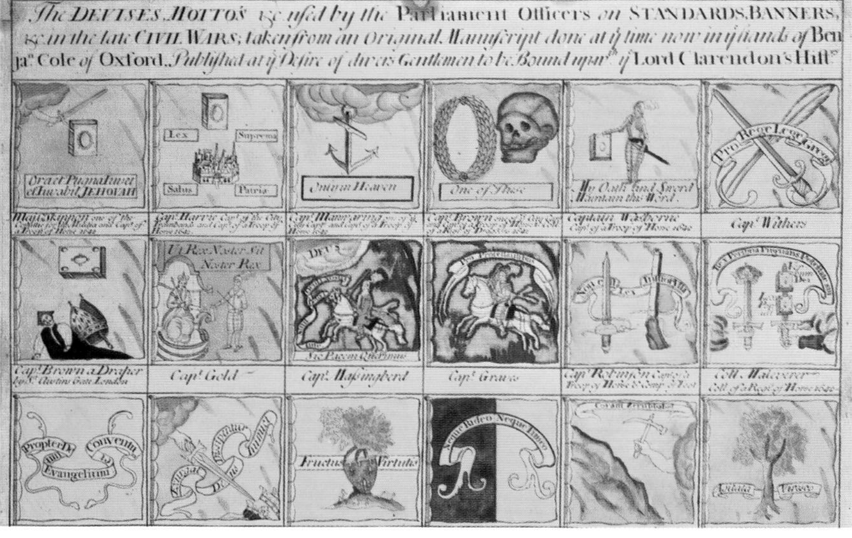

Personal standards used by various Parliamentary commanders during the Civil War.

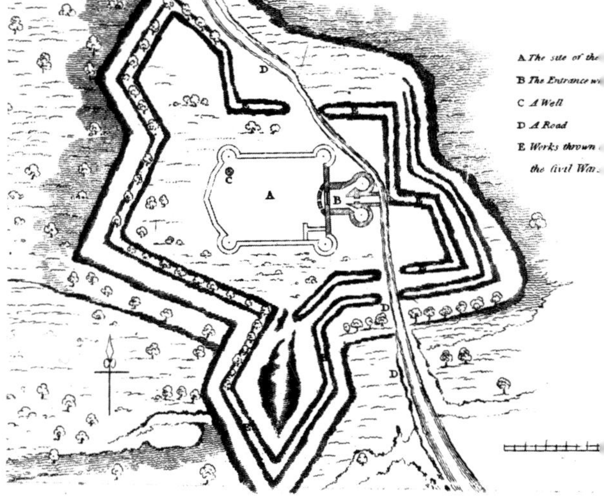

Above right: Donnington Castle, Berkshire, from an early 19th-century print. This medieval fortress was transformed into a Royalist garrison in the Civil War, controlling one of the main roads from the West to London. The five-pointed star fortress was built during the Civil War.

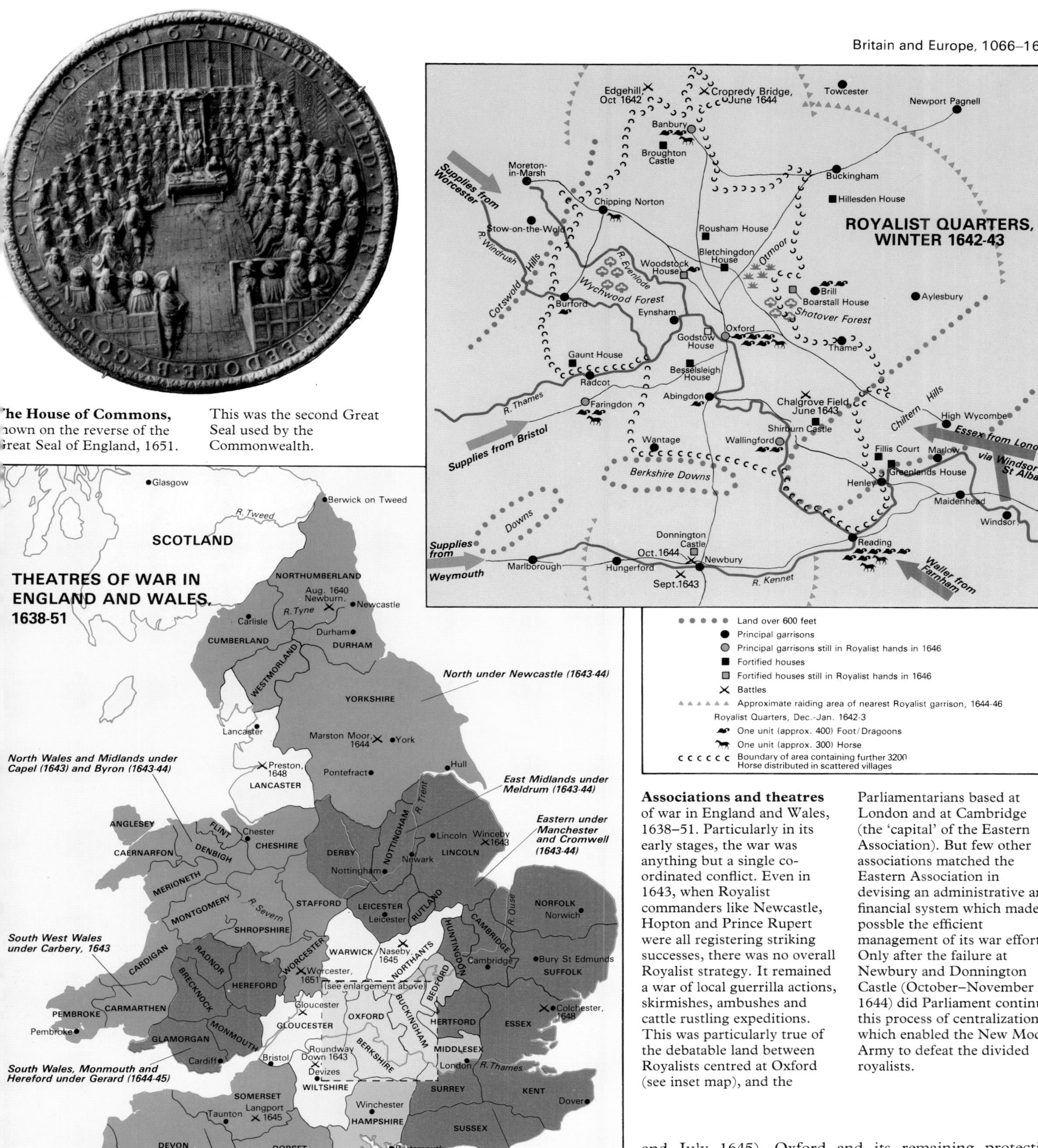

The House of Commons, shown on the reverse of the Great Seal of England, 1651. This was the second Great Seal used by the Commonwealth.

Associations and theatres of war in England and Wales, 1638–51. Particularly in its early stages, the war was anything but a single co-ordinated conflict. Even in 1643, when Royalist commanders like Newcastle, Hopton and Prince Rupert were all registering striking successes, there was no overall Royalist strategy. It remained a war of local guerrilla actions, skirmishes, ambushes and cattle rustling expeditions. This was particularly true of the debatable land between Royalists centred at Oxford (see inset map), and the Parliamentarians based at London and at Cambridge (the 'capital' of the Eastern Association). But few other associations matched the Eastern Association in devising an administrative and financial system which made possble the efficient management of its war effort. Only after the failure at Newbury and Donnington Castle (October–November 1644) did Parliament continue this process of centralization which enabled the New Model Army to defeat the divided royalists.

and July 1645). Oxford and its remaining protective garrisons surrendered in 1646.

The Second Civil War, when, in the summer of 1648, Cromwell defeated a Scots invasion at Preston, and Fairfax captured Royalist-held Colchester, did not reverse the earlier judgement. The trial and execution of Charles I followed. Cromwell secured the new English republic with successful campaigns against the Scots and Irish.

Chapter Four
THE EXPANSION OF ENGLAND, 1660-1815

The years which lie roughly between 1660 and 1815 see the expansion of England in two directions. Scotland and Ireland became formally tied to England, while the overseas empire developed apace. In Europe, French dominance was ended during the Napoleonic Wars, while at home prosperity and industrial development provided the background for the peaceful evolution of constitutional government.

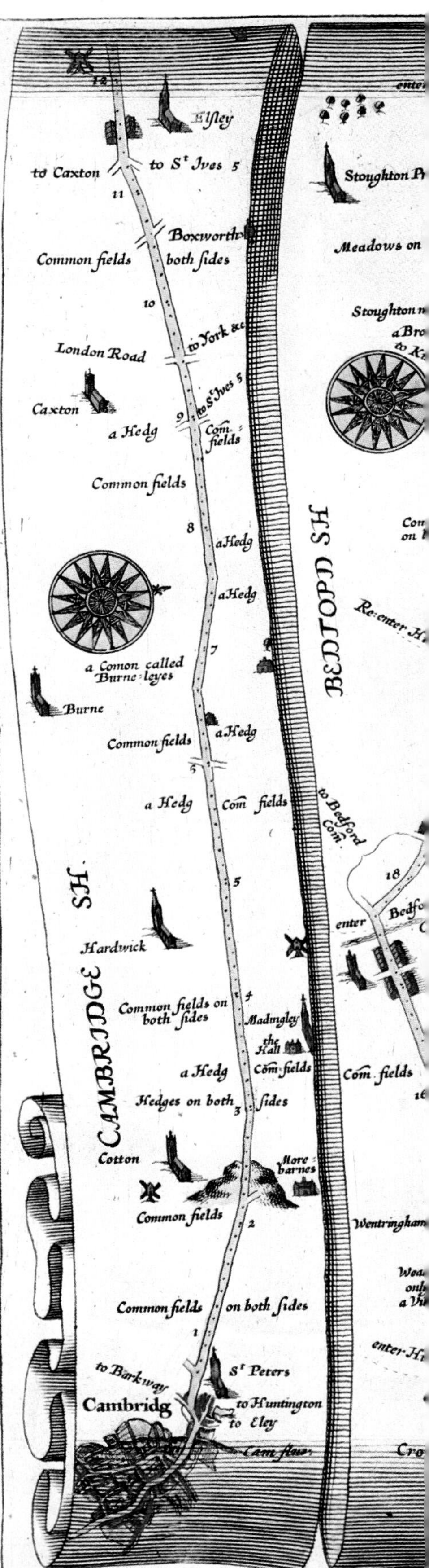

Strip map showing the road from Cambridge to Coventry by John Ogilby.

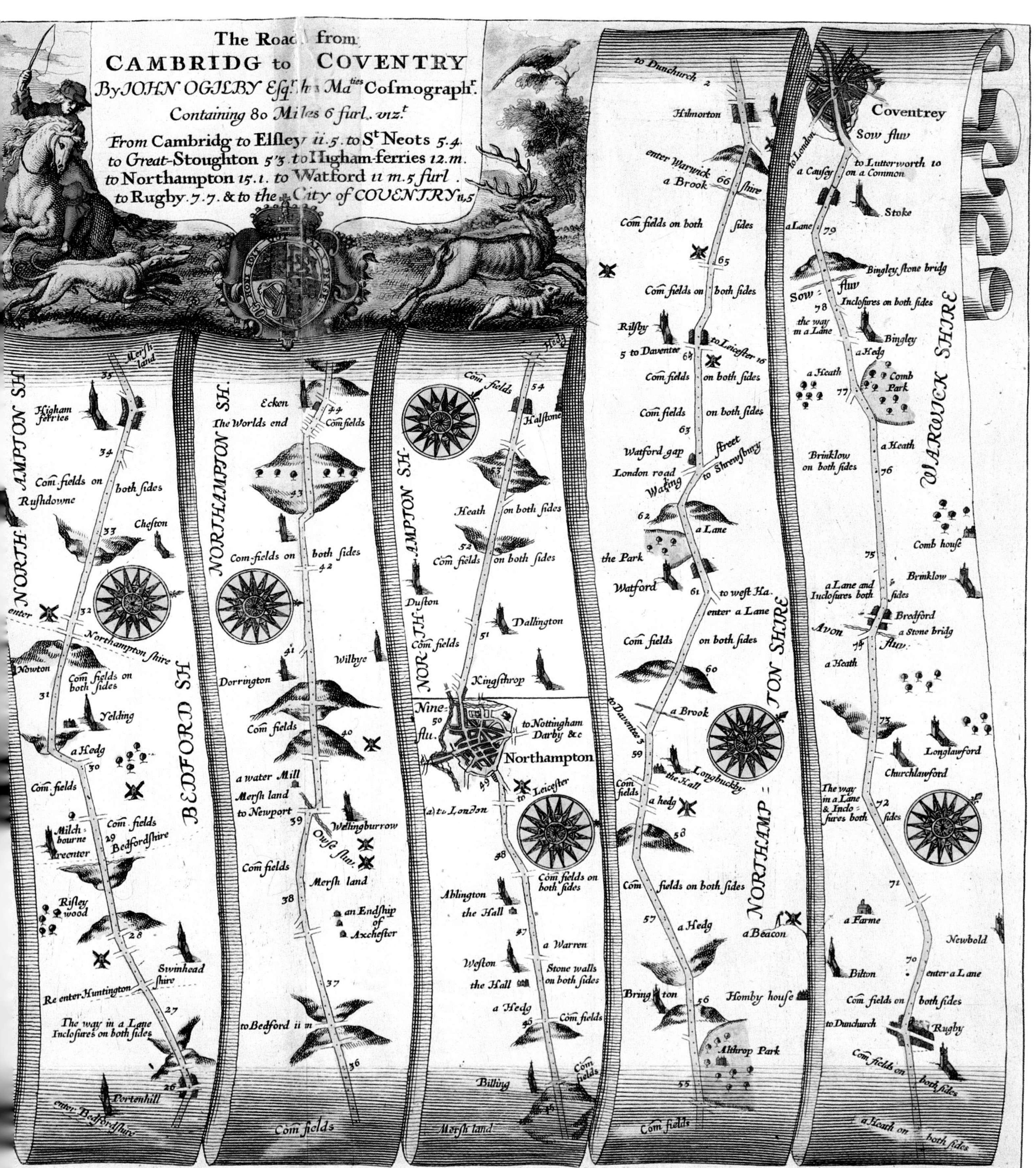
The Road from
CAMBRIDG to COVENTRY
By JOHN OGILBY Esq. his Maties Cosmograph.
Containing 80 Miles 6 furl. viz.
From Cambridg to Elsley 11.5. to St Neots 5.4.
to Great-Stoughton 5.3. to Higham-ferries 12.m.
to Northampton 15.1. to Watford 11 m.5 furl.
to Rugby. 7.7. & to the City of COVENTRY 11.5
NORTHAMPTON SH.
BEDFORD SH.
NORTHAMPTON SHIRE
WARWICK SHIRE
Mersh land
Higham ferries
Com fields on both sides
Rushdowne
Cheston
Northampton shire
Nowton
Yelding
a Hedg
Com fields
Milchbourne
Bedfordshire
Reenter
Risley wood
Swinhead shire
Re enter Huntington
The way in a Lane
Inclosures on both sides
Portenhill
enter Bedfordshire
Ecken
The Worlds end
Com fields
Com-fields on both sides
Dorrington
a water Mill
Mersh land
to Newport
Wellingburrow
Ouse fluv.
an Endship of Axchester
to Bedford 11 m
Halstone
Heath on both sides
Duston
Dallington
Wilbye
Kingsthrop
Nine flu.
to Nottingham Darby &c
Northampton
to Leicester
(a) to London
Ablington
the Hall
a Warren
Weston
Stone walls on both sides
a Hedg
Billing
to Dunchurch
Hilmorton
enter Warwick shire
a Brook
Rilsby
to Daventee
to Leicester
Watford gap
London road
Watling street
to Shrewsbury
a Lane
the Park
Watford
to west Ha.
enter a Lane
a Brook
to Daventee
Longbuckby
the Hall
a hedg
a Beacon
Bring ton
Homby house
Althrop Park
Coventrey
Sow fluv
to London
to Lutterworth
to a Causey on a Common
Stoke
a Lane
Bingley stone bridg
Inclosures on both sides
the way in a Lane
Bingley
a Heath
Comb Park
Brinklow on both sides
Comb house
Brinklow
a Lane and Inclosures both sides
Bredford
Avon fluv
a Stone bridg
Longlawford
Churchlawford
The way in a Lane & Inclosures both sides
a Farme
Newbold
Bilton
enter a Lane
to Dunchurch
Rugby
a Heath on both sides

Restoration and Revolution, 1660–1815

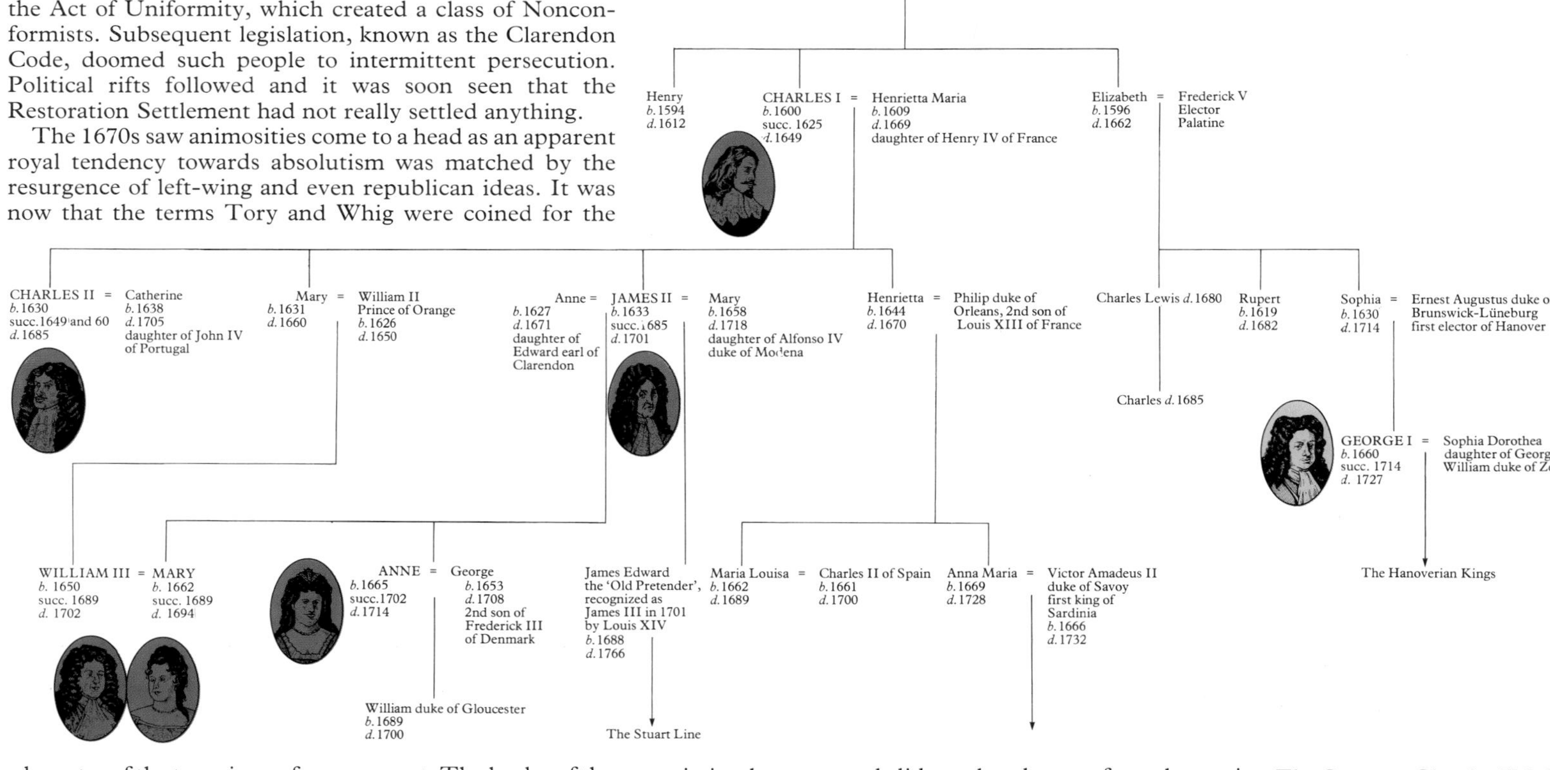

The restoration of Charles II in 1660 was warmly welcomed by a people tired by the divisions of the past two decades. The King tried to promote harmony by pardoning nearly all his former enemies in the Act of Indemnity and advocating a policy of religious toleration, but the continuing divisions among his people were too strong. In 1662, the loyalist 'Cavalier' Parliament passed the Act of Uniformity, which created a class of Nonconformists. Subsequent legislation, known as the Clarendon Code, doomed such people to intermittent persecution. Political rifts followed and it was soon seen that the Restoration Settlement had not really settled anything.

The 1670s saw animosities come to a head as an apparent royal tendency towards absolutism was matched by the resurgence of left-wing and even republican ideas. It was now that the terms Tory and Whig were coined for the advocates of the two views of government. The leader of the Whigs was the Earl of Shaftesbury. He exploited popular fears of Catholicism to acquire a massive following after the exposure in 1678 of the so-called Popish Plot, a fictitious Jesuit-inspired plot to murder the King and take over the government. Shaftesbury used his popular backing in a campaign to exclude the King's Catholic brother and heir, James, from the succession but, in the end, the King outwitted him. From 1681 till his death in 1685, Charles was able to rule without Parliament, while the Whigs and their Nonconformist allies suffered severe persecution in the inevitable backlash.

In 1685, the Catholic James II was welcomed to the throne by the now dominant Tories. His position was strengthened by the easy suppression of a Whig rebellion led by the Duke of Monmouth, bastard son of Charles II. James used the rebellion as an excuse to increase his army and then proceeded to alienate almost every section of the population, including the Tories, by ruling without Parliament, appointing Catholics to positions of power, undermining the authority of the Established Church and manipulating the personnel of local government. Fear of his army prevented resistance until 1688, when the birth of a male heir, the future Old Pretender, made it likely that the Catholic, absolutist régime might be perpetuated. An invitation to invade the country was sent to William of Orange, James's nephew and the husband of his Protestant daughter Mary.

William's invasion met practically no opposition and he and Mary were offered the Crown jointly. The Revolution Settlement which inaugurated this new régime was pragmatic in character and did not lay down a formal constitution. A measure of toleration was granted to Protestant dissenters and a Bill of Rights excluded Catholics from the succession. In theory, the King could still act arbitrarily but, in practice, his need for money to fight the war against Louis XIV which was his major interest ensured that Parliament should meet every year, as it has done ever since. The Act of Settlement in 1701 defined the succession further, ensuring that, after the death of Mary's younger sister Anne, the Crown should go to her closest Protestant relative, the Dowager Electress Sophia of Hanover.

The reign of Queen Anne (1702–14) saw the Crown's actions more closely circumscribed by the activities of Parliament, but it was far from being a period of political peace as Tory and Whig struggled for dominance. The electorate was such that the Tories were normally in power and their opposition to toleration, and belief in a strong royal prerogative, threatened to undermine the settlement of 1688. Ironically, this was prevented because the right wing of the Party was so Tory that they considered the Old Pretender to be the legitimate heir to the throne. Their incompetent efforts to upset the Act of Settlement on Queen Anne's death in 1714 and, even more, their association with the very poorly organized Jacobite rebellion of 1715, doomed them as a party for the next 45 years. The Whigs ensured the succession of Princess Sophia's son, George I, and they were long to enjoy the rewards of their loyalty. Britain was to enjoy a period of relative stability in which most people paid at least lip-service to the Protestant and parliamentary ideals of the Revolution of 1688.

The Stuarts: Charles II left no legitimate children, and the crown passed to his brother whose unpopularity soon became so great that English nobles invited his son-in-law and nephew, William of Orange, to come 'to the rescue of the laws and religion of England'. William and his wife Mary were proclaimed joint sovereigns as William III and Mary II. Again they left no heirs, and the throne passed to James's younger daughter Anne. None of her children survived her; and the next Stuart heir was Princess Sophia, Electress of Hanover. But she died shortly before her cousin and in the event it was her son George, Elector of Hanover, who succeeded to the throne of Great Britain. Hanover and Britain remained under the same rule until the accession of Queen Victoria.

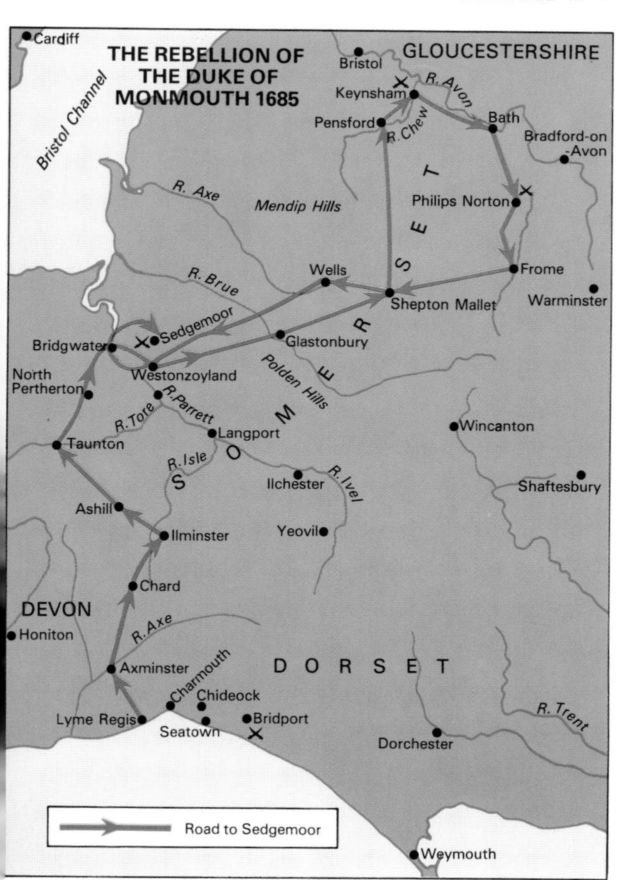

The Rebellion of the Duke of Monmouth. He landed in Dorset with 82 followers in June 1685 but despite popular support failed to gain the backing of the gentry. Monmouth delayed his advance on Bristol and gave the King's forces time to close in on him. He fell back on Bridgwater where he just failed in a night attack on the royal army's encampment at Sedgemoor. His followers were punished with great savagery in what were known as the Bloody Assizes.

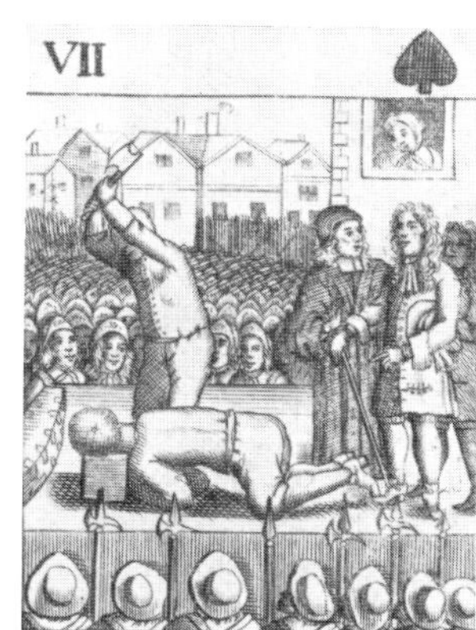

Above: The landing of William of Orange with a Dutch army in 1688 heralded the 'Glorious Revolution'. Parliament offered him and his wife Mary the throne jointly.

A playing card showing the execution of Charles II's illegitimate son, James, Duke of Monmouth, after his unsuccessful rebellion.

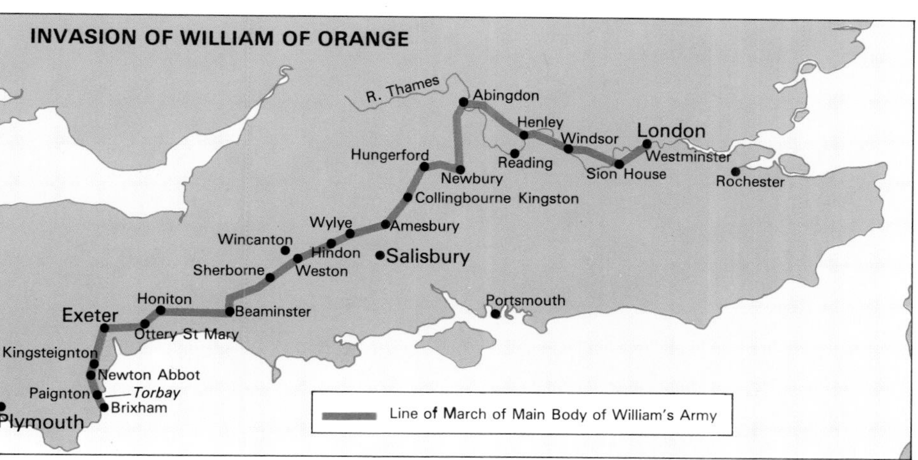

Wars and Warfare, 1660–1715

The period 1660–1715 sees England transformed from an off-shore island of little military significance into a major European power. However, there was little sign of this transformation during the first two wars, which were a continuation of the Cromwellian struggle against the Dutch for naval supremacy. In the Second Dutch War, which broke out in 1665, England won the major naval battle of Lowestoft, but shortage of funds and Dutch power soon cancelled the early gains and England was to suffer the humiliation of the famous Dutch raid on Chatham dockyard in June 1667. The Treaty of Breda (1667) completed England's chain of colonies in North America by confirming the capture of New Amsterdam (New York), but did little to resolve the original causes of conflict.

The Third Dutch War (1672–4) was fought in alliance with the French. A joint attack was planned to extinguish the Dutch Republic and divide their territories, but the English had few successes to compare with those of her French allies who threatened to overwhelm the United Provinces and were only checked by the personal leadership of William of Orange. A skilful propaganda campaign by the Dutch reinforced a growing fear in England that the French under Louis XIV were a threat to the liberties of all Europe and led to a demand for an early end to the war which was met by the inconclusive Treaty of Westminster in 1674.

When William became King in 1689, he brought England into the Grand Alliance which he had built up to combat the growing power of France and so inaugurated the series of French wars which lasted till 1815. King William's War (1689–97) was a defensive war, fought mainly in Flanders, and was England's first experience of major campaigns on the Continent. Defensive tactics were successful, despite English losses at Steinkirk (1692) and Landen (1693), and the Peace of Ryswick (1697) was the product of mutual exhaustion. This war saw the creation of a funded national debt guaranteed by Parliament, an innovation of major importance in the financing of future wars.

Right: Alliances in The War of the Spanish Succession. This war was primarily over the rival Hapsburg and Bourbon claim to the Spanish throne, and th possible solution of a partitio of the Spanish Empire to preserve a balance of power i Europe.

A British grenadier, from a tapestry depicting the battle of Blenheim. Companies of these élite troops, equipped with grenades in addition to their muskets, were attached to infantry regiments until the mid-18th century, when they formed regiments of their own.

The battle of Blenheim, at which the French and Bavarian army, some 56,000 troops and 90 guns strong, was defeated by a joint army of Austrians and Britons commanded by the Duke of Marlborough and the Austrian commander Prince Eugene of Savoy. This was the greatest victory by a British general since Agincourt. Prince Eugene was considered by Napoleon to be one of the seven great commanders of all time.

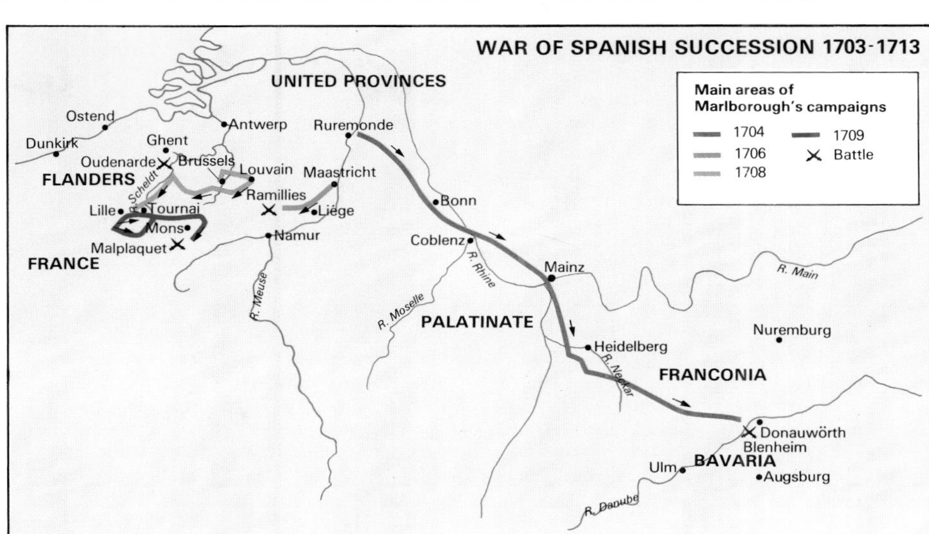

Peace did not last long. In 1700, the childless King Carlos II of Spain died, leaving his entire inheritance to Louis XIV's grandson, Philip, thus threatening French hegemony both in Europe and America. In 1701, James II of England died and Louis XIV recognized his son as James III, forcing a reluctant England to go to war with France to defend the Protestant succession. England's principal allies in the War of the Spanish Succession (1702–13) were the Dutch and the Austrians, while the French enjoyed the support of most of Spain and Bavaria.

Marlborough's campaigns

The war was dominated for England by the campaigns of the Duke of Marlborough, who acquired a military reputation greater than that of any Englishman since the days of Henry V. He was a superb administrator as well as a brilliant strategist and tactician who could always surprise his enemies. The main fighting took place in Bavaria and on the borders of France and Flanders. Marlborough's great victories, especially Blenheim (1704) and Ramillies (1706), shattered the military reputation of France and made Louis XIV ready to make large concessions in return for peace.

But victory made the allies greedy and the war dragged on until 1713, by which time the Duke of Marlborough had been replaced and the allies had got seriously bogged down in Spain. The Treaty of Utrecht (1713) was not as unfavourable for France as peace in 1706 or 1708 would have been. Philip remained King of Spain and the Indies, with an undertaking that the crowns of Spain and France would never be united. The rest of Spain's European empire was divided between Savoy and the Hapsburg Emperor.

The English naval effort was not to be so important in the wars of 1689–1713 as it was to be later in the 18th century. Victory at La Hogue (1692) guaranteed security against French invasion and the French made no further effort to acquire mastery of the sea, concentrating their attention on a very successful privateering campaign. The Spanish side of the war provided the English with two important acquisitions, Gibraltar (1704) and Minorca (1708), which laid the basis for a Mediterranean naval policy. In America, an attempted invasion of Canada failed, but Nova Scotia and Newfoundland were acquired from France, while English traders acquired the rights to break into Spain's monopoly of trade with her South American empire. The Treaty of Utrecht recognized England's position as a major power not only in Europe but in the world.

Britain and America, 1600–1783

The British were slow to follow the example of the Spaniards and Portuguese in establishing colonies in America but, by the end of the 16th century, slave-trading, privateering, fishing and deliberate exploration had made them familiar with much of the West Indies and the Atlantic seaboard of North America. Permanent settlement began in Virginia in 1607. The early settlers experienced problems which were to be shared by many who followed them – dislike of hard work, shortage of food, Indian hostility and the inability to find the means to pay for European imports being the most important. By about 1620, most of these problems had been solved and Virginia was a going concern, growing and exporting tobacco to pay for such things as could not be produced locally.

The next decade saw the settlement of Barbados, St Kitts and other islands in the West Indies, and the beginnings of

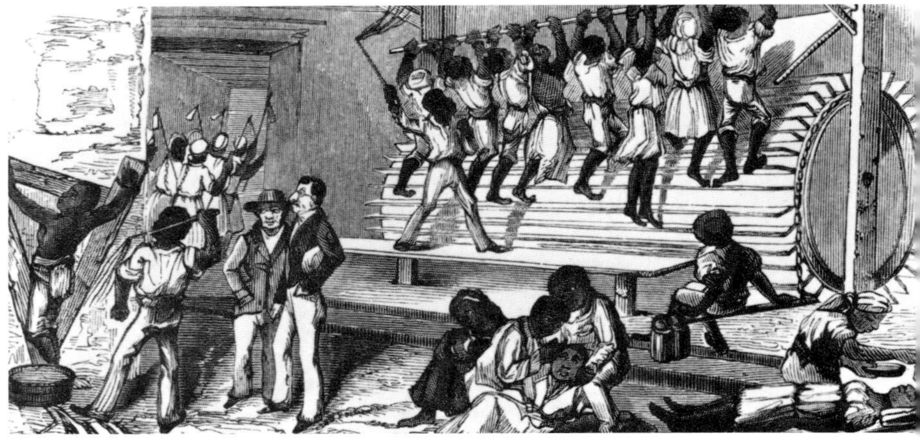

Above right: Slaves on a tread-wheel on a West Indies plantation. The first slaves were taken from Africa to the New World by Sir John Hawkins in 1562.

America in 1758, when France and Spain still controlled considerable areas. War broke out in America between France and Britain in 1754, both countries claiming the vast area between the Allegheny Mountains and the Mississippi. The struggle continued until the British took Montreal in 1760.

At the Treaty of Paris all French possessions in Canada and east of the Mississippi were ceded to Britain, while Louisiana went from France to Spain. The Proclamation Line was a westward limit set to colonial settlement, intended to placate the Indians. It failed completely to halt encroachment on Indian land.

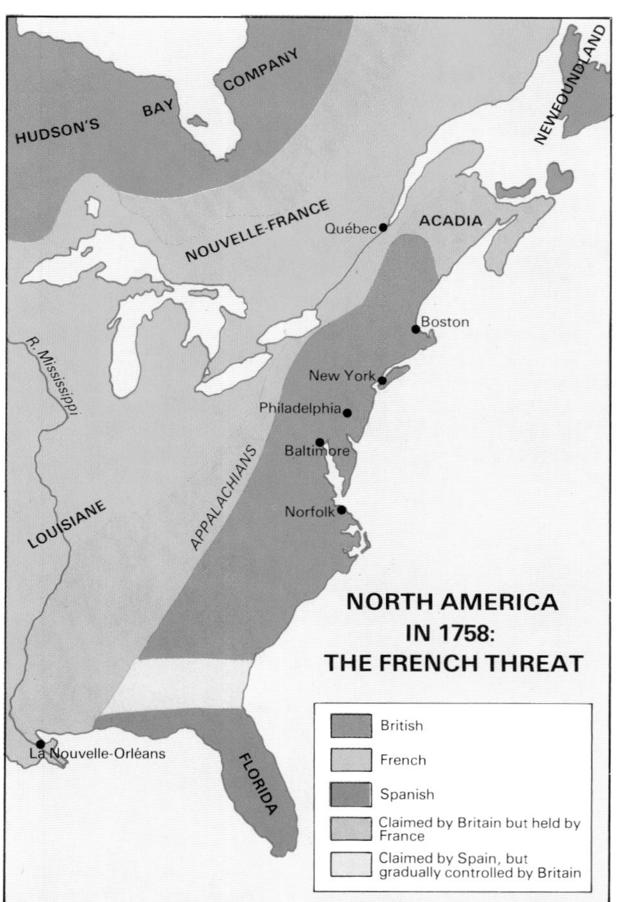

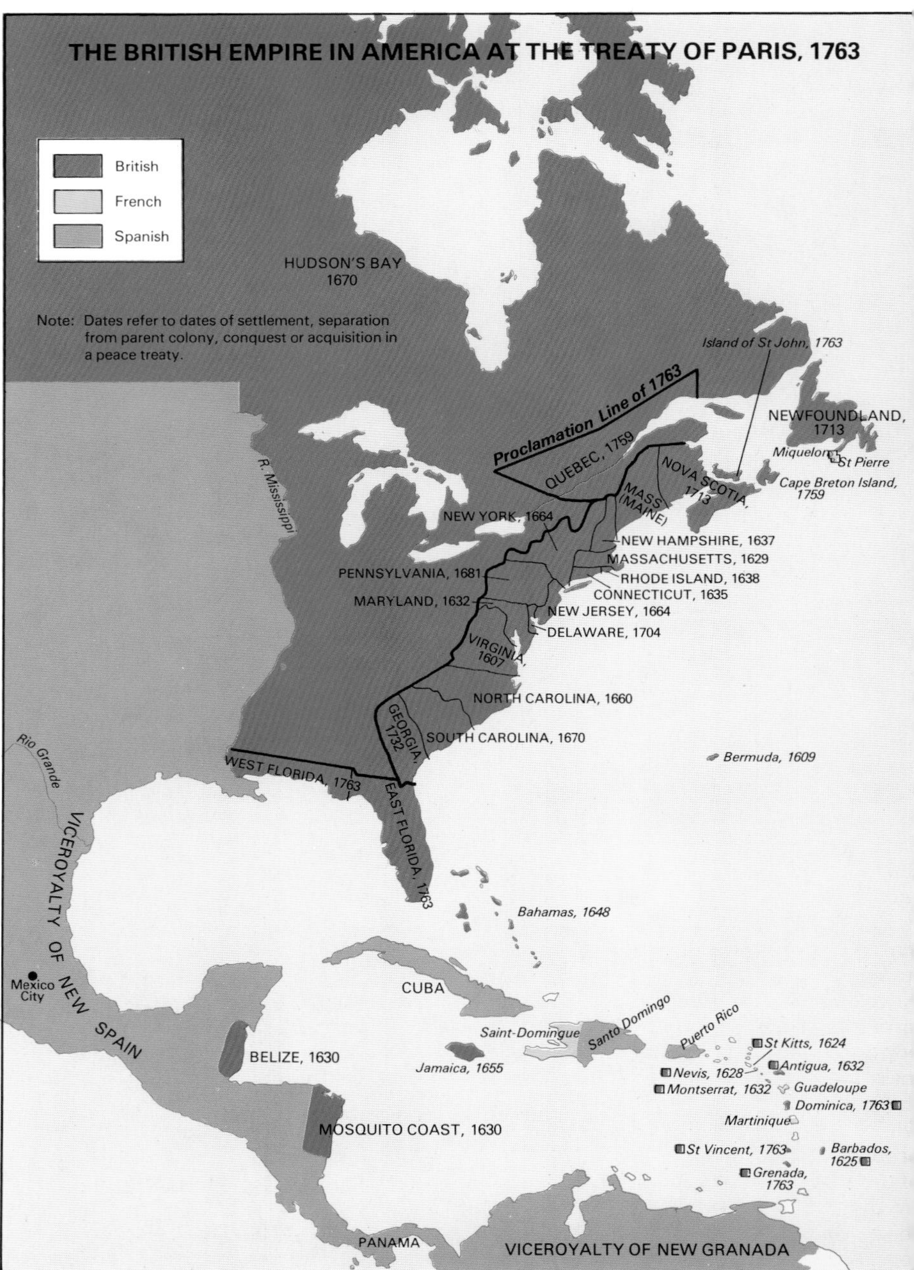

ıe Puritan exodus to New England. The Pilgrim Fathers migrated in 1620; Massachusetts, the parent of Rhode sland and Connecticut, was founded in 1629. By 1640, early 20,000 emigrants had sailed to New England to seek new life and attempt to establish a Bible commonwealth in ıe wilderness. The experiment prospered and New ngland was to have a very different society and economy om the colonies to the south.

Once a pattern had been established, more colonies were ettled, some established by conquest, such as Jamaica and lew York, some by proprietary grant, such as Maryland, outh Carolina and Pennsylvania. As population increased apidly, settlement moved inland from the tidewater into ıe piedmont and exploration continued across the Appachian mountains.

By 1700, all the original 13 North American colonies xcept Georgia had been settled, a start had been made in

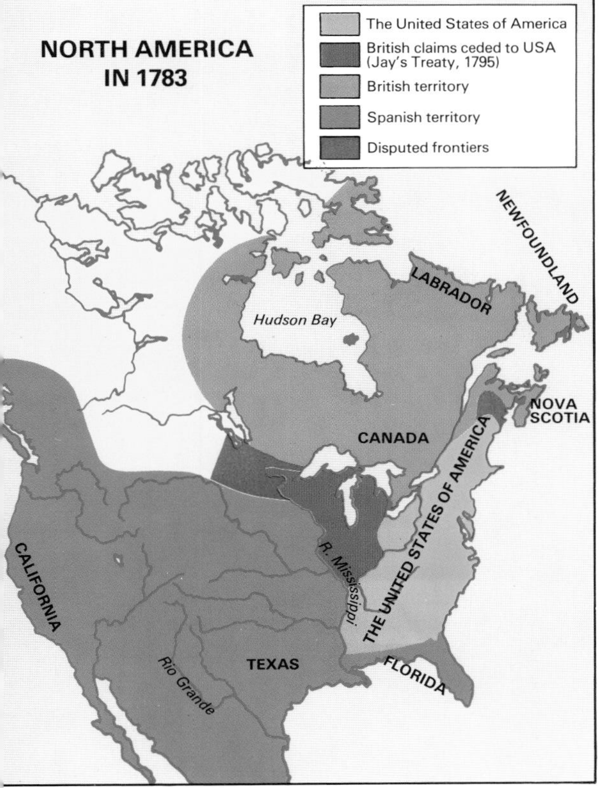

Canada with the Hudson's Bay Company, and the main entres of British settlement in the West Indies, Bahamas nd Bermuda had been established. The population of British America was already nearly half a million, almost a enth of that of England itself, and a pattern of imperial rade and economy within the restrictive English Navigation Laws had been developed which was to last ntil the end of the period, by which time the white opulation was nearly three million. England produced nanufactured goods which were exchanged for sugar from he West Indies and tobacco from Virginia and Maryland, while New England and the Middle Atlantic colonies roduced fish, foodstuffs and shipping services for the rest f the empire. In the 17th century, labour was found mainly y the indenture system, in which white men delivered hemselves into slavery for a fixed period of time in return or their passage and a stake in the country when their time was up. But, as the period continued, permanent black slavery increased rapidly, particularly in the sugar and tobacco colonies, and by 1775 there were an estimated 800,000 slaves, of whom rather more than half were in North America and the rest in the West Indies.

A huge addition was made to the British North American empire in the Seven Years' War (1756–63) when, after the capture of Quebec (1759) and Montreal (1760), Canada was taken from the French and French influence was eliminated beyond the Appalachians, leaving the way clear for eventual settlement up to the Mississippi. But this very success was to lead to a much greater loss of empire, for the Americans no longer needed British military and naval assistance, a fact which encouraged a minority of the colonists to resist British attempts to tax them for their own defence. The radical cry 'no taxation without representation' brought popular support, but it was probably the fact that conservative Virginian aristocrats and Bostonians were prepared to lead the revolt, together with the bungling, arrogance and incompetence of the British government, which ensured success. Serious friction began with the Stamp Act (1765) and led almost inexorably to the first armed clashes in 1775 and the Declaration of Independence in 1776. Only about a third of the colonists supported the revolt, but this was sufficient to nullify British attempts to reimpose authority by force, especially after the French joined the Americans in 1778. A preliminary treaty, signed late in 1782, recognized the independence of the United States and this was confirmed at the Peace of Paris (3 September 1783), the date which sees the formal ending of the 'First British Empire'.

North America in 1783, after the confirmation of the independence of the United States. Canada remained British and after independence some 40,000 people loyal to Britain moved there from the United States.

The 'Boston Tea Party' in December 1773 presaged the conflict between the British and the colonists. It was a raid by American colonists on three ships in Boston harbour – a protest against the system of taxation and a new monopoly on the sale of tea. When the tea-laden ships arrived in harbour some 7000 people petitioned the governor to order them to England unloaded; on his refusal about 50 men boarded the ships and dumped the tea in the harbour.

Scotland, 1603–1800

With the death of Elizabeth of England on 24 March 1603, King James VI of Scotland became also James I of England, Ireland, and (notionally) France. Thus the last of the Scottish House of Stewart was also the first Anglo-Scottish Stuart (the spelling of the name had been altered by his mother Mary Queen of Scots). Proclaimed in London within eight hours of the death of Elizabeth on a Thursday, James was informed of his succession late on the Saturday evening by the hard-riding Sir Richard Carey. Official news reached him five days after his proclamation in his new capital. Almost immediately James set off for London, having achieved the central obsession of his dynasty at least since the 1550s. Scotland had become a mere footstool to the mounting ambition of its royal family. It now had an absentee king. James promised the subjects of 'our ancient kingdom', in a speech in the High Kirk of St Giles in Edinburgh before his departure, that he would come back every third year and grant the meanest of them ready access. In fact he returned precisely once – in 1617 – and apart from lack of interest there were hard financial reasons for this. Moving the royal entourage was expensive and the revenues of the Crown of Scotland could only with difficulty cope with the repairs to the royal palaces necessary if the sovereign made any sort of tour in Scotland.

It is quite wrong to search the years between 1603 and the death of James in 1625 with one eye on the Great Civil War and the other feverishly trying to identify the 'causes' of the Covenanting Movement in Scotland. After 1638 Scotland was a storm centre, but between 1603 and 1625 James operated an acceptable form of government based on a fast courier service between Edinburgh and London, and on the Scots Privy Council. The Privy Council was the real ruler of a very decentralized group of regional societies. Its membership, combining royal officials and great magnates, virtually guaranteed accommodating, realistic government. The Kirk, that other great engine of governance, combined presbyterian forms with a mild conservative episcopacy craftily upheld by King James. Latterly, that British Solomon rather lost touch with the feelings of his northern realm. Increasingly arrogant and occasionally stupid letters disturbed the Lords of the Privy Council while the liturgical innovations designed to narrow the gap between the Kirk and the Church of England and known as the Five Articles of Perth, though pushed through into technical validity in 1618, proved a tactical blunder and scarcely enforceable. Nor should historians treat as seriously as they have James's propaganda about reducing the turbulent Borders to perfect peace as the 'Middle Shires'. Sir William Cranston's much-vaunted mounted police force had only 25 men in it.

The reign of Charles I started disastrously with an Act of Revocation (1625) cancelling all grants of Crown and ecclesiastical property since 1540. It is futile to point out that Charles never intended to resume all these grants, merely to negotiate for a more adequate remuneration for the clergy, and that Scots kings habitually issued such revocations at the end of their minorities. Charles never was a minor. Arrogant insensitivity was the new ruler's supreme failing. Having threatened the property of virtually every noble, he went on to outrage their sense of status by giving the bishops what his father had never allowed them except in peripheral areas like Orkney or the Hebrides – a central role in government. They began to dominate the Privy Council. In 1633 Charles came north to be crowned. The Anglican service alienated many. The creation of a Bishopric of Edinburgh out of the vast Archbishopric of St Andrews cost Edinburgh more than it wished to pay. With the issue of a new liturgy and set of canons in 1637 and 1636 respectively, both authorized, most offensively, purely by royal fiat, the Scottish ruling classes decided the time had come to remind Charles of reality. From encouraging rioting their pressure mounted to the formation of a provisional government and the signing in 1638 of the National Covenant.

Sincere concessions would probably have arrested the drift to war. Charles, however, combined disastrously stubbornness and a transparent deviousness. By 1639 he hoped to invade Scotland from the South while the Marquis of Hamilton, his leading 'Court Scot', landed on the east coast and Lord Antrim, head of 'Clan Donald South' invaded on the west. The Grand Design aborted. By 1640 the Scots had invaded England, won a skirmish at Newburn and occupied Newcastle, cutting London's vital coal supply. Episcopacy (not denounced in the National Covenant) had been swept away by a Glasgow General Assembly in 1638. By 1641, led by Archibald 8th Earl and 1st Marquis of Argyll, High Chief of Clan Campbell, the Scots had carried through a radical parliamentary revolution making the Scots Parliament or Estates the real ruler of Scotland. They were undone by division in the English Long Parliament (which they had insisted be summoned). Rebellion in Ireland followed by civil war in England left the Scots in a hopeless dilemma. Argyll knew they could not afford to let Charles win his war, lest he crush the Scottish Revolution. By the Solemn League and Covenant of 1643 the Scots tried to save their Presbyterian revolution by exporting it to England. Their army certainly saved the English Parliament which before the Battle of Marston Moor was losing its war. However, the Marquis of Montrose, a deadly rival of Argyll and indeed of Hamilton, unleashed in 1644–5 a hurricane rebellion based on the Highlands and MacDonalds from Ulster, and fatally wounded the status of the Covenanting régime before its main army crushed him at Philliphaugh on the Borders. Hamilton in 1647 persuaded the Scots nobility to invade England to rescue their monarch from captivity. Rooted in a conservative reaction, 'The Engagement' with Charles led to total military disaster at Preston in Lancashire. Argyll

Scotland and the Civil Wars, 1639–1650. The wars began as a result of Charles I' alienation of the Scottish aristocracy. Declaring against arbitrary royal authority, the Scots signed the National Covenant in 1638. In the ensuing 'Bishops' Wars' the Covenanter armies, under the leadership of Argyll, invaded England as far as Newcastle, which they occupied in 1640. In 1647, however, forced to choose between the Royalist and Parliamentary causes, Argyll fatally decided for Charles. The result was defea by Cromwellian forces at Dunbar (1650). The last Scot force was defeated at Worcester in the same year.

The Souldiers in their paſsage to York turn unto
reformers pull down Popiſh pictures, break dow
rayles, turn altars into Tables.

Parliamentary troops wreck a church, from a contemporary woodcut. Initially, the Presbyterian Scots saw Parliamentary forces as natural allies against the Crown.

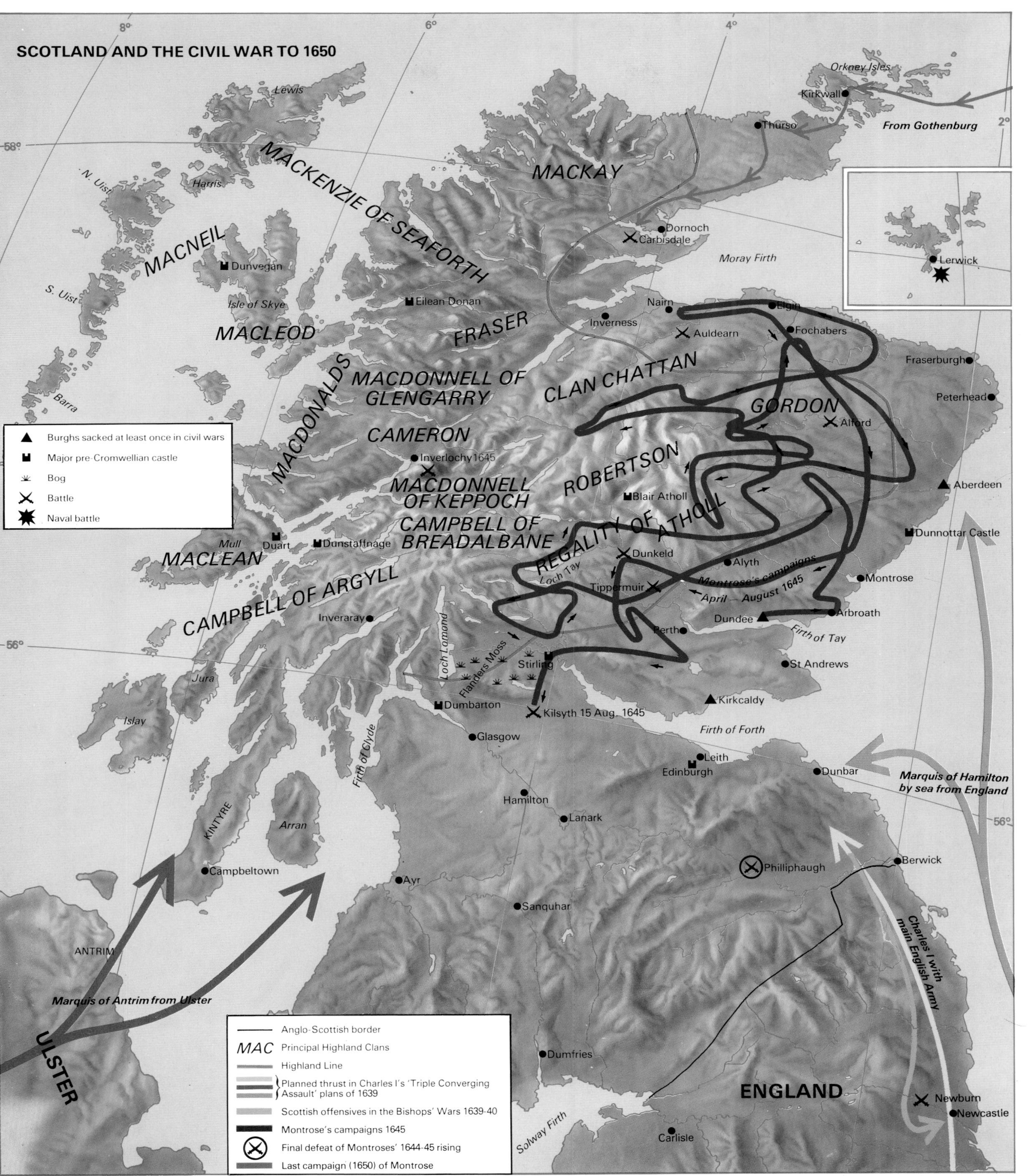
SCOTLAND AND THE CIVIL WAR TO 1650
Orkney Isles
Kirkwall
From Gothenburg
Thurso
Lewis
MACKENZIE OF SEAFORTH
MACKAY
N. Uist
Harris
MACNEIL
Dunvegan
Dornoch
Carbisdale
Moray Firth
Lerwick
S. Uist
Isle of Skye
Eilean Donan
MACLEOD
FRASER
Nairn
Inverness
Elgin
Auldearn
Fochabers
Fraserburgh
Barra
MACDONALDS
MACDONNELL OF GLENGARRY
CLAN CHATTAN
GORDON
Peterhead
Alford
CAMERON
Inverlochy 1645
MACDONNELL OF KEPPOCH
ROBERTSON
Blair Atholl
Aberdeen
CAMPBELL OF BREADALBANE
REGALITY OF ATHOLL
Dunnottar Castle
Mull
Duart
Dunstaffnage
MACLEAN
Dunkeld
Alyth
Loch Tay
Montrose's campaigns April – August 1645
Montrose
Tippermuir
CAMPBELL OF ARGYLL
Inveraray
Dundee
Arbroath
Perth
Firth of Tay
Loch Lomond
Flanders Moss
Stirling
St Andrews
Jura
Kirkcaldy
Islay
Dumbarton
Kilsyth 15 Aug. 1645
Firth of Forth
Glasgow
Firth of Clyde
Leith
Edinburgh
Dunbar
Marquis of Hamilton by sea from England
Hamilton
Lanark
KINTYRE
Arran
Berwick
Philliphaugh
Campbeltown
Ayr
Sanquhar
Charles I with main English Army
ANTRIM
Marquis of Antrim from Ulster
ULSTER
Dumfries
ENGLAND
Newburn
Newcastle
Solway Firth
Carlisle
Burghs sacked at least once in civil wars
Major pre-Cromwellian castle
Bog
Battle
Naval battle
Anglo-Scottish border
MAC Principal Highland Clans
Highland Line
Planned thrust in Charles I's 'Triple Converging Assault' plans of 1639
Scottish offensives in the Bishops' Wars 1639-40
Montrose's campaigns 1645
Final defeat of Montroses' 1644-45 rising
Last campaign (1650) of Montrose

tried to save an autonomous Scotland but the execution of the King in 1649 forced him into war with England. Argyll's power was destroyed by Cromwell's invasion and victory at Dunbar. The last Scots army was annihilated deep in England at Worcester. By 1651 Scotland was prostrate under the New Model Army.

Prosperous Jacobean Scotland had been stricken by war, war-taxation, plague, famine and deep economic recession. Nor did the first Anglo-Dutch war of 1652–4 help a Scottish economy whose main overseas trading partner was the Netherlands. General Monck brilliantly suppressed the royalist Glencairn's Rising in the Highlands. From its citadels the garrison army ruled sensibly and moderately a Scotland formally united in one Commonwealth with England and Ireland. Nevertheless, the Restoration of 1660 was hailed joyfully in Scotland, once again a distinct kingdom, and one in which the nobles, chastened by the horrors of the 1650s, were restored to effective social and political power. Charles II restored a Jacobean episcopacy in a still recognizably Presbyterian Kirk and with the help of most of the nobles wore down religious dissent from major rebellion defeated in battles like Bothwell Bridge (1679), to quite small radical groups. These latter, in the Sanquhar Declaration of 1681, finally rose above the instinctive loyalty to the House of Stuart displayed by even the most radical Covenanter of the 1630s or 40s. Charles II ruled under a very reactionary constitution which swept away all the achievements of the period 1638–41, although in practice he was in tacit alliance with the local rulers, the nobles and lairds who still enjoyed extensive private jurisdictions up to the level of a regality or 'petty kingdom'.

James VII and II succeeded to this tacit alliance in 1685 and used it to defeat a rebellion by the exiled 9th Earl of Argyll, whom he executed. The economic upswing of the reign of Charles II was flattening out, but it was the Catholicizing policies of James and the high-handed denial of local and especially burghal self-government which shattered the basis of the régime by alienating the local ruling classes. Scotland followed, in its own fashion, the English Glorious Revolution of 1688 and Scottish history entered a new phase which lasted until the mid-18th century.

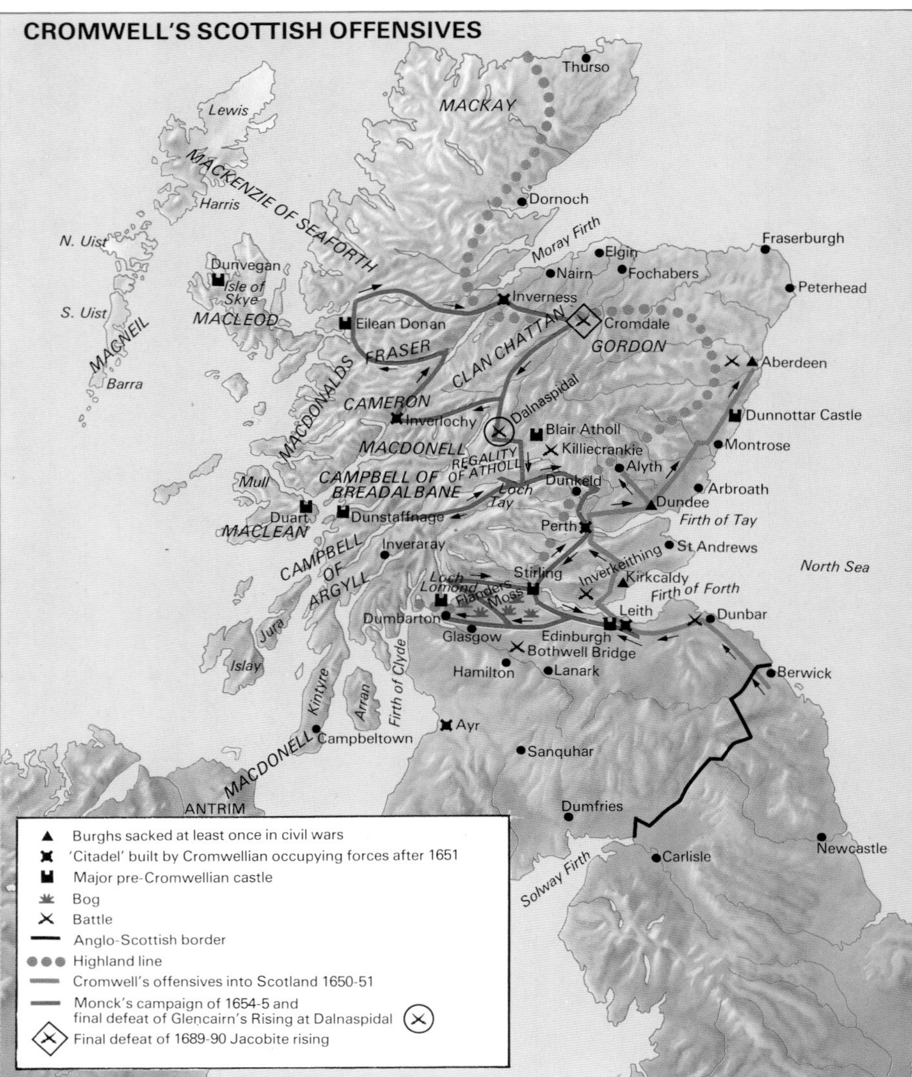

Above: The Civil Wars and their aftermath in Scotland. Cromwell's New Model Army dealt efficiently with Scottish resistance. Monck's garrison army governed Scotland well, responding quickly to the Royalist Glencairn's Rising in the Highlands in 1655. After the Restoration, Charles II revived something of the old alliance between the King and the Scottish ruling classes. However, the Catholic James VII and II insensitively attempted to impose a new order, goading radical sections of the Lowland bourgeoisie into support of the Glorious Revolution of 1688–9. By this James was expelled in favour of William of Orange. A Jacobite faction, under Viscount Dundee (John Graham of Claverhouse), arose in the Highlands, but its revolt in 1689–90 did not long survive its leader's death at the battle of Killiecrankie.

The battle of Bothwell Brig (Bridge), 22 June 1679. A Highland army under Dundee and the Duke of Monmouth defeat Covenanter forces at the start of the Jacobite uprising of 1689–90.

The Revolution of 1688–9 in Scotland was a curiously incoherent process which proved much more radical in nature than its English counterpart. Its political theory was very radical. Embodied in the Claim of Right, it flatly stated that James had been deposed for tyranny and it strongly implied that monarchy in Scotland was contractual. Due to the intransigent Jacobitism of the bishops of the Kirk by Law Established, King William, who would have preferred to keep them, had by 1690 been forced to accept a Presbyterian Settlement in the Kirk. Apathy seems to have been the majority attitude among the Scottish ruling classes whom James had so alienated. A radical minority made the Revolution. An even smaller minority opposed it. Lieutenant-General John Graham of Claverhouse, Viscount Dundee, led this Jacobite opposition with a small army drawn mainly from the lesser clans of the Central Highlands. Victorious but slain at Killiecrankie

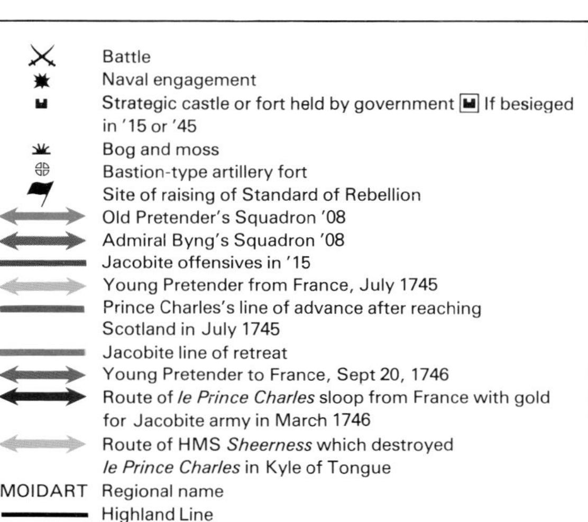

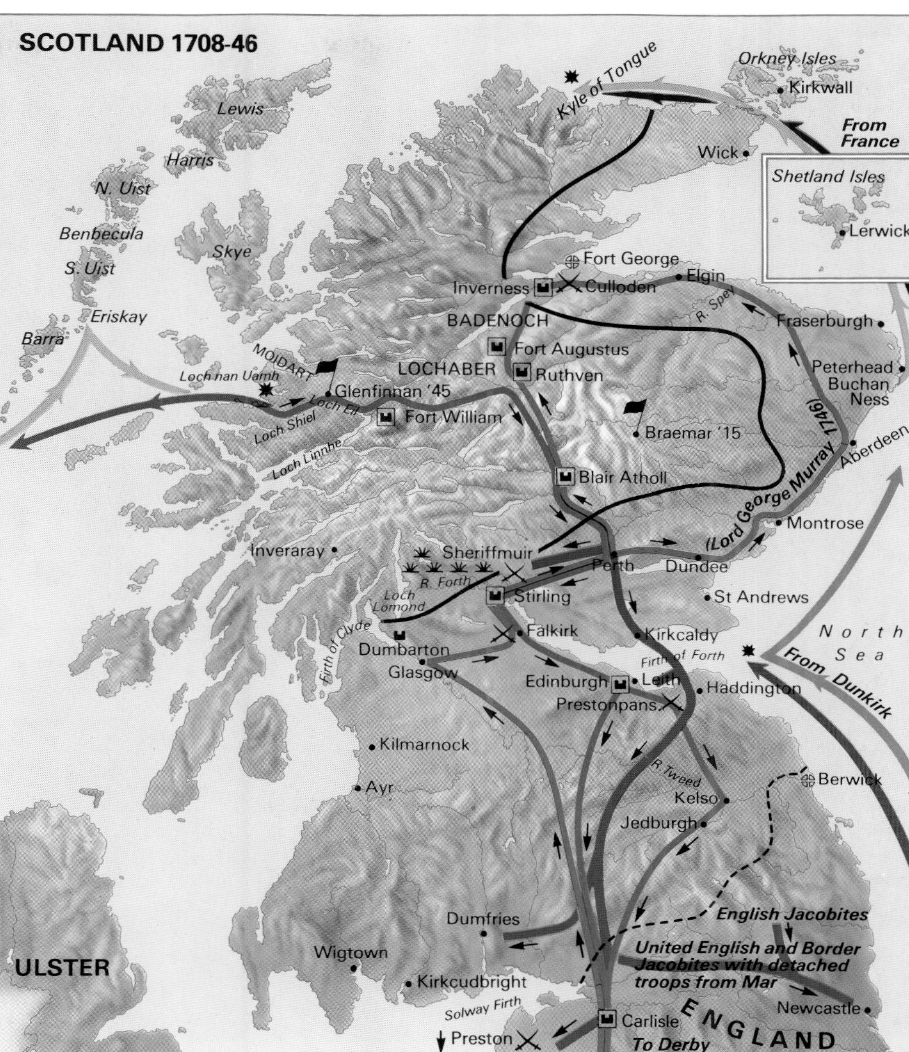

Above: Rebellion in Scotland, 1708–45. Economic decline under William, and the emptiness of the terms promised under the Act of Union (1707), caused a revival of Jacobitism, expressed in a series of revolts. The 1715 Rebellion, in favour of James VII and II's son James Francis Stuart (the Old Pretender), was the most serious of these. It failed ultimately because of the incompetence of its leader, the Earl of Mar. The 1745 rebellion, on behalf of the Young Pretender, Charles Edward Stuart, was a slighter affair, utterly crushed by Cumberland at Culloden in 1746.

Engraved portrait of Charles Edward Stuart ('Bonnie Prince Charlie') in 1745.

Right: The capture of the rebel Jacobite Lord Lovat during the 1745 uprising.

Glencoe, Argyllshire. The infamous massacre of the MacDonalds by Campbells and English troops took place here in 1692. This brutal and incompetent attempt to control the Highlanders by terror typified the inadequacy of William's military policy in Scotland. The Highlands were to be more effectively reduced by the abolition of local lordships in 1707, and by the clearances enforced by great landowners to make way for the growth in sheep farming. Rural depopulation continued apace into the 19th century.

near the strategic heart of the Highlands, he left an army whose attempt to break into the Lowlands was checked in battle at Dunkeld. At the Haughs of Cromdale on Speyside it was routed by Williamite cavalry.

William's reign in a Scotland he never visited was unsuccessful, partly for reasons he had no control over and partly because of his own attitudes. Uninterested in the country save as a source of soldiers and taxes, he was not even willing to provide adequate garrisons for the Highlands. Inverlochy Fort, renamed Fort William, was reactivated under its old Cromwellian commander Colonel John Hill, but an attempt to substitute terror for effective power led to the appallingly counter-productive episode of the Massacre of Glencoe of February 1692, when soldiers of Argyll's Regiment made an incompetent but bloody bid to wipe out the MacDonalds of Glencoe on the dubious grounds that their chief had failed to take an oath of loyalty to the government in time. William's wars with France from 1689 to 1697 and again from 1702 had a catastrophic impact on the overseas trade of Scotland. Furthermore, for a four-year period from 1695, Scotland experienced its last great famine which reached peaks of severity in 1696 and 1699 with a relative respite between 1697–8.

After William's death in 1702, Queen Anne's ministers inherited his policy. They were able to hijack Scotland illegally by executive action into the War of the Spanish Succession (1702–13), but the problems of controlling the Scots Parliament and of imposing the English Act of Settlement of 1701 (which secured the Hanoverian succession) on Scotland led to moves for incorporating Scotland in a union with England. By buying the Duke of Hamilton, the nominal leader of the opposition, Queen Anne's English ministers were able to pass through the Scots Parliament the carefully prearranged package-deal embodied in the Act of Union of 1707. At the highest level Scottish politics were simply abolished with the absorption into the English Parliament of 45 Scots M.P.s and 16 Representative Peers. The peculiar political tradition of the Scottish Parliament vanished. At local level a large measure of autonomy was guaranteed in the Act, as it had to be to secure its passage. The self-government and privileges of the royal burghs were specifically secured, as was the peculiar Scots legal tradition and central court structure. More dramatic was the confirmation of all hereditary offices and jurisdictions which meant that the very extensive private franchises of Scotland continued to function.

The upshot of these dramatic changes was a series of rebellions in Scotland, led by the committed Jacobite minority, but expressing far more general discontent. In 1708 the 'Old Pretender' James Francis Stuart, the son of James VII and II, and then a young man, was carried to the mouth of the Firth of Forth by a French fleet which fled north at the approach of Admiral Byng. In 1715 a disgruntled Scottish politician, the Earl of Mar, led by far the most serious Jacobite rising, which should have succeeded but for his own incompetence. The pro-government Duke of Argyll kept the main Jacobite army north of the Forth-Clyde line by a drawn battle at Sheriffmuir, while a Border rising and the crossing of the Forth by the troops of the Jacobite Macintosh of Borlum culminated in disaster at Preston in Lancashire where the Scots had linked up with English Jacobites. Early in 1716 Mar and James fled from Montrose by sea for France. Ineffective legislation tried to disarm the Highland clans while General Wade supervized the construction of a network of military roads in the Highlands which ultimately helped nobody very much except 'Bonnie Prince Charlie' in 1745. That rebellion was always a madcap scheme driven on by the stubborn egotism of the Young Pretender and supported by only a tiny minority in Scotland. Seizing Edinburgh with no serious fighting, the Jacobites routed the luckless Cope at Prestonpans (whence he had come from Aberdeen). On their retreat from England the Jacobites scored a last major victory at Falkirk over the brutal General Hawley, but were utterly crushed in the spring of 1746 by the Duke of Cumberland at Culloden outside Inverness. The banning of Highland dress and more effective disarming were perhaps less significant than the Abolition of Heritable Jurisdictions Act (Scotland) 1747, which marked the end of a process begun in 1603, accelerated in 1707, and culminating in the abolition of the distinctive Scots polity.

Thereafter Scotland, in political terms, vanished. Even the Highland landlords soon accepted that their future was as North Britons. The vast artillery fort, Fort George, built on Ardersier Point north of Inverness to check a future rebellion was irrelevant before it was finished. Scottish politics ceased to exist, in the sense that the last thing M.P.s or peers wished to do was trouble Westminster with specifically Scottish problems. That would have endangered their own good standing with, and hence eligibility for, patronage from the government of the day. Gradually a system of 'management' was evolved which first reached a peak of maturity under the Earl of Islay (later Duke of Argyll) in the 1750s and which was carried to its ultimate stage of development under the Dundas of Armiston family in the shape of the first and second Viscounts Melville. They were allowed to monopolize government patronage in Scotland in exchange for delivering an obedient phalanx of M.P.s to support the governments of the Younger Pitt and Lord Liverpool. The job was all the easier with only a few thousand county voters and votes in burghs confined to the self-perpetuating oligarchs

Scottish counties
1 Aberdeen
2 Argyll
3 Ayr
4 Banff
5 Berwick
6 Bute
6a Caithness
7 Clackmannan
7a Kinross
8 Cromarty
8a Nairn
9 Dumbarton
10 Dumfries
11 Edinburgh
12 Elgin
13 Fife
14 Forfar
15 Haddington
16 Inverness
17 Kincardine
18 Kirkcudbright
19 Lanark
20 Linlithgow
21 Orkney & Shetlands
22 Peebles
23 Perth
24 Renfrew
25 Ross
26 Roxburgh
27 Selkirk
28 Stirling
29 Sutherland
30 Wigtown

Note:
Counties with the same number took turns electing an M.P. before 1832

Left: The distribution of Scottish industry in the 18th century. With the exceptions of woollens and linen, the development of industry and urbanization in Scotland was essentially confined to the Lowlands. Canal building continued until the arrival of railways in the 19th century.

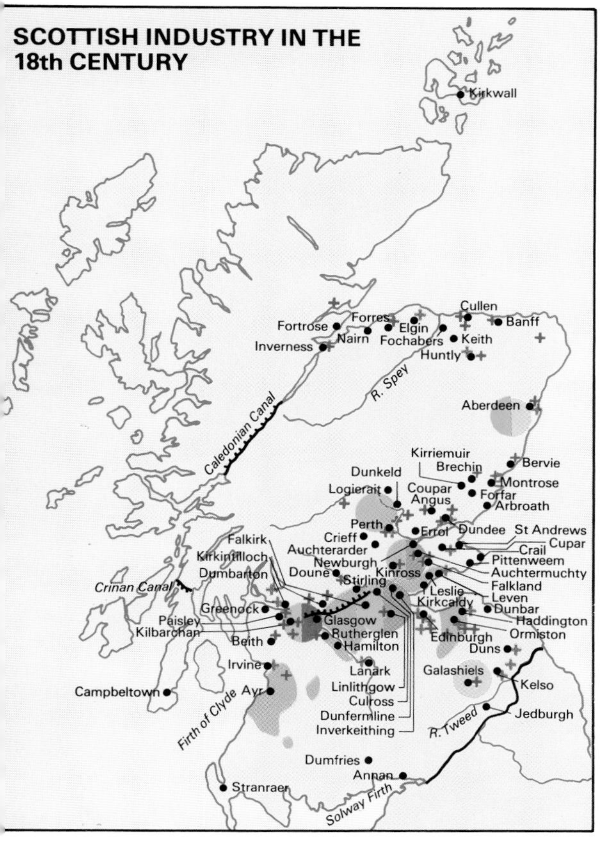

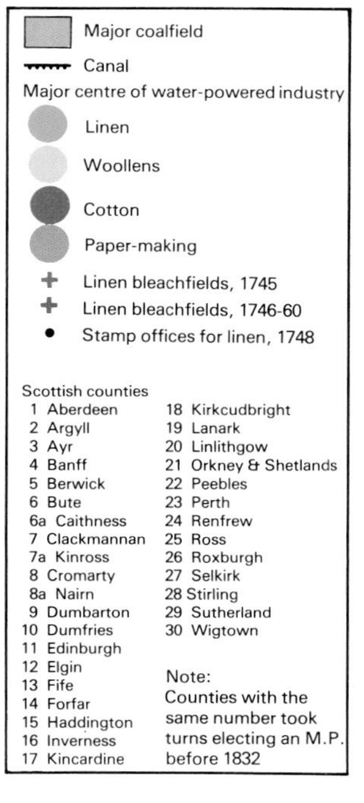

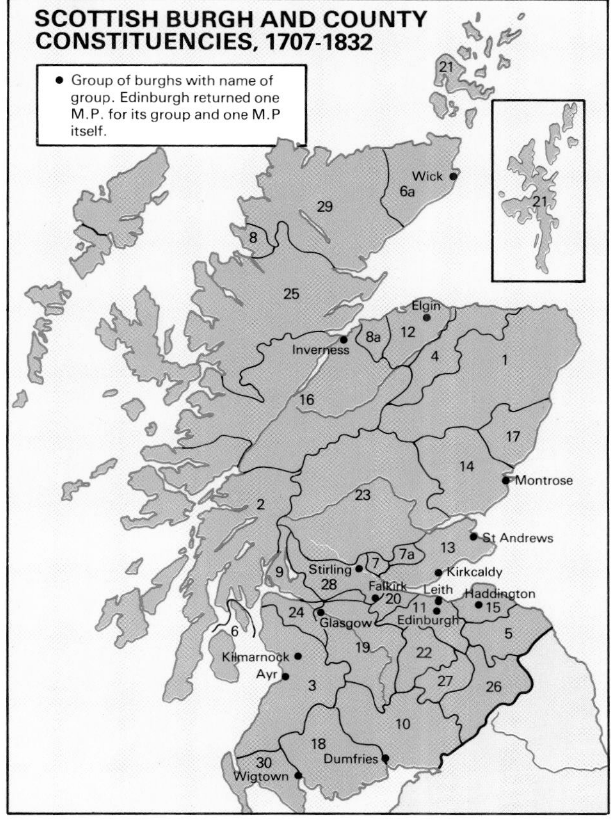

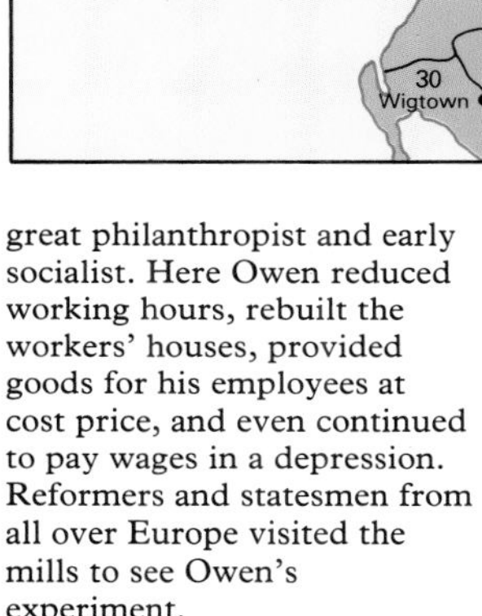

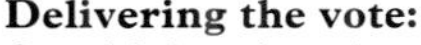

Delivering the vote: Scottish burgh and county constituencies, 1707–1832. Aristocratic vote fixers like the Earl of Islay and the Dundas of Armiston family ensured the election of pliant members to the Westminster Parliament.

n the town councils. Representative peers were elected by process which from the start was totally rigged by the overnment.

Economic development, ultimately incompatible with ne landed ascendancy which staffed the Dundas machine, athered pace after 1750. Linen was the first spectacular rowth area, though until the American Revolution Glasgow built up a great trade in the import and re-export f tobacco. After 1783 the boom in water-powered cotton-pinning to some extent compensated for the collapse of obacco re-exports. Iron founding and coal mining, and the alt-production associated with coal workings all developed otably. By 1799, in an attempt to persuade cheap labour nto the mines, the servile status of Scottish colliers and alters was finally abolished. However, only with the ombination of the hot-blast process in iron foundries and ne exploitation of Lowland reserves of black band onstone from about 1830 can the second stage of the cottish industrial revolution be said to have started, on the asis of specialization in heavy metallurgy.

By then, clearances for sheep farms had already caused xtensive disruption in the Highlands. The collapse of kelp rices after 1815 destroyed the seaweed-burning 'industry' hich had helped many Highland estates and peasants to urvive. Population growth and urbanization were by 1810 unprecedented levels. Scotland was becoming essentially ne Lowlands, in human terms. Politically it was, and emained after the 1832 enfranchisement act, North ritain. It is ironic that in a land devoid of meaningful ationalism the politically very reactionary Sir Walter cott (a pillar of the Dundas Interest) spearheaded a omantic movement which created an image of a feudal Caledonia stern and wild', at odds with the past (and totally nrepresentative of the present and future) but neverthe-ess infinitely seductive.

The New Lanark Mills, near Glasgow, created in the 1780s. This famous cotton spinning factory was later (in 1800) managed and part-owned by Robert Owen, the great philanthropist and early socialist. Here Owen reduced working hours, rebuilt the workers' houses, provided goods for his employees at cost price, and even continued to pay wages in a depression. Reformers and statesmen from all over Europe visited the mills to see Owen's experiment.

Ireland, 1640–1801

Relations between Ireland and England for much of the 17th and 18th centuries were strife-torn and unhappy. Successive English governments sought solutions to the Irish problem through repression, which further exacerbated the dilemma. Rebellions in 1567, 1579 and 1595, in the names of Catholicism and Irish nationalism, confirmed English fears that Ireland might become a base for a Spanish invasion and that the Irish were not to be entrusted with self-government. After each rebellion, the estates of the leaders were confiscated and millions of acres handed over to English and Scottish Protestant immigrants.

During Charles I's reign Ireland was 'ruled' by Stafford, under whose harsh administration Ireland became more settled and prosperous. Then in 1640 Stafford was recalled to England to help the King in his struggle with Parliament. His recall became the signal for the rebellion of 1641 in which thousands of Protestants were killed by the Catholic peasantry. The Catholic rebels sent help to Charles I in the Civil War and after his execution (1649) recognized the young King, Charles II.

Cromwell and Ireton led English troops to put down the Irish rebellion with a policy of 'thorough'. Irish garrisons at Wexford and Drogheda were massacred, every priest found by the Puritan soldiery slaughtered, and the remaining Irish landowners banished to Connaught. Their estates were divided among the soldiers and those financiers who had provided the money to pay for the expedition. Under Cromwell's rule law and order was imposed, trade and industry slowly revived and towns grew. But for the Catholic peasantry there was little consolation in all this. They paid high rents for their small plots of land and their religion was savagely repressed.

The Restoration of 1660 did not lead to much improvement for the Irish who had been the first to recognize Charles II. Few of those who had lost their estates got them back, although the Catholic religion was now tolerated.

Ulster: The Origins of the Conflict

Ireland, whose traditional, independent culture and language were of great antiquity by 1500, underwent rapid change in the century and a half following, brought about by increasingly close contact with England and English settlers and administrators. Its four provinces were shired in the English manner after 1500, the 'Old English' (landowners of medieval English origin) were dominant, especially in the 'Pale' (four counties round Dublin), and direct rule from Dublin by representatives of the English Crown, the Lord Lieutenant and his Deputy, was extended. The Protestant Reformation and the Elizabethan government further extended English influence, in the Church, in law, in farming and in commerce and the use of English spread. But the mountains and rivers, woods and bogs of much of Ireland beyond the east and south-east plain, preserved intact both the old Gaelic lordships, the Irish language and the old ways of life. In particular Connaught, west of the Shannon, and Ulster, remained little affected by these changes. The rebellion of the Ulster chieftains, Tyrone and Tyrconnell, in the 1590s, required much expense of time and money to overcome. The North was impenetrable apart from passes at Ballyshannon in the west and the Moyry pass in the east; and a Spanish landing in aid of the rebels had to be combatted at Kinsale in the South. The defeat of the earls, however, gave James VI and I the opportunity to settle his Scots subjects in the six Ulster counties forfeited to the Crown, and to encourage unofficial immigration to Antrim and Down. This 'Ulster Plantation' was successful. By 1640 some 30–40,000 new Scots and English settlers had been established in Ireland.

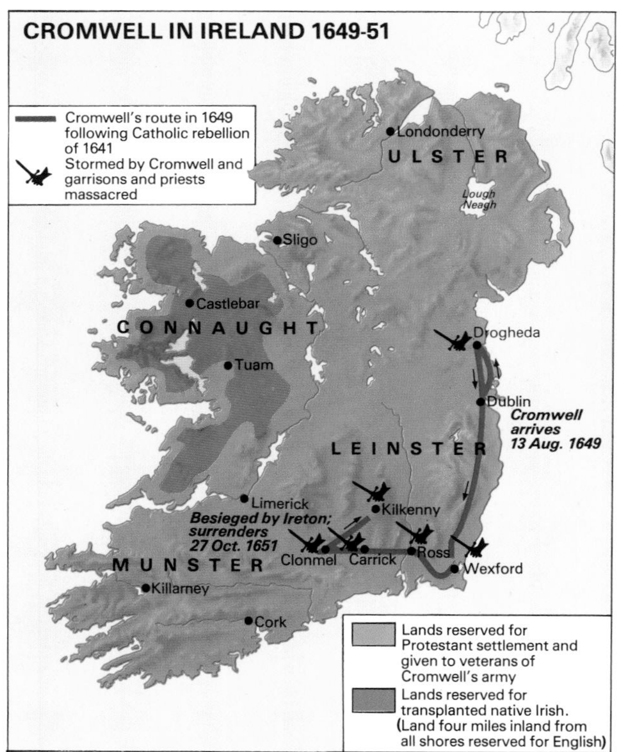

Cromwell's campaign through eastern Ireland to quell the Catholic uprising left a legacy of lasting bitterness. Much of the country was granted by him to veterans of his Parliamentary Army. From now on large landowners were Protestant, while small farmers and peasants were Catholic.

Above: In the early 17th century large numbers of Protestant immigrants, mainly from Scotland, were encouraged to move to northern Ireland and settle there. They built up a flourishing linen industry. This late 18th-century picture shows linen workers on the Earl of Moira's estate in County Down, where over half the population was Protestant.

he accession of the Catholic King James II was widely elcomed, although Irish merchants and traders resented .e way in which the English Parliament hampered eland's economic development. Measures were passed rbidding the export of Irish dairy produce while also cluding the Irish from that colonial trade which contri- ited to England's own economic development.

The Glorious Revolution of 1688 led to the renewal of ›stilities between the Catholics and Protestants, partic- arly in Ulster. A Catholic Irish army led by Sarsfield llied to James II when he landed at Kinsale. Londonderry d Enniskillen were besieged, while the Catholic South clared against William of Orange. However, London- rry was relieved by the English fleet after a four months' ege, while the garrison at Enniskillen broke out and won .e battle of Newtownbutler. In 1690 the English won the ittle of the Boyne following which James II fled to ance. Cork and Kinsale were captured, the Catholics feated at the battle of Aughrim and the rebellion finally ded by the surrender of Sarsfield at Limerick (1691).

The ensuing Treaty of Limerick allowed the Irish eedom to leave to serve in the French army and promised ligious freedom to the Catholics. But the Westminster irliament went on to pass a series of anti-Catholic laws, iown as the Penal Code. It was forbidden to hold Catholic rvices or to open Catholic schools; Catholics were rbidden to own land, to wear a sword (the mark of a ntleman) or to hold jobs in local or national government. he Catholic, a second-class citizen socially and economic- ly, was also forbidden to vote in parliamentary elections. it the Protestant Irish were also oppressed; they were rbidden to trade freely and their Parliament had no real wer. The country was governed from Dublin Castle by a ord Lieutenant, a member of the English Cabinet, aided an English army. He controlled the system of patronage hich made the Irish parliamentary system even more rrupt than the English one, while Poynings' Law and the 'estminster Act (1714) ensured English control of an tensibly independent Irish Parliament.

A Protestant oligarchy dominated the Irish Parliament, vned most of the land, controlled industry and commerce it slowly became discontented with the economic and ›litical oppression exercised by England. During the merican War (1776–83) English troops were withdrawn om Ireland, which was thus exposed to the threat of a ench invasion. A local Volunteer force was raised for eland's defence. At the same time Henry Grattan rsuaded the hitherto supine Irish Parliament that the merican arguments against English domination could also used by the Irish. English politicians feared a Protestant- d Irish rising and, in fear, passed a series of ameliorating ws. The Irish were allowed a share in colonial trade 780); the more severe of the anti-Catholic laws were laxed (1781); and the Irish Parliament was granted its dependence (1782) by the repeal of Poynings' Law. This d not provide Home Rule for Ireland, which was still verned by 'the Castle'.

The onset of the French Revolution had important fects in Ireland. Grattan led the demand for a reform of .e parliamentary system; Wolfe Tone, a Protestant lawyer om Belfast, founded the United Irishmen and demanded ome Rule for Ireland. At first, Tone's society consisted of ›th Catholics and Protestants, but Catholics, their anger used by Pitt's refusal to give them complete civil, ligious and social liberty, attacked Protestant property d people. This led to Protestants leaving the United ishmen and to the formation of the Orange Society 795).

Pitt's refusal to grant further concessions to Catholics led Tone to ask for French help. Two French attempts (1796 and 1797) to invade Ireland were failures, but frightened the government into a policy of savage repression against Catholics suspected of having helped the invaders. This cruelty precipitated a rebellion in 1798. Badly organized, poorly armed and with their plans well known to the authorities, the rebels were easily, if savagely, repressed. Once again French help came – but, once again, too late.

Pitt realized that the Irish problem was a mixture of Catholic anger, Protestant fears and English ignorance. He tried to solve this problem with his proposals for a Union of the Irish and Westminster Parliaments. In this Union the Catholics would always be a small minority, and could be allowed their freedom (to stand in elections etc) without fear of their being able to organize effective anti-Protestant campaigns. The Irish Protestant oligarchy did not want to lose their independence, but were bribed or cajoled into passing the legislation needed to bring about the Union (1801). But King George III refused to agree to Catholic Emancipation; Pitt resigned on the grounds that he had promised this to the Irish Catholics. The Union got off to a bad start with Protestant reluctance allied to Catholic conviction that they had been betrayed, again, by a Protestant politician.

The rebellion of the 1790s, inspired by the French Revolution, was at first both Protestant and Catholic, though their uneasy alliance broke down in 1795. A French fleet sailed into Bantry Bay but was scattered by storms and no troops landed. Another French expedition in 1798 was more successful, but by this time the rebellion had been put down by government troops.

Wales, 1604–1850

Welsh topography and geography largely explain its modern development. Until the middle of the 18th century, Wales remained a backward country completely lacking an industrial tradition and any real sense of social modernization. Agrarian activities predominated, with hill farming and sheep rearing on the upland interior, which comprises 90 per cent of the land area, and incursions into arable and pastoral farming on the flatter coastal plains. Population was sparse and evenly distributed, the only concentration being where land was particularly fertile, such as the Vale of Towy, or in favourable coastal locations, such as Swansea. Topography determined also the limited extent of integration between North and South, the latter being by far the most significant region, resulting in the two halves functioning as separate entities for most practical economic and social purposes. It determined too the isolation which generally characterized Wales as a mountainous, unattractive appendage to the western parts of England, accentuated by its different language, culture and poor communications.

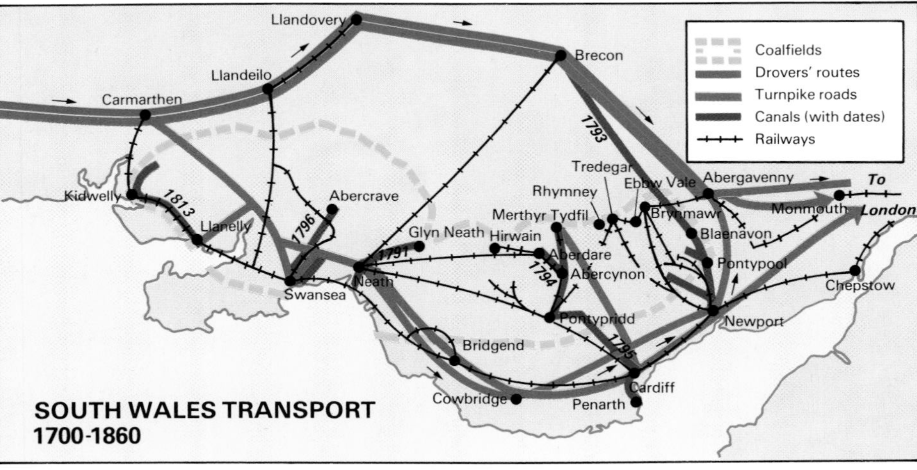

The development of transport in South Wales, 1700–1860. Industrialization demanded effective means of bulk carriage. This need was met initially by a system of canals linking the Coalfield to the coast. By the 1840s, a growing network of railways was carrying coal down the valleys to the ports of Swansea, Cardiff and Newport.

Economic and social life tended to be more advanced in the small ports dotted round the coastal plains which skirted the upland interior, where commercial contacts with London, Bristol or Liverpool occurred. The only other 'civilizing' activity was the regular contact made by the drovers, who since the 14th century had driven cattle for sale and slaughter in the markets of the English Midlands and London. Thus the drovers were instrumental in establishing the first banks in Wales, such as Banc y Ddafad Ddu (Black Sheep Bank) of Aberystwyth. The only industrial activities in the mid 18th-century were essentially small-scale and closely linked to the rural background. Woollens were manufactured in most areas by farmers and their families; coal was sporadically mined in both North and South Wales; non-ferrous metal smelting had begun to concentrate in the south-west corner of the South Wales Coalfield where an organized sale-coal industry had also started; lead-mining and copper-mining both gave portents of more significant developments to come; and small iron forges and foundries were dotted over the face of the country to serve the basic agrarian economy.

Thus industrial growth came in the middle of the 18th century, not spontaneously from within the domestic economy, but rather as an implant from outside, attracted by the variety of riches in Wales's geological structure. Beginning in the 1750s, with Isaac Wilkinson's coming to Hirwaun, the second half of the 18th century and the early 19th century saw a number of English entrepreneurs turn the northern rim of the South Wales Coalfield into Britain major iron-producing district. The two foremost ente prises, the Dowlais Works (1759) and Cyfartha (1765) we both located in Merthyr, but the iron works by the 184 stretched right across the north of the coalfield fro Ystalyfera in the west to Blaenavon in the east. T immigrant entrepreneurs provided what the region lacke sufficient capital for the initial establishment of a larg scale activity, and commercial connections, particular through London and Bristol. These ensured the expansic of industry which supplemented the large-scale ploughir back of profits on which most firms depended. T juxtaposition of ironstone and coal ensured the response the district to its first major challenge, the war-tin demands of the late 18th century and early 19th centur Later, the concentration of the bigger works on t manufacture of rails for the rapidly expanding railw networks of Britain, and the world, consolidated th progress. With the advent of steel, the industry declin during the last three decades of the century and, as a great reliance upon imported haematite ore necessitated maj regional shifts, it became increasingly relocated on t coast.

The other significant industrial development in Sou Wales saw the south-western corner of the Coalfield emer as a centre of non-ferrous metal smelting (particularly copper). Entrepreneurs were attracted into the district b the availability of good smelting coal, and the ease importing ores from Anglesey and Cornwall. The mov ment of tinplate manufacture from the Pontypool area Swansea and Llanelly furthered the region's significance a metalliferous centre. Coalmining also expanded, as t growth of metal smelting required ever increasing qua tities of coal, and during this period coal was mined main for this purpose. It was not until the 1850s that the era sale-coal mining really began and witnessed a half centu or so which completely transformed the rural valleys of t Coalfield into crowded, vibrant strips of settlement a intense economic activity.

With its general lack of an industrial base, South Wal was ill-fitted for the sudden requirements made of it. addition to a paucity of capital the region suffered from unsatisfactory supply of labour; a sparse, unskilled a widely distributed population was not conducive to t creation of a viable industrial labour force. Thus to inordinate degree the industrial growth of South Wales w dependent upon the large-scale movement of people in the coalfield areas. Up until the middle of the 19th centu people came chiefly from the surrounding rural area supplemented by a specific movement of Irish, especially Merthyr Tydfil. As knowledge and communications in proved, and as markets for coal dramatically expande more workers were needed. After 1850, England becan the main source of the immigrant population, a trend whi brought about the erosion of the native Welsh language.

The other early drawback to industrial growth was t poor condition of the transport network. The turnpi roads helped improve communications in the rural areas not without their problems, as evidenced in the Rebec Riots – but industrialization demanded a more effecti means of bulk carriage. This was afforded by the co struction of a number of canals which linked the northe rim of the Coalfield to the coast, an improvement whi sufficed until the 1840s, when, with the advent of stea technology, railways began to replace the canals. Ra traffic provided outlets for the produce of the emergi coal-mining valleys by way of the ports of Swansea, Card and Newport.

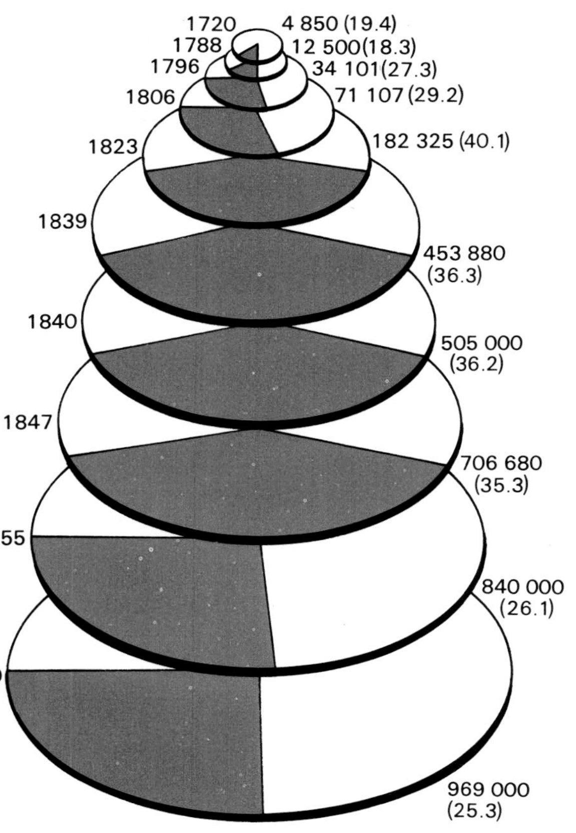

Pig iron output in South Wales 1720–1869, expressed as a proportion of total British production. Figures are given in tons. The percentage of the South Wales output is shown in brackets.

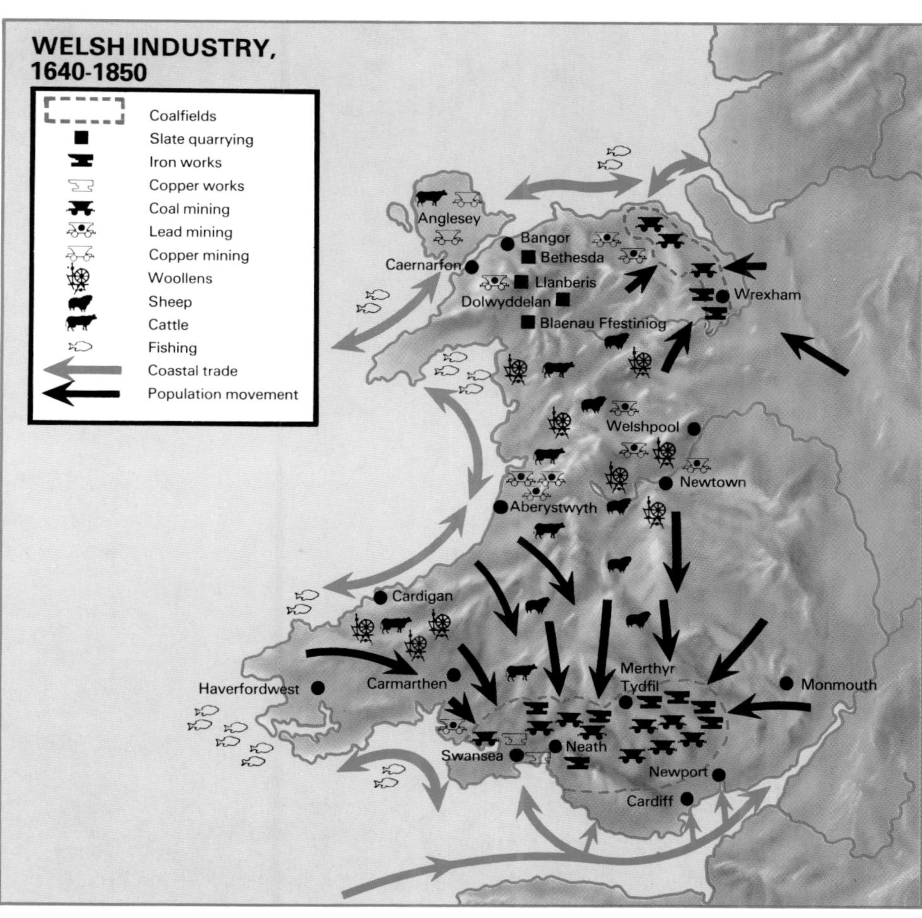

The progress of Welsh industry, 1640–1850. The main areas of heavy industry were in the North-East and, by the 1850s, within the South Wales Coalfield.

North-east Wales also saw more intensive activity as the vantages of a coalfield location increased, and by the iddle of the 19th century a belt of iron works had formed a all 'Black Country' between Brymbo and Acrefair, with rexham as the commercial centre. Coalmining had also dergone a substantial growth and in 1840 there were ore miners employed than in South Wales, a lead which s very rapidly eclipsed during the following decade. ıtside the coalfields, industrial activity included lead ning which was still fairly widely distributed but with an creasing concentration in north Cardiganshire; copper ning in Anglesey, which like that of lead, had undergone bstantial developments since the early 18th century; slate arrying, which grew into the major single economic ivity of north-west Wales during the early 19th century; d woollen manufacture, which made rapid progress up to e end of the 18th century, especially in Montgomeryshire d Merionethshire.

Thus, by the middle of the 19th century, the complexion Wales had changed. Though the major part of the land a remained of necessity backward, rural and sedentary, attraction of easily mined coal had created in the north-t corner and over a large part of the south of the country, more varied society. Industrialization had come into les from outside, but as yet it had not undermined the ive tongue, nor transformed Welsh culture. Though this s to occur to a greater extent in the South than in the rth as the English moved in to supply a work-force for phenomenal expansion of the sale-coal industry after 50, the South Wales Coalfield succeeded in holding on to Nonconformist values which made it a distinctly erent industrial region from its English counterparts.

Below: Copper workings at Holywell, Flintshire, in the Welsh Marches.

Politics and Domestic Affairs, 1715–1815

Within the bewildering patchwork of political and domestic events which marked this century, several broad threads can be discerned. First, the opening of the period saw the very last of a long series of crises over the succession to the English throne. Henceforth, except for Scottish dissidents, disputes were largely to be about what powers the monarch should have rather than whom he or she should be. And this is the second theme: the evolution of a constitutional monarchy with a correspondingly powerful Parliament. The transition was not easy. Not until the last two decades of the 18th century was royal power eroded to an extent which would make the term constitutional monarchy appropriate. Third, we see the evolution of cabinet government, the effective establishment of the office of Prime Minister, and the clearer demarcation of political parties. Fourth, and fundamentally, the period stood in sharp contrast to the turbulent affairs of the previous century.

Notwithstanding the Jacobite rebellions, troubles in Ireland, and various popular disturbances from time to time, the period was one of domestic tranquillity. During this period architecture, music, literature and drama flourished (over 100 provincial theatres were built): Georgian has come to have a special meaning of its own, denoting elegance, cultivation and stability. And finally, we may note the momentous rise in Britain's prosperity, based on industrial and commercial advances, with all the social problems and economic opportunities these provided. Wealth, too, lay behind Great Britain's growing national strength, which manifested itself in the forging of an empire and defeat at Waterloo of France, Britain's traditional foe.

At the risk of oversimplifying a complex episode, the accession to the throne in 1714 by George of Hanover, as King George I of England, after Queen Anne's death can be described as a victory for the liberal Whigs over the traditional High Church Tories (some were suspected of Catholic sympathies), who were generally supporters of monarchical power. Simplifying even further, we can say that the first half of the 18th century was marked by Whig ascendancy and a relative rise in parliamentary power and prestige at the expense of the Crown. After the accession of George III (1760), the King reasserted a large measure of personal rule until a series of disastrous policies in the 1770s, the effective parliamentary leadership of Pitt and the King's failing health, reversed the process.

During the period, too, the House of Commons gradually gained influence relative to the House of Lords, especially in questions of taxation and finance. The opening of the Hanoverian era was inauspicious. In 1715 came the first Jacobite rebellion, and for a time opposition to the new king threatened to reach dangerous proportions. But internal peace and prosperity helped to promote stability. Georgian England was the great era of the country house, designed by Vanbrugh, Hawksmoor, the Adam brothers and their imitators. Chippendale and others designed the furniture for these houses, whose gardens were laid out by men such as Capability Brown and whose rooms were decorated with the works of the British School of artists – Reynolds, Gainsborough, Constable and Turner. The English theatre also enjoyed a renaissance with Goldsmith and Sheridan heading a list of British dramatists. The elegant music of Handel, Arne and Boyce filled fashionable churches and aristocratic drawing rooms.

But such development of national life and prosperity depended upon political stability and internal peace. Once the Jacobite rising of 1715–6 had been put down, the Whigs, successful in the 1716 elections, rushed through the Septennial Act which prolonged the life of Parliament from

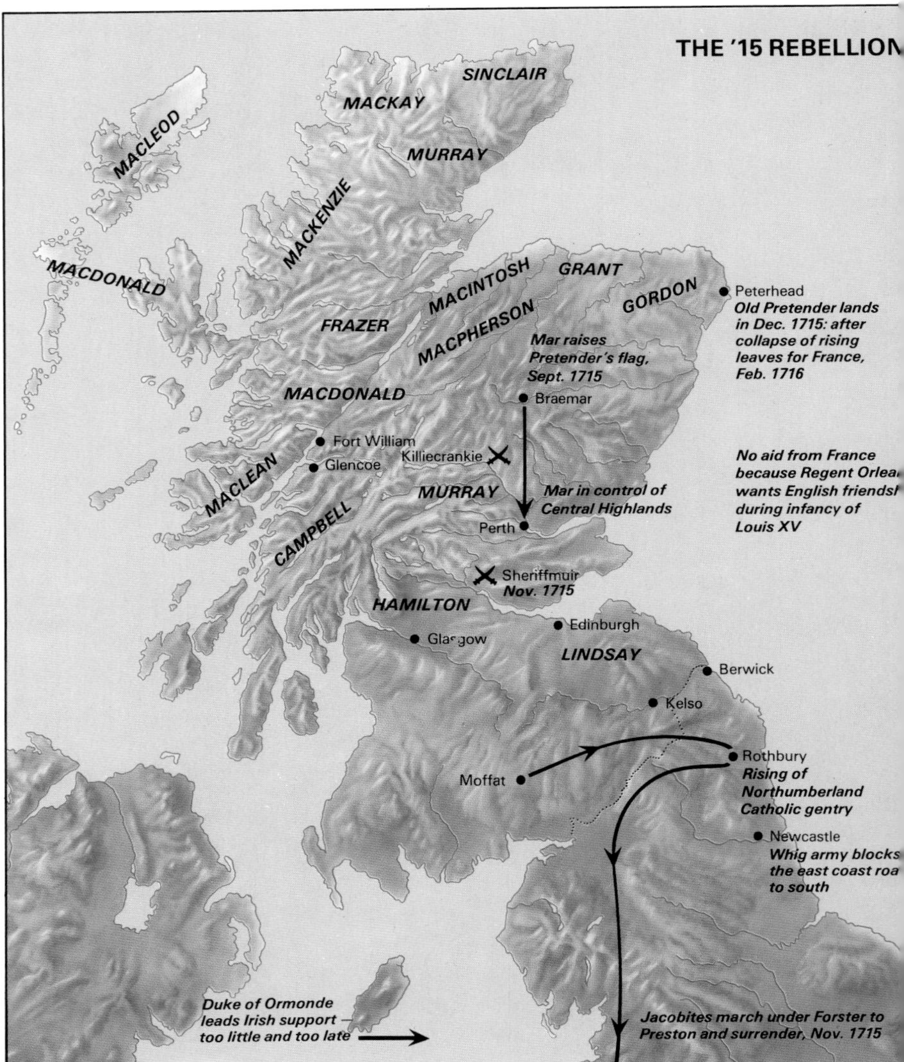

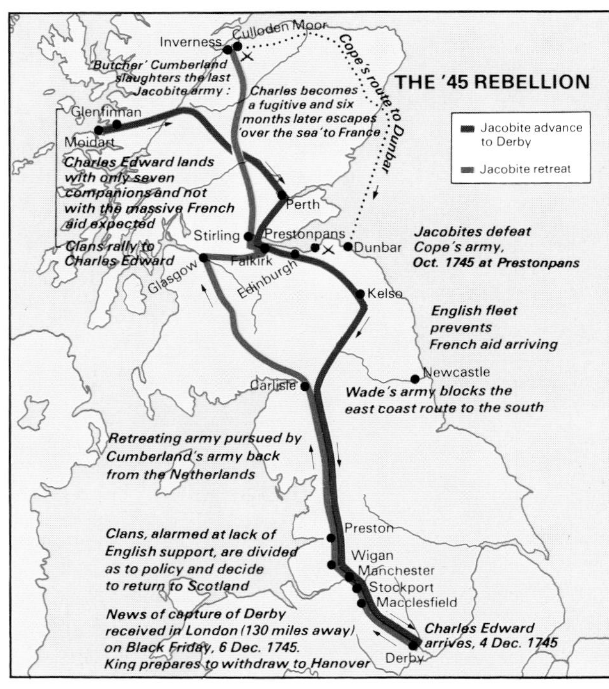

Prince George of Hanove accession to the English throne in 1714 heralded the first Jacobite rebellion in support of 'James III', son James II. The Jacobite area of northern England, the South-West and Scotland agreed to rise together, but only the Highland rebellion proved of real significance. There the Earl of Mar collected an army of about 12,000, largely untrained Highlanders, but was defea by the Duke of Argyll at Sheriffmuir.

In 1745 Prince Charles Edward Stuart landed from France with seven followers He raised an initially successful army. After victo at Prestonpans he led his ar as far south as Derby but w then forced to retreat. The revolt finally ended on 16 April 1746 on Culloden Mo

ree to seven years. This gave them time to ensure the
orking of their two main policies: lowering taxes to attract
e support of the landed gentry, and religious toleration to
n the support of the Nonconformists.
George I found it difficult to understand English, and did
t preside over meetings of his Cabinet as Queen Anne
d done. He left that duty to his first, or Prime, Minister.
ter a series of short-lived ministries, George I handed
wer to a Norfolk squire, Sir Robert Walpole, who had
fended the King, his mistresses and fellow-ministers
m public attack after the collapse of the South Sea
bble in 1720. Walpole, the first effective Prime Minister,
minated politics throughout the 1720s and 1730s. He
countered, nonetheless, growing parliamentary oppo-
ion which wanted commercial expansion at the expenses
Spanish interests in South America, and French interests
India, Canada, West Africa and the West Indies. William
t (later Earl of Chatham), a powerful orator, became
okesman for this opposition and the clamour for action
ally forced an unwilling Walpole to declare war on Spain
1739 and on France in 1740. Initial military setbacks and
wing unrest in Scotland (leading eventually to the
ond Jacobite Rebellion) caused Walpole's resignation in
42. Subsequently, however, British fortunes improved,

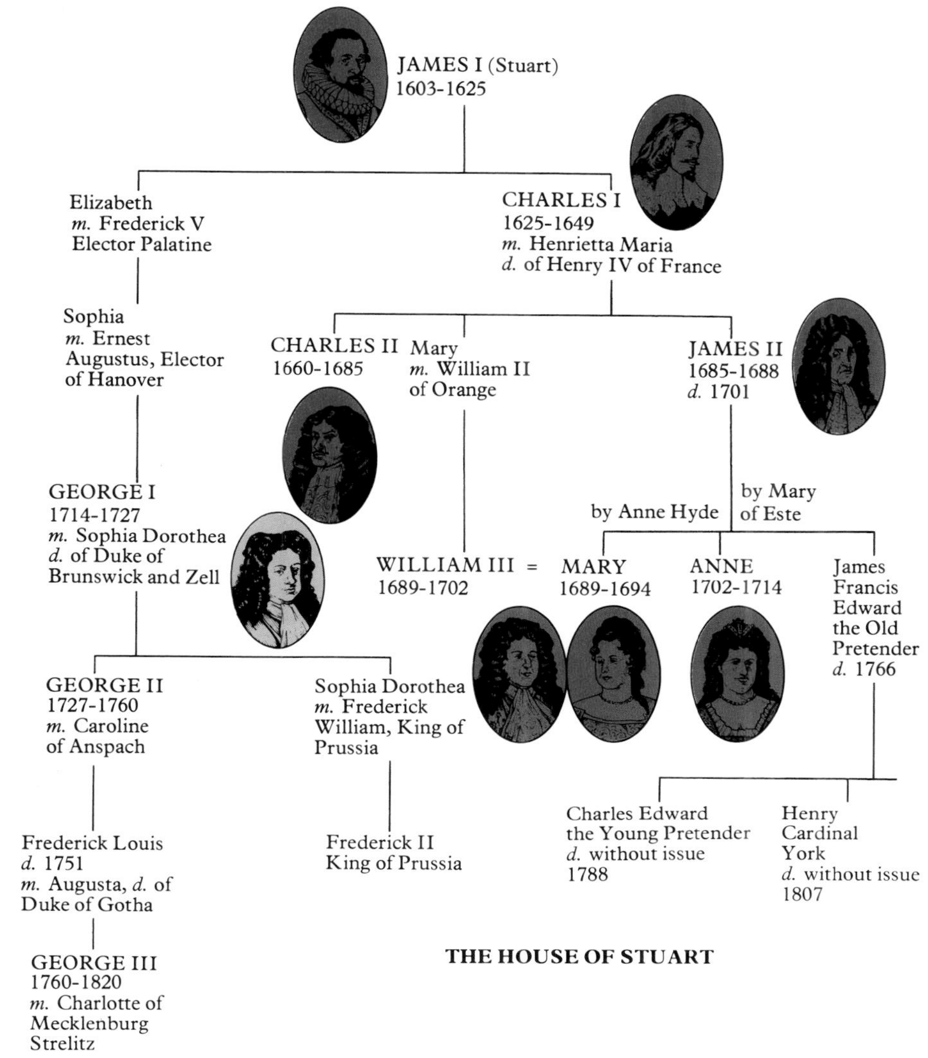

THE HOUSE OF STUART

and by the death of George II, in 1760, the basis had been laid for the future development of an Empire in India and Canada, the West Indies and West Africa.

George III, grandson of George II, succeeded to the throne at the age of 22. He soon clashed both with Parliament and with public opinion. Opposition to the King's reassertion of monarchical power became widespread, and protests centred around the figure of John Wilkes, who attacked royal policies in *The North Briton*. Wilkes became the popular champion of 'Liberty', and disturbances flared in various parts of the country.

It was really the loss of the American colonies that brought opposition to a head, and in 1780 there was a parliamentary majority for John Dunning's famous resolution 'that the influence of the Crown has increased, is increasing, and ought to be diminished'.

In the wake of a deep constitutional crisis, during which the King forced the resignation of the Fox–North coalition in 1783, the brilliant younger Pitt became Prime Minister at the age of 24. Pitt's astute policies, coupled with Britain's commercial strength, the ill-health of the King (who suffered bouts of insanity from 1788 and was finally obliged to accede to a Regency in 1811), and the national unity forged during the French and Napoleonic Wars between 1793 and 1815, all combined to produce an environment of constitutional stability and national purpose.

Above: The Stuart and Hanoverian successions.

Above left: Cartoon of George III showing the King studying a miniature of Cromwell – a reference to the belief that he was trying to set himself up as an absolute ruler. In fact he was merely using his royal power as laid down in the various acts which made up the Revolutionary Settlement after 1688.

Far left: Vauxhall Gardens, the fashionable pleasure park beside the Thames in London, in 1809.

Wars and Warfare, 1715–83

Opposite: The world in 1713–15 and in 1763. In Europe the Seven Years' War (1756–63) brought little change in the balance of power but it settled the rivalry of France and Britain in America and India, decisively in Britain's favour.

Great Britain's main interest in wars of this period was to employ her wealth and naval power to win colonies. Continental commitments had a lower priority, but were necessary to defend the territory of Britain's Hanoverian kings and to remove French manpower from the colonial conflict. Such objectives were achieved by subsidies to allies, the employment of mercenaries and of small, but significant, British contingents.

The period opens for Britain with 25 years of almost total peace but, by the 1730s, rivalry with the French in India and clashes with Spain in America foreshadowed the ensuing world struggle for empire. In 1739, Britain went to war with Spain (War of Jenkins' Ear) and this conflict soon merged into the general European war of Austrian Succession (1740–8) in which Britain, Hanover and Austria were opposed to France, Spain and the rising power of Prussia. The continental war was distinguished for Britain by the victory of the allies commanded by King George II at Dettingen (1743), the last battle fought by a king of England, and the defeat of Fontenoy (1745) which was followed by the withdrawal of the British troops to combat the French-inspired Jacobite Rebellion led by the Young Pretender. Overseas, the French were successful in southern India, capturing Madras in 1746, while the English captured the French naval base of Louisburg at the mouth of the St Lawrence. Both conquests were restored by the Treaty of Aix-la-Chapelle in 1748 and this war must be seen as a dress rehearsal for the contest that was to come.

The Seven Years' War (1756–63) saw a change of partners, Prussia now allied to Britain and Austria to France. The continental war was centred on the brilliant campaigns of Frederick the Great to save Prussia from the combined attentions of France, Austria and Russia, while an Anglo-Hanoverian army intermittently guarded his west flank and won the battle of Minden in 1759. The main British interest, however, was overseas where, after a poor start, the global strategy of William Pitt the Elder was brilliantly successful. In the East, Robert Clive conquered Bengal after the battle of Plassey in 1757 and opened northern India to eventual British control, while Fren power in southern India was eliminated after the battle Wandiwash in 1760. In America, the French were driv out of Canada after the capture of Quebec in 1759 and Montreal in 1760. The key to these far-flung victories, a to many others from the West Indies to as far afield as t Philippines, was Britain's complete mastery of the seas af the naval victories over the French at Lagos and Quiber Bay in 1759. British interest in the war declined after th successes and, to her shame, she deserted Prussia in 17 The Treaty of Paris (1763) confirmed most of the Brit conquests and was an expression of the fact that Britain v now unchallenged as a naval and colonial power.

Retribution was to follow. With the end of the dan from French Canada, the American colonists no lon needed British military assistance and bitterly resen attempts to tax them to pay for their defence. Argument a armed clashes led to the War of American Independe (1775–83), in which British and mercenary troops soon bogged down in the immense task of forcing the rebels return to their allegiance. American success was assu after the surrender of General Burgoyne's army at Sarat in 1777 led to the entry of the French on the American si an example soon followed by most other European powe eager to avenge past humiliations at British hands. Brit survived alone remarkably well, but a temporary loss control of the sea allowed a French naval squadron a French and American troops to force the surrender General Cornwallis at Yorktown in 1781. Britain n recognized American independence in order to concentr on a successful defence of the rest of her empire, losing o Minorca and Florida to Spain by the Peace of Versai (1783). A marvellous opportunity to humble their ri even to invade Britain itself, had been lost by the muddl and indecision of France and Spain and their allies, w before the end of the war Britain had regained that cont of the sea on which her success depended.

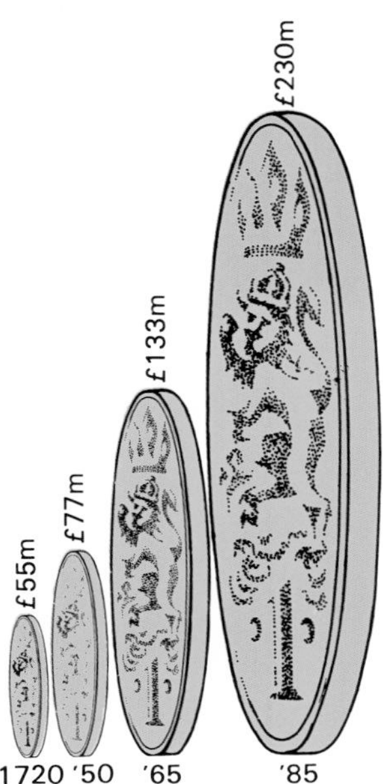

National Debt growth between 1715 and 1783. England's success in her 18th-century wars depended heavily on the government's ability to borrow money to pay for men and munitions and to subsidize her allies. Each coin marks a post-war period.

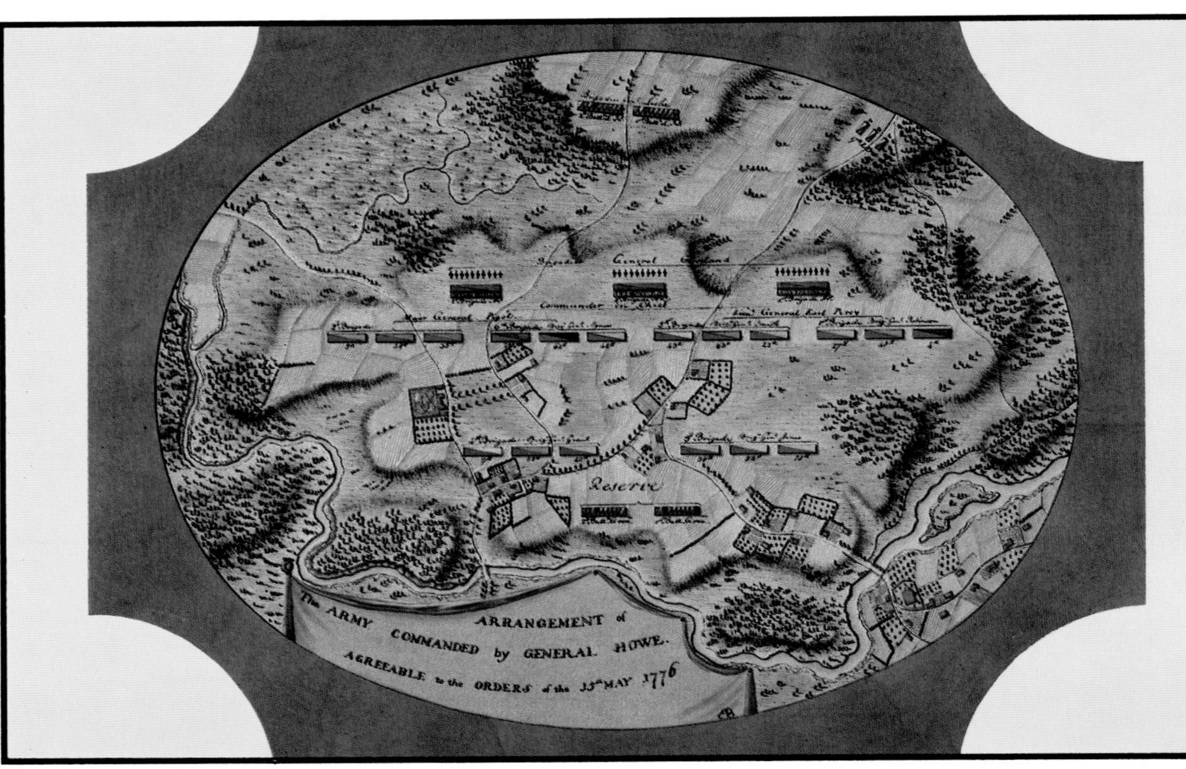

Disposition of troops by the British General Howe during the American Revolution. The British forces, although more experienced, were almost always outnumbered by the Patriot soldiers, while the British had serious problems of supply and communications. The Patriots were able to withdraw into the interior and were familiar with the countryside, and were motivated by burning ideals, while the British had no strong commitment.

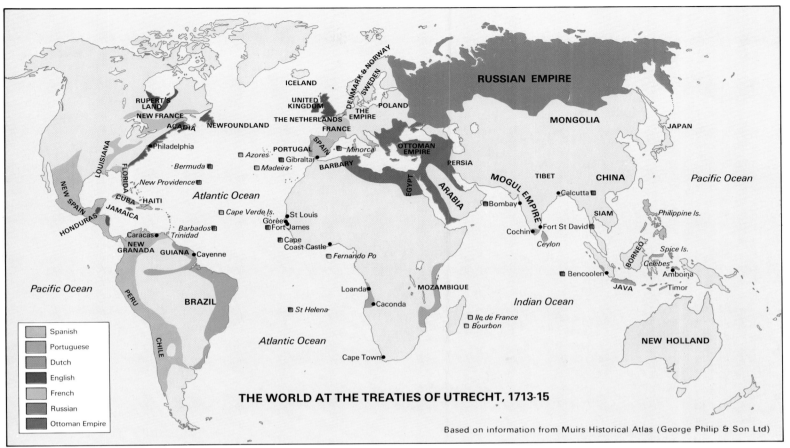

THE WORLD AT THE TREATIES OF UTRECHT, 1713-15

- Spanish
- Portuguese
- Dutch
- English
- French
- Russian
- Ottoman Empire

Based on information from Muirs Historical Atlas (George Philip & Son Ltd)

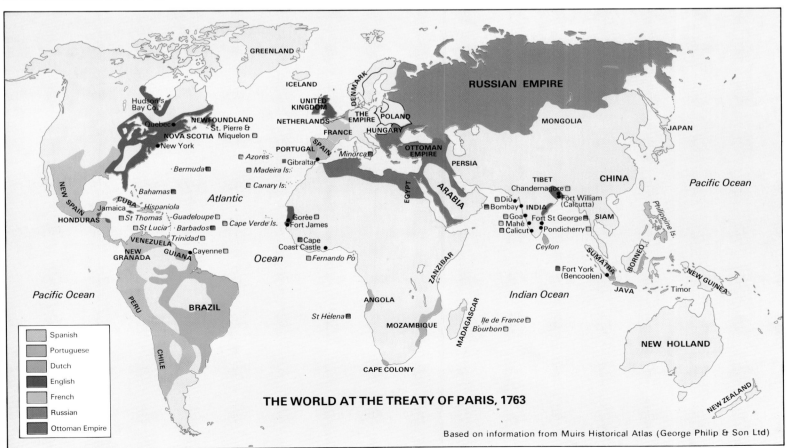

THE WORLD AT THE TREATY OF PARIS, 1763

- Spanish
- Portuguese
- Dutch
- English
- French
- Russian
- Ottoman Empire

Based on information from Muirs Historical Atlas (George Philip & Son Ltd)

Britain and the Napoleonic Wars, 1793–1815

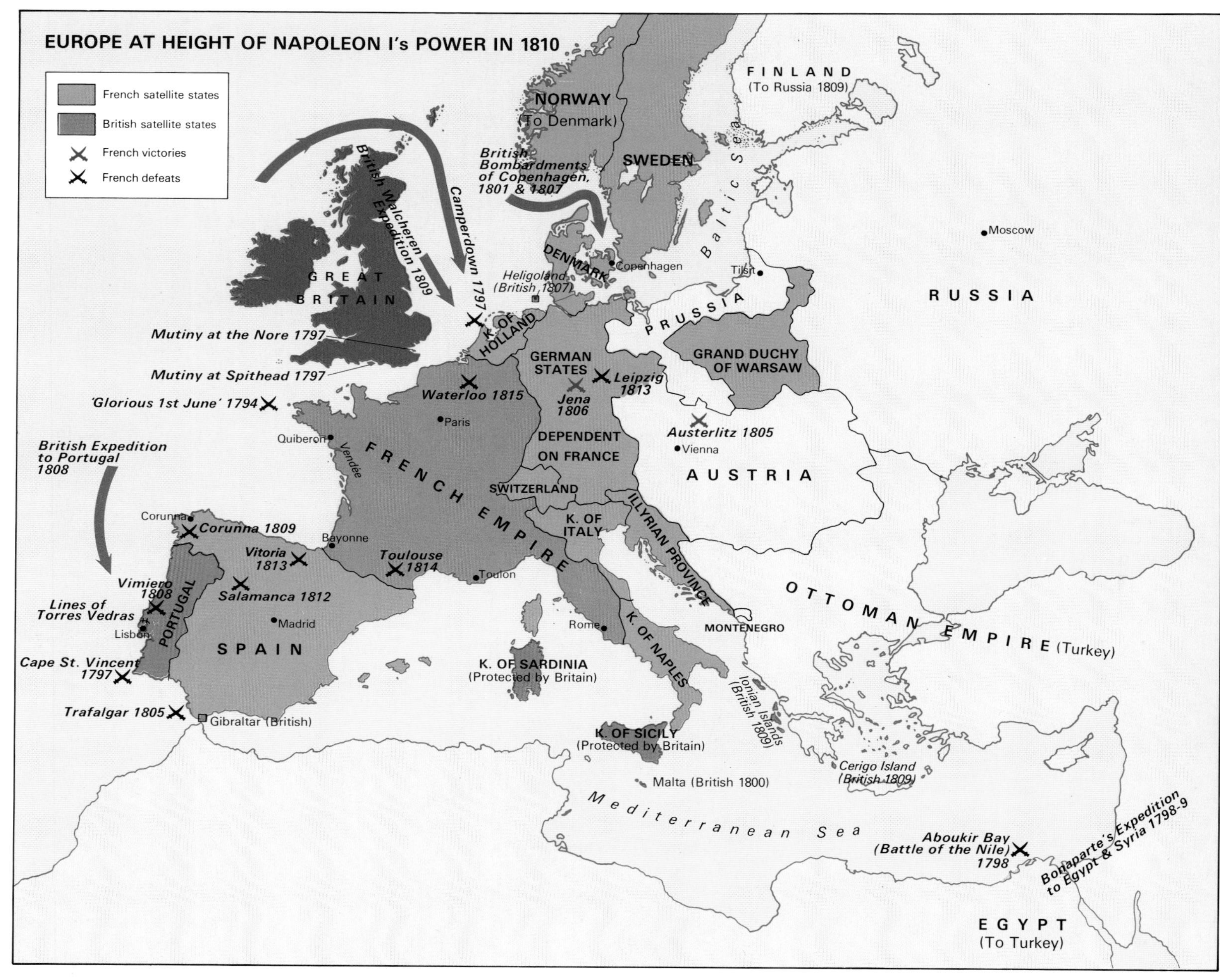

Europe in 1810. British policy was to use her naval power to prevent neutral nations from trading with France and French satellite states. British naval supremacy was established by major victories at Aboukir Bay in 1798 and Cape Trafalgar in 1805. Napoleon's response was to construct his 'continental system', designed to cut British trade with those European markets dominated by France. Nationalist revolts against French occupation of Portugal and Spain enabled Britain to land and supply the Peninsular army commanded by Wellington.

Great Britain was at first indifferent or even sympathetic to the French Revolution (1789). William Pitt the Younger (Prime Minister, 1783–1801) was preoccupied with financial reform and believed that the Revolution would weaken France. So, when France declared war on Austria and Prussia in 1792, he stood aside. But the French Republic's encouragement of revolutions elsewhere, its occupation of Belgium and the execution of Louis XVI at the beginning of 1793 led to war in February of that year. Britain formed an unstable coalition with Austria, Prussia, Sardinia, Spain and Holland, and adopted the policy she was to follow for two decades of subsidizing continental allies and using her navy to blockade France and seize French colonies. Direct intervention was limited to a tiny expedition to Belgium and to ineffective help to revolts in France. Although the victory of 'The Glorious First of June' (1794) confirmed British naval supremacy, by 1795 France's mass armies had forced Prussia, Spain and Holland to peace. Spain and Holland then joined France's naval and colonial war against Britain. After Napoleon Bonaparte's victorious Italian campaign, Austria also concluded peace (Campo Formio, October 1797), recognizing France's annexation of Belgium and accepting the creation of French satellite 'sister republics' in western Europe. Britain therefore had to oppose French power on her own.

In 1797, despite mutinies in the fleets at Spithead and the Nore, a threat of invasion was avoided by naval victories over Spain off Cape St Vincent in February and over Holland off Camperdown in October. In 1798 France attacked Britain indirectly when Napoleon undertook his expedition to Egypt to threaten the land route to India. However, Nelson's destruction of the French fleet at Aboukir Bay in August and the failure of his own Syrian campaign, compelled Napoleon to return to France. Here, in November 1799, he seized power and began his rule as

First Consul and later, in 1804, as Emperor.

Napoleon's Egyptian expedition had allowed Britain to build and subsidize a Second Coalition with Austria and Russia early in 1799. But Austro-Russian campaigns in Switzerland and Italy collapsed amid mutual recriminations, and Russia withdrew from the war. Decisive military defeats forced Austria to peace in February 1801 and to recognize French control of western Europe. British isolation increased when Russia, Denmark, and Sweden formed the Armed Neutrality (1800) against British interference with neutral shipping to enforce her permanent blockade of France. The death of Tsar Paul and Nelson's bombardment of the Danish fleet at Copenhagen in April 1801 – an event repeated in 1807 – broke up this association, but Britain had to make peace with France at Amiens in March 1802.

The Third and Fourth Coalitions

The peace was merely a truce. Britain could not accept France's hegemony in western Europe and war broke out again in May 1803. The formation by Pitt (Prime Minister, 1804–6) of a Third Coalition with Austria and Russia forced Napoleon to abandon his plans to invade Britain – just a month before Nelson destroyed a Franco-Spanish fleet off Trafalgar on 21 October 1805. This naval victory showed France could not inflict direct military defeat on Britain. From 1805 to 1807 Napoleon entrenched and extended his power, establishing his family as rulers as far east as Poland: first Austria (1805), then Prussia (1806) and finally Russia (1807) were defeated. These victories over the European powers encouraged Napoleon to try to ruin Britain's economic power through his 'continental system'. From 1806 he prohibited the import of British goods into France or French dependents. British industry suffered badly, especially in 1811, as exports slumped, although expanding South American markets provided some relief. Britain retaliated with 'Orders in Council' (1807), which prevented neutrals trading with Napoleon's empire, action which eventually caused war with the United States of America (1812–14).

To enforce the 'continental system', Napoleon invaded Portugal in 1808 and imposed his brother on Spain as king in 1809. The widespread national revolts there allowed Britain to use her naval power to mount and supply a major continental campaign. In 1808 Wellington was sent to Portugal and defeated the French at Vimiero; in 1809, after the Walcheren expedition to seize Antwerp failed, Wellington returned. For two years he occupied large numbers of French in the Iberian peninsula by retreating continually behind the defensive lines of Torres Vedras outside Lisbon and waging a skilful war of attrition. In July 1812 Napoleon's withdrawal of troops for his ill-fated Russian campaign enabled Wellington to win an important victory at Salamanca.

After Napoleon's disaster in Russia, Prussia and then Austria allied with Russia and Britain. This Fourth Coalition, heavily subsidized by Britain, decisively defeated Napoleon at Leipzig in October 1813. Wellington meanwhile defeated the French at Vittoria in June, expelled them from Spain and invaded France, winning the battle of Toulouse in April 1814. But it was the invasion of Britain's allies which forced Napoleon's abdication in April. Britain's Foreign Secretary, Lord Castlereagh, had largely kept the coalition together and Britain showed most determination in resisting Napoleon's attempt to regain power in 1815. It was also Wellington's army which played the greater part in Napoleon's final defeat at Waterloo on 18 June 1815.

The charge of the Life Guards at the Battle of Waterloo, after the painting by L. Clennell.

THE WATERLOO CAMPAIGN IN BELGIUM, 16-18 JUNE 1815
Prussians
British
French
Primary roads
Brussels
N
Waterloo
Wavre
Battle of 18 June
Wellington
Blücher
La Haye Sainte
Napoleon
Napoleon's Advance
Quatre Bras
Gembloux
Wellington
Blücher
Ney
Ligny
Battles of 16 June
Napoleon
Mons
Namur
Charleroi
To Paris

Left: Plan of the Waterloo campaign in Belgium, 16–18 June 1815. In the preliminary battles of Quatre Bras and Ligny, Napoleon had successfully divided the superior allied forces by defeating Blücher's Prussians. By 18 June, Napoleon's troops were concentrated against Wellington, whose army had retreated northwards toward Waterloo under leisurely pressure from Ney. French failure to account finally for Blücher's forces, the result of confused communications, allowed the Prussians to regroup and advance to rejoin Wellington. Despite a last charge by Ney, the combined allied forces proved too strong and by 8.15 pm victory was assured.

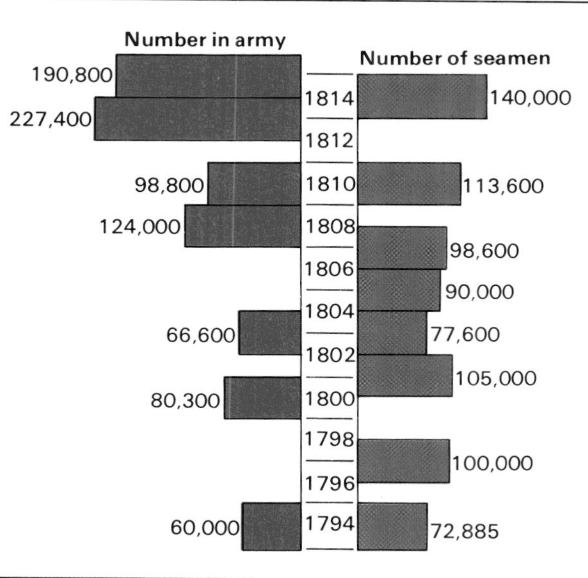

Growth of number of recruits in British Army (left-hand column) and Navy during the French and Napoleonic Wars.

India, 1700–1858

The death in 1707 of Aurangzeb, the last great Mughal Emperor, left a power vacuum in India which warring Mughal officials and northern invaders were eager to fill. British interests in the area were represented by the East India Company, a private trading company founded in 1601 whose territories were limited to the immediate surroundings of its trading posts at Bombay, Madras and Calcutta. The Company employed soldiers for defence and had diplomatic relations with local rulers, but was interested only in profits and not in territorial expansion.

It was intervention by the French in local rivalries in the Carnatic, the province surrounding Madras, and their capture of Madras itself in 1746, that inaugurated the process which led to British paramountcy. Madras was restored in 1748, but Anglo-French rivalry continued. Victories by Robert Clive at Arcot (1751) and Eyre Coote at Wandiwash (1760) assured British dominance in south-east India. The experience demonstrated the territorial and trading advantages of interference in local politics, the overwhelming superiority of European arms and military discipline against traditional Indian troops, and the significance of British sea power.

The seizure of Calcutta by the Nawab (Governor) of Bengal in 1756 led to much greater British intervention and demonstrated how defence of British interests led almost inevitably to territorial acquisition. Clive recaptured Calcutta and then defeated the Nawab at Plassey (1757), a victory consolidated at Buxar (1764). In 1765, Clive's treaty with the Mughal Emperor gave the Company financial, and hence in practice political, control of Bengal and Bihar, the richest region of India. Corruption and exploitation followed this sudden expansion of power and wealth, but was brought under control by Warren Hastings, the first Governor-General (1772–85), who also improved the administration and successfully defended British India against the French during the War of American Independence. The British government, alarmed that a private company should have such power, passed the Regulating Act (1773) and the India Act (1784) which introduced a considerable measure of government control over the Company.

Official policy opposed further territorial expansion, but this changed in the 1790s with the realization that only British control could end the constant wars and provide satisfactory conditions for trade, a belief given urgency by the threat of a French invasion of India after Napoleon's Egyptian expedition (1798–9). The architect of the new policy of aggression was Lord Wellesley (Governor-General, 1798–1805) who expanded British territory in the North-East to beyond Delhi and brought most of southern India under direct rule. He also perfected the subsidiary system which deprived independent states, such as Hyderabad (1798) and Oudh (1801), of all real power by treaties which placed their defence and foreign relations under British control in return for a guarantee of protection against foreign attack.

Ultimate supremacy was now inevitable, although Wellesley was recalled before he was able to subdue the Marathas, whose loose confederacy dominated most of central India. This was achieved by the Marquess of Hastings (Governor-General, 1813–23) who defeated the Marathas, suppressed the roving bands of freebooters called Pindaris and brought Rajputana under British protection. Britain's only potential enemies were now on the periphery. The most dangerous of these was the great Sikh state of the Punjab which was finally defeated and annexed in 1849.

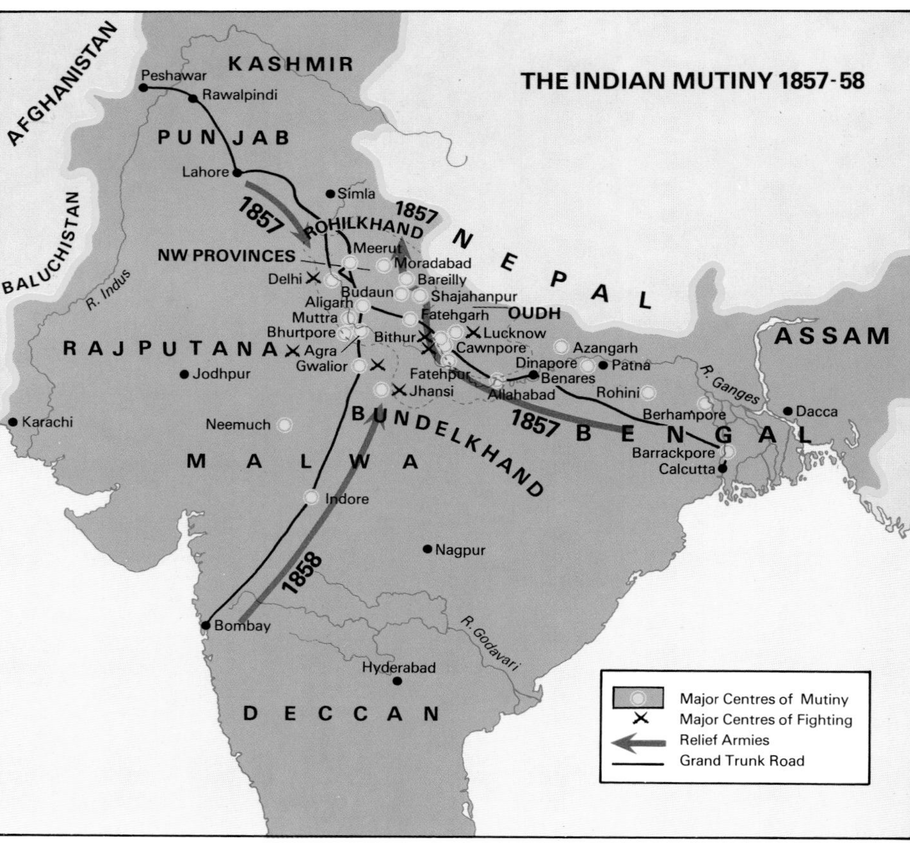

The extension of British control coincided with the opening up of India as an important market for British exports. The major growth took place after 1860, but already by the early 1850s the export of cotton textiles had grown from an insignificant level in 1815 to more than £6 million. In 1839 came the first shipment of Assam tea to Britain, though not until the 1860s did India and Ceylon make serious inroads into China's monopoly of the British tea market.

The huge area of British India was still ruled by the East India Company who increasingly became administrators pure and simple, as their trading monopoly was curtailed in 1813 and finally abolished in 1833. Administration became more efficient, but also more supercilious, as the 18th-century adventurers gave way to a new type of well-trained civil servant with an innate belief in the superiority of European culture and technology. English replaced Persian as the language of administration and a conscious effort was made to introduce Western ideas, a process which was accelerated by the impact of the machine-made goods and technology of the Industrial Revolution on the traditional Indian economy. Conservative reaction to such rapid westernization and jealousy of British power were important factors in the clash of civilizations and mutual barbarism which followed the mutiny of the Bengal army in 1857. But, although the Indian Mutiny briefly threatened British paramountcy, its suppression with the aid of loyal Indian troops, such as the recently conquered Sikhs, demonstrated that India was so divided in religion, politics and culture that many, if not most, Indians preferred British rule to that of their neighbours. The Mutiny brought an end to Company rule and the beginning of direct control by the Crown in 1858.

In 1857 there was less than one British soldier to every six Indian soldiers in India. Discipline in the Bengal Army was notoriously slack. On 10 May sepoys at Meerut, 40 miles north of Delhi, shot their British officers and then captured Delhi, where they proclaimed the elderly and bewildered Bahadur Shah II, the titular Mughal emperor, as their leader. The mutiny, sparked off by the introduction of new cartridges greased with fat which were unclean for both Muslims and Hindus, spread quickly through the Bengal Army. But Bombay, Bengal and the Punjab were held by the British who disarmed troops of doubtful loyalty. Relief armies, of British and loyal Indian troops (especially Sikhs and Gurkhas), advanced on the rebellious regions and by 20 June 1858 the Mutiny was virtually over.

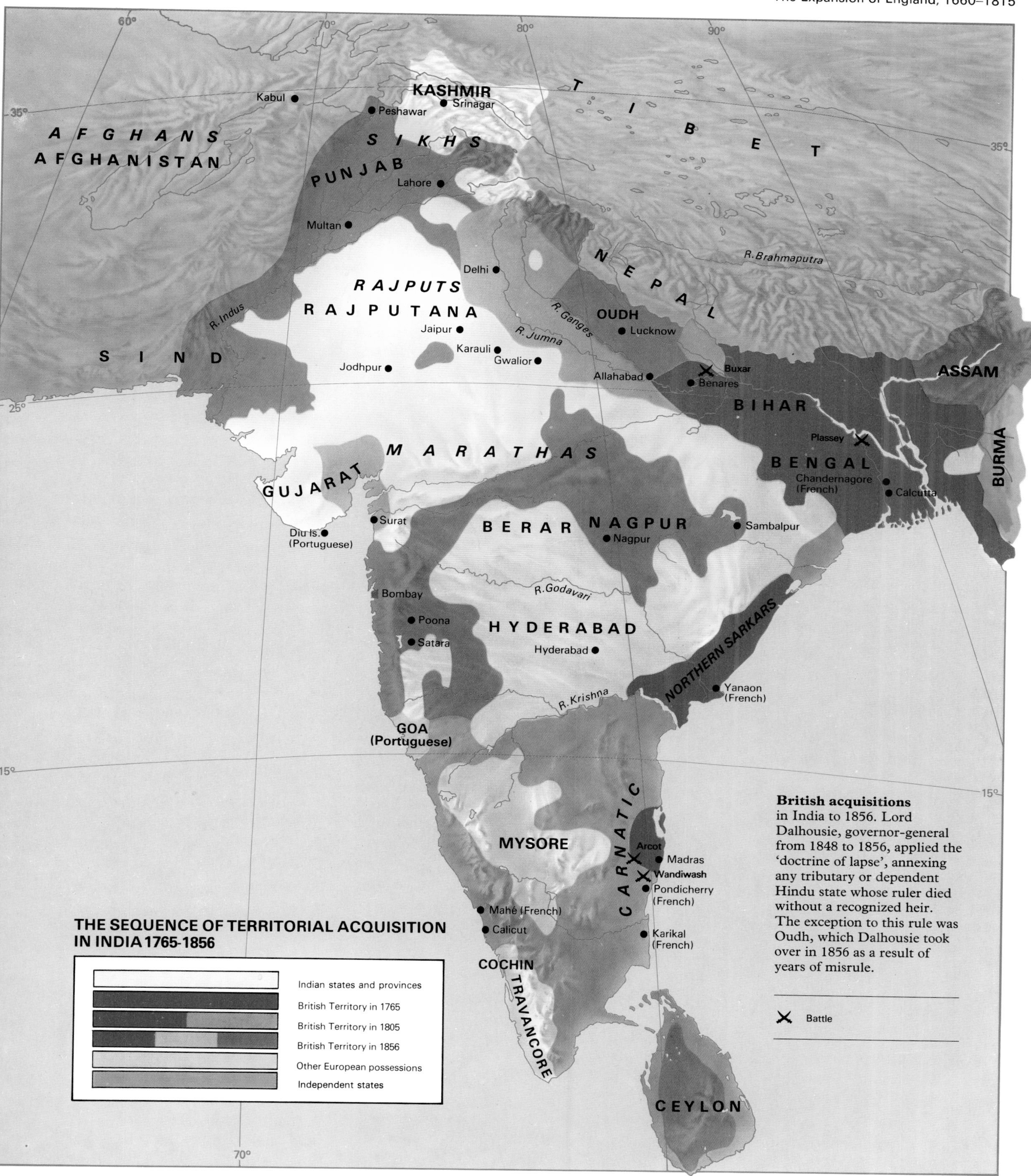

British acquisitions in India to 1856. Lord Dalhousie, governor-general from 1848 to 1856, applied the 'doctrine of lapse', annexing any tributary or dependent Hindu state whose ruler died without a recognized heir. The exception to this rule was Oudh, which Dalhousie took over in 1856 as a result of years of misrule.

Chapter Five

POWER, PEACE AND PROSPERITY, 1815-1914

For nearly a century following the Battle of Waterloo in 1815 Britain enjoyed a period of relative peace during which her industries flourished, her Empire expanded, and her navy safeguarded British interests throughout the world. Neither the Crimean War nor the numerous colonial wars made perceptible inroads into Britain's financial strength, while her influence and power grew for much of the 19th century. By the turn of the century, however, the growth of European rivals and unexpected reverses in the Boer War cast a shadow over Britain's role and position in world affairs.

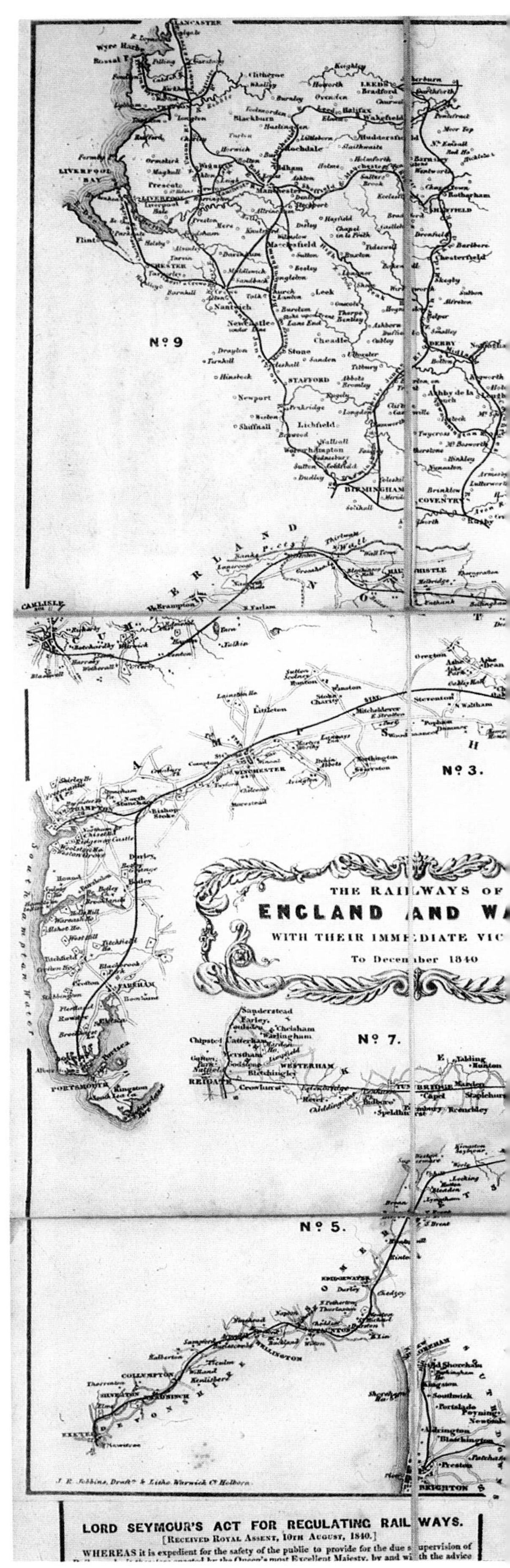

A contemporary map of the railways of England and Wales in 1841.

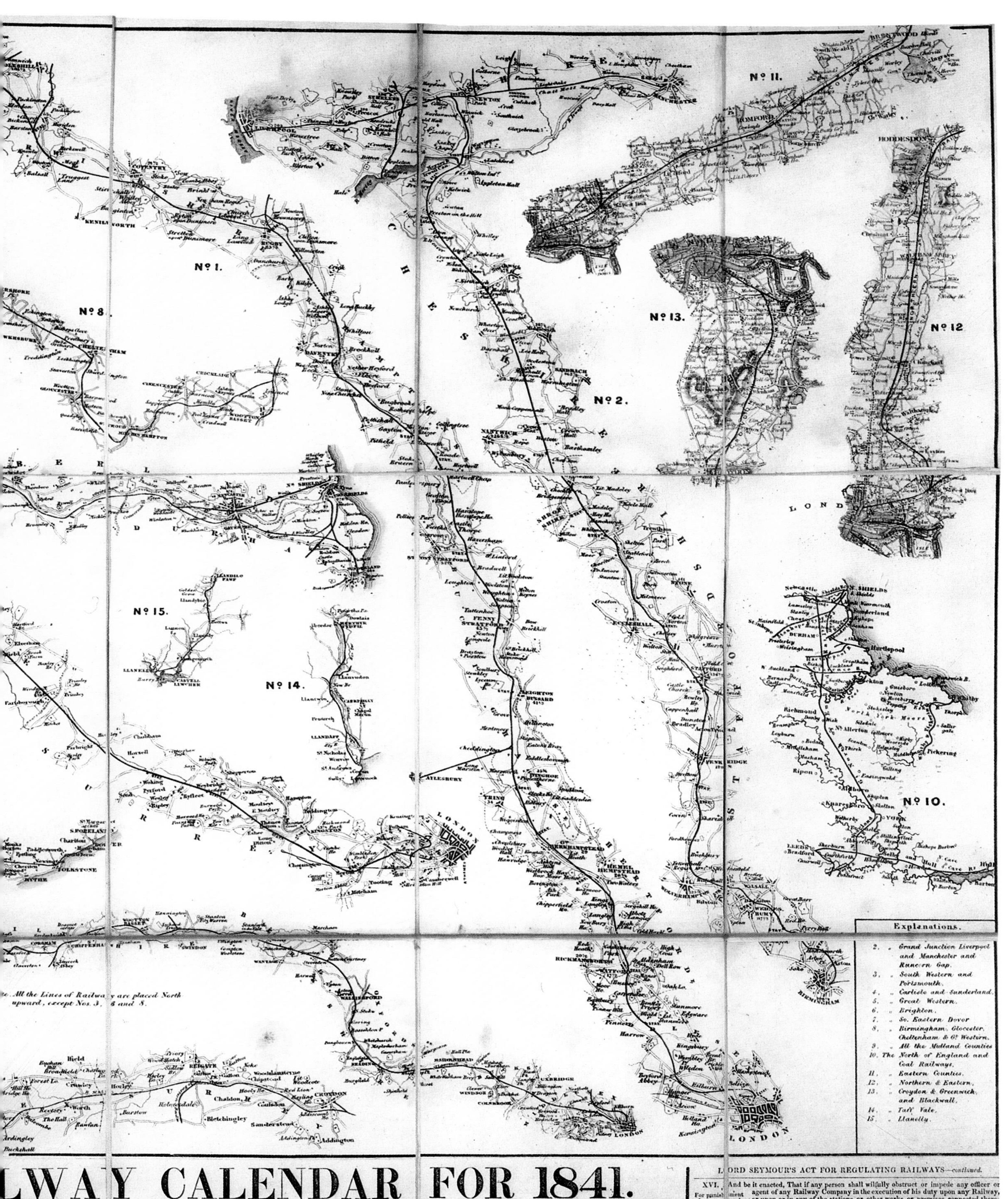
Nº 1.
Nº 2.
Nº 8.
Nº 10.
Nº 11.
Nº 12.
Nº 13.
Nº 14.
Nº 15.
LIVERPOOL
MANCHESTER
ROMFORD
BRENTWOOD
HODDESDON
LONDON
YORK
BIRMINGHAM
STAFFORD
AYLESBURY
FOLKSTONE
CROYDON
…te. All the Lines of Railway are placed North upward, except Nos. 3, 6 and 8.
Explanations.
2. " Grand Junction Liverpool and Manchester and Runcorn Gap.
3. " South Western and Portsmouth.
4. " Carlisle and Sunderland.
5. " Great Western.
6. " Brighton.
7. " So. Eastern Dover
8. " Birmingham, Glocester, Cheltenham & Gt. Western.
9. " All the Midland Counties
10. The North of England and Coal Railways.
11. " Eastern Counties.
12. " Northern & Eastern.
13. " Croydon & Greenwich, and Blackwall.
14. " Taff Vale.
15. " Llanelly.
…LWAY CALENDAR FOR 1841.
LORD SEYMOUR'S ACT FOR REGULATING RAILWAYS—continued.
XVI. And be it enacted, That if any person shall wilfully obstruct or impede any officer or agent of any Railway Company in the execution of his duty upon any Railway, or upon or in any of the stations or other works or premises connected there-
For punishment of persons ob-

Politics and Domestic Affairs, 1815–55

The period of peace between Waterloo and the outbreak of the Crimean War in 1854 has been called the Age of Reform. As the nation digested the political, social, and economic consequences of such momentous forces of change as the French Revolution, industrial and urban expansion and rapid population growth, so a series of fundamental reforms were carried through, many in the remarkable decades of the 1830s. These affected nearly all segments of Britain's varied society: institutions like Parliament, local authorities and the Church, and countless individuals from landowners, farmers, factory owners and merchants, to factory workers, miners and paupers.

Domestic affairs were influenced by four dominant themes, each the product of complex causes. First, there was the social unrest which flared periodically, especially in the troubled years after 1815, in the early 1830s, and again in the late 1840s when much of Europe was engulfed in revolution. Second, and related to this, were the unprecedented problems imposed on an archaic structure of local government by the evils of huge, insanitary towns containing large numbers of low-paid workers and paupers. Third was the enhanced role of central government as politicians tried to provide solutions to these problems. Finally, there was the rise of new classes. The middle classes, the newly prosperous commercial, industrial and professional men whose wealth reflected Britain's industrial revolution, naturally sought political influence and government policies attuned to their own enhanced status. The working classes included men whose crafts were made redundant by the industrial revolution as well as men who learned the new skills demanded by that revolution and who slowly learned to articulate their demands for a say in parliamentary affairs and an influence on the policies of the government.

Upsurge of Social Unrest

Immediately after Waterloo there was an upsurge of social unrest resulting from the large-scale unemployment caused by the two dislocations of the Napoleonic Wars, the spread of factory machines and by the deflationary policies of the government. At meetings and demonstrations resolutions were passed in favour of political and economic reform. To this the government, the memory of the excesses of the French Revolution fresh in mind, responded with a series of repressive measures aimed at increasing the powers of land-owning magistrates and impeding the freedom of radical spokesmen.

A period of 'enlightened Toryism' between 1822 and 1830 saw the prison, penal and legal reforms directed by Peel, whose Metropolitan Police Force served as a model for later provincial forces. Canning, the leader of these liberal Tories, supported the campaign for religious emancipation for Nonconformists, Jews and Catholics which came to a head between 1827 and 1829 and revealed the fluid nature of political loyalties and party affiliations. Wellington and Peel refused to serve under Canning in 1827 only to find that, on his death, Canningites, such as Huskisson and Palmerston, refused to serve under Wellington because of his opposition to emancipation. Eventually Wellington was forced to bring in the Catholic Emancipation Bill which further divided the Tories by alienating the die-hards.

Divisions in Tory ranks helped the Whigs to win the election of 1830 and so enabled them to bring in the Reform Bill. The Bill breached the traditional electoral system in favour of the middle classes, while ensuring that both that system and Parliament remained under the control of landowners. The reformed Parliament tackled some of the major problems of industrialized Britain and in so doing followed a Benthamite pattern: the Report of a Commission of Enquiry, followed by a debate leading to legislation setting up central and local authorities to administer the new law whose implementation was to be ensured by government-appointed inspectors and officials (whose further Reports might lead to additional legislation). This was the process followed for the passage of the first effective Factory and Mines Acts, of the Municipal Corporations Act which democratized local government, of the first Public Health Act which allowed the establishment of local boards of health empowered to deal with the problems of insanitary towns, and of the Poor Law Amendment Act aimed at ending the costly Speenhamland system of outdoor relief.

A significant feature of much of this legislation was the creation of Boards in Whitehall to supervise the work of the local authorities and government-appointed inspectors. Some critics saw this as the growth of an unpopular Leviathan, but it might be better seen as a tentative attempt to find the right administrative structures to cope with the problems found in towns of the world's first industrial nation, as well as the basis for the later extension of the role of the state.

In the late 1830s two major reform campaigns were launched. The Chartist movement, largely working-class, aimed at social improvements through political and parliamentary reform. Formed in the wake of the 1832 Act, it gained some support during the periods of trade recession in 1837, 1841–2, but it collapsed in 1848, the year of European revolutions, due partly to internal dissension and partly to resolute action by the government which brought about improved economic conditions.

An Anti-Corn Law League was a largely middle-class movement, with its simple aim which was in line with the free trade trend pursued by Huskisson, Gladstone and Peel. The Corn Laws had been instituted in 1815 to protect farmers. Their repeal in 1846 was the economic counterpart of the political changes of 1832; a new, middle-class piper was now calling the tune.

The repeal of the Corn Laws, the work of a Tory government dependent on the votes of landowners and farmers, split the Tory Party into a Peelite majority, including future Prime Ministers in Aberdeen and Gladstone, and a rump of backbenchers led by landowners such as Stanley and romantics such as Disraeli. The Peelites continued to be a force even after their leader's death in 1850, serving under Whig Prime Ministers such as Russell and Palmerston and providing their own Prime Minister of a Whig–Peelite coalition in Aberdeen. The gradual merger of the Peelites into the Whig party changed the nature of that party and won for it the title of Liberal.

The accession of Queen Victoria in 1837 was of some significance. The 18-year old Queen relied on her ministers for advice, and in particular she looked to Melbourne as to a father-figure. This eased the transition towards a constitutional monarchy, a process helped by the influence of Prince Albert. The Queen's marriage to the German Prince in 1840 had initially provoked hostility, but Albert came to understand the limitations of the sovereign's powers in his adopted country. He persuaded her to overcome her natural antipathy for Peel, Melbourne's opponent, and to accept him as a Prime Minister in 1841. Albert was also aware of the growing importance of industry throughout Europe and in organizing the Great Exhibition he hoped not only to enable British industrialists to show off but to provide them with a warning of overseas competition.

Inset: Lord John Russell, shown stalking over 'boroug mongers' in a cartoon from the period of the 1832 Refor Act, of which he was one of the framers.

Industrial unrest was widespread during this peric as new machinery and factories brought new worki methods and conditions and fear of unemployment. Anti-machinery riots took place, especially around the factory districts of Yorkshire, Lancashire and Nottinghamshire, between 1811 and 1816. The rioters were known as 'Luddites', taking the name from a half-witted Leicestershire boy, Ned Ludd, who had destroy two stocking-frames some 2 years earlier.

On 10 March 1817 a grou of Manchester workmen me intending to join rioters in Derby and march to Londor They were known as Blanketeers since each carrie a blanket or greatcoat. Their march was broken up near Stockport.

In 1830 agricultural riots against the use of machinery took place. Threatening lett under the name of the mythical Captain Swing wer sent to proprietors using machinery.

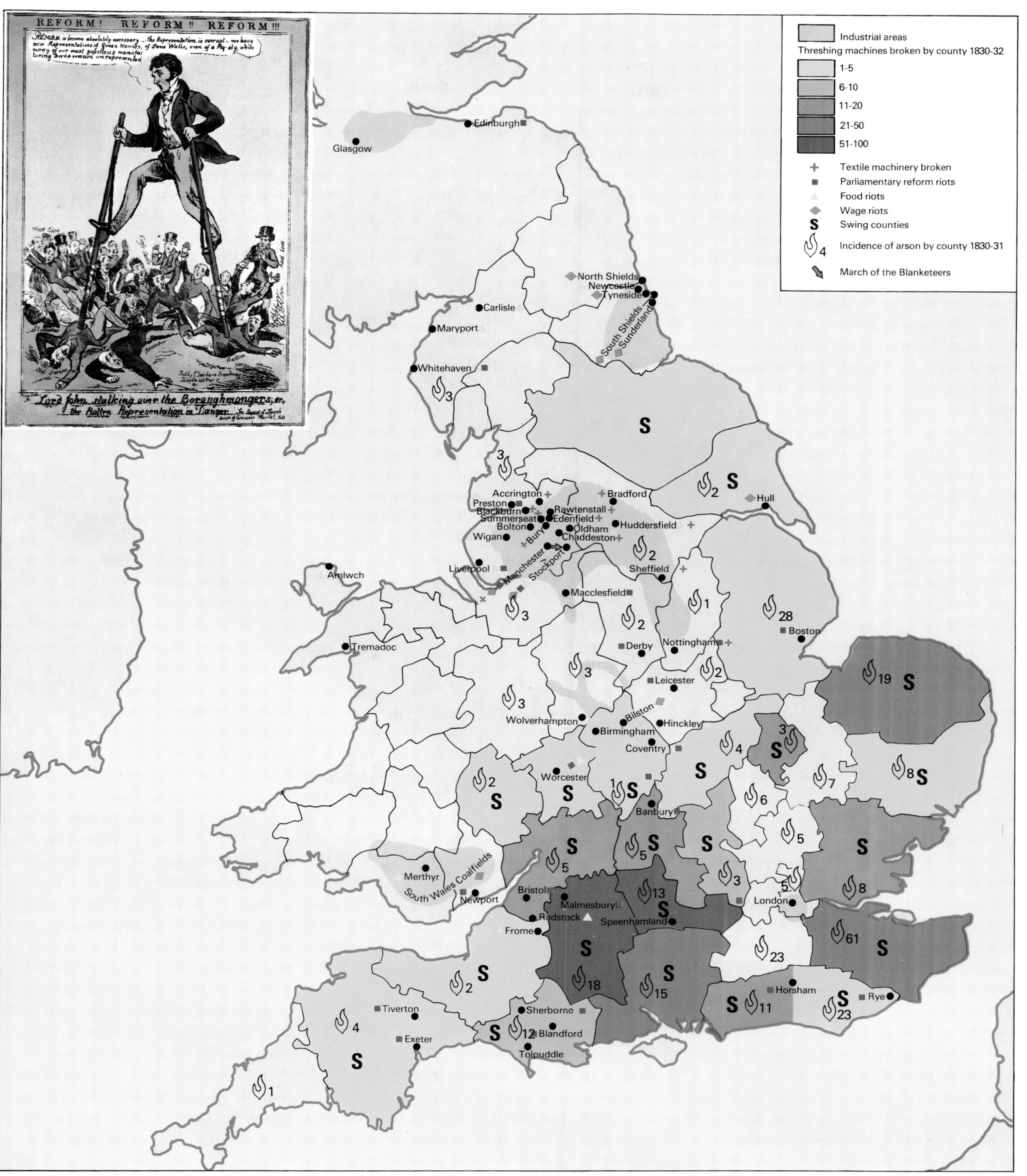

REFORM! REFORM!! REFORM!!!
Lord John stalking over the Boroughmongers; or, the Rotten Representation in Danger
Industrial areas
Threshing machines broken by county 1830-32
1-5
6-10
11-20
21-50
51-100
Textile machinery broken
Parliamentary reform riots
Food riots
Wage riots
Swing counties
Incidence of arson by county 1830-31
March of the Blanketeers
Edinburgh
Glasgow
North Shields
Newcastle
Tyneside
South Shields
Sunderland
Carlisle
Maryport
Whitehaven
Accrington
Bradford
Preston
Blackburn
Rawtenstall
Summerseat
Edenfield
Bolton
Oldham
Huddersfield
Wigan
Bury
Chaddeston
Hull
Sheffield
Liverpool
Manchester
Stockport
Amlwch
Macclesfield
Boston
Tremadoc
Derby
Nottingham
Leicester
Wolverhampton
Bilston
Hinckley
Birmingham
Coventry
Worcester
Banbury
Merthyr
South Wales Coalfields
Newport
Bristol
Malmesbury
Radstock
Speenhamland
London
Frome
Horsham
Rye
Sherborne
Tiverton
Blandford
Exeter
Tolpuddle

Parliamentary Reform, 1780–1928

The electoral system remained unreformed during the 18th century. By 1800 still only three percent of adult males possessed the vote. The ten counties south of Bristol and the lower Thames elected two-fifths of the House of Commons, and in individual constituencies the 'influence' of the land-owning class was as pervasive as ever in determining the outcome of elections. Pitt in 1785 sought to make the system more representative by proposing to chop away 36 of the more 'rotten' boroughs, but was defeated by a mixture of royal-cum-parliamentary opposition and prevailing public indifference.

By the 1820s the climate of expectations was quite different. A burgeoning commercial and professional middle class now explicitly demanded its own formal role on the political stage; a newly self-conscious working class sought as an end in itself the erosion of the aristocratic monopoly of power; and organizations like the Birmingham Political Union (led by the banker Thomas Attwood) emerged to channel these aspirations. The response to this on the part of Grey's Whig ministry was essentially one of shrewd calculation, with the result that the ensuing Reform Act of 1832 proved of decidedly mixed character and consequence. With the Act the old anomalies and abuses were modified rather than eradicated; and the rapidly expanding industrial cities in the North were still palpably under-represented. But the very fact that popular agitation had brought about parliamentary reform was undoubtedly instrumental in bringing the political class at Westminster to accept a more responsive relationship with public opinion as a whole. The subsequent verdict, attributed to Bright, that 'it was not a good Bill, but it was a great Act when it was passed' remains a telling assessment.

Further parliamentary reform was temporarily blocked as, over the next two decades, the bulk of the newly enfranchised middle class, successfully detached from their erstwhile radical associates, joined with the traditional governing order in resisting Chartist demands for such innovations as universal manhood suffrage, paid MPs and the secret ballot – demands that only died down with the general prosperity of the 1850s.

When the next round of franchise reform came, it did so partly because of renewed working-class agitation, especially in the shape of the Reform League. At the same time, a group of middle-class politicians (headed by Gladstone) was becoming aware that giving the vote to the now unimpeachably sober and responsible artisan element would help to bind tight not just the community at large but also a wide range of progressive opinion in the nascent Liberal Party. On the whole these hopes were justified, even though, following internal Liberal dissension in 1866 led by Lowe, the eventual Second Reform Act of 1867 was introduced by the Conservative Party under Derby and Disraeli. In introducing the Act the Conservatives sought to 'dish the Whigs', bid for the artisan vote, and arrange the redistribution of seats to benefit the landed interest.

Subsequent instalments of parliamentary reform were brought about in less contentious circumstances. In 1872 Gladstone's ministry passed the Ballot Act, overcoming the age-old argument that open voting was more 'manly', however turbulent the election. In 1883 the Corrupt and Secret Practices Act continued the process towards fairer elections by, among other measures, imposing a restriction on election expenses. The following year the Third Reform Act enfranchised, broadly speaking, miners and agricultural workers. And in 1885 the Redistribution of Seats Act ironed out most of the outstanding problems of over- and under-representation. Even so, by the eve of the First World War, with the Liberal government obdurately resisting the pressures of the suffragette movement, less than a third of the total adult population possessed the vote, while in many outlying districts land-owning 'influence' persisted. But ineluctably the 'peers' were giving way to the 'people'. This was made dramatically clear by the Parliament Act of 1911 that followed the Lords' opposition to Lloyd George's radical Budget of 1909. By this Act the blocking powers of the Lords were emaciated. In the same year payment for MPs became a reality.

The final steps towards a modern parliamentary democracy came at the end of the First World War. The Representation of the People Act of 1918 gave all adult males the vote and introduced the principle of female suffrage, completed by legislation ten years later. For the first time in Britain there existed a genuinely mass electorate ready to be wooed and won.

Houses of Parliament before they were almost completely burned down in 1834. A competition was held for the present buildings; all designs had to be in the Gothic or Elizabethan styles. It was won by Charles Barry who, as he was not familiar with the finer points of the Gothic style, procured the help of Augustus Welby Pugin for the detailed designing.

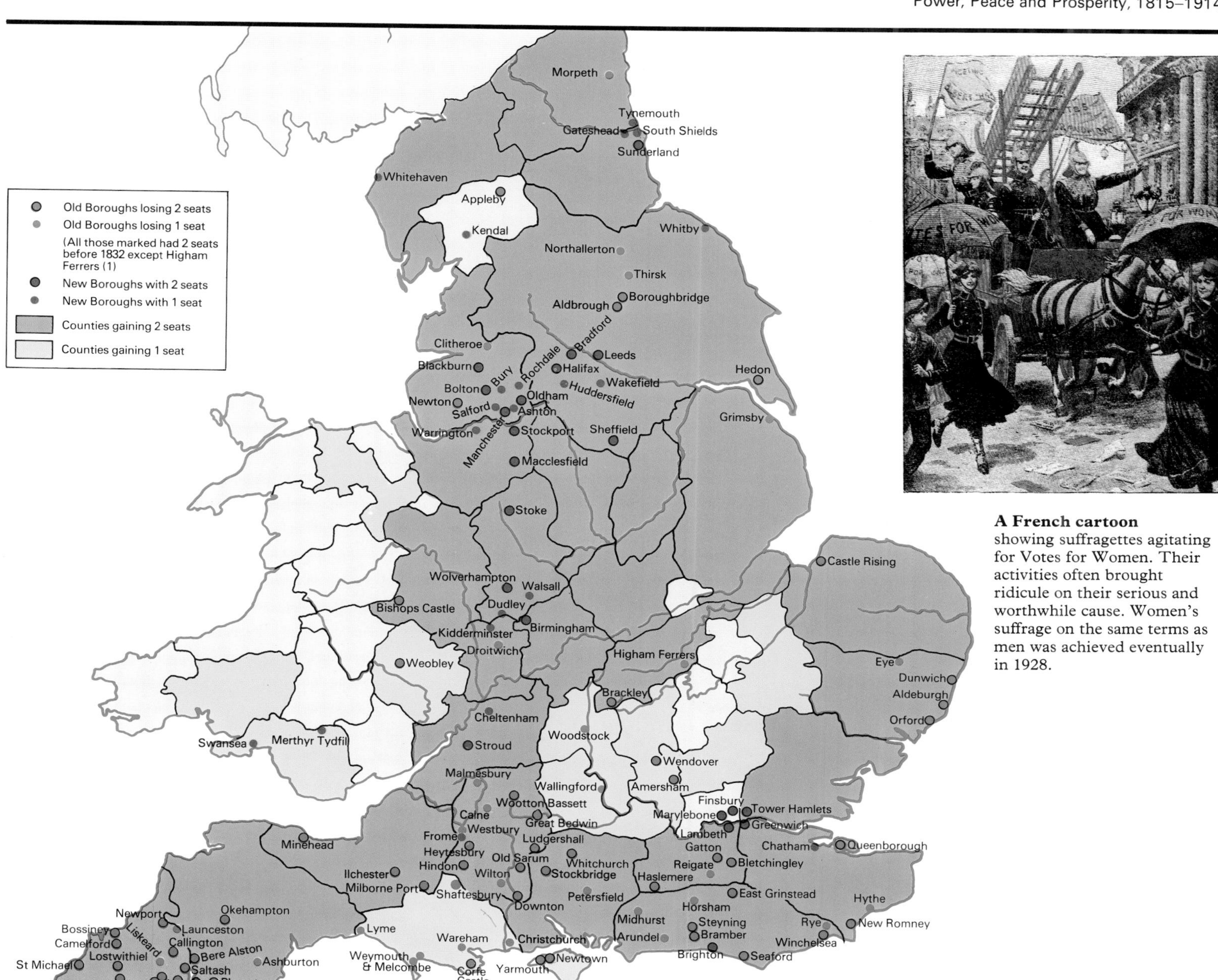

A French cartoon showing suffragettes agitating for Votes for Women. Their activities often brought ridicule on their serious and worthwhile cause. Women's suffrage on the same terms as men was achieved eventually in 1928.

Until the Reform Bill of 1832, members of the House of Commons came largely from the South and their election was strongly influenced by landlords. The map shows boroughs and counties that gained or lost seats in the great Reform Bill of 1832. The anomalies by which tiny hamlets had returned two seats and large cities none were modified and new boroughs were created, although the rapidly growing industrial centres of northern England were still inadequately represented.

Principal Franchise Qualifications

Before 1832	Boroughs:	Various qualifications. Counties: 40 shilling freeholders.
1832–67	Boroughs:	£10 property owners. £10 lodgers (if sharing a house and the landlord not in residence).
	Counties:	40 shilling freeholders. £10 copyholders. £50 tenants. £10 long leaseholders (60 years). £50 medium leaseholders.
1867–84	Boroughs:	Householders and £10 lodgers resident.
	Counties:	£12 occupiers (£14 in Scotland) and £5 property owners.
1884–1918		The introduction of single-member constituencies ends the distinction between boroughs and counties, with the principal qualification becoming that of the 1867 borough franchise.

British Foreign Policy, 1815–56

Nineteenth-century British governments, unlike their continental counterparts, pursued a foreign policy responsive to Parliament and public opinion. This invariably meant upholding British economic and naval supremacy, a policy which demanded peace in Europe. In 1814–5 at the Congress of Vienna, which reshaped the continent after Napoleon's defeat, Britain's Tory Foreign Secretary, Lord Castlereagh, successfully reaffirmed British naval and commercial hegemony outside Europe. In the settlement Britain acquired useful bases on the world's major trade routes. In Europe Castlereagh worked with the Austrians in the hope that they would balance and restrain France and Russia, and his view that these were the restless powers dominated British foreign policy for almost a century. This accounts for British concern over western Europe, particularly the Netherlands, and over the Near East, particularly the survival of Turkey, for decades to come.

Castlereagh hoped periodic great-power congresses would solve future disputes and maintain the 1815 settlement. The other powers, however, especially Austria and Russia, wanted international co-operation to defend absolute monarchies against liberal and nationalistic revolutions as well as to preserve the territorial settlement. Castlereagh disapproved of indiscriminate intervention by the great-power alliance, except in France, and suspected the powers might use intervention to extend their own influence. Consequently he refused to attend the congress of Troppau-Laibach (1820–1) which met to discuss suppressing revolts in Spain, Portugal and Italy. After Castlereagh's death in 1822, the liberal and publicity-minded George Canning followed an overtly nationalistic policy with successes in South America, Portugal and the eastern Mediterranean. Although he could not prevent France's putting down the Spanish revolution in 1823, British naval supremacy meant Spain's former American colonies could be defended. These had revolted during the Napoleonic Wars and were now important trading partners for Britain. After welcoming the U.S. President Monroe's declaration in 1823 against European interference in the Americas, Canning recognized their independence in 1824. A fleet and troops were then sent to protect Portugal's constitutional government from Spanish attack in 1826. Earlier, in 1821, the Greeks had rebelled against the Muslim Turks. As Tsar Nicholas I (1825–55) wanted to help his co-religionists and British opinion supported them, Canning seized the chance to breach the solidarity of Europe's absolutist rulers. In July 1827 he secured Russian and French agreement to Greek self-government, and the three powers destroyed a Turkish-Egyptian fleet at Navarino Bay in October, shortly after the death of Canning.

In autumn 1830 the Whigs came to power with Lord Palmerston as Foreign Secretary. He soon proved a flamboyant champion of liberalism and an enemy of despotism abroad, and he was to dominate British foreign policy for 35 years. In July 1830 the French established the constitutional monarchy of Louis Philippe; in August the Belgians revolted, demanded independence from Holland and eventually, in June 1831, elected Leopold of Saxe-Coburg as constitutional king. By co-operating with France, Palmerston forestalled possible French annexation and protected Belgium against Holland and the other powers, who finally agreed to recognize Belgian independence in 1839.

Anglo-French co-operation developed further in 1834 when their forces defended the liberal Isabella of Spain and Maria of Portugal against reactionary pretenders. However, their association collapsed over the Near East. In 1831 Mehemet Ali of Egypt had attacked his Turkish overlord; the following year he seized Syria and advanced on Constantinople. Tsar Nicholas protected Turkey but forced her, through the Unkiar Skelessi Treaty in 1833, to close the Straits to foreign warships. Palmerston felt Turkish integrity had to be preserved: he was determined to reverse what he believed was Russian control of the Straits and also to undermine France's growing influence with Mehemet Ali. In July 1840 he persuaded Austria, Prussia and Russia to limit Mehemet Ali to Egypt; a British fleet and Anglo-Austrian forces then compelled him to restore Syria. Although the French supported Egypt, they eventually backed down, fearing war with Palmerston's European coalition. In July 1841 the powers signed the Straits Convention, closing the Straits to foreign warships but letting Turkey open them to her allies in wartime. This new settlement suited all the powers.

The policies of Sir Robert Peel's Tory government (1841–6) were more pacific. In 1846 a settlement was achieved of the U.S.-Canadian western boundaries, while in Europe a close entente was established with France. However, on Palmerston's return to office in 1846, relations quickly deteriorated: Palmerston vehemently opposed Louis Philippe's attempts to extend his influence in Spain through dynastic marriages. In 1848 revolutions erupted throughout Europe. Although Palmerston and British opinion openly sympathized with the short-lived constitutional régimes, he did not intervene and used British influence to prevent general war. Two years later Britain blockaded Greece to enforce payment of the claims of the Gibraltar-born Jew, Don Pacifico, because of Palmerston's insistence that British subjects should receive protection everywhere. In 1851, Aberdeen formed a coalition government, which soon faced, despite its pacifism, a further eastern crisis. The British feared Russia intended to dismember Turkey, fears which led ultimately to the Crimean War.

British troops seizing the Chinese town of Chinkiang on the Grand Canal in 1842. This illustration was sketched on the spot by a Royal Navy captain. In the Far East, British principles of Free Trade and the right to protection of British subjects led to the first Opium War (1839–42). It arose out of attempts by Chinese Imperial authorities to enforce a ban on the illegal sale of opium by British merchants, who appealed to the British government for protection. As a result of the war, Britain won important trading concessions from the Chinese and a lease on the port of Hong Kong.

Right: The delegates meet at the Congress of Vienna, 1815

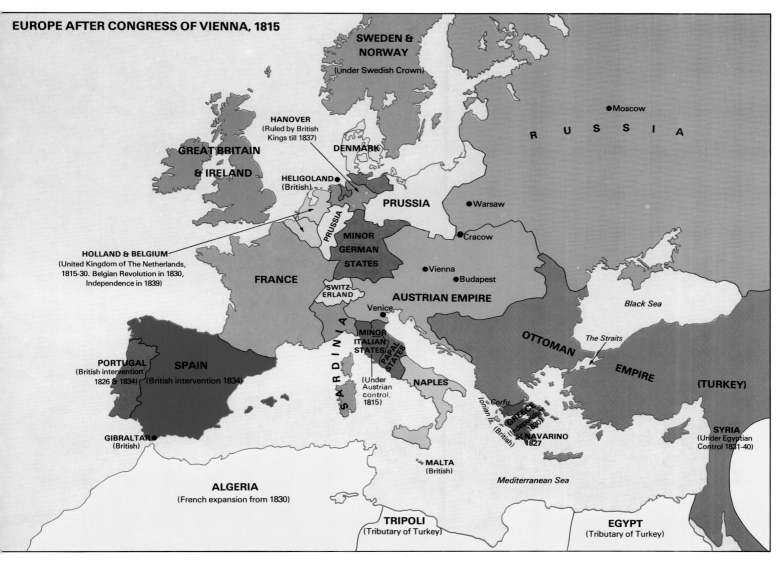

EUROPE AFTER CONGRESS OF VIENNA, 1815

SWEDEN & NORWAY
(Under Swedish Crown)
HANOVER
(Ruled by British Kings till 1837)
GREAT BRITAIN & IRELAND
DENMARK
HELIGOLAND
(British)
PRUSSIA
RUSSIA
Moscow
Warsaw
Cracow
PRUSSIA
MINOR GERMAN STATES
HOLLAND & BELGIUM
(United Kingdom of The Netherlands, 1815-30. Belgian Revolution in 1830, Independence in 1839)
FRANCE
Vienna
Budapest
SWITZERLAND
AUSTRIAN EMPIRE
Venice
Black Sea
SARDINIA
MINOR ITALIAN STATES
PAPAL STATES
(Under Austrian control, 1815)
OTTOMAN EMPIRE
(TURKEY)
The Straits
PORTUGAL
(British intervention 1826 & 1834)
SPAIN
(British intervention 1834)
NAPLES
Corfu
Ionian Is. (British)
GREECE
(Independent 1830)
NAVARINO
1827
SYRIA
(Under Egyptian Control 1831-40)
GIBRALTAR
(British)
MALTA
(British)
Mediterranean Sea
ALGERIA
(French expansion from 1830)
TRIPOLI
(Tributary of Turkey)
EGYPT
(Tributary of Turkey)

The balance of power in Europe after the Congress of Vienna, 1815. In the eyes of the British Foreign Secretary, Castlereagh, British interests lay in supporting great-power alliances in order to contain the 'restless powers' of France and Russia. He resisted attempts by absolutist regimes in Austria and Russia to invoke the alliance in order to deal with nationalist revolts throughout Europe. Later British foreign policy was sometimes more, sometimes less strongly in sympathy with nationalist uprisings. But it was always directed to upholding British economic and naval supremacy.

The Crimean War, 1854–56

The Crimean War, the first between the great powers since 1815, arose from a trivial dispute between Napoleon III of France and Nicholas I of Russia over guardianship of the Holy Places in Palestine, still part of Muslim Turkey. In February 1853 Nicholas insisted on Russia's right to protect Turkey's Balkan Christians as well. He ultimately hoped to partition Turkey and seize control of Constantinople and the Straits. In July his troops occupied Turkey's dependencies of Moldavia and Wallachia. Turkish resistance was encouraged by Great Britain and France, who sent a joint fleet to Constantinople. Napoleon III took the lead, wanting prestige abroad and an excuse to humble Russia. In London, Aberdeen's coalition government of Peelites and Whigs drifted with events: it wanted peace, but desired also to preserve the crumbling Turkish Empire to safeguard overland routes to India and keep Russia from the Mediterranean. But Anglo-French support only encouraged Turkey to declare war in October and when in November her fleet was destroyed by Russia at Sinope, there was an outcry in the West. As Nicholas refused to withdraw from Moldavia and Wallachia, Great Britain and France declared war on 28 March 1854. Threats of intervention by Austria finally forced Russian withdrawal in June and Austria occupied both provinces throughout the war.

Their reason for war had disappeared, but Great Britain and France still went ahead with an expedition to the Crimea to seize the naval base at Sevastopol, the foundation of Russian power in the Black Sea. The British force of 27,000 was commanded by the incompetent Lord Raglan, who was 75 and had not seen action for 40 years. The slightly larger French army was better organized but its leadership was as poor. The allies landed north of Sevastopol on 14 September 1854, but their advance was immediately opposed on the River Alma. A frontal attack by British troops forced a Russian retreat six days lat
The Russians' smooth-bore muskets proved no match f
the allies' rifled weapons: they lost 9,000 men to 2,0
British. However, the allies failed to press their advanta
and allowed the Russian engineer Todleben to complete t
fortifications of Sevastopol, while Russia's field arm
retreated to the eastern Crimea. As the harbour was block
by sunken ships and a naval bombardment was impossib
the allied armies moved to the south to besiege the city. C
25 October the Russian army unsuccessfully attacked t
British around their supply port of Balaclava. During t
battle muddled orders led to Cardigan's disastrous char
of the Light Brigade. The Russians renewed their atta
farther north across the River Chernaya – the battle
Inkerman (5 November). Once more the full weight fell
the British, who successfully repelled them. Milita
deadlock followed: Sevastopol held out while the Russi
army continually harassed the besiegers from the east. T
opposing armies now had to endure a savage winter wi
little food or shelter, although control of the sea meant t
allies fared better. Typhus and cholera devastated t
armies and the British death rate from these diseas
reached 190 per 1000 compared with about 35 per 10
killed and wounded.

News of the suffering was brought to the British pub
through the reports of *The Times* war correspondent W.
Russell. The radical John Bright had already condemn

Below: The Battle of Balaclava, 25 October 1854, from a contemporary painting. Largely through the efforts of *The Times* war correspondent W. H. Russell, the Crimean War became notorious for the muddle and incompetence of its British commanders. At Balaclava a crack brigade of light cavalry under Cardigan was ordered to deal with an isolated enemy outpost. In the disastrous confusion, Cardigan instead led the Light Brigade against the main Russian artillery positions, with predictable results.

Below: The comparative composition of British war funding in the American Wa of Independence, the Napoleonic Wars and the Crimean War.

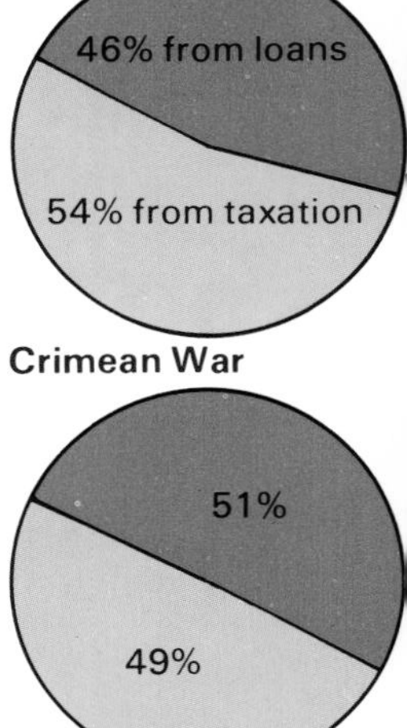

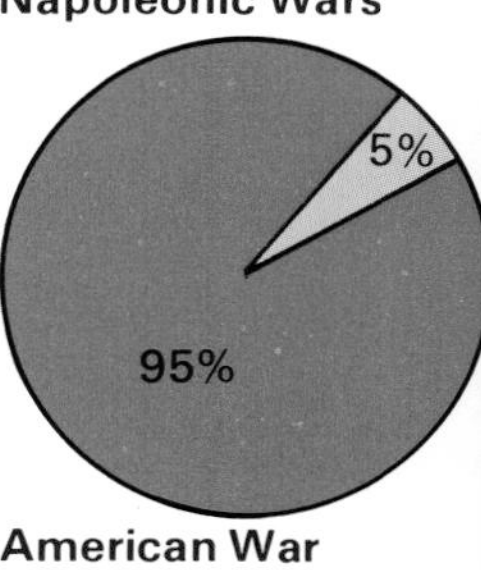

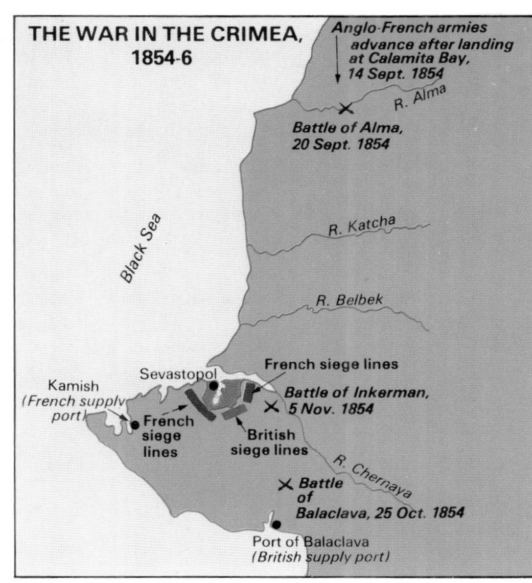

Above: The Crimean War 1854–6: the Anglo- French advance and the siege of Sevastopol.

Left: Political division in the eastern Mediterranean and Black Sea region, 1853–6. The major beneficiaries of the Crimean War were the former Turkish provinces of Moldavia and Wallachia which, together with an area of Southern Bessarabia, were formed into a new state of Romania. Otherwise, little or nothing was achieved. (Note: Orange areas on the map were tributaries of Turkey.)

Below: Panoramic view of the Anglo-French allied armies at the siege of Sevastopol 1854–5.

the war for its inhumanity and disruption of trade; but the angry public wanted victory not peace. In February 1855 Aberdeen fell because of the conduct of the war: Palmerston's new Whig ministry brought some order into sending supplies to the Crimea. Moreover, the arrival in November 1854 of Florence Nightingale, with 38 nurses, at Scutari in Turkey and her introduction of basic hygiene and nursing in the military hospitals there and in the Crimea produced a dramatic drop in the death rate among the wounded. By spring 1855 the British army was in much better shape, but the heavily reinforced French now did the bulk of the fighting. Throughout spring and summer the allies bombarded Sevastopol and frustrated Russian relief attempts.

In September Sevastopol finally fell and peace moves followed. In March 1855 Tsar Nicholas had died and his son Alexander II wanted to undertake domestic reform. Moreover neither Great Britain nor France knew how to continue the war. Some desultory naval operations in the Baltic had only led to shelling of the Åland Islands and Finnish coast. Therefore on 30 March 1856 the Treaty of Paris was signed. Turkish independence was confirmed; Russia ceded southern Bessarabia to Moldavia which, together with Wallachia, became independent Rumania in 1859; the Black Sea was neutralized and Russia forbidden a fleet or bases there. Ostensibly the allies had triumphed, but Russia renounced the Black Sea clauses in 1870 and continued her pressure on Turkey for the rest of the century. The war itself showed all the powers involved that they needed urgent military reforms, while the naval engagements proved the superiority of steamships and the vulnerability of wooden vessels without iron-cladding to shell fire.

Ireland, 1801–1922

After the passing of the Act of Union in 1801 the three problems of land, religion and government still remained to be solved. The demand for self-government took the form of agitation for the repeal of the Act of Union. Throughout the period Ireland was disturbed by agrarian outrages and political agitations.

Daniel O'Connell, a Catholic lawyer and a moderate reformer opposed to violence, led the struggle for Catholic emancipation. He formed the Catholic Association in 1823 to mobilize Catholic opinion, collecting a 'rent' of a penny a month from the peasants. In 1828 he stood, illegally, as a candidate in the by-election in County Clare. His victory posed a problem for Wellington and Peel, both of whom had refused to serve under Canning because of his favourable attitude towards Catholic emancipation. They might have refused to allow O'Connell to take his seat – and so be accused of disfranchising the voters of Clare and face the risk of civil war in Ireland. They decided to allow O'Connell to take his seat after persuading Parliament to pass the Catholic Emancipation Act of 1829. This laid them open to attacks from hard-line Tories, opponents of emancipation who feared that it would be the cause of increased Papal influence.

For a time O'Connell co-operated with the Whigs but, disappointed by their limited reforms, he formed the Repeal Association in 1840. 'Monster meetings' throughout Ireland whipped up popular support and frightened the government. Peel forbade the holding of a meeting to take place at Clontarf, near Dublin, in 1843. O'Connell called off the meeting, a decision which caused a radical section of his supporters to form the Young Ireland movement, advocating the use of violent methods to drive the English out of Ireland. An attempted rebellion in 1848 was a complete failure.

In 1845 and the following few years a blight attacked the potato crop – the principal food of the Irish peasants. Private charity, relief works, emigration and finally the repeal of the Corn Laws failed to save thousands of peasants from starvation. Peasants unable to pay their rents were evicted amid scenes of violence; resentment against landlords increased, with their property being attacked as they united holdings to make larger, more profitable farms.

The Irish emigrants to America carried their bitterness with them. Many of them 'made good' and contributed financially to the growth of the Fenian movement, an American-based society which aimed at establishing an independent republic of Ireland. Others fought in the armies involved in the American Civil War and brought their military expertise to the Fenian movement. Armies were trained, raids into Canada organized in 1866–7 and attacks made on public and private property throughout England and Ireland.

It was against this background that Gladstone came to office in 1868, declaring 'My mission is to pacify Ireland'. In this first Ministry he disestablished the Irish Church and put through the First Land Act which protected a tenant who paid his rent – but failed to deal with the problems of high rents and the eviction of tenants.

Charles Stewart Parnell, a Protestant landowner, took over the leadership of the Irish Party in Parliament in 1880. He pledged this tightly disciplined group to securing the independence of Ireland. He received financial support from America and massive support throughout Ireland of which he became 'the uncrowned king'.

Parnell was helped by Michael Davitt, a former Fenian, who had formed the Land League of 1879 to fight landlordism and to win better conditions for tenants. Parnell became President of the Land League, using his

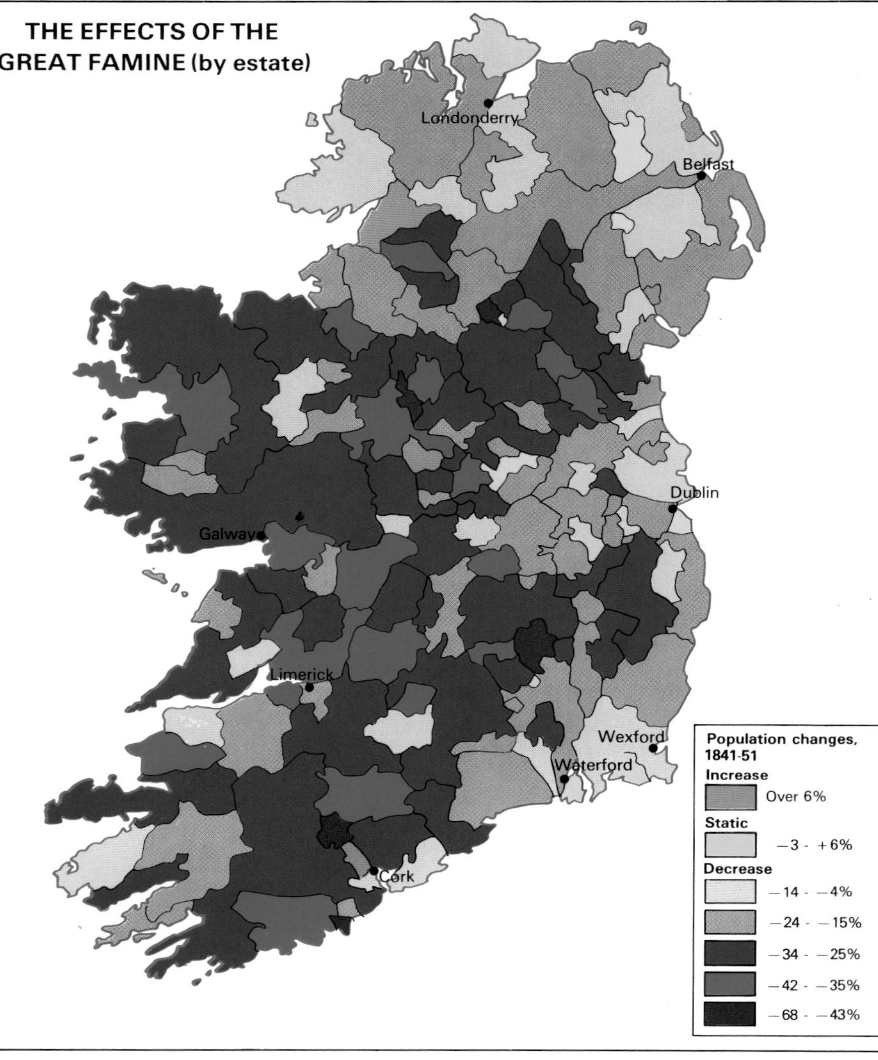

The effects of the great potato famine of the 1840s. In a few areas the population more than doubled, but in most places it diminished, from immigration and from death. The failure of the potato crop, on which the peasants completely depended for food, was followed by typhus, and despite relief measures hundreds of thousands of people died. The illustration on the right shows starving peasants at the gates of a workhouse in 1846.

position to preach a 'no rents' campaign and the policy of 'boycott' against anyone taking over farms from which tenants had been evicted. While Parnell was opposed to violence, crime and murder were commonplace as a frustrated peasantry took matters into their own hands.

During his second Ministry (1880–5), Gladstone first tried to combat the violence with Coercion Acts which allowed the arrest of Parnell for advocating the non-payment of rents. Gladstone also passed a Second Land Act which led to a 20 per cent reduction in rents, guaranteed tenants freedom from eviction and gave them the opportunity of obtaining from landlords payments for any improvements which they made in the farm during a tenancy. But by this time falling grain prices were adding to agrarian distress. The 'no rents' campaign went on while Parnell was in prison. Finally Gladstone had to arrange the Kilmainham Treaty with the Irish Leader who was released after promising to call off his campaign. But the subsequent murder of the new Chief Secretary in Phoenix Park led again to the Coercion Acts.

Following the election of 1885 Parnell's Irish Party held the balance of power in the Commons. Gladstone, anxious to win Parnell's support, declared his conversion to Home Rule. His first Home Rule Bill (1886) was defeated in the Commons, largely owing to the defection of a Chamberlain-led group of Liberal Unionists. His second Home Rule Bill (1893) was defeated in the Lords.

The Conservatives, in power from 1886 to 1892 and from 1894 to 1906, tried to kill Home Rule by kindness and firmness. They put down disorder with a firm hand while bringing in a series of Land Purchase Acts which advanced money to enable tenants to purchase their farms. This improvement in the land situation did not lessen the demand for Home Rule. After Parnell's death in 1891 the Irish Party was led by John Redmond who took advantage of the political situation in 1910 to demand a price for supporting the Liberal government. Part of that price was the promise of a Home Rule Bill (1912), another was the Parliament Act (1911) which limited the power of the Lords.

In 1886 Lord Randolph Churchill had 'played the Orange card' by inviting Ulster Protestants to prepare to make war against Gladstone's proposed Home Rule Bill. He coined the slogan, 'Ulster will fight, and Ulster will be right'. In 1912 the Protestants of Ulster were mobilized by Sir Edward Carson who hoped that Ulster's opposition to Home Rule would force the government to drop the scheme. With the active support of the Conservative Party, armies were trained, munitions brought in from Europe and the British Army in Ireland rendered less effective by the Curragh mutiny while the Home Rule Bill made its way through the Commons and Lords. The Commons approved the Bill for the third time in September 1914 but its operation was suspended until the end of the War.

Some Irishmen joined the British forces but others joined the Sinn Fein Party which rose in rebellion in Easter 1916. Some public buildings in Dublin were seized and a Provisional government of the Irish Republic was proclaimed. The rebellion was put down in five days and a number of the ringleaders shot by the British. In the 1918 'Coupon' election Sinn Fein candidates won 73 of the 106 Irish seats; they refused to go to Westminster, setting up their own Parliament or 'Dail' in Dublin with Eamon de Valera, one of the leaders of the 1916 rising, as President.

There followed three years of bitter warfare as the British fought the Sinn Fein forces. During this time the British Parliament passed the Government of Ireland Act which established two Parliaments in Ireland – one for Southern (Catholic) Ireland, which would have Dominion status within the Empire, the other an Ulster (Protestant) Parliament for the six counties where Protestants formed a majority of the population.

In July 1921 a truce was called and a Conference held in London at which, in October, the leaders of Sinn Fein agreed to accept the terms of the 1920 Act. In December 1921 the Irish Dail voted to accept the truce and the terms of the agreement and the Irish Free State came into being. De Valera and a minority of Sinn Fein refused to accept the division of Ireland and fought their own Civil War against the 'Staters' only calling off their struggle in 1923. Ireland, it seemed, had ceased to be a major British problem – until the resurgence of the Ulster problem in the 1960s.

Sackville Street, Dublin, after the Easter Week Rising of 1916 when the Sinn Fein Party led a rebellion proclaiming an Irish Republic. For nearly a week Dublin was paralysed by street fighting.

Politics and Domestic Affairs, 1855–1914

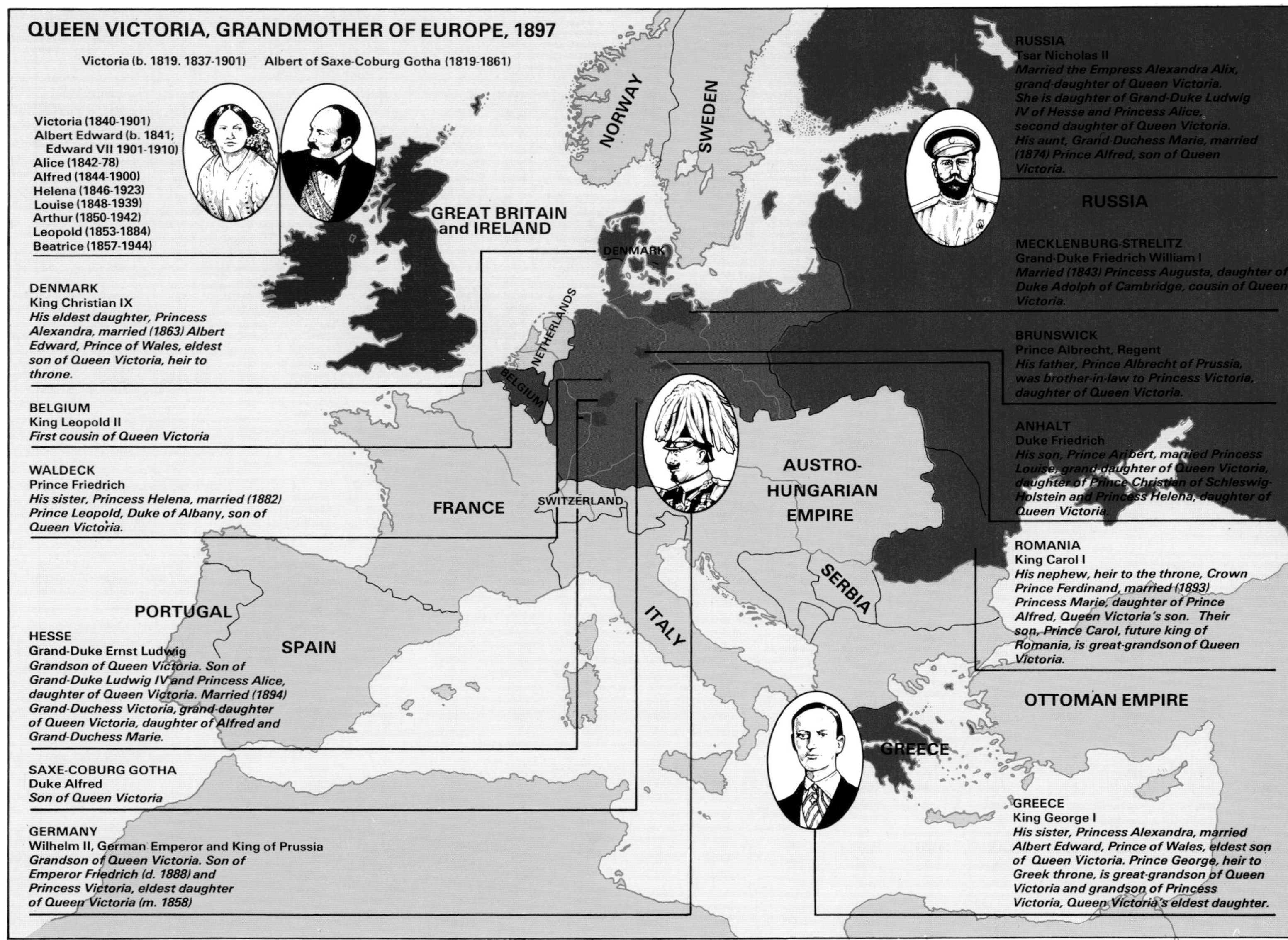

QUEEN VICTORIA, GRANDMOTHER OF EUROPE, 1897
Victoria (b. 1819. 1837-1901)
Albert of Saxe-Coburg Gotha (1819-1861)
Victoria (1840-1901)
Albert Edward (b. 1841; Edward VII 1901-1910)
Alice (1842-78)
Alfred (1844-1900)
Helena (1846-1923)
Louise (1848-1939)
Arthur (1850-1942)
Leopold (1853-1884)
Beatrice (1857-1944)
DENMARK
King Christian IX
His eldest daughter, Princess Alexandra, married (1863) Albert Edward, Prince of Wales, eldest son of Queen Victoria, heir to throne.
BELGIUM
King Leopold II
First cousin of Queen Victoria
WALDECK
Prince Friedrich
His sister, Princess Helena, married (1882) Prince Leopold, Duke of Albany, son of Queen Victoria.
HESSE
Grand-Duke Ernst Ludwig
Grandson of Queen Victoria. Son of Grand-Duke Ludwig IV and Princess Alice, daughter of Queen Victoria. Married (1894) Grand-Duchess Victoria, grand-daughter of Queen Victoria, daughter of Alfred and Grand-Duchess Marie.
SAXE-COBURG GOTHA
Duke Alfred
Son of Queen Victoria
GERMANY
Wilhelm II, German Emperor and King of Prussia
Grandson of Queen Victoria. Son of Emperor Friedrich (d. 1888) and Princess Victoria, eldest daughter of Queen Victoria (m. 1858)
NORWAY
SWEDEN
GREAT BRITAIN and IRELAND
DENMARK
NETHERLANDS
BELGIUM
FRANCE
SWITZERLAND
PORTUGAL
SPAIN
ITALY
AUSTRO-HUNGARIAN EMPIRE
SERBIA
GREECE
OTTOMAN EMPIRE
RUSSIA
RUSSIA
Tsar Nicholas II
Married the Empress Alexandra Alix, grand-daughter of Queen Victoria. She is daughter of Grand-Duke Ludwig IV of Hesse and Princess Alice, second daughter of Queen Victoria. His aunt, Grand-Duchess Marie, married (1874) Prince Alfred, son of Queen Victoria.
MECKLENBURG-STRELITZ
Grand-Duke Friedrich William I
Married (1843) Princess Augusta, daughter of Duke Adolph of Cambridge, cousin of Queen Victoria.
BRUNSWICK
Prince Albrecht, Regent
His father, Prince Albrecht of Prussia, was brother-in-law to Princess Victoria, daughter of Queen Victoria.
ANHALT
Duke Friedrich
His son, Prince Aribert, married Princess Louise, grand-daughter of Queen Victoria, daughter of Prince Christian of Schleswig-Holstein and Princess Helena, daughter of Queen Victoria.
ROMANIA
King Carol I
His nephew, heir to the throne, Crown Prince Ferdinand, married (1893) Princess Marie, daughter of Prince Alfred, Queen Victoria's son. Their son, Prince Carol, future king of Romania, is great-grandson of Queen Victoria.
GREECE
King George I
His sister, Princess Alexandra, married Albert Edward, Prince of Wales, eldest son of Queen Victoria. Prince George, heir to Greek throne, is great-grandson of Queen Victoria and grandson of Princess Victoria, Queen Victoria's eldest daughter.

Europe's royal families were closely related through marriage. Such relationships could be significant, for although some monarchies were constitutional (as in the United Kingdom) there were countries like Russia where the sovereign had autocratic power. Queen Victoria was called 'the mother of Europe' because she was related to so many members of foreign royal houses through her four sons, five daughters, 40 grandchildren and 29 great grandchildren. Relationships were closest with Protestant royal houses in northern and central Europe, but extended to Russia, Romania, and Greece. The map shows how the hereditary rulers of various states were related to Queen Victoria in 1897.

In the history of this period two major and two minor themes can be discerned – the former now noted with nostalgia, the latter providing a foretaste of major themes of the 20th century. The first major theme has been encapsulated in such terms as 'the Workshop of the World' and Pax Britannica. For during part of this period Britain – the first industrial nation – dominated the world. And it continued to make the running until the 1870s, as it found new markets in the ever expanding Empire. It seemed natural that the unrewarding task of exploring the interior of Africa should have been tackled from the world's leading power.

The second major theme follows almost naturally from the first. A great power exercising great influence was, not surprisingly, governed by a series of great politicians debating major issues. Gladstone dominated the Liberal Party until his retirement in 1893, long before which even his enemies accorded him the affectionate title of The Grand Old Man. The Tories were led by Disraeli until his retirement in 1880, and his rivalry with Gladstone seems in retrospect to be the clash of giants. After 1880 the Tories were led by Lord Salisbury, whose large frame and massive head seems fitting for the Prime Minister who was also Foreign Secretary of the world's leading power.

Even minor players on this political stage now appea[r] larger than modern politicians. Joseph Chamberlain an[d] Lord Randolph Churchill fighting against their respectiv[e] leaders and against each other in the new political worl[d] following the enfranchisement of about half the adul[t] males; Charles Stuart Parnell using a variety of weapons i[n] his fight for Home Rule for Ireland; A. J. Balfour succeed[-] ing his uncle as Tory Prime Minister in 1902; Asquith[,] Lloyd George, the ebullient young Winston Churchill – th[e] roll call of Victorian and Edwardian 'greats' seems to b[e] almost endless.

While these giants spent part of their time discussin[g] trivial affairs and while modern research shows that man[y] of them had feet of clay, they also debated and decided grea[t] issues. The completion of the Free Trade programme, th[e] major reform of the Civil Service and the creation of a[n] equally competent administration for the new counties an[d] older boroughs, the creation of a system of state educatio[n] and major developments in the Welfare State – these ar[e] only some among the issues decided then which stil[l] influence life in Britain today.

But beneath these major themes are the minor theme[s]

which became increasingly strident towards the end of the period and which have developed into the major themes of the 20th century. There was, for example, the evidence that Britain was falling behind in the industrial race. For some people, like Chamberlain, this was proof that the Free Trade Policy ought to be abandoned in favour of tariffs. It was Chamberlain, too, who first learned the lesson of the Boer War: that Britain could no longer afford the luxury of her 'splendid isolation', but would have to join one or other of the Armed Camps into which Europe was divided.

Chamberlain's attack on the sacred cow of Free Trade was condemned by many in his own party and was a major cause of the Tory defeat in the 1906 election. But he was not alone in casting doubt on long-held beliefs. By 1900 an increasing number of intellectuals and of urban workers were calling attention to the manifestly unfair results of the working of the free market economy which provided great wealth for a small minority – who measured their incomes in tens or hundreds of thousands a year – but which condemned the mass of the population to live below, on or just above a pitifully low poverty line. The findings of Liberals such as Charles Booth and Seebohm Rowntree confirmed the findings of Mrs Pemberton Reeves whose *Round About a Pound a Week* both described the lives of the majority of workers and, in its title, captured the unfair distribution of incomes.

The newly enfranchised working class was slow to use its political power. At first it was content with ameliorating laws and, in particular, with laws which ensured the legal position of trade unions. The members of the old craft unions, the 'aristocrats of labour', believed in the market economy which had provided them and their members with the opportunity to earn relatively high wages and to found their own union-based welfare system. But the mass of workers could not afford the high fees charged by these unions, nor did they have any skill to offer an employer. Lowly paid, frequently unemployed or underemployed – they gained little from the market economy and proved fertile soil for the growing socialist ideals.

The formation of the Labour Party in 1900 was, indeed, opposed by the leaders of the old craft unions. But these unions enrolled in the new Labour Party after 1903, and the greater wealth, experience, and qualities of leadership they brought greatly strengthened the Labour movement.

In 1906 the Liberal Party won a massive overall majority in the House of Commons, but Balfour noted the fact that 53 Labour MPs had been elected: 'We have to do here with something bigger than a Liberal victory'. For in the success of the Labour Party lay the seeds of the decline in the fortunes of the seemingly powerful Liberal Party, driven after 1906 to pursue socialist policies which managed to offend traditional Liberals while failing to satisfy the demands of the increasingly militant working class.

Balfour was more perceptive than the majority of people and politicians who continued to behave as if Britain were still the leading world power whose sons would extend 'wider still and wider' that Empire which was seen as a gift of a benevolent 'God who made thee mighty'.

Above right: Queen Victoria is driven through London during the celebrations of her Diamond Jubilee in 1897. After a period of unpopularity, when she withdrew from public life following Prince Albert's death in 1861, the Queen became a much loved figure.

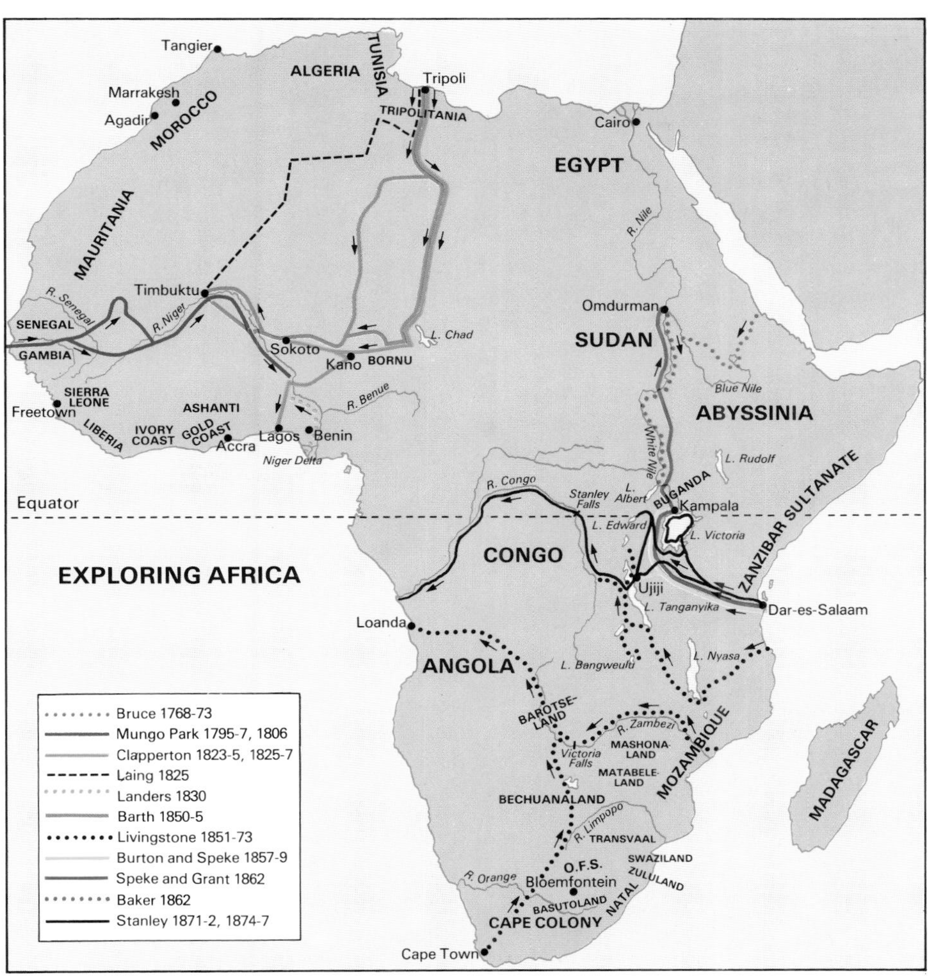

The 19th century saw the opening up of the African continent. Many of the explorers were British. They went with a variety of motives – curiosity, adventure, commercial gain, missionary work. By the 1880s Africa had become a focus of colonial rivalry.

British Foreign Policy, 1856–1914

British foreign policy during the decade after the Crimean War was largely conducted by Palmerston. Although continuing to fear Russian expansion in the Near East and in Central Asia, he was equally wary of France in western Europe. Fear of the latter as well as sympathy for Italian nationalism led to active British diplomatic support for Italian unification in 1859–60. Palmerston condemned the Austrian and Prussian attack on Denmark in 1864, but after his death in 1865 Britain cautiously welcomed the German Empire created by Bismarck following Prussia's victories over Austria in 1866 and over France in 1870–1: the new Germany, Britain suspected, would check France and Russia. While British intervention could hardly have changed events on the Continent, her naval power could have been decisive in the American Civil War (1861–5). However, British opinion was deeply split over the war and neutrality was maintained, despite quarrels with the North over the seizure of Southern envoys from the British ship, *Trent*, and over the British-built Southern raider, *Alabama*.

Gladstone as Prime Minister (1868–74) pursued non-intervention abroad and merely forced Russia to submit her renunciation in 1871 of the Black Sea clause of the Peace of Paris to international agreement. But Disraeli returned to traditional policies. His enthusiasm for imperialism, purchase of Suez Canal shares in 1875 and the creation of Victoria as Empress of India in 1876 made him determined to contain Russia whom he saw as a threat to India. Disraeli therefore supported Turkey when Russia attacked that country in 1877 after the Sultan had brutally suppressed a revolt in Bulgaria in 1876. While Gladstone publicly condemned Turkey, Disraeli sent the fleet to Constantinople to support her. Although Russia forced Turkey to sign the Peace of San Stefano in March 1878, creating a huge Russian satellite state in Bulgaria, British threats of war produced changes at the Congress of Berlin which met the following June. With Austrian support, Disraeli successfully reduced the size of Bulgaria, denying her access to the Aegean, and checked Russia by Britain's occupation of Cyprus and Austria's of Bosnia. British interest in the Eastern Mediterranean and the route to the East increased further when Gladstone reluctantly occupied Egypt to suppress internal disorder there in 1882. This action antagonized France and throughout the 1880s and 1890s British governments, particularly under Salisbury, co-operated informally with Germany, Austria and Italy against France and Russia in the Mediterranean. The growing British and European enthusiasm for imperialism and the frenzy of colonization in these decades merely carried British hostility towards France and Russia into the continents of Africa and Asia. In 1898 Britain and France almost went to war in the Fashoda Crisis over control of the Upper Nile.

Britain's concentration on imperialism and confidence in her naval supremacy led to indifference towards Europe as during the 1890s it divided into hostile military blocs, the Dual Alliance of France and Russia against the Triple Alliance of Germany, Austria and Italy. However, British confidence in her 'splendid isolation' was badly shaken by the Boer War (1899–1902). Early defeats and European hostility brought home the dangers of isolation. In 1902 an alliance was concluded with Japan for support against Russia in the Far East. In 1904 colonial differences with France were settled by the *Entente Cordiale*, recognizing British dominance in Egypt and French dominance in Morocco. Although it was not intended to support France in her quarrels with Germany, German action led to this. Germany was rapidly overtaking Britain industrially and in 1898 began building a navy which would make her a world power. The policy was soon interpreted as a direct threat to Britain, a threat which Germany's inept, blustering diplomacy seemed to confirm. In 1905 Germany tried to test the recent Anglo-French agreement and weaken France's position in Morocco. But in the Algeçiras Conference (January 1906) Britain supported France.

The Liberal government formed in December 1905 with Grey as Foreign Secretary continued the new direction of policy of its Conservative-Unionist predecessor, and in 1907 Britain signed a convention with Russia, settling differences over Central Asia. Although not formally allied to France or Russia, Britain increasingly associated with them in their confrontations with Germany and Austria (Italy was uncommitted). This was largely because of Germany's insistence on enlarging her navy: an Anglo-German naval race developed alongside the arms race on the Continent. In 1911, when Germany again challenged France's position in Morocco by sending a gunboat to Agadir, Britain forced her withdrawal. A year later Britain agreed with France to concentrate her navy in the Channel and North Sea while France covered the Mediterranean. Although Britain's interests hardly seemed involved in the fatal Austro-Russian quarrel over the Balkans and Serbian independence in July 1914, Germany's support for Austria and declaration of war against Russia (1 August) and then France (3 August) made British intervention inevitable: Britain's survival seemed bound up with that of France. Germany's invasion of Belgium to attack France from the north removed all doubts, as it breached Belgian neutrality. Britain formally entered the war on 4 August 1914.

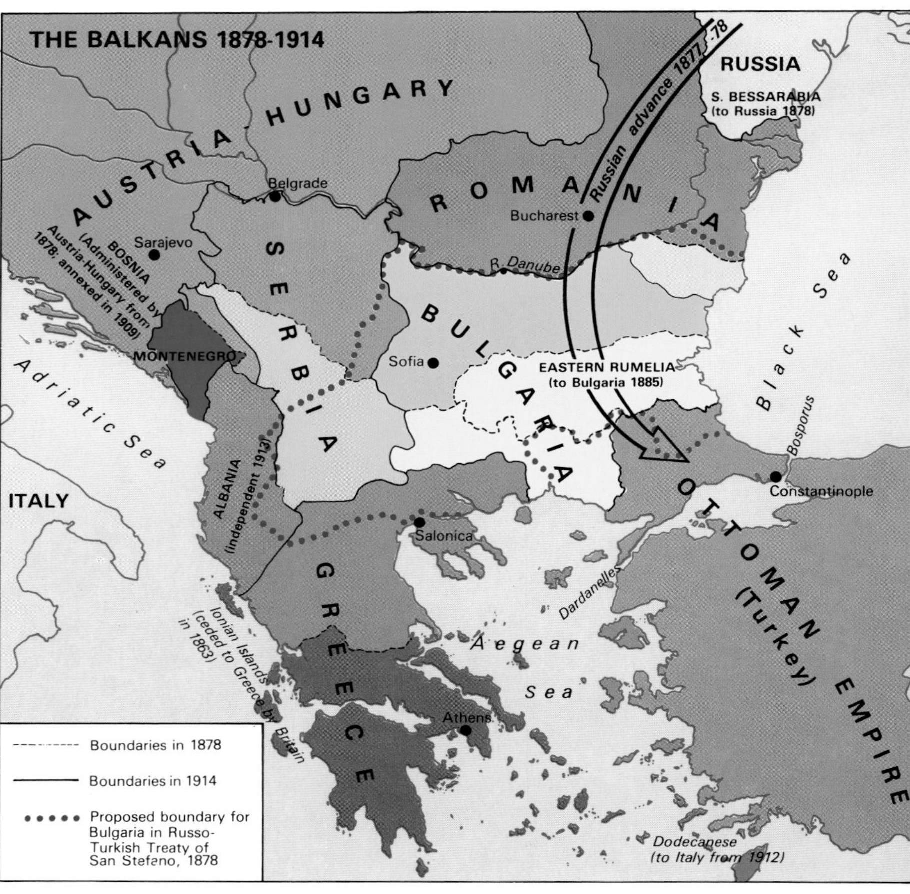

The cockpit of rivalries between the Austro-Hungarian and Russian empires, the Balkans were to prove the flashpoint of the 1914–18 conflict.

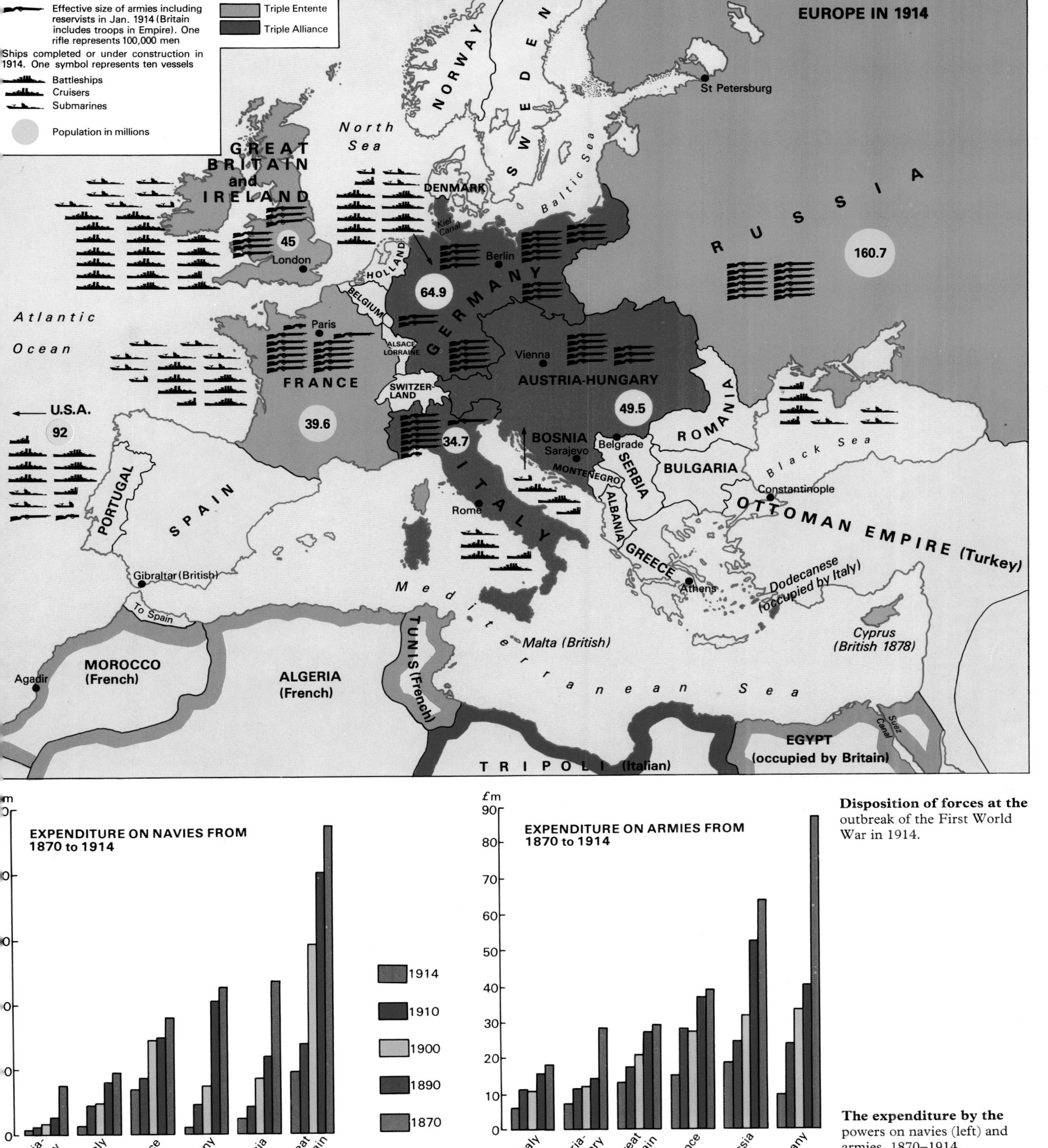

Disposition of forces at the outbreak of the First World War in 1914.

The expenditure by the powers on navies (left) and armies, 1870–1914.

The Boer War, 1899–1902

In the 1850s Dutch settlers, the Boers, founded two states in southern Africa, the Orange Free State and the Transvaal (or South African Republic). The founders had trekked northwards to escape British domination and to preserve their Afrikaner identity. On their journey they had to defend themselves repeatedly against the British and powerful African tribes. By the 1890s British imperialists felt the two states obstructed complete British control of South Africa and threatened the security of the route to the East. The discovery of huge gold deposits in the Transvaal in 1886 had increased the danger: the poor Boer farmers now had the chance to expand industrially and even territorially. In 1899 Joseph Chamberlain, Colonial Secretary in Salisbury's Conservative-Unionist government, was determined to annex the two republics. Together with the Governor of Cape Colony, Milner, he tried to force their collapse. A plausible excuse existed in the refusal of the patriarchal Transvaal president, Paul Kruger, to grant political rights to the *Uitlanders*, the foreign, mainly British, entrepreneurs and workers who had developed the gold mines and now outnumbered the Boers. Increasing pressure was put on Kruger to emancipate them and British military intervention was just a matter of time. The Transvaal and Orange Free State leaders concluded they had to fight to preserve their independence and declared war on 12 October 1899.

The Boers had 45,000 troops against British forces less than half as strong and scattered throughout Cape Colony and Natal: they hoped quick victories would destroy British ambitions. One Boer army therefore advanced westwards, invested Mafeking and the diamond centre of Kimberley and entered Cape Colony; another invaded Natal and besieged Ladysmith. The British commander-in-chief, Buller, countered by splitting his forces and trying to raise all three sieges. This led to three British defeats in the 'black week' of December, at Stormberg, Magersfontein and Colenso. The Boers rode rapidly through country they knew and, when dismounted, used long-range rifles from the protection of trenches with deadly effect. The defeats evoked outbursts of jingoism in Britain and determinatic to continue the war. Early in 1900 large reinforcemen arrived from Britain and the Empire, led by a ne commander-in-chief, Lord Roberts, with Kitchener unde him. These generals followed a more imaginative an mobile strategy, less tied to the vulnerable railway beginning a counter-offensive in February. With fa greater numbers Roberts surrounded General Cron outside Kimberley, forced him to lift the siege and the surrender at Paardeberg (27 February). He then seize Bloemfontein, the Orange Free State capital (13 March Meanwhile Buller, after a costly drawn battle at Spion Ko (24 January), relieved Ladysmith (28 February) and drov the enemy from Natal. Everywhere the vastly outnumbere Boers had to retreat. In May Roberts assembled 100,00 men at Bloemfontein to invade the Transvaal. Th campaign opened with the relief of Mafeking, defended fo 217 days by Colonel Baden-Powell, later of Boy Scou fame. On 5 June the Transvaal capital Pretoria fell an Kruger escaped for exile in Europe. Roberts himsel returned home in November 1900, convinced the war wa over. His victories allowed the Conservatives and Unionist to win the 'khaki election' and another six years' power.

The war, however, was not over and now entered its mos savage stage. The Transvaal commander, Botha, and th Free State leaders, de Wet and Steyn, dispersed thei armies in small units, hoping to wear out the British b guerrilla raids. Their mounted commandos, only abou 30,000 altogether, harried British communication throughout South Africa. Kitchener, now in comman with 250,000 men, countered by building a system o numerous corrugated-iron block-houses to guard th railways and criss-cross the countryside, and by scorched earth warfare. Boer farms were systematically destroye and Boer families herded into 'concentration camps', wher poor sanitation and epidemics caused 20,000 deaths British troops also suffered badly from typhoid: diseas accounted for two thirds of their 22,000 war losses. Th Boers were ultimately forced to peace at Vereeniging on 3

'Mafeking' by R. Caton-Woodville. The siege of Mafeking was an episode which triggered off the most jingoistic sentiments on the part of the British population. The inscription on this painting reads: 'On the morning the relief force arrived, Commander Eloff, after capturing a force within the British lines, was surrounded and taken prisoner by the Mafeking garrison.'

Лay 1902 and to accept annexation of their republics. To often the blow £3 million was granted to restore their evastated farms. By 1910 the former republics were joined vith Cape Colony and Natal in the self-governing Union of outh Africa. Although moderate Boer leaders like Botha nd Smuts became reconciled to the Crown, the conflict left eep and lasting scars and largely strengthened Afrikaner ationalism.

The war cost Britain £200 million and produced bitter ivisions at home, particularly in the Liberal party, where nany, such as Lloyd George, were openly pro-Boer. Kitchener's brutal methods caused a revulsion against nperialism and renewed interest in social reform. The umiliating defeats resulted in a shake-up in military dministration and thinking. Although Britain's Navy revented outside help reaching the Boers, all Europe was ostile and British statesmen now realized the dangers of splendid isolation'.

The setting for the campaigns of the Boer War, 1899–1902. Initial successes by irregular Boer volunteers were met by a strong counter-offensive under Kitchener and Roberts. The sieges of Ladysmith and Mafeking were lifted and Bloemfontein, the Boer capital of the Orange Free State, was captured. A new campaign of guerrilla warfare by the Boers was countered by a British policy of savage reprisals. This culminated in the confinement of large sections of the Boer population in concentration camps.

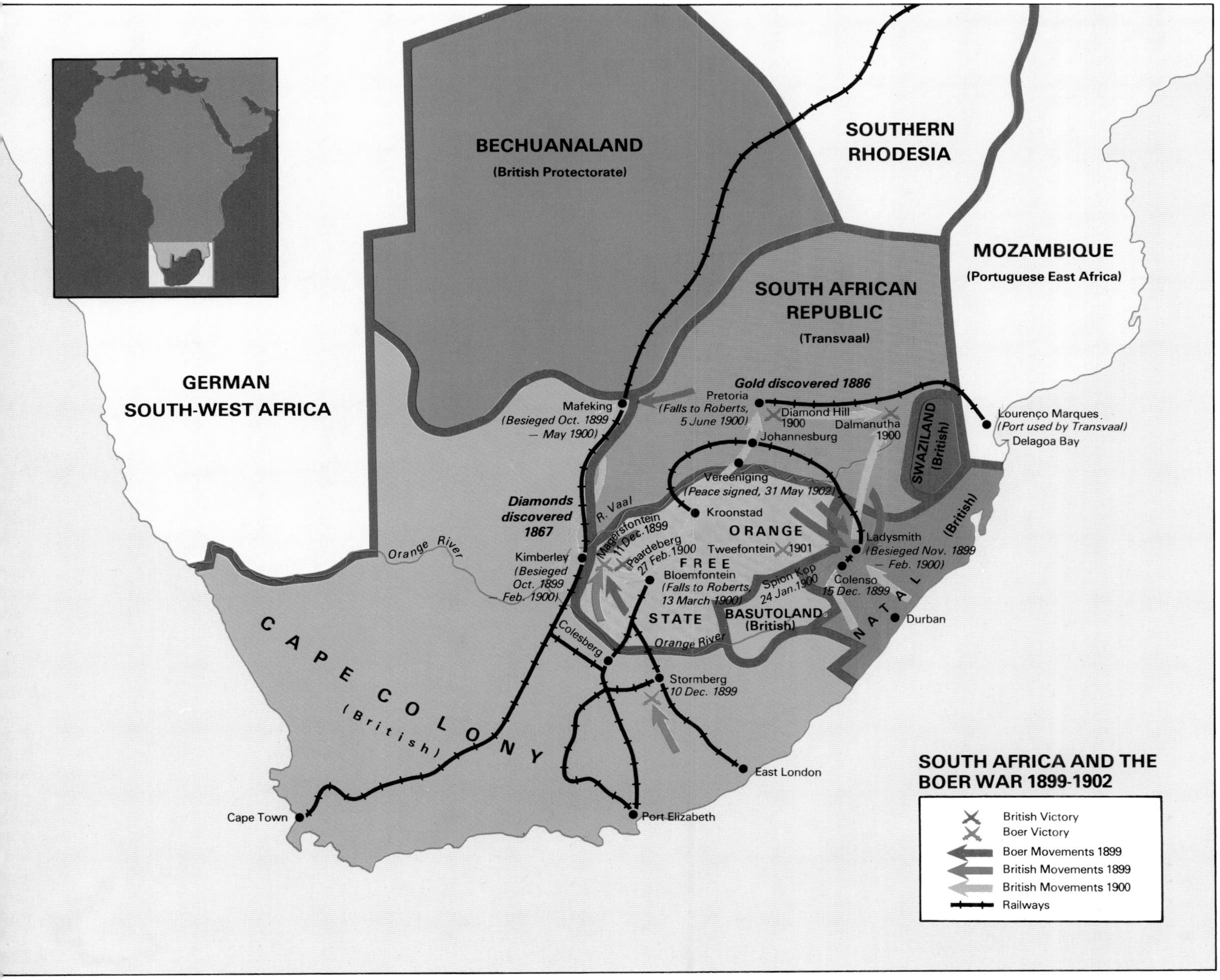

SOUTH AFRICA AND THE BOER WAR 1899-1902

British Victory
Boer Victory
Boer Movements 1899
British Movements 1899
British Movements 1900
Railways

India, 1857–1947

The Mutiny delivered a severe blow to British self-confidence in India. The fear of provoking a second uprising turned a potentially revolutionary Empire into a consciously conservative one. Before the Mutiny philosophic radicals and evangelical Christians might dream of remaking Indian society in a European mould: but in the aftermath of the revolt stability seemed more important than reform – and stability meant contracting alliances with politically powerful groups in Indian society, like the landlords and native princes. There were to be no more 'revolutions from above' comparable with the great land tenure systems set up when the East India Company first became a territorial power, and no more annexations of native states like the unfortunate Oudh.

The growth of nationalism confirmed these conservative alliances. The great landowners and the princes were loyal counterpoises to the 'sedition' of a new class growing up in the towns: the Western-educated professional men. The first universities were set up – in the three 'presidency towns' – in 1857: by 1947 there were 20 universities and over 200,000 university students in India. It was from this service class of lawyers, doctors, journalists, schoolteachers and civil servants that the first generation of nationalistic politicians was drawn. Later they were joined by the business community, and later still by rich peasants. Congress was formed in 1885, and the steady growth of popular support and party organization made it possible to launch a series of mass agitations, each more widespread and violent than the last. In 1920–2 the Government of India stood aside and let the first non-cooperation movement burn itself out; in 1930–2 they were forced to employ a judicious mixture of force and diplomacy to restore order; and in 1942, at the height of the 'Quit India' movement, they lost control of large areas in the northern part of the country.

Successive British governments shrank from the coercion necessary to maintain an undiluted autocracy, and made constitutional concessions designed to conciliate 'moderate' opinion. The two major bouts of constitutional reform – the Montague-Chelmsford reforms of 1919, and the 1935 Government of India Act – widened the franchise, set up legislatures with elective majorities, and transferred power to Indian ministers in the provinces. By 1937 Congress ministries were in office in every major province, bar the Punjab and Bengal. But their very success at the polls – coupled with the reluctance of the Congress leadership to share power with the Muslim League – intensified the Muslims' dread of Hindu domination; and in the vital 1946 elections the Muslims voted overwhelmingly for a separate Pakistan and partition. In the massacres that followed – as millions of Muslim refugees fled to Pakistan, and millions of Hindus and Sikhs sought refuge in India – half a million people were estimated to have died, sowing the seeds of later Indo-Pakistani wars.

The development of the Indian economy over the same period was patchy. Whether agricultural output kept pace with population growth is unknown and – because the statistics are so unreliable – probably unknowable. But it is certain that some provinces – such as Bihar – stagnated, while in others agricultural productivity rose. The Punjab, for instance, benefited from the construction of the largest irrigation schemes in the world and the introduction of higher-yielding varieties of wheat and cotton. Here the settlers on the irrigation canals became the richest peasants on the sub-continent, if not in Asia. The Green Revolution of the 1970s duplicated this historic pattern of growth and stagnation, increasing the differentials between the most favoured and the least favoured areas.

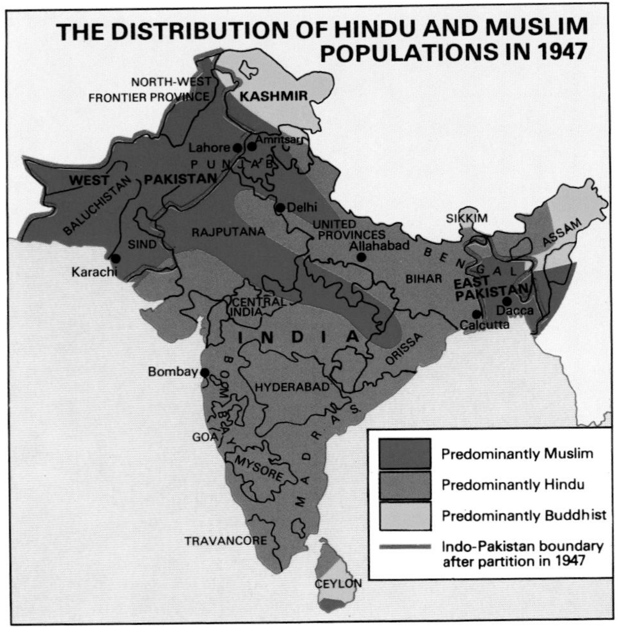

The distribution of Hindus and Muslims in 1947. The Sikhs were mainly concentrated in the Punjab; when the western part of the Punjab became part of Pakistan about $2\frac{1}{2}$ million Sikhs moved to India. The mass exchange of Muslim, Hindu and Sikh populations was accompanied by great violence, and hundreds of thousands of people were killed.

Opposite: India before partition. The annexation of states by Britain ceased after the Mutiny. The native states comprised about a third of the sub-continent, and were ruled by nearly 600 princes and minor rulers. These princely states had treaties with the British, who were responsible for their defence, external affairs, and communications, but did not in theory meddle in their internal affairs.

Improvements in communications tended to level out inequalities in prices and wages. The trans-continental railway network was complemented by the substitution of steam for sail on India's external trade-routes and, internally, by the extension of carting to areas in which wheeled transport had been unknown, and the development of road transport in the 1920s. This improved transportation was once supposed to have destroyed Indian handicrafts by exposing them to competition from factory-made imports; but recent research suggests that some cottage industries (such as handloom weaving) held their own, while others prospered – or collapsed. Foreign competition clearly failed to prevent the development of two great factory industries: cotton, at first centred on Bombay, and the iron and steel industry dependent on the ores and coal of Bihar. Growth rates in the modern industrial sector were remarkably buoyant right through the inter-war years, partly because the advent of protective tariffs encouraged diversification through import-substitution. As a result, India had become a major industrial power by 1947, with a sophisticated industrial base capable of indefinite expansion without many imported raw materials. Exports were still dominated by raw materials; but the range of raw materials was so wide, and the proportion of domestic output exported so small, that the Indian economy was never destabilized by violent fluctuations in the prices of a small number of primary products.

In fact the British and Indian economies were already so independent of one another in 1947 that their political separation only enhanced existing trends. It was the loss of India as a military base, rather than an export market or a source of primary produce, that fatally weakened the British Empire. The sub-continent had served as a British arsenal in an oriental sea: an inexhaustible reservoir of manpower and revenue that made Britain an Asiatic power. Without the Indian Army to police the Indian Ocean and fight 'small colonial wars', it was too costly to maintain a 'presence' east of Suez; and there was now less need to protect the historic sea-routes to the Indies via Suez and the Cape, which had drawn Britain into Africa. Once India had gone, it was only a matter of time before Africa – and all the remaining colonies – followed suit.

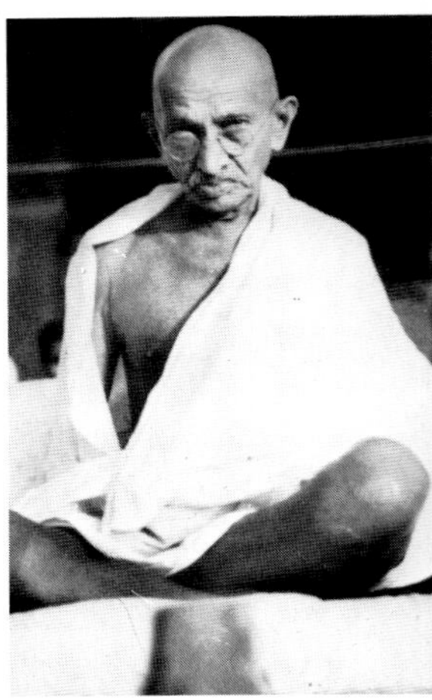

Mohandas Karamchand Gandhi, known as Mahatma ('great-souled'), was a leader in the Indian independence movement. He stressed the importance of non-violence. He was shot by a Hindu fanatic in 1948.

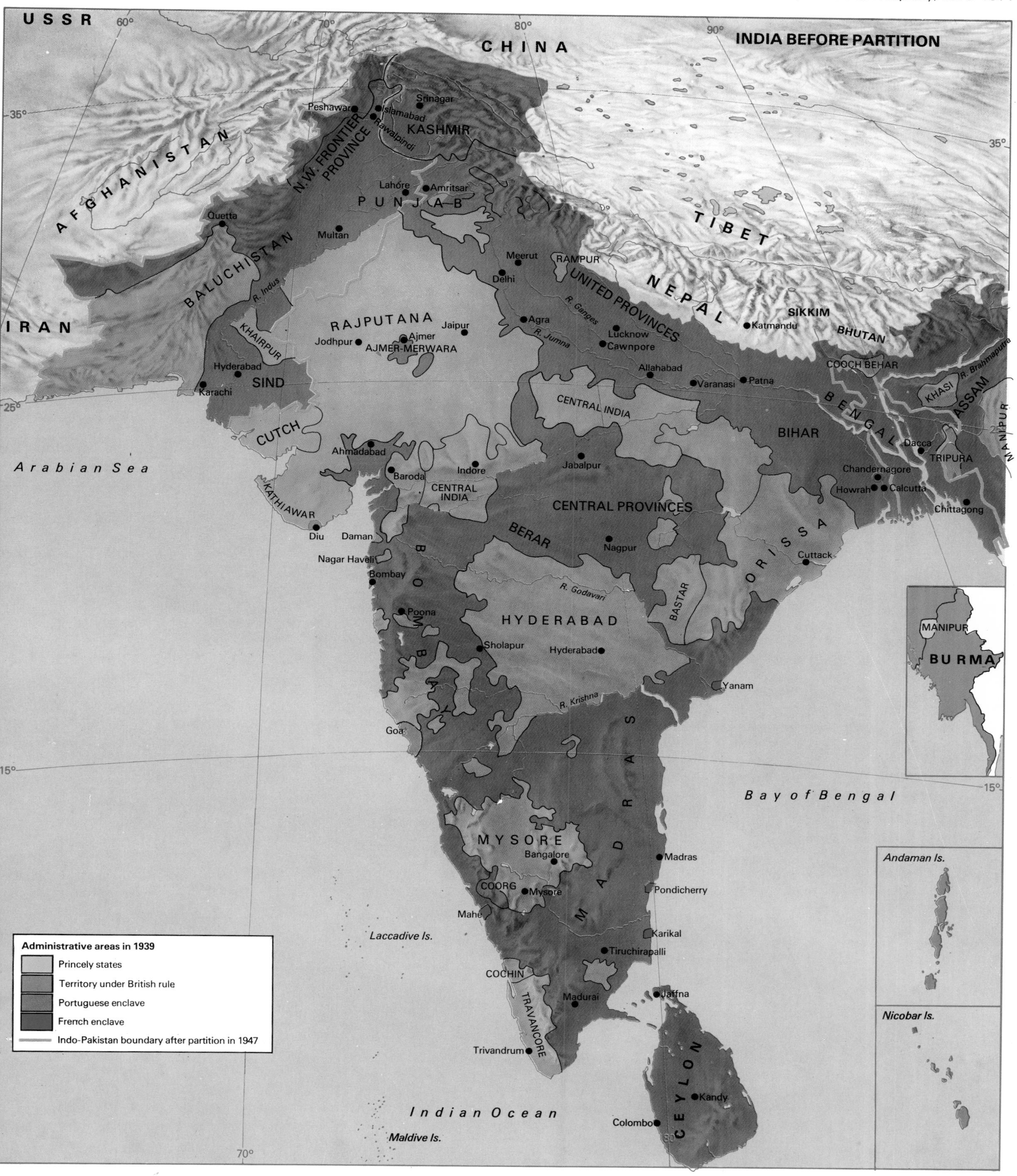
INDIA BEFORE PARTITION
USSR
CHINA
TIBET
NEPAL
SIKKIM
BHUTAN
AFGHANISTAN
IRAN
BURMA
Arabian Sea
Bay of Bengal
Indian Ocean
Laccadive Is.
Maldive Is.
Andaman Is.
Nicobar Is.
N.W. FRONTIER PROVINCE
KASHMIR
PUNJAB
BALUCHISTAN
RAJPUTANA
AJMER-MERWARA
KHAIRPUR
SIND
CUTCH
KATHIAWAR
CENTRAL INDIA
UNITED PROVINCES
RAMPUR
CENTRAL PROVINCES
BERAR
BIHAR
BENGAL
COOCH BEHAR
KHASI
ASSAM
MANIPUR
TRIPURA
ORISSA
BASTAR
HYDERABAD
BOMBAY
MYSORE
COORG
MADRAS
COCHIN
TRAVANCORE
CEYLON
Peshawar
Islamabad
Rawalpindi
Srinagar
Lahore
Amritsar
Quetta
Multan
Meerut
Delhi
Agra
Lucknow
Cawnpore
Allahabad
Varanasi
Patna
Katmandu
Jaipur
Ajmer
Jodhpur
Hyderabad
Karachi
Ahmadabad
Baroda
Indore
Jabalpur
Diu
Daman
Nagar Haveli
Bombay
Nagpur
Cuttack
Chandernagore
Howrah
Calcutta
Dacca
Chittagong
Poona
Sholapur
Hyderabad
Yanam
Goa
Bangalore
Mysore
Madras
Pondicherry
Mahe
Karikal
Tiruchirapalli
Madurai
Jaffna
Trivandrum
Kandy
Colombo
R. Indus
R. Ganges
R. Jumna
R. Brahmaputra
R. Godavari
R. Krishna
60°
70°
80°
90°
35°
25°
15°
Administrative areas in 1939
Princely states
Territory under British rule
Portuguese enclave
French enclave
Indo-Pakistan boundary after partition in 1947

The British Empire, 1815–1914

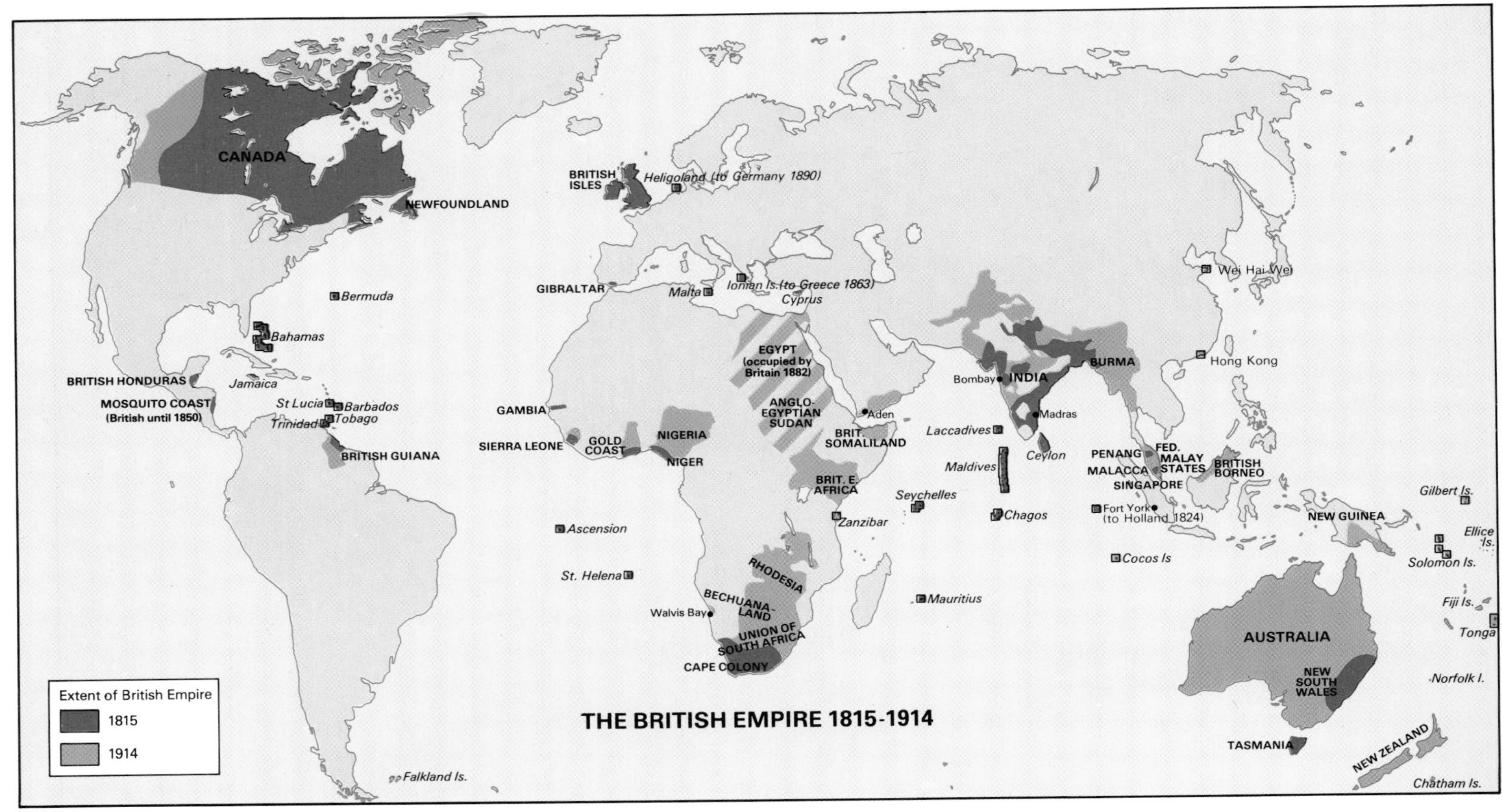

The expansion of the British Empire. The period from 1870 to 1914 saw the acquisition of territory in Africa, much of Burma, Malaya and Borneo, and a number of islands in the Pacific.

The history of the British Empire before 1914, when it reached an apex of power and influence, can be divided, for convenience, into three periods. First, from the late 16th century to the 1780s the Empire was concentrated in the American Colonies and the West Indies – sometimes called the Old Colonial System. The next hundred years, roughly from the loss of the American Colonies and the acquisition of Quebec to the creation of the Dominion of Canada (1867) and the opening of the Suez Canal (1869), was the Second Empire. The years 1870–1914, sometimes referred to as the 'new imperialism', saw the most dramatic expansion. In area, the Empire more than doubled from 4.5 million square miles to 11.1 million square miles, a growth of population from 202 million to 372 million; and the number of territories increased approximately (according to the definition used) from 47 to 73. In the first half of the 19th century the most important feature was the consolidation of the territories that later became the Dominions; Australia, New Zealand, Canada and the Cape Colony; and in the latter part of the century Africa became the principal area of extension. The trade of slaves, bullion and spices at the end of the 18th century had been replaced by wheat, wool, meat and dairy products by the end of the 19th century.

Explanations abound for such developments. In the first period the prevailing mercantilist philosophy of wealth being increased through trade, with protection and colonies following, is a useful summary. Free trade and the liberal economics of the late 18th and early 19th centuries led away from the Old Empire, and a potent, though disputed, source of explanation for the second period has been found in the 'imperialism of free trade' – that, as the leading manufacturing nation, Britain used free trade to open up the world to further British influence or control. The final burst of territorial acquisitiveness threw up other explanations of both the economic and political variety. Three broad areas of explanation have emerged. Economic explanations concentrate on the need of the imperial power in terms of sources and outlets for trade and investment. Political explanations embrace all manner of expressions of nationalism, as well as Schumpeter's atavistic theory of an objectless disposition on the part of the state to unlimited frontier expansion, and actions at the periphery that led to formal annexation. A third source has been sociological, the spreading of 'civilization', associated with notions of racial superiority, social organization, culture and religion.

All of these explanations have some application somewhere but no one of them can stand alone in so complex a process. The Empire grew for varied reasons: out of individual traders' needs, from subduing trouble at the periphery, for strategic considerations, the promotion of free trade, the transporting of convicts to Australia, the planned settlement of New Zealand, and so on.

It has sometimes been found useful to have a broader view of Empire and see it in terms of British influence, to speak of 'informal' Empire. The informal Empire extends into Latin America and parts of the Far East that have never been painted red on the map. Aggressive trading often secured British traders a dominant position. Sometimes friction and outright conflict resulted, as in the Opium Wars in the 1840s or in the Boxer Rising of 1900 when the Chinese actively opposed foreign intrusion. Against this, the example of Peru is often quoted as a country keen to associate closely with Britain but never formally tied in any way. Trade dominates in the discussion of informal Empire in the 19th century and the economic ties of trade, capital flows and migration were very strong, particularly with the white dominions and parts of the informal Empire. Many other territories then acquired a strategic importance in keeping open crucial trade routes.

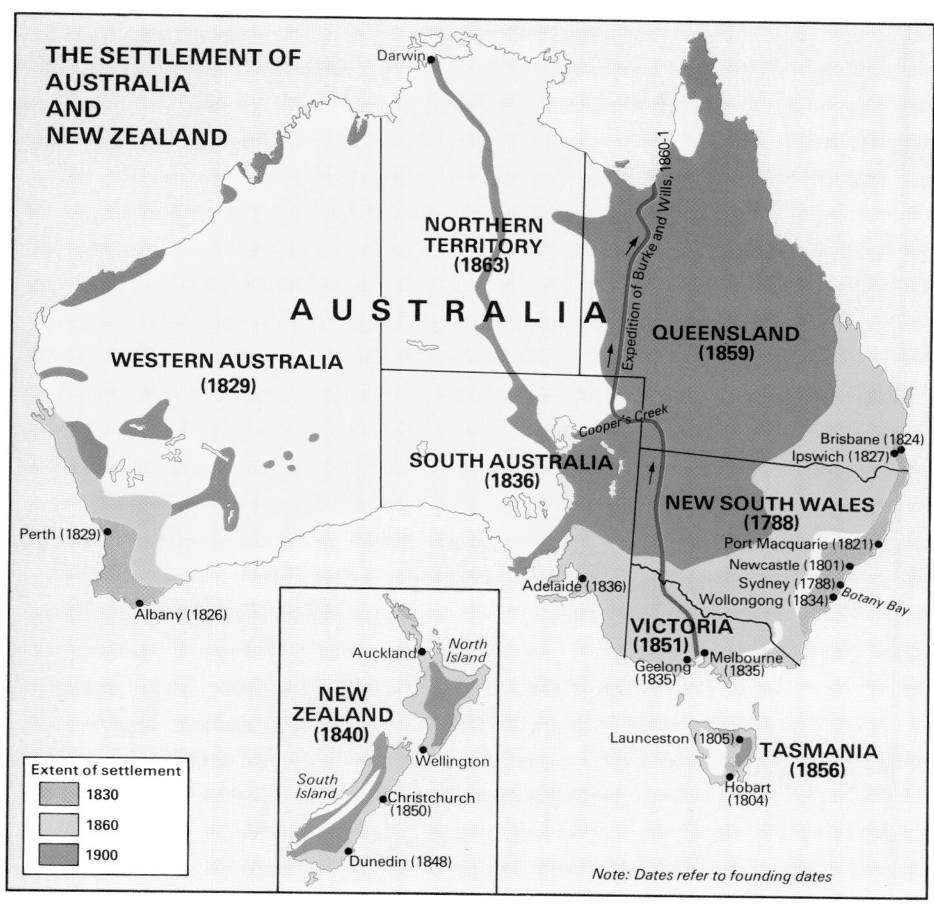

The settlement of Australia and New Zealand. The earliest settlements in Australia were penal colonies, but from the 1820s, when a way had been found across the mountains behind Sydney into the plains beyond, free settlers arrived to exploit the agricultural potential. The discovery of rich gold deposits in Victoria in 1851 led to a massive influx of immigrants, most of whom eventually settled in the main cities.

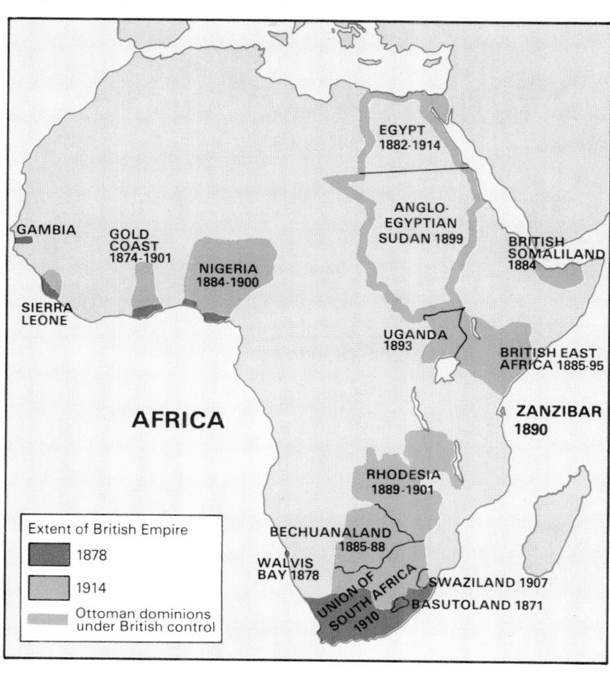

GOVERNOR DAVEY'S PROCLAMATION TO THE ABORIGINES 1816

Left: Thomas Davey governed Tasmania from 1813 to 1817. Between 1803 and 1830 numbers of Aborigines there dropped from 2000 to 200

British possessions in Africa. In 1889 the British South Africa Company was formed by Cecil Rhodes and Alfred Beit; it allowed British rule to expand in Central Africa without involving the government in expense or responsibility. The Company acquired the right to administer what is now Zimbabwe (Rhodesia) and Zambia (Northern Rhodesia) although it did not manage to gain control of Malawi (Nyasaland).

The British gained control of the Dutch South African colony in 1814 and from the beginning there was considerable hostility between British and Boers. To escape from British rule the Boers began to trek northwards in 1835, in the face of Zulu opposition. After their victory at Blood River in 1838, the Boers founded independent settlements in Natal, the Orange Free State, and the Transvaal; but these too were to be mopped up by the British Empire following the South African Wars.

British Elections, 1832–1980

The search for the election-winning 'middle ground' that has preoccupied so many 20th-century politicians was also the key to early Victorian politics in the wake of the Reform Act of 1832. By 1841 the Whigs had lost the sanely reforming impetus that had gained them widespread middle-class support in the early 1830s; instead that support went to Peel, who now attempted in his reforming ministry to broaden the basis of the Tory Party, hitherto almost solely identified with the interests of 'backwoodsmen' squires. His strategy proved premature – scuppered finally by the Party's revolt in 1846 against the repeal of the Corn Laws. So instead the way was left open to two decades of more or less Whig dominance, pending fundamental realignments of party policies and allegiances. The elections of the mid-Victorian period tended as a result to be rather muddled affairs, often pivoting on local rather than national issues. Nevertheless, the election of 1857, following the Crimean War, showed a clear vote of confidence in the 'forward' stance of Palmerston as against the 'Little Englander' outlook of Cobden and Bright.

By 1868 a more recognizably 'modern' pattern had emerged: the Whigs had been joined by the Radicals and the Gladstone-led Peelites to form the Liberal Party; the Tories now tended to be called the Conservative Party, reflecting the lesson taught by 20 years virtually out of office that naked reaction was no longer practical politics; and the passing of the Second Reform Act in 1867 confirmed earlier tendencies that political parties would have to be organized more systematically in the face of an enlarged electorate.

The year 1868 marked a notable triumph for the Gladstonian Liberal Party, as popular Nonconformity responded to the promise of disestablishing the Irish Church and the artisan class thanked Gladstone, not Disraeli, for extending the franchise. But for the rest of the century elections were dominated by the severe difficulties the Liberal Party found itself under in appealing simultaneously to its diverse elements. On the one hand, Anglican middle-class support became increasingly doubtful. This was revealed first in 1874 by the distinct mood of suburban retrenchment that followed the major reforms of Gladstone's first ministry. And it was confirmed by the elections of 1886 and 1895, when on both occasions Gladstone's espousal of Irish Home Rule was strongly opposed by propertied opinion (including the Liberal Unionists within the Liberal Party's own ranks). On the other hand, the emergence of an organized working class (both skilled and unskilled) created a sense of class identity that undermined labour's unquestioning allegiance to a Party that was dominated – especially at local level – by moral but insensitive middle-class Nonconformity.

The process was fluctuating and drawn out: for if Gladstone in 1892 achieved only a muted success by his continuing commitment to the Irish cause – in comparison with his triumph in 1880 over the Bulgarian and Afghanistan questions – the Liberal Party in 1906 was able to win a landslide victory. The Liberals won this election precisely by standing for such 'moral' mid-Victorian precepts as humanitarianism and Free Trade. Yet it was significant that when in 1910 two elections were held to try to resolve 'the Peers versus the People' question following the attempt by the House of Lords to block Lloyd George's radical fiscal proposals, the Liberal Party was unable to engender that degree of middle-cum-working class enthusiasm that would have been the case even a quarter of a century earlier. Instead, the middle class as a whole was almost as resentful as the peers about the new taxes, while the organized working class, now tentatively represented in Parliament by the infant Labour Party, showed little

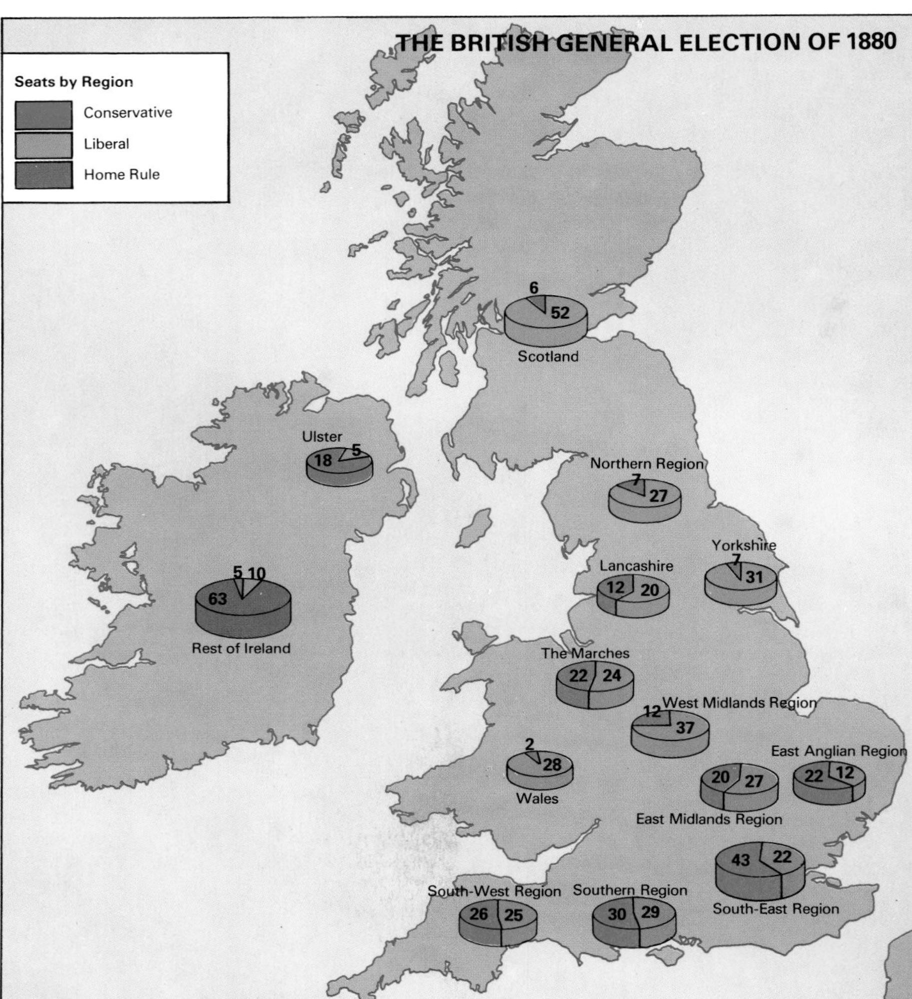

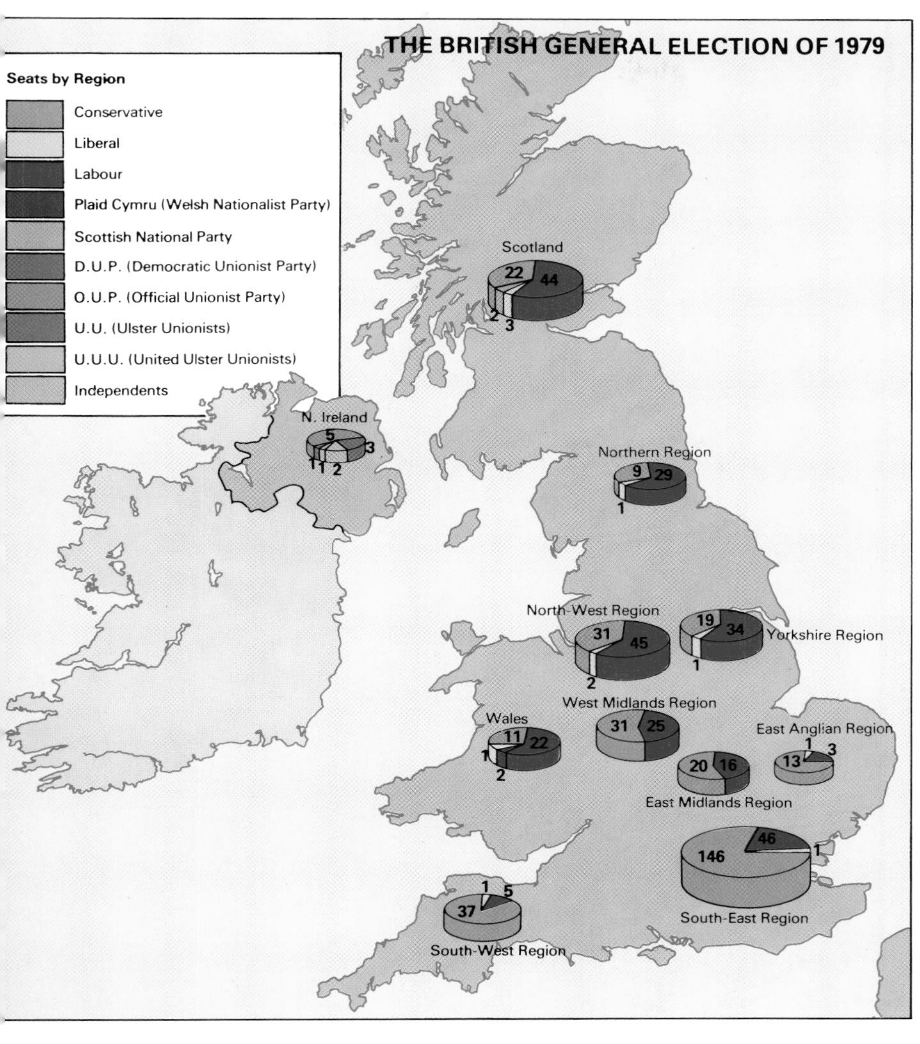

British Elections 1832–1980

(seats gained by each party)

	C	L		
1832 Dec	185	473		
1835 Jan	279	379		
1837 Aug	314	344		
1841 July	367	291		
			P	
1847 July	243	324	89	
1852 July	290	319	45	
1857 March	256	372	26	
1859 May	306	348		
1865 July	300	358		
1868 Nov	279	379		
			IN	
1874 Feb	352	243	57	
1880 April	238	352	62	
1885 Nov	250	334	86	
			IN	**LU**
1886 July	316	191	85	78
1892 July	268	274	81	47
1895 July	341	177	82	70
1900 Oct	334	186	82	68
	C&LU		**IN**	**Lab**
1906 Jan	156	379	83	52
1910 Jan	273	275	82	40
1910 Dec	272	272	84	42

	Coal.	Opp.		
1918 Dec	478	229		
	C	**Lab**	**L**	**Others**
1922 Nov	345	142	116	12
1923 Dec	258	191	159	7
1924 Oct	419	151	40	5
1929 May	260	288	59	8
	Coal.	**Lab**		
1931 Oct	554	52		11
1935 Nov	429	154	21	11
	C	**Lab**	**L**	**Others**
1945 July	213	393	12	22
1950 Feb	298	315	9	3
1951 Oct	321	295	6	3
1955 May	344	277	6	3
1959 Oct	365	258	6	1
1964 Oct	304	317	9	0
1966 March	253	363	12	2
1970 June	330	288	6	6
1974 Feb	297	301	14	23
1974 Oct	277	319	13	26
1979 May	339	269	11	16

C Conservative; IN Irish Nationalist
L Liberal; LU Liberal Unionist
P Peelite; Lab Labour

Note: 'Liberal' pre-1865 denotes a loose group of Whigs, Liberals, Radicals and Peelites, and Irish, often held together only by being anti-Conservative.

Far left and left: Election results in 1880 and 1979, showing the proportion of seats held by the different parties in each region.

In 1909 the House of Lords tried to block Lloyd George's tax reforms. He countered with the threat to create enough Liberal peers to overtake the Conservative majority. Two general elections followed before the Parliament Act was passed in 1911, which limited the powers of the Lords.

interest in questions of constitutional principle in comparison with more immediate matters of wages and hours.

The events of the First World War, hastened these underlying pre-1914 tendencies. By the mid-1920s, following a series of elections, it was apparent that the Liberal Party was no longer a major force in British politics. It had been ousted by a Conservative Party under Baldwin and a now nationally based Labour Party under Ramsay MacDonald that represented the respective interests of capital and labour. Thus was the electoral mould set that has broadly persisted to this day.

Since the Second World War there have been four elections of unusual significance. In 1945 the Labour landslide embodied the hopes of a generation afflicted first by economic depression and then war that there would in the future be a greater measure of social security. In 1951 the Conservatives entered a lengthy period of office on the premise that the twin ideas of Welfare State and nationalized industry had been taken by Attlee's government as far as they could reasonably go. In 1964 Labour returned to power, taking up Macmillan's 'You've never had it so good' mantle of 1959 and adding a certain socially concerned, technologically progressive colouring to it. And in 1979 Labour's claim to be the 'natural party of government' was abruptly shaken when a markedly *laissez-faire*, anti-collectivist stance brought a decisive victory to the Conservative Party, and brought Britain its first woman Prime Minister.

Chapter Six

CONFRONTATION AND CHANGE: BRITAIN SINCE 1914

Between 1914 and 1945 Britain fought in two World Wars, suffered a catastrophic economic depression, and saw the beginning of the end o her colonial Empire. Since 1945 Britain's role in world affairs ha continued to shrink, while the Empire has all but disappeared. In thes changed circumstances Britain has sought both political and economi security in wider groupings, and her relations both with the Unite States and with Europe have left far behind that 'splendid isolation which was the hallmark of British foreign policy at the close of the las century.

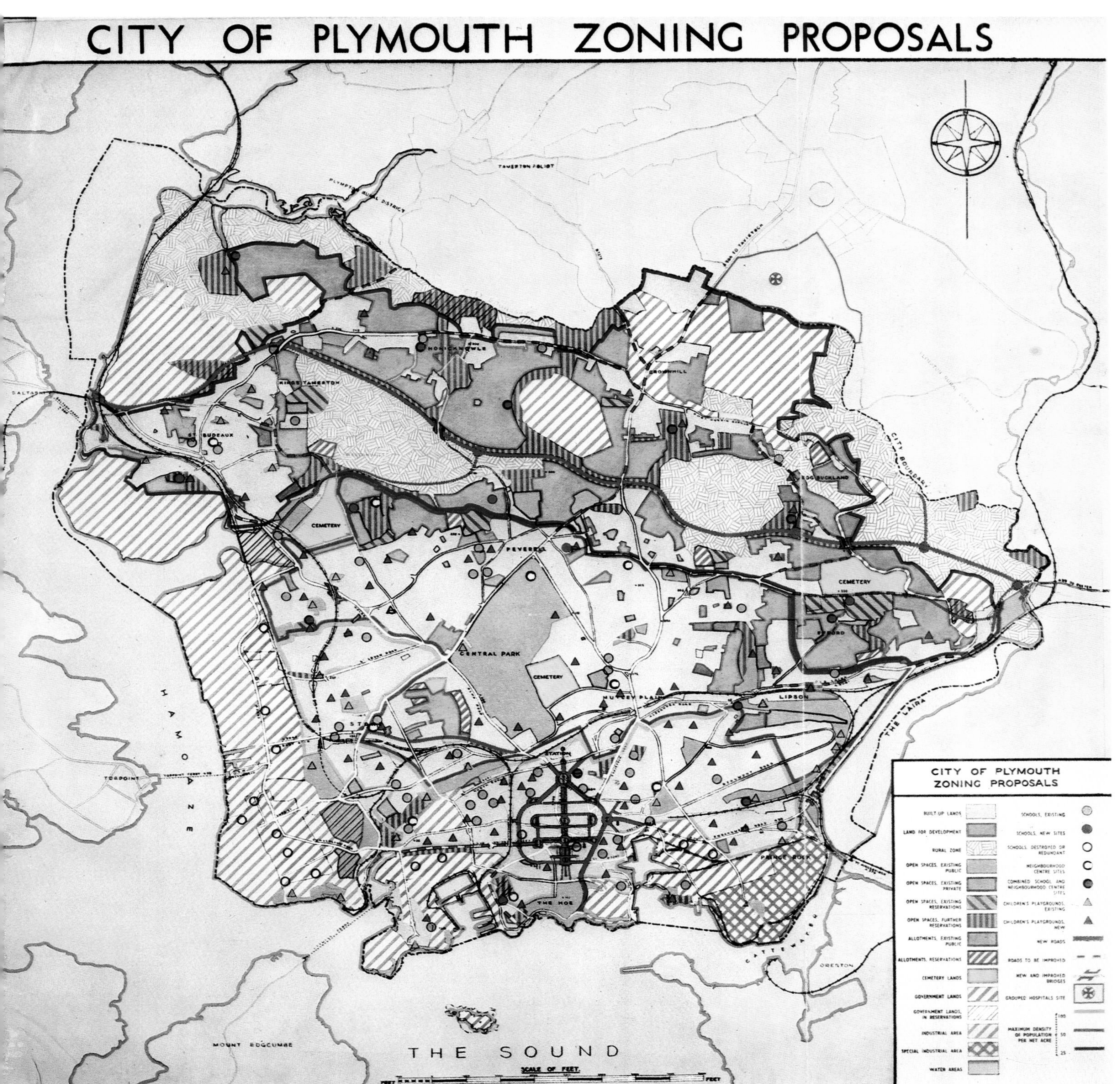

'A Plan for Plymouth' (1943) by P. Abercrombie. Red arrows show blitz damage with buildings demolished or damaged beyond repair.

The First World War

In August 1914 massive German armies swept through Belgium and northern France: they aimed to surround Paris, encircle France's armies and destroy them before turning to face Russia in the East. The hastily despatched, but highly trained, British Regular Army, 100,000 strong, met the full weight of the German right wing at Mons on 23 August and had to retreat. The British then joined the vastly superior French army in a counter-attack on the Marne, from 9–16 September, which forced the over-extended Germans to retreat when 15 miles (25 km) from Paris. In October and November Anglo-French troops saved the French ports by the battle of Ypres, with 50,000 British casualties. By late 1914 Allied and German armies stood in parallel lines of trenches stretching across France from the Channel to Switzerland. These lines moved only a few miles either way throughout the war, with the British holding the Allied left wing. Deadlock resulted because trench warfare favoured defence: barbed wire and machine guns could withstand cavalry and infantry attack.

In 1915, controlling Belgium and France's industrial North, Germany stood on the defensive, repelling futile and costly Allied attacks. She concentrated instead, with Austrian help, on the East, seizing most of Poland from Russia. France bore the brunt of the war in the West, although Britain had 600,000 men there by May 1915. The British War Secretary Kitchener began to build a huge volunteer army and in 18 months had 2.5 million volunteers. Britain's dominions and India had declared war and were also mobilized. Empire troops conquered Germany's colonies but were also deployed in France and against Turkey, which joined Germany in October 1914.

Britain's economy was gradually regulated for total warfare; from May 1915 Lloyd George, munitions minister, ensured adequate armaments were available. It was Lloyd George, with Churchill at the Admiralty, who initiated an expedition to attack Turkey and push supplies through the Straits to Russia. In April 1915 (as Italy joined the Allied side) Allied troops, mainly Australian, New

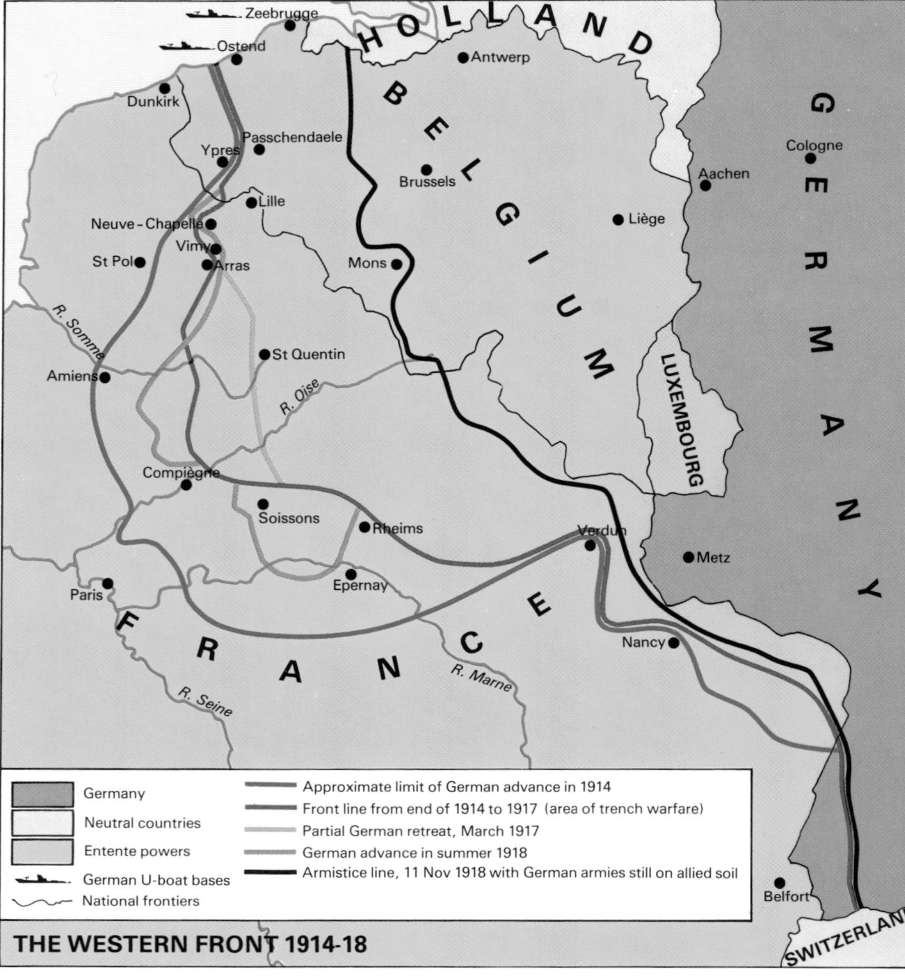

The Western Front. From the end of 1914 to 1917 the front line altered little; troops were dug into trenches and battles costing hundreds of thousands of lives achieved gains of only a few miles.

Woman at work in an English factory. The war brought thousands of women into industry, many doing jobs hitherto thought suitable only for men. By the end of the war their presence was taken for granted and their struggle for emancipation, at a stalemate for so long, was significantly advanced.

The Eastern European and Middle Eastern theatres. British and Empire troops fought the Turks disastrously at Gallipoli and, successfully, in Mesopotamia and in Palestine. There they incited the Arabs to rebel against their Turkish rulers by promising to create independent Arab states – a promise largely broken after the war, which was to cause much bitterness.

Zealand and Indian, landed on the Gallipoli peninsula but failed to advance from the beaches before being evacuated by January 1916. Britain's one success at this stage was her navy's almost total blockade of Germany. The Germans retaliated with submarine attacks on Allied shipping, but the sinking of the British liner, *Lusitania*, in April 1915, caused American protests and the prospect of intervention. Germany consequently limited her attacks. However, in May 1916 Germany's fleet left its North Sea ports to challenge the British under Jellicoe in the battle of Jutland, off the Danish coast. Although Britain suffered the heavier losses the Germans returned to harbour and stayed there throughout the war.

In 1916 Germany tried to win decisive victories in the West. From February to July her armies attacked the fortress of Verdun, calculating France would bleed herself white defending it. But both sides lost over 300,000 men. By 1916 the British army, commanded by Haig since late 1915, was over a million strong and increasing as conscription was imposed (May 1916) and women entered industry, transport and agriculture. In May 1916 Haig launched a major British offensive on the Somme. This failed with appalling slaughter: by the close, in November, British casualties reached 400,000. Although Lloyd George brought more vigour into the war effort as Prime Minister (December 1916), the generals could not solve the stalemate in the West, despite having more troops there than the Germans in 1917. In March 1917, following a partial German withdrawal to a shorter front line, France launched a disastrous spring offensive which caused mutinies in her armies. A British attack around Ypres (battle of Passchendaele, July to November) won five miles (8 km)for 400,000 losses.

In February 1917 Germany declared unrestricted submarine warfare, hoping to starve Britain into surrender. But America's entry into the war in April and the use of convoys and anti-submarine devices gradually beat the U-boat threat. It was now vital for Germany to win in the West before enough American troops arrived. The Russian Revolution in 1917 had led to the collapse of Russia's war effort and peace with Bolshevik Russia (March 1918) gave Germany temporary numerical superiority in France. In March 1918 Germany attacked the junction of the British and French lines. The Allied front buckled but held and with continual American reinforcements they counter-attacked in August. Haig's British troops dominated this decisive campaign, at last using tanks effectively to breach German defences. The exhausted and outnumbered Germans retreated and, although still on foreign soil, were forced to make peace on 11 November. Germany had collapsed internally and her allies, Austria, Turkey and Bulgaria, were already surrendering. Austria collapsed before Italian attacks and an Anglo-French offensive through the Balkans from Salonika. The Turkish Empire was also disintegrating: Anglo-Indian forces in Mesopotamia had taken Baghdad in March 1917 and in October 1918 Arab irregulars and a British expedition from Egypt seized Damascus.

Post-battle devastation on the Western Front. Farmland and forests were reduced to mud and sticks.

Politics and Domestic Affairs, 1914–39

A London bus leaves its depot under police escort during the General Strike of 1926. The failure of negotiations between the government and the Trades Union Congress on wages and conditions in the coal mines triggered off the strike, for which the government was far better prepared than the unions. Troops were brought in, and many strikers were arrested but the strike was on the whole peaceful; volunteers kept essential services running and after nine days the strike was called off. The miners, however, continued their strike until the autumn when lack of funds forced them back to work.

In party political terms the single great fact of the years 1914 to 1939 was the almost complete eclipse of the Liberal Party. Although the signs of the decline had been apparent before 1914, the political events following the outbreak of the Great War had their own dramatic momentum. Almost from the start of the war it became clear that the traditional Liberal *laissez-faire* approach to government (summed up by the slogan 'Business as usual') was inappropriate to what for Britain was an entirely new kind of war. And so, in May 1915, following a scandal over the shortage of shells, Asquith was forced to bring the Conservatives into a coalition. Asquith's leadership of the war effort remained ineffectual, and in December 1916 Conservative pressure compelled his resignation in favour of Lloyd George. This created a schism between Asquith and Lloyd George which, by the time it was healed in the mid-1920s, had left the Liberal Party as the merest shadow of its former self.

With the Liberals thus split, and in particular Lloyd George entrapped from 1916 to 1922 as leader of a Conservative-dominated coalition, the anti-Conservative vacuum in party politics was instead filled by the Labour Party, especially in the wake of the introduction in 1918 of near-universal suffrage.

The First Labour government

Under Ramsay MacDonald's leadership, and with a solid foundation laid by Arthur Henderson's organization, the Labour Party in this period was able to form two governments, both minority, first in 1924 and then in 1929. Neither proved particularly successful. By 1931 the second Labour ministry had met such a severe financial crisis that a section of the Party under MacDonald himself splintered off to form a 'National' government, dominated by the Conservatives. But by the eve of the Second World War it was clear that the Labour Party, despite its problems in office, had come to stay and that for the foreseeable future would represent the main alternative to the Conservative Party.

In domestic terms the inter-war period will perhaps best be remembered for three issues: Ireland, the Abdication, and the slump.

The Irish Question was finally 'settled', on paper at least, by Lloyd George in December 1921 through a treaty which created an Irish Free State, thereby giving Ireland Dominion status and virtual independence, while allowing six counties of Ulster to remain part of the Union.

Fifteen years later King Edward VIII's decision to choose the woman he loved in preference to retaining the Crown hardly had the same momentous import. To many contemporaries, however, even if sympathetic to the dilemma of the man, it marked a significant regression from the high Victorian standards of public duty.

Overriding everything were the grave economic difficulties, particularly affecting traditional heavy staple industries, in which Britain found herself enmeshed. These

Hunger marchers from Jarrow on their way south to present a petition in London in 1936. Jarrow, in north-east England, was dependent on ship-building and steel manufacture, and was in one of the worst-hit regions in the depression of the 1930s.

followed the catastrophic effects of the war, on top of a certain decline which had begun even before 1914. In the election of 1918 Lloyd George had boldly pledged 'to make Britain a fit country for heroes to live in'. But mounting unemployment, and financial difficulties that took an especially heavy toll of Addison's housing programme, made a mockery of Lloyd George's promise during the course of the ministry's life. The General Strike of 1926, which pivoted on the dire straits of the coal-mining industry, and the Hunger Marches of the 1930s were palpable signs of deep economic and social malaise. The politicians in office did relatively little that was positive to remedy the situation, but concentrated, in impeccably Gladstonian fashion, on balancing the books and redeeming the National Debt.

Levelling of society

Nevertheless, by no means everyone suffered during these years. If the industrial North bore the brunt, the service-providing South in many instances actually flourished, especially with the development of mass-produced consumer goods. Walter Greenwood's *Love on the Dole* (1933) evoked a twilight northern townscape, but population was drifting southwards and the leafy suburban world of Metroland was growing apace. In many ways this was a period of implicitly profound social change in which many of the 19th-century barriers finally came down. In terms of the transition to a more genuinely democratic society, nothing was more important than the enhanced status of women. Their active role during the war was first meagrely rewarded in 1918, with the vote being given to women over the age of 30, and then more properly being given its due in 1928 with the enfranchisement of all women over 21. Other examples of the levelling tendencies now beginning to operate included the decline of domestic service, the first widespread use of contraceptives among the working class, the advent of the holiday camp, the spread of the cheap motor car, and in 1936 the beginning of the world's first television service, ironically enough in the same month that fire destroyed Crystal Palace, symbol of the leisure of another age. But then, once *The Times* had decided in 1922 to omit the prefix 'Mr' before the names of amateur cricketers it was obvious that nothing was sacrosanct.

British Foreign Policy since Versailles to 1939

At the end of 1918, British forces and British influence were extended farther than ever in British history. The Russian civil war had brought British forces to Archangel, the northern Baltic, the Caucasus, the Caspian Sea and Vladivostok. The Ottoman surrender was observed by British forces in the Dardanelles and at Constantinople. Mixed Arab, Indian, British and Commonwealth forces had 'liberated' Palestine, Syria, the Lebanon, Mesopotamia and the Hejaz itself. The German colonies in Africa, Tanganyika, the Cameroons and South-West Africa were occupied by British African or South African forces. But Britain's reach was much further than her grasp, exhausted by the war's losses in money and men, could sustain. Moreover the extent of British gains awoke ancestral nationalist suspicions in France and the United States. Between 1919 and 1922 there was a rapid contraction of British power which ameliorated, though it did not basically improve, relations between the three war-time partners. With America Britain was forced, by the usual mixture of need and sentiment, to compromise. A generous, (over-generous as it was to prove) offer settled the issue of Britain's war-debts to the United States in 1922. That same year a mixture of American pressure and Canadian anxiety saw the Anglo-Japanese alliance transmuted into a four-power Pacific pact, and Anglo-American naval competition frozen in a naval disarmament agreement signed at Washington. It was to be extended in 1930 and 1936 in successive treaties signed in London.

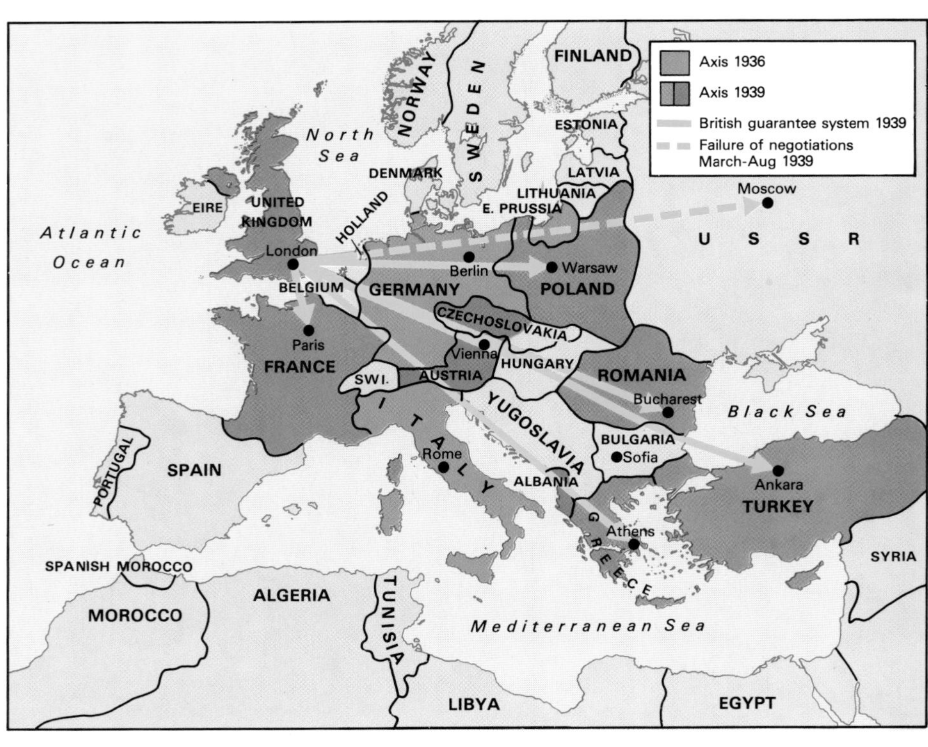

British foreign policy between the wars. Through a series of alliances and guarantees, Britain sought to contain the growing power of Nazi Germany.

Lausanne and Locarno

In the Middle East, British, American and French oil interests reached an accommodation over the exploitation of oil in the former Ottoman territories of Mesopotamia and the Gulf (it did not cover Saudi Arabia). In the Near East the revival of Turkish nationalism under Ataturk led, after a confrontation at Chanak on the Dardanelles in 1922, to the Treaty of Lausanne that same year which was to put British relations with Turkey on a permanently friendly basis. Anglo-French rivalry was temporarily appeased by the assignment of Syria to France (the Arab revolt was suppressed) and Mesopotamia and Palestine to Britain as mandates.

Disagreement remained, however, over the policy to be followed towards Germany. Britain regarded a revival of Germany's economy as an essential concomitant of her own, while French fears of Germany led her to use the reparations issue to keep Germany weak, until this French policy collapsed in 1923–4. Britain was now able to play her part in the Franco-German *détente* that followed by guaranteeing France's, Germany's and Belgium's common frontiers in the Treaty of Locarno (1925). This was a symbolic rather than a real commitment to a new intervention in Europe. British opinion had swung towards an isolationism cloaked by the illusion of 'collective security' provided by the League of Nations. Through the long drawn-out and weary disarmament negotiations of 1925–34, Britain proved unable or unwilling to provide any guarantees for France's security adequate to allow France to accept the removal of Versailles' restrictions on German power. In the meantime Britain's own armed forces were reduced to a mere shadow. The world economic crisis of 1931, which forced Britain to abandon her efforts to recover the position of world supremacy in finance she had enjoyed before 1914, saw further cuts in arms expenditure and a mutiny in the Royal Navy.

This revelation of British weakness coincided with the collapse of peace in the Far East. Here, renascent Chinese nationalism, with which Britain was quietly accommodat-

Lloyd George, Orlando, Clemenceau and Wilson at the Peace Conference of Versailles, 1919.

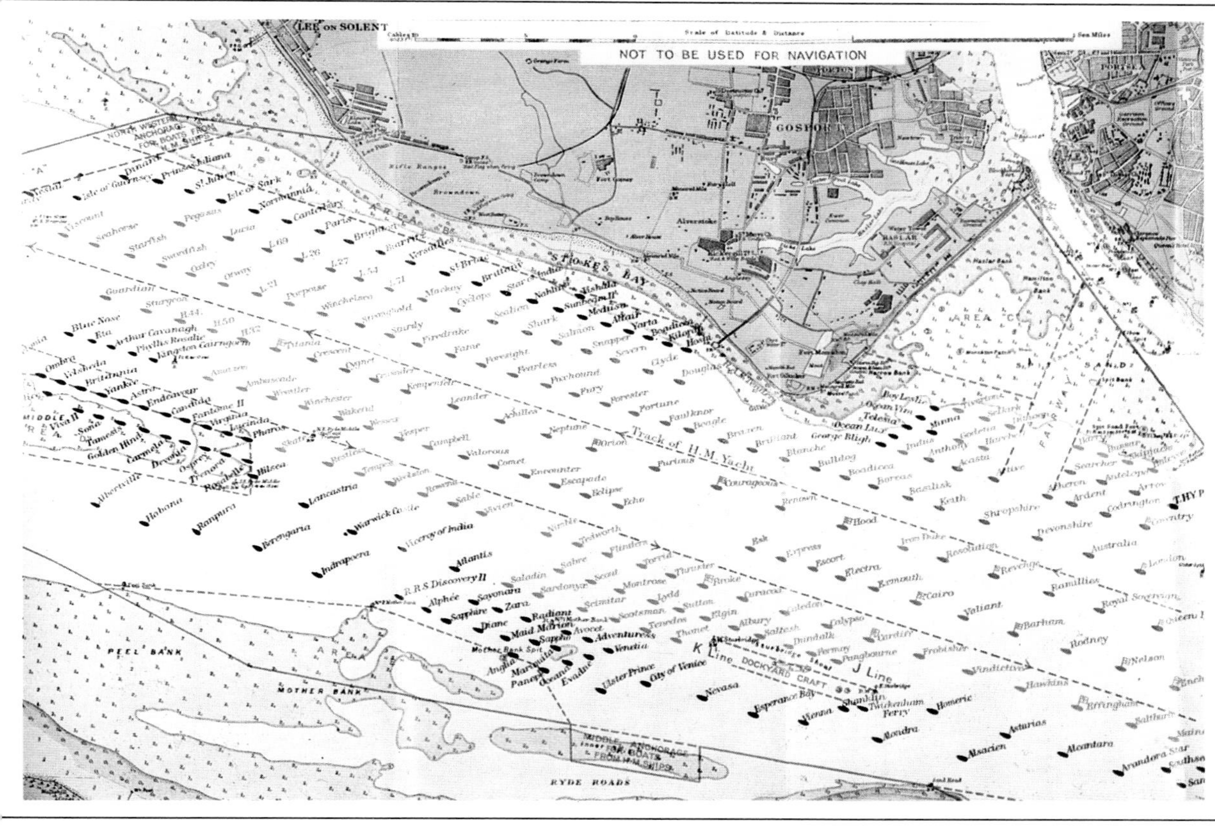

Plan of the Spithead royal naval review of 1935. British naval power, supposedly the cornerstone of a global British foreign policy, was effectively limited by agreements designed to allay American suspicions of a resurgent British Empire. To American eyes, Britain appeared as a potential rival for Great Power status.

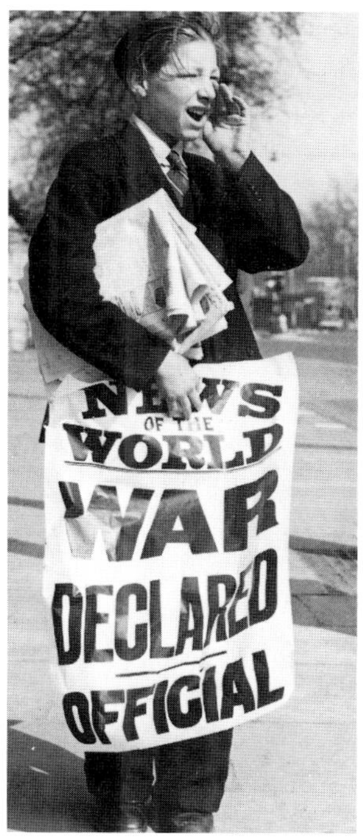

The announcement of war, 3 September 1939.

ıg her enormous trading interests in China, clashed irectly with Japanese militarism in Manchuria. The ,eague of Nations proved powerless; America acted on her wn, but with words not deeds. Britain realized that her 'hole strategic position in the Far East, supposedly ounded on a new and still uncompleted base at Singapore, 'as threatened. The threat was to grow throughout the ext eight years, providing a constant, distracting and 'eakening influence on Britain's position in Europe. Iitler, German Chancellor from 1933, was apparently ommitted to the establishment of German supremacy in urope, come what might. And Britain's policy makers ecognized her inability to contain Germany until Britain's ilitary weakness, especially to attack from the air, had een repaired. Until then, concessions to German na-onalist claims against Versailles (claims that commanded uch sympathy among British opinion), were essential. 'he 'appeasement' of Germany moved from inaction when Iitler threw off restraint on German armaments in 1935, arched into the demilitarized Rhineland in 1936, sup-orted the Spanish nationalist revolutionaries in the panish Civil War from 1936–8 and annexed Austria in Iarch 1938, to negotiating away Czechoslovakia's western orders at Munich in September 1938 to avoid a general ar in Europe.

Parallel clashes with Fascist Italy over the invasion of thiopia (1935–6), pirate submarine activities in the Iediterranean and support of the Arab revolt in Palestine .936), and with Japan once the Sino-Japanese conflict had ared up into war in 1937, made the British position weaker ather than stronger and the need to control and contain ermany even more urgent. In January 1939 baseless eports of German plans to invade the Low Countries and) bomb London swung the Cabinet toward the military ommitment to Europe they had hitherto refused. A German–Polish clash in March and an alleged threat to Romania led the British government, in an effort to deter Hitler from further action, into a series of guarantees and alliances with Poland, Romania, Turkey and Greece, in which France participated. Britain and France failed to secure Soviet Russian adhesion to these guarantees. Instead Stalin compacted with Hitler; and Hitler, incredulous of Britain's new-found resolution, attacked Poland. The Anglo-French declaration of war followed three days later on 3 September 1939.

British Prime Minister Neville Chamberlain leaves to meet Hitler at Berchtesgaden in September, 1938. Chamberlain's three missions formed the last throw of a policy which had aimed at maintaining peace in Europe. Despite receiving substantial concessions, Hitler contemptuously ignored the terms of what became known as the Munich agreement.

The End of Britain's Empire, 1919–80

Independence for the new Zimbabwe as the Union Flag is lowered outside Government House in Salisbury, 17 April 1980. Decolonization in Britain's African territories was on the whole peaceful, but the struggle between the white settler community in Rhodesia and the black majority (where Ian Smith's Rhodesian Front Party ruled illegally for 15 years, following the Unilateral Declaration of Independence on 11 November 1965) was a bitter exception.

In 1919 Great Britain acquired the last territories to be added to the Empire. These were the mandates over Germany's former colonies in Africa and elsewhere, and over parts of the Arab territories of the Ottoman empire. These new possessions made up a fourth category of territories under British sovereignty, the first three comprising: the self-governing Dominions, including, though they were not Dominions as such, India and Southern Rhodesia (self-governing from 1922); Crown colonies; and protected states of various kinds, mainly in the Middle and Near East. Official British doctrine saw these as sharing a common British citizenship, though their natural progress was towards economic self-support and political self-government under the British Crown. Britain, through the British Colonial Service, saw herself as playing a tutelary role in this process. At the same time British governing circles saw the Empire as the continuing basis of world power. The Dominions had made a major contribution, in blood and treasure, to Britain's victory in 1918. Most of British mass opinion tolerated rather than approved or understood the Empire. One section of those that did, hoped that the Empire would become a tariff union and an organization which would develop institutions to maintain a common defence and foreign policy. They were to succeed only in the sphere of defence. The Imperial Conferences of 1921, 1923 and 1926 revealed, especially on the part of Canada and South Africa, a total unwillingness to be bound by anything but their own parliaments. And as for a tariff union, the infant industries of the Dominions were none too happy about facing British industry unprotected; whereas the dominant faith in Britain was still placed in free trade and cheap food. The Empire Exhibition at Wembley in 1923, and the constant pan-Imperial voyaging of the Prince of Wales and his brothers, kept the more colourful aspects of empire before British eyes. But except by extreme left-wing societies, and by some right-wing newspaper proprietors, the failure of hopes of an economic and foreign policy union passed unnoticed. Indeed, the establishment of the British Commonwealth, by the Statute of Westminster in 1931, was regarded more as a matter for congratulation than regret.

Among the colonies, protectorates and mandates were, of course, areas of trouble. The mandate over Iraq was transformed very easily into a military alliance and Iraq became independent in 1928. There were troubles between Jews and Arabs in Palestine, where the terms of the mandate imposed on Britain the impossible task of supervising the establishment of a Jewish 'national home' in an area which Arab nationalism regarded as its own. This flared into full-scale revolt in 1936. There were troubles with a militant Catholic Church in Malta; between Greek and Turk in Cyprus; and with nascent trades unionism in the West Indies – condemned by British free trade dogma to squalid, if picturesque, stagnation. There were continual troubles in Egypt, nominally independent in 1922, but with real autonomy only after 1936. Above all there were troubles in India, with the Congress Party united behind the improbable figure of Mahatma Gandhi, whose own doctrine of non-violence only intermittently dampened down the simmering sectarian violence of Indian urban life. The Government of India Act of 1935 went a long way towards Indian provincial self-government, but nothing like fast enough for Indian aspirations.

The Japanese occupation of Burma and Malaya in 1942, and the alliance with the United States, whose people still saw the Empire as inspired by the spirit of George III, brought the British to deal directly with the vision of Indian self-government. Muslim nationalist distrust of the Hindu

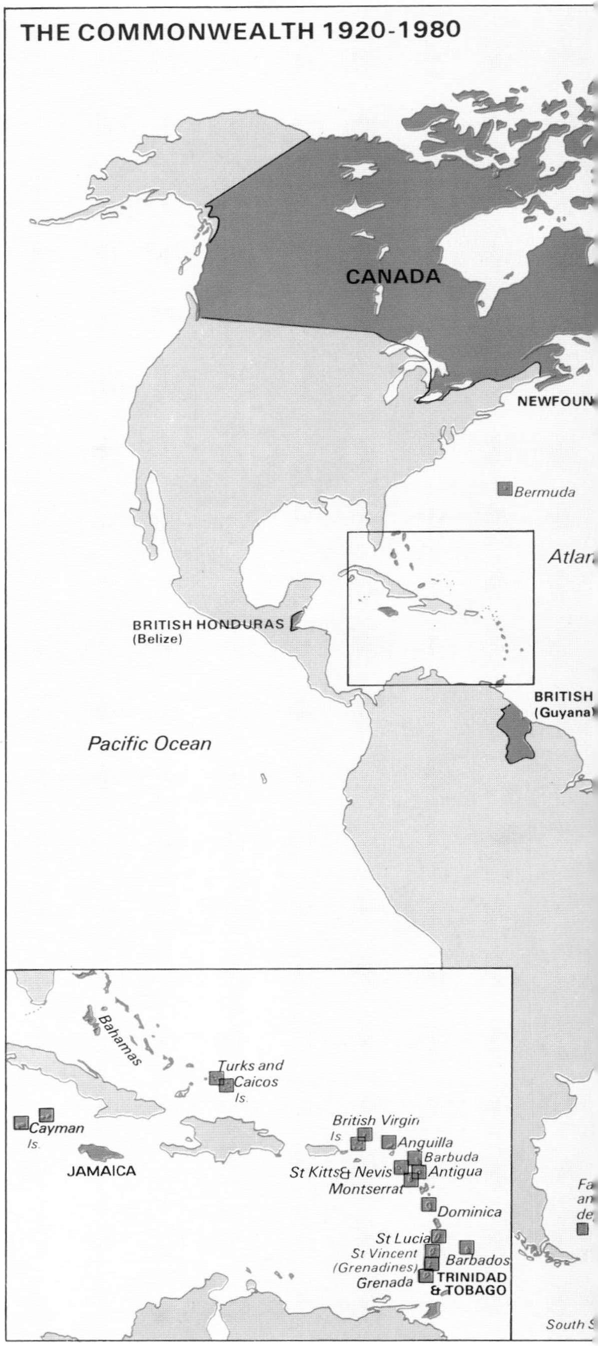

majority and Gandhi's militant pacificism proved incon patible with British aims. In Burma nationalist leaders fir collaborated with then turned against the Japanese. Malaya, Chinese communists led the resistance to Japa The Japanese defeat restored British rule, and took Britis and Indian troops into Indo-China and Indonesia. Britis forces had occupied the former Italian colonies of Liby and Somalia leading them painlessly to independence. Th incoming Labour Government of 1945 was determined do the same with India. In 1947 the last Viceroy, Lor Louis Mountbatten, presided over the independence Ceylon, India and Muslim Pakistan, East and West, having proved impossible to maintain Indian unity. A ne formula was found to reconcile Indian republicanism wi the role of the British Crown, as the bond uniting t

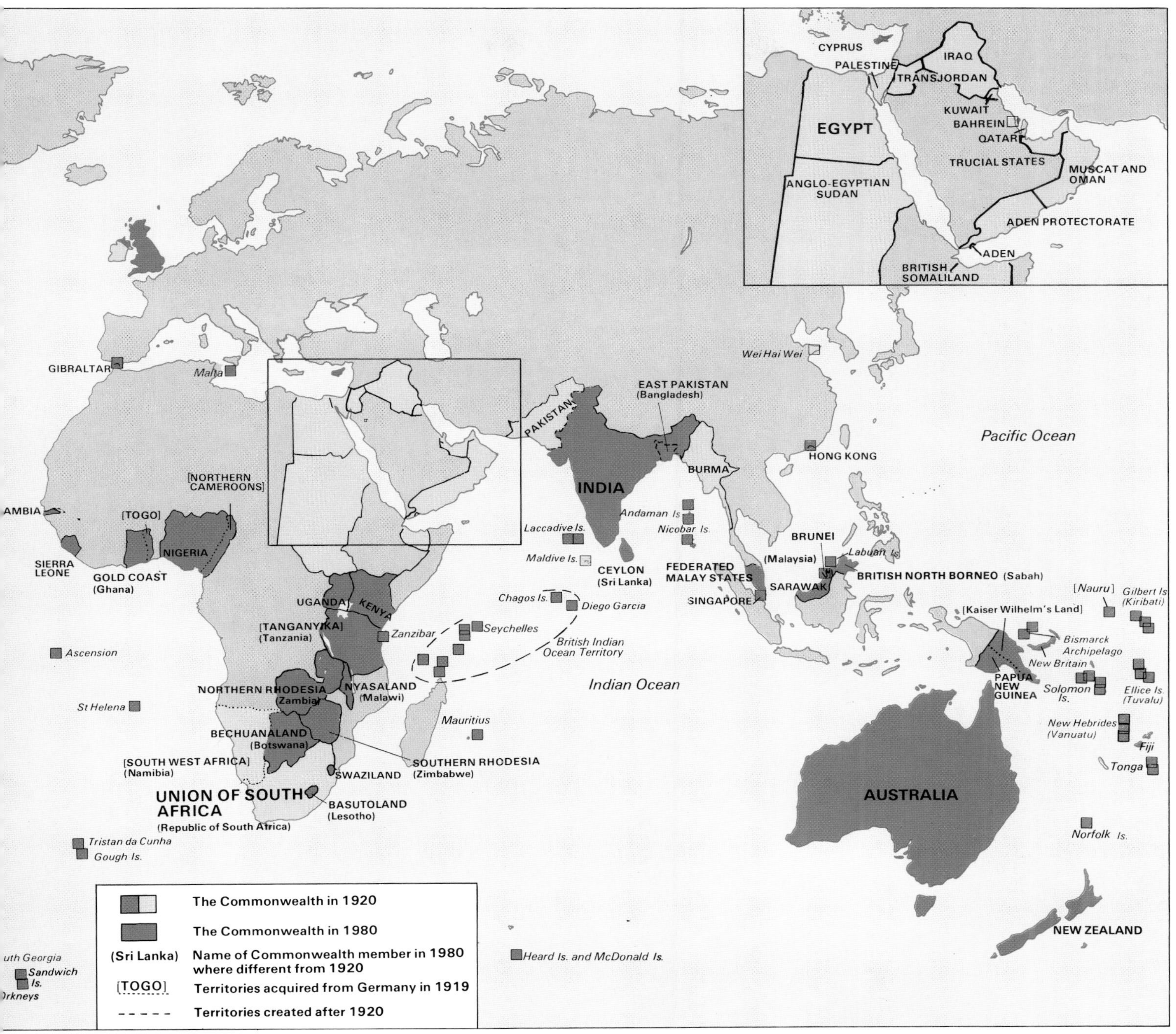

From Empire to Commonwealth. Since the end of the Second World War almost the entire Empire has achieved independence and most of the countries have remained within the Commonwealth.

ommonwealth. But the price of Indian membership urma left the Commonwealth entirely) was the end of the ommonwealth as a defence community.

The single force which now united the Commonwealth, art from the Crown, whose Imperial tours grew more portant, was the British system of higher education. om 1932 hopes had again been growing in the economic d financial field. The Ottawa treaties had set up a system economic preference for Commonwealth goods entering protected British market and regular freedom of entry of ommonwealth citizens to Britain continued, but there was real reciprocity in either case. The Sterling Area nbraced much of the Commonwealth (and much else sides), but not Canada. After the British withdrawal from lestine in 1948, the 'informal empire' in the Middle East and the Gulf readily melted away. All British troops east of Suez were withdrawn in 1969. From 1957 the 'winds of change' began to blow in Africa, forcing South Africa to leave the Commonwealth. In 1965 Rhodesia declared its independence unilaterally to avoid the same principle, a revolt which lasted until 1980. War between India and Pakistan, and the transformation of East Pakistan into the separate state of Bangladesh, caused Pakistan to withdraw in 1972. British opinion swung sharply against unrestricted immigration from the Commonwealth, destroying the common citizenship basis of membership. In place of the ideals and apparatus of the greatest empire in modern history there remained only the Commonwealth Secretariat, the Crown and the still strong links of education, language and culture.

Britain and the Second World War

Great Britain's declaration of war on Germany was followed by a long period of inactivity on land and in the air. Britain's expeditionary force (the B.E.F.) was bound by France's defensive strategy. In the air, each side was reluctant to be the first to begin a major bombing offensive. Nothing was done to prevent the swift German conquest of Poland. At sea, however, German submarines struck the day war opened, sinking the liner *Athenia*. German heavy ships raided into the Atlantic, searching for convoys to destroy. A British squadron caught the pocket battleship *Graf Spee*, driving her into shelter and ultimate scuttling in the River Plate; the remaining ships and submarine attacks were more or less contained. British military engagement really began with the German attack on Norway on 10 April 1940, which forestalled a British move to lay mines in Norwegian waters to interfere with iron ore shipments to Germany. British troops coming to Norway's aid proved unable to contain or eliminate the invaders in the face of the German air superiority, and were withdrawn in June. The Royal Navy lost some ships but the German navy was temporarily crippled, both of its battlecruisers being damaged, and one cruiser and twelve of her twenty-five destroyers sunk.

The British failure brought down the Conservative government of Neville Chamberlain. It was replaced by an all-party coalition led by Winston Churchill. The fall of the Chamberlain government coincided with the German invasion of the Netherlands, Belgium and France. The bulk of the B.E.F. covering the Franco-Belgian border moved into Belgium to resist the German onrush. But the German break-through in the Ardennes towards the Channel and the subsequent Belgian surrender threatened to encircle the B.E.F. and cut it off from the sea. A rapid fighting retreat, one counter-attack at Arras, the sacrifice of British garrisons in Boulogne and Calais, and Hitler's error in halting his armour for a vital two days enabled the evacuation of the B.E.F, together with 112,000 French and Belgian soldiers, from Dunkirk. This 'miracle' did not stop the German drive into France. Churchill offered France union with Britain but would not commit the remaining RAF fighter reserves.

The Second World War involved the whole population of Britain to an extent unimagined in earlier conflicts. Children like these, from areas vulnerable to attack, were evacuated to safer areas in the countryside.

Britain Stands Alone

On 10 June, Italy entered the war, Mussolini, the Italian dictator, being anxious for his share of the spoils. On 21 June 1940 France capitulated and Britain now stood alone. Hitler had made no plans for invading Britain; but Churchill's rejection of his 'peace offer', his rallying of Free French, Norwegian, Dutch, Belgian and Polish forces against Nazism, and the aid which the United States was now persuaded to give Britain made further action essential. To invade Britain Hitler needed to destroy the Royal Air Force. The air battles over Britain began early in August: but with radar to spot German aircraft well offshore, ground-to-air control to mass the fighter squadrons to attack them, and a recovery rate of pilots much greater than the Germans, the RAF held fast. At the end of September Hitler called off his invasion preparations and the Luftwaffe turned to a campaign of night attacks on Britain's cities, the *Blitz*. Nearly 100,000 British civilians were killed and wounded, but morale held.

Meanwhile, Britain's forces in Africa went over to the offensive against the Italian forces in Libya and in the Italian colonies of Eritrea, Abyssinia and Somalia. By February 1941 they had destroyed the Italian army in Cyrenaica. In May, the Italian forces in East Africa surrendered. In an air attack on the Italian naval base at Taranto in November 1940 and at the battle off Cape Matapan (28 March 1941) the Italian surface navy wa crippled. But the British no longer had to deal with th Italians alone, for an anti-German coup in Yugoslavia an the landing of British troops in Greece in March 194 resulted in a major German offensive in the Mediterranea In April, Greece was captured, the British forces bein evacuated. In May the Germans attacked Crete wit airborne troops. The *Luftwaffe* drove British surface shi from the central Mediterranean entirely, and submarine mines and human torpedo attacks on Alexandria reduce the British Mediterranean fleet to three cruisers and handful of destroyers.

In the western desert the German general Rommel drov the British forces, weakened by the dispatch of their be forces to Greece, from Cyrenaica; though a second Britis offensive in December 1941 recaptured all that had bee lost. In the meantime, spurred by reports of Fifth Colum activities, British forces put down a pro-Axis coup in Ira (May 1941), overran the French armies in Syria which we loyal to the defeated French government of Marshal Péta (June–July 1941), and divided Iran with the Russia (August 1941). The German attack on Russia (June 194 had now diverted the main German air and land forc eastwards: and American aid, though increasing enorm ously, now had to be divided with Russia.

Pearl Harbor

In December 1941 Japan entered the war, smashing th American Pacific Fleet at Pearl Harbor, sinking the *Prin of Wales* and the *Repulse* off Malaya, overrunning Malay and Singapore in February 1942 and driving the British o of Burma up to the Indian border by May 1942. In th meantime, the Japanese navy cleared the East Indian seas the remaining British, Dutch and American warship raiding as far afield as Darwin in Northern Austral (February 1942) and Colombo in Ceylon (April 1942).

In January 1942 Rommel attacked again in Cyrenaic recapturing the western half of the province. In May–Jun he drove the Eighth Army, after bitter fighting, to within 6 miles of Alexandria and the Nile Delta, taking Tobruk. I September his attack on Alam Halfa was repulsed, and the end of October his forces were decisively defeated b General Montgomery and pursued all the way back Tunisia. The British victory coincided with an Angl American invasion of Morocco and Algeria and a driv from the landings into Tunisia. Desperate German mea ures held Tunisia for six months, while Rommel's retrea ing forces linked up with them. But in May 1943, a quart of a million German and Italian troops surrendered. An by May 1943, also, British and American forces (though th bulk of the effort was British) had overcome the mo serious of all threats to Britain's survival, the Germa attacks with surface raiders, submarines and long-rang aircraft against Britain's vital sea supply routes. Th sinking of the battleship *Bismarck* in May 1941 had helpe to end the threat of surface raids by heavy ships save fo those on the northern supply route to Russia. Not until th end of 1943, with the second German navy battleshi *Tirpitz* damaged by British midget submarine attack i September 1943, and the *Scharnhorst* sunk in batt (December), was the Russian convoy route freed from tha threat. The submarine threat was at its worst in mid-194 and in the first four months of 1943, when Britain wa reduced to three months' supplies. But the British ability t read the German ciphers, coupled with the use of long range aircraft and escort carriers, harried the U-boats s effectively that 62 convoys crossed the Atlantic betwee May and September 1943 without the loss of a single shi

The European and North African theatres. Churchill described Italy as the 'soft underbelly of Europe', but resistance to the Allied invasion proved unexpectedly severe.

ıt the same time the Germans were losing three out of very five U-boats to leave German ports.

The British victory over the German U-boat offensive ʼas matched by the German victory over the Anglo-ɹmerican strategic bombing offensive against Germany, ne Americans by day, the RAF by night. The strategic ffensive from the air had begun in strength in May 1942 ʼith the first 1000-bomber raid on the Ruhr; the aim ventually was to damage German heavy industry and to ripple civilian morale. In the summer of 1943 mass raids n Hamburg killed upwards of 40,000 people and reduced he city to rubble: but as the attack shifted deeper into Germany the German air defences got the upper hand. In October the USAF lost over half the 288 aircraft attacking he Schweinfurt ball-bearing works, and in November an RAF raid on Nuremburg suffered similarly heavy casualties. The German success was concealed by the shift, early n 1944, of Allied aircraft to preparation for the invasion of Europe.

In September 1943, after the Anglo-American forces had overrun Sicily and the Fascist Grand Council had removed

Bomb damage in a London suburban back garden. Many houses had Anderson bomb shelters.

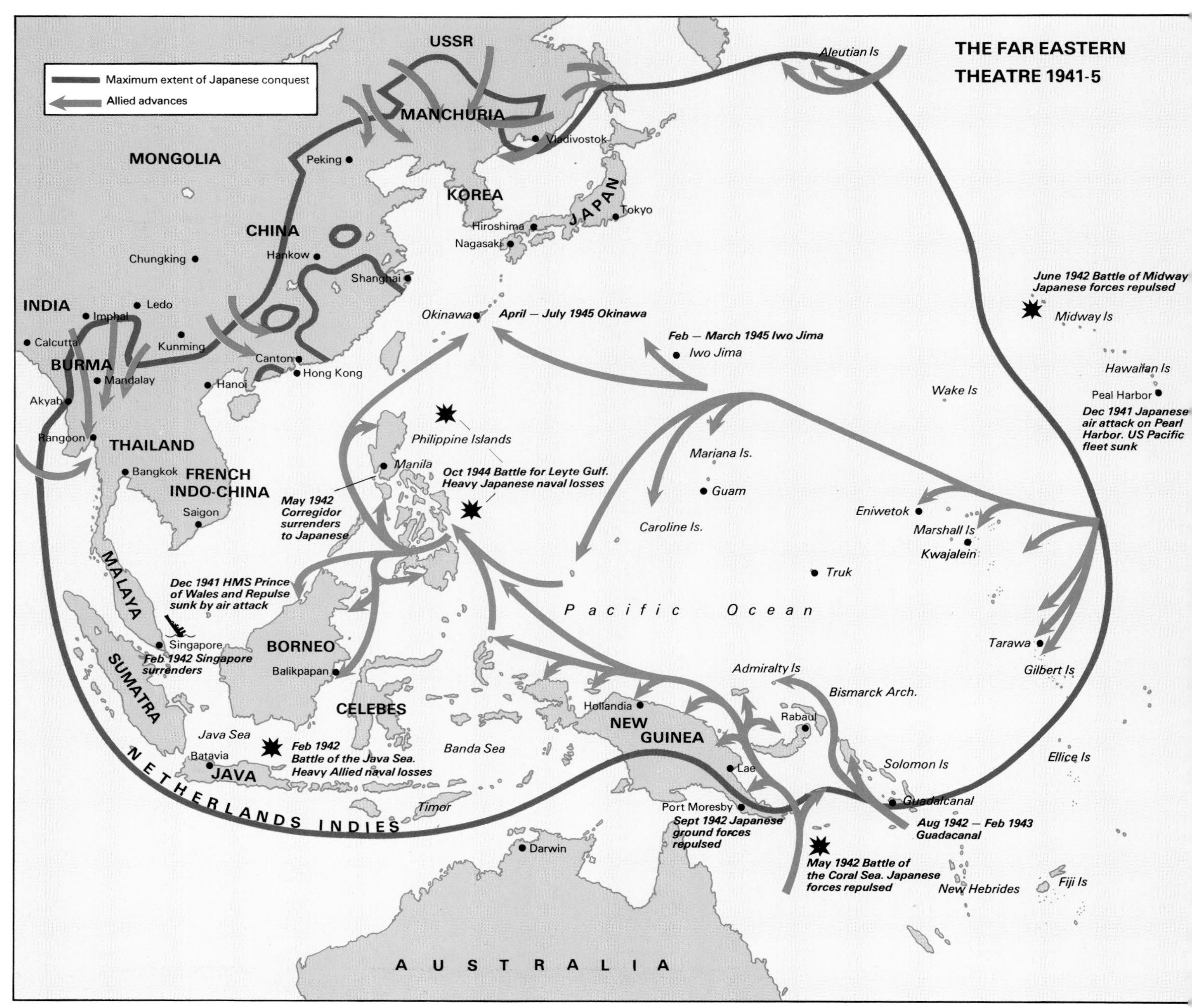

The War in the Far East. Between December 1941 and May 1942 the Japanese overran Malaya, the Dutch East Indies, Burma, Hong Kong and the Philippines. In June 1942 they were defeated by the Americans at Midway Island. Before Midway the Japanese had never lost a battle in the Pacific; afterwards they never won one.

Mussolini from office, the Italians signed a secret armistice with the Allies. Alerted by their cipher intelligence the Germans rushed forces to Italy, came within a hairsbreadth of defeating the Allied landings at Salerno near Naples and forced the Anglo-American Fifth and Eighth armies to face a long 20 months' slog up the mountainous length of the Italian peninsula. A British attempt to seize the Aegean islands of Kos, Samos and Leros failed in the face of German control of the air. Allied Forces in Italy only broke through the German defences south of Rome in May 1944, entering Rome in June, but being brought to a halt on fresh German defences south of Bologna (the Gothic Line) in October. The final breakthrough came only in April 1945, in the last month of the war. That victory was missed in 1944 was less the fault of the British than the slowness and inflexibility of policy inseparable from waging war by coalition.

By the end of 1943 the American share of the war effor (including very substantial support of the British war effor through Lend Lease, without which bankruptcy migh have induced British withdrawal from active participatio in the war in 1941) was so great as to give the United State the dominant voice in the coalition over Britain. The join military command in the war worked excellently so far a the planning and execution of planning phases of th invasion of Europe were concerned. The landings i Normandy in June 1944, the defeat of the German force Hitler massed to repel the invasion, and the break-out fron the lodgement established in Normandy were militar masterpieces. But when the pursuit of the surviving force began across France, involving a second landing i southern France, the political exigencies of coalitior warfare made concentration on either the British o American wings of the pursuit impracticable. Th

American wing ran out of supplies on the German border, the British failed to clear the Scheldt approaches to the great port of Antwerp and attempting to seize a clear route across the rivers of Belgium with airborne troops, failed at the last bridge, that over the Rhine at Arnhem, necessitating a long and bitter winter attack to clear the north bank of the Scheldt. The Germans won time not only to man a continuous front along their frontiers, but even to stage a massive counter-attack on the American position in the Ardennes in December 1944. With British aid the U.S. forces rode out and defeated this last gambler's throw, clearing the way for the last offensives which took the Anglo-American forces across the Rhine in March, taking the British 2nd Army into Hamburg and Lübeck and up to the Elbe by the time of the German surrender on 7 May to Montgomery of all forces in Holland, Denmark, Schleswig and North-West Germany, one day before the unconditional surrender of all German forces was staged.

But by this time Germany was in ruins. Her last hope at sea, the new submarines equipped with so-called *Schnorkel*, or breathing tubes, failed to reach adequate strength. The pilotless flying bombs, the *V-1*s, and the rocket missiles, the *V-2*s, did much damage in south-east England in the summer of 1944 before the main firing sites of these weapons were overrun. As for the introduction of jet-propelled fighters by the Germans early in 1945, the Messerschmidt 262 came too late to save Germany from a resumption of the strategic bombing offensive abandoned at the end of 1943. German heavy industries, German cities were destroyed one after the other, the worst attacks being those on Dresden in February 1945.

War in the Pacific

In the meantime the US forces had been carrying the main burden of the war against Japan in the Pacific. British forces had occupied Madagascar in 1942 to deny the Japanese bases in this Vichy France-controlled island. Fighting on the Burma–Indian front in 1943 had been largely inconclusive, the main British success being scored by the first Chindit raid into Japanese-held territory. In the first three months of 1944 the British 14th Army defeated a Japanese probing attack at the southern end of the front. In April they withstood a full-dress attempt by the Japanese 15th Army to cross the Chindwin river into India, holding the towns of Imphal and Kohima against a prolonged siege with the aid of airborne supplies, and destroying the Japanese airforces over Burma. The real British offensives in Burma, hitherto starved of supplies and landing craft in comparison with the European theatre, came in the first five months of 1945 when the 14th Army reopened the Burma Road to China, crossed the Irrawaddy, eluded a Japanese trap, broke the Japanese Burma Area Army completely, liberated Rangoon (2 May) and pursued the Japanese survivors into Thailand. Australian and American forces spent 1943 and 1944 fighting their way up the east coast of New Guinea, landing in the summer of 1945 to recover the oil-bearing areas of Borneo, Brunei and Balikpapan. The dropping of the atomic bombs on Hiroshima and Nagasaki (6 and 9 August 1945) and the Japanese offer to surrender (10 August 1945) brought all subsequent military operations to an end, British and British–Indian troops of South-East Asia Command taking over from the Japanese occupation forces in Malaya, Singapore, Indonesia and southern Indo-China.

British casualties in the Second World War, 400,000 dead and 500,000 wounded, were less than a third of those suffered in the 1914–18 war, but the cost to Britain was over three times as great in direct costs alone. The British mobilization of men and resources was as total as that of the Soviet Union and much greater than that practised by Germany, at least until 1944 or so. For twelve months (June 1940–June 1941) she faced a victorious Germany and her Italian allies alone, save for the military aid of the Commonwealth. But without the money and arms provided by US Lend Lease (in return for which she contributed to the alliance the scientific and decipherment leads that she, the occupied European states of France and Poland, and the refugee scientists of central Europe had together developed, together with the uranium of Canada and the Congo), her survival in the long term would have been at best uncertain. American money and manpower, and the long and bitter struggle of the Soviet people on the Eastern Front, made the defeat of Nazism inevitable.

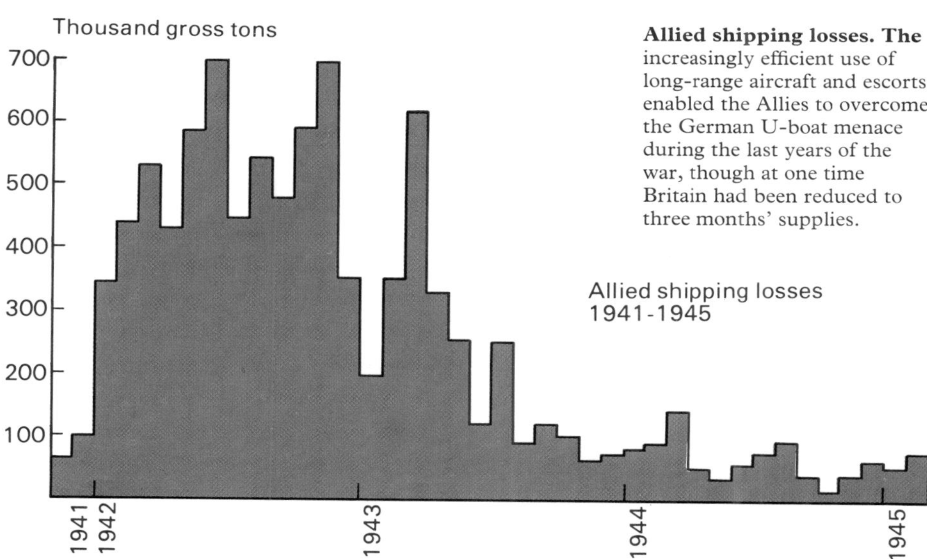

Allied shipping losses. The increasingly efficient use of long-range aircraft and escorts enabled the Allies to overcome the German U-boat menace during the last years of the war, though at one time Britain had been reduced to three months' supplies.

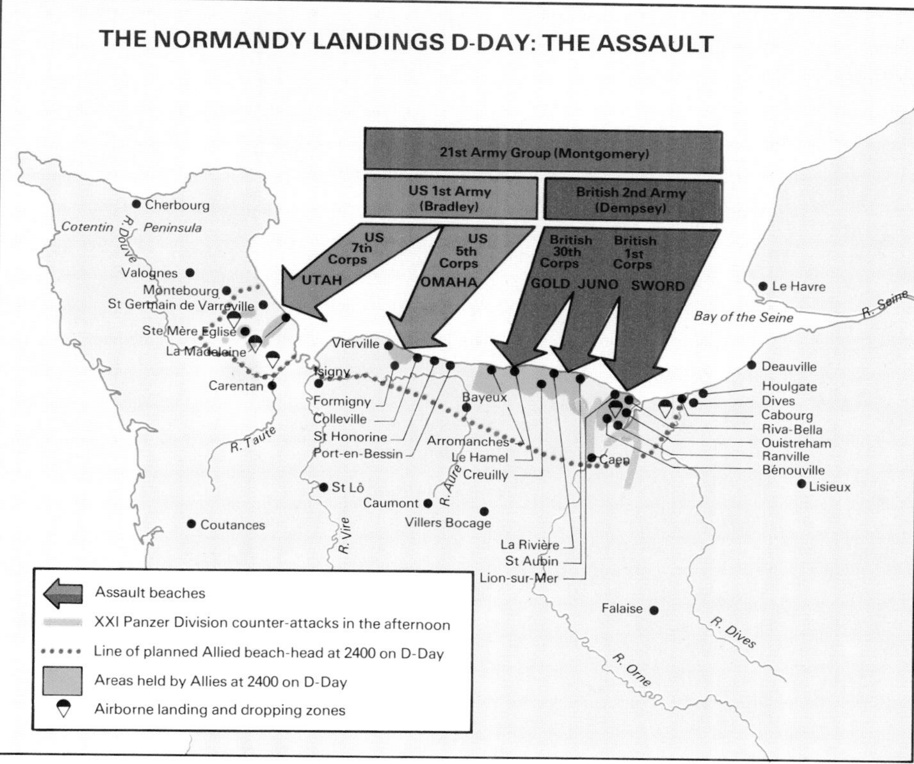

The Allied invasion of Normandy. The Germans were deceived into thinking that the landings would take place farther east and were taken by surprise. Fortunately for the Allies Rommel's plans for defending the coastline with underwater obstructions and mining the beaches were not wholeheartedly supported or carried out, while the British had developed specially adapted vehicles which were able to beat paths through the minefields.

Britain and Europe since 1945

The history of Britain's relationship with Europe since 1945 has been one of failure to realize European hopes after first raising them; of rejection of opportunities to become the leading power in the European movement only to become latterly an unsuccessful applicant for membership of the European Economic Community (EEC) and now an uneasy and reluctant member of that Community.

The movement for European unity – as distinct from mere co-operation – grew out of the Second World War. By 1946 there were about 25 million refugees living in camps, cellars or ruins; industry and commerce had been destroyed, governments overthrown and the fabric of society broken down. And over this war-shattered Europe loomed the threat of an even greater war between the two new super-powers. It was then that Churchill called for 'a kind of United States of Europe' as the only means whereby European recovery could be ensured and a powerful third grouping created.

For even after economic recovery had taken place, no individual European power would be able to match the super-powers – whereas, collectively, the states of Europe with their common cultural background, their long tradition of industrial and commercial development and a collective population of some 250 million would form the richest and most powerful bloc in the world.

In 1946 Britain was the most powerful of the European powers – the only one not to have been occupied by invading forces. Inspired by Churchill's call, political leaders from ten democratic European countries met at The Hague in May 1948 to produce a plan for a European parliament which, they hoped, would be directly elected by the people of the member states and be the springboard for that unity of which Churchill had spoken. But British politicians of both major parties were unwilling to help create a potentially powerful and supra-national organization; members of the proposed parliament would be merely delegates from the national parliaments. The resulting assembly, the Council of Europe, became, what its opponents wanted it to be, a mere debating chamber.

The threat from Russia led to closer military co-operation. Under the Treaty of Brussels (1948), the Benelux countries joined Great Britain and France in an alliance which was the forerunner to the much more important North Atlantic Treaty Organization (NATO) formed in 1949. But even here Britain proved a 'reluctant European', rejecting the plans for a European Army as part of an EDC (European Defence Community) proposed by Schuman of France in 1951 but abandoned in 1954.

The United States of America had provided the bulk of the funds for the United Nations Relief and Rehabilitation Organization (UNRRA) between 1945 and 1947 and so helped Europe's slow recovery. When that scheme came to an end, the US Secretary of State, George Marshall, proposed an even more massive aid for Europe, provided that the European powers agreed on a co-operative recovery programme. Once again Britain took the lead when Ernest Bevin, Labour Foreign Minister, helped create the Organization for European Economic Co-operation (OEEC) which initially covered 16 nations of Western Europe with West Germany as an associate member. The benefits of this co-operation were quickly evident and led many to believe that European unity might be achieved by means of economic collaboration.

In 1950 Schuman proposed that France and Germany should pool their coal and steel resources under a joint supra-national authority (ECSC). He realized that France could not prevent the development of German industry and considered that European recovery, started by Marshall Aid, stood a better chance if European heavy industry came under a single authority than if each country pursued its own path.

Schuman argued that the development of Europe's industrial heartland would be greatly stimulated if it served a vast European market, rather than a series of smaller national markets. Britain was then the largest coal producer and the second largest steel producer in Europe, and Schuman hoped that she would join France, Germany, Italy and the Benelux countries in this scheme. But Labour and Conservative governments were opposed to handing real power to a controlling organization which would have real independence. So it was that in June 1952 the European Coal and Steel Community came into being.

The development of Euratom was similar to that of the European Coal and Steel Community (ECSC). The advantages of co-operation in the field of nuclear research were obvious – only through such co-operation could Europe hope to keep pace with Russia and the United States of America. Britain was the most advanced European state in this field but proved unwilling to share her knowledge with less advanced countries or to hand over control to an international commission. So in 1957 the six countries of the ECSC went ahead with their own scheme.

The success of the ECSC and the proof that European states could hand over, with benefit, part of their sovereignty to a supra-national Commission, led European politicians to open discussion in 1955 on the proposal for a wider European Economic Community. Britain was invited to take part at Messina – but whereas the other European countries sent powerful politicians to speak on their behalf, Britain sent only low-grade civil servants.

The Treaty of Rome

The six countries formulated plans for a customs union with a common external tariff, for a powerful Commission which would control the trade, commerce and, in time, the financial fiscal and social policies of the member states.

Britain, however, was not enthusiastic about these proposals and instead tried to get agreement for a projected Free Trade Area. Within this area there would be the gradual abolition of protective tariffs on manufactured goods. Each member country, however, would retain the right to maintain its trading links with outside countries (such as the Commonwealth), while the FTA would have no supra-national Commission. The six were not interested in this idea. In 1957 they signed the Treaty of Rome which established the European Economic Community (EEC). Britain then set up the much more limited European Free Trade Association (EFTA) consisting of seven member nations. While the Six enjoyed an unprecedented boom so that their peoples' living standards rose rapidly, Britain lurched from economic crisis to economic crisis. In 1961 Britain formally applied to join the Common Market, but negotiations foundered on such issues as Commonwealth trade and agriculture. In January 1963 Charles de Gaulle vetoed Britain's application. At the end of the 1960s Britain tried again, and in 1971, under Edward Heath's leadership, Britain finally became a member of an enlarged EEC. But there was a good deal of opposition – from Left and Right – to this late move into Europe. The positive result of the referendum in June 1975 failed to end this opposition; the groundswell of criticism rose as Britain's economy deteriorated at the opening of the new decade.

Since the Second World War the countries of Europe have grouped themselves in varied defensive, economic and political alliances. Britai often remained aloof, becaus public opinion favoured clos ties with the Commonwealth rather than with Europe. Bu despite Britain's late entry t the EEC her trade with the Common Market countries now exceeds her trade with the rest of the world. The Communist countries of Eastern Europe have also grouped into political and economic blocs.

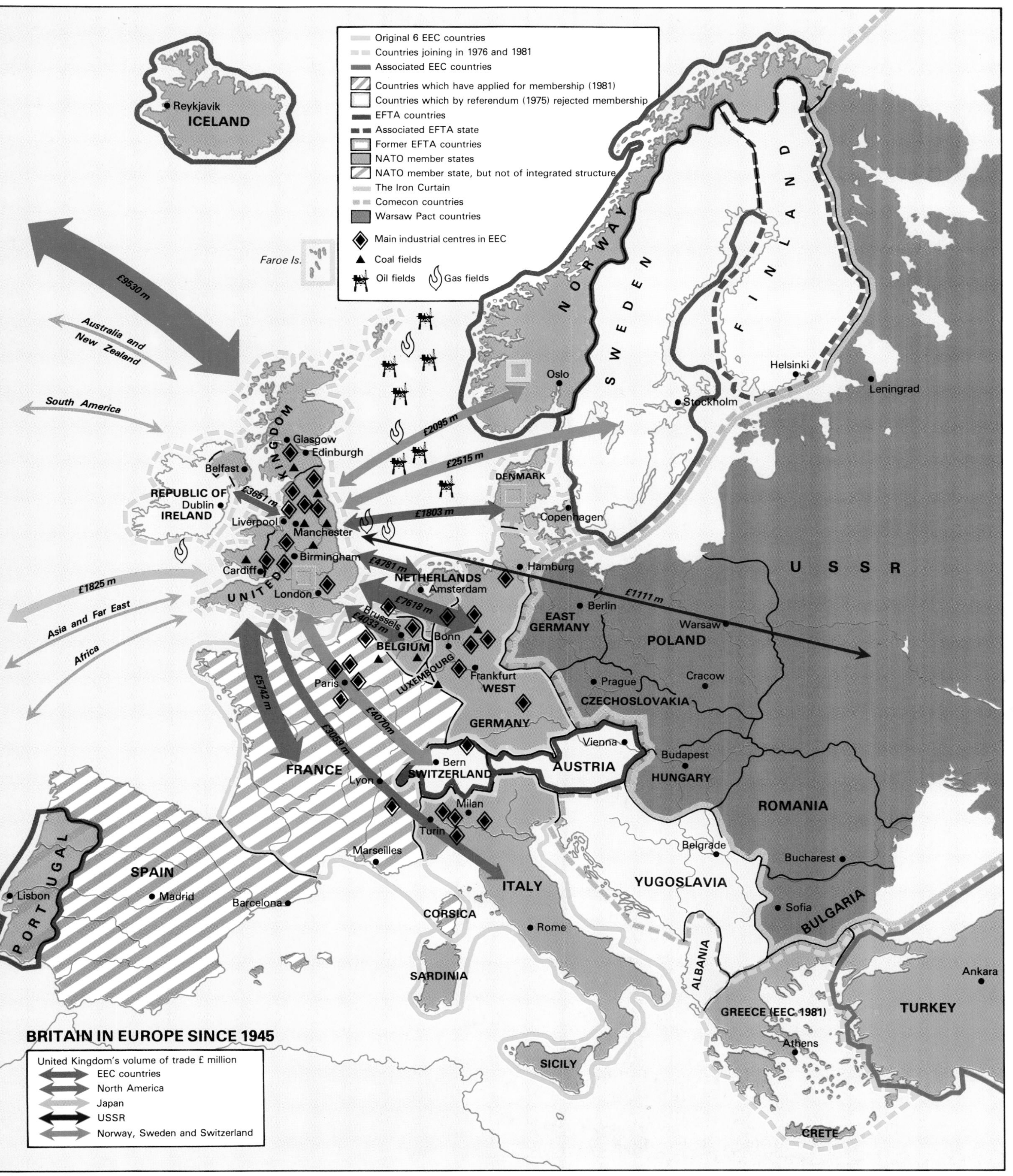
Original 6 EEC countries
Countries joining in 1976 and 1981
Associated EEC countries
Countries which have applied for membership (1981)
Countries which by referendum (1975) rejected membership
EFTA countries
Associated EFTA state
Former EFTA countries
NATO member states
NATO member state, but not of integrated structure
The Iron Curtain
Comecon countries
Warsaw Pact countries
Main industrial centres in EEC
Coal fields
Oil fields
Gas fields
BRITAIN IN EUROPE SINCE 1945
United Kingdom's volume of trade £ million
EEC countries
North America
Japan
USSR
Norway, Sweden and Switzerland
ICELAND
Reykjavik
Faroe Is.
NORWAY
SWEDEN
FINLAND
Oslo
Stockholm
Helsinki
Leningrad
UNITED KINGDOM
Glasgow
Edinburgh
Belfast
REPUBLIC OF IRELAND
Dublin
Liverpool
Manchester
Birmingham
Cardiff
London
DENMARK
Copenhagen
Hamburg
NETHERLANDS
Amsterdam
BELGIUM
Brussels
LUXEMBOURG
Bonn
Frankfurt
WEST GERMANY
EAST GERMANY
Berlin
POLAND
Warsaw
Cracow
USSR
Prague
CZECHOSLOVAKIA
Vienna
AUSTRIA
Budapest
HUNGARY
ROMANIA
Bucharest
Bern
SWITZERLAND
FRANCE
Paris
Lyon
Marseilles
Milan
Turin
ITALY
Rome
CORSICA
SARDINIA
SICILY
SPAIN
Madrid
Barcelona
PORTUGAL
Lisbon
YUGOSLAVIA
Belgrade
BULGARIA
Sofia
ALBANIA
GREECE (EEC 1981)
Athens
CRETE
TURKEY
Ankara
£9530 m
Australia and New Zealand
South America
£1825 m
Asia and Far East
Africa
£2095 m
£2515 m
£1803 m
£3651 m
£4781 m
£7618 m
£4033 m
£1111 m
£5742 m
£3059 m
£4070 m

Northern Ireland since 1922

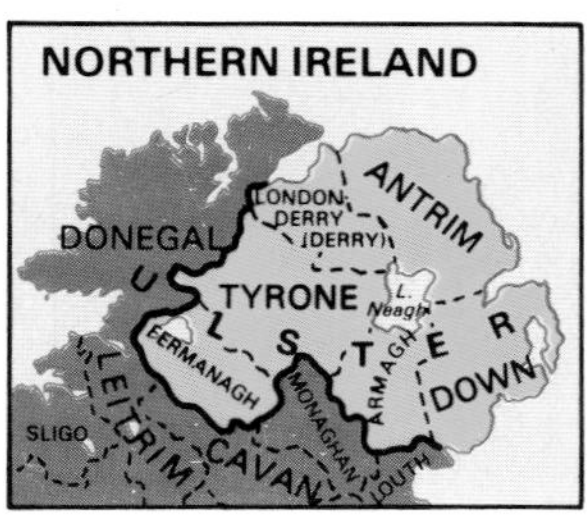

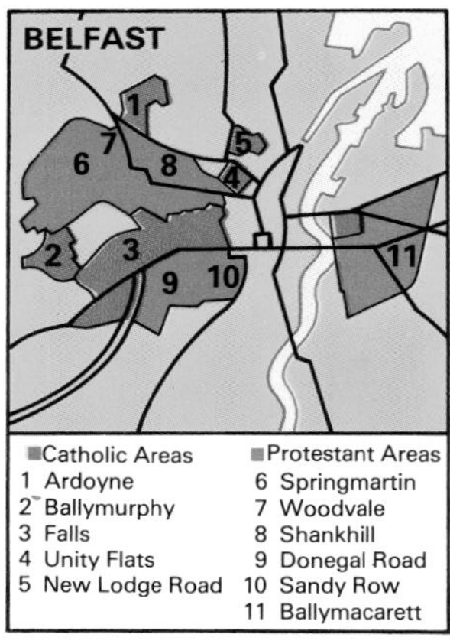

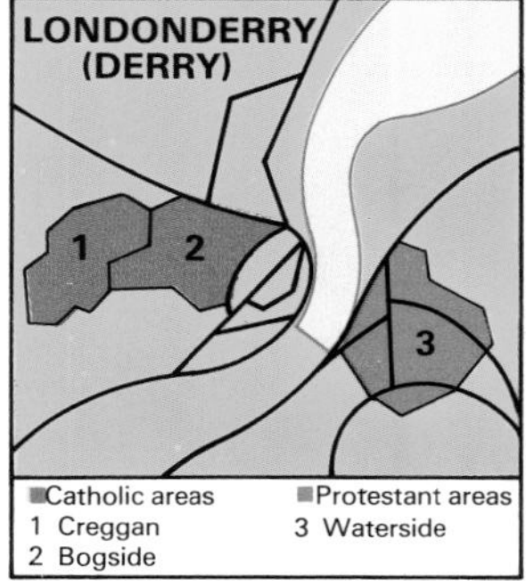

In 1922 Ireland was partitioned, the six north-eastern countries remaining within the United Kingdom but with their own parliament at Stormont (right). They also returned 12 members to the United Kingdom Parliament. The area was heavily settled by Protestants during the 17th and 18th centuries, and at the time of partition the Protestants were a substantial majority. In the last 60 years, however, the Catholics have increased, by virtue of a higher birth rate and by immigration from the Republic, until a voting majority of Catholics in Ulster is probable by the end of the century.

Inevitably the history of Northern Ireland has been dominated by 'the troubles' which flared during the 1970s. During the 1960s a generation of increasingly well educated and articulate Catholics, influenced, no doubt, by 'independence' movements in the Third World and by a wave of student-led anti-authoritarian protests in many developed countries, began to demand a better deal for the minority. But the response from the Irish Parliament at Stormont was tentative and lukewarm.

In February 1967 a predominantly Catholic Civil Rights Movement was set up to channel Catholic demands for electoral and social reform and the abolition of the B-Special security force. A series of Province-wide marches roused support among the hitherto apathetic Catholic minority and deepened Protestant fears and suspicions. Sectarian violence became commonplace until, in August 1969, Protestant gangs 'invaded' the Catholic Bogside, burning, looting and wrecking as they went. Reports of this 'invasion' led to sectarian fighting in Belfast, and the British government was forced to send in detachments of the Army to defend the Catholics and restore order. This angered the Protestants while failing to mollify the Catholics who then formed their own militant gangs for self-protection. Indeed, Catholic resentment of the presence of British troops, and opposition to various security methods imposed by the authorities, have been a further source of seething discontent.

The British government urged the Prime Minister of Northern Ireland, Captain O'Neill, to make speedier and more sweeping reforms and to disband the B-Specials (accomplished in October 1969). These modest reforms raised Protestant fears on which extremist politicians such as the Reverend Ian Paisley built their support. The Catholic minority also turned to more active political leaders, and the Social Democratic and Labour Party replaced the traditional Nationalist Party. By this time the peaceful methods and relatively modest demands of the Civil Rights Movement had been left far behind. Catholics were now lending sympathetic support to the Official Irish Republican Party and the more violent-minded Provisional IRA, whose campaigns of bombing and shooting led to innumerable clashes between Catholics and the British Army.

Protestant politicians united to drive O'Neill from power but were quickly dissatisfied by the inability of his successor, Chichester-Clark, to solve the problems. He was followed by the 'tougher' Brian Faulkner who banned sectarian marches, allowed the internment without trial of political suspects, but who quickly realized the need of a political settlement of the problems. In September 1971 he met the Prime Ministers of Great Britain and Eire at Chequers where they agreed on their support for a United Ireland – provided the majority in Ulster would agree to it. But division grew and violence intensified. Belfast, Armagh and other towns and cities were devastated by IRA bombing campaigns; in January 1972 there occurred the massacre of 'Bloody Sunday' when British forces fired on Catholics taking part in a peaceful – but illegal – march in Londonderry.

The British government now announced the abolition of the Ulster Parliament at Stormont and the establishment of Direct Rule. This angered the Protestants, of whom some, led by William Craig, advocated the creation of an Independent Ulster, while others, led by Paisley, argu for the complete integration of Ulster in the Unit Kingdom. At the same time, in May 1972, Protestan formed the Protestant Ulster Reform Association and t Ulster Defence Volunteer Force – the para-milita counterparts of the Official and Provisional wing of t IRA. Sectarian battles and bombings threatened to lead an all-out civil war.

In yet another attempt to find a political solution to t problem the British then experimented with 'Pow Sharing', a system in which Catholics were to have a sha in the Provincial decision-making processes. But t elections for the new Assembly showed that there w greater support for the hardliners such as Craig and Paisl than for the moderates such as Faulkner.

The result of the 1974 election showed clearly that t Protestants were unwilling to accept any step towar agreement with the South. Anti-Faulkner candidat standing on behalf of the United Ulster Unionist Coun won the Protestant seats, and in May 1974 a strike by t Ulster Workers' Council forced the resignation of t power-sharing executive.

The 'troubles' are far from over, and no solution see yet in sight. Perhaps the best hope lies in co-operati between the British and Irish governments. But, in the lig of Ireland's tortured history, it seems clear that the ro will be long and hard.

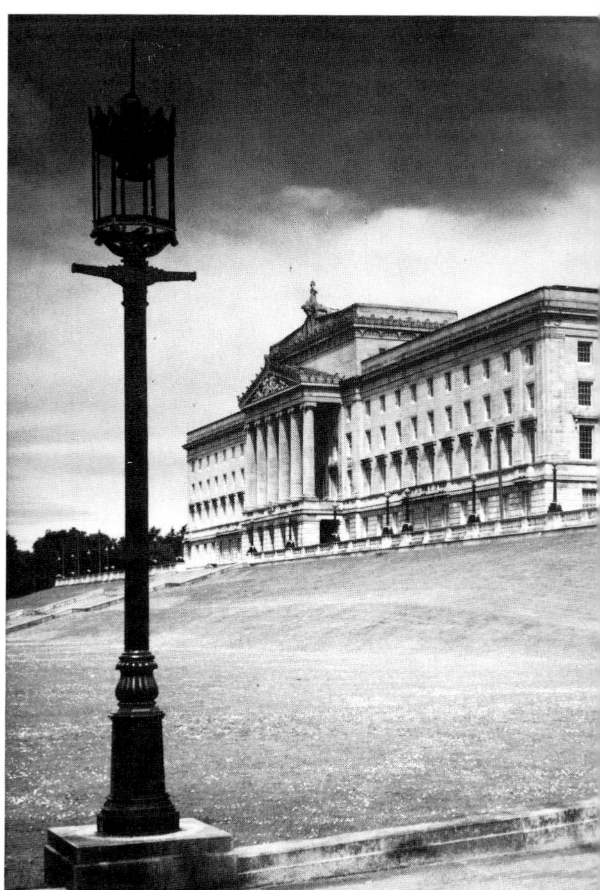

PART TWO: THE SOCIAL AND ECONOMIC HISTORY OF BRITAIN

Chapter Seven
'A FAIR FIELD FULL OF FOLK'

At the end of the 14th century Piers Plowman dreamed of the England he knew, 'a fair field full of folk' – a well-settled countryside of small farms, market towns and just one major city; a landscape which – as the Domesday Survey had already shown – was long familiar with the plough, the sheepfold and the water-mill. Despite the Black Death, perhaps the greatest single disaster in English history, these were centuries of progress in every sphere of economic life, rural and urban, on land and water, at home and overseas. By the end of the period Britain was showing signs of becoming the most advanced economy in the world.

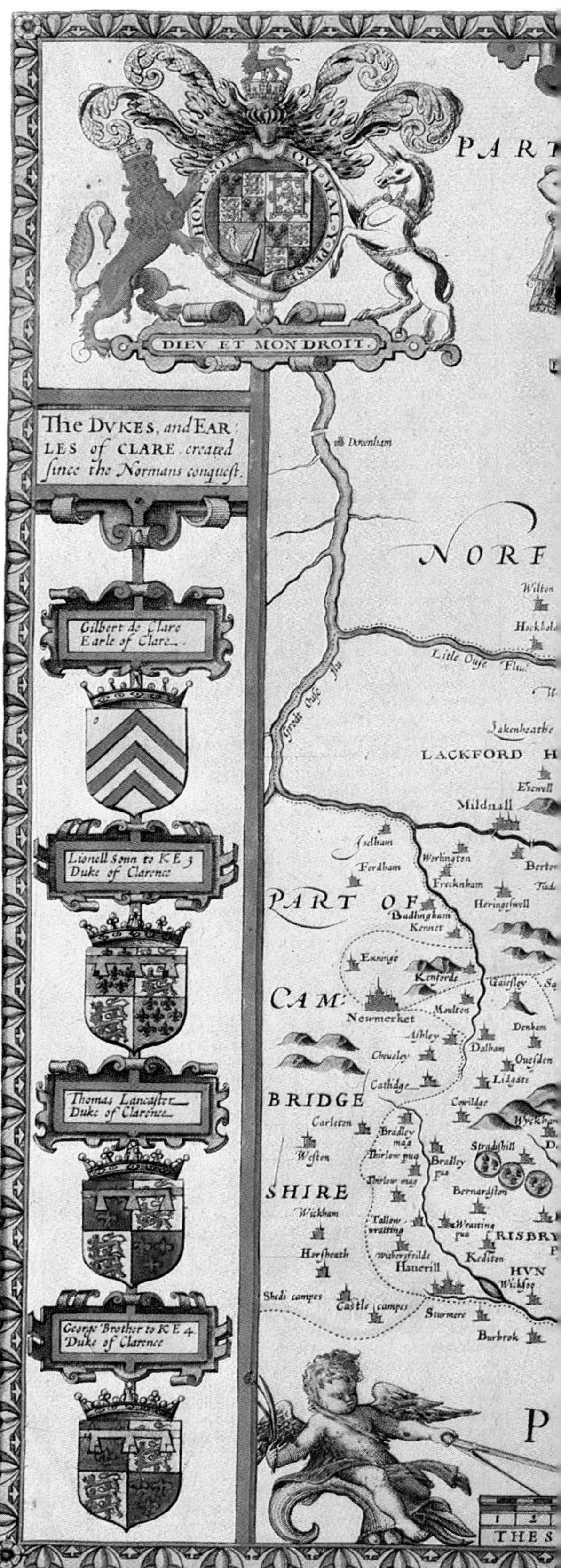

Map of Suffolk in 1610 by the English antiquarian and cartographer John Speed. Speed published a series of 54 maps of various parts of England and Wales between 1608 and 1610.

IPSWICHE
A SCALE OF PASES
SUFFOLKE described and divided into Hundreds, The situation of the fayre towne IPSWICH shewed, with the ARMES of the most noble families that have bene either DUKES, or EARLES both of that Countie as also of Clare
THE DUKES and EARLES of SUFFOLK Created since the Normās conquest
Robert Vfford. Erle of Suffolk
William de la poole Duke of Suffolk
Charles brandon duke of Suffolk
Henry Gray duke of Suffolk
Thomas Howard Earle of Suffolke
BOADICIA
OF
OF
ESSEX
MILES
Cum Privilegio Anno 1610.
Performed by Iohn Speede and are to be solde in Popes-head alley against the Exchang by George Humble

The English Population before and after the Black Death

Long centuries of colonization had by 1086, the date of the Domesday survey, substantially modified the natural landscape of England, but settlement was far from complete or uniform. Large parts of the country were only sparsely settled: the density of population appears to diminish as the land rises from the plain to the moorland, and as one progresses from the South and East to northern and western regions. In addition to expanses of under-populated moorland there were huge areas of under-utilized forest, woodland, and marshland.

Despite the immense amount of information contained in Domesday Book, it is not possible to calculate the total population of England with any great certainty; but a figure somewhere between 1.75 and 2.25 million is probably of the right order of magnitude. So few people meant not only much empty ground but a thin spread of inhabitants even in settled areas; the average density of settlement throughout the country was probably around 30 persons per square mile (2.6 km²). The map of 1086 clearly shows the uneven distribution of population.

Average number of sons per household among English noble and gentry families, 1255–1505. For more than a century after the Black Death, the number of sons surviving their fathers scarcely reached an average of one per household. The depleted stock of surviving children led to a steady decline in population.

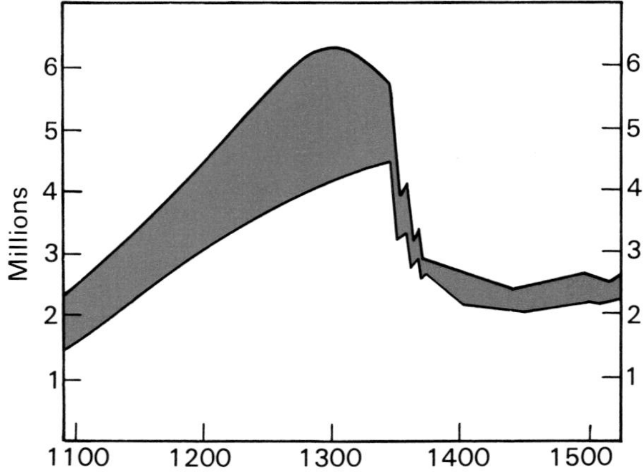

Right: Population of England, 1110–1525. Within an estimated range, this diagram shows the steady rise prior to the Black Death, and the dramatic decline which followed.

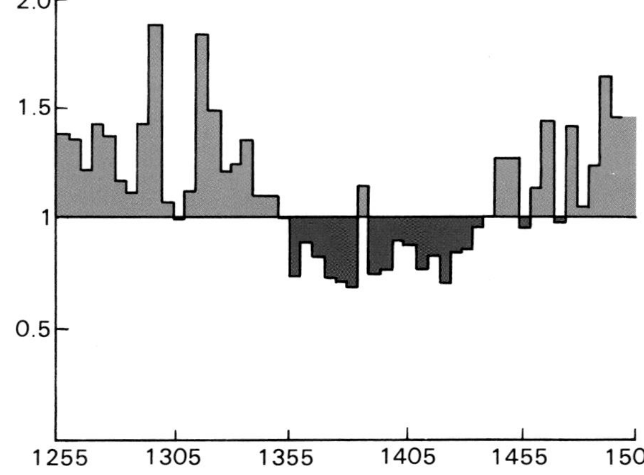

Measurement of the level of population, and of the direction and scale of its movements, before the first national census of 1801, is a speculative undertaking. In the era before the mid-16th century, when the keeping of registers of births, deaths and marriages in each parish became common, such measurement must depend largely upon indirect evidence, including settlement and wage and price levels, supported by a small range of direct data which are often difficult to interpret. Nonetheless, there is some measure of broad agreement among historians about the course of population change in the half millenium and more after the Norman Conquest. These were two protracted periods of substantially rising numbers, and two of falling or only marginally rising numbers.

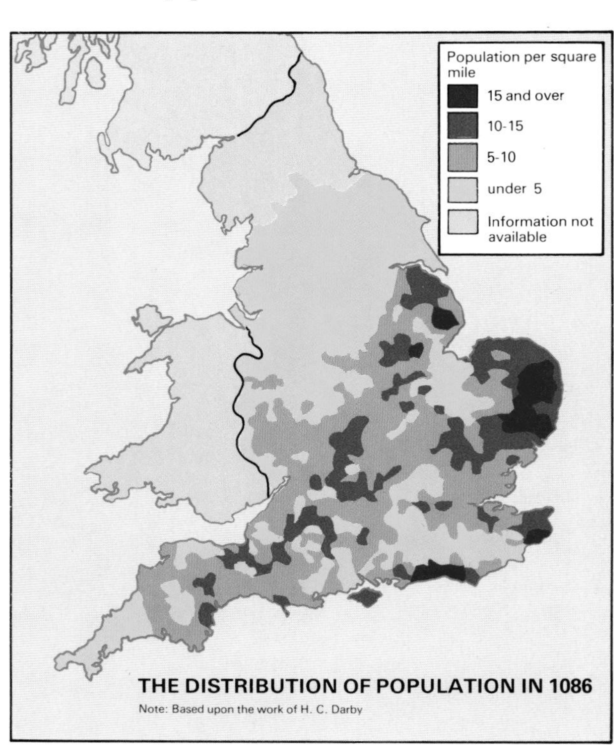

Right: Distribution of population in England at the time of the Domesday survey, 1086. The uneven variations in density can be clearly seen. Lincolnshire, Norfolk and Suffolk accommodated almost a quarter of the whole population. Essex, Oxfordshire, Berkshire and Wiltshire were more thickly populated than average. In some parts of the North there were only four or five people per square mile. Note, too, tracts of low density even within relatively densely settled areas such as Lincolnshire, Norfolk and Kent.

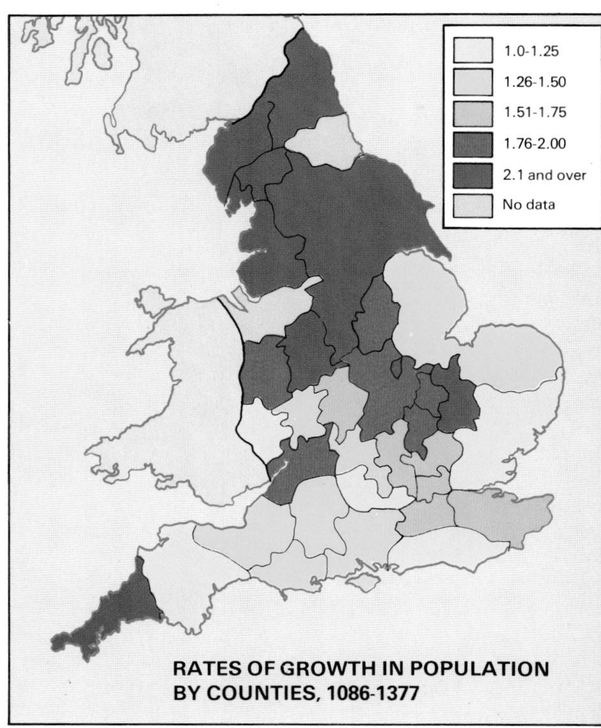

Far right: Comparative rates of population growth, 1086–1377. The contrasting rates of increase of English counties reveal the progress of colonization and settlement. Most notably, the fastest rates of growth tended to occur in those counties which were lightly settled in 1066. These had the largest reserves of colonizable land to be brought into productive use.

The impact of the plague at Tournai, Flanders, 1349. The victims were buried in their thousands in mass graves.

The map of population growth between 1086 and 1377 has been compiled from the demographic landmarks provided by Domesday Book and the Poll Tax returns of 1377. Thus it covers the long period of population growth of the central Middle Ages. For some northern counties, Domesday Book lacks precise information, but there can be no doubt of the very rapid growth in their populations in the centuries which followed. The Poll Tax, of course, was levied almost 30 years after the arrival of the plague, well into the era of declining numbers, making it difficult to estimate the precise scale of growth.

The progressive increase in the two and a half centuries after the Norman Conquest may well have taken England's population up to a peak of somewhere between four and six millions before the Black Death. The ensuing decline was even more dramatic; by the mid-15th century, when the population was probably at its lowest point, there may well have been fewer than 2.5 million people in the country. The Black Death seems to have wiped out about a third of England's population at a single stroke. Despite attempts at recovery, subsequent epidemics in 1360–2, 1369 and 1375 forced the level even farther down. In the next 100 years there were at least a further 13 major national epidemics. But perhaps of even greater significance was the fact that the plague became endemic, flaring up in local outbreaks.

The downward course of population was not caused by simple mortality alone. It seems likely that plague, and many other virulent diseases present in the 15th century, struck hard at the young. Future child-bearing cohorts were thereby depleted. In addition, it is possible that the age at marriage increased, that fewer people married, and that many marriages were interrupted by the death of one of the partners. Whatever the causes, we have clear evidence that not enough children were surviving to maintain, still less increase, the population.

By the time that Thomas Cromwell instigated a system of parochial registration in 1538, the population had embarked upon a strong recovery. Nonetheless, mortality peaks recurred: growth was periodically arrested or even, as in the influenza outbreak of 1557–8, violently reversed. The net result, by the mid-17th century, was a population of around five to six millions. Thereafter, for a time at least, deaths once again regularly began to exceed births.

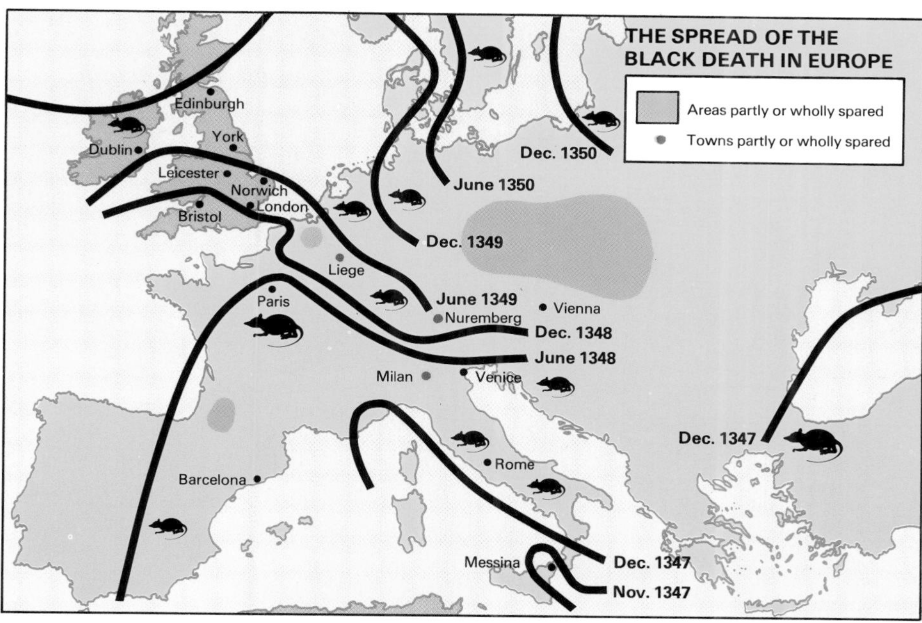

The progress of the Black Death westwards across Europe. It is unlikely that more than two-thirds of Europe's population survived into 1350. Cities and regions which escaped the first outbreak were hit especially severely in the next epidemic, ten years later.

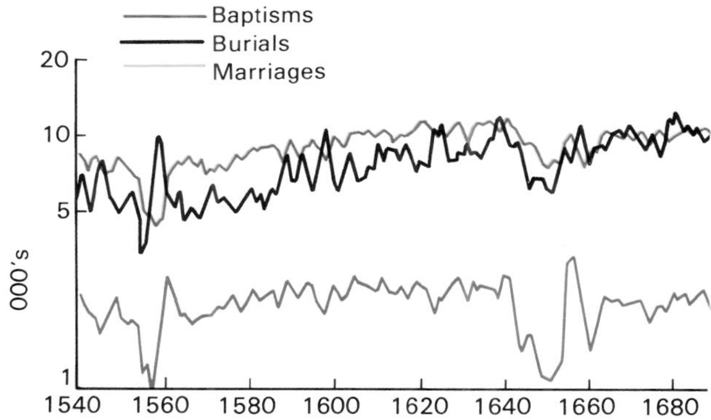

Births, marriages and deaths in England and Wales 1540–1680. Compiled from parish registers, this diagram clearly shows that births were exceeding deaths by a very substantial margin, despite recurring peaks of high mortality.

Manors, Fields and Flocks: Farming in Medieval England

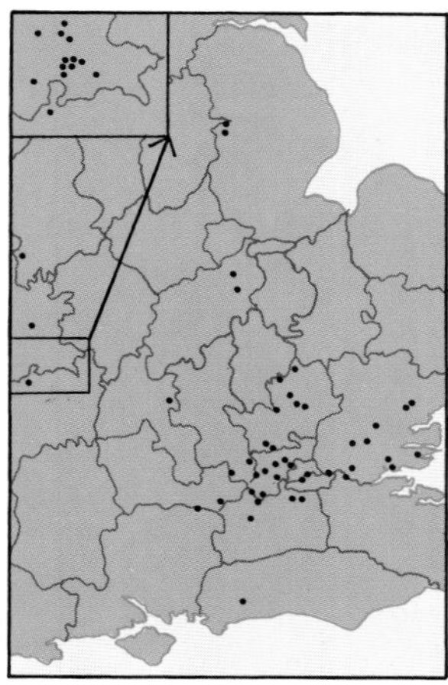

Manors belonging to Westminster Abbey in 1086. The map shows how widespread the distribution of a great ecclesiastical estate's possession could be.

The estate or fief was the unit of large-scale exploitation supporting the ruling class, and the manor was the constituent cell of which the fiefs and estates were composed. Each manor in turn consisted of land called the demesne, which could be managed and cultivated directly by the lord, and land in the hands of rent-paying tenants, predominantly in small plots.

If we examine the manor in detail we soon find that it displayed an almost infinite variety of structures, each one dependent upon a wide range of jurisdictional, topographical and agricultural variables. Yet there were a number of common features which assist the grouping of manors into broad categories. Most notably we have manors with nuclear or with scattered settlement, and this distinction went hand in hand with either strip farming in open fields or with the cultivation of small enclosures. Two examples illustrate these two main forms of manorial and farming structure. Wigston Magna in Leicestershire was an open-field village of the classic type, and its three great fields remained virtually unchanged until 1776. The bulk of the 70 or more families in medieval Wigston lived in cottages lining the two main streets, close to the village green and between the two churches. The lands held by each family would be scattered in small strips, often of an acre or less, in the three fields. By contrast, the upland terrain of Cornwall was ill-suited to open-field farming and tightly clustered villages. At Stoke Climsland in the east of the county we find the 100 or more families on the manor living in scattered hamlets and cultivating compact enclosed pieces of land. There were over 40 different settlements, and they were interspersed with expanses of rough pasture and unimproved downland.

In open-field villages the freedom of the individual farmer was limited by the need to conform to communal routine, for his lands were intermingled and interlocked with those of other tenements. Under an orthodox, three-field system, each field would experience a three-year rotation consisting of winter-sown crops (wheat and rye), spring-sown crops (oats or barley) and fallow.

The cultivation of small enclosed fields by individual families could by contrast be very flexible. Generally

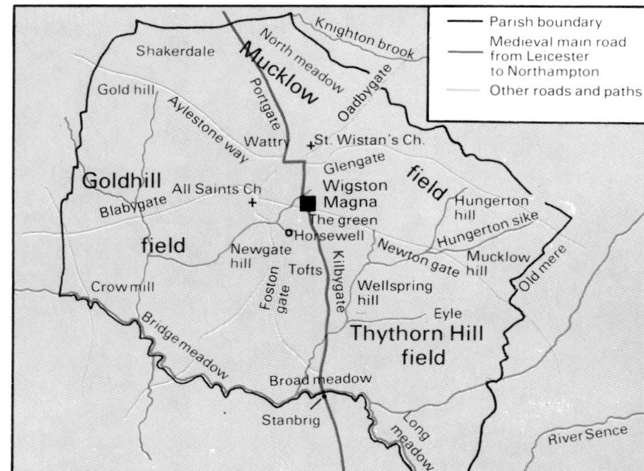

Right: Two types of manorial settlement and cultivation. At Wigston Magna (top) in Leicestershire, good-quality land was farmed on the three-field system from a central settlement. At Stoke Climsland in Cornwall more marginal land led to a pattern of scattered settlements.

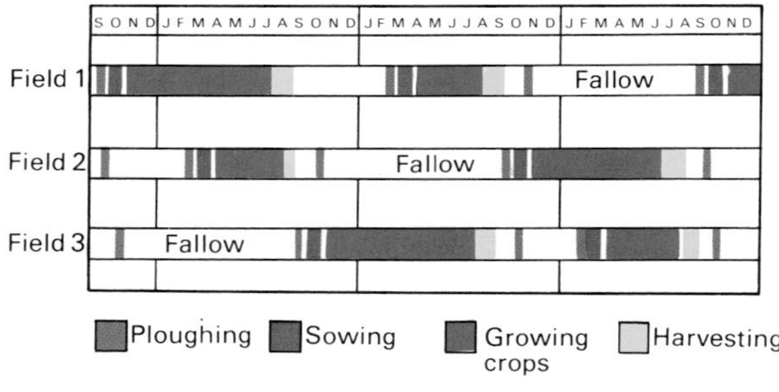

The operation of the classic open field system.

enclosures were prominent in hilly terrain and where land was being taken in small parcels from moorlands, woodlands, and marshlands. Often convertible husbandry was pursued, in which the plots were subjected to rotation of crops followed by a number of years under grass. The length of the grain and grass cycles could be altered to suit the needs of the farmer and the quality of the soil; moreover, the rotation helped to improve both crop yields and the quality of pasture.

Although there were some places, especially in the remote colonizing frontiers, where fields were of minor importance and enterprise was primarily pastoral, mixed farming predominated throughout most of England. Consequently, the right to pasture animals on village fields and wastes was highly prized. Even in those regions particularly suitable for arable, beasts had to be reared to draw ploughs and carry produce and people and, of course, livestock was essential to arable farming as the prime source of fertilizer. Most peasants aspired to possess plough-beasts, and a few cows, pigs, sheep and poultry, though their limited resources usually meant that they attained far less. Landlords, however, frequently built up large herds and vast flocks. During the wool-production boom of the 13th century a large number of estates kept flocks of many thousands of animals. In Edward I's reign the export trade alone absorbed the fleeces of eight million sheep a year.

English wool was among the finest in Europe. The diagram provides a guide to the relative quality of the wool produced throughout the country in the first half of the 14th century. Altogether the prices fixed in 1343 relate to over 50 different grades of wool, varying in price from £9. 7s. 6d a sack down to £2. 10s. 0d. At one end of the spectrum we have the very best wool from the Shropshire and Herefordshire borderlands, followed by fine fleeces of Lindsey and the Cotswolds, and at the other end we have Cornish wool, described contemptuously by contemporaries as 'Cornish hair'.

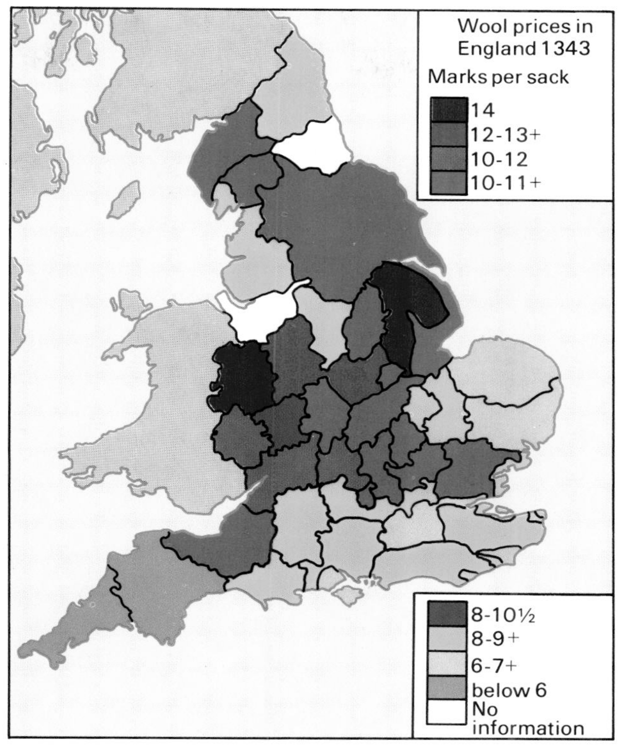

Above left: Agricultural prosperity: wool prices in England in 1343, shortly before the first outbreak of the Black Death. Contemporaries were well aware of the value of English wool: 'half the wealth of the kingdom' was how one of them described it in the late 13th century.

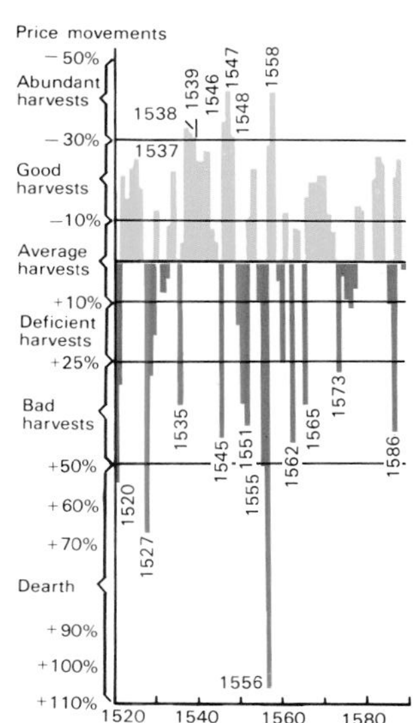

Grain price movements, 1520–90. Prices oscillated wildly as yields fluctuated. Until the great agrarian improvements of later centuries, and the development of an international trade in foodstuffs, all sectors of the economy were deeply affected by the quality of the harvest.

Landlords untroubled by the stark struggle for subsistence which characterized peasant farming, had much greater freedom of choice as to how to manage the land which they controlled directly, their demesnes. While one choice was the balance between arable and pastoral, a more fundamental choice was between direct exploitation and leasing. The 13th century, with its strongly rising prices for agrarian produce and cheap labour, was the age of direct management, the age, as it is called, of 'high farming', when landlords marketed increasing quantities of grain, dairy produce and wool. The 14th century, with its famines and plague, was a far more difficult period for the large-scale farmer. But it was not until the last quarter of that century that prices turned decisively downwards. Thereafter, falling prices for both grain and wool, combined with rising wages and associated labour problems, undermined demesne profits and encouraged leasing.

By modern standards, yields in the Middle Ages of both arable and livestock husbandry were low. Even the rather optimistic estimates of contemporary farming treatises put the return of oats at around only four-fold the seed sown, wheat five-fold, and barley eight-fold. The average yields actually achieved on the extensive demesne farms of the Bishops of Winchester never approached even these modest targets. At these levels wheat and barley would have yielded less than one-third of today's crops, and oats less than one-fifth. A variety of measures were taken to improve returns, including in many places the digging in of marl and seaweed. Many villages also switched from a two-field regime, in which half the land lay fallow each year, to a three-field system, but the adoption of legumes, which improved fertility by fixing nitrogen in the soil, was not rapid. It is possible that, in comparison with modern standards, livestock farming was relatively more efficient than arable.

Land Enclosure

The adoption of enclosure, associated with improved crop rotations, was perhaps the single most important development in agriculture. Whatever advantages the open fields may have had for the communities which farmed them in earlier centuries, the greater efficiency and productivity of enclosed land ensured a progressive abandonment of the open-field system. Nonetheless, looked at over the centuries, progress was relatively slow. Open fields seem always to have been less in evidence in the Highland Zone of the North and in the South-West, in Wales, in Kent, and parts of Essex and in those areas where land had been reclaimed from forest, waste and marsh. In later medieval and early modern times enclosure of fields and commons for both pasture and arable progressed even further in these regions, as well as in others where open fields had predominated. The later 15th century was a period of widespread enclosure for pasture, and in the following two centuries we can discern that the progress of enclosures was most rapid in the North-West, the Welsh borders, the Vales of Gloucester and Glamorgan, the north-west Midlands, west Yorkshire, and parts of Norfolk, with each region adopting the type of enclosure best suited to its needs (see p. 185). By the later 17th century the greater part of land was enclosed in northern and western regions, and in the South-East; but open fields were still dominant in a broad swathe of central England. Attention must also be drawn to the other major agricultural improvement, engrossment. The concentration of land into larger farms and the decline of the smallholder were to be powerful forces in raising agricultural efficiency.

It was only after long centuries of agrarian improvement and the opening up of international trades in foodstuffs on an unprecedented scale, that the dependence of Englishmen and women upon the state of the harvest was substantially lessened. During the medieval and early modern centuries the quality and quantity of the harvest was of paramount importance to the whole population and to all sectors of the economy. A poor harvest meant that smallholders had less to eat; a bad harvest forced them to purchase food in order to survive, and might also entail the sale or slaughter of essential livestock. Poor yields also meant high prices, so that all those who had to buy food were left with less money to spend on manufactures and non-essential items. Thus harvest failures not only struck rural communities; they adversely affected craftsmen and merchants. The harvest was at the very heart of the economy and its health was determined by the vagaries of the weather. Prices oscillated wildly as yields fluctuated. Such instability severely limited the potential for development and progress in the nation's economy.

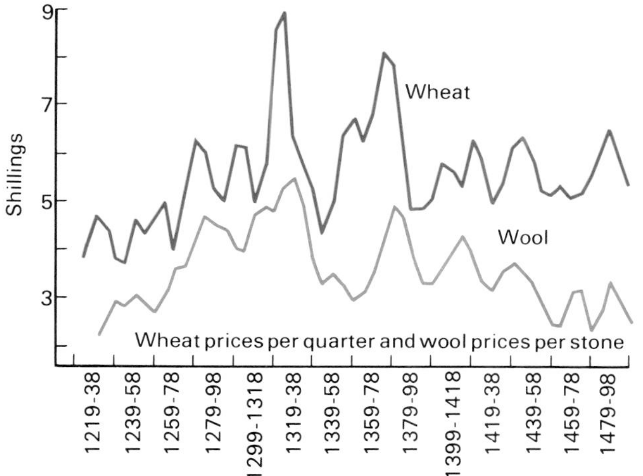

The underlying trends revealed by this graph show steadily rising prices both for wheat and wool during the 13th century followed by a period of stable or declining prices in the following two centuries.

Six Centuries of English Towns

Looked at through modern eyes Norman England was a backward, underdeveloped land. Techniques of production were primitive, *per capita* output was low, and much land and much labour were needed to sustain a population which was relatively tiny. Moreover, the vast majority of the people subsisted at standards of life which were abysmally low. Yet if we were tempted to hold this view, it was not shared by contemporaries. To the conquerors, England was richer and more advanced than many if not most European societies. To the Normans, England was a land 'fertile by virtue of its fecundity, the wealth of which merchants have increased by bringing in riches. Treasures have been amassed there which ar remarkable for their number, their quality and thei workmanship'. Indeed, it would be wrong to stres backwardness to the neglect of the burgeoning network c boroughs, ports, markets, and fairs, the intensification c trade, local, regional and international, and the develop ment of industries and crafts.

The 12th and 13th centuries experienced an expansion c the urban sector which paralleled that in the countryside Established towns grew in size: the population of York ma well have doubled between 1086 and 1300, and that c Leicester increased by more than half. But probably of sti greater significance was the accretion of urban characteris tics by villages, many of which evolved into fully fledge towns. Often such transformations were natural processes but often they owed much to the initiative of landlords; fo the foundation of towns was an enterprise which attracte many medieval lords. It has been estimated that some 14 new towns were 'planted' between 1100 and 1300. By n means all of these tender plants flourished, but among th more successful was Stratford-upon-Avon. There were n burgesses at Stratford in 1182, but by 1252 there wer around 300. The map of immigration into Stratford show clearly that the growth of such towns depended upon constant influx of people from the countryside. In Strat ford's case we can see that the main bulk of the immigrant probably came from within a radius of about ten mile (16 km).

London necessarily attracted immigrants from muc farther afield. In addition to the large numbers who cam from neighbouring counties, there was a very substantia influx from East Anglia and the East Midlands. Indeed, i has been argued that the influx from these two regions wa on a great enough scale to ensure that their dialect pushe out the old southern speech which had been hithert current in the capital.

Three maps together show a broad picture of England' leading cities and towns over six centuries, and indicate th

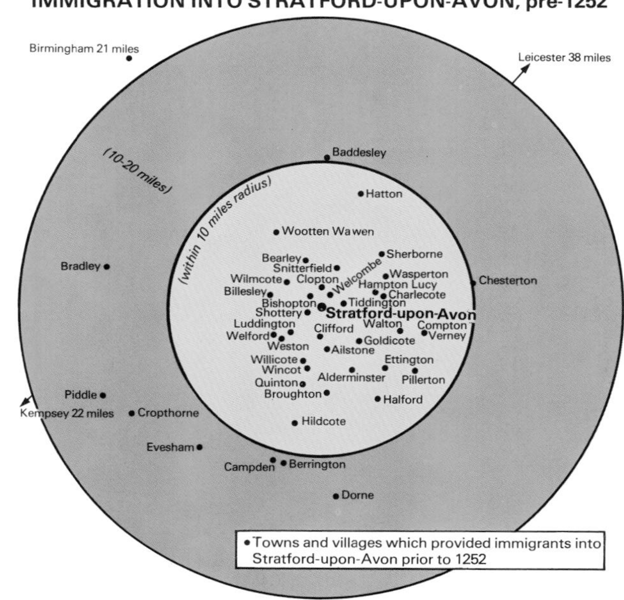

Rural immigration into Stratford-upon-Avon before 1252. This diagram is based on an analysis of surnames of Stratford burgesses which links them to the villages and hamlets of Stratford's hinterland.

Below: Three maps showing the leading cities and towns of England over six centuries. The pattern remains surprisingly constant – although the rise of new centres in the manufacturing Midlands and North is significant.

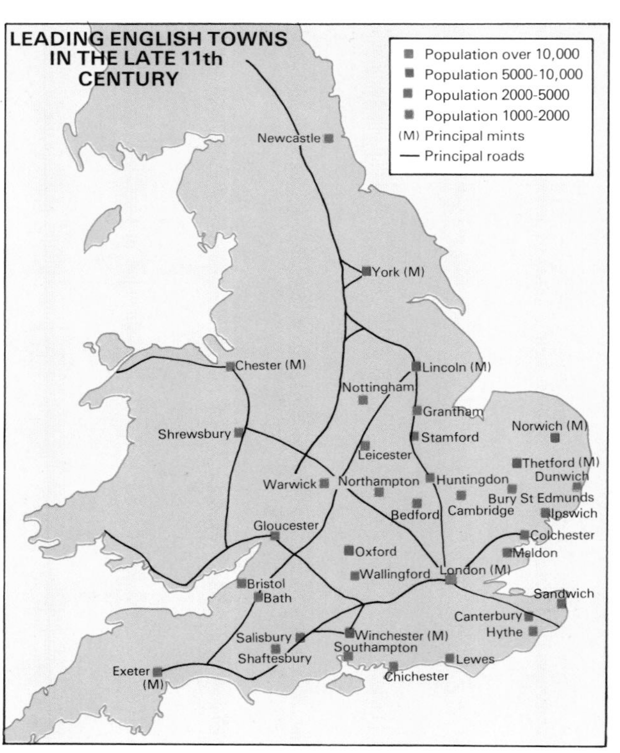

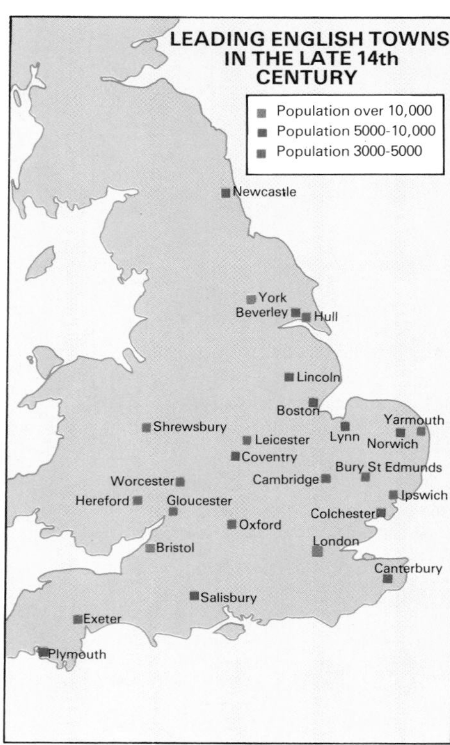

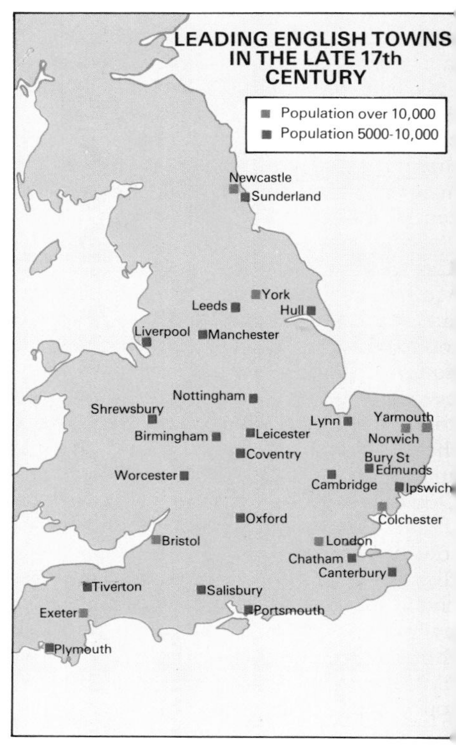

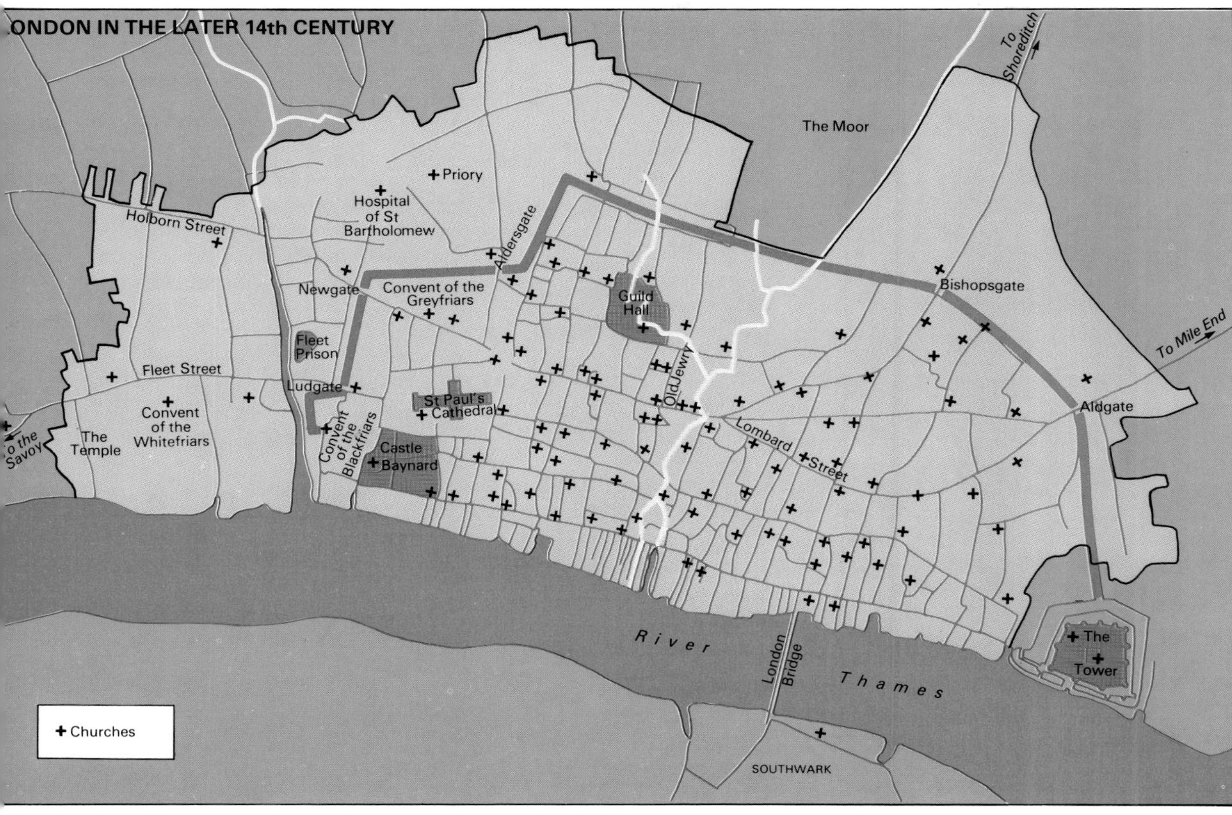

A sketch map of London in the later 14th century. The physical expansion of Chaucer's London can be seen from the growth of the suburbs, particularly to the West, towards the royal courts at Westminster. The City's administrative nucleus was around Guildhall, but its heart lay along the riverside. Here were the wharves and warehouses which linked London with all the economic centres of Europe.

Below: Map of Bristol in the 17th century, by the cartographer John Speed. From very early times Bristol maintained its importance as the great port city of the West.

hanges which took place in their relative standing. There re some examples of spectacular transformations in ortune. At the time of the Norman Conquest Dunwich, ow a tiny village on the Suffolk coast, Lewes in Sussex and Vallingford in Berkshire were among the top 20 English owns, while Thetford in Norfolk may well have been in the op six. The fortunes of other towns, Exeter, for example, ollowed a cyclical rather than a linear pattern; the Devon apital lost much ground between Domesday Book and the ater 14th century, but staged major recoveries in the later 5th century and in the 17th century. Most notable among eclining cities in the later Middle Ages were the leading loth centres of the 12th and 13th centuries, such as tamford and Lincoln, while over the same period the najor wool port of Boston declined step by step with the ontracting wool exports of East Anglia.

he 'New' Towns

Aost notable among the rapidly urbanizing centres of the ater 16th and 17th centuries were the 'new' industrial owns, such as Leeds, Manchester and Birmingham, and ockyard towns like Chatham and Portsmouth. But erhaps most striking of all is the strong measure of ontinuity, particularly among England's largest towns. Of he eight largest towns in the late 17th century, at least five, nd probably more, had been among the 20 largest towns of Domesday England.

London seems always to have towered over other English owns. As early as 1183, William Fitz Stephen reported that here were 13 great conventual churches and 126 parish hurches in the city, and that the port of London was visited y 'merchants from every nation that is under heaven'. By he mid-14th century the population of the capital may well ave exceeded 50,000 and, as the map of London shows, the opography of the centre had taken on an appearance which s clearly recognizable today.

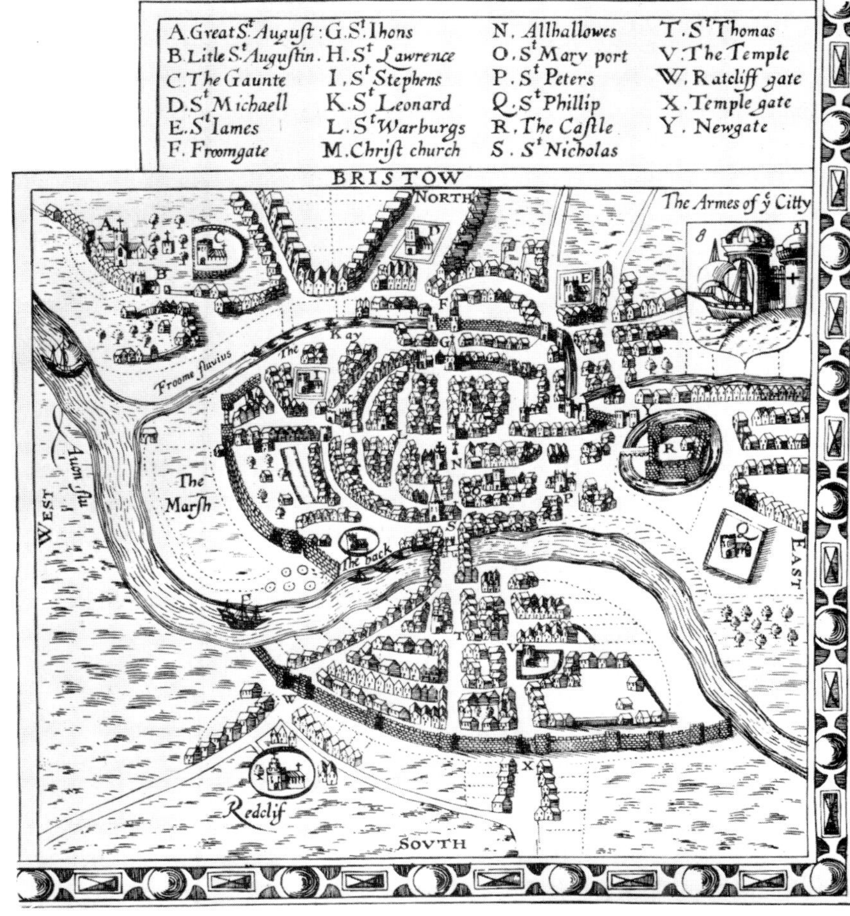

The Textile Industry in Town and Country

Industry in medieval and early modern England was limited by many factors. For most people, incomes were low and spent largely on food. As a result, the development of anything approaching a mass market, except for a tiny range of basic products, was severely curtailed. Annual variations in the harvest, too, inevitably produced sharp fluctuations in levels of output and incomes. On the other hand, the complete natural economy – in which prices and incomes are determined solely by food production – seems never to have been a reality, at least in this period. Towns, trade and industry were always of importance. Peasant farmers needed to exchange foodstuffs for cash with which to pay rents, and for essential items such as clothing, metalwares and household and farming equipment which could not be produced at home. In addition there were always the richer members of society, small in number, but exerting a powerful influence through the disposal of their enormous incomes. In consequence, from earliest times we find both ubiquitous local craftsmen, operating often on a tiny scale to serve the needs of local communities for low-priced basic manufactures, and the highly organized and centralized production of luxury and semi-luxury goods.

The textile industry illustrates this state of affairs. In the early Middle Ages it fell into two distinct branches, which served two distinct markets. The most renowned was the highly regulated urban industry which specialized in the production of luxurious and very expensive cloth for sale to rich customers at home and abroad. It was an industry which was necessarily limited in scale, and it was primarily concentrated in a small range of towns, most notably Lincoln, York, Beverley, Stamford, Huntingdon, Northampton, Leicester, Oxford and Gloucester. In addition to these urban industrial centres making fine-quality cloths we might also add other towns which made somewhat cheaper cloths, such as the burels of London and Winchester, and the russets of Colchester. Famous as this English industry was, it was overshadowed by the great industrial centres of the Low Countries; and in terms of total scale and output i was also overshadowed by ever present, but seldor recorded, village clothworking, which was suited to loca needs for cheaper cloth of lower quality.

Yet we should not draw too sharp a dividing line betwee town and country production. From the late 12th centur we know that townsmen were using rural labour for th preliminary stages of cloth production, such as washing combing, and spinning wool; and, as the map shows, by th late 13th century water mills for the mechanical fulling o felting of cloth were widely distributed. They were built o the banks of the fast-flowing streams in many parts of th English countryside.

The facilities offered by cheap rural labour could assis the urban manufacturer, but in the long run they could als undermine the town's central rôle. After suffering th effects of increased foreign competition, which resulted i declining fortunes for many cloth towns, the Englis industry embarked upon a remarkable era of expansio from the mid-14th century onwards. Although this expansion for a time gave a boost to the older centres, its mai base became the countryside. The less restrictive atmosphere of the village and hamlet, with their ample supplies c unregulated and largely part-time labour, suited the need of a rapidly developing industry and the entrepreneurs wh ran it. Thus York enjoyed a resurgence of prosperity in th later 14th century, but this was followed by a long period c decline during which much of the city's cloth trade wa taken by nearby industrial villages, including Ripor Leeds, Wakefield and Bradford.

During the later Middle Ages commercial cloth makin spread widely throughout the country. Nonetheless, thre regions emerged clearly pre-eminent by the 15th century Perhaps the most important of all was in the West Country where clusters of thriving villages stretched along the rive valleys of Gloucestershire, Wiltshire and North Somerset producing such famous cloths as 'Stroudwaters' an 'Castlecombes'. Farther west, new centres concentratin

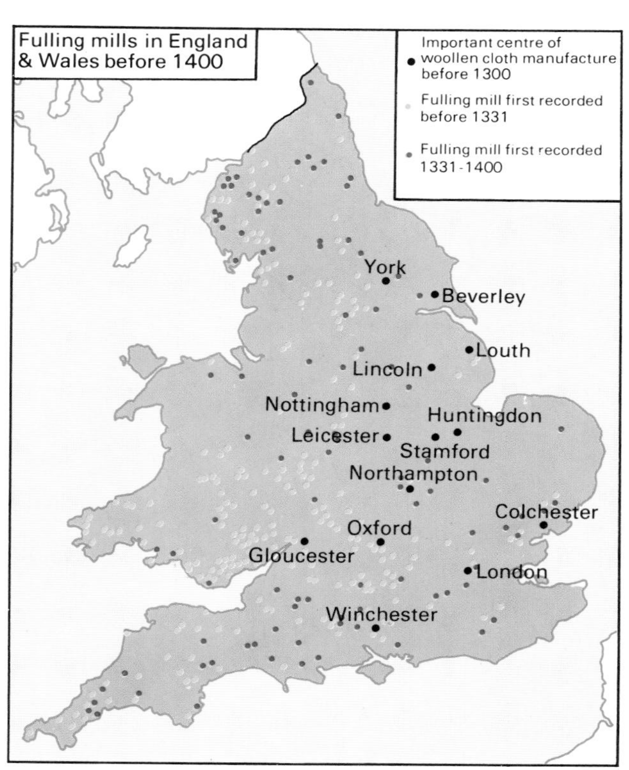

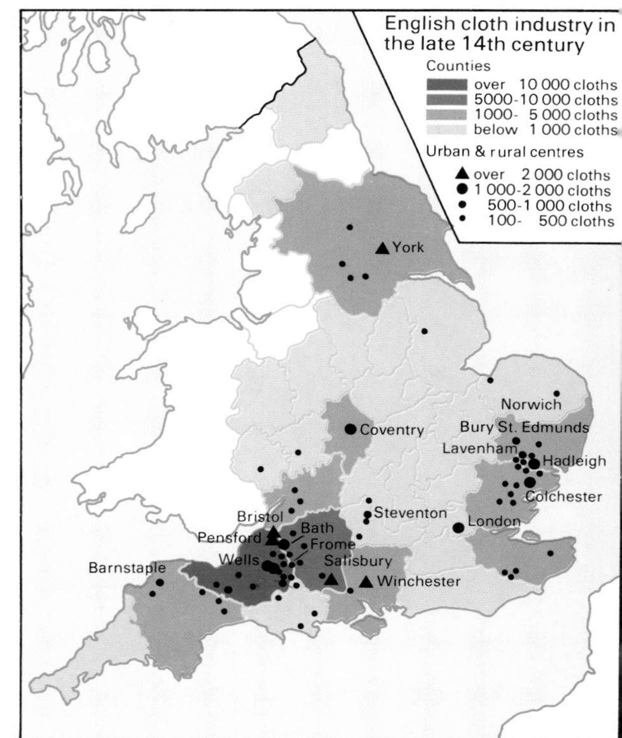

Right: The English cloth industry – fulling mills in existence before 1400. At these water-powered mills, cloth was beaten or compressed in water to shrink it. In this way, the density of the cloth was increased, making it more weatherproof. The earliest mills were operating in the late 12th century.

Far right: The English cloth industry – production in the later 14th century. Symbols give only an approximate guide to output; they are based upon aulnage accounts (tax paid on cloth produced for sale) which do not include worsted cloth. Royal customs accounts do, however, enable us to measure with some precision the amount of cloth manufactured for export.

A happy rural scene with women weaving is contrasted with the tortures of hell in this composite illustration from a medieval manuscript. Wool and woollen cloths were England's most important exports in the Middle Ages.

n medium and coarser quality cloths arose around arnstaple and Exeter, and over the county border in east Cornwall. At the opposite end of the country, in East nglia, lay the important coloured broadcloth and kersey egion centred on the Suffolk and Essex border villages of avenham, Clare, Sudbury, Hadleigh, Long Melford, Nayland, Coggeshall and Kersey itself. The third major egion was the West Riding of Yorkshire and the eastern arts of Lancashire which bordered it. Here, in the upper eaches of the Aire and Calder valleys, abundant quantities f coarse woollens were produced.

From the later 16th century onwards, the English textile ndustry underwent a transformation. This was initially timulated by severe slumps in the demand for traditional roadcloths and kersies and further aided by an influx of killed Protestant artisans fleeing from persecution in the Netherlands. While some of the long-established regions, otably Essex, faded and decayed, new regions such as Kent, Norfolk and the East Midlands rose to prominence. Moreover, many of the old-established cloth-working areas managed to switch to new products with some success, such as the West Country with its medley cloths and worsteds, and Suffolk with its worsteds.

Finally, development in the Lancashire industry must be stressed (see map below). This is not because of the scale of manufacture, but because of its variety and most particularly its precocity. In the 17th century Lancashire continued to produce cheap and coarse woollens, but it was her smallwares, linens and fustians which presaged the future. Soon after 1600 we learn that fustians had a linen warp and cotton weft, and before 1700, in the linen area around Manchester, cotton was used in association with flax yarn to produce a lighter cloth than fustian. The complex process of expansion, which had begun in the mid-14th century, had turned England into the most important cloth-producing country in Europe.

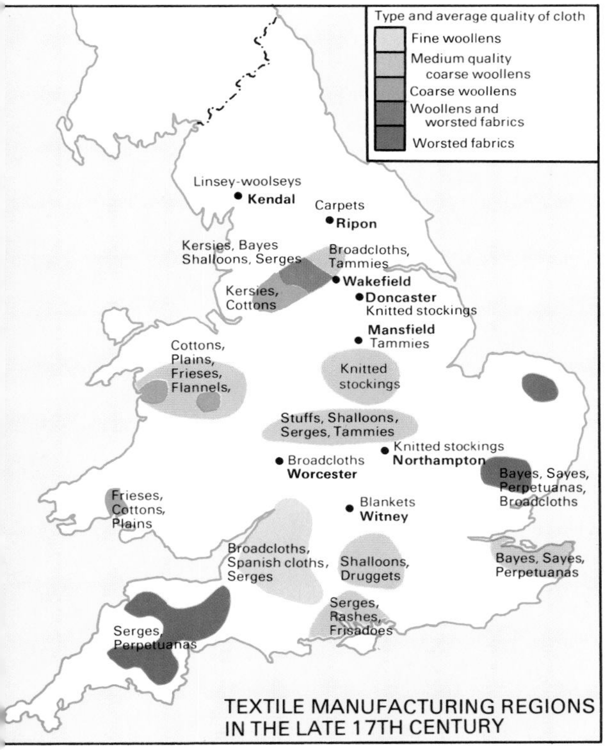

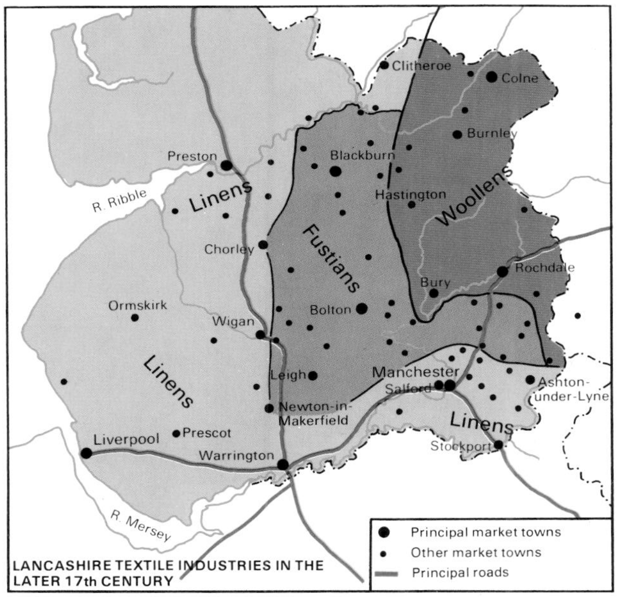

Far left: Types of cloth produced by the various manufacturing regions *c*.1350–1700.

Left: Lancashire textile industries in the later 17th century.

Minerals in Medieval and Early Modern England

A medieval illustrated calendar for the month of July showing trees being felled. Huge quantities of timber were used for the production of charcoal. In the 16th and 17th centuries coal production soared due to the shortage and high price of timber and coal replaced wood and charcoal in a long succession of industrial processes.

Right: Tin output in Cornwall. By the 14th century, Cornwall was the major production area of the Devon and Cornwall region. These figures are derived from amounts on which royal duty was paid.

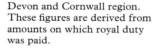

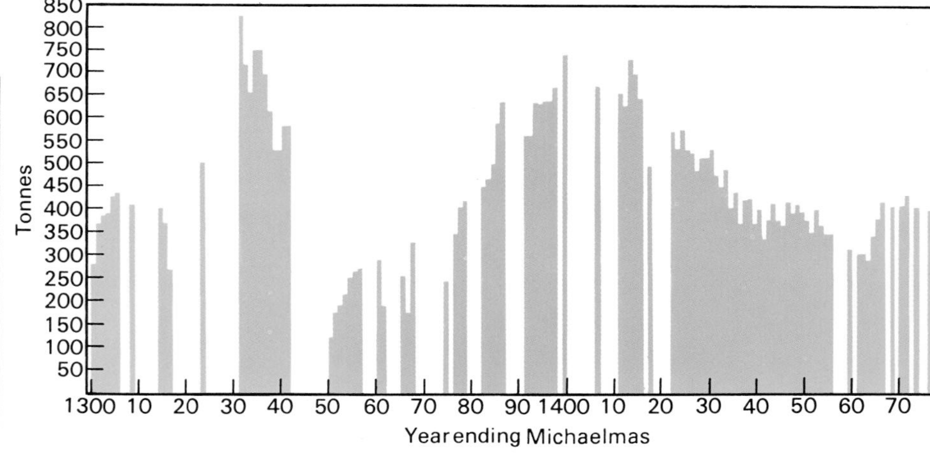

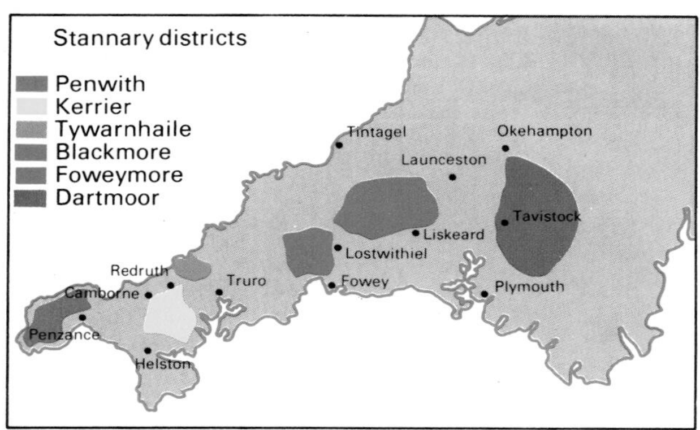

Above: Tin production in Cornwall. The extent of the stannary districts (mining franchises) was never defined in the Middle Ages, and the areas shown give only an approximate guide to tin-working regions. It should also be noted that the area of a stannary bore little relation to its productivity.

Most larger-scale industrial production in the medieval and early modern eras fell into one of three major categories: guild or craft; domestic or 'putting out'; and centralized.

Guilds were associations of master craftsmen whose power rested on local monopolies. They were of necessity strictly regulated urban institutions. The household of the master was both the unit of production and living. It housed not only the master and his family, and usually any apprentices and journeymen, but also a workshop and retail shop. The domestic system, as the name suggests, was also centred on the household, but it was the household of the employee rather than the employer. This system rested in large measure upon the part-time labour of families in their own homes, who worked for piece-rates on raw material supplied by an organizer or entrepreneur. The advantages of this system, which helped to account for its popularity and durability, lay in the low labour costs and capital investment, and great flexibility. Centralized production was usually determined by particular factors – in the case of mining the location of mineral deposits and, in that of building, the nature of the site. By the later 16th century some industrial processes required expensive capital equipment, as in the manufacture of soap, glass and paper; but even so the individual units of production were often not large. In short, centralized production was most often determined by technical factors rather than any inherent returns to scale.

England's mineral and metal-working industries were second only to her cloth industries in international repute. England was blessed with rich deposits of a wide range of valuable minerals. Tin, lead, iron and coal were extensively worked in the Middle Ages, although copper seems not to have been mined before the 16th century. There are relatively few deposits of tin in Europe, and those of the south-west peninsula were the 'best and most abundant' of all, and the tin itself was widely judged to be the finest quality available. Indeed, Devon and Cornwall possessed a virtual monopoly of production. Even after the exploitation of tin deposits in Central Europe and the Far East, English tin retained a strong hold of the international trade in Europe and the Middle East until well into the 17th century.

Below: Industries and communications in 17th-century Kent.

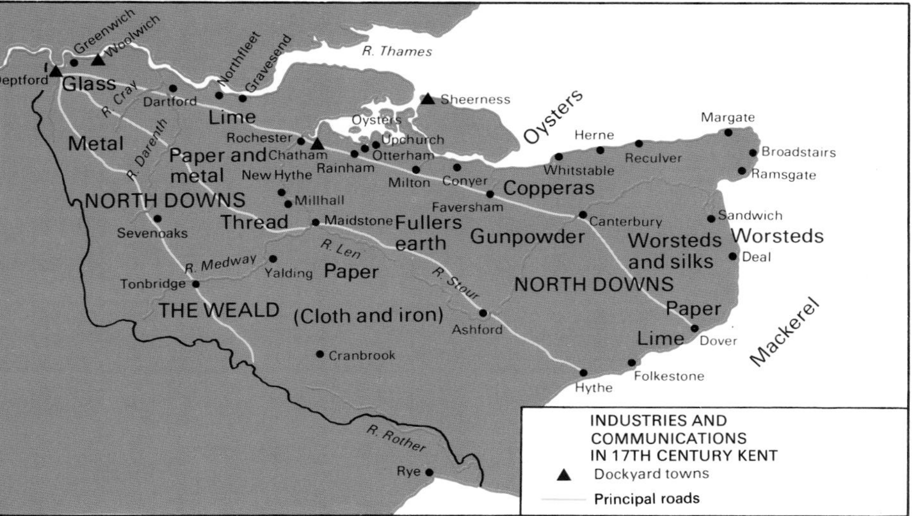

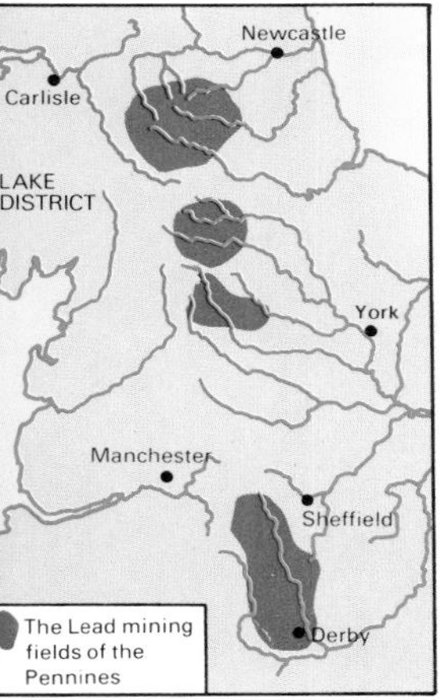

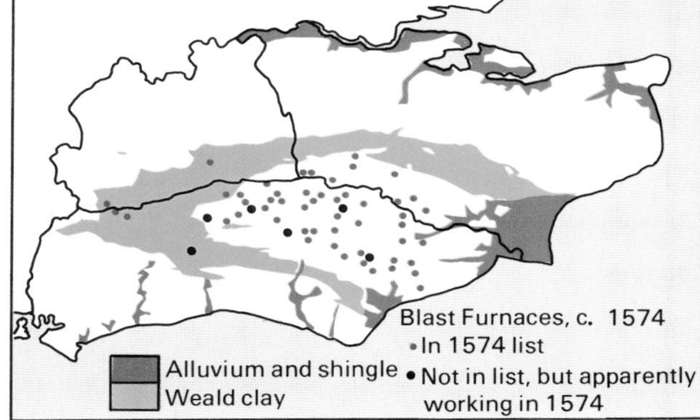

Above left: The lead-mining fields of the Pennines.

Above: Charcoal blast furnaces in Sussex, Kent and Surrey, *c.*1574. Government contracts for the manufacture of cast-iron guns – significantly cheaper than bronze artillery pieces – provided an important impetus for the development of the Wealden iron industry in the 16th century.

Right: A 15th-century blacksmith, woodcut illustration from Caxton's *Game and Play of Chess*, 1488.

Tin in various forms and alloys had a wide variety of uses, from the illumination of manuscripts to the manufacture of organ pipes, but by far the largest quantities went into the production of pewter and bronze. Tin is the only commodity for which we have national output figures. During the Middle Ages there were three phases of rising output: the first phase occurred in the latter half of the 12th century; the second and third took place respectively in the early and later 14th century, interrupted by a severe recession occasioned by plague. Succeeding the final phase of expansion was an era of falling output which lasted into the last quarter of the 15th century.

Lead deposits were much more widely distributed than tin, and by the 16th century total output exceeded that of tin. Lead was extensively used in building, for roofing and water pipes, and in pewter manufacture; by the Tudor period increasing quantities were being consumed for bullets and shot, and in sheathing the hulls of men-of-war. The major lead fields were situated in the Mendips, and in the Cumberland, Yorkshire and Derbyshire Pennines.

The soaring production of coal in the 16th and 17th centuries, to meet the increasing demand for domestic and industrial fuel at home and overseas, was to have far more profound consequences for England's economy. The shortage and high price of timber ensured a ready market for coal as a domestic fuel and, during these centuries, coal replaced wood and charcoal in a long succession of industrial processes, including brewing, dyeing, salt-making, lime-burning, soap-boiling and brick-making. Although coal could not be used for smelting iron ore until the 18th century, it was used for working a variety of metals, including iron, lead, zinc, copper and tin. By the late 17th century all the major coalfields had a wide range of manufacturing industries gathered around them, most notably those specializing in the production of metalwares of all sorts: locks, nails, needles, chains, cutlery, scythes, ploughshares and so on.

Like coal mining, iron mining and working had a long history, but entered upon a phase of rapid expansion from the later 15th century. Iron production was stimulated by the increased demand for iron-wares for peace and war, and the invention and spread of the blast furnace. The presence of both iron ore and abundant timber in the Wealden areas of Kent, Sussex and Surrey led to a prodigious concentration of charcoal blast furnaces and forges by the 1570s. But thereafter iron-smelting established itself in Yorkshire, Wales and the Forest of Dean. This was less in response to the availability of charcoal than to the demand for smelted iron from coal-based metalworking industries located round the coalfields in these regions.

In industrial terms, Kent was undoubtedly a precocious county, but the number and variety of its manufactures are powerful testimony to the degree of industrial development which took place well away from coalfields and well before the Industrial Revolution. In addition to the substantial textile and iron industries which have already been noted, we find in Kent by the later 17th century the nation's most important naval dockyards at Chatham, lime-burning on the chalk Downs, copperas manufactured on the Thames Estuary, paper-making near Dover and Dartford, and gunpowder plants at Faversham.

Rich and Poor in Medieval and Early Modern England

Most of the wealth and power of post-Conquest England was concentrated in the hands of a relatively small class of landlords, headed by the King, his barons, and leading churchmen and ecclesiastical institutions. As yet the significance of those engaged in trade and manufacture was relatively limited. Land was the basis of almost all wealth and income, and the vast bulk of the population gained their sustenance directly from farming. Consequently, the possession of land provides an excellent guide to economic standing. Domesday Book enables us to calculate with accuracy how the land of England was distributed and how the income derived from it was shared. In 1086 the total annual income produced by the land was assessed at around £37,000. The King and his immediate family received just under one-fifth; about 100 priories, abbeys and bishoprics with their dependents received a little over a quarter, and some 170 lay barons and their men got just under a half. The final portion of less than a tenth was shared by a mixed assortment of royal officials and servants, and a few surviving Old English lords.

The diagrams provide a comparison of the proportions of the various categories of tenant with the amounts of land which they held. In the middle were the *villani* who comprised around two-fifths of the listed population an
occupied around two-fifths of the land. By contrast th
cottagers, who made up almost a third of the Domesda
population, held only 5 per cent of the land. At the opposi
extreme was the 14 per cent of the population who we
designated free, for they had a fifth of the land. The 10 p
cent of the population who were slaves held no land, whi
the remaining third of England was under the dire
management of the landlords themselves.

Although Domesday Book provides some indication
the geographical distribution of wealth, we are on firm
ground from the late 12th century with the introduction
taxation based upon the assessed value of 'moveable good
of individuals. Such personal taxation, which rested upo
an agreed proportion, commonly a tenth or fifteenth, of th
value of crops, livestock and other possessions, had becom
a frequent method of revenue-raising by the close of th
13th century. The changes over time in the assessmen
which were made are suggestive of changes in the relati
wealth of towns, counties and regions. Such data have r
pretence to complete accuracy for, as with all early ta
gathering, evasion, extortion and inefficiency were rife. O
a legitimate level there were also many exemptions; mo

Three diagrams showing income from the land and its tenants, *c.*1086. These diagrams are based on information from the Domesday Book which normally lists only heads of households, not total population.

Far right and top right: Two maps showing the distribution of wealth in England according to the fifteenths of 1225 and 1334. By comparing these annual tax assessments, we can obtain a useful general guide to changes in the regional distribution of wealth.

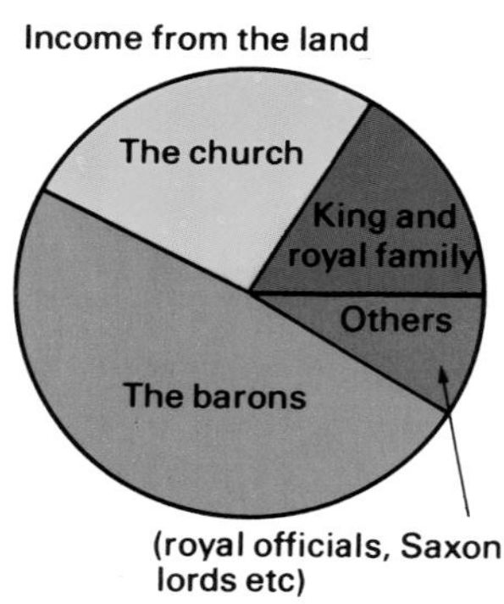

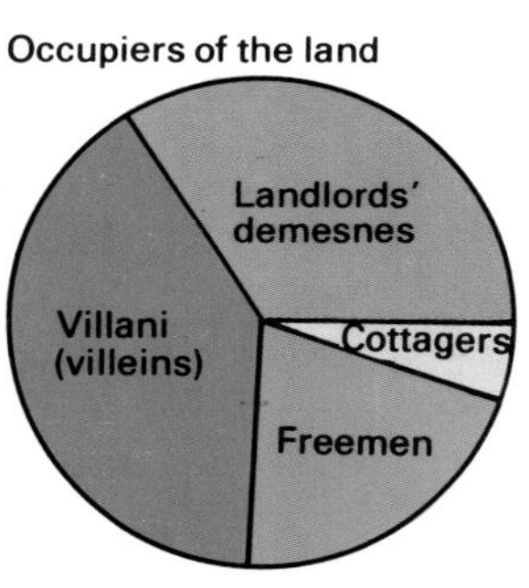

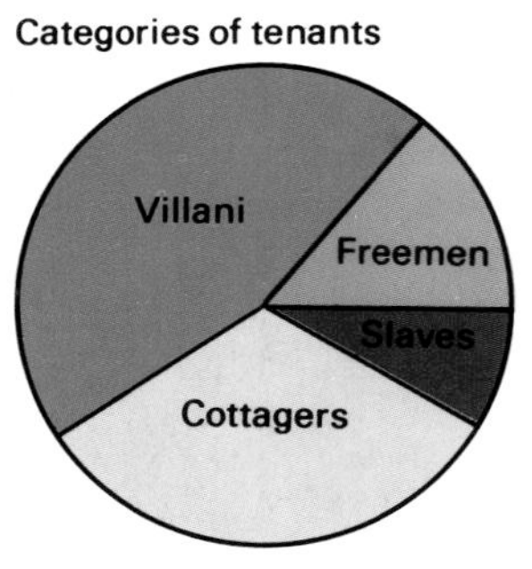

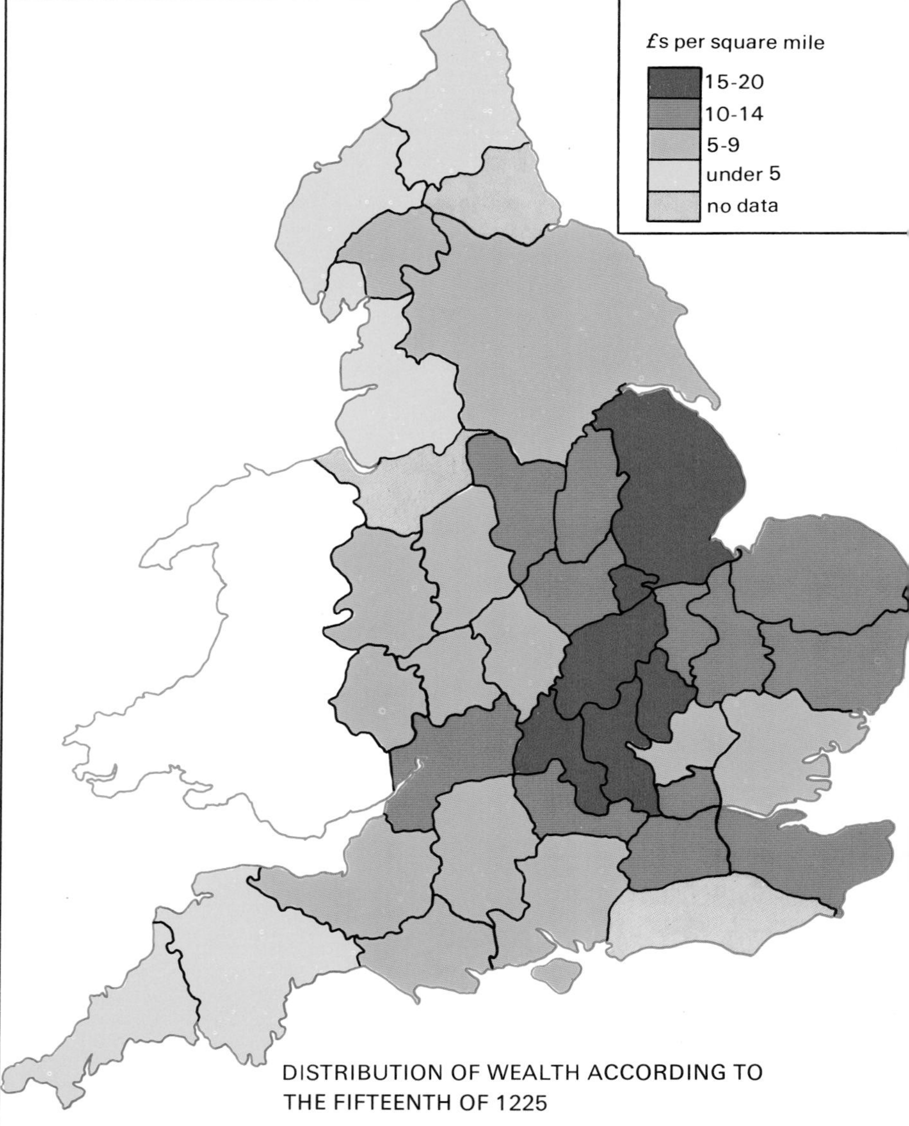

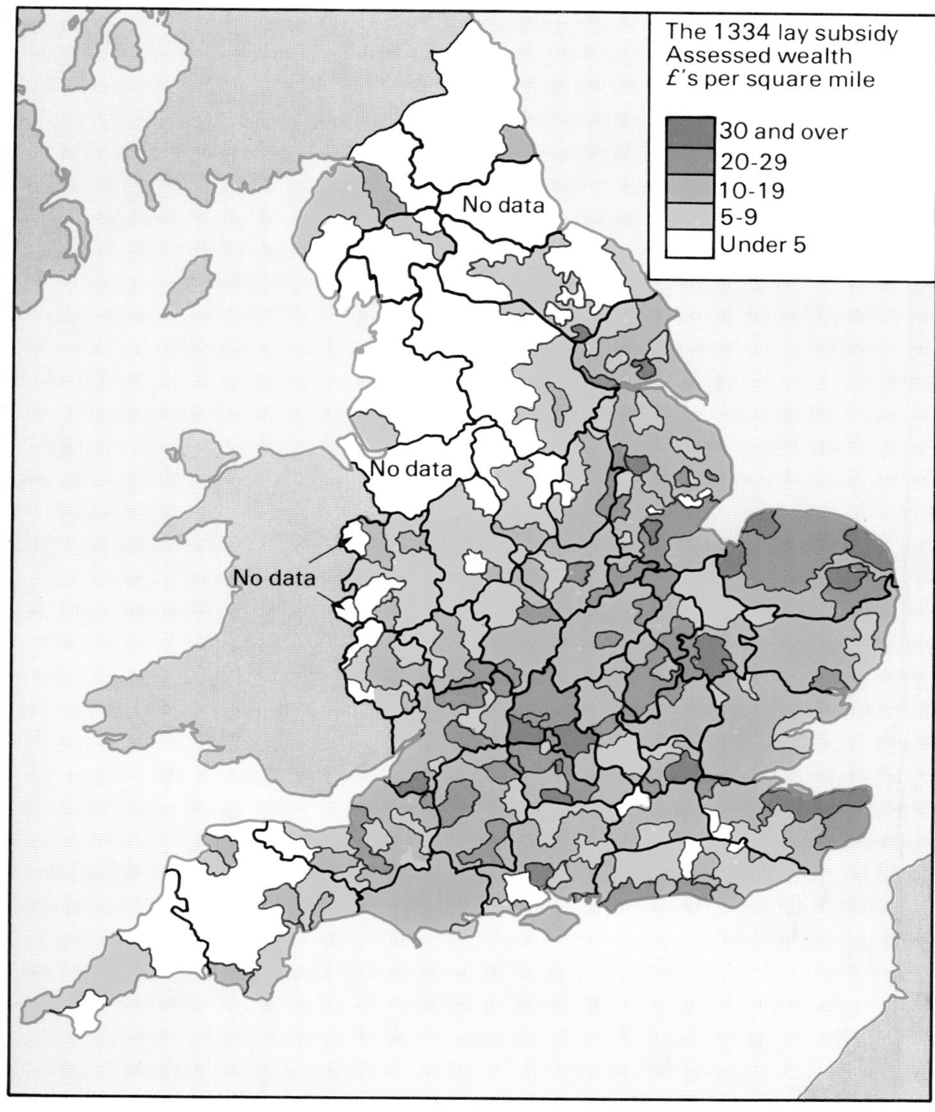

importantly Church wealth, but also including the Cinque Ports, the tinners of Devon and Cornwall, and the Palatinates of Durham and Chester. Nonetheless they have much to tell us.

Using the assessment of a fifteenth in 1225, we can see a marked concentration of wealthy counties in a band running from the Severn to the Wash. The wealthiest counties of all, excluding Middlesex which benefited greatly from London, lay in the very heart of England. By 1334, the date of a thorough reassessment of wealth, we can discern that the band of rich counties and regions had considerably expanded. At this date a line drawn from Exeter to York would neatly divide England into two countries with contrasting levels of wealth. The farther north and west of the line that one went, the poorer and less populous the county became until, in Cumberland and elsewhere, the assessed wealth was less than £5 per square mile. By contrast, between 1225 and 1334 there was a particularly rapid accumulation in Wiltshire, Somerset and Dorset, and a further advance of Norfolk and many central counties. The highest county assessments, of over £20 per square mile, were to be found in Oxfordshire, Norfolk, Bedfordshire, Berkshire and Rutland. As a general rule the richest regions were the great corn-growing lands of lowland England.

Thanks to the researches of Dr Glasscock and many local historians, we now know a great deal about variations within counties and regions in 1334. Indeed, comparisons between counties often mask differences within shires. Areas of especial wealth and poverty could be very localized. Naturally, heavy clays and light chalks were poor, as were the lightly settled wooded regions, such as the Wealden areas of Kent, Sussex and Surrey. Moorlands, too, were inevitably less productive than more fruitful lands, and the boundaries of the wild south-western moors of Bodmin, Dartmoor and Exmoor can easily be discerned from their exiguous assessments. However, some of the wealth of Bodmin Moor and Dartmoor rested with the tin miners, who were not taxed. Enclaves of extreme wealth are also in evidence, such as the Vale of Taunton, the coastal regions of east Kent and parts of Norfolk and Lincolnshire.

Below: Heriots and prices on five Winchester manors, 1270–1350. A heriot in the form of the best animal or money, depending upon wealth, was paid to the lord of the manor on the death of each customary tenant. In broad terms, therefore, the diagram shows the correlation between deaths and prices.

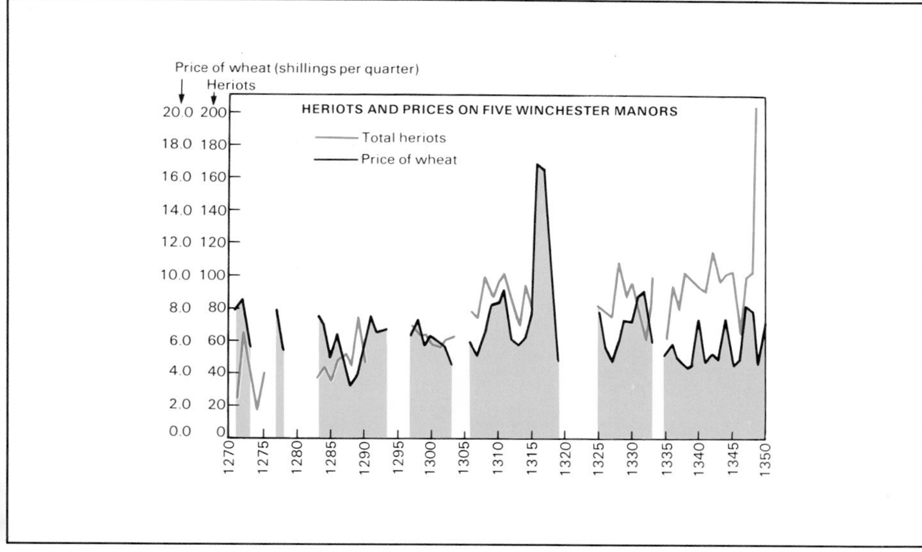

Standard of Living

In medieval and early modern England, the great mass of people gained their livelihoods from agriculture. Technical progress was limited and the size of the population was one of the most important determinants of aggregate output and individual prosperity. The number of people in the country also exercised considerable influence over the structure of society and the distribution of wealth. The ratio of men to land was always critical. Consequently, because the supply of land was relatively inelastic, a rising population posed threats to the well-being of the majority. Inevitably, the long rise in population of the central Middle Ages eventually began to outstrip the ability of the land to support it. By the later 13th century it appears that over half of the rural families had insufficient land with which to maintain themselves with any security. The gap between what their land produced and what was needed to provide for those families had to be bridged by earnings from casual labouring. But these were low in an age of labour surplus. The impact of increasing poverty on mortality is highlighted in the diagram on the left. The significance of these dates is not only that death rates rose when harvests failed, for this is a common feature of pre-industrial societies, but that the population of these Winchester bishopric manors became progressively more sensitive to variations in yields. ▶

A 15th-century market-place from contemporary illustration.

Below: Comparison between levels of English population and the real wage-rates of craftsmen, 1250–1750.

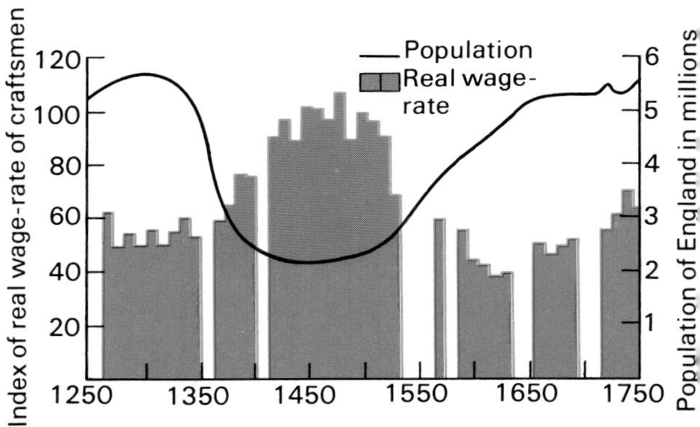

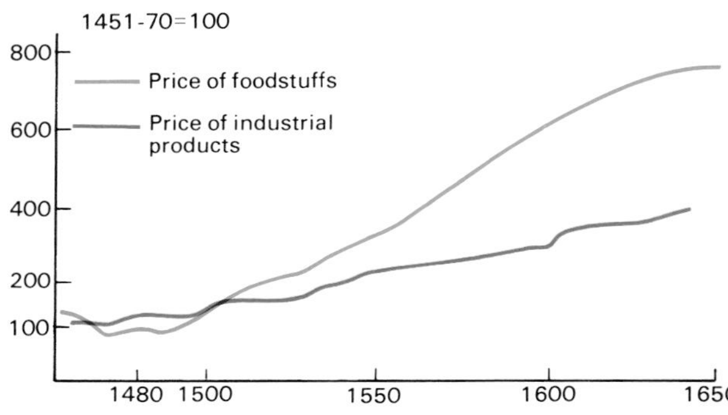

Above: The prices of food-stuffs and industrial products 1450–1650. The price of foodstuffs is an index of the prices of certain grains, malt, butter, cheese, meat and fish in the proportions likely to be consumed by a building worker in southern England. The price of industrial products is an unweighted index of the prices of charcoal, candles, oil, canvas, shirting, woollen cloth, some building materials, lead and solder.

In the late 13th and 14th centuries, every shortfall resulted in an appreciable rise in deaths. The first two decades of the 14th century, which included the Europe-wide harvest failures and livestock epidemics of 1315–22, were an era of very high mortality.

The relationship between the numbers of people and their standards of life is succinctly demonstrated in the diagram (top right).

We can see that the high levels of population and low living standards at the turn of the 13th century were succeeded, after the famines and the arrival of the plague, by an era of low population in which most people enjoyed substantially enhanced incomes. Indeed, the later 14th and the 15th centuries were, in pre-industrial terms at least, an age of remarkable affluence for the great majority of people. We can also see, however, that this age was succeeded by one of demographic recovery during which rising numbers inevitably went hand in hand with increasing poverty.

The appalling consequences of the increasing abundance of labour and shortage of food are revealed in the sharp fall in the level of real wage rates in 16th-century England, a process which reached its nadir in 1596, the year in which Shakespeare wrote *A Midsummer's Night Dream*, but also the year when real wages reached their lowest recorded level in English history. They remained low during the opening decades of the 17th century.

Another perspective on the same phenomenon is revealed in the diagram above: between the 1450s and the 1650s food prices rose more than twice as steeply as the prices of industrial products. Part of the explanation lies in the far greater ease with which the supply of manufactured goods could be increased, and part in the fact that, as the prices of grain, meat, drink and dairy produce soared, so the bulk of the population spent a greater part of their increasingly inadequate incomes on these items of sustenance, and were thereby forced to cut expenditure on manufactures.

If the standard of living of the mass of the population varied greatly over the centuries of medieval and early modern England, the social distribution of income and wealth appears to have displayed much greater stability. Analysis of the subsidy returns of 1522–5 suggests that the top five per cent of the taxable population possessed at least half of the total wealth assessed for the whole country, while the lowest 60 per cent, not including the poor who paid no tax at all, possessed only 20 per cent. According to the calculations of Gregory King in 1688, the combined income of the top two per cent of families in his day was as large as that which had to be shared by the bottom 63 per cent.

Going to Market

The growth in economic activity in the central Middle Ages demanded an increasingly dense network of markets and fairs, both in towns and in villages. Complementing the more specialized trading activities of the larger towns were the more basic, but by no means less

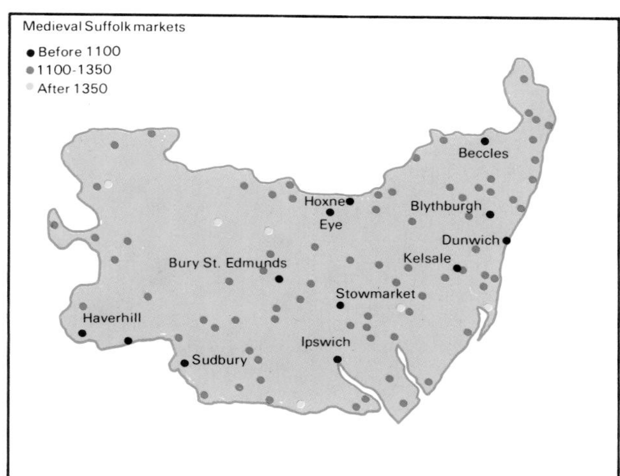

The growth of medieval markets in Suffolk, from the late 11th to late 14th century.

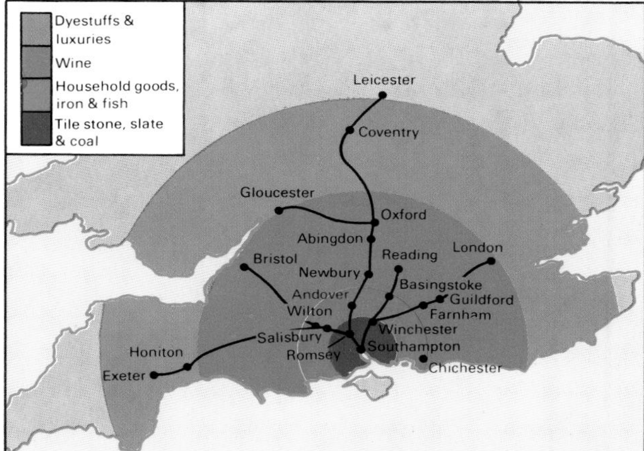

The area served by 15th-century Southampton.

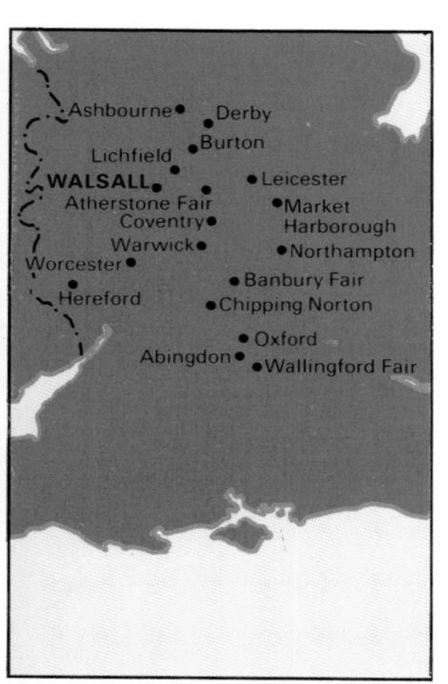

Below: Distribution of Walsall pewter in 1640. Although the source for this map lists only substandard pewter, the pattern confirms the existence of a widespread trade in manufactured goods.

vital, exchanges of agrarian produce and necessities in local markets. Between 1227 and 1350 the Crown granted the right to hold markets to some 1200 places in England and Wales. The spectacular proliferation of Suffolk markets, was repeated in many other counties. These markets were an essential part of the equipment of a developing economy.

The fortunate survival of the local toll-books of Southampton enable us to study the overland distribution of goods from one of England's major ports in the later Middle Ages. Through all the seasons of the year a steady traffic of carts came and went, linking Southampton by road to towns over 100 miles (160 km) distant. Coventry, a Midlands cloth-producing centre, for example, regularly received woad, alum, and madder for its industry, as well as wine and a wide variety of Mediterranean luxuries for consumption by its richer citizens. When the carts returned to Southampton they were frequently laden with cloth and wool bound for overseas markets. We can be certain that, despite the absence of such informative records for other ports, Southampton's pattern of transport communications was repeated many times throughout the country.

In addition to the necessarily long-distance trades in imports and exports and in specialized products and luxuries, was the vital network of regional trades centred upon provincial towns and markets, in which each town serviced the requirements of its hinterland. In the case of Worcester, the market area extended approximately 25 miles (40 km) to the east and west, and 15 miles (24 km) to the north and south. In broad terms the size of the market region was determined by the presence of other market centres, and by convenient travelling distances.

For some products we have records which show their distribution to shops and consumers over a wide area. Pewter is one such product. Although pewterers could be found in virtually every sizeable provincial town, the fact that pewter was used in nearly every household in the realm encouraged specialization. The search records of the

Far right: Main road and river communications in England and Wales *c.*1600.

London Pewterers' Company provide evidence of considerable specialization by the 17th century, with the products of particular centres and makers being widely disseminated.

So highly developed a marketing and transport system was of necessity based upon an efficient network of roads and navigable rivers. The major roads and rivers of England at the turn of the 16th and 17th centuries are outlined on the above map. The dominance of London is exemplified by its focal position in the road and river network, with all the major routes to the North, West, South and East radiating from the capital. But no less striking are the ample road and river systems of the major provincial towns and cities. York, Bristol and Coventry, for example, had excellent main road links, not only with London, but with many other towns as well. In fact, all leading towns had four to six main roads converging on them. Water transport played a significant role almost everywhere, and coastal trade was often of prime importance. The sea has been aptly described as 'merely a river round England'. London in particular benefited greatly from its ideal location for water-borne trade. Its insatiable appetite for food and fuel, for example, meant a constant flow of grain and dairy produce from East Anglia and Kentish ports, and coal from Newcastle.

England's Treasure by Foreign Trade

The beginnings of England's international commerce long ante-date the Norman Conquest. During the late Saxon era a Western European economy was emerging, of which England became an integral part. One beneficial consequence of the Viking raids and Cnut's conquests was the development of strong trading links with Scandinavia.

This Scandinavian trade remained important well after the Conquest and, as the German merchants of the Hanse established economic dominance over the whole of the Baltic area, so England's links with this region were strengthened and added to those with the Cologne region. The Conquest itself provided an impetus to trade with Normandy and northern France and, during the course of the 12th century, Flanders came to depend upon England's wool.

Direct trade with southern Europe was a later development, at first concentrated on Bordeaux, but by the 13th century taking in Spain and Portugal and, by overland routes, many Mediterranean ports. This trade was given an immense boost at the turn of the 13th and 14th centuries when Italian merchants opened up direct sea contact with north-west Europe.

Baltic came silvan products and naval stores, such as timber, furs, potash, hemp, flax and linen, as well as large quantities of fish. From Cologne and the industrial towns of the Meuse valley came metalware and a variety of small manufactures. The main products of southern and Mediterranean Europe fell into the luxury or semi-luxury category: fine textiles (including silks and cloths of gold), fine foodstuffs and wine, spices, exotic fruits, sugar and rice. But some Mediterranean exports were raw materials vital to England's thriving cloth industry, notably dyestuffs such as woad and alum. Finally, we must stress the importance of the wine trade with France and to a lesser extent Germany, and of imports of salt from the Bay of Bourgneuf.

The importance of the wine trade in the Middle Ages is revealed in the abundant customs accounts of Bordeaux and numerous English ports. At its peak in the early 14th century 90–100,000 tons of wine were exported annually from Bordeaux. The proportion of these exports which came to England cannot be precisely quantified, but there can be no doubt that, although Bordeaux wine was consumed in most of the countries of north-western Europe, England was the principal single market. It has

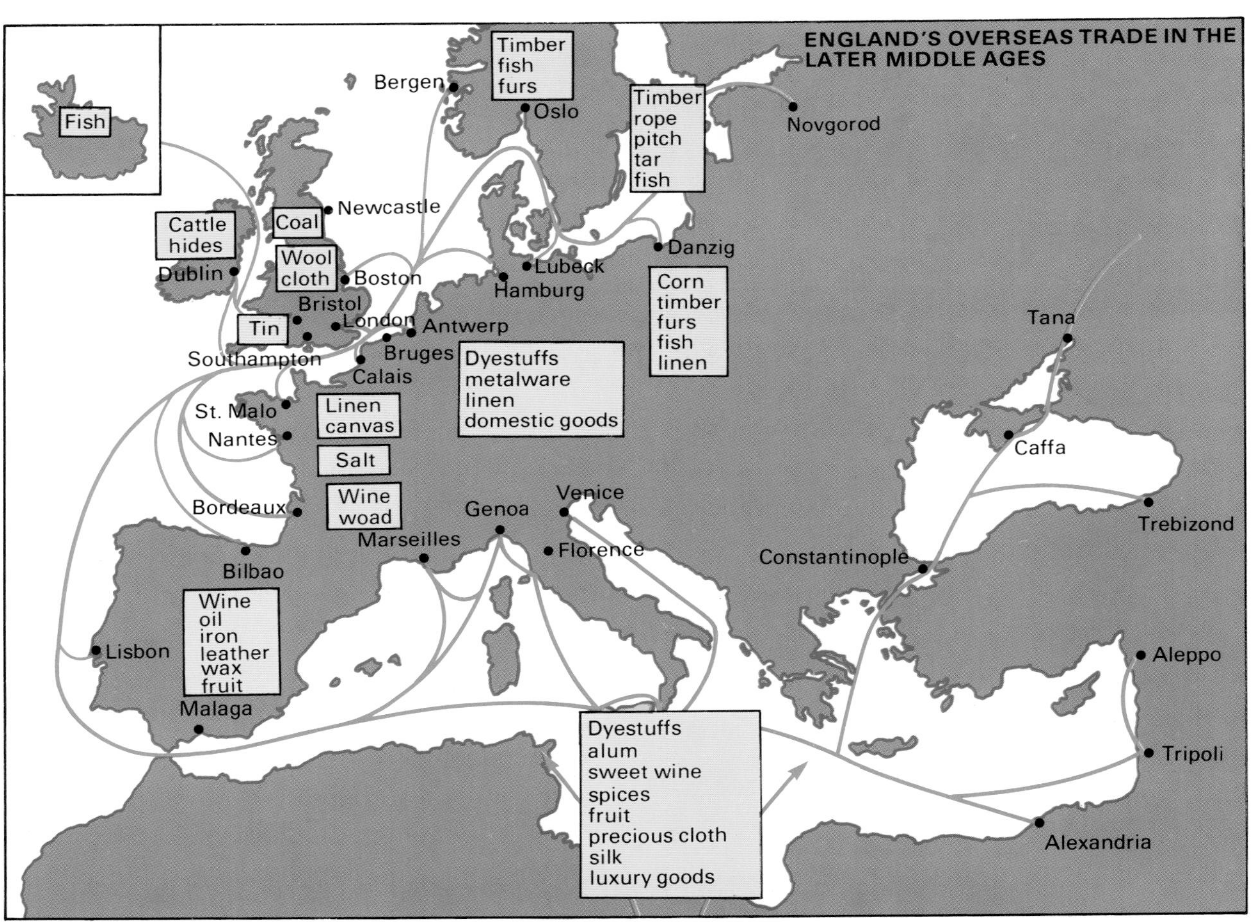

England's overseas trade in the later Middle Ages. In the early Middle Ages, the bulk of England's export trade had been in primary products, raw materials which were then processed in economically more advanced regions like the Low Countries and north Italy. Thus the development of exports of manufactured cloth in the 14th century marks a significant shift in emphasis. England was now exporting industrial products.

England's overseas trade in the Middle Ages and the Tudor period can be divided into three geographical sectors: the northern trades with Scandinavia and the Baltic nations; the southern and Mediterranean trades with Spain, Italy and the East; and the cross-Channel trades with France, the Low Countries and inland Germany.

England was ideally located at the confluence of the northern and southern trades. From Scandinavia and the

been suggested that England's imports at this time may have exceeded 20,000 tons per annum. During the course of the 14th and 15th centuries the trade contracted in the face of a variety of economic and political factors, including plague and the Hundred Years' War, until by the beginning of the 15th century imports averaged 9–10,000 tons per annum. The trade contracted further thereafter, but by the close of the century it was back to the level of 1400s. In addition to fluctuations in the scale of imports of wine, significant changes occurred in the patterns of its distribution. At the beginning of the 14th century, every port in the realm was engaged directly in the wine trade. The smaller ports served their immediate hinterland, while the larger distributed wine over a wide inland area. By the late 15th century there was much greater specialization and concentration. The trade of many eastern and southern ports – most notably Hull, King's Lynn, Sandwich, and Southampton – shrank, to leave London as the sole regional centre of the East, while that of Bristol and the ports of Devon and Cornwall expanded to serve the needs of western markets.

England's Wool Exports

If imports were striking for their diversity, exports were concentrated into a narrow range dominated by wool, cloth, tin, lead and coal. Of these, the first three at least had a long history as exported products. English cloaks were sold in Charlemagne's Gaul in the late 8th century, and tentative references make it seem likely that English tin was also sent abroad in these early times. Yet it was wool which from the 12th to the 14th centuries was the export commodity without rival. From the mid-12th century exports of raw wool began to expand rapidly, and by the late 13th century an average of 30,000 sacks of wool were exported every year. Each sack contained the fleeces of more than 250 sheep.

Thanks to the unparalleled series of English customs accounts we can chart the progress of wool exports from 1275 and cloth exports from 1347, in an almost unbroken sequence through to the end of Henry VIII's reign. Our diagram shows the long-term decline of wool exports and the massive rise of cloth exports. Because cloth was worth substantially more than raw wool, the total value of the exports of these two commodities was almost twice as great in Henry VIII's reign as it had been in that of Edward II, two centuries before.

By the midddle of the 17th century elements of both continuity and change in the pattern of English overseas trade can be discerned. Cloth was still overwhelmingly the most important export, accounting for perhaps as much as 75 per cent of all exports by value. But by 1640 'new draperies' were almost as important as traditional broadcloths, and moreover they were being carried by English merchants into the Mediterranean and the Levant. New trading links had been established with lands to the far East and West; the East India Company had set up trading posts in the East Indies or Spice Islands (now Indonesia) and on the coasts of India, and settlers were founding thriving communities in New England and the West Indies. Yet if these regions were to prove instrumental in the transformation of England's overseas trade in future generations, by the mid-17th century it seems that just under two-thirds of total imports still came from north and north-west Europe, just under one-third from the Mediterranean, with Asia and America accounting for a mere 5–7 per cent.

Below left: The wine trade with south-west France – average annual imports of Gascon wine in the 15th century. Each ton contained around 210 gallons (945 litres). The figures do not include German and Mediterranean wine imports.

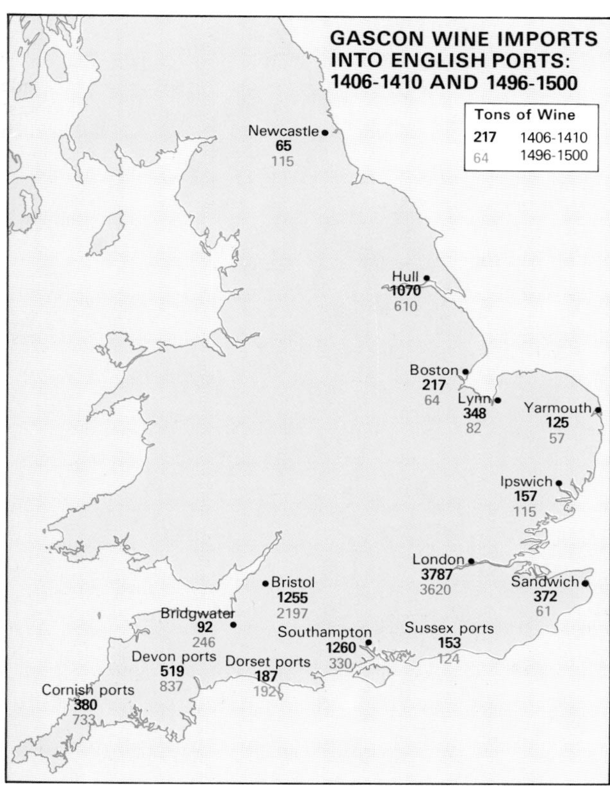

Bottom: England's exports of raw wool and woollen cloth 1347–1544. Although the value of the export trade increased in the later Middle Ages, royal customs revenue declined. This was because merchants paid only a light duty on cloth, in contrast to the heavy duty levied on wool from the 1340s onwards.

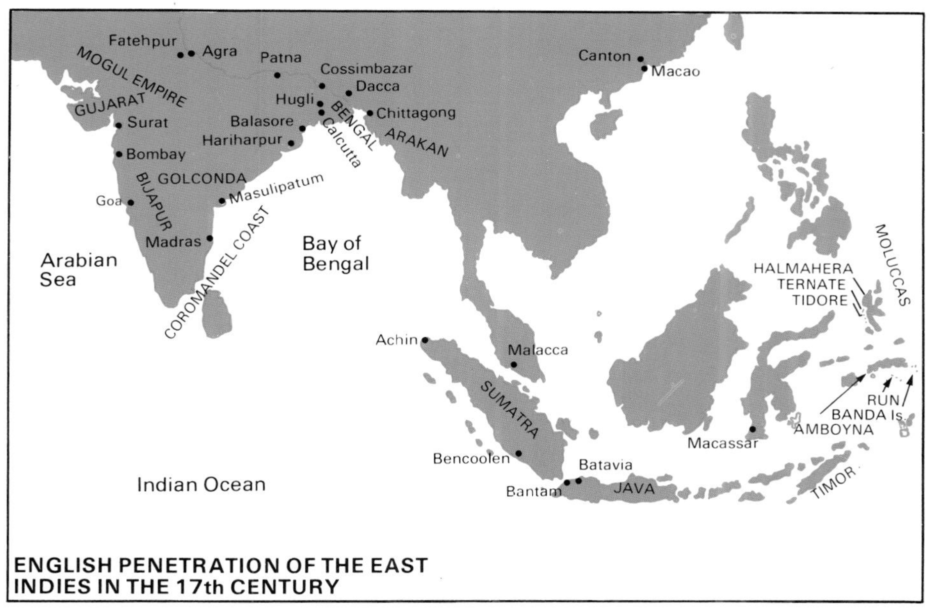

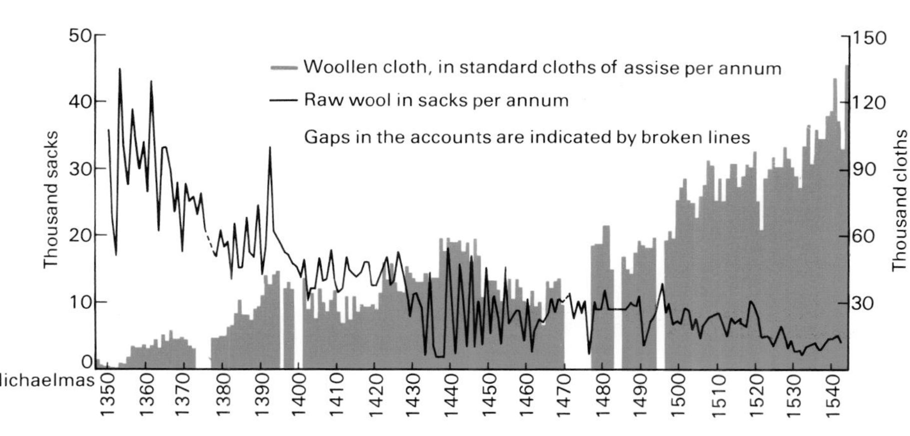

Chapter Eight

THE GREAT TRANSFORMATION: THE RISE OF INDUSTRY AND ITS AFTERMATH

Britain was the first country in the world to experience an 'industrial revolution', and so to reap both the benefits of rising incomes and wealth and the miseries from the social dislocation this involved. By the 1870s there were already visible signs that Britain's astonishing economic paramountcy would be challenged, and the succeeding years have seen the gradual erosion of Britain's early dominance. At the same time society in Britain, as elsewhere, has undergone a profound transformation, accelerated in this century by the crises of war and depression and by the impact of massive technological advances.

The social structure of London, 1898–99. One of twelve contemporary maps surveying the living standards of Londoners.

MAP DESCRIPTIVE OF LONDON POVERTY, 1898-9

(IN 12 SHEETS)

SHEET 12.
SOUTH-EASTERN DISTRICT

THE STREETS ARE COLOURED ACCORDING TO THE GENERAL CONDITION OF THE INHABITANTS, AS UNDER:—

Black	Lowest class. Vicious, semi-criminal.
Dark blue	Very poor, casual. Chronic want.
Light blue	Poor. 18s. to 21s. a week for a moderate family.
Purple	Mixed. Some comfortable, others poor.
Pink	Fairly comfortable. Good ordinary earnings.
Red	Middle class. Well-to-do.
Yellow	Upper-middle and Upper classes. Wealthy.

A combination of colours—as dark blue and black, or pink and red—indicates that the street contains a fair proportion of each of the classes represented by the respective colours.

Agrarian Change, 1660–1850

Between the years 1660 and 1850 British agriculture scored a double achievement in expanding sufficiently fast to feed a population which grew four times, with very little recourse to imported foodstuffs, while at the same time improving the quality of much of the food produced, especially meat. The period was once known as the Agricultural Revolution, but this expression is now not often used, because it is realized that agricultural change was by no means revolutionary but was an almost continuous process extending over some three centuries.

A 19th-century painting of a prize ram. During the 18th and 19th centuries there was great interest in developing and improving breeds of sheep, pigs and cattle, and in selective breeding to develop desired characteristics.

Agricultural improvement was brought about by a very considerable extension of the area under cultivation, involving deforestation, drainage of fens and marshes and the conversion of rough grazing on common land to arable cultivation, by a radical change in the structure of landholding and by the generalization of improved methods of husbandry, nearly all of which were known before 1660.

The Spread of Enclosures

A major factor in the extension of the cultivated area was the spread of enclosure, a process which had been carried on in a piecemeal manner up to 1700, by which time about half of all land had been enclosed, but which was accelerated in the 18th and early 19th centuries. Enclosure was often by agreement between the landowners in an area, but from the middle of the 18th century there was frequent resort to enclosure by Act of Parliament, which was conditional on the agreement of the owners of three-quarters of the total acreage. The parliamentary enclosure movement, which was at its peak during the period of high prices in the Napoleonic Wars, resulted in the enclosure of about a quarter of the acreage of England, mainly in the Midlands. Enclosure led to more efficient farming by individual farmers, who were no longer restricted in their methods of husbandry by the need to get communal agreement for change. It also made for intensive use of formerly under-utilized comons and wastelands.

The same period saw a concentration of land in fewer hands and a decline in the number of owner-occupiers and peasants. The new large estates were divided in turn into large farms worked by farmers who specialized in production for the market rather than for the sustenance of their own families, a process which was accelerated by the reorganization of land that was possible after enclosure.

The growth in the number of large enclosed farms worked by capitalist farmers with hired labour was the background to the technical changes in husbandry, a process which was encouraged by the great contemporary interest in improvement and the dissemination of information by well-known publicists and writers. The most important technical change was the virtual elimination of the fallowing system which had meant that about a third of all arable land was out of cultivation in any one year. The key factors in this vital change were the development of the system called convertible husbandry, by which land remained under grain cultivation for three or more years in succession and was then sown to grass for six or seven years, and the introduction into arable rotations of turnips and artificial grasses, such as clover. Experiments with rotations led to the development of the alternate or Norfolk system, which was a rotation of wheat-turnips-barley-clover or wheat-barley-turnips-barley-clover-rye-grass. Such systems, which greatly increased the production of both grain and livestock, were most effective in areas of light soils and good natural drainage. In heavy soil areas, development waited for the introduction of cheap drainage in the mid-19th century and most land was laid down to permanent pasture.

Systema
Agriculturæ.
Being
The Mystery of Husbandry
Discovered and
layd Open
by
J W
H Van Hove sculp
Printed for Tho. Dring at ye Corner of Chancery lane in Fleetstreet. 1675

Other important changes included the much greater use of fertilizer, including dung from the increased number of animals on the farm and materials imported from outside, such as town waste and seaweed. Soils were also improved

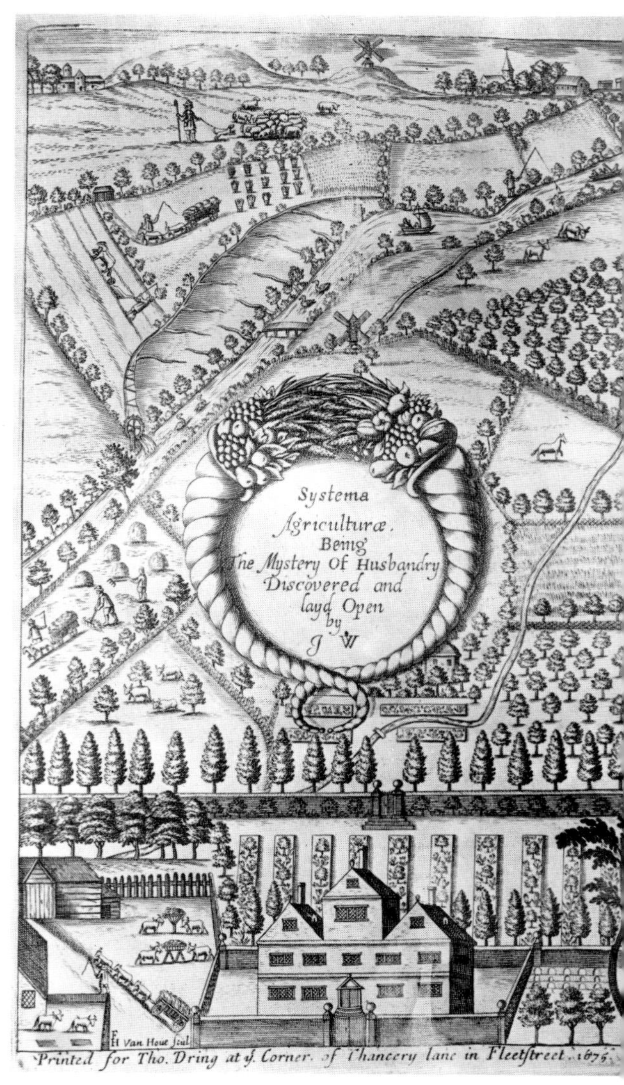

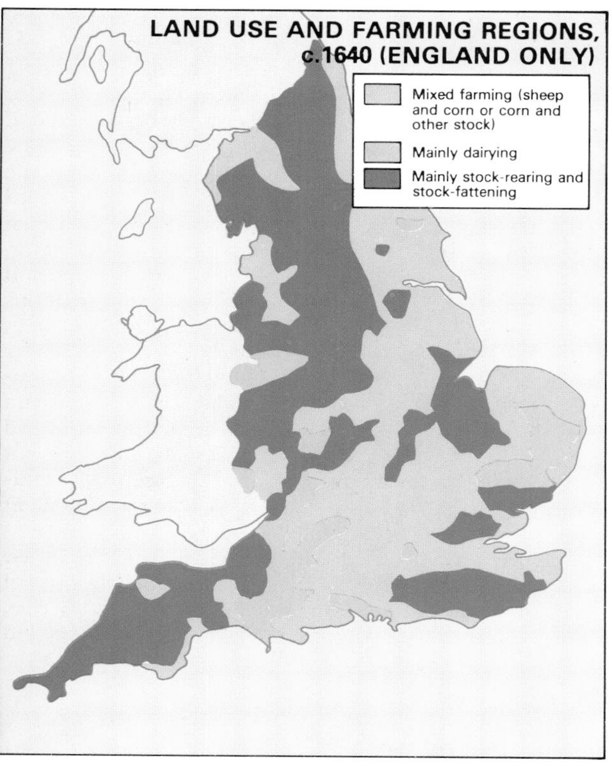

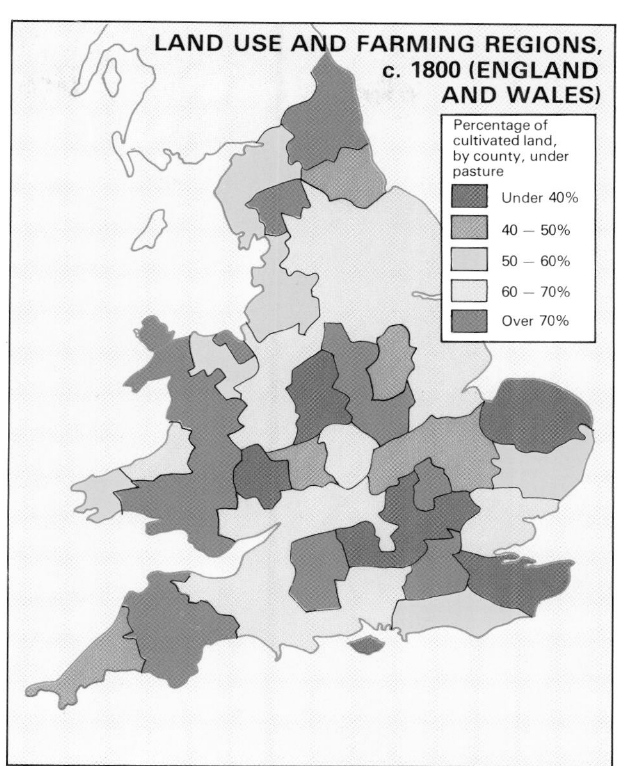

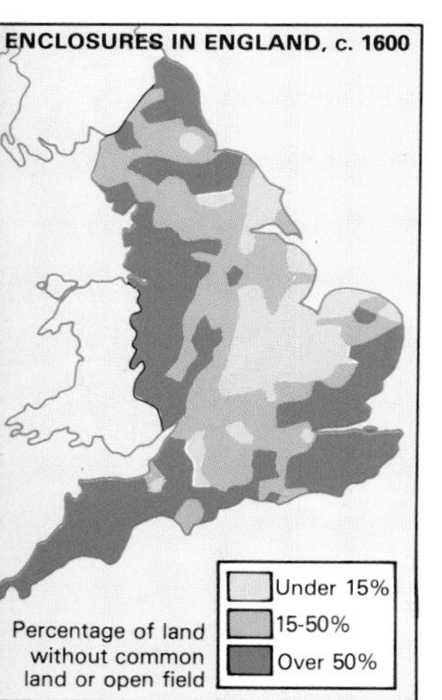

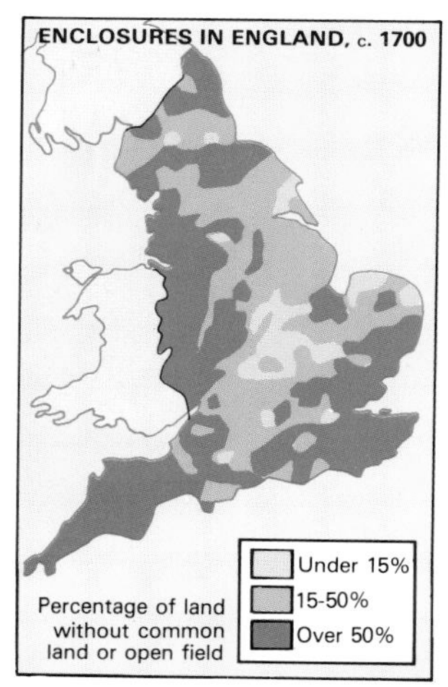

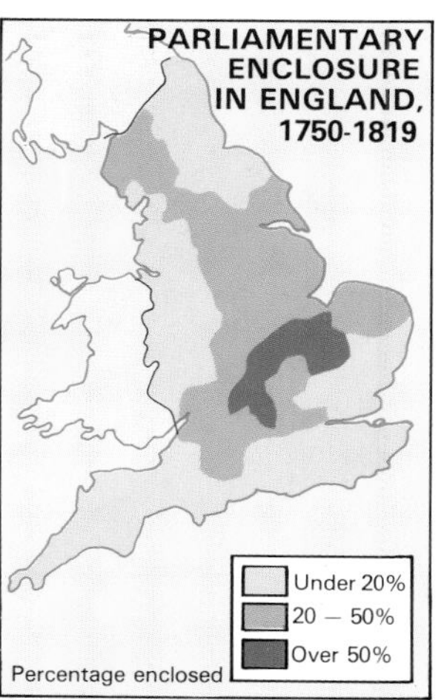

Between 1600 and 1800 much of the unenclosed land remaining was gradually consolidated and enclosed. After 1750 enclosure by Act of Parliament, often of common grazing land, was rapid, especially in the Midlands. Both the causes and consequences of enclosure are controversial, but 18th-century enclosure probably aided agricultural efficiency, encouraged larger farms, but impoverished some of the poorest farmers who had need of the common land and also dispossessed some who had no clear title to the land they traditionally used.

by the spreading of marl on light soils and lime on heavy soils. Such changes, together with heavier crops and the increased production for the market, required a much greater investment in carts and waggons and an increase in the number of horses and oxen required, both for carrying and for husbandry itself.

Every one of these changes had been known since the late Middle Ages and their introduction was a gradual process of dissemination. The 18th and early 19th centuries saw some new developments, especially in the breeding of sheep and cattle, and in the early development of agricultural machinery, such as the seed-drill and the threshing machine, but it is not till the second half of the 19th century that investment in machinery becomes really important. But, long prior to that, British agriculture had improved sufficiently to feed a much larger population and to allow that process of urbanization which accompanied the early stages of the Industrial Revolution.

The Structure of Agricultural Employment in England and Wales, 1851

Occupations

Males	226,515	Farmers and Graziers
	10,561	Farm baliffs
	908,678	Agricultural labourers (outdoor)
	12,517	Shepherds
	189,116	Farm servants (indoors)
Females	22,916	Farmers and Graziers
	44,310	Agricultural labourers (outdoor)
	99,156	Farm servants
Total	1,513,778	

In 1851 agriculture still occupied more than one fifth of the total population. In 1700 the proportion had been around three-quarters and already by 1800 this had fallen to one third. After 1851 not only the share but the absolute numbers of those working on the land declined.

Agrarian Change, 1850–1980

By 1850 Britain was well on the road to becoming an industrial economy and an urban society. Urban population surpassed rural population for the first time in 1851. Agriculture still remained important, providing employment for over two million people, or more than a fifth of the occupied population; and it still produced one-fifth of national income. Agriculture was not only the largest single occupation in the country, but the one which was widely regarded as having a social duty to find work for all those who could not find other means to support themselves.

Agriculture had been in relative decline – in comparison with the industrial, commercial, and service sectors – for about 150 years before 1850. Despite this, in terms of acreage cultivated, numbers employed, and physical output it had been steadily growing in size. But, from the middle years of the 19th century, even this growth halted and turned into decline. Since the Second World War, agriculture has more or less stabilized its position at between 3 and 4 per cent of both workforce and national income. During this prolonged period of relative and absolute decline, agriculture has shed excess numbers and divested itself of uncompetitive functions, often at the price of much social dislocation and political clamour.

The broad chronology of agricultural fortunes is well-established: depression after 1815; recovery from the late 1830s, and then high prosperity in the 1850s and 1860s; severe depression and near-ruin from the late 1870s to the 1890s; partial recovery before 1914; prosperity in the First World War, rudely turned into slump in the 1920s; revival in the Second World War, with generally continued and rising prosperity since 1945 thanks to government help, a prosperity somewhat disturbed since Britain entered the Common Market. But such a broad catalogue of alternating periods of depression and prosperity should not conceal the continued major changes and adjustments within the structure of farming that in the long view have made it into a slimmer and more efficient sector of the national economy.

The simple view of the prosperity of the 1850s and 1860s is that Britain enjoyed a lucky interlude between the coming of free trade in 1846 and the flood of cheap imported grains from Russia and North America in the late 1870s, due to the time it took to open up new areas of cereal production by building railway networks and developing ocean shipping. In fact, while the stable grain prices certainly helped British farmers, the growing size and purchasing power of their urban consumer market was reflected in rising demand for meat, butter, and cheese, rather than for cereals. The successful farmers were those who met this demand by increasing their output of livestock products within a mixed farming system. In such a system stock consumed the crops of part of the arable acreage and sustained the yields of grains with their manure. The capital-intensive 'high farming' which was a feature of this period involved the injection into such a mixed farming

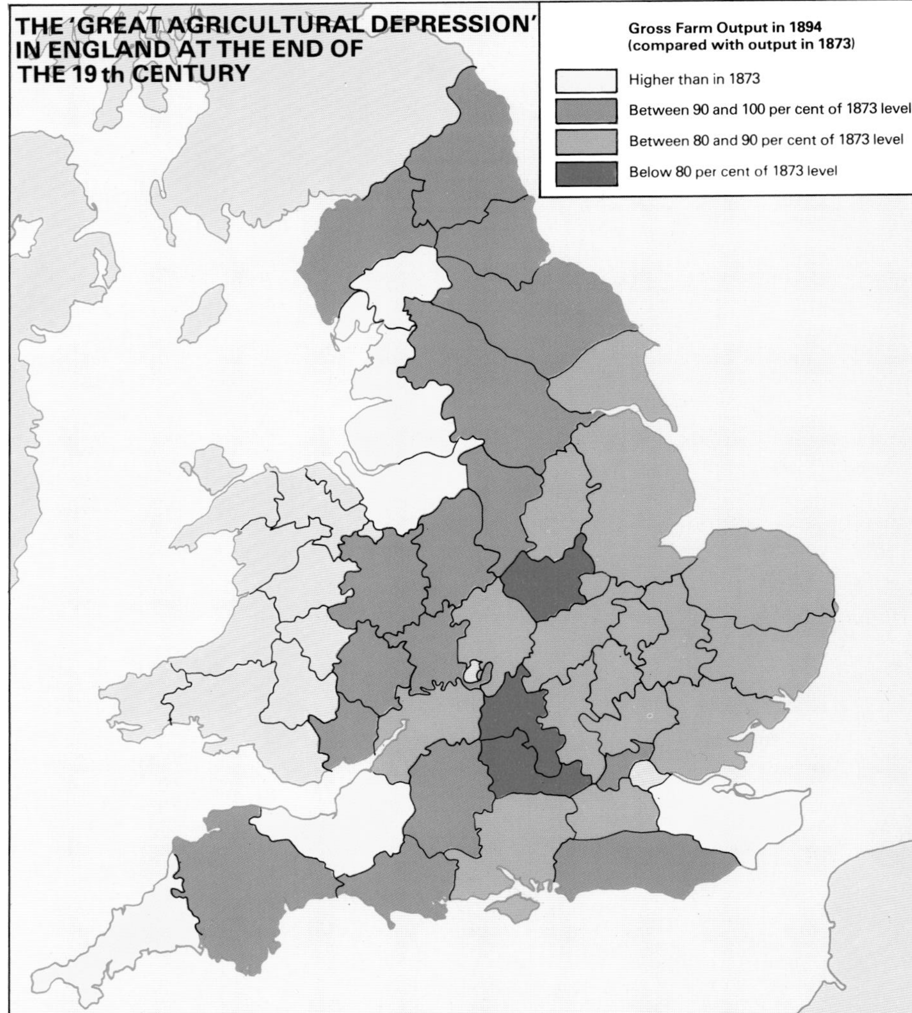

Right: How farm output dropped during the last quarter of the 19th century. The areas worst affected were the exclusively arable regions. At the same time the market for meat and dairy products was increasing, so farmers in the dairying counties of Lancashire, Cheshire, Somerset, and Cornwall prospered, helped by the low cost of feed grain. Western and upland areas where stock breeding or fattening were important also suffered relatively little.

Below: The meat market at Smithfield Market in London, in the 19th century.

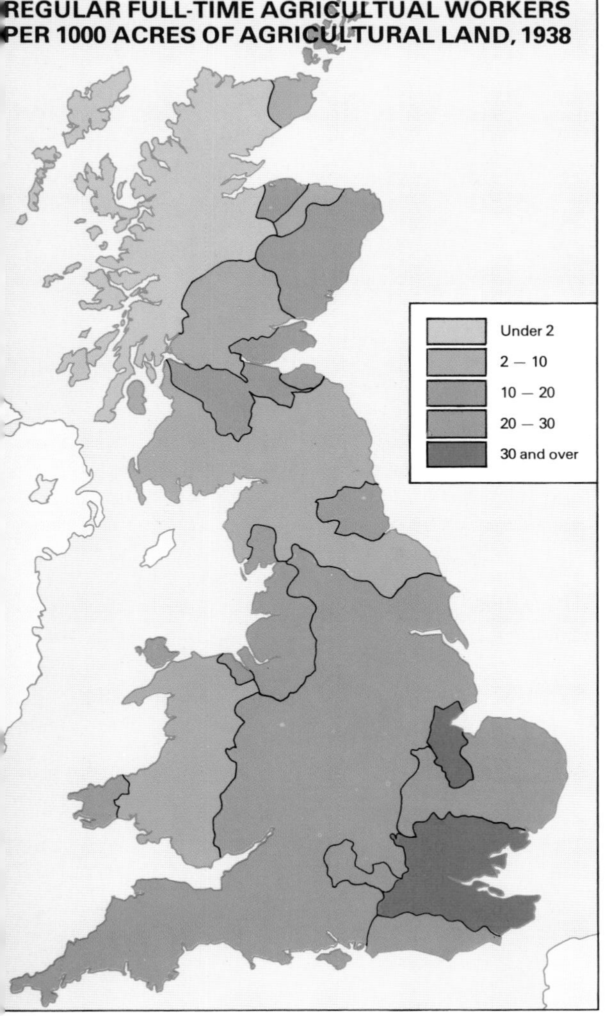

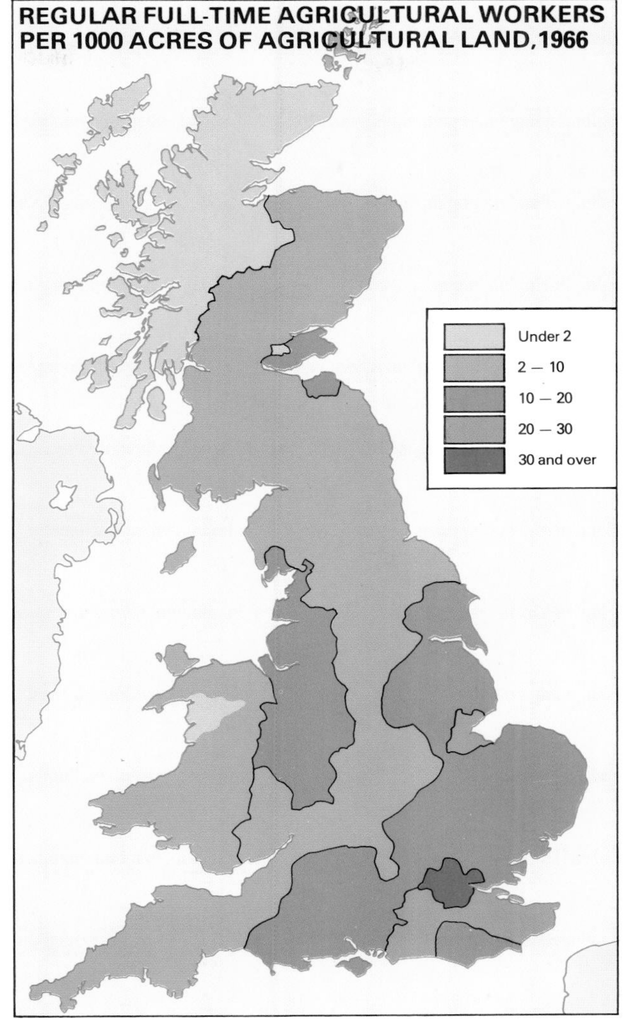

The number of agricultural workers per 1000 acres of land has declined sharply with increasing mechanization. The high level of agricultural workers in the London area is accounted for by the concentration of market gardens.

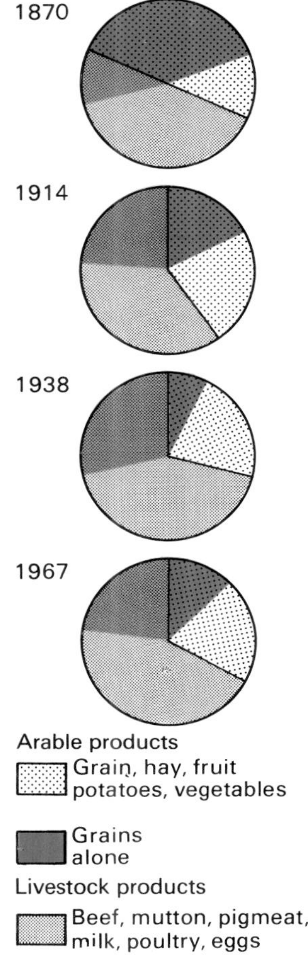

The changing composition of British agricultural output.

system of extra quantities of feeding stuffs and fertilizers as purchased inputs. As a result, it was those regions suited by soil and climate to the sheep-corn, or turnip-barley, type of farming – broadly speaking, eastern and southern England and the Midlothians and eastern coastal areas in Scotland – which experienced prosperity, contrasting with the more pastoral western districts and the midland clay areas.

The flood of imported grains, which caused the price of wheat to fall by half and of barley by a third between the early 1870s and the mid-1890s, undermined the economy of mixed farming. Wheat acreages tumbled, flocks of arable-sheep dwindled, land went out of cultivation, farmers went bankrupt, rents collapsed. But all these signs of distress were localized in eastern and southern England; non-arable farmers often did well in these years. The decline in arable farming was briefly reversed during the Great War, but it continued thereafter. After 1918 livestock farmers now suffered competition from Australia, South America and Denmark, while cereal farmers lost their wartime guaranteed grain prices in 1921. Grain farmers also suffered from intense foreign competition which drove down grain prices in the 1930s to levels unequalled since Tudor times. The inter-war years were the one period when virtually the whole of agriculture was in depression and decline.

In the 1920s and 1930s the ground was being laid for full-scale mechanization and for the intensified application of agricultural chemistry in fertilizers and pest and weed controls. These developments came into their own during the Second World War and into full fruition thereafter. Between 1940 and 1945, efforts to increase the home production of food were more successful and better balanced than in the First World War; the output of wheat, barley, and potatoes was doubled during the war, and that of oats increased by 50 per cent. At the same time, the output of milk was also increased, the production of beef was well maintained, and only the output of mutton and lamb declined significantly.

Agricultural prosperity continued and increased after 1945 through systematic state subsidies. This system was painless for consumers, who paid for their food at world price levels in the shops and, as it happened, not too expensive for taxpayers. This was because technological changes in machinery, agricultural chemistry, and plant strains increased yields dramatically, raised labour productivity, and kept down costs of production. But the system for protecting and subsidizing agriculture was radically altered by Britain's entry into the Common Market in 1972. Prices were now fixed by the EEC, the price being at once the amount actually paid by consumers and the price at which the EEC would buy as much as farmers chose to produce. Thus arose the notorious beef and butter 'mountains'. At the same time, high tariffs have been imposed on agricultural goods coming from outside the Common Market.

The Growth of London, 1500–1750

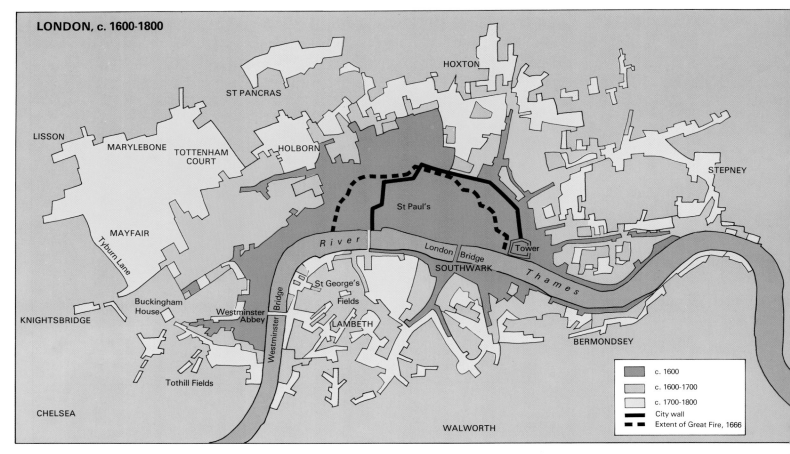

LONDON, c. 1600-1800

HOXTON
ST PANCRAS
LISSON
MARYLEBONE
TOTTENHAM COURT
HOLBORN
STEPNEY
St Paul's
MAYFAIR
Tyburn Lane
River Thames
London Bridge
Tower
SOUTHWARK
St George's Fields
Buckingham House
Westminster Abbey
Westminster Bridge
KNIGHTSBRIDGE
LAMBETH
BERMONDSEY
Tothill Fields
CHELSEA
WALWORTH

c. 1600
c. 1600-1700
c. 1700-1800
City wall
Extent of Great Fire, 1666

London grew in population from less than 200,000 in 1600 to about one million in 1800. As population grew, and as London developed as a port, a centre of industry and as a place of entertainment, so the city made increasing inroads into the surrounding regions. Laws were enacted in the 17th century to prevent further building in London, but in vain.

The famous Covent Garden fruit and vegetable market grew spectacularly from the gathering place of fruit and flower sellers in the early years of the 17th century. The Earl of Bedford, whose gardens adjoined the area, built shelters for them in 1632, shown in this picture. In 1828 a new market was built and remained in use until 1976.

London in 1500 had a population of 60,000–70,000, quite small for a capital city by the standards of the day. By 1750, the city was the second largest in Europe, after Istanbul, with a population of 675,000, over 0 per cent of the total population of England and Wales and over 10 times as big as any other English town. The capital's growth was a vital factor in the economic development of the country as a whole, encouraging specialization in food production for the market through an ever-widening area, stimulating the development of coastal shipping and inland transport and acting as a funnel for the exports and imports of most of the country. London, as the country's major centre of both consumption and industry, also acted as a disseminator of new ideas, new tastes and techniques.

The city's phenomenal growth was probably at its fastest in the 16th century, a period when population was growing everywhere. Many people were attracted to the rapidly growing port which handled up to 90 per cent of total English foreign trade and gave rise to a wide range of ancillary industries. Others provided goods and services for the Court, which now settled permanently in the capital, and for the growing numbers of the rich and ambitious who were attracted by the Court's presence. This concentration of the wealthy made London a great leisure centre and the main purveyor of professional services, especially in medicine and law. Population growth now tended to become cumulative. More people needed ever more people to provide them with the goods and services which they required to survive in a large city.

London was always an unhealthy place and mortality rates were much higher than elsewhere in the country, sometimes rising to catastrophic heights as in the terrible plagues of 1603, 1625 and 1665, the last of which probably killed 80,000 people, a sixth of the total population of the city. Such high death rates, coupled with rather low fertility, meant that London could never grow by its own natural increase. In the century after 1650, when London continued to grow but the English population remained fairly stable, immigration to the city drained the country-side of people and gave London its highest-yet proportion of the total population. It was probably then, in the early 18th-century London of Defoe and Gay and Hogarth that the city also had its greatest significance as a cultural centre and as a school of manners and ideas for the rest of the country.

Early Georgian London was a very different city from the London of Elizabethan times. The central part of the metropolis had been burned down in the Great Fire of 1666 and was re-built in brick and stone and, although full advantage was not taken of the opportunity to plan a fine, modern city, the streets were made wider and were better paved and lit, while Wren and his colleagues crowned the new city with magnificent churches, culminating in the great new cathedral of St Paul's (completed in 1710).

In the West End, a whole new and spacious city of squares and fine brick houses had been built in St James's, Bloomsbury and Piccadilly for the rich and famous, while development was extensive in the north and east of the old city where the port and local industries continued to expand. It is estimated that the population of this area grew from approximately 20,000 to nearly 100,000 during the course of the 17th century, much faster than the growth of the city as a whole.

The growth of London did not lack critics. Already, in Elizabethan and Jacobean times, people were frightened that the city would swallow up the whole country and unsuccessful attempts were made to check growth by something approaching a modern 'green belt' policy. Outside London, there were continuous complaints of the way in which the city dominated the country's trade and business and absorbed so much of the nation's capital and talent. But such complaints became muted after the Restoration as towns generally began to grow and as other regions, particularly in the North and West, began to undergo economic development. In Georgian England the provinces were still jealous of London, but they soon paid the metropolis the compliment of imitation. Small-scale copies of the London season, complete with theatres and assembly rooms became common in ambitious provincial towns as each strove to become the little London of its region.

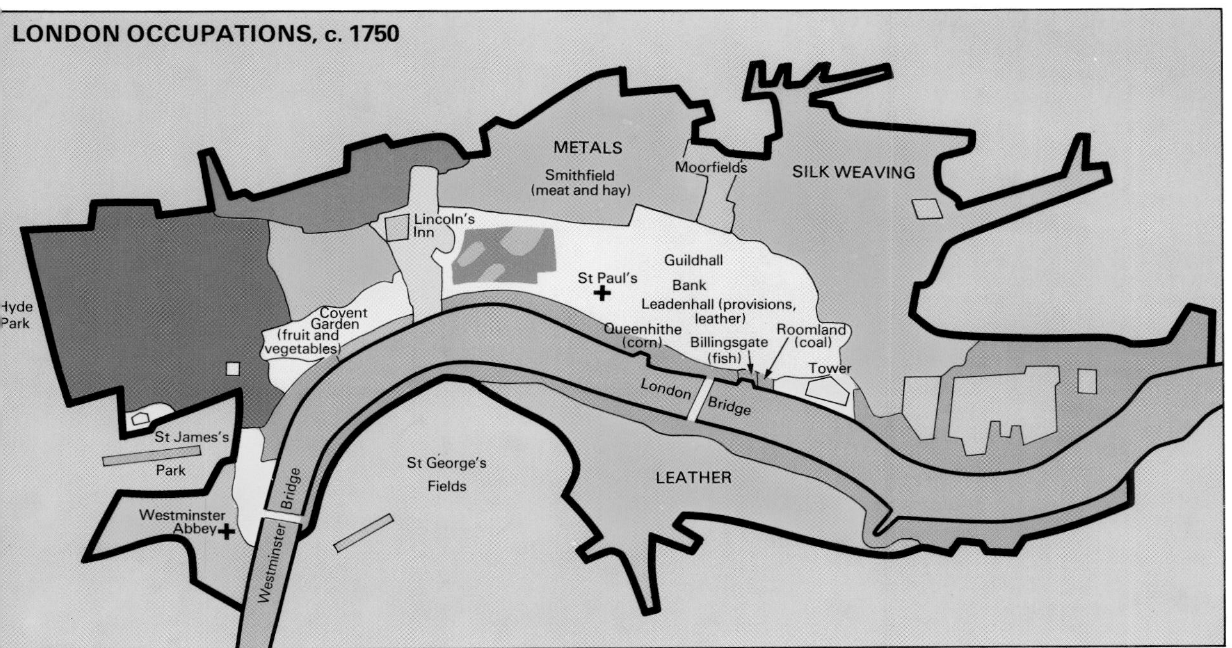

The map shows the approximate boundaries of industrial, commercial and residential districts in the built-up areas of London around 1750. Surrounding the small tradesmen, the financial offices and the wholesale markets of the City were three principal industrial areas: 1. The great variety of trades, especially jewellery, clock-making and general metal-working found in Clerkenwell, Shoreditch and Bishopsgate; 2. The silk-weaving district of Spitalfields with its rows of small weavers' cottages; and 3. south of the river, the tanneries, timber yards and many other trades stretching between Lambeth and Deptford.

Industrial and Commercial Change, 1660–1851

In the 1720s Daniel Defoe could describe England as 'the most flourishing and opulent country in the world'. Such a view contains a salutary warning to those who would see subsequent developments, especially the so-called 'industrial revolution', traditionally dated between 1760 and 1830, as a complete break with the past.

Nevertheless, England at the opening of the 18th century was still predominantly an agricultural country, with some two-thirds of the population working on the land. Most industrial occupations were bound up with agriculture; agricultural raw materials like timber, wool, flax, hides and tallow provided much of industry's requirements while spinners, weavers, tanners, blacksmiths, and a host of other industrial workers laboured in their rural cottages or in village workshops. Woollen textiles were overwhelmingly the main manufacturing industry, as they had been a century earlier. In 1730 woollen and worsted manufacture probably comprised more than one-third of the nation's total industrial output. In addition, there was a vast range of manufacturing activities scattered throughout the country, such as processed sugar and tobacco, beer and spirits, paper, glass, musical instruments, ferrous and non-ferrous metal goods, ships, clocks and watches, as well as a great many others.

By the close of the 18th century a remarkable transformation was taking place. New industries were established, and new processes applied to the manufacture of traditional products. Inexorably, Britain was becoming the first industrial nation, although even in 1830 factories were by no means typical units of production, and power-driven machinery was dominant only in a few sectors, such as cotton-spinning.

The industrial revolution was, in essence, the rise of a narrow range of manufacturing industries which became highly concentrated in certain localities. Such changes were supported by parallel changes in transport, overseas trade, banking, agriculture, and in a variety of other ways at all levels of economy and society.

The Cotton Industry Transformed

Cotton textiles provide the most impressive, and most important, example of this industrial transformation. Here was an industry of relatively little significance before the 1780s, yet in a period of little more than 20 years it became Britain's leading industry and major export earner, employing many thousands in the south Lancashire factory towns. This striking growth was in part the result of the application of machinery to spinning; at first water-powered mills in rural valleys in Lancashire and the east Midlands, but after the 1790s increasingly steam-powered in the fast-growing urban centres. After spinning, weaving, too, was adapted to power-driven machinery so that by the 1840s the entire cotton industry was characterized by factory production based on steam power. Later than cotton, and more slowly, the woollen and worsted cloth industry became mechanized and was increasingly concentrated in the West Riding of Yorkshire.

Other industries also showed considerable growth. Iron making, like textiles, was transformed with the help of new technology. The breakthrough here was the ability to smelt iron ore with coke rather than with expensive and increasingly scarce charcoal from timber. The main period of expansion came after the 1780s as a result of Henry Cort's patents for puddling and rolling iron, and it was now possible to have cheap iron in all forms except steel.

It would be a mistake to concentrate too much on textiles and the iron industry. Many other industries, metal goods in the Black Country and around Sheffield, clothing, soap boiling, glass making, steam engine construction, an others grew rapidly, some using new technologies, other still based on methods of organization and processes use for centuries. Completely new industries emerged. Gas lighting made its appearance in the first decade of the 19t century, while by the 1830s a wide variety of industrie connected with the new railways were developing quickly

Alongside this industrial revolution went a no les momentous growth of overseas trade. Trade became a increasingly important element in Britain's overall growth as exports of manufactured commodities were exchange for raw materials and foodstuffs the expanding industrie and urban populations demanded. The first half of the 19t century saw a decisive movement towards 'free trade', an this did much to foster Britain's commerce.

The causes of Britain's industrial transformation ar complex, and remain the subject of much controversy. I understanding the phenomenon a few points must b emphasized. First, the transformation owed much t favourable geographic features. Relatively abundant an easily accessible supplies of coal, iron, and other minera enabled Britain to adapt quickly to the new technologie

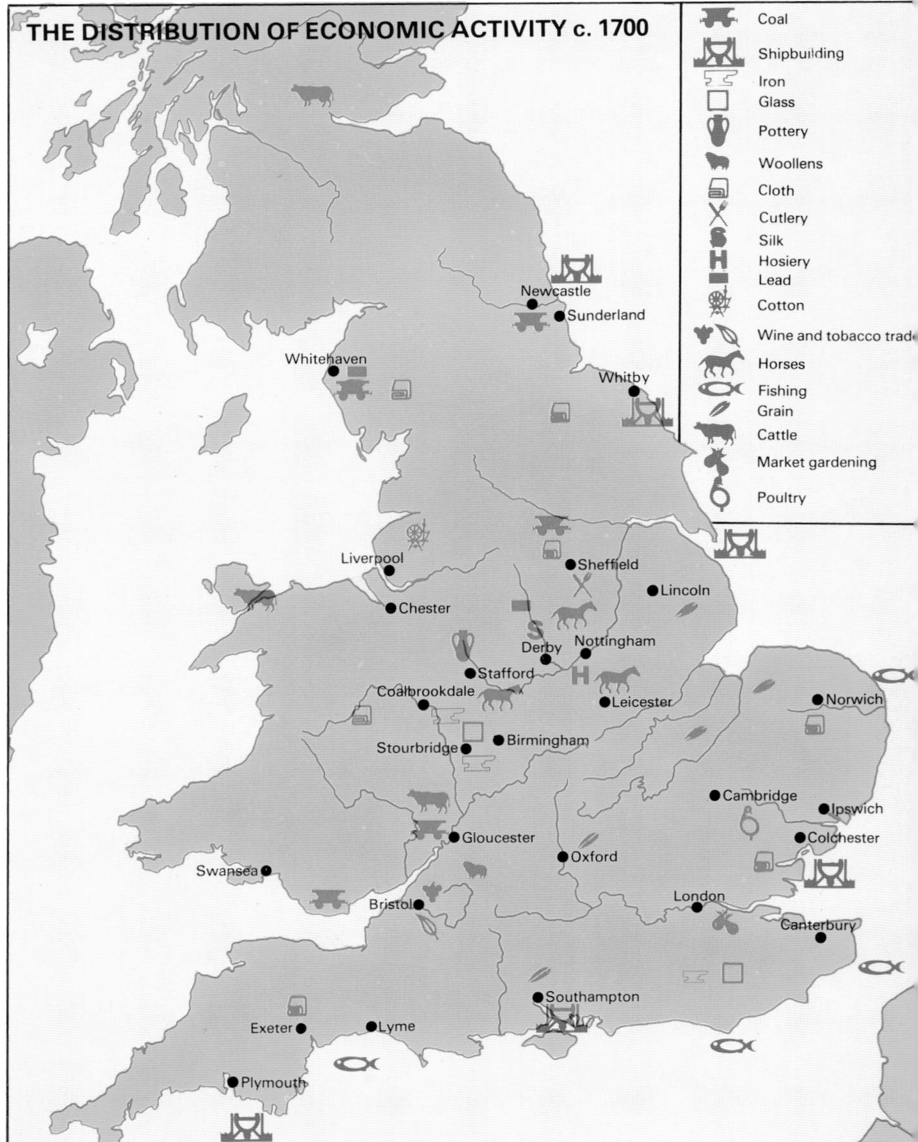

In 1700 the major areas of Britain's industrial activity were still concentrated around the great woollen textile regions of the West Country, East Anglia, and the West Riding. Mining regions were other centres of activity, but coal had yet to transform the face of industrial England.

Landmarks in the Industrial Revolution

1719 Lombe's silk factory at Derby
1733 Kay's flying shuttle
1740 Huntsman produces cast steel
1761 Bridgewater Canal constructed
1767 Hargreaves' spinning jenny
1769 Arkwright's water-frame
1776 Adam Smith's *Wealth of Nations* published
1779 Crompton's mule
1782 Watt's rotary steam engine
1783 Cort's development of puddling and rolling iron
1785 Cartwright's power-loom
1812 First gaslight company established in London
1825 Stockton to Darlington railway built
1828 Neilson's hot-air blast for iron manufacture
1838 Atlantic steamship service starts
1839 The electric telegraph developed
1851 Channel underwater cable for telegraph
1856 Bessemer's hot-air blast for steel manufacture

Commercial Developments, 1600–1849

1600 Foundation of the East India Company
1651–96 Navigation Acts passed
1689 The New East India Company formed
1700 Act prohibiting the importation of calico and silks passed
1703 Methuen Treaty with Portugal signed
1750 Prohibition of iron refining in North American colonies
1756 The Seven Years War begins
1776 The Publication of Adam Smith's *The Wealth of Nations*
1793 The Napoleonic Wars – to 1815
1802 Cotton exports exceed woollens in value
1807 Slave trade declared illegal
1813 Ending of East India Company's trading monopoly with India
1815 Passing of the Corn Laws
1824 Removal of prohibition on export of machinery
1825 Removal of prohibition on emigration of skilled artisans
1826 William Huskisson's 'sliding scale': modification of the Corn Laws
1839 Foundation of the anti-Corn Law League
1842 Robert Peel's Budget: substantial reduction of import duties
1846 Repeal of the Corn Laws
1849 Repeal of the Navigation Acts

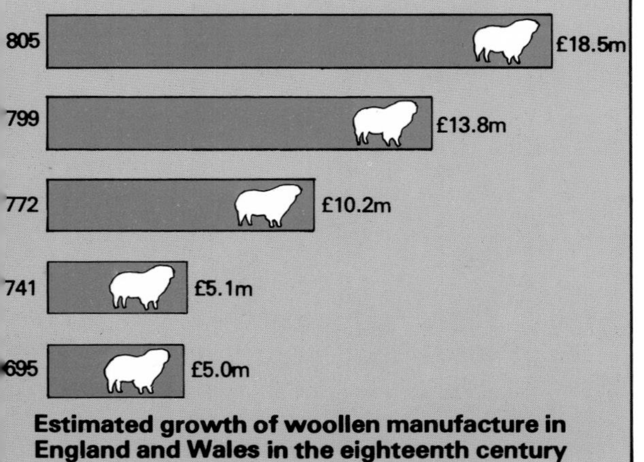

Estimated growth of woollen manufacture in England and Wales in the eighteenth century

'oollen textiles remained ritain's major manufacturing dustry in terms of value of tput, employment, and ports, until the opening decade of the 19th century. But cotton textiles then rapidly became the foremost industry and major export earner.

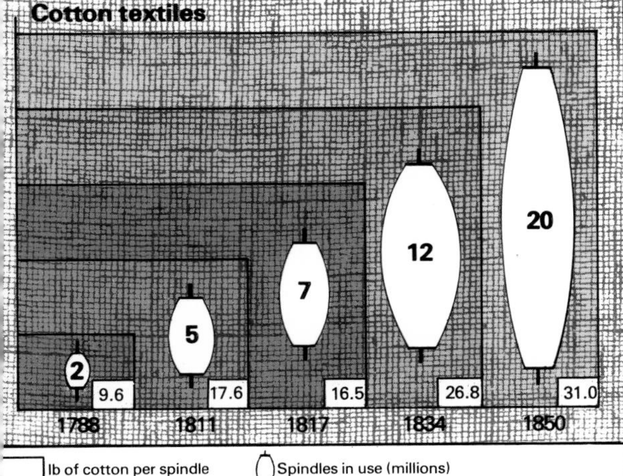

Commodity Structure of Foreign Trade (percentage)

Principal Imports	Textiles	Groceries	Corn	Raw Cotton	Linens	Other textile raw materials	Other raw materials
1663/9(1)	32.2	29.2	—	—	7.3	17.3	7.3
1700(2)	25.2	25.9	—	—	15.6	16.2	6.4
1750(2)	21.3	32.6	—	0.9	14.8	16.4	5.8
1780(2)	8.7	37.3	2.8	4.6	9.6	21.2	5.2
1800(3)	6.3	34.9	5.2	6.0	5.6	15.4	5.9
1820(3)	4.1	37.6	3.1	14.6	4.6	9.6	9.8
1850(3)	2.7	17.8	10.8	21.1	2.1	7.3	11.3

Principal Exports	Woollen and worsted goods	Cotton Textiles	Other Textiles	Corn	Non-ferrous metals	Iron and Iron goods
1663/9(1)	74	—	1.7	2	3.2	—
1770(2)	70.4	—	2.4	3.7	5.1	1.6
1750(2)	45.9	—	6.2	19.6	5.4	4.4
1780(2)	38.6	4.7	8.9	1.6	7.2	7.5
1800(3)	28.5	24.2	6.1	—	4.3	6.1
1820(3)	13.9	56.8	4.8	—	2.3	4.2
1850(3)	12.7	39.4	8.6	—	1.6	16.4

(1) London only
(2) England and Wales
(3) Great Britain

Corn: includes all grains and flour.
Groceries: includes coffee, sugar, tea, tobacco and wine.
Other textile raw materials: includes wool, silk, flax, hemp.
Other raw materials: includes timber, hides, skins, oils, iron.

Overseas Trade: Annual Averages [Figures in £mill. Official Values]

	1663/9 (1)	1700/9 (2)	1750/9 (2)	1780/9 (2)	1800/9 (3)	1820/9 (3)	1840/9 (3)
Exports	3.0	4.4	8.8	10.2	25.4	46.5	124.5
Re-Exports	0.9	1.6	3.5	4.3	12.2	10.0	16.7
Imports	4.0	4.8	8.3	13.8	28.7	38.3	79.4

(1) London only
(2) England and Wales
(3) Great Britain

Britain's trade developed considerably during the 18th century, and even faster in the opening decades of the 19th. Between 1700 and 1800 the volumes of trade (imports plus exports) grew approximately five-fold, while there was roughly a six-fold expansion between 1800 and 1850. During the 1820s there were moves to dismantle tariffs and other forms of protection, and by the 1860s Britain had adopted a free-trade policy.

based on steam-power and iron goods. Fertile soil, too, helped create agricultural wealth. Overseas trade was fostered by Britain's accessible and safe ports and by her crucial location lying between the New World and the European continent. From such sources of wealth could be drawn the capital necessary to finance such improvements as canals, roads and harbours, as well as factories and mines. After 1760, too, Britain's population grew rapidly, providing ready supplies of cheap labour at a time when labour was still overwhelmingly the chief productive force in industry.

During the 18th century Bristol was England's leading provincial city in terms of wealth, population, and commerce. Its commercial prosperity rested on the growing Atlantic trade with the West Indies and North America: imports of tobacco, sugar and Newfoundland cod, and exports of various manufactured goods; the triangular slave trade between the Guinea Coast, England, and the West Indies; and trade with Ireland.

The transformation of Britain's industries was closel bound up with the adoption of new technologies, especiall the textile innovation associated with such men as Kay Hargreaves and Arkwright, with the steam-engine, as sociated with James Watt and manufactured by the gre Birmingham firm of Boulton and Watt, and with th improvements in iron manufacture introduced by th Darbys at Coalbrookdale after 1713 and by Henry Cort i the 1780s. We should be wary of attributing too much t these innovations and their processes. Often, innovatior were as much a consequence of economic change as a caus of it. Thus, for example, the growing productivity c weavers after the invention of Kay's flying shuttle in 173 led to concerted efforts to apply machinery to spinnin Some inventions, like the steam-engine itself, had a lon ancestry. Thus in the late 17th century 'atmospher engines' were being used to pump water from Cornish ti mines. Moreover, innovations often spread only slowl and subsequent improvements were often of the greate economic significance. The simple 'heroic' view of th industrial revolution, attributing Britain's transformatio to the genius of a few individuals, is now discredited.

The significance of industrial growth (which, after a lon period of steady growth, began to progress rapidly aft about 1780) was great. Such growth underlay and pe mitted a sustained increase in overall incomes and wealt even if the poorer classes for a long time shared little in th prosperity. Industrialization, in other words, led to eco omic growth. And, despite the hesitant and less tha complete move towards what Clapham called an 'indust state', British industry was the first to undergo th transformation. Thus Britain's manufactured goods textiles and metal goods above all – found outlets throug out the world. By the time of the Great Exhibition in 18 Britain could truly be called 'the Workshop of the World

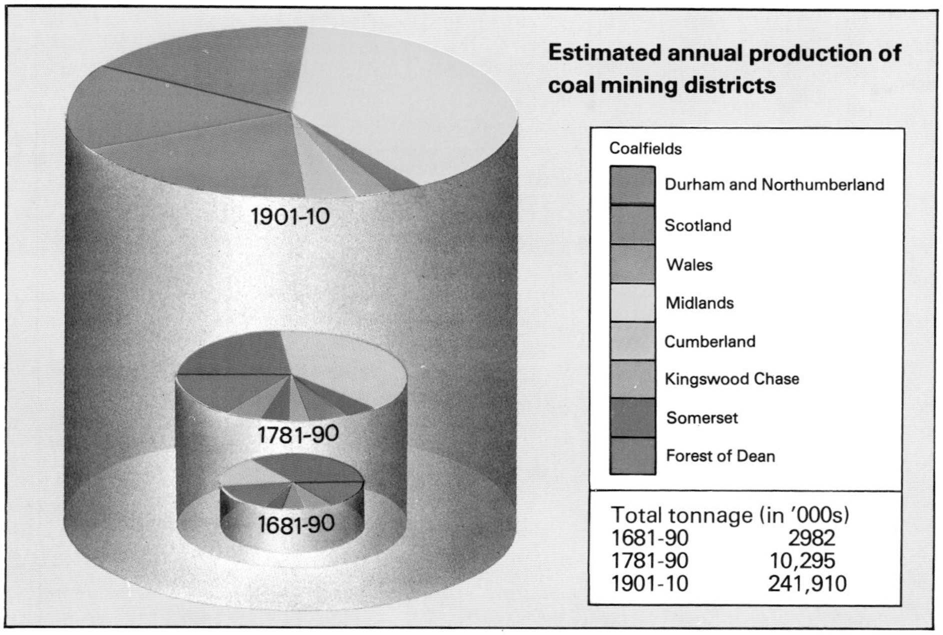

Abundant supplies of accessible coal lay at the heart of the Industrial Revolution. The north-eastern collieries were traditionally the main producers, but after 1900 they were overtaken by the Yorkshire and Nottinghamshire field, and, a few years later, by South Wales. In 1913 more than one-third of the record production of 287 million tons was exported.

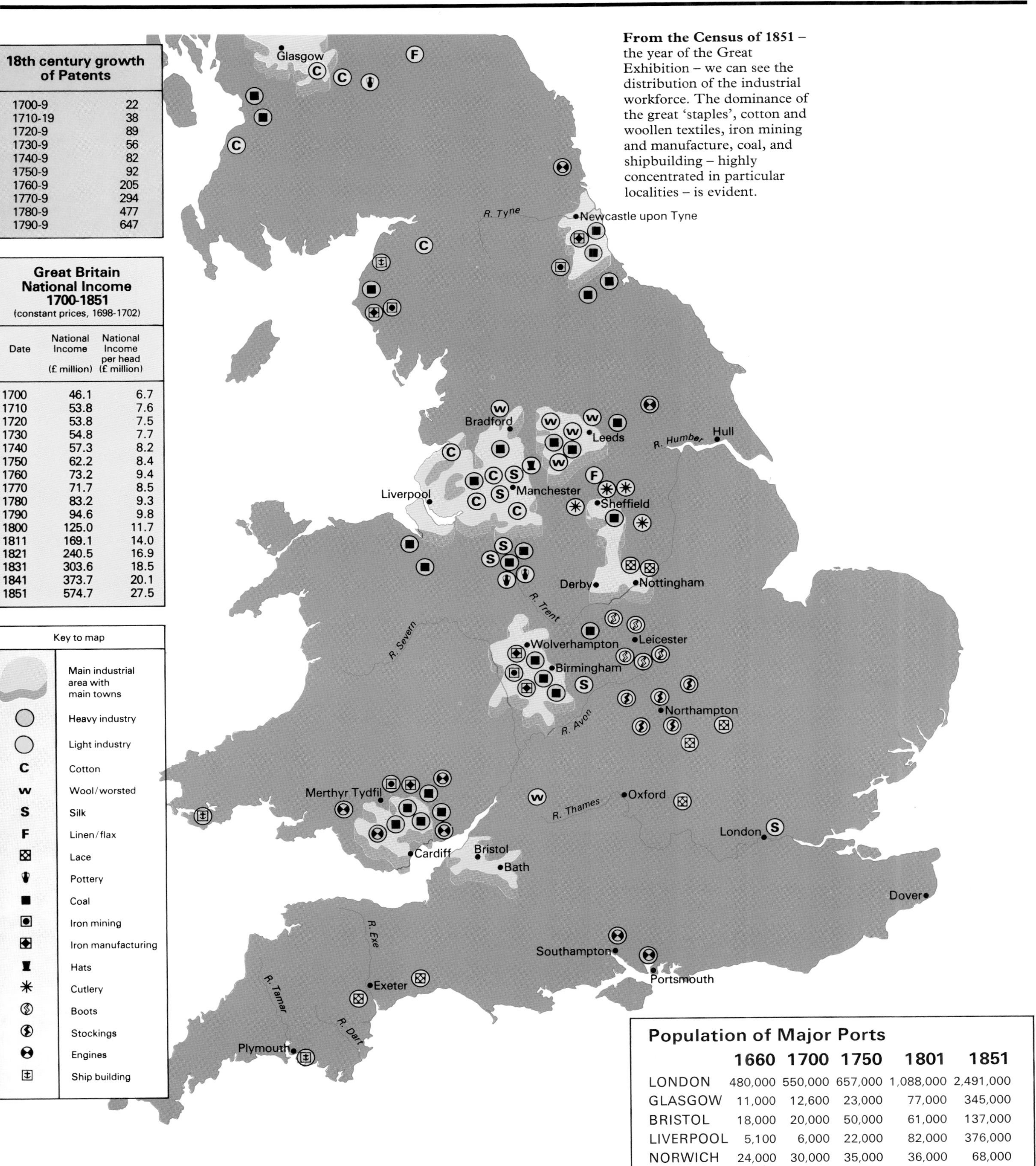

From the Census of 1851 – the year of the Great Exhibition – we can see the distribution of the industrial workforce. The dominance of the great 'staples', cotton and woollen textiles, iron mining and manufacture, coal, and shipbuilding – highly concentrated in particular localities – is evident.

18th century growth of Patents

1700-9	22
1710-19	38
1720-9	89
1730-9	56
1740-9	82
1750-9	92
1760-9	205
1770-9	294
1780-9	477
1790-9	647

Great Britain National Income 1700-1851
(constant prices, 1698-1702)

Date	National Income (£ million)	National Income per head (£ million)
1700	46.1	6.7
1710	53.8	7.6
1720	53.8	7.5
1730	54.8	7.7
1740	57.3	8.2
1750	62.2	8.4
1760	73.2	9.4
1770	71.7	8.5
1780	83.2	9.3
1790	94.6	9.8
1800	125.0	11.7
1811	169.1	14.0
1821	240.5	16.9
1831	303.6	18.5
1841	373.7	20.1
1851	574.7	27.5

Population of Major Ports

	1660	1700	1750	1801	1851
LONDON	480,000	550,000	657,000	1,088,000	2,491,000
GLASGOW	11,000	12,600	23,000	77,000	345,000
BRISTOL	18,000	20,000	50,000	61,000	137,000
LIVERPOOL	5,100	6,000	22,000	82,000	376,000
NORWICH	24,000	30,000	35,000	36,000	68,000

English Society, 1600–1800

English society in this period was in a transitional stage. The long-established hierarchy based on a man's relationship to the land he owned or worked was being undermined by the growth of towns and urban occupations which did not fit easily into such a system, and by the gradual development of a more modern class structure based on the division between capital and labour. England remained an aristocratic society where the ownership of a large estate and a title was an assured sign of power and prestige, where the *nouveau riche* bought land and called himself a gentleman; but already the middle-class way of life was becoming respectable and was given a stimulating lead by an increasingly confident bourgeois London society. Trade, industry, the professions and government service provided a wide range of occupations for the new and aspiring middle class, while a minor revolution in education produced many new academies, both Anglican and Nonconformist, which undertook to train people for these occupations and to give them a much more 'modern' schooling. English was substituted for Latin as the language of instruction and subjects such as mathematics, science and foreign languages were introduced into the curriculum for the first time. The rapidly growing middle class was also catered for by the huge contemporary increase in the output of the printing press, which produced newspapers, novels and works of moral

'The Coffee house Mob': (left) from a contemporary engraving. The coffee house's function was as much to disseminate news as to serve refreshment.

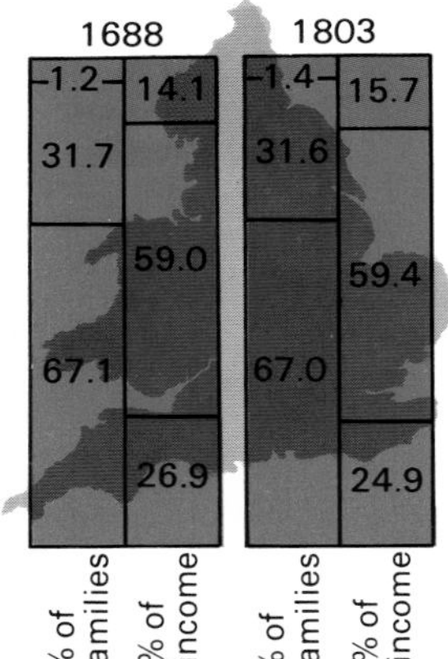

Distribution of wealth in England and Wales in 1688 and 1803.

Right: *The Gin Shop.* During the 18th century and later, gin drinking became a social evil in British society. The warmth and light of the 'gin palaces' encouraged the ill-housed poor to flock there. Gin was cheap and consumption rose from 0.5 million gallons to 8 million gallons between 1690 and 1740.

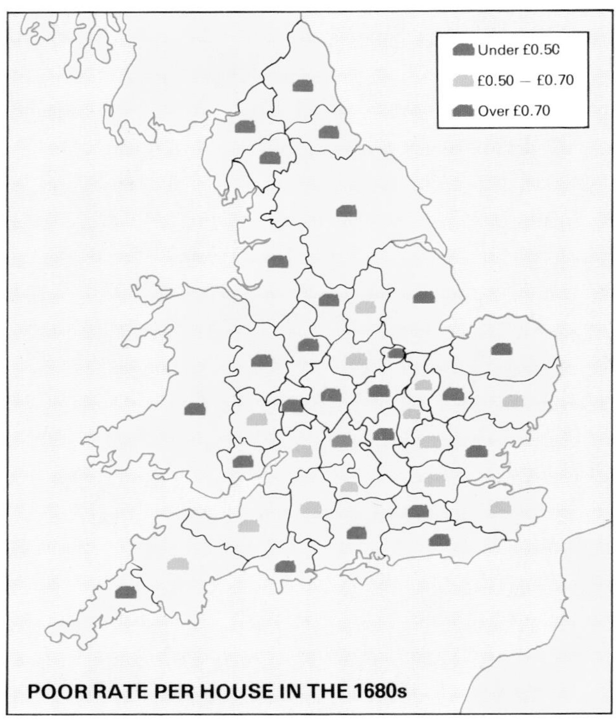

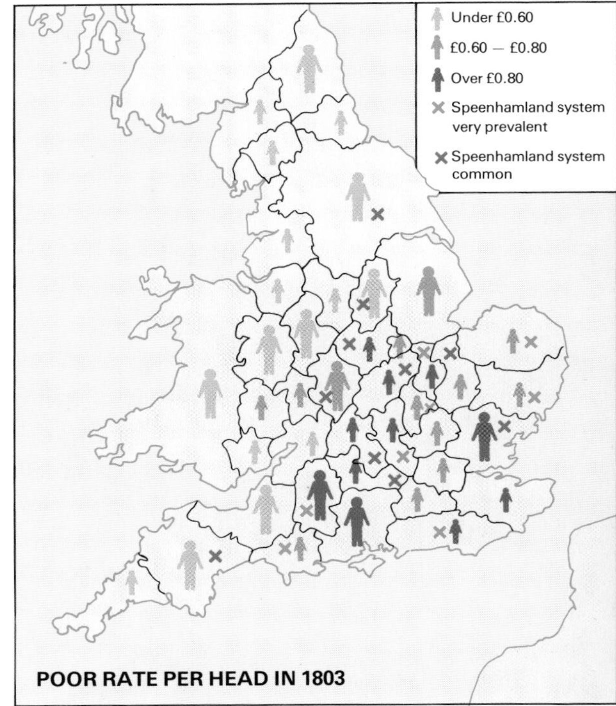

These four maps illustrate the regional spread of wealth and poverty around the 1690s and 1800s. The amount of poor rate levied reflects the relative local need for poor relief. The assessments for the 1692 land tax and the 1804 Schedule D income tax are used as indicators of wealth. The maps provide a comparison of living standards at the two periods.

Left to right: Poor rate per house in the 1680s and per head in 1803. The range in the 1680s was from £1.02 (Rutland) to £0.15 (Lancashire). Assuming that there was a population of five million, the average poor rate per head was £0.13 compared with £0.60 in the 1803 assessment. In 1803, the main generalization one can make is that the poor rate was likely to be higher in counties with a large number of agricultural labourers and little rural industry. In such counties, too, the Speenhamland system was likely to be introduced.

and intellectual improvement for an increasingly literate public, and also by the development of the theatre and the assembly room, the coffee house and club, both in London and the provinces.

Just as the men of the middle class aspired to gentility, so those in the ranks of the artisans and shopkeepers aspired to middle-class respectability, and this period is one in which contemporary observers were constantly complaining of the lower orders, and especially servants, aping their betters in matters of dress and social behaviour. It is this drive towards upward social mobility and the conspicuous consumption that went with it that provided much of the demand, as well as the hard work and enterprise, which is associated with the early Industrial Revolution.

Aristocracy and gentry, middle class and aspiring middle class, can have comprised at the most only about a third of England's population. As for the remaining two-thirds, life remained one of drudgery and hardship which tended to get worse as the period continued. More and more people found themselves divorced from the land and from that ownership of the means of production which had given them self-respect, if not economic security, in the past. By the early 18th century, probably well over half the adult male population relied on wages or piecework for their living and were increasingly vulnerable to accidents, such as bad harvests, wars, new techniques of production or changes of fashion, which could throw them out of work. Real wages were rising in the first half of the period, but became increasingly subject to high food prices as population rose rapidly after 1750. The workman's income was only a third or a quarter of incomes in the lower middle classes; he was only able to buy bare necessities, with cheap drink as almost the only form of entertainment.

In such circumstances, it was almost impossible to save for periods of sickness or unemployment and many people found themselves regularly forced to seek charity or poor relief but, as the applications and the poor-rates grew, so did the attitude towards the poor harden. The early 18th century sees the widespread introduction of workhouses whose object was to make life so unpleasant for their inmates that no-one would apply unless absolutely destitute. Despite this, poor-rates continued to rise, particularly in the harsh years of war and high prices in the 1790s. Real wages were then so low in some rural areas that the Speenhamland system was introduced to subsidize wages from the poor-rates, an indication of just how much living standards had deteriorated in some parts of the country in the course of the century. By this date the old hierarchy of England was being threatened by the more obvious class divisions of a society in which wealthy farmer and impoverished farm labourer faced each other on the land, and master and man made a glaringly unequal division of the product of the new industries.

Portrait of the Warde family, 1735. Confidently at ease, the landowner displays his house, his estate and his family for our admiration.

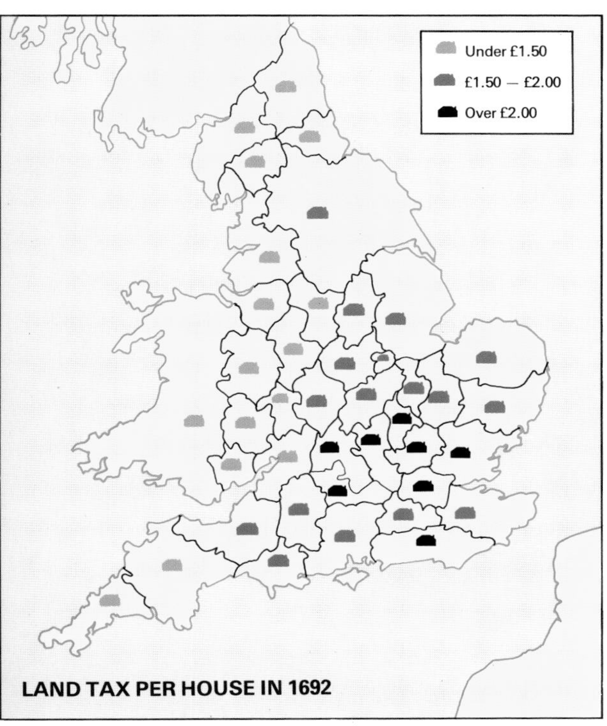

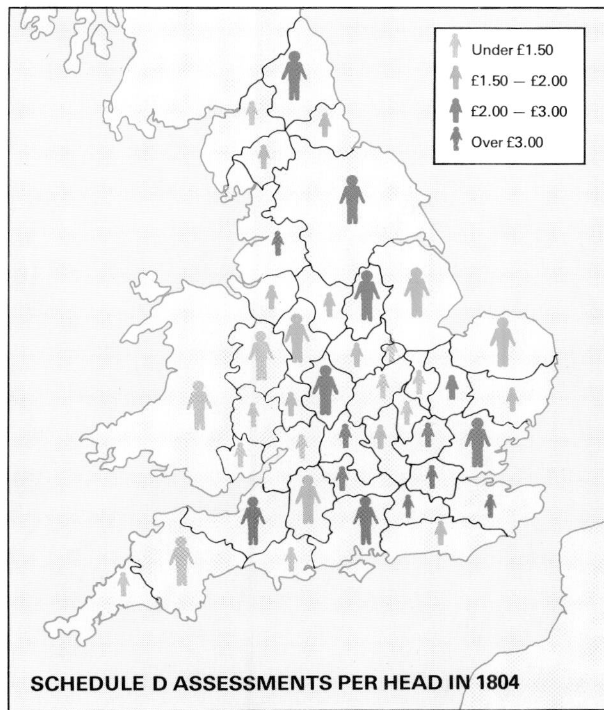

Land tax assessment per house for 1692. The range was from £2.76 (Middlesex, including London) to £0.24 (Cumberland). Note that contemporaries believed that the North and West were under-assessed in the land tax, so that this map probably exaggerates the comparative poverty of those areas. The map on the left shows the Schedule D income tax assessment per head for 1804. The range was from £17.41 (Middlesex, including London) to £0.48 (Herefordshire). This map shows the growing relative importance of business in the North and Midlands, while at the same time demonstrating the significance of London and the Home Counties.

Internal Trade and Transport, 1500–1760

The economy of 16th century England was still extremely localized. Most trade took place within small, self-sufficient regions and most exchanges occurred in face-to-face transactions in the very widely distributed market towns. Trade between regions was on a small scale and was mostly conducted at the periodic fairs, though carters and packmen distributed imports and specialized products by means of an extensive, if primitive, road and track system all over the country.

The growth of London from a small town to a city with 10 per cent of England's population, the growth of population generally, a breakdown in self-sufficiency through regional specialization and the wider use of heavy products such as coal, bricks, building materials and lime, all increased the scale of inter-regional trade and put pressure on the existing transport system which ultimately led to a considerable improvement.

In the 16th century, the main emphasis was on the development of the coasting trade to supply London with coal, corn and building materials. East coast ports, such as East Lynn, Hull and Newcastle, developed to satisfy this

Above: Perils of travel in the early 18th century. Regular provision for the carriage of passengers and mail was improving, but was still very slow (see map on the right). Highwaymen and a lack of springs could make for an uncomfortable journey.

Top right: A coach and waggon of the second half of the 17th century from Loggan's *Oxonia Illustrata*. The waggon and coach were the vehicles of the future, but depended on improvements in road surfaces to be fully effective. Rapid improvements came with the turnpike boom of the next century.

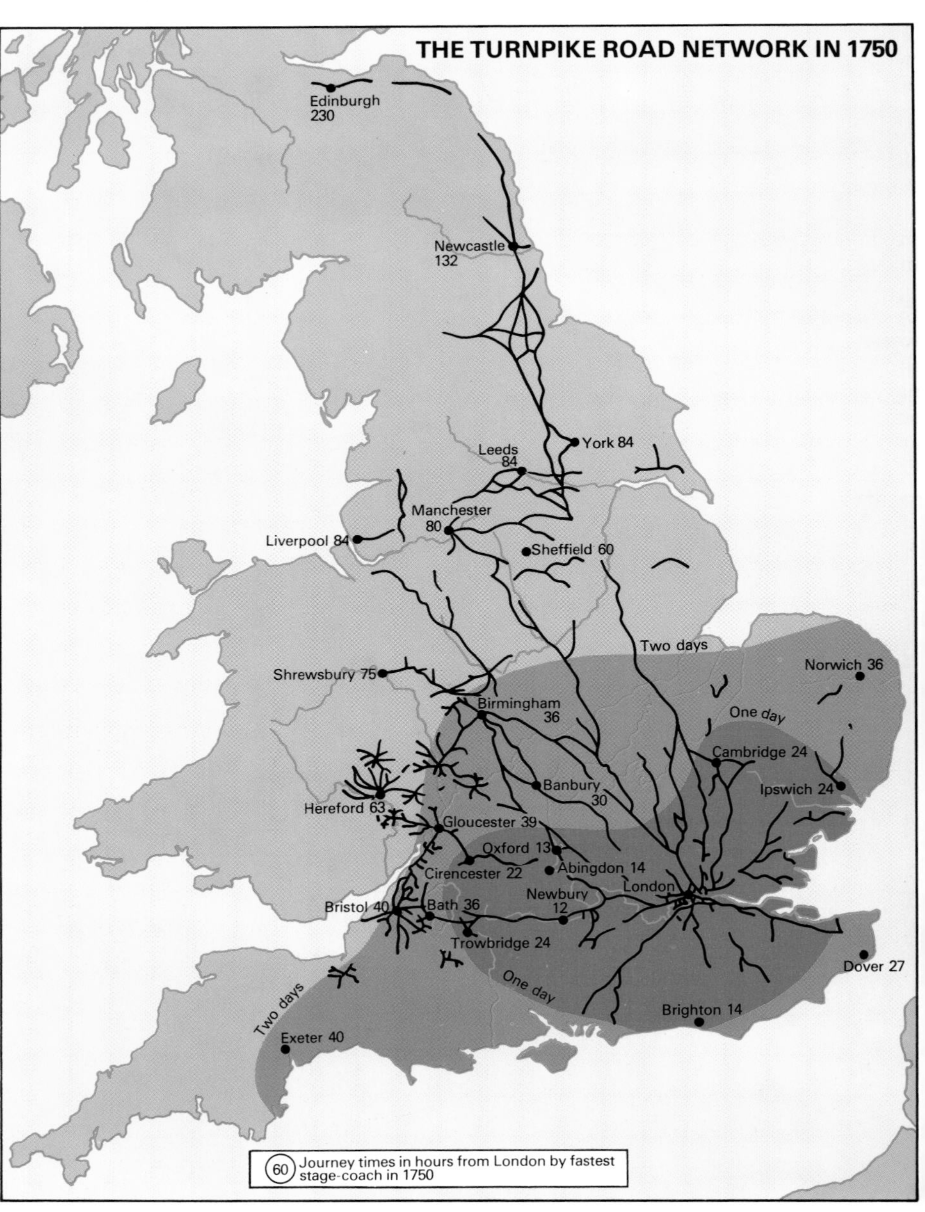

The turnpike road network in Britain, 1750. Turnpike trusts charged tolls to road users, and were thus provided with funds to maintain and improve the road network. The main era of construction came after 1750; by the 1830s, more than 20,000 miles (32,000km) of turnpike road were collecting more than £0.5 million annually. Better roads and stage coaches rapidly reduced journey times. Bristol was a journey of nearly two days from London in 1750; by 1785, it took a mere 19 hours.

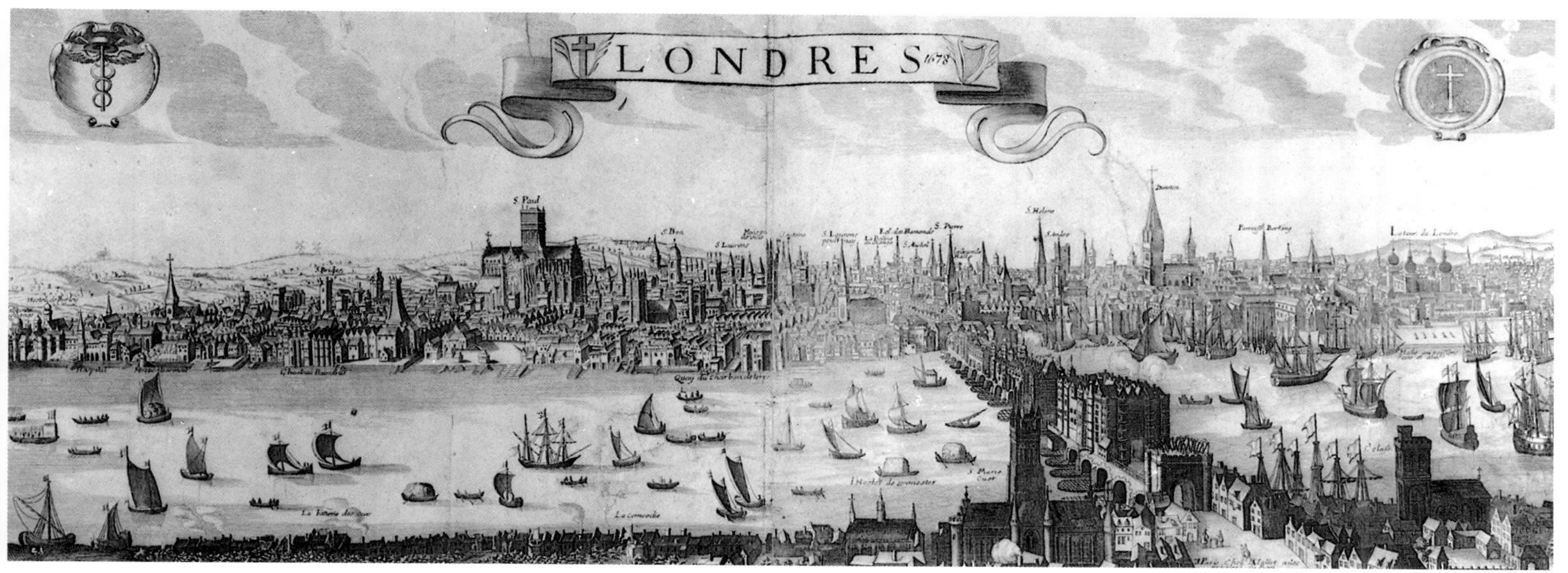

A 1678 view of the Thames near London Bridge, London's only road over the river until Westminster Bridge was built in 1728. London was by now England's principal port and the river was the most crowded of London's highways with passengers in boats threading through the heavy commercial traffic. Much of London's trade was still carried on at the great City fairs.

need and were helped by the requirement that ships engaged in the coasting trade should be English. The period saw the continuous development of coasting; ships got larger, docks and harbours were improved, the southern and western coasts were brought into the system and the range of goods traded became more varied, though coal and corn remained the most important and their carriers provided a high proportion of the total English merchant marine.

England was well-favoured by her system of rivers and, by 1600, there were already 500 miles (800 km) of navigable waterway, but the increase in internal trade soon exposed the deficiencies of the system. Many of the existing navigations were hampered by obstructions, some natural, such as bends, shallows and a tendency to silting, others artificial, such as corn-mills with their systems of weirs and flash locks.

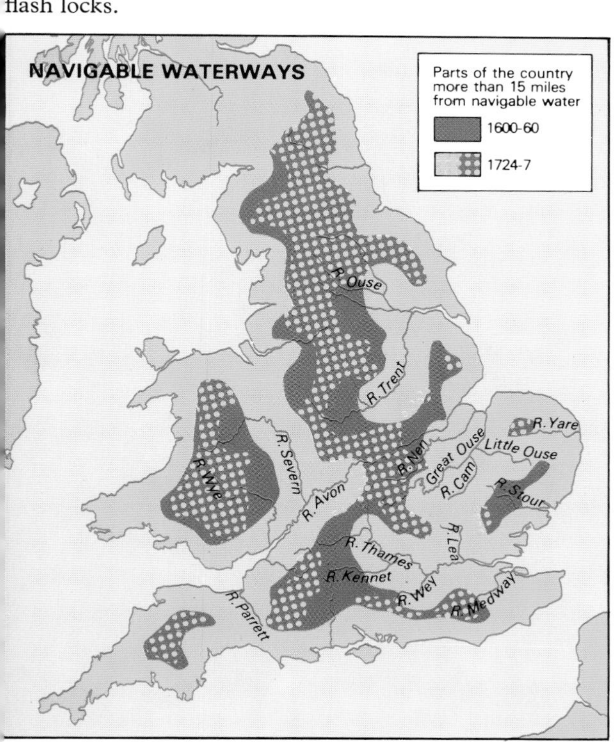

Navigable waterways in Britain. The period 1600–1760 saw major extensions to Britain's navigable rivers. The 700 miles (1120km) or so of naturally navigable rivers were doubled through the work of engineers – an important prelude to the great age of canals which followed.

The 17th century saw many attempts to improve and increase the mileage of river navigation, but these were often thwarted by opposition of riparian owners or by technical or financial problems. From the 1660s, however, improvements became more successful, and by the 1720s there were 1160 miles (1856 km) of navigable waterway, double the figure for a century earlier. Acts of Parliament enabled local opposition to be defeated and owners bought out or compensated, while Dutch experience in river improvement and drainage could be exploited to solve technical problems. Capital was usually raised locally to finance the improvement, while the management of the navigation and the collection of tolls was often farmed out to independent syndicates of businessmen. Improved waterways brought down the distribution costs of heavy goods and hence led to a further increase in internal trade which, by 1750, was making renewed demands on the improved system.

The first half of the 18th century also saw a considerable improvement in the roads. Increased inland transport, and especially the rapid increase of waggon traffic, had a serious effect on the primitive roads and tracks which had been sufficient in earlier periods. The maintenance of roads was a parish responsibility, a fact which meant that long-distance users paid nothing for destroying the roads they travelled on. In 1663, provision was made for tolls to be levied on a very heavily used part of the Great North Road and the money was used to supplement repair work of the local parish. This, the first 'turnpike', remained a solitary measure until 1696 but, from then on, there was a continuous series of Turnpike Acts leading to a boom in the 1720s. By 1750, there were 143 turnpike trusts responsible for the collection of tolls and maintenance of 3386 miles (5410 km) of road, mainly in and around London and in the Severn Valley and the West Midlands. The standard of improvement varied enormously; some turnpikes had no drains and consisted merely of piles of rubble thrown on to the highway, but few people thought that a turnpike was worse than what it replaced. Turnpikes did not lower transport costs, but they considerably increased the speed of movement between towns and their very existence often made transport possible. This simultaneous development of the road and river systems in the early 18th century was an essential contributing factor in that increase in internal trade which foreshadowed the Industrial Revolution.

The Transport Revolution, 1760–1914

The sustained expansion of the British economy in the later 18th century necessitated radical changes in the transport system which, despite improvements in the preceding century, had reached the limits of its capacity. The two major improvements which took place in the industrial revolution (*c*.1770–1830) were adaptations of existing modes, namely the turnpiking of roads and the construction of canals.

Turnpiking involved an attempt to improve the parochial system of road administration by creating turnpike trusts for selected stretches of roads which were financed from the collection of tolls. The half century before 1750 brought a stream of Turnpike Acts after which the pace of development slackened markedly. By the late 1830s, when new turnpikes had become a rarity, there were some 100 separate turnpike trusts controlling about 22,000 miles of road, ranging from major trunk routes to by-roads and suburban streets. Even at their peak, the turnpike trusts accounted for less than one-fifth of the English road system, the remainder being the responsibility of the parishes. After 1830 their importance diminished and road improvements were not to feature prominently again until the age of the motor car in the 20th century.

While road improvement greatly facilitated the movement of goods and people, they were not able to cope with the growing need to move large volumes of bulky commodities such as coal. Nor had the existing river system, despite the extensive improvement to river navigation in the century prior to 1750, the capacity to meet such a demand. The logical solution therefore was the cutting of deadwater canals, the commercial success of which was demonstrated, in the early 1760s, when the Duke of Bridgewater's Canal halved the cost of delivering coal to Manchester. Subsequently a network of canals was built throughout the country and at the end of the construction period (*c*.1830) Britain had some 4000 miles (6500 km) of navigable waterway, as against nearly 1400 miles (2250 km) in 1760 (in England and Wales).

These improvements were important in terms of increasing the capacity of the transport system and reducing costs, and without them Britain's industrial development would have been seriously hampered. Road transport and water navigation provided the chief means of conveyance during the first phase of the country's industrialization. Coastal shipping also played an important part in the movement of bulky freight, though in this case there were few technical improvements, the main change being a significant rise in capacity as more coastal ships were brought into service. In time the system again became inadequate to cope with the demands of an ever-growing economy. During the second phase of the development, from the 1830s onwards, therefore, the older forms of transport were partly eclipsed by the rise of an entirely new form, the steam railway.

The iron rail has long antecedents but the start of the modern railway system dates effectively from 1830 when the first major line, the Liverpool to Manchester Railway,

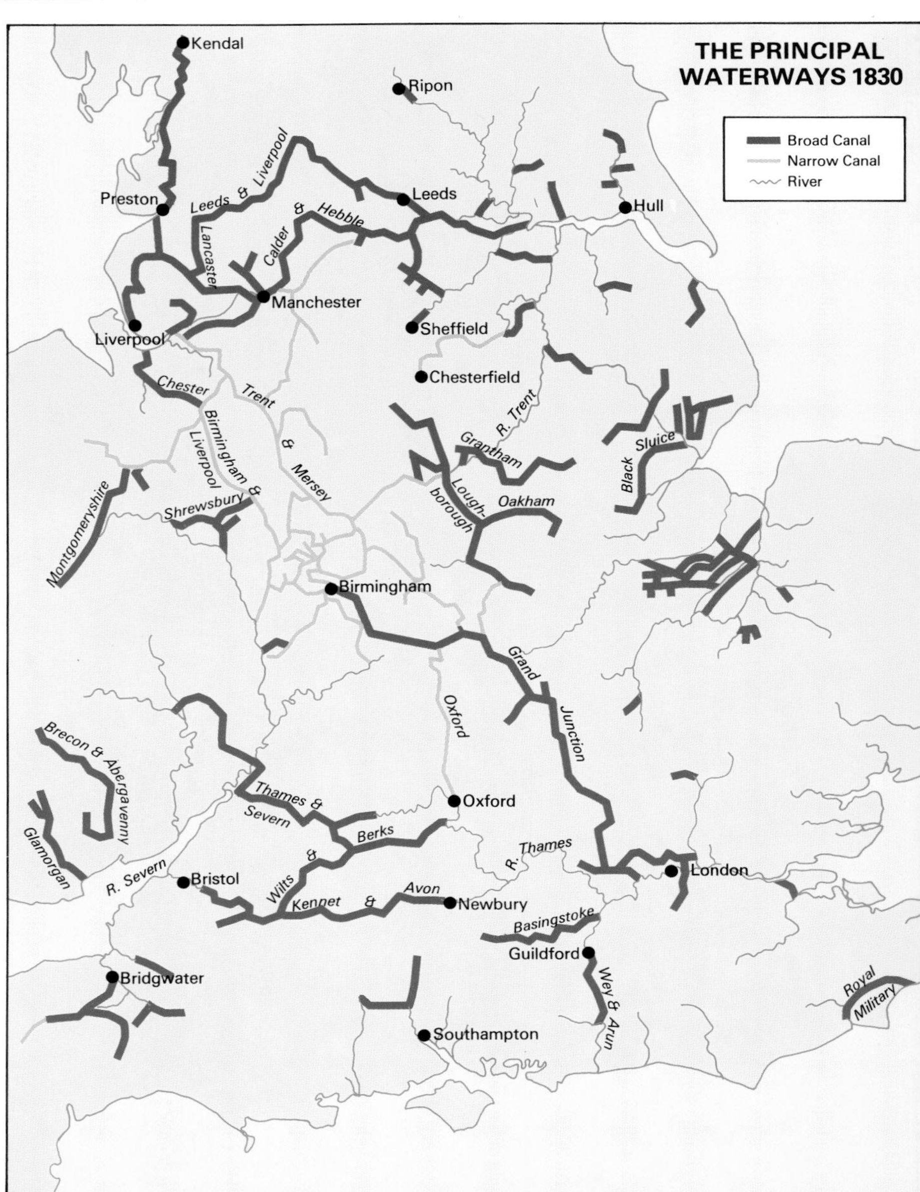

Above right: The network of waterways constructed in England by 1830 allowed bulky goods to be transported easily and cheaply, though slowly; its importance was diminished later in the century by the growing railway system.

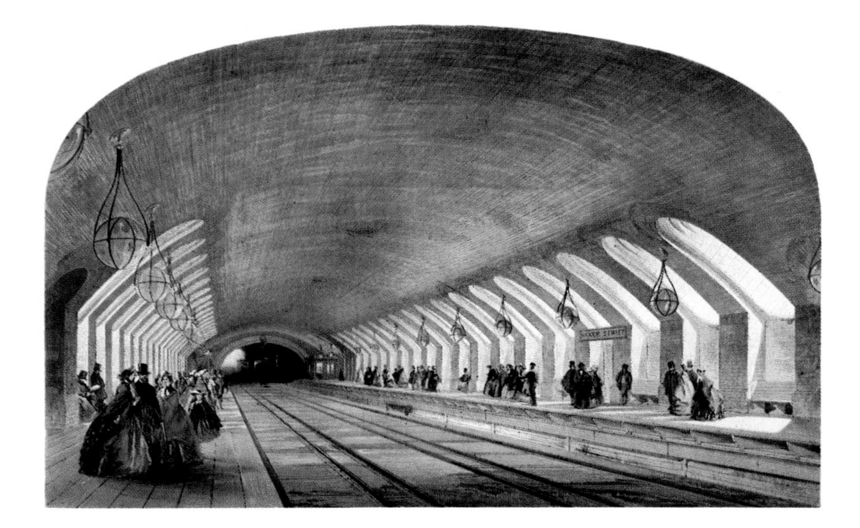

Right: Baker Street station in London, on the Metropolitan Railway. Its network of stations north and west of the city brought a home in the country within reach of many city workers. This picture shows the three-rail tracks laid so that they could be used by both standard- and broad-gauge locomotives.

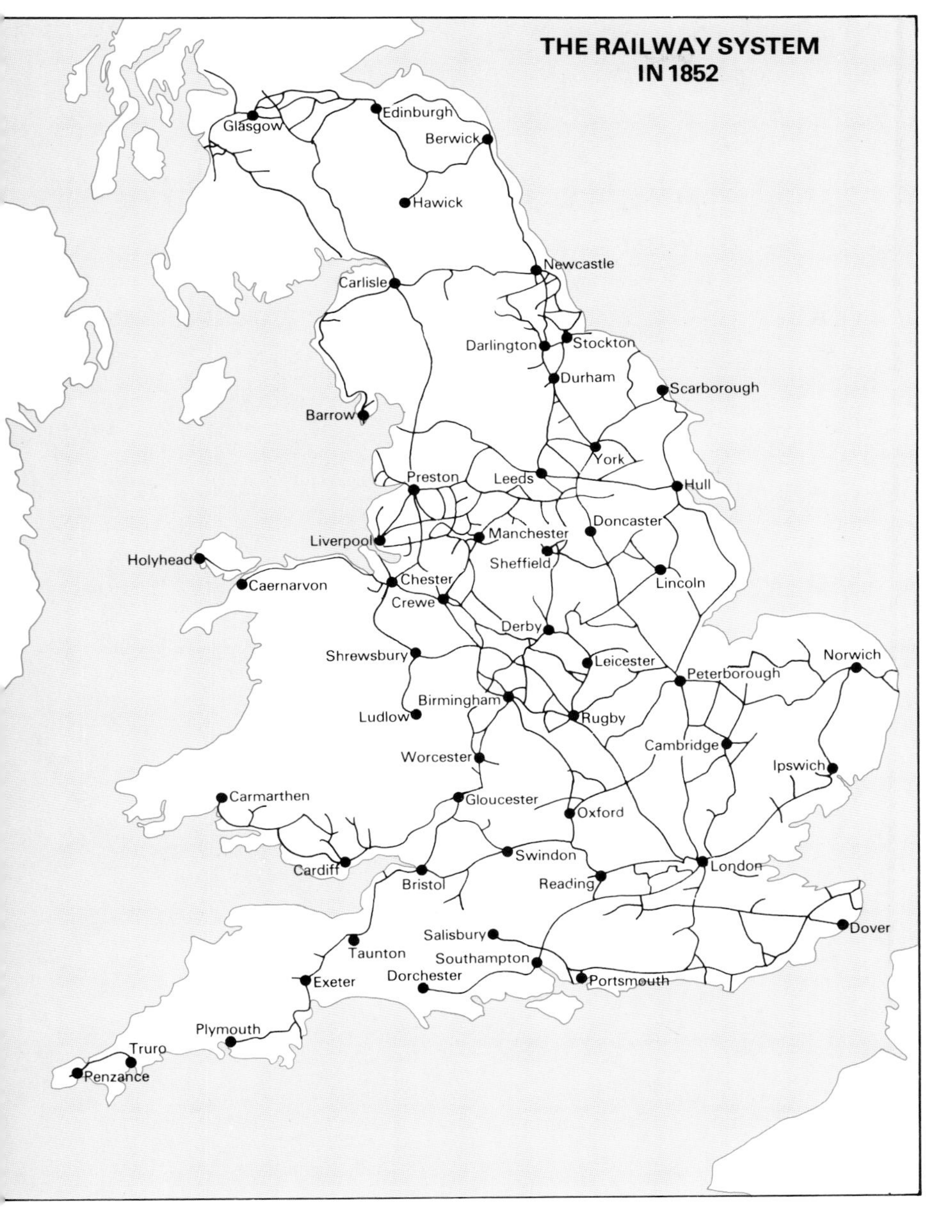

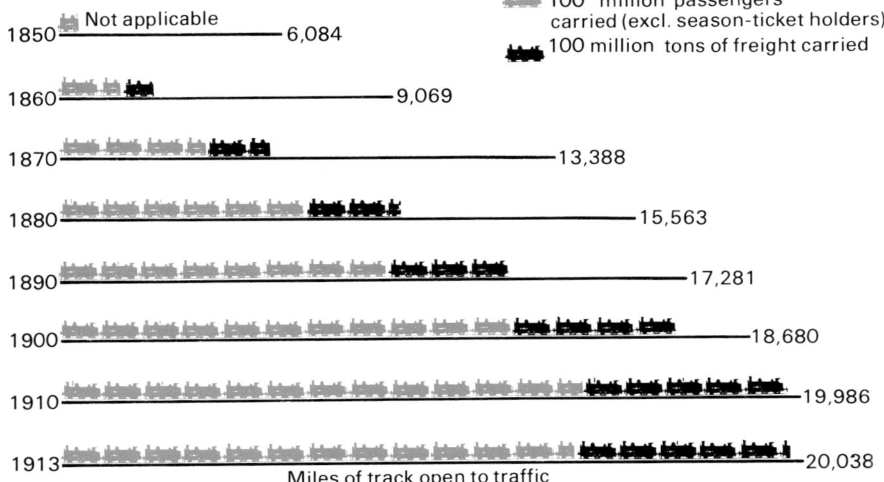

began operations. The 1830s and 1840s saw two massive waves of railway building which provided the country with a skeletal system of inter-city routes. During the next 20 years the main line system was completed, until by the early 1870s over 13,000 miles (21,000 km) were open to traffic. Though one-third of the railway mileage still remained to be built, most of the additions after 1870 consisted of branch and local lines, feeder lines, loops and cut-offs, to fill in the network. The enormous growth in traffic volumes, both passenger and freight, demonstrates their importance to the national economy down to 1914, when they had a semi-monopoly of the transport system. For long-distance conveyance, road transport and navigable waterways were insignificant, though coastal shipping for some time retained a competitive edge in the movement of bulk freight.

In the years after 1870 the railways also played an important role in promoting suburban development around the major cities and towns. This process was complemented by the building of underground railways (London) and the development of extensive tramway networks in many parts of the country. By 1913–14 there were some 2700 miles (4300 km) of tramway route carrying around 3400 million passengers annually, compared with 151 million in 1879. At the later date there were more than twice as many tram journeys as train journeys.

The 19th century saw an enormous growth in communications to which the railways made a significant contribution. Prior to the 1830s postal services relied on the mail coach system: an extensive and tolerably efficient network of mail coach services had been built up in the later 18th and early 19th centuries, but inevitably the facilities offered were slow and expensive, while capacity restraints set limits to the volume of bulky mail items that could be transported.

The rapidly growing demands of the Post Office led, therefore, to early collaboration with the railways, as did the spread of the electric telegraph in the later 1830s, while the reduction in newspaper duties in 1836 and the introduction of the penny post in 1840, did much to stimulate the flow of written correspondence. The combined effect of these factors led to a substantial upsurge in the quantity of mail and newspaper deliveries during the 1840s and 1850s, which would have been physically impossible but for the provisions made by the railways to convey these items. Until 1914 the volume of mail generated continued to expand rapidly, and the speedy cheap services offered by the railways and Post Office did much to improve the commercial efficiency and enhance the social life of Britain. Indeed, in terms of the quality of service – same day delivery in many larger towns and even some evening delivery – postal services in the 19th century were better than those of today. In the latter part of this period telegrams and telephone calls made an increasing contribution to the communications system.

Above left: By 1852 the essential inter-city links had been completed; by 1914 the system had grown to link remote areas, with numerous cross-country lines. Even small villages had their own stations.

Urbanization and Population Growth, 1660–1841

In the late 18th century the British Isles experienced a demographic transition which was to be a forerunner for population growth around the world. Until the mid-18th century the population was growing slowly. Since there was no national census until 1801 it is necessary to rely on estimates, but these suggest that the population of the British Isles increased from about 9.5 million in 1700 to 10.5 million in 1750. Thereafter the rate of population growth increased rapidly and the population reached 15.75 million in 1801 and 27.5 million in 1841. The exact means and causes for this great increase in population have received much interest, but the absence of firm statistical information provides scope for considerable debate and the absence of definitive conclusions. In any case it is likely that there is no simple explanation for the increase in population. It seems likely that both the birth rate increased and the death rate decreased. In both cases improved food supply – the result of agricultural innovations, and perhaps good weather – may have been a factor. At the same time there were improvements in hygiene and health care which contributed to a fall in general mortality. The rise in the birth rate may also have been partly caused by earlier and higher rates of marriage, and this in turn may have been caused by greater prosperity.

The increase in population which took place between 1750 and 1841 affected all areas of the country, and rural as well as urban and industrial regions. The highest rates of increase occurred in the London area, in the textile districts of Lancashire and Yorkshire, and in industrial areas around Birmingham and Glasgow. There were also high rates of increase in some of the mining areas like those of Durham, Derbyshire and Cornwall. However, some rural areas grew rapidly in population, the most spectacular of these being Ireland. Between 1750 and 1841 the population of Ireland increased by five million, a result of the introduction of the potato, the subdivision of land-holdings and earlier marriage. Although detailed county figures are not available, it appears likely that the increase was greatest in the western parts of the country. Already by the early 19th century there was overpopulation and migration both overseas and to the rest of Britain. In the other rural areas of the country the expansion of agriculture and the traditional craft industries were able to sustain population growth, but once again there was some outward migration to the growing towns and industrial districts. In general, with the exception of Ireland and skilled workers, migration took place over short distances to the nearest growing area rather than from south to north.

The outstanding growth centre of the country was London, which grew from about 450,000 in 1660, to 575,000 in 1700, to 675,000 in 1750, to 980,000 in 1801 and two million in 1841, a result of its expanding role both within the country and overseas. Its growth was only possible because of very large-scale migration, particularly necessary in the early 18th century when its death rates were high.

Outside London the principal urban growth centres were Manchester, Glasgow and Liverpool. There was considerable urban growth in the industrial areas, but often the new industrial settlements of the early industrial revolution were small-scale and scattered, a result of the need to be near either mineral deposits or water power. Outside these areas the county towns often showed growth, reflecting the growing prosperity of their regions. In southern England the naval bases of Chatham, Portsmouth and Devonport (Plymouth) grew rapidly and there was also the development of health resorts, most noticeably at Bath, Brighton and Cheltenham.

Three views of the port of Liverpool: in 1680, 1728 and 1830. Before 1660, Liverpool was a tiny village, its population probably at no time exceeding 1000 or so. After that, the rise of textile manufacturing in the North-West, and the development of trade with the Americas, the West Indies and Ireland, set Liverpool on the road to growth and prosperity.

Right: Centres of population and average growth of population by region, 1750–1841.

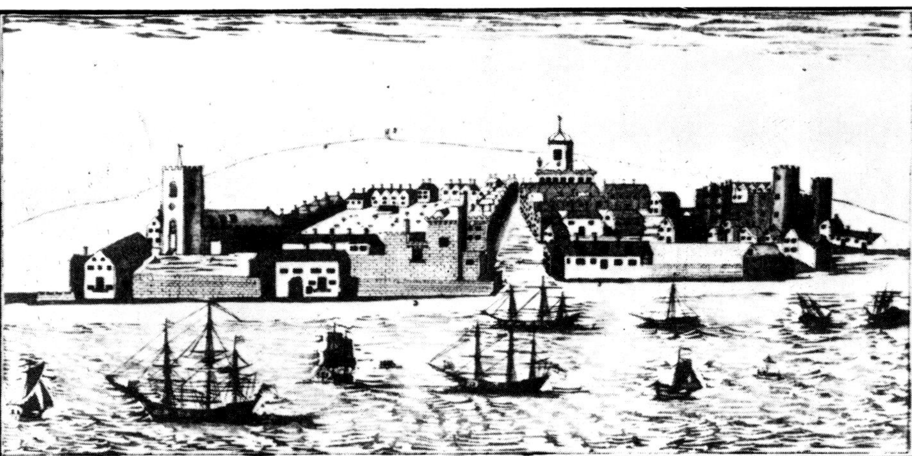

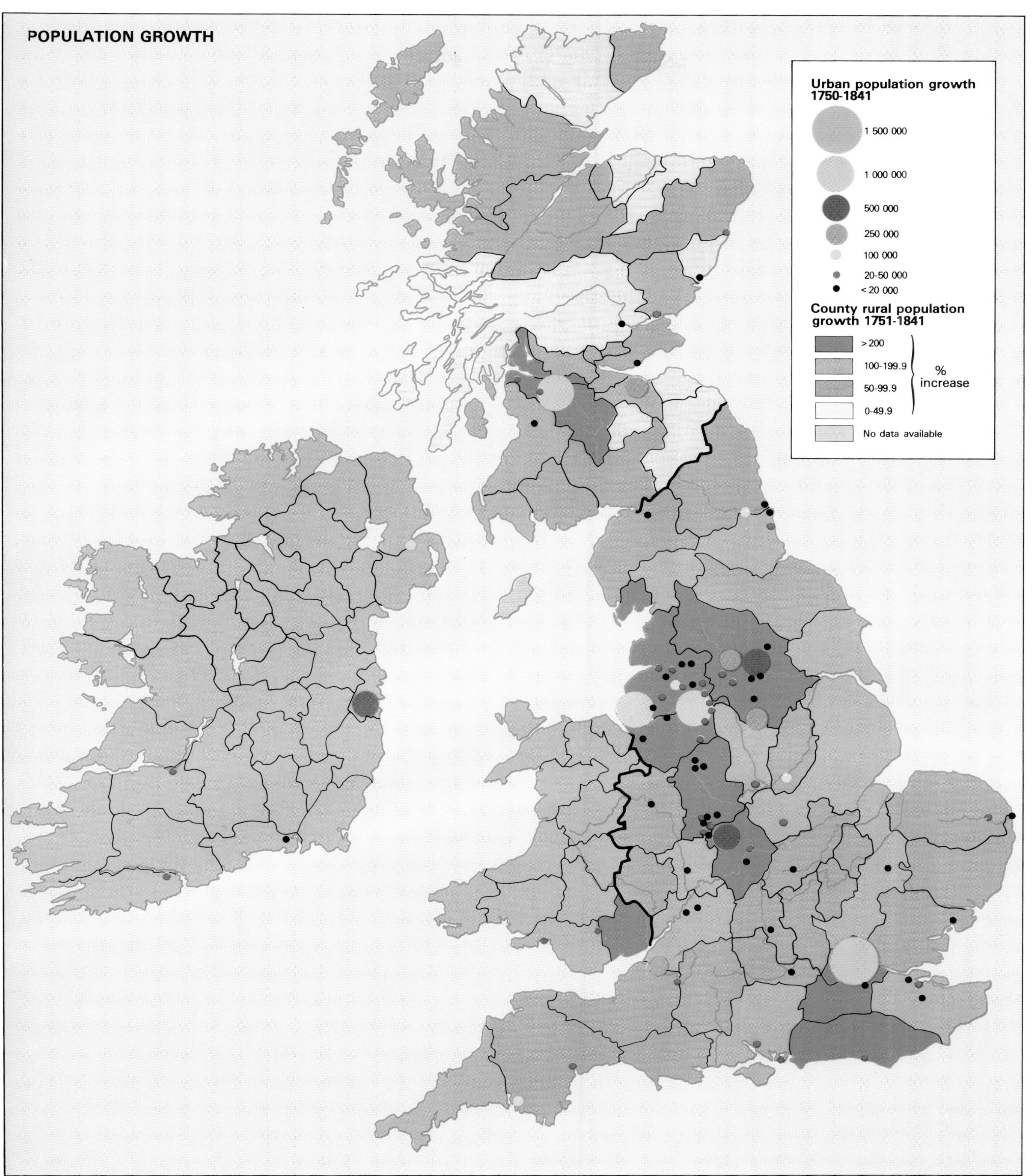
POPULATION GROWTH
Urban population growth 1750-1841
1 500 000
1 000 000
500 000
250 000
100 000
20-50 000
< 20 000
County rural population growth 1751-1841
> 200
100-199.9
50-99.9
0-49.9
% increase
No data available

Population Change, 1841–1951

The population of the British Isles increased from over 27 million in 1841 to 45 million in 1911 and 53 million in 1951. In the 19th century there was a high rate of natural increase, births exceeding deaths, but towards the end of the century the birth rate began to fall so that in the 20th century, and particularly in the inter-war period, there has only been a small natural increase, if any at all. Throughout the period until the 1930s there was also heavy net outward migration, particularly from Ireland, mainly towards North America and the British colonies. Only in the period around the Second World War has there been net inward migration, this being from Europe.

In the period from 1841 to the First World War population growth was focused on the industrial regions of Central Scotland, North-East England, West Yorkshire, South Lancashire, Birmingham and the Black Country, South Wales and also in London, while the remaining rural regions either grew slowly or actually declined. Decline occurred spectacularly in Ireland where the population reached a peak of 8.5 million in 1845, but following the potato famine of that year fell rapidly and by 1911 was only 4.4 million. Ireland and the other rural regions lost people either abroad or to the growing industrial areas. Generally, migrants preferred to move to the nearest growing urban and industrial centres so that for each industrial region the bulk of the migrants came from the surrounding regions. However, in the case of Ireland there was migration to all the major centres including Merseyside, Clydeside and London.

Throughout the period the share of the urban population continued to increase, rising from 37 per cent in 1841 to 74 per cent in 1911. London continued to dominate the urban structure, growing from 2 million in 1841 to 6.5 million in 1911, but there was also massive growth in Liverpool, Glasgow, Birmingham and Manchester where populations were either just above or nearly one million. Urban growth was concentrated in the industrial regions. In such regions there was a mixture of sizeable towns (like Sunderland, Bolton and Wolverhampton, for example), combined with a very large number of small urban settlements. The latter were either industrial towns, often based on textiles or mining villages. A characteristic feature of many urban settlements in the 19th century was the dominance of one industry or activity. Outside the industrial districts some of the traditional regional centres grew, attracting industry; in addition a new type of town came into being, the sea-side resort, made possible by the development of railways. Away from the urban districts there was rural depopulation – reflecting the declining demand for agricultural labour, the decline in rural craft industry and the resulting decline in the supporting population. This rural depopulation was highest in Ireland and some of the highland areas, and least in the lowland areas and near the growing centres.

Since the First World War the spatial pattern of population change has altered. Growth has been focused in the South and the Midlands, while there has been stagnation and occasionally decline in the industrial regions of the North and West. This is a reflection of the decline of economic activities in these regions and the growth of new activities in the South and Midlands. Consequently, the population has tended to move southwards and eastwards with particularly large movements from South Wales to the London area in the inter-war period. The pattern of urban growth, which has continued, reflects these changes. Most urban expansion has been in the South-East and Midlands. By the Second World War London had a population of over eight million and was surrounded by a ring of satellite towns. Throughout the country the lower density of development and the need for more houses to reflect the smaller household size has meant a sprawl of towns. In the heavily populated districts this has often meant a joining or fusion of previously independent towns to form conurbations. Since the First World War rural depopulation has been much less and confined to the remoter parts of the country. Near the major centres the rural areas have been repopulated as commuters have taken the opportunity of the motor car to combine the benefits of town and country.

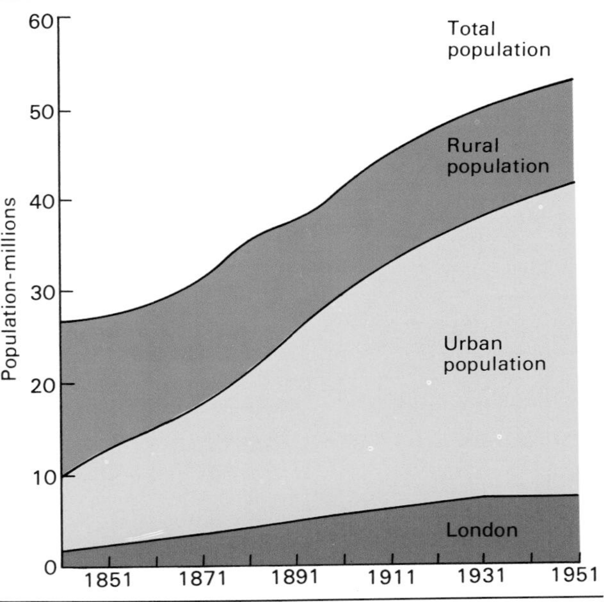

Left: Comparative growth of population 1841–1951. The enormous increase in the number of town- and city-dwellers can be clearly seen. London has maintained its historical position as the most populous urban centre.

Right: London Underground poster, early 1900s. As electrified railways reached into the countryside surrounding London, it became possible for commuters to live in the rural suburbs and work in the city.

London slum, 1912. All big cities at this time displayed the evils of wretched housing, squalor and poverty. Private individuals made attempts to improve conditions: examples include the beginnings of the garden city movement around 1900, and the construction of model industrial towns such as Port Sunlight, begun by Lever in 1888. But these efforts were on too small a scale to do much more than call attention to deeply entrenched problems.

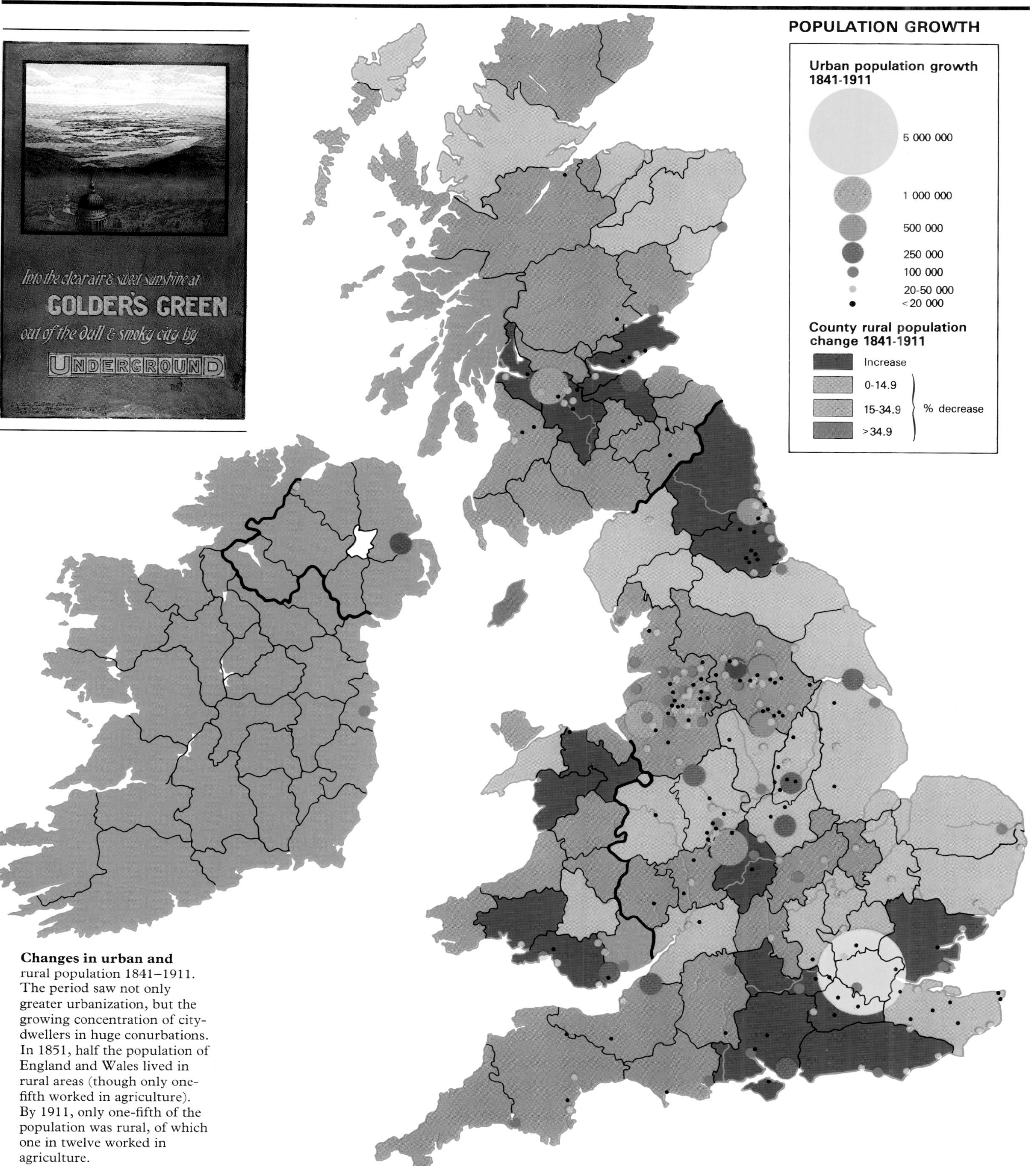

Changes in urban and rural population 1841–1911. The period saw not only greater urbanization, but the growing concentration of city-dwellers in huge conurbations. In 1851, half the population of England and Wales lived in rural areas (though only one-fifth worked in agriculture). By 1911, only one-fifth of the population was rural, of which one in twelve worked in agriculture.

The Economy after the Industrial Revolution

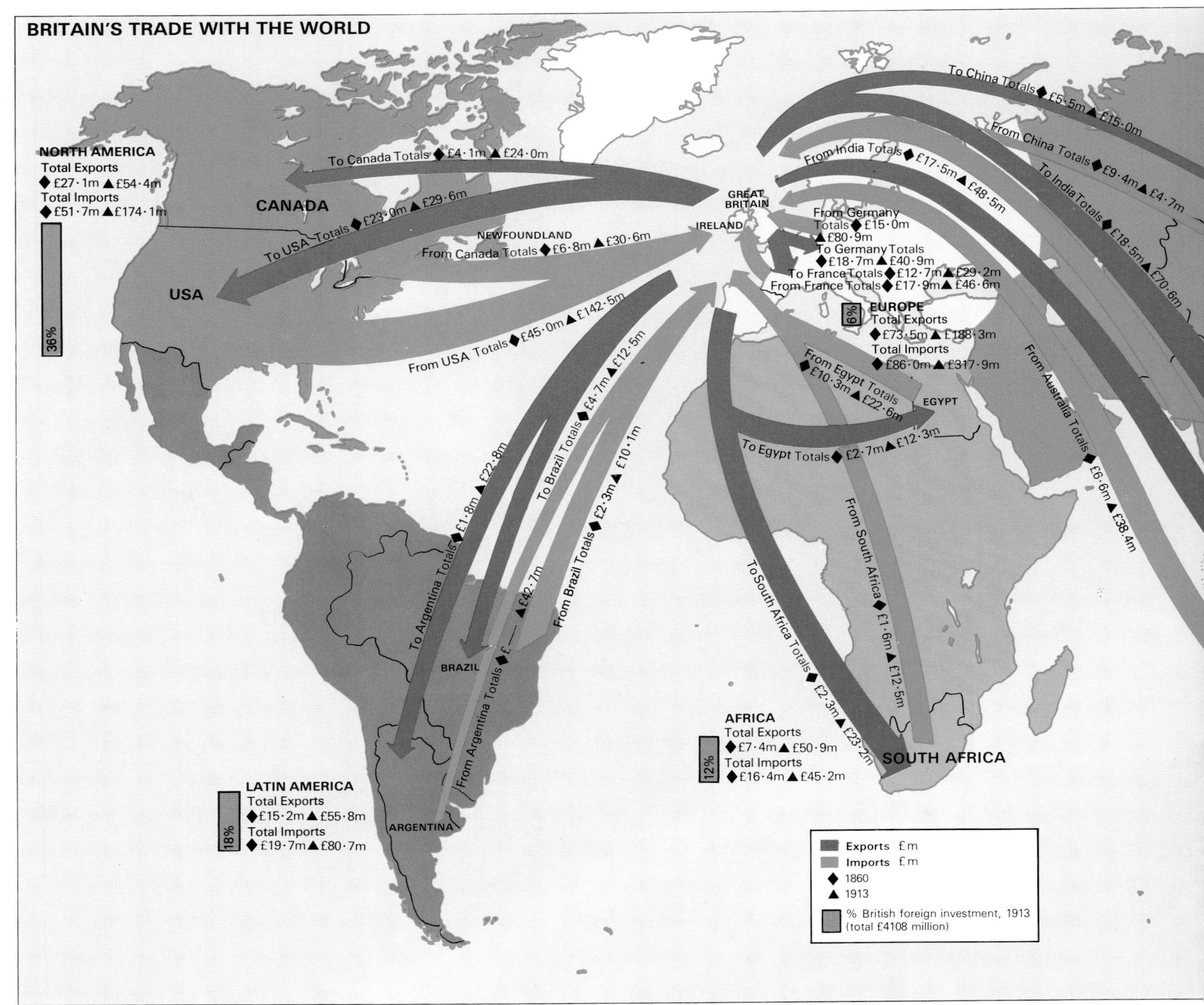

In 1914 Britain was still the world's leading trading nation and easily the leading foreign investor. Between 1860 and 1914 a growing share both of trade and investment was with the countries of the Empire.

The mid-Victorian years – from the repeal of the Corn laws in 1846 to the boom of the early 1870s – are generally regarded as a period of prosperity and expansion. This was the great era of gold discoveries, railway building, commercial expansion and free trade. It was a time when restrictions on commerce were lifted or modified in many countries following the lead set by Britain in a series of measures from the 1840s. These measures included the repeal of the Corn Laws, abandonment of the Navigation Acts as well as the removal of most import duties.

In 1850 Britain was the world's only major industrial nation, and was called the 'workshop of the world'. Industry and commerce expanded rapidly and even agriculture flourished without protection. Britain remained faithful to free trade (with a few exceptions) until 1931 – but its advantages appeared to wane after the 1870s. Now other countries were industrializing, and a flood of cheap food imports from the New World undermined the security of Britain's agriculture. Industry, too, found the going more difficult and complained about depressed conditions and foreign competition. Although the original concept of a 'Great Depression' in the late 19th century has now been greatly modified, it is clear that British industry was slow to adapt to the more difficult and competitive trading conditions of the period and, as a result, it experienced retardation and a loss of market shares. On the other hand, many of the service trades – financial, commercial and shipping – continued to thrive under free trade, and in 1914 Britain still dominated the world in these fields.

During the 50 years or so before 1914, the British economy had continued to expand steadily. But, in sharp

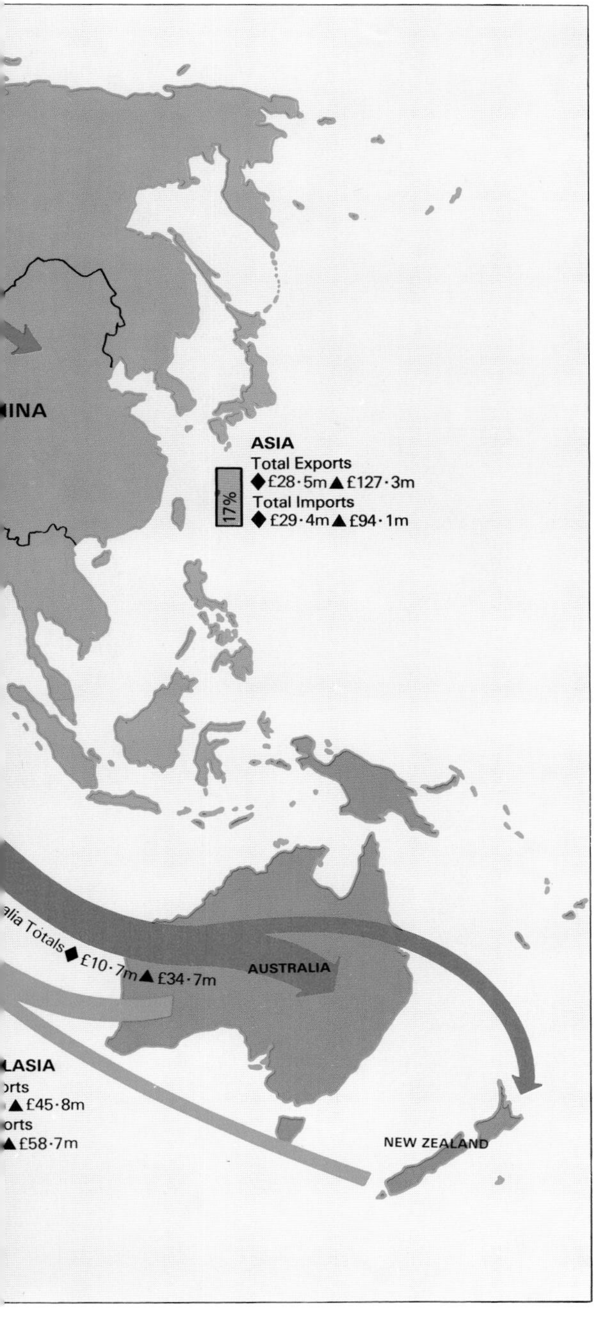

ontrast to the years before 1870, the period saw a slowing own in the pace of expansion and a relative decline in ritain's economic importance in the world. This slowing own was most noticeable in manufacturing in which, as ther countries industrialized and put up tariffs, the rate of xpansion slackened markedly. Britain's share of world nanufacturing production, for example, declined from early 32 per cent in 1870 to only 14 per cent in 1913. And ritain's imports were now including, ominously, a growng share of manufactured goods.

This increasing loss of market shares was partly to be xpected, given Britain's extraordinary early dominance. It vas not, in itself, necessarily a sign of weakness. Rather nore disturbing was the fact that from the 1870s to 1914 ritain recorded one of the slowest rates of growth among he major developing countries. Out of 16 countries for which data are available, only Australia, Italy and the Netherlands had lower rates of growth in total output per head of population between 1870 and 1914. Britain had also one of the lowest rates of export growth in the period. Again, in the middle of the 19th century Britain had – with the possible exception of Australia – by far the highest level of per capita income of any country in the world. But, by 1914, she had been overtaken by Canada and the United States, while several countries, notably France, Denmark, Sweden, Germany, Switzerland and Belgium, were catching up. This period thus marks the start of Britain's relative long-term economic decline which, with short intermissions, has continued to this day.

The Service Trades

Sluggish industrial growth in the period 1870–1914 was in part compensated for by the growth of service trades – in particular those of insurance, banking, finance, commercial activities and shipping services – which were related to thriving world trade. A large proportion of the world's financial, commercial and shipping services were transacted through United Kingdom institutions. London's financial centre, the City, became the pivot of the international gold standard, and sterling came to be the world's paramount currency.

As a maritime nation Britain was still without equal: in 1913 nearly one half of the world's steam tonnage was under the British flag (four times as large as the nearest rival, Germany); one-half of the seaborne trade of the world was carried in British vessels; and, during the 25 years prior to the First World War, about two-thirds of new ships launched were built in Britain.

Britain was also by far the largest foreign investor. In 1914 Britain's overseas assets totalled £4000 million, which was approaching the combined overseas investments of all other leading countries. From her vast investments, spread over every corner of the globe – with heavy concentrations in North America, Latin America, Asia and Africa – Britain derived an increasing stream of income. This, together with earnings from shipping, financial and other services, more than compensated for the growing deficit on her physical trade account.

From the 1870s Britain's lending and trade became increasingly concentrated in the Empire. This may be seen as a further indication of Britain's declining competitive strength. British exports were heavily concentrated on a relatively narrow range of products – textiles, clothing, iron and steel products, coal, ships and railway rolling stock. But this meant that opportunities for trade expansion with the rich and rapidly expanding markets of Western Europe and North America diminished, as these areas became increasingly efficient in producing such products themselves and at the same time protected their home markets with tariff barriers.

So, on the eve of the First World War, Britain still ranked as a major economic power. But her former supremacy had been seriously challenged, especially on the industrial side. And there were evident signs that the British economy lacked the flexibility to meet the challenge. At the time, the continued expansion of world trade and economic activity, and with it the prosperity of Britain's staple industries together with her flourishing financial and service sectors, lulled the country into a sense of false security. It was not until the vastly different and more difficult international economic conditions which followed the First World that the underlying weaknesses in Britain's economy became apparent.

British Society in the 19th Century

British society in the 19th century changed from a hierarchical and deferential structure, acknowledging an aristocracy ruling by right of birth, to a society conscious of class distinctions. Alienation was at the root of it. There had always been a concept of duties owed to each other by landlords, farmers and servants in agriculture, but people deriving their living from the land declined in numbers. Aristocrats lost predominance to entrepreneurs – people successful in industry and trade, who employed others, recognizing no obligation beyond the terms of the contract. The greatest increase took place, not in occupations of people making goods, but among those providing services – professional services at the top end, humble clerical or transport services at the bottom. The middle class discovered the value of education; public schools, hitherto the preserve of aristocratic youth, were required to prepare middle-class sons not only for executive, but also for administrative responsibility within the community. Daughters never received as good an education as sons because they were expected to play a purely decorative role, leading in due course to marriage and motherhood. Many intelligent middle-class women smarted under the insignificance of the contribution they made to the community; gaps in social provision created an opportunity for them to initiate activities hitherto unknown, namely the social services out of which the Welfare State has grown.

Mechanics' Institutes, set up by well-intentioned middle-class people to increase the workers' understanding of physical science and to raise their social and cultural standards, had only very limited success among those whom they were meant to benefit: they had insufficient funds to pay for good lecturers or to replace worn-out books, and they kept clear of political and religious controversy, thus rendering much discussion insipid. The lower middle class, however, found them useful to supplement a basic education received, up to 1870, entirely in voluntary schools provided by religious denominations and, after 1870, increasingly in board schools (which were financed from the rates). Literacy, always higher in Scotland and probably in Wales than in England, rose greatly during the century. The penny post, initiated in 1840, led to an overwhelming flood of correspondence. Stamp duties on newspapers were reduced in 1836 and abolished in 1854, benefiting the Press as much as did the invention of rapid mechanical methods of printing, especially the rotary cylinder press, later in the century. A very large public, both middle-class and working-class, waited anxiously to read the periodical instalments in which Dickens first published his novels.

There has been much argument how the changes up to the middle of the century affected the workers' standard of living; the most that can be said is that, if it rose at all, the rise was disappointingly slow and small. But there is general agreement that workers greatly improved their standards of living in the second half of the century: the fall in the mortality rate, increase of consumption and of savings all point in that direction. Improvements in retail trading in the last quarter of the century caused sales of necessities of life to be made in larger quantities at lower rates of profit. Fewer children per family reduced the number of people dependent on the average worker's wage. For the middle class, on the other hand, life became less easy in the last quarter. Business profits declined, leading to loss of self-confidence on the entrepreneur's part and to growing demand for state intervention. The model of a self-reliant community paled before the ideal of a caring society.

Religious fervour ran high in the 19th century, but found

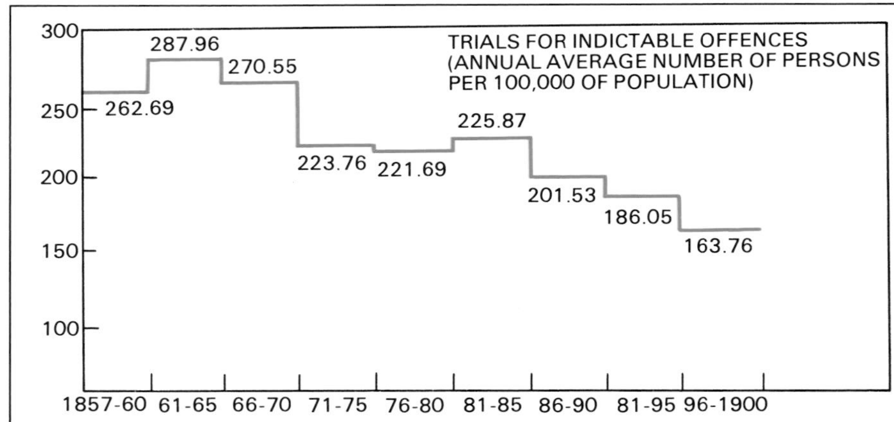

Annual average number of people per 100,000 of population tried for indictable offences in England and Wales between 1857 and 1900.

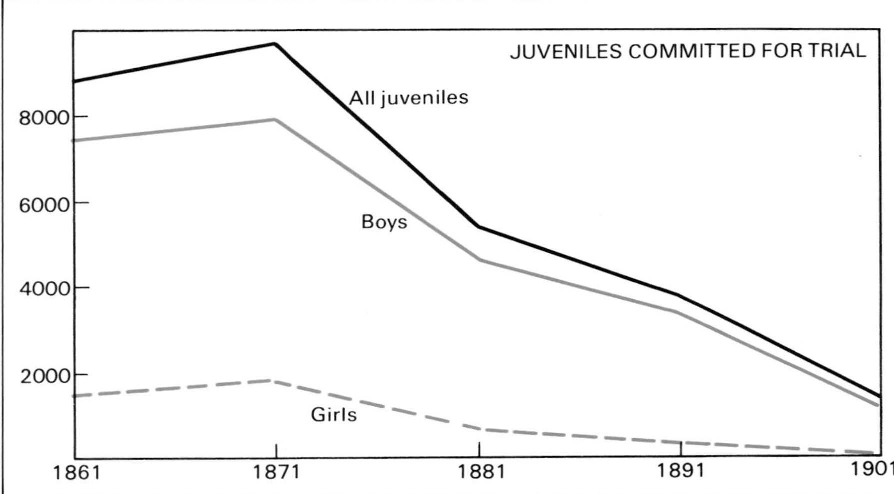

Number of children under 16 committed for trial in England and Wales between 1861 and 1901.

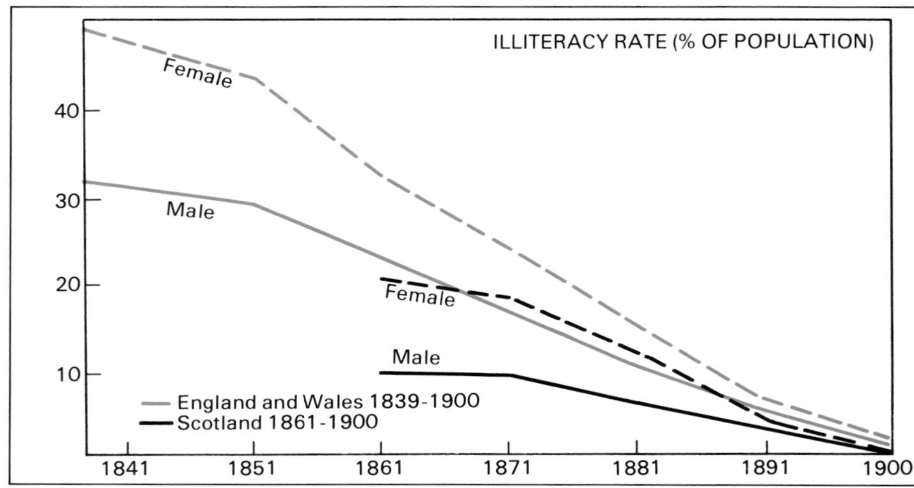

Illiteracy in England and Wales, and in Scotland, between 1839 and 1900. Always rarer in Scotland, it had almost disappeared there by the end of the century, and in England and Wales, too, the decline was very steep.

risoners in Wandsworth il at the end of the 19th :ntury.

Below: Education increased not only in academic subjects but also in aspects of health; this lesson, around 1898, is in dental hygiene.

s counterpart in criticism of the Bible. Standards of living ten determined membership of denominational groups, ough not of minority religions: rarely did Jews or atholics convert. The latter increased the number of their ligious houses, priests and places of worship faster than d Protestants. But the highest and lowest income groups nded to belong to the Church of England, whereas the iddle class was largely Nonconformist. Not that the orking class went to church to any considerable extent: at time when population flocked to the towns, more urches were built in the countryside than in urban rroundings, a policy which did little to induce urban orkers to attend; they mistrusted paid ministers of ligion, disliked the social distinctions within congre- tions and the indifference of the Church to social nditions. Though the number and variety of associations ganized for religious purposes greatly increased during e first half of the century, only one-third of all those who ould reasonably be expected to attend a place of worship n any Sunday actually did so.

Victorian society was a society of extremes. When Booth nd Rowntree made their famous surveys of London and ork at the turn of the century, they found a great many ving in abject poverty and near starvation. By contrast, the ealthy enjoyed elegance and extravagance on a scale that oubled the consciences of many and provided a focal point r growing socialist discontent as the century progressed. he First World War provided a devastating blow to a orld still sharply divided between those 'upstairs' and ose 'downstairs'.

GROWTH OF EDUCATIONAL CENTRES IN GREAT BRITAIN

Notes:

1. Public schools are attributed to the first location they, or their oldest constituent school, had in this country.
2. The university colleges of Aberystwyth, Cardiff, Bangor and Lampeter constituted the University of Wales.

Boys' Public Schools—
- founded before 1800
- London, 15 schools
- founded 1800-1850
- London, 6 schools
- founded 1860-1869
- founded 1870-1913
- Universities existing in 1800
- Universities established between 1800 and 1914
- University Colleges established between 1800 and 1914
- Mechanics' Institutes established between 1820 and 1825

The education movement expanded at all levels during the 19th century. The map gives a picture of this for the major British cities: public schools, Mechanics' Institutes and universities. Note in particular, the large number of public schools established after 1860.

The Labour Movement

The history of the British labour movement is today far more open to debate and controversy than has been the case in the past. This holds true even in respect to the origins of trade unionism. Early historians denied any lineage between the 'trade clubs' of the 18th century and the medieval guild system. But more recently this has been seen as being at the very least an over-generalization and it is now argued that the early trade unions were successful in preserving many of the guild's regulatory devices, such as the apprenticeship system.

During the first quarter of the 19th century, combinations of both employers and workmen were declared illegal by legislation; this appears, however, to have resulted in many workers' organizations being forced underground, or masquerading as friendly societies. But even with the repeal of the Combination Acts in 1824, trade unions continued to experience a precarious existence. As late as 1834, a group of agricultural labourers from Dorset was sentenced to transportation to Australia, ostensibly as a result of swearing an illegal oath, and the village of Tolpuddle was written indelibly into the annals of Trade Union history. Around this time also, attempts were being made at organizing working men on broader geographical and ideological fronts, but the National Association for the Protection of Labour, established by John Doherty in 1830, and the Grand National Consolidated Trades Union (1834), which embraced Robert Owen's socialism, were premature and fraught with inconsistencies.

It was not until the first half of the 1870s, after a few years of intense unrest, that trade unions appear to have secured respectability, symbolized in the change in legal nomenclature from 'Master and Servant' to 'Employer and Workman'. The London Trades Council set up in 1860 and the Junta which emerged out of it; and the establishment of the first Trades Union Congress in 1868 at Manchester, which saw the beginning of a more effective national organization of provincial trade unions, both undoubtedly contributed to this process. At this time most unions were of the exclusive, craft type, with some developing nationally alon the lines of the 'New Model Unions', such as th Amalgamated Society of Engineers (1851) and the Amalga mated Society of Carpenters (1860). Apart from th beginnings of the organization of agricultural workers b Joseph Arch in the early 1870s, the movement did n experience any significant change in its composition, an grew steadily until the late 1880s, when there emerged new wave of union organization on a mass scale. Th resulted in the formation of a different type of associatio the 'unskilled' union. Some of these, by way of a process c amalgamation, came to have a marked impact upon th industrial relations of the 20th century, as in the case of th Transport and General Workers Union (formed in 1922)

The 'general' unions, as they became known, were bor in a period of significant strike activity, most notably amon the dockers and matchgirls of East London. But the followed two decades of relative industrial peace, unt another wave of labour unrest erupted in the yea immediately preceding the First World War. It wa

The banner of the National Union of Gas Workers and General Labourers, one of the new mass organizations of the late 1880s.

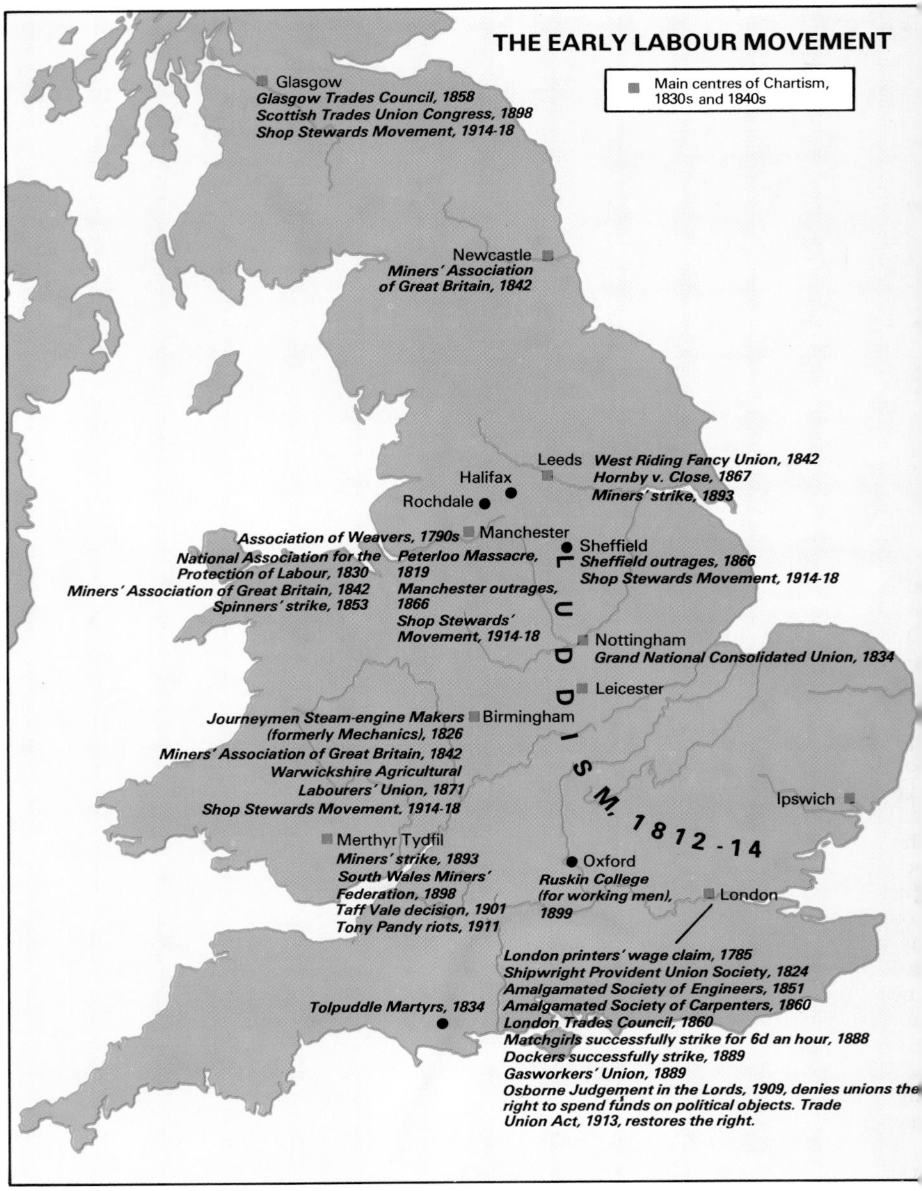

A procession in support of the 'Tolpuddle Martyrs', a group of six agricultural workers sentenced in 1834 to seven years' transportation for swearing an illegal oath; they had in fact established a lodge of the Friendly Society of Agricultural Labourers.

erhaps during these years, and those immediately follow- ıg the War, that trade union members came closest to rticulating a desire for radical social and political change.)uring the War these aspirations were reinforced by an nofficial 'shop-steward movement', which saw power hannelled into the hands of unofficial rank-and-file leaders vho did not consider themselves bound by the leadership's greements. The War undoubtedly strengthened the ormal institutions of collective bargaining and saw a ignificant increase in union membership.

The 1920s, and economic depression, served to intensify he industrial struggle, particularly in those sectors of the conomy such as coal-mining, where exports had been lost uring the War. In 1926, after a few years during which the oal-owners attempted to solve their industry's problems y reducing the miners' wages, a general strike, which asted nine days, was called and, although the coal-miners tayed out, they eventually returned to work having gained othing. In some ways the strike could be seen as the ulmination of the conflict between capital and labour.

Meanwhile, in the law courts, the unions had lost another ignificant skirmish in 1901 when the 'Taff Vale Decision' ad declared that unions were liable for the losses incurred by a business as a result of strike action. Parliament quickly changed the position with the 1906 Trades Disputes Act, and it was not until the 1960s that the unions again found themselves effectively under attack from legal quarters. A combination of numerous short, unofficial strikes, accelerating inflation and Britain's poor general economic performance caused governments of both major political parties to consider some form of legal restraint on union actions, despite the fact that a Royal Commission under Lord Donovan had, in 1968, advised against this. Shop-stewards had also become prominent once more, though now they did not constitute a movement as such, but were rather the local representatives of shop-floor aspirations. At the same time, many union members occupied office and other white-collar jobs as the scope of trade union recruitment spread even wider. It is possible to argue that, when an Industrial Relations Act was introduced in 1971, it was partly aimed at restoring the control of union behaviour to the hands of union officials and out of the hands of unofficial local leaders. However, the Act was dealt a severe blow when five unofficial dockers' leaders were gaoled for defying some of its provisions, and it was repealed in 1974.

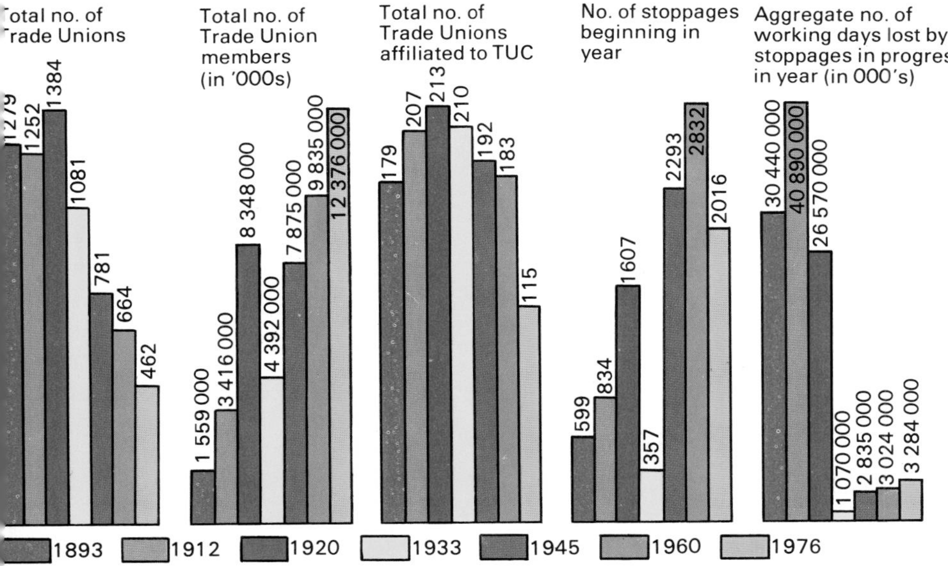

Trade Unions and their effects. The number of unions has decreased through rationalization and amalgamation. The effect of the economic difficulties of the inter-war years stands out clearly.

Inland Transport since 1914

Before the First World War the railways dominated inland transport in Britain. However, their ability to translate this dominance into profits was progressively weakened by the demand, voiced by hard-pressed traders and industrialists, that the companies should act more as 'public service' corporations than as profit-making businesses. Government regulation increased to satisfy this expectation and, by 1914, there was a considerable body of legislation dealing with services, charges, safety and labour relations. During the War, the industry was brought under full state control, and in the post-War planning debates nationalization was considered seriously. However, after spirited lobbying on both sides, this formula was rejected in favour of regulated, regional monopolies. Most of the companies – 123 of them – were amalgamated to form four 'Main-line' railways. They were the Great Western, London and North Eastern, London Midland and Scottish, and Southern. The government thus demonstrated its final rejection of inter-railway competition as a protection for consumers, but it missed the opportunity to go beyond regulation and co-ordinate all forms of transport while the motor vehicle was still in its infancy.

With the rapid development of road transport in the inter-war years, regulated monopoly became an increasingly irrelevant concept on the railways. There was a tenfold increase in the number of motor vehicles between 1919 and 1938, the biggest advance coming from the private car. Goods vehicles, both 'public' (road haulage firms) and 'private' ('C' licence), also experienced spectacular growth. Together they began to challenge railways in a number of markets, but especially in the short-distance passenger and short- and medium-distance freight. The government responded in the 1930s by imposing an element of control on the newcomers. The Acts of 1930 and 1933 established new licensing systems which restricted entry into road passenger transport and road haulage, while further legislation in 1933 created the London Passenger Transport Board as a public authority with a controlled monopoly of passenger transport in the capital.

Nevertheless, the co-ordination of inland transport remained a rather remote concept. In the 'Square Deal Campaign' of 1938, the railway companies were able to show that their obligations to carry and charge for transport were still very much more restrictive than those faced by their more flexible rivals. By 1938, it is probable that a half of total passenger traffic and a fifth of freight traffic were being carried on the roads. Railway profits, already dented by the contraction in Britain's staple industries, suffered accordingly. The 'standard revenue' of £45 million, envisaged for the main-line companies by the Act of 1921, was never attained: the average for 1934–8 was only £33 million, representing a rate of return on capital expenditure of under three per cent.

The Second World War provided a temporary boost for railway profits by disrupting both road and coastal shipping operations. But the price of a substantial increase in railway traffic was a worn-out and inadequately maintained system which could not be restored to its pre-war state in the austerity conditions which followed peace. There is no doubt at all that the railways were, in Dalton's phrase, 'a very poor bag of physical assets' when they were taken into state ownership in 1948. Road transport suffered, too. The number of private cars, for example, fell from 2 million in 1939 to 1.8 million in 1946. However, recovery here was comparatively easy to achieve once fuel became more plentiful.

The election of a Labour government in July 1945 led

Railway cutbacks since 1954. Many small branch lines have been completely axed, while other lines have lost their freight-handling facilities. These cutbacks in the interests of economy have greatly increased road traffic, and are altering the patterns of employment in areas now almost devoid of public transport.

Licensed Cars (000)

1903	1920	1939	1854	1979
8	187	2034	3100	14,568

Licensed haulage vehicles (000)

1903	1920	1939	1954	1979
4	101	488	1033	1788

An early traffic jam: a farm cart, car and coach on a country lane in the 1920s. Since the early days of motoring it has been a struggle for roads to carry the ever-increasing load of traffic, a situation exacerbated by the cutback in the railway network and the consequent increase of heavy goods traffic to be borne by the roads.

naturally to the nationalization of a great deal of inland transport. Under the Transport Act of 1947 the British Transport Commission was given the challenging responsibility of presiding over a vast undertaking comprising the railways, London Transport, long-distance road haulage, some important bus companies, the docks and inland waterways, and the railway hotels. The Commission's duty to provide a 'properly integrated system' of transport was difficult to fulfil with an independent sector of private cars, bus operators, coastal shipping, and 'C' licence (own-account) lorries, which became increasingly popular in the period of cheap oil. Furthermore, a large part of road haulage was denationalized after the Conservative return to power in 1951.

The railways kept their operating account in the black until 1956, despite problems caused by under-investment and antiquated pricing controls. However, they continued to lose traffic to the roads, and the rapid expansion of the latter from the mid-1950s had predictable effects on their market share. By 1977 this had fallen to 18 per cent of freight ton-mileage and 7 per cent of passenger-mileage. The rail network was also reduced: by 1977, it was only 55 per cent of what it had been in 1914. There is no doubt that the contraction would have been speedier had the government given the industry firmer and more consistent guidelines before the Transport Act of 1962, which attempted to establish a more commercial approach to railway operation.

The 1962 Act was followed in 1963 by the abolition of the British Transport Commission, and the creation of the British Railways Board. But financial losses continued to be heavy, despite rationalization. It was left to the Labour government of 1964–70 to resolve, in part at least, the conflict between those expecting the industry to adopt strict commercial criteria and those demanding that it fulfil 'social service' obligations. Barbara Castle, the Transport Minister, identified a basic network for development, and the Transport Act of 1968 introduced Treasury grants for specified loss-making passenger services.

Road transport has continued to make steady progress. About 33,000 miles (53,000 km) of new road, including 1,500 miles (2,400 km) of motorway have been added since 1950, and the number of vehicles has increased four-fold (private cars six-fold). Road transport now accounts for 93 per cent of passenger-mileage and 64 per cent of freight ton-mileage, although it is noticeable that the flexibility of private motoring, despite rising fuel costs, has affected public transport, i.e. trams (until 1960), buses and coaches. The market share of this sector has fallen from 39 per cent in 1955 to only 12 per cent in 1977.

Passenger Transport in Great Britain (000 million passenger-km)

	1954	%	1974	%
Private road transport	76	38.8	350	79.1
Rail	39	19.9	36	8.2
Bus and coach	81	41.1	54	12.2
Air	0.3	0.2	2.3	0.5
All passenger transport	196	100.0	442	100.0

Freight Transport in Great Britain (000 million tonne-km)

	1954	%	1974	%
Road	34.5	37.4	89.9	65.1
Rail	36.1	39.2	24.2	17.5
Coastal shipping	21.1	22.1	20.5	14.8
Pipeline	0.2	0.2	3.4	2.5
Inland Waterways	0.3	0.3	0.1	0.1
All freight transport	92.2	100.0	138.1	100.0

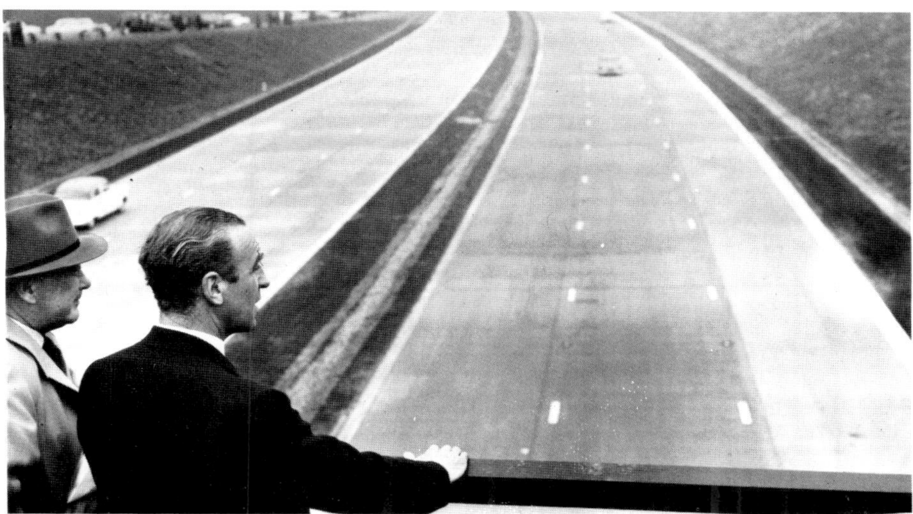
Britain's first major motorway, the M1, was opened in November 1969. Britain, along with Switzerland, was one of the last west European countries to build a comprehensive motorway system.

The Great Depression between the Wars

When the Duke of Manchester arrived in New York towards the end of 1931, he told reporters 'affairs in England are too bad to talk about'. They might well have seemed so. It was a sad, tense winter in a Britain still stunned by the effects of the summer financial storm and the continuing world depression. Less than two years earlier, millions had hopefully looked forward to a new era of prosperity. When the second minority Labour government under Ramsay MacDonald took office in June 1929, the outlook was as promising as at any time in the decade. Unemployment, the scourge of the post-war years, was lower than it had been a year before and remained so until November.

From that time England was sucked into the whirlpool of recession, slowly at first, and then with a headlong rush. As winter gave way to spring, the normal increase in employment did not take place. Instead, throughout 1930 unemployment grew steadily. In April it reached 1,761,000. In July it passed two million and, by the end of the year, stood at 2.5 million. In June 1931 it was over 2.7 million, and by this time it was reported that about one worker in five was without a job.

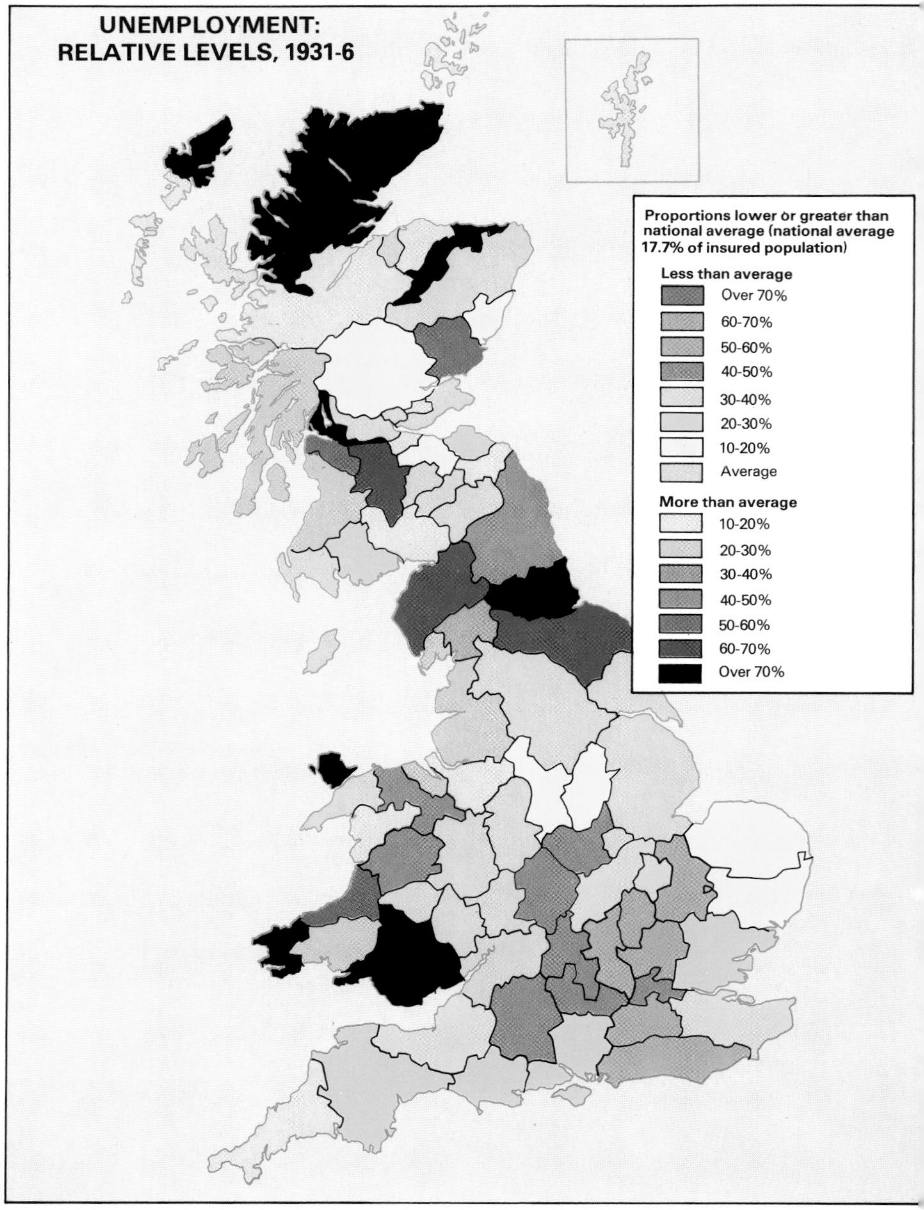

All regions suffered from high levels of unemployment during the depression, but some fared far better than others. Even when national recovery took place after 1932, some areas remained intensely depressed. The map shows clearly the 'two nations' – the relatively prosperous Midlands and South-East, and the deeply depressed North and Wales.

Endemic Unemployment

Mass unemployment was something which Britain, alone of the great nations, had suffered ever since the end of the First World War. In no year had the register of unemployed fallen below one million. Only in 1927 did the percentage of unemployed fall below one-tenth of the total workforce, and then only just. The cause of this affliction lay in the weaknesses of Britain's traditional staple industries. These industries – coal, cotton and woollen textiles, shipbuilding, and iron and steel – had formed the foundation of Britain's pre-war economic strength. But during the 1920s they languished, and a half-hearted improvement at the end of the decade was soon swamped by the great depression. Most of the difficulties of these industries can be traced back to the war years, though some went beyond. The necessities of war, and the subsequent armoury of protective devices, encouraged some countries to produce for themselves where previously they had imported. India, for example, increasingly produced at home cotton textiles once bought from Britain. Also, new competitors, such as Japan, emerged. Their success was helped by the inefficiency and technical backwardness that unhappily characterized a number of Britain's leading industries at this time. Another problem was that these major exporting industries produced commodities for which world demand was anyway not expanding rapidly, some, such as coal, because of the development of substitutes. Finally, the return to gold at the old parity in 1925 had left Britain's exports relatively overpriced in world markets.

Not surprisingly, this combination of misfortunes left many of Britain's industries with excess capacity. Despite the fact that the registered labour force contracted in all the depressed industries, unemployment remained severe. Moreover, the older industries were highly concentrated. The eclipse of one industry meant intense hardship in a particular region. The worst hit areas were in South Wales, South Lancashire, the West Riding, the Tyne-Tees, and the industrial belt of Scotland.

Britain therefore entered the great depression with a poorly functioning economy. Nothing of the American boom had occurred there. The general international prosperity of 1925–9 had found only a muted echo in the country that had at one time been the workshop of the world.

The Labour Government was totally unable to check the creeping depression, the closing factories, the growing queues of unemployed men waiting for the dole or standing without hope at the labour exchanges. Conditions were worst in the great export industries and in the regions that depended upon them. The volume of Britain's exports fell from £839 million to £657 million. Steel production fell from 9.6 million tons in 1928 to 5.2 million in 1931. By June 1932 nearly one in every two steel workers were unemployed. Shipbuilding fared even worse. In 1930 over 1.4 million tons had been launched in British yards; in 1933, a mere 133,000. And nearly two out of three of the industry's workforce were unemployed. Similar depression was felt throughout the nation's older industrial districts. In 1930 unemployment averaged 31.2 per cent in Wales, 29.3 per cent in the North-West of England, and only 9.8 per cent in London.

In the summer of 1931 a financial hurricane swept across from Vienna to Berlin and soon reached the shores of Britain. Swift and tumultuous events followed: the des-

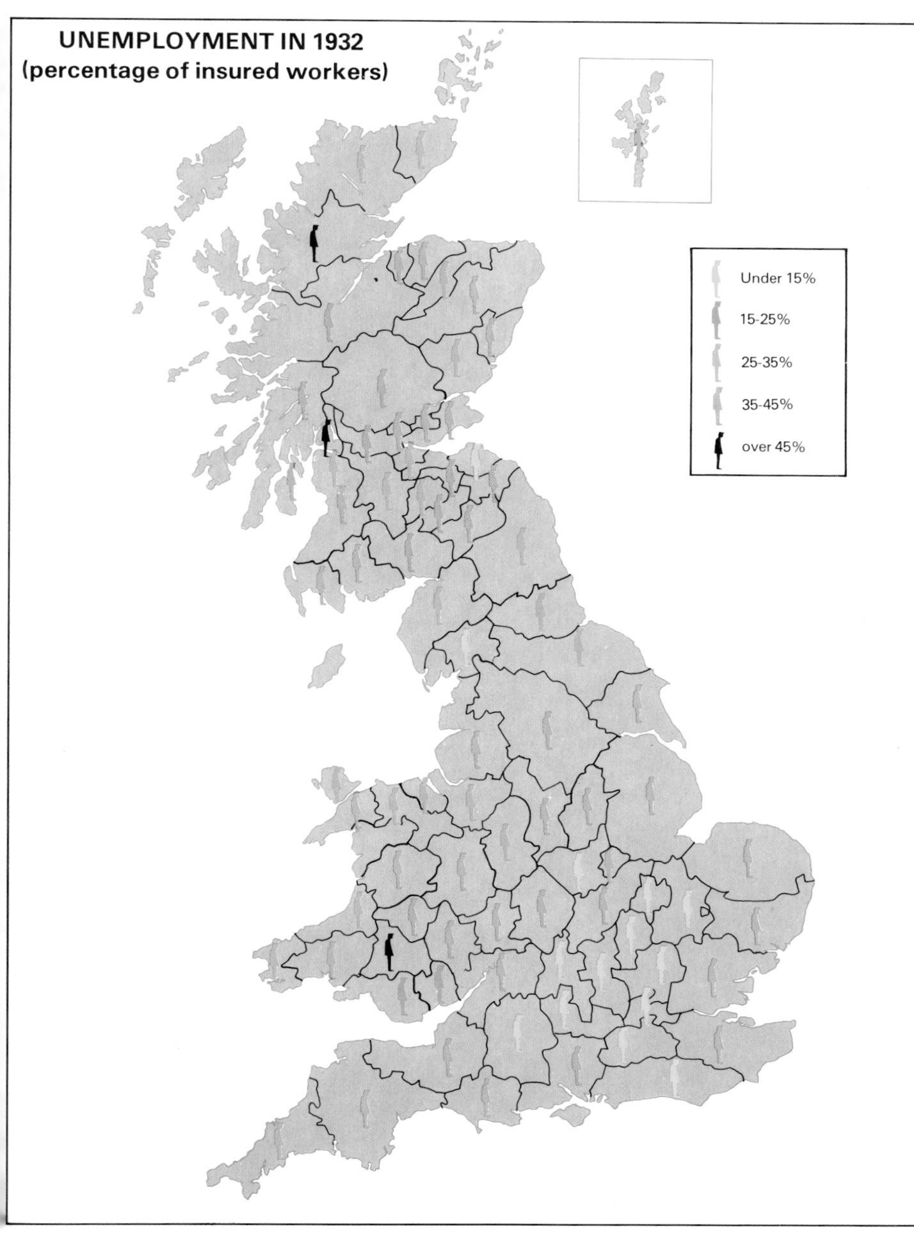

perate endeavours to save the pound; the foreign borrowing; the fall of the Labour Government on 23 August and the formation of the coalition National Government the following day; Snowden's drastic budget on 10 September; the Invergordon mutiny; and, ultimately, the devaluation on 18 September, when Britain at last abandoned the gold standard. A few months later another great British institution, free trade, was finally swept away, too, in the great depression.

1932 was the worst year of the depression. The regional impact is brought out by the varying incidence of unemployment in this particular year.

Although, as 1931 gave way to 1932, the economic outlook seemed grim, the country as a whole was, remarkably, past the worst. In contrast to Germany, the United States, France and many others, unemployment rose little in 1932. Nor did the percentage of unemployment go so high as it did in most other countries. The number of insured workers without work stayed below three million, reaching a peak of 2,955,000 in January 1933. Then came a steady improvement. In August 1933 under 2.5 million were unemployed for the first time since December 1930; in July 1935 the numbers fell below two million and a year later unemployment was 1.6 million.

Total industrial production declined no further during 1932. From the middle of that year there was a significant advance, checked by the American troubles of the winter and spring of 1933, but resumed afterwards. By 1937 output was one-fifth greater than it had been in 1929. Imports, too, increased once more. And, by 1936, they had reached their pre-depression volume – although in value they were one-third lower.

Britain's recovery, however, was neither general nor complete. Unemployment continued throughout the 1930s at a higher level than in the previous decade. Although the staple industries improved a little, unemployment remained high. Conditions in the depressed industrial towns and mining villages were frequently tragic and demoralizing. When prosperity returned elsewhere, these areas did not participate. Men in their forties or fifties came to realize they would never work again: living on the dole became a way of life. Thus, in 1934, only 6.4 per cent were unemployed in Birmingham, 5.1 per cent in Coventry. But in Jarrow, where Palmer's Shipyard had closed down, 67.8 per cent were without work. There was little hope for these men; in October 1936, when 200 of them marched to London, more than two in every three still had no job. Jarrow was one of the worst cases, but by no means stood alone. In 1934, unemployment in Merthyr Tydfil was 61.9 per cent, in Maryport 57 per cent.

Why Britain Recovered

Why did recovery occur in Britain? Recovery certainly owed a little to government policy. Rearmament made some contribution after 1936 but Chamberlain, who had succeeded Snowden in October 1932, pursued the same policies of balanced budgets. Devaluation helped to lift the internal price level and gave protection to Britain's industries. More significant was the lowering of interest rates for 'cheap money', which encouraged borrowers and stimulated investment, most notably in the building of houses.

But the real springs of recovery were generated within Britain itself. Most important, real wages for those in work improved. Wages hardly fell at all but prices, especially of imported food, dropped sharply. One reason why wages were high was that productivity increased in many industries. Also the terms of trade moved appreciably in Britain's favour. Even in 1929 a given volume of British exports was buying 14 per cent more imports than before the First World War. By the mid-1930s, 40 per cent more could be bought. Thus Britain could maintain her imports and still have more unemployment. Improved living standards took place at the expense of foreign suppliers and Britain's own unemployed. The South-East and the Midlands gained, while the northern districts and South Wales languished.

Britain's experience in the great world depression was unique. No great policy upheaval resulted. There was nothing like Hitler's Reich, Roosevelt's New Deal, Leon Blum's Popular Front, or Japan's policy of military conquest. Alone among the great powers no life was lost in Britain in any political or industrial disturbance. At the height of the crisis in 1931 the British electorate chose the path of safety. No radical alternative, fascist or communist, made much headway. And mainly in spite of, not because of, the government, Britain began recovering earlier than most – and from a level which had never sunk to the depths reached in many countries all over the world.

Society and Change since 1945

The years since 1945 have seen profound social and economic changes in Britain. Despite recurrent economic crises and the relative decline in Britain's economic standing in comparison with the achievements of other western European countries, these years have seen significant general improvements in national wealth and living standards. Both income and wealth have become more evenly distributed so that a greater proportion of the population has shared in the 'affluent society'.

Prosperity was stimulated by a remarkable period of full employment which lasted until the end of the 1960s. Only in the 1970s, and especially after 1979, has unemployment soared to levels which recall the abyss of 1931–2. And, as in the earlier depression, so in recent years has the brunt of recession fallen with particular severity on certain vulnerable industrial regions: the North-West, North-East, South Wales, Northern Ireland, and Southern Scotland.

The physical symbols of prosperity, allied often to major technological developments, have been manifested in many ways – for example in the mass ownership of motor cars, washing machines, and televisions; in the rise in the numbers taking foreign holidays; in improved housing standards, as slums have been cleared and such luxuries as central heating have become increasingly common.

Rising levels of consumption, both cause and effect of mass advertising, have been visible throughout different segments of society. In the 1950s, for example, the term 'teenager' came into prominence as affluent youth spawned a new era in pop music and clothing fashions. There was a succession of distinctive cults, associated with 'teddy boys', 'mods and rockers', and the like. Women, too, have become an increasingly powerful consumer group as opportunities for employment have grown – partly from the rise of appropriate jobs and partly through the increasing tendency of married women to go out to work.

The rise of new forms of entertainment and occupations has been balanced by declines in traditional areas. Thus after a period of post-war revival the cinemas, professional cricket and football matches, and even the familiar seaside 'boarding house', have fallen in popularity. Domestic service has largely disappeared.

A further major change has been the arrival of a long period of sustained inflation, in contrast to the generally falling prices of the inter-war years. The introduction of the new decimal currency in February 1971 happened to usher in a period of soaring prices, but even earlier the value of money was being steadily eroded.

Underlying many of the social and economic developments since 1945 has been the influence of government. The war itself markedly accelerated those forces which were already pointing towards a welfare state. The famous Beveridge Report in 1942 and the subsequent government White Paper in 1944 held out the promise of government initiative to promote social equality through changes in education, health, town planning, and national insurance. In 1944 Butler's Education Act was passed, installing the system of grammar and secondary modern schools which was to be undermined by the spread of comprehensive schools in the 1970s. State intervention was facilitated by the introduction of the PAYE system of taxation at the beginning of the war, and by the collection of better economic statistics. The return of the Labour government in 1945 marked a period of considerable economic and social legislation. The years 1945–51 saw the nationalization of major industries (and consequently the further rise of the 'public sector'), the establishment of the National Health Service, and many other welfare measures. These were still years of rationing and other forms of controls as Britain readjusted painfully to the post-war world. But by the early 1950s, under a Conservative government committed to relaxing many of Labour's controls, rationing came to an end. Favourable international circumstances helped promote a period of considerable prosperity. A vigorous housing programme helped remedy one of the worst legacies of the war.

Economic difficulties became increasingly evident during the 1960s and 1970s, and have tended to mask continued material progress. Areas of social tensions have grown. Movements for devolution in Scotland and Wales, the misery of Ulster, growing fears over coloured immigration, violent outbreaks on picket lines – all are symptomatic of a malaise which is neither easy to pinpoint nor to analyse, nor to control. Successive governments have tried, with little success, to defeat inflation and the subsequent industrial troubles to which their policies have given rise.

Few would doubt that the post-war years have brought revolutionary changes. Some would emphasize the economic consequences of affluence and government intervention, and the mounting impact of large firms and multinational companies. Others might emphasize social changes: the Welfare State, the decline of religious observance, changing attitudes to authority, the emergence of a cosmopolitan society, or the influence of American values and culture through the powerful medium of television. But of the depth and significance of a vast array of inter-related movements and changes, there can be no argument.

Britain's standard of living

	1951	1966	1976
Dwellings (per 1000 of population)	275	333	368
TV licences (ditto)	15	249	322
Car licences (ditto)	48	179	257
Telephones (ditto)	103	197	392
Students in higher education (ditto)	3.7	7.9	11.6
Real personal disposal income per head (1970 prices)	£383	£583	£735
Average prices of new dwelling on mortgage	100	174.6	578

The post-war years have seen a significant rise in the standard of living for most people in Britain. Possession of cars, televisions and refrigerators and the ability to take foreign holidays are now taken for granted by a high percentage of the population, where once they were regarded as luxuries.

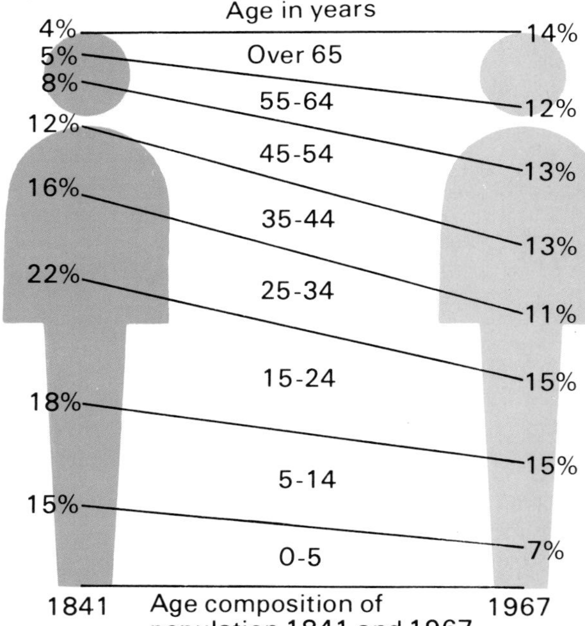

The changing age composition of the population. The very significant increase in the upper age range is largely due to better health and living conditions but has brought with it considerable problems in caring and paying for the aged.

Photographic Acknowledgements

Aerofilms Pages 15, 17 top, 81 top. Ashmolean Museum 39. British & Foreign Bible Society 89. British Museum 20 top left, 22 bottom left, 29, 41 left 95 top, 175. British Tourist Authority 6 right, 9 right, 17, 23 top, 26, 44, 56, 64 right, 72, 108. Cambridgeshire Collection 96/97. Cooper-Bridgeman Library 8 left, 30, 31, 34, 43, 52 right, 110, 115, 116, 126, 138, 153 top 186, 192. Mary Evans 196 left. Fotomas Index 12/13, 55, 59, 81, 92 bottom, 94 left, 99 right 106, 107 right, 109, 113, 145, 196 top 197, 200, 208, 209. Michael Holford 7 left 57, 164/5. Alan Hutchison 8 right. Imperial War Museum 149. India Office Library 7 right. Library of Congress 103. Mansell Collection Cover, centre, 9 left 23 top right, 25 bottom, 33, 48, 61, 69 bottom, 99 top, 101, 102, 104, 115 top, 119, 125 insert, 127 insert, 129, 130, 131, 139, 140, 144, 148, 178, 184, 194, 207 top & bottom. National Army Museum 100, 128. Picturepoint 17 right, 21, 25 centre 27 top, 32, 36, 47, 50, 62 top, 66, 68, 76, 78, 92 top, 143 right & left, 173, 174, 188, 195, 203. Photo Library International 6 left. Radio Times Hulton Picture Library 132, 133, 135, 150, 151, 152, 153 both, 156, 164, 167, 202, 211 top. Robert Hunt Library 157. Science Museum, London 198. John Topham 154, 211 bottom. Zefa (UK) 87.

The Editors gratefully acknowledge the following sources which were used in the preparation of the maps and diagrams in this work:
p.17 – Iron Age Square Barrows on the Yorkshire Wolds – After H. Ramm. *The Parisi* (Duckworth); Hill Forts on the South Downs – After B. Cunliffe. *Iron Age Communities in Britain* (Routledge and Kegan Paul). p.69 – Wine Production in Gascony – After Y. Renouard. *Bordeaux sous les Rois d'Angleterre* – Based on analysis of K.R.A.V. made by M. K. Jones. p.99 – The Rebellion of the Duke of Monmouth – After Sir George Clark. *The Western Rising* (Longman). Invasion of William of Orange – After Sir George Clark. *The Later Stuarts* 1660–1714. (Clarendon Press). pp 103–103 – North America in 1758: North America in 1783 – Martin Gilbert, *American History Atlas* (Weidenfeld & Nicolson). p.110 – Cromwell in Ireland – Martin Gilbert, *British History Atlas* (Weidenfeld & Nicolson). p.117 – World at Treaty of Utrecht: World at Treaty of Paris, 1763 – Based upon *Muir's Historical Atlas*. p.127 – 1832 Reform Bill – From R. J. Evans, *The Victorian Age* (Edware and Arnold). p.166 – Distribution of Population, 1086 – Based on the work of H. C. Darby as in R. A. Dodgshon & R. A. Butlin (eds.), *An Historical Geography of England and Wales* (Academic Press) p. 166 – Population in England (diagram) – After John Hatcher. *Plague, Population and the Economy, 1348–1530. (Macmillan)* p. 168 – Manors Belonging to Westminster Abbey – From B. Harvey, *Westminster Abbey and Its Estates in the Middle Ages (Oxford University Press)*. p.168 – Wigston Magna Manorial Settlement – From W. G. Hoskins. *The Midland Peasant: the Economic and Social History of a Leicestershire Village*. (Macmillan). p.168 – Open Field System (diagram) – From N. J. G. Pounds, *An Economic History of Western Europe* (Longman). p.169 – Harvests during the 16th century (diagram) – From W. G. Hoskins, *The Age of Plunder* (Longman). p.170 – Leading Towns in the Late 17th Century – P. Clark & P. Slack, *English Towns in Transition*. p. 170 – Immigration into Stratford-upon-Avon (diagram) – From E. M. Carus-Wilson, *The First Half-century of the Borough of Stratford-upon-Avon* (Economic History Review, 2nd series XVIII, 1965). p. 171 – London in the Later 14th century – From R. Bird, *The Turbulent London of Richard II*. (Longman). p.172 – Fulling Mills in England and Wales – From R. A. Pelham, *Fulling Mills: a Study in Application of Water Power to the Woollen Industry* (S.P.A.B. Wind and Watermills, section no. 5). p.172 – English Cloth Industry, Late 14th century – H. C. Darby (ed.), *An Historical Geography of England before AD 1800* (Cambridge University Press) p. 173 – Textile Manufacturing regions, late 17th Century – From R. A. Dodghson and R. A. Butlin, *Historical Geography of England and Wales* (Academic Press). p.173 – Lancashire Textile Industries in later 17th century – From A. P. Wadsworth and J. de l.Mann, *The Cotton Trade and Industrial Lancashire, 1600–1780* (Manchester University Press). p.174 – Tin Output in Cornwall – From J. Hatcher, *Rural Society and Economy in the Duchy of Cornwall, 1300*–1500 (C.U.P). p.175 – Lead Mining Fields of the Pennines – From A. Raistrick and B. Jennings, *A History of Lead Mining in the Pennines* (Longman). p.175 – Industries and Communications – From C. W. Chalkin, *17th Century Kent: a Social and Economic History* (Longman). p.175 – Charcoal Blast Furnaces – From H. C. Darby (ed.), *New Historical Geography*. p.177 – Heriots and Prices of Five Winchester Manors (diagram) – From M. M. Postan and J. Z. Titon, *Heriots and Prices of Winchester Manors* (Economic History Review, 2nd series, XI, 1959). p.178 – Prices of Foodstuffs – Based on table 4, E. H. Phelps Brown and S. V. Hopkins, *Wage, Rates and Prices: Evidence for Population Pressure in the 16th Century* (Economica, 1957). p.178 – English Population and Real Wage Rates – From J. Hatcher, *Plague, Population and the English Economy, 1348–1530* (Macmillan). p.179 – Medieval Suffolk Markets – Based on N. Scarfe, *The Suffolk Landscape*. p.179 – Walsall Pewter – From J. Hatcher and T. C. Barker, *A History of British Pewter* (Longman). p.179 – Road and River Communications – From H. C. Darby, *New Historical Geography of England* (C.U.P.). p.179 – Area served by 15th-century Southampton – From C. Platt, *English Medieval Towns*. p.181 – Gascon Wine Imports – Based on M. K. James, *Studies in Medieval Wine Trade* (O.U.P.). p. 181 – England's exports of Woollen Cloth – From E. M. Carus-Wilson, *Medieval Merchant Venturers* (Methuen). p.188 – London c.1600–1800 – From H. C. Darby, *A New Historical Geography of England* (C.U.P.). p.189 – London Occupations c.1750 – From H. C. Darby, *An Historical Geography of England before AD 1800* (C.U.P.). pp 194–5 – Poor Rate and Land Tax 1680s & 1692 – From J. Thirsk and J. Cooper, *17th Century Economic Documents* (Clarendon Press). p. 194 – Poor Rate, 1803 – From J. Marshall, *A Digest of all the accounts*. p.195 – Schedule D, 1804 – From Mark Blaug, *The Myth of the Old Poor Law and the making of the New* (Journal of Economic History XXIII, 1963). p.196 – Turnpike Network, 1750 – From Eric Pawson, *Transport and Economy: the Turnpike Roads of 18th Century Britain* (Academic Press). p.197 – Navigable Waterways – From Charles Hadfield, *British Canals: an Illustrated History* (David and Charles). p.212 – Unemployment: Relative Levels, 1931–6 – From M. P. Fogarty, *Prospects of the Industrial Areas of Great Britain*.

CHRONOLOGY OF WORLD HISTORY

BRITAIN

BC

*c.*4000	Farming develops in Britain
*c.*2000–1300	Wessex Culture in Southern Britain
*c.*1300	Building of hill-forts begins
*c.*120	Beginning of Belgic immigration

AD

43	Roman Conquest begins
61	Rebellion of Boudica
122	Hadrian's Wall begun
287–96	Revolt of Carausius and Allectus
367	Invasion of Picts and Scots
408	Final withdrawal of Roman troops
*c.*400–*c.*600	Migration and settlement of Angles, Saxons and Jutes
563	Columba arrives at Iona
597	Augustine arrives in Kent
*c.*610–55	Reign of Penda of Mercia
672	Council of Hertford
731	Bede completes his *Ecclesiastical History*
757–96	Reign of Offa of Mercia
832–60	Reign of Kenneth MacAlpin in Scotland
865	Danish Great Army overruns East Anglia, Northumbria and Eastern Mercia
871–99	Reign of Alfred of Wessex
899–939	Reconquest of Danelaw by Wessex kings
1014	Battle of Clontarf: victory of Brian Boru over Vikings
1016–35	Reign of Cnut
1066	Norman Conquest; Foundation of Anglo-Norman Empire
1086	Domesday Survey
1139–54	Intermittent civil war in Stephen's reign
1170	Murder of Thomas à Becket
1215	Magna Carta
1264–5	Barons' war against Henry III; Simon de Montfort killed

EUROPE

BC

*c.*6500	Farming begins in Greece and the Aegean
*c.*2000–1200	Minoan and Mycenean civilization in Crete and Greece
*c.*750–*c.*550	Greek and Phoenician colonization in Mediterranean and Black Sea
490–479	Battles of the Persian Wars
431–404	Peloponnesian War
*c.*380–300	Work of Plato, Euclid and Aristotle
*c.*327–300	Main period of Roman expansion
27	Octavian takes title of Augustus: end of Roman republic

AD

284–305	Reign of Diocletian. Imperial reorganization and partition
378	Valens defeated by Visigoths at Adrianople. Movement of Germanic peoples into Europe
410	Sack of Rome
476	Baptism of Clovis, king of Franks
535–40	Reconquest of Italy under Justinian
542	Outbreak of bubonic plague
568	Lombards begin to settle in Italy
*c.*600	Slavs move into Balkans
711	Muslim invasion of Spain
732	Battle of Poitiers. Charles Martel defeats Arab raiding army
800	Charlemagne crowned
843	Treaty of Verdun: partition of Carolingian empire
886	Viking siege of Paris
911	Vikings granted duchy of Normandy
962	Otto I crowned emperor at Rome
1054	Beginning of schism between Greek and Latin churches
1073–85	Pontificate of Gregory VII. Quarrel between Empire and Papacy begins
1130	Roger II establishes Norman Kingdom of Sicily
1202–4	Philip II of France captures Normandy and Anjou
1204	Fourth Crusade. Latins capture Constantinople
1209–29	Albigensian crusade against heretics
1215	Pope Innocent III presides over Fourth Lateran Council
1261	Greek Empire restored at Constantinople

NEAR EAST AND NORTH AFRICA

BC

*c.*8000	Domestication of plants and animals: farming begins
*c.*4000–3500	Invention of wheel, plough and sail in Mesopotamia and Egypt
*c.*3000	Early development of writing in Mesopotamia and Egypt
*c.*2700–*c.*2200	Age of pyramids in Egypt
*c.*2000–*c.*1200	Hittite civilization in Turkey
*c.*1200–*c.*650	Period of domination of Assyrian Empire
*c.*550–330	Achaemenid Empire in Persia; Zoroastrianism the state religion
334–323	The campaigns of Alexander the Great

AD

*c.*30	Crucifixion of Jesus, founder of Christianity
226–636	Sassanid Empire in Persia
312	Freedom of Christian worship in Roman Empire
429–44	Vandals occupy North Africa
533–4	Belisarius re-conquers North Africa for Justinian
540	Persian-Byzantine war begins
542	Outbreak of bubonic plague
622	Mohammed goes to Medina
636–43	Arab conquest of Syria, Egypt and Persia
658	Ommayyad dynasty established in Damascus
750	Abbasid caliphate established at Baghdad
969	Fatimids conquer Egypt
1055	Seljuk Turks capture Baghdad
1071	Seljuks defeat Byzantine army
1096–99	First Crusade; establishment of Kingdom of Jerusalem
1187	Battle of Hattin; Saladin overruns Kingdom of Jerusalem
1250	Mamluks seize power in Egypt
1258	Mongols sack Baghdad
1260	Mamluks defeat Mongol detachment at Ain Jalut

ASIA AND AMERICA

BC

*c.*6000	Beginnings of rice cultivation in Far East
*c.*2700–1700	Harappan civilization in Indus Valley
*c.*1500–*c.*1000	Shang dynasty in China
*c.*1000–*c.*500	Chou dynasty in China
*c.*480–*c.*220	The age of warring states in China
*c.*320	Mauryan Empire in India (Ashoka's reign 272–231)
*c.*200 BC–*c.*220 AD	Han dynasty in China

AD

*c.*300–*c.*900	Mayan civilization in central America
304/8	Huns invade China
*c.*320	Gupta Empire in Ganges Valley: traditional 'Golden Age' of Hindu culture
*c.*300–500	Main period of spread of Buddhism in China
*c.*520	Decimal system invented in India
618–906	T'ang dynasty in China
646	Taika reform in Japan
711–13	Muslim conquest of Samarkand and Indus Valley
794	Japanese capital moved to Kyoto
?960–1280	Sung dynasty in China
966–1027	Climax of Fugiwara regency
*c.*1000	Greenland Vikings reach America
1206	Sultanate of Delhi founded. Temujin (Chingis Khan) unites Mongol tribes
1206–80	Period of Mongol conquests

BRITAIN

1277–83	Edward I annexes the Principality of Wales
1296–1336	Ango-Scottish Wars
1327	Deposition and murder of Edward II
1348	Black Death in England
1381	Peasants' Revolt
1399	Deposition of Richard II. Henry IV establishes Lancastrian dynasty
1455–87	The Wars of the Roses
1529–39	Henry VIII's Reformation Parliament and the dissolution of monasteries
1554–58	Brief Catholic restoration under Mary Tudor
1588	Dispersal of Spanish Armada
***c.*1590–*c.*1613**	Shakespeare writes his plays
1603	James VI of Scotland succeeds to English throne
1642–48	Civil Wars in England
1649	Execution of Charles I
1660	Restoration of monarchy under Charles II
1688	Deposition of James II
1707	Union of England and Scotland
***c.*1730**	Wesley brothers found Methodism
***c.*1785–1800**	First steam powered cotton mills
1800	Union of England and Ireland
1825	Stockton-Darlington railway completed
1832	Great Reform Act
1845	Irish famine
1846	Repeal of Corn Laws
1851	Great Exhibition, London
1863	Building of first underground railway, London. Darwin's *Origin of Species*
1922	Irish Free State established
1926	General Strike
1940	Battle of Britain
1945	Labour government elected on programme of nationalization and social welfare
1973	Britain enters Common Market

EUROPE

1307	Suppression of Order of Templars
1309–78	Papacy at Avignon
1337	Beginning of Hundred Years' War in France
1347–50	Black Death
1378	Great Papal schism
1397	Union of Kalmar (Scandinavia united)
1419–36	Hussite rebellion in Bohemia
***c.*1450**	Gutenberg starts printing
1450–53	English driven out of France
1453	Constantinople falls to Ottoman Turks
1462–1505	Reign of Ivan III (establishment of Grand Duchy of Muscovy)
1521	Condemnation of Martin Luther. Beginning of Protestantism
1526	Battle of Mohacs; Turks overrun Hungary
1545–63	Council of Trent
1572	Beginning of Dutch revolt against Spain
***c.*1600–1650**	Scientific work of Kepler, Galileo and Descartes
1618–48	Thirty Years'War
1661–1715	Reign of Louis XIV
1682–1725	Reign of Peter the Great, Tsar of Russia
1740–86	Reign of Frederick the Great, King of Prussia
1756–63	Seven Years'War
1789	Outbreak of French Revolution
1799	Napoleon seizes power in France
1815	Battle of Waterloo; Congress of Vienna
1821–29	Greek War of Liberation
1848	Year of Revolutions throughout Europe. Publication of *Communist Manifesto*
1854–6	Crimean War
1870	Completion of Italian *Risorgimento*
1870–71	Franco-Prussian War. Proclamation of German *Reich*
1885–95	Daimler and Benz work on automobile; Marconi's wireless
1900	Freud publishes *Interpretation of Dreams*
1914	Outbreak of WW1
1917	Bolshevik revolution in Russia
1922	Mussolini takes power in Italy
1926	Salazar takes power in Portugal
1933	Hitler becomes German Chancellor
1936	Outbreak of Spanish Civil War
1939	Outbreak of WW2
1941	Germany invades Russia
1945	Defeat of Germany. Cold War begins
1957	Russia launches first space satellite. Treaty of Rome: formation of 'Common Market'

AMERICA AND AUSTRALASIA

***c.*1325–1520**	Aztec empire in Mexico
***c.*1400–1525**	Inca civilization in Andes
1492	Columbus reaches America
1493	Treaty of Tordesillas between Spain and Portugal
1519	Cortes begins conquest of Aztec Empire
1532	Pizarro begins conquest of Inca Empire
1545	Discovery of silver in Mexico and Peru
1608	French colonists found Quebec
1620	*Mayflower* Puritans settle in New England
1645	Tasman discovers New Zealand
1776	American War of Independence
1788	British colony founded at Botany Bay, Australia
1793	Development of cotton gin in America
1803	Louisiana purchase
1817–24	Careers of Simon Bolivar and José de San Martin
1840	Britain annexes New Zealand
1846–8	USA-Mexico War
1859	Oil well drilled in Pennsylvania
1861–65	American Civil War
1869	Completion of first trans-continental railway in USA
1876	Alexander Bell patents telephone
1898	Spanish-American War
1903	Wright brothers: first powered flight
1911	Mexican Revolution
1913	Henry Ford's assembly line begins to roll
1914	Panama Canal opened
1929	Wall Street Crash ushers in Great Depression
1933	Roosevelt introduces New Deal Program
1941	USA enters WW2
1952	Contraception pill developed
1959	Cuban revolution
1963	Assassination of President Kennedy
1969	Neil Armstrong lands on Moon
1981	First Space shuttle

ASIA AND AFRICA

***c.*1200–*c.*1600**	Zimbabwe states in Africa
1271–95	Travels of Marco Polo
***c.*1300**	Beginnings of Ottoman Turk expansion
1368–1644	Ming dynasty in China
1380–1405	Career and conquests of Timur (Tamerlane)
1405–33	Voyages of Cheng-Ho to East Africa and East Indies
1486–98	Voyages of Bartholomew Diaz and Vasco da Gama
1500–1736	Safavid dynasty in Persia
***c.*1500–1870**	African slave trade
1522–1680	Mughal expansion in India (reign of Akbar I 1556–1603)
***c.*1550–*c.*1650**	Russians colonize Siberia
1603	Tokugawa establishes shogunate at Edo (Tokyo)
1619	Dutch found Batavia (Jakarta)
1630s	Japan isolates herself from rest of world
1644–1911	Manchu dynasty in China
1652	Dutch found Cape Colony
1757	Battle of Plassey; British defeat French in India
1805	Establishment of East India Company's dominance in India
1806	Britain takes control of Cape Colony
1818–28	Shaka rules Zulu Kingdom
1839–42	Opium War; Britain takes Hong Kong
1853	Commander Perry forces entry into Japan
1857–9	Indian Mutiny
1868	Meiji restoration in Japan
1869	Suez Canal opened
1880–1900	'Scramble for Africa'; 'Scramble for China': Boxer Rebellion (1900)
1899–1902	Boer War
1911	Republic established in China under Sun-yat-Sen
1920–38	Career of Mustafa Kemal Atatürk
1937	Japan invades China
1941	Japanese attack Pearl Harbor
1945	USA drops atomic bombs on Japan
1947	India obtains independence
1948	State of Israel founded; Series of Arab-Israel wars begin
1949	Communist victory in China. Doctrine of Apartheid formulated in South Africa
1952–62	African states win independence

INDEX